BUSINESS
COMMUNICATION

Process and Product

First Canadian Edition

BUSINESS
COMMUNICATION

Process and Product

Mary Ellen Guffey
Los Angeles Pierce College

Kathleen Rhodes
Durham College

Patricia Rogin
Durham College

Nelson Canada

I(T)P An International Thomson Publishing Company

Toronto • Albany • Bonn • Boston • Cincinnati • Detroit • London • Madrid • Melbourne
Mexico City • New York • Pacific Grove • Paris • San Francisco • Singapore • Tokyo • Washington

I(T)P™
International Thomson Publishing
The ITP logo is a trademark under licence

© Nelson Canada
A division of Thomson Canada Limited, 1996

Published in 1996 by
Nelson Canada
A division of Thomson Canada Limited
1120 Birchmount Road, Scarborough, Ontario M1K 5G4

Canadian Cataloguing in Publication Data

Guffey, Mary Ellen
  Business communication : process and product

1st Canadian ed.
Includes bibliographical references and index.
ISBN 0-17-605570-3 (bound) ISBN 0-17-605601-7 (pbk.)

1. Business writing.   2. English language –
Business English.   3. Business communication.
I. Rogin, Pat, 1958–   . II. Rhodes, Kathy,
1951–   . III. Title

HF5718.3.G838 1996   808'.066651   C95-933078-X

Team Leader and Publisher	Michael Young
Acquisitions Editor	Andrew Livingston
Senior Production Editor	Tracy Bordian
Project Editor	Joanne Scattolon
Editorial and Market Assistant	Evan Turner
Production Coordinator	Brad Horning
Art Director	Liz Harasymczuk
Cover Design	Liz Harasymczuk
Cover Illustration	Mick Wiggins
Lead Composition Analyst	Zenaida Diores

Printed and bound in Canada

3 4 (ML) 99 98 97

Brief Contents

Detailed Contents

Preface

This first Canadian edition builds upon the success of Mary Ellen Guffey's *Business Communication: Process and Product.* Using a unique teaching/learning package that solves a major problem for instructors and students today, this text provides the atmosphere of an exciting real-life business environment for business communication—without sacrificing sound pedagogy. This means that students experience the enrichment of real people and real business situations while learning a hands-on process that they can carry with them long after they leave the classroom. While the basic structure of the text has been retained, examples and exercises have been adapted to include experiences familiar to our Canadian students.

The first Canadian edition of *Business Communication: Process and Product* takes students inside many well-run and respected organizations such as Canadian Airlines, Seagull Pewter, and Tilley Endurables. More importantly, though, it balances this exposure with a well-developed and consistently applied process approach to communication. Students need more than real business settings in which to frame their learning. They need a process that outlines specific steps to follow in solving future communication problems, a tangible strategy they can apply in their careers. In addition to a process, we provide ample products of that process.

Features that Build Career Skills Quickly

Today's students know they must have top-notch career skills to succeed in an increasingly competitive, diverse, and global business environment. This book includes numerous features that supply both process and product—the two keys to developing successful communication skills. Briefly described here, selected features are illustrated in the Visual Guide to the Book that follows.

3 × 3 writing process. This rational, comprehensive process outlines a plan that guides both oral and written composition. Developed in Chapters 3, 4, and 5, the process is then applied in all following chapters. Phase 1 includes analyzing, anticipating, and adapting. Phase 2 covers researching, organizing, and composing. Phase 3 presents revising, proofreading, and evaluating. In addition to explaining the writing process, these chapters teach basic writing techniques. They also provide plenty of reinforcement exercises, thus enabling students to develop facility with working tools they will need on the job.

Career Track Profiles. Each chapter begins with an interview of a front-line employee from a leading company. These interviews provide insights, tips, and, in many instances, role models for readers. Interviewees like Lise Andrews at Tilley Endurables and James Paterson at the Toronto Raptors Basketball Club, Inc. discuss their careers and supply practical advice for beginning business communicators. Because most interviewees are entry-level or mid-career employees and not CEOs or company presidents, readers can relate to their experiences and identify with them readily.

Process visualizers. Many model documents illustrate the 3 × 3 writing process graphics. Readers immediately see how the process relates to a specific letter, memo, or report. For today's visually oriented audiences, these process visualizers emphasize and demonstrate the most important part of the course—a strategy and basic pattern to follow in solving communication problems.

Career Track feature boxes. Colourful boxes discuss topics in four areas: ethics, cross-cultural issues, technology, and career skills. These enrichment boxes keep readers current with fast-paced articles providing career tips, communication strategies, and stimulating insights on current issues.

Integration of ethics and cross-cultural issues. Instead of treating these topics in separate chapters or in appendices, we introduce ethics and cross-cultural issues early and in all relevant chapters thereafter. Each chapter also includes one or more ethical questions to stimulate discussion and focus attention.

CLUE: Competent Language Usage Essentials. Students can review and reinforce grammar and language principles by using the CLUE program. This business writer's handbook contains 50 of the most used and abused writing concepts, along with reinforcement and learning exercises. After completing the diagnostic test (located in the *Instructor's Manual*), students may study the CLUE program independently or together in class, as the instructor directs. Chapters 1 through 10 contain CLUE checkups for class instruction and review.

Complete but concise coverage. In just 16 succinct chapters (instead of 18 to 24 in other books), all the traditional business communication topics are covered. Additionally, students will find career communication extras like how to write performance appraisals, employee warnings, and letters of recommendation.

Powerful employment chapter. Practical and up-to-date model résumés, letters of application, and job-search suggestions led reviewer after reviewer to commend Chapter 16. Two veteran business communication professors said that this chapter was among the best they had ever seen in any textbook. This edition also discusses the impact of technology on the job search and offers valuable suggestions for adapting to it.

Efficient report treatment. In only four chapters, we present comprehensive report-writing techniques and fully formatted reports. Moreover, our long analytical report illustrates a real campus problem in which college students collect data, analyze solutions, draw conclusions, and make recommendations. Instead of a corporate problem far beyond the experience of students, this book shows a realistic problem typical of student research.

Textual Aids that Promote Learning and Retention

The message of this book centres on both process and product. To deliver that message most effectively to readers, we introduce a unique pedagogical program featuring **visualization**. More than ever, today's sophisticated audiences respond to visual cues. Moreover, visualization is an important part of learning theory, helping readers understand and retain concepts. Therefore, the following textual aids contain many elements that involve showing as well as telling:

- Dozens of fully formatted memos, letters, reports, résumés, and other documents

- Targeted annotations on model documents that direct the eye to specific strategies, applications, and examples (instead of unfocused marginal comments)

- Numerous bulleted items highlighting important strategies, such as the components of a persuasive message

- Colourful graphics to emphasize important strategies, such as the components of a persuasive message

- Tips boxes to spotlight and summarize practical, "how-to" advice

- Colour photos with provocative images and relevant captions

- Draft documents to stimulate discussion and provide revision practice

- Checklists that capsulize relevant concepts for rapid review

- Lively end-of-chapter activities with a variety of short and long cases and at least one collaborative problem for each chapter

- Up-to-date advice on communication technology and software so that students know what to expect in today's offices and how to best use current tools

- Learning goals coordinated with chapter summaries so that students can check their comprehension

Instructional Resources that Facilitate Dynamic Teaching

A rich variety of instructional resources supplement and support the book, giving every instructor working tools to create a dynamic, exciting, and effective course.

Canadian Resources

Instructor's Resource. This package contains an Instructor's Manual, hard copy Test Item File, Transparency Masters, and Video Vantage Points.

Instructor's Manual. This helpful guide includes model course schedules, sample syllabi, teaching ideas, classroom management techniques, focus for chapter lectures, chapter outlines, answers for chapter review questions, suggested responses for discussion questions, and ideas for using chapter activities.

Test Item File. Instructors may generate their own tests from a test-item file containing 50 questions for each chapter. These questions include true-false, multiple choice, and fill-in items.

Transparency Masters. These masters summarize, supplement, and highlight course concepts. Lecture outlines for every chapter and solutions to key problems are included.

Video Vantage Points. A set of questions are provided for each of the five videos to stimulate class discussion and application.

Computerized Test Bank. The hard copy test item file found in the Instructor's Resource is also available on disk.

PowerPoint Presentation Slides. Using your personal computer and LCD technology, you can project colour slides that contain flying bullets, fade-outs, and other dazzling effects. With your own PowerPoint software, you can easily customize any slide to fit your lecture. These slides are available on 3 ½" disks. Handouts and transparency masters can also be created using this resource.

All Canadian support materials are available free to adoptors by contacting their Nelson Canada sales representatives.

Additional Support Material

Student Study Guide, Videotapes, and the **Business Communication Newsletter and Free Teaching Materials** are additional support materials corresponding to *Business Communication: Process and Product*, Second Edition, by Mary Ellen Guffey (Cincinnati: Southwestern Publishing, 1996).

Videotapes. Specially filmed to supplement the book, this set of five videotapes introduces each book part: communication foundations, the process of writing, letters and memos, reports and proposals, and presentation skills.

Student Study Guide. This hands-on study guide provides students with a variety of exercises and sample test questions that review chapter concepts and key terms. The study guide also helps students enrich their vocabularies, master frequently misspelled words, and develop language competency with bonus CLUE exercises. Nearly all exercises are self-checked so that students receive immediate feedback.

Adoptors may inquire about the videotapes and Student Study Guide materials by contacting their Nelson Canada sales representatives.

Business Communication Newsletter (*Business Communication News***) and Free Teaching Materials.** In addition to highlighting current issues and news of interest in the business communication course, the newsletter announces various free teaching materials that may be ordered directly from the author. You may reach Dr. Guffey in the following ways:

Mail:
Dr. Mary Ellen Guffey, 23715 W. Malibu Road, Ste. 307, Malibu, CA 90265

Voice Mail: 1-800-876-2350,2, ext. 814

Fax: 1-805-964-8614

Internet: meguffey@rain.org

World Wide Web: http://www/rain.org/~meguffey/

Acknowledgments

Our first acknowledgment must, of course, go to Dr. Mary Ellen Guffey. Her comprehensive coverage and innovative approach provided a firm foundation for this first Canadian edition.

Appreciation is extended to the Nelson team of Tracy Bordian, Andrew Livingston, and Joanne Scattolon. In addition, thanks must go to the many Canadian reviewers who helped direct us with this text.

Finally, we would like to thank David Napier for his professionalism and journalistic insight in researching and interviewing individuals from Canadian companies for the Career Track Profiles.

Kathy Rhodes and Pat Rogin
Durham College

A Visual Guide to the Book

In successful business communication, process and product are closely related. This book presents a consistent, logical process approach that you can apply to solve communication problems and create successful communication products—both written and oral. And the manner of presentation is innovative. The authors introduce unique visualization techniques to involve you *actively* in learning communication skills and applying them effectively. In addition to state-of-the-art graphics, you'll find model documents and inside tips from some of the country's best-run and most-respected organizations.

Process is a strategy developed early and applied consistently throughout the book. Easy-to-follow models translate theory into concrete visuals so that you can see the process in action and apply it yourself. You'll learn to analyze a problem, organize your ideas logically, and express your ideas correctly and persuasively. **Product** represents the wide range of communication skills and applications today's successful businesspeople must have at their command. Both process and product are presented visually for quick comprehension and lasting retention.

Model documents appear in every chapter. They include résumés that work for job hunters, memos that monitor operations and gain support, business letters that satisfy customers and deliver information, and reports that analyze problems and offer solutions.

On the next seven pages, you will find specific features of the book that will help you learn the essentials of successful business communication by mastering the principles, applying them consistently, and visualizing yourself as an effective business communicator.

EMPHASIS ON PROCESS VISUALIZATION

The **3 × 3 process**, a practical and helpful approach to written and oral communication, is developed fully and applied consistently. With the book's strong graphics to guide you, you'll understand and remember this multi-stage process of *analyzing-anticipating-adapting, researching-organizing-composing,* and *revising-proofreading-evaluating.* After detailed discussion of each of these nine steps (in Chapters 3, 4, and 5), the 3 × 3 process is then applied to create communication products in all the chapters that follow. **Process visualizers** are colourful graphics that summarize the writing process and show how to apply it in solving specific problems. By consistent repetition and application of the process, you will learn and retain an invaluable problem-solving strategy you can take with you and use every day in your future career. Visualizing makes the process easy to understand and easy to remember.

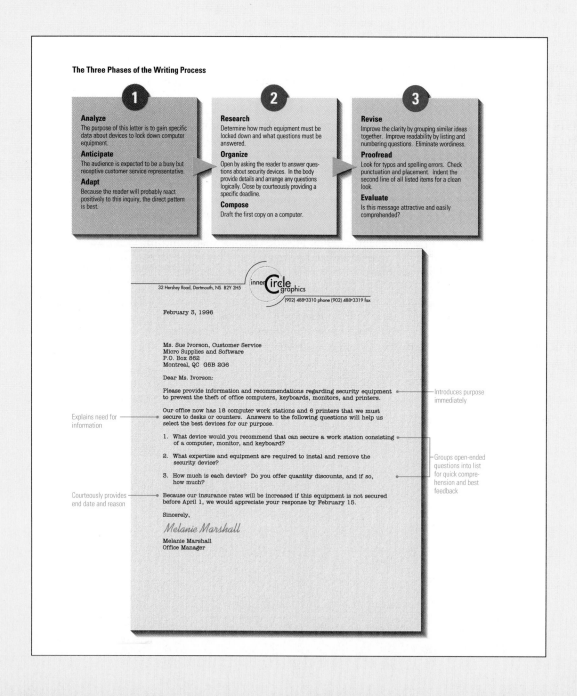

The Three Phases of the Writing Process

1

Analyze
The purpose of this letter is to gain specific data about devices to lock down computer equipment.

Anticipate
The audience is expected to be a busy but receptive customer service representative.

Adapt
Because the reader will probably react positively to this inquiry, the direct pattern is best.

2

Research
Determine how much equipment must be locked down and what questions must be answered.

Organize
Open by asking the reader to answer questions about security devices. In the body provide details and arrange any questions logically. Close by courteously providing a specific deadline.

Compose
Draft the first copy on a computer.

3

Revise
Improve the clarity by grouping similar ideas together. Improve readability by listing and numbering questions. Eliminate wordiness.

Proofread
Look for typos and spelling errors. Check punctuation and placement. Indent the second line of all listed items for a clean look.

Evaluate
Is this message attractive and easily comprehended?

inner **Circle** graphics

32 Hershey Road, Dartmouth, NS B2Y 2H5

(902) 488·3310 phone (902) 488·3319 fax

February 3, 1996

Ms. Sue Ivorson, Customer Service
Micro Supplies and Software
P.O. Box 862
Montreal, QC G5B 2G6

Dear Ms. Ivorson:

Please provide information and recommendations regarding security equipment to prevent the theft of office computers, keyboards, monitors, and printers. — Introduces purpose immediately

Explains need for information — Our office now has 18 computer work stations and 6 printers that we must secure to desks or counters. Answers to the following questions will help us select the best devices for our purpose.

1. What device would you recommend that can secure a work station consisting of a computer, monitor, and keyboard?

2. What expertise and equipment are required to instal and remove the security device?

3. How much is each device? Do you offer quantity discounts, and if so, how much?

— Groups open-ended questions into list for quick comprehension and best feedback

Courteously provides end date and reason — Because our insurance rates will be increased if this equipment is not secured before April 1, we would appreciate your response by February 15.

Sincerely,

Melanie Marshall

Melanie Marshall
Office Manager

ROLE MODELS AND RELEVANCE FOR CAREER SUCCESS

Bank of Montreal

When she first came to work at the Bank of Montreal in the mortgage department, Johanne Totta took her ability to communicate for granted. Of course, she was glad to be able to speak, listen, and negotiate well, but the graduate of McGill University's commerce program had no idea that it would shape her entire career. These days, communication describes the 38-year-old's full-time job—whether it be arbitrating a dispute between employees or speaking at an international conference.

As one of Canada's largest banks, which handles billions of dollars and employs some 37 000 people, the Bank of Montreal is first and foremost a service-oriented business. Its staff, from front-line bank tellers to loan officers, is its most important resource. When the bank realized that it was not making the most of its employees, it identified four areas that needed improvement—the advancement of women, of people with disabilities, of natives, and of visible minorities—then chose Johanne to head the project. "The people who had worked with me gave me very favourable reviews for my communication skills, particularly listening. That, combined with the fact that I had spent some time implementing policy, was the reason I was chosen for this position."

Now Johanne heads the program responsible for workplace equity. This requires extensive internal communication to understand the needs of the bank's employees, as well as external communication to share some of the ideas they have developed.

"Things have changed a great deal at the bank," she says. "Communication wasn't considered terribl[y] ... [recog]nized as essential. Now, as part of the int[erviewing process] ... Interviews which put the interviewee in a ... judge his or her skill in speaking, listening ... sis on communicating now." Body languag[e] ... employee will communicate with custome[rs] ... elements of communicating," Johanne exp[lains] ... someone, it is almost as important as wha[t they are saying.]

Johanne divides the kind of commu[nication] ... external, internal, and individual—and has ... to put myself in the other person's shoes, ... do is treat each employee exactly the same ... a unique perspective to the table. By liste[ning] ... the complementary ideas and not miss an[y] ...

> *"Body language is one of the most important elements of communicating.... When you are sitting across a table from someone, it is almost as important as what they are saying."*

36

Career track profiles—in-depth interviews with successful business communicators—open each chapter. Since most of those profiled are front-line employees in entry-level or mid-career positions, you can relate to their "in-the-trenches" experiences easily. These interviewees discuss their careers and employers, offering practical advice that directly relates to the material covered in the chapter. As you discover how strong communication skills helped these communicators move into rewarding and often unexpected new careers, you can look to the profiles to inspire you and serve as role models for your own career track ascent.

Career track feature boxes keep you current with topics relevant to career success. These boxes provide communication strategies, career tips, and up-to-date information about effective business communication. Each box contains a **Career Track Application** that challenges you to apply what you have just learned so that you can be immediately productive on the job.

CAREER SKILLS

NINE POOR LISTENING HABITS THAT CAN SIDETRACK YOUR CAREER

Listening is a vital business skill, yet most of us have such underdeveloped listening skills that we fail to retain 75 percent of what we hear. The following poor habits cost businesses millions of dollars in mistakes and lost productivity. They can also retard your own career advancement if you are unable to recognize and correct them. How many of these apply to you?

- **Reacting to the speaker's appearance and speech mannerisms.** It's easy to be distracted by a speaker's looks, attire, age, or mannerisms. Poor listeners refuse to make the effort to overcome personal biases that block objective reception.

- **Failing to control distractions.** Some listeners yield easily to external and internal distractions. They fail to control or block out surrounding noises, or they fail to resist thoughts that interfere with their concentration.

- **Listening to evaluate rather than to understand.** Too often we listen only to determine if the speaker's ideas fit our frame of reference and beliefs. Listening for immediate evaluation interferes with hearing and understanding the speaker's ideas.

- **Daydreaming and pretending to listen.** We all know how to fix our gaze and look intently at the speaker while hearing nothing being said. This pseudolistening is one of the most serious of the bad listening habits.

- **Assuming the speaker wants input or advice.** Some listeners feel compelled to interrupt a speaker with comments like "Well, here's what I think about it" or "What you ought to do is ... " Unless the speaker requests it, keep your advice to yourself.

- **Avoiding listening to anything difficult.** Many listeners prefer light, recreational listening. They automatically tune out serious topics. In doing so, they deprive themselves of the opportunity to learn something new and to develop listening techniques for coping with complex issues.

- **Waiting to jump in and grab the limelight.** Too many listeners are uncomfortable in the role; they much prefer to be speaking. The result? They fail to concentrate on what's being said, but instead are mentally preparing their next comments to be interjected at the first pause.

- **Pretending to understand.** Fear of appearing stupid, impolite, or uninformed may cause us to nod in agreement when we don't really understand. Equally bad is presuming we already know what the speaker means, perhaps because we are familiar with the topic. In either case always ask clarifying questions to ensure that you understand.

- **Listening for facts only.** Failing to observe nonverbal cues can be crucial in one-to-one conversations. Poor listeners fail to pick up on voice intonation, eye movement, and body language. These cues help skilful listeners detect subtle meanings.

Career Track Application

During the next week complete two activities aimed at improving your listening skills. First, conduct a reality check. Ask your closest friends and family to evaluate your listening skill. And be grateful for their honest feedback! Second, evaluate your conversational style using the "50/50" rule. Do you listen 50 percent of the time?

summarizing a message in your own words. Effective listeners do this during lag time—the pause that naturally occurs when the listener is waiting for the speaker's next idea. A final technique for improving retention is selective note-taking. Good listeners jot down key points, especially if they know they will be responsible for the information later.

Improving Your Listening Effectiveness

Positive attitude, involvement, openness, and retention are key factors that influence effective listening, but people who want to improve their listening skills usually need pointers or specific techniques. The following checklist

LEARNING FROM LEADERS

FIGURE 3.3 ■ Successful Customer Response Letter

February 23, 1996

Mrs. Elaine Hough
2175 Edenwood Road
Brandon, MB R7A 6A9

Dear Mrs. Hough:

Your letter was a strong endorsement of our belief that we made the right choice when we devoted our company to comfort, ease of care, durability, and a smart appearance — and that it's still the right choice.

It's true we've made changes. In the past few years, with the markets soft and tastes changing, we reexamined our merchandise with a view to continuing to serve valued customers while introducing ourselves to new ones. We decided we want to give you more choices for more occasions.

Our commitment to the classics hasn't weakened, as I hope you'd agree, having seen recent catalogues. But we've defined "classic" more inclusively than in the past. We're using new fabrics, new colours, a more relaxed fit. There's more imagination in our product mix now, but the hats, pants, vests, jackets, and other basics for which you've relied on us are still here. You may not find each one in every catalogue, and you may notice the new products more than those you've seen before. The classics are still here, and the selection will be growing.

I've arranged to send you just the four catalogues a year you wanted. I hope you'll keep an eye out for them. I think that, more and more, you'll be able to come to us for the styles you want.

Sincerely,

Lise Andrews

Lise Andrews
Customer Service

Annotations:
- Explains evolving merchandise line from company's and reader's view
- Emphasizes areas of agreement
- Opens response to inquiry by agreeing with customer
- Uses conversational language to convey warmth and sincerity
- Concludes by giving customer what she wants and promoting future business

The Human Resources Department requires that the enclosed questionnaire be completed immediately so that we can allocate our training resources funds.

You can be one of the first [e]sign up for the new career [development] program. Fill out the attache[d] questionnaire and return it [...] immediately.

Cultivating the "you" view. Notice how many of the previo[us] focused messages included the word *you*. In concentrating on receiv[ers], skilled communicators naturally develop the "you" view. They [use] second-person pronouns (*you*, *your*) instead of first-person pronou[ns (we,] *our*). Whether your goal is to inform, persuade, or promote g[oodwill, the] catchiest words you can use are *you* and *your*. Compare the followi[ng...]

Sophisticated visualization techniques reinforce your understanding of the principles involved. Colourful pointers on the letters, memos, and reports lead to concise annotations that point out communication strategies and applications of theory. In addition, helpful **Tips** boxes appear with many of the documents, spotlighting and summarizing key procedures. These concise Tips boxes supply you with a valuable reference resource when you are on the job and need fast answers.

FIGURE 6.7 ■ Adjustment Letter

Tips for Letter Formatting

- Single-space business letters. Double-space between paragraphs.
- Place the date on line 13 or 2 lines below the letterhead.
- Set margins so that letter looks centred on the page.
- Leave three blank lines for the handwritten signature.
- Use a colon after the salutation and a comma after the complimentary close.
- Be consistent in letter format. For example, use full block with all lines starting at the left margin or modified block as shown here.

Rose World
One Rose Lane
Beamsville, ON L0R 1B1
1-800-543-2000

June 3, 1996

Mr. James Bronski
68 Wingate Crescent
Richmond Hill, ON L4B 2Y9

Dear Mr. Bronski:

We're happy to replace the six rose bushes you purchased or return your money in full.

The quality of our plants and the careful handling they receive assure you of healthy, viable roses for your garden. Even so, plants sometimes fail without apparent cause. That's why we guarantee every plant to grow and to establish itself in your garden.

Along with this letter is a copy of our current catalogue for you to select six new roses or reorder the favourites you chose last year. Two of your previous selections—Red Velvet and Rose Princess—were last season's best-selling roses. For fragrance and old-rose charm, you might like to try the new David Austin English Roses. These enormously popular hybrids resulted from crossing full-petaled old garden roses with modern repeat-flowering shrub roses.

Since we want you to enjoy your roses to the fullest, Mr. Bronski, we're also sending a copy of our authoritative Home Gardener's Guide to Roses. This comprehensive booklet provides easy-to-follow planting tips as well as sound advice about sun, soil, and drainage requirements for roses.

To receive your free replacement order, just fill out the order form inside the catalogue and attach the enclosed certificate. Or return the certificate, and we'll refund your full purchase price.

We're proud of our roses. The quality of these plants reflects the expertise we've gained in over a century of hybridizing, growing, harvesting, and shipping top-quality garden stock. Through the years we've also learned something about service. We know that if you're not happy, we're not happy. To ensure your satisfaction and your respect, we maintain our 100 percent guarantee policy.

Sincerely,

Michael Vanderer

Michael Vanderer
General Manager

meg
Enclosures

Annotations:
- Tactfully skirts the issue of what caused plants to die
- Offers resale information to assure customer he has made a wise choice
- Projects personal, conversational tone by using contractions and reader's name
- Shows pride in the company's products and concern for its customers
- Approves customer's claim immediately
- Avoids blaming customer
- Includes some sales promotion without overkill
- Tells reader clearly what to do next
- Strives to regain customer's confidence in both products and service

COMMUNICATION IN MANY FORMS

As a business communicator, you must be able to direct messages in different formats to diverse audiences. This book goes beyond traditional topics to provide **strategic coverage** in several crucial areas. A full chapter is devoted to **memos**, the most commonly written business document. Examples include information, procedure, request, reply, and confirmation memos—plus an extensive discussion of electronic memos.

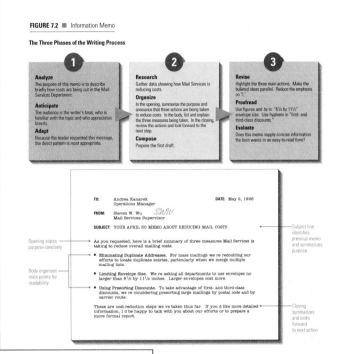

FIGURE 7.2 ■ Information Memo

The Three Phases of the Writing Process

1

Analyze
The purpose of this memo is to describe briefly how costs are being cut in the Mail Services Department.

Anticipate
The audience is the writer's boss, who is familiar with the topic and who appreciates brevity.

Adapt
Because the reader requested this message, the direct pattern is most appropriate.

2

Research
Gather data showing how Mail Services is reducing costs.

Organize
In the opening, summarize the purpose and announce that three actions are being taken to reduce costs. In the body, list and explain the three measures being taken. In the closing, review the actions and look forward to the next step.

Compose
Prepare the first draft.

3

Revise
Highlight the three main actions. Make the bulleted ideas parallel. Reduce the emphasis on "I."

Proofread
Use figures and *by in* "6⅛ by 11½" envelope size. Use hyphens in "first- and third-class discounts."

Evaluate
Does this memo supply concise information the boss wants in an easy-to-read form?

TO: Andrea Kanarek   DATE: May 2, 1996
        Operations Manager

FROM: Steven W. Wu   *SWW*
        Mail Services Supervisor

SUBJECT: YOUR APRIL 30 MEMO ABOUT REDUCING MAIL COSTS

Opening states purpose concisely
As you requested, here is a brief summary of three measures Mail Services is taking to reduce overall mailing costs.

Body organizes main points for readability
■ **Eliminating Duplicate Addresses.** For mass mailings we're redoubling our efforts to locate duplicate entries, particularly when we merge multiple mailing lists.

■ **Limiting Envelope Size.** We're asking all departments to use envelopes no larger than 6⅛ by 11½ inches. Larger envelopes cost more.

■ **Using Presorting Discounts.** To take advantage of first- and third-class discounts, we're considering presorting large mailings by postal code and by carrier route.

These are cost-reduction steps we've taken thus far. If you'd like more detailed information, I'd be happy to talk with you about our efforts or to prepare a more formal report.

Subject line identifies previous memo and summarizes purpose

Closing summarizes and looks forward to next action

[M]ail Memos

[amo]ng memos printed on paper, increasing numbers of business-[co]mmunicating by electronic mail (E-mail). E-mail requires [syst]ems, and software. Messages travel electronically over networks [te]lephone lines and satellites. Almost instantly, a keyboarded [... t]o another computer—whether on the next desk or halfway [worl]d. The message remains stored in the receiver's mailbox until [...] the receiver may edit, store, delete, print, or forward the [... a]ll without paper.

[Am]erica's larger business organizations are rapidly embracing [...] by E-mail (called "messaging" as in "Why don't you 'message'

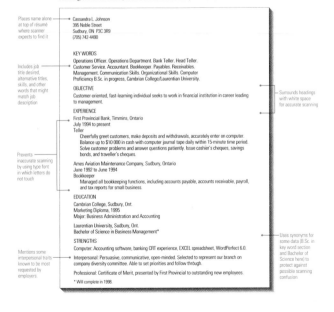

FIGURE 16.11 ■ Computer-Friendly Résumé

Cassandra prepared this computer-friendly résumé (free of graphics and fancy formatting) so that it would scan well if read by a computer. Notice that she begins with a key word summary that contains job titles, skills, traits, and other descriptive words. She hopes that some of these key words will match those submitted by an employer. To improve accurate scanning, she avoids italics, vertical and horizontal lines, and double columns.

Places name alone at top of résumé where scanner expects to find it
Cassandra L. Johnson
395 Noble Street
Sudbury, ON P3C 3R9
(705) 742-4490

KEY WORDS
Includes job title desired, alternative titles, skills, and other words that might match job description
Operations Officer. Operations Department. Bank Teller. Head Teller. Customer Service. Accountant. Bookkeeper. Payables. Receivables. Management. Communication Skills. Organizational Skills. Computer Proficiency B.Sc. in progress, Cambrian College/Laurentian University.

OBJECTIVE
Customer-oriented, fast-learning individual seeks to work in financial institution in career leading to management.

EXPERIENCE
First Provincial Bank, Timmins, Ontario
July 1994 to present
Teller
Prevents inaccurate scanning by using type font in which letters do not touch
Cheerfully greet customers, make deposits and withdrawals, accurately enter on computer. Balance up to $10 000 in cash with computer journal tape daily within 15-minute time period. Solve customer problems and answer questions patiently. Issue cashier's cheques, savings bonds, and traveller's cheques.

Ames Aviation Maintenance Company, Sudbury, Ontario
June 1992 to June 1994
Bookkeeper
Managed all bookkeeping functions, including accounts payable, accounts receivable, payroll, and tax reports for small business.

EDUCATION
Cambrian College, Sudbury, Ont.
Marketing Diploma, 1995
Major: Business Administration and Accounting

Laurentian University, Sudbury, Ont.
Bachelor of Science in Business Management*

STRENGTHS
Computer: Accounting software, banking CRT experience, EXCEL spreadsheet, WordPerfect 6.0.
Mentions some interpersonal traits known to be most requested by employers
Interpersonal: Persuasive, communicative, open-minded. Selected to represent our branch on company diversity committee. Able to set priorities and follow through.
Professional: Certificate of Merit, presented by First Provincial to outstanding new employees.

* Will complete in 1998.

Surrounds headings with white space for accurate scanning

Uses synonyms for some data (B.Sc. in key word section and Bachelor of Science here) to protect against possible scanning confusion

---

Education

✓ **Name your degree, date of graduation, and institution.** Emphasize your education if your experience is limited.

✓ **List your major and your average.** Give information about your studies, but don't list all your courses.

Chapter 16
Employment Messages

501

A powerful employment communication chapter contains on-target advice for job-hunting, along with twice the number of model **résumés** found in other leading texts. And all model résumés are fully annotated.

Comprehensive, yet concise, material on **report-writing** is included, with excellent, fully annotated models of reports and proposals. This book contains nearly three times as many complete and fully formatted reports as other leading texts.

Personnel communication is covered, including **performance appraisals**, which are increasingly important in business today. Employee warnings and operational instructions are also illustrated.

ETHICAL AND CROSS-CULTURAL CONSIDERATIONS

FOUR ETHICAL GUIDELINES BUSINESS COMMUNICATORS SHOULD KNOW

Pressures on people and on organizations today can create dilemmas that require, in addition to communication skills, an ability to make ethical decisions. Often, the dilemmas have no clear-cut right or wrong answers.

Assume that Carolyn Song and you are competing for a promotion to regional manager in Surrey, B.C. In the past year Carolyn has been quite successful at her work. Although you acknowledge that Carolyn is doing a good job, you have been with the company longer and believe you deserve the position. Moreover, you feel threatened by her; and frankly, you don't like her. This promotion is important to you not only professionally but personally: your elderly parents live in the Surrey area, and you want to be close to help them out.

One day you happen to meet an old friend who has known Carolyn for some time. Over a cup of coffee you learn that Carolyn never graduated from the University of British Columbia, as stated on her résumé. In fact, she never attended university at all.

What should you do? Say nothing and, in effect, allow Carolyn to be rewarded for lying? Head straight to the vice president and expose the truth—which might, at the same time, conveniently eliminate a rival? Each action has possible consequences that make the decision difficult. Frequently, say ethicists, the "right" action is the one you can live with. But how do you arrive at that decision? Here are four simple guidelines that can help any business communicator make ethical choices:

- **Visualize the desired outcome.** What would you like to see happen as a result of resolving this issue? Will your choice produce the goal you seek?

- **Weigh the interests of all stakeholders.** Who will be affected by your choice? Consider the consequences for you and your fellow employees, your boss, the organization, your family, and the community. What effect will it have on Carolyn? Can you live with the consequences? Whose interests are most important?

- **Take the public-scrutiny test.** How would you feel about revealing your choice to your colleagues, friends, or family?

- **Balance your professional and personal goals.** Consider each choice and its effect on your career. Also consider its personal effects. Is there a choice that reconciles your professional goals with your personal values?

Career Track Application

Determine three or four actions you could take regarding Carolyn's dark secret. Then, evaluate each choice according to the four guidelines here. Be prepared to discuss your final choice and the reasoning behind it in class. Additional ethical guidelines will be presented in Chapter 3.

—talk back and forth within the organization, up and down the hierarchy— may well be more important to a company's success than external communications." Free-flowing information in an organization enables management "to identify and attack problems fast, say, when customer service representatives first get an earful about some quality [problem or when sales reps] encounter a new competitor."[33] Open [communication can foster an] atmosphere of trust and employee goo[dwill. By sharing information,] organizations can reduce barriers to com[munication.]

Encouraging an open environment [To develop a healthy communication] climate an organization cultivates g[ood relationships with employees. At] Microsoft small groups of employees [meet regularly with CEO Bill Gates. At] Chrysler, Lee Iacocca used to hold "t[own hall" meetings with randomly] selected employees. "I talk for five minu[tes; then I invite them to come after me and] to knock my head in," he said.[34] Ag[ri-food Canada, an organization with] 1700 staff and 24 production sites in Qu[ebec, realizes that open, candid] communication with members is esse[ntial.]

To help you recognize and apply ethical principles and intercultural sensitivity in all communication settings, the authors integrate these concepts throughout the book. This integrative approach puts ethical conduct and cross-cultural tolerance in context, rather than isolating these increasingly important considerations from the reality of day-to-day business interactions. Discussion appears in the text wherever relevant, along with **Ethics** and **Cross-Culture boxes**. An **"Ethical Issues" question** for class discussion also appears in the chapter exercises.

SEVEN WAYS COMPUTER SOFTWARE CAN HELP YOU BECOME A BETTER BUSINESS WRITER AND COMMUNICATOR

Although computers and software programs cannot actually do the writing for you, they provide powerful tools that make the composition process easier and the results more professional. Here are seven ways your computer can help you be a better business communicator.

- **Fighting writer's block.** Because word processors enable ideas to flow almost effortlessly from your brain to a screen, you can expect fewer delays resulting from writer's block. You can compose rapidly, and you can experiment with structure and phrasing, later keeping and polishing your most promising thoughts. Many authors "sprint-write," recording unedited ideas quickly, to start the composition process and also to brainstorm for ideas on a project. Then they tag important ideas and use computer outlining programs to organize those ideas into logical sequences.

- **Collecting information electronically.** As a knowledge worker in an information economy, you will need to find information quickly. Much of the world's information is now accessible by computer. You can find the titles of books, magazine and newspaper articles, and government publications by using on-line services or CD-ROM (compact disks) that hold massive data collections. Through specialized information-retrieval services (such as *InfoGlobe Online*) you can have at your fingertips up-to-the-minute legal, scientific, scholarly, and business information. By subscribing to Rose Media, CRS Online, CompuServe, or Prodigy, you gain access to many electronic services including databases and special-interest forums. And the Internet, a loose collection of voluntarily linked global computer networks, is opening additional vast information treasures. You'll learn more about exciting, dynamic electronic resources in Chapter 11.

- **Outlining and organizing ideas.** Most high-end word processors include some form of "outliner," a feature that enables you to divide a topic into a hierarchical order with main and subpoints. Your computer keeps track of the levels of ideas automatically so that you can easily add, cut, or rearrange points in the outline. This feature is particularly handy when you're preparing a report or organizing a presentation. Some programs even enable you to transfer your outline directly to slide frames to be used as visual aids in a talk.

- **Improving correctness and precision.** Nearly all word processing programs today can catch and correct spelling and typographical errors. Poor spellers and weak typists universally bless their spell checkers for repeatedly saving them from humiliation. Still, writers must recognize that misused words (*affect/effect*) and confusing words (*its/it's*) will escape detection by the spell check. Other writing tools include grammar and style checkers. These programs make suggestions about word usage, readability, jargon, and various other writing problems. Thesaurus programs help you choose precise words that say exactly what you intend.

- **Adding graphics for emphasis.** Your letters, memos, and reports may be improved by the addition of graphs and artwork to clarify and illustrate data. You can import charts, diagrams, and illustrations created in database, spreadsheet, graphics, and draw-and-paint programs. Moreover, ready-made pictures, called "clip art," can be used to symbolize or illustrate ideas.

- **Designing and producing professional-looking documents and presentations.** Gone are the days when writers were forced to take their copy to printers or in-house art departments for professional effects. Most high-end word processing programs today include scalable fonts (for different type sizes and styles), italics, boldface, and other print features to aid you in producing professional-looking results. Moreover, today's presentation software enables you to incorporate colour, sound, pictures, and even movies into your talks before management or customers.

- **Using collaborative software for team writing.** Assume you are part of a group preparing a lengthy proposal to secure a government contract. You expect to write one segment of the proposal yourself and help revise parts written by others. Special word processing programs with commenting and strikeout features allow you to revise easily and to identify each team member's editing. These collaborative programs, called "groupware," also include decision-support tools to help groups generate, organize, and analyze ideas more efficiently than in traditional meetings.

Career Track Application

Individually or in teams, identify specific software programs that perform the tasks described here. Prepare a table naming each program, its major functions, and its advantages and disadvantages for business writers in your field.

Technology feature boxes help to keep you up-to-date with the latest issues and trends. Discussions of E-mail and Internet communication technologies are included.

INTEGRATED AIDS TO LEARNING

The authors have included a number of carefully thought-out elements to help you understand and remember important concepts and techniques. **Learning goals** correlate with **chapter summaries** to focus your attention on the key points set forth in the chapter, thus enabling you to confirm that you have accomplished those goals.

CHAPTER

2

Expanding Communication Power

L E A R N I N G   G O A L S

After studying this chapter, you should be able to

... name

... ell as
ve listen-

from

... hance

5   Explain the importance of intercultural sensitivity and clarify pivotal North American cultural values.

6   Describe three key attitudes that help overcome cultural barriers.

7   Employ 10 specific procedures for adapting messages to intercultural audiences.

CHAPTER REVIEW

1. What purpose do most reports serve? (Goal 1)
2. List nine kinds of typical business reports. (Goal 1)
3. How do informational and analytical reports differ? (Goal 2)
4. How do the direct and indirect patterns of development differ? (Goal 2)
5. Under what circumstances would an analytical report be organized directly? Indirectly? (Goal 2)
6. Identify four common report formats. (Goal 3)
7. List the seven steps in the report-writing process. (Goal 4)
8. What is factoring? (Goal 4)
9. How do primary data differ from secondary data? Give an original example of each. (Goals 5, 6)
10. Should data collection for most business reports begin with primary or secondary research? Why? (Goal 5)
11. What major sources of print and electronic data could you expect to find in most libraries today? (Goal 5)
12. Name four major sources of primary data. (Goal 6)
13. In questionnaires what kind of questions produce quantifiable answers? (Goal 6)
14. What is documentation, and why is it necessary in reports? (Goal 7)
15. What kind of data require no documentation? (Goal 7)

DISCUSSION

1. What kinds of reports typically flow upward in an organization? What kinds flow downward? Why? (Goal 1)
2. Discuss this statement, made by three well-known professional business writers: "Nothing you write will be completely new."[7] (Goals 5, 6)
3. For long reports, why is it a wise idea to have a written work plan? (Goal 4)
4. How can a researcher improve the generalizability of collected data? (Goal 6)
5. **Ethical Issue:** Discuss this statement: "Let the facts speak for themselves." Are facts always truthful?

EXERCISES

11.1   Report Types, Functions, Writing Styles, and Formats (Goals 1, 2, 3)

For the following reports, (1) name the report's primary function (informational or analytical), (2) recommend a direct or indirect pattern of development, and (3) select a report format (memo, letter, or manuscript).

a. A persuasive proposal from a construction firm to the Ontario College of Art describing the contractor's bid to renovate and convert the school's newly purchased 1930s art deco office building into offices, studios, and classrooms.
b. A situational report submitted by a sales rep to her manager describing her attendance at a sports products trade show, including the reactions of visitors to a new noncarbonated sports drink.
c. A recommendation report from a technical specialist to the vice-president, Product Development, analyzing ways to prevent piracy of the software company's latest game program. The vice-president values straight talk and is familiar with the project.
d. A progress report from a location manager to a Hollywood production company describing safety, fire, and environmental precautions taken for the shooting of a stunt involving blowing up a boat off Toronto Island.
e. A feasibility report prepared by an outside consultant examining whether a company should invest in a health and fitness centre for its employees.
f. A compliance report from a national moving company telling provincial authorities how it has improved its safety program so that its trucks now comply with provincial regulations. The report describes but doesn't interpret the program.

11.2   Collaborative Project: Report Portfolio (Goals 1, 2, 3)

In student teams of four or five, collect four or more sample business reports illustrating at least three report types described in this chapter. (Don't forget corporate annual reports.) For each report identify and discuss the following characteristics:

338

Lively, realistic, and practical end-of-chapter activities include **chapter review questions, discussion topics, exercises,** and **problems.** Each chapter also provides at least one collaborative project to accustom you to the type of teamwork efforts often required in business today.

OTHER INTEGRATED AIDS TO LEARNING

This text includes many other features that are specifically designed to help you get full value from this book. Concise, yet insightful, **marginal notes** draw your attention to important material; informative **photo captions** advance ideas that are presented in the text; and **checklists** summarize text discussions to help you integrate, review, and apply concepts.

Smart companies know their customers' needs and concerns. The Body Shop serves the needs of its environmentally responsible customers by living by the motto "Reduce, Reuse, Recycle." More than 45 of The Body Shop products can be refilled, and a discount is given to those customers who take advantage of the offer.

less than one customer in twenty with a major problem will complain. Customers give the following reasons for not complaining:

It's not worth the trouble.

I don't know to whom to complain.

Nothing will be done anyway.

I don't want to be victimized.

Furthermore, of the customers who do complain, up to 80 percent are dissatisfied with the way their complaint was handled.[10]

Therefore, it is important to welcome complaints from customers as a way of ensuring repeat business and loyal customers. The Strategic Planning Institute found that companies that are seen by customers as offering good service achieve a 12 percent return on sales, compared with a 1 percent return on sales for companies that do not offer good service.[11]

Favourable responses to customer claims follow the direct pattern; unfavourable responses follow the indirect.

In responding to customer claims, you must first decide whether to grant the claim or not. Unless the claim is obviously fraudulent or represents an excessive sum, you'll probably grant it. When you say yes, your adjustment letter will be good news to the reader, so [...] When your response is no, the indire[...] discusses the indirect pattern for conveyi[...]

You'll have three goals in adjustment[...]

• Rectifying the wrong, if one exists

• Regaining the confidence of the cust[...]

• Promoting further business

Part III
Letters and Memos

166

The opening of a positive adjustment[...] claim immediately. Notice how quickly[...] good news:

Part III
Letters and Memos

FIGURE 4.7 ■ Transitional Expressions to Build Coherence

To Add or Strengthen	To Show Time or Order	To Clarify	To Show Cause and Effect	To Contradict	To Contrast
additionally	after	for example	accordingly	actually	as opposed to
again	before	for instance	as a result	but	at the same time
also	earlier	I mean	consequently	however	by contrast
besides	finally	in other words	for this reason	in fact	conversely
likewise	first	that is	so	instead	on the contrary
moreover	meanwhile	this means	therefore	rather	on the other hand
further	next	thus	thus	still	
furthermore	now	to put it another	under the circum-	though	
	previously	way	stances	yet	
	then				

Composing short paragraphs. Although no rule regulates the length of paragraphs, business writers recognize the value of short paragraphs. Paragraphs with fewer than eight lines look inviting and readable, whereas long, solid hunks of print appear formidable. If a topic can't be covered in fewer than ten printed lines (not sentences), consider breaking it up into smaller segments.

The following checklist summarizes the key points of writing a first draft.

Paragraphs with fewer than ten lines are attractive and readable.

■ Checklist for Composing Sentences and Paragraphs

For Effective Sentences

✓ **Use short sentences.** Keep in mind that sentences with fewer than 20 words are easier to read. Use longer sentences occasionally, but rely on short sentences.

✓ **Emphasize important ideas.** Place main ideas at the beginning of short sentences for emphasis.

✓ **Apply active and passive verbs carefully.** Use active verbs (*She wrote the letter* instead of *The letter was written by her*) most frequently; they immediately identify the doer. Use passive verbs to be tactful, to emphasize an action, or to conceal the performer.

✓ **Eliminate misplaced modifiers.** Be sure that introductory verbal phrases are followed by the words that can logically modify them. To check the placement of modifiers, ask Who? or What? after such phrases.

For Effective Paragraphs

✓ **Develop one idea.** Use main, supporting, and limiting sentences to develop a single idea within each paragraph.

Chapter 4
Researching, Organizing, and Composing

111

In addition, the **CLUE program,** a handy review and reference guide, appears as an appendix to the text. CLUE (an acronym for Competent Language Usage Essentials) focuses on frequently used and abused elements of grammar and usage, as well as words that are often misspelled or misused. You will feel more confident about the correctness of your language by brushing up your skills. Use the self-checked CLUE exercise within the guide itself or complete the exercises at the ends of Chapters 1 through 10.

BUSINESS

COMMUNICATION

Process and Product

Communication Foundations

Communicating in the New World of Work

L E A R N I N G   G O A L S

After studying this chapter, you should be able to

1 Explain the importance of communication skills for knowledge workers in the new world of work.

2 Describe the process of communication.

3 Discuss barriers to interpersonal communication.

4 Identify methods of overcoming barriers to interpersonal communication.

5 Analyze the purposes and forms of organizational communication.

6 Discuss the flow of organizational communication.

7 Describe barriers to organizational communication.

8 Name methods of surmounting barriers to organizational communication.

Microsoft Corporation

"I remember being 22, right out of college, and thinking, 'I'm not successful right now, and I'm pretty sure I'm not going to be successful next year. My life is a failure.' "

Like many college graduates, Mario Juarez despaired when his degree (in journalism and mass communication) didn't immediately unlock the doors to a secure career. Without a clear career path in sight, he followed his heart and his dreams, developing writing and journalism skills in adventurous spots. He worked as a reporter for radio stations in Alaska, travelled in Europe and New England, and, when he needed quick cash, wrote computer documentation for various companies. Settling on the West Coast, Mario signed on as a temporary technical writer at the Microsoft Corporation eight years after graduation.

Based in Redmond, just outside Seattle, Washington, Microsoft was soon to become the largest and most profitable software company in the world. It designs, develops, markets, and supports software for personal computers. The company's immense profits result largely from its MS/DOS and Windows programs, which account for nearly 90 percent of the world's PC operating software. And its youthful co-founder and chairman, Bill Gates, became the richest man in America.

> *"Our future contribution will be in the form of better thinking and better use of existing resources. Instead of physical work, we'll be doing brain work."*

Mario joined Microsoft during its most explosive growth period. Building on his writing, journalism, and computer skills, he moved from a temporary position and eventually became manager of Employee Communications. He also serves as editor of MicroNews, the weekly company newspaper. "One of the intangible benefits of my job is that I get to see Bill Gates in action. And I am in awe of the guy," confesses Mario. "Blessed with an incredible business mind, he's also one of the best engineers in the company. Some people regard him as ruthless; actually, he's aggressive—and also extremely efficient and knowledgeable."

Mario has watched Microsoft grow into a huge company with over 17 000 employees, including 330 at Microsoft's Canadian headquarters in Mississauga, Ontario. Keeping the lines of communication open and information flowing in such a large organization is a difficult but critical task. Bill Gates particularly wants communication to be open and free of regulation. The right things must be communicated to the right people at the right time without excessive channels of approval or restrictions.

One tool that facilitates open communication at Microsoft is electronic mail (E-mail). Every new employee gets a computer and is automatically connected to the company network. "E-mail is a great equalizer," says Mario. "At Microsoft there's always been a feeling that anyone can ask anything of anyone. The lowliest technical writer or adminis-

trative assistant can E-mail a suggestion to one of our senior VPs or even to Bill Gates—and look forward to a response. It might take a while, but all senior people read their E-mail personally and respond."

Employees are expected to analyze the way things are being done and offer suggestions for improvement. "We have a very flat hierarchy of command here," says Mario. "I'm sure Bill Gates would be dismayed if any employee did not feel free to come to him with an idea or suggestion."

Recently Microsoft underwent a major reorganization. How to communicate the company's redefined goals and new structure to all employees represented a significant challenge to senior management. One vice-president suggested E-mailing a short general announcement to all employees. Details of the reorganization would then be sent to managers only; they in turn would explain the specifics to their workers. Immediately, another vice-president objected, saying that such a plan implied that managers were smarter or more important than line people. "And this simply is not the case at Microsoft," says Mario. "Company news doesn't have to be filtered through managers. Everybody in the company is bright, and all are capable of dealing with information that pertains to their jobs." In the end, everyone received a personal E-mail message describing the reorganization. Official information flowed directly from senior management to workers. Such a short line of communication avoids possible distortions, omissions, and misunderstandings.

Mario recognizes that Microsoft is a knowledge company operating in a knowledge society. "Having depleted its resources, this country doesn't have a lot left to pull out of the ground. Our future contribution will be in the form of better thinking and better use of existing resources. Instead of physical work, we'll be doing brain work. I used to think that the software industry was a big scam—kind of like cheating. Software products don't actually exist; they're just a lot of blips and beeps packaged on a disk. Now I've come to understand that computer software programs represent remarkably well-defined thought processes. They are brain work. And these programs are among the few products that we in this country can deliver that no other country can produce right now."

When Mario graduated from college, the software industry didn't even exist. That's why he has some rather unconventional advice for today's college students. "Avoid marrying yourself to a specific job that you think you should be doing when you graduate," cautions Mario. "Instead, develop an enormous willingness to try new things. View yourself as adaptable, flexible, and smart enough to take on new challenges. Above all, consciously push yourself out of your comfort zone, and get ready for life in the knowledge society."[1] ▪

Surrounding the main buildings of Microsoft headquarters are soccer and softball fields, a brook, a pond, and nature trails that wind through moss-covered hardwoods and towering pines. The atmosphere resonates a corporate culture encouraging open communication, collaboration, and team projects.

■ Communication Power for Knowledge Workers

In many ways Mario's experiences at Microsoft reflect the bigger picture facing you and others preparing for careers. You will be entering a work environment that has undergone profound changes. Today's economy and globalization have changed the way business is done. Process improvement, re-engineering, information technology, and other innovations abound, and companies are looking for ways to reduce costs and retain quality and service. Research indicates that 90 percent of attempts to change fail because human factors were not taken into account.[2] Like Mario, you may be using tools and working in industries that do not now exist. As part of the Information Age, you will doubtless become a knowledge worker. And communication skills will be critical to your success. Before we discuss the communication process and how organizations communicate, let's look more closely at the new world of work and the powerful role that communication skills will play in your future as a knowledge worker.

The New World of Work

A new world of work has emerged in the past decade. To survive in a highly competitive global economy, businesses have been flattening their management hierarchies and "delayering." This means that fewer management levels separate decision-makers (owners and executives) from workers. As businesses restructure, they are laying off workers and squeezing budgets for maximum efficiency. You're likely to see continued downsizing and job consolidation for some time to come, predict the experts. As a result, competition for jobs will continue to be strong. According to Statistics Canada, workers now spend 37.5 hours per week in the workplace. This is up three hours from the decade before.[3] Many people are working longer and perhaps harder for the same amount of money as before. But the reassuring note is that knowledge workers seem to be better able to retain their jobs than others in the labour force and the jobless rate for knowledge workers is a mere 2 to 3 percent.[4]

The good news is that as businesses downsize and decentralize, they are increasingly empowering workers to participate in decision-making. This means you'll have more control over what you do. Nearly 80 percent of employers in all industries have adopted some form of quality circles and team-based systems. These arrangements make workers more self-directed. It is beneficial when employees are involved at all levels in decisions that affect them. One successful organization used a team of employees to make decisions on job-termination options and alternatives both in Canadian and American operations. The approach seemed more successful in Canada, where organizations appear to adapt to a more participatory style of management. Regardless, the employee involvement gives control back to the employees, resulting in improved productivity and fewer managers.[5] More employers across the country now expect employees to share in managing, planning, and decision making. Accompanying this trend toward employee empowerment is a movement to provide more information directly to employees. Instead of hoarding information at the top, progressive companies like Microsoft are working to open the lines of communication.

Surviving in the Knowledge Society

Seeing these momentous changes taking place in the world of work, we become more aware of an advanced economy based on information and knowledge. Physical labour, raw materials, and capital are no longer the essential ingredients in the creation of wealth. According to Toronto economist Nuala Beck, everyone agrees that knowledge is the most highly prized asset of the nineties.[6] The world of mass-manufacturing of the past has been replaced by technology: industries, employees, communities, and economies must adjust to the new realities or be doomed.[7] Knowledge-intensive industries created nearly 304 000 jobs between 1984 and 1991 in Canada, equal to 89.5 percent of all new employment. They account for 26 percent of total employment in Canada.[8] Tomorrow's wealth depends on the development and exchange of knowledge. And people entering the workforce offer their knowledge, not their muscles. Knowledge workers, says management guru Peter Drucker, get paid for their education and their ability to learn.[9] They engage in mind work. They deal with symbols: words, figures, and data. Beck reports that 70 percent of Canadians are already employed in the new economy, a figure that shows how well the country has adjusted.[10]

What does all this mean for you? As a future knowledge worker, you can expect to be generating, processing, and exchanging information. Currently, three out of four jobs involve some form of mind work, and that number will rise sharply in the future. Management and employees alike will be making decisions in such areas as product development, quality control, and customer satisfaction.

> **Knowledge workers are people who generate, process, and exchange information.**

You'll be asked to think critically. This means having opinions that are backed up by reasons and evidence. When your boss or team leader asks, "What do you think we ought to do?", you want to be able to supply good ideas. The Career Skills box on page 8 gives you a five-point critical-thinking plan to help you solve problems and make decisions.

In the new world of work, you can expect to be in constant training to acquire new skills that keep up with improved technologies and procedures. You can also expect to be taking greater control of your career. Don't presume that companies will provide you with clearly defined career paths or planned developmental experiences.[11] And instead of thinking of lifetime employment with a company, you should be thinking of *lifetime employability* and *lifelong learning*. To survive in the new world of work, you must be flexible and willing to continually learn new skills to supplement the strong foundation of basic skills you acquire in college or university.

Communication Skills as a Foundation

Probably the most important foundation skill for knowledge workers in the new world of work is the ability to communicate. This means being able to express your ideas effectively in writing and speaking.

> **Employers value effective communication skills because good communicators make and save money.**

Actually, most students today don't need to be advised by a futurist that communication skills will be important to their success in a career. When they look through employment classified ads, they see job listings like those shown in Figure 1.1. The Conference Board of Canada outlines the following critical employability skills that employers look for in new employees.[12]

SHARPENING YOUR SKILLS FOR CRITICAL THINKING, PROBLEM-SOLVING, AND DECISION-MAKING

Gone are the days when management expected workers to check their brains at the door and do only as told. As a knowledge worker, you'll be expected to use your brains to think critically. You'll be solving problems and making decisions. Much of this book is devoted to solving problems and communicating those decisions to management, fellow workers, clients, government, and the public. Shortly you'll learn the specifics of effective communication. First, though, let's examine the processes of critical thinking and problem-solving.

Faced with a problem or an issue, most of us do a lot of worrying before separating the issues or making a decision. All that worrying can become directed thinking by channelling it into the following procedure. To make the best decisions and to become a valuable knowledge worker, try this plan to develop your critical thinking skills.

1. Identify and clarify the problem. Your first task is to recognize that a problem exists. Some problems are big and unmistakable, such as the failure of an air-freight delivery service to get packages to its customers on time. Other problems may be continuing annoyances, such as regularly running out of toner for an office copy machine. The first step in reaching a solution is to pinpoint the problem.

2. Gather information. Learn more about the problem. Look for possible causes and solutions. This step may mean checking files, calling suppliers, or brainstorming with fellow workers. For example, the air-freight delivery service would investigate the tracking systems of the commercial airlines carrying its packages to determine what went wrong.

3. Evaluate the evidence. Where did the information come from? Does it represent various points of view? What biases could be expected from each source? How accurate is the information gathered? Is it fact or opinion? For example, it is a fact that packages are missing; it is an opinion that they are merely lost and will turn up eventually.

4. Consider alternatives and implications. Draw conclusions from the evidence gathered and propose solutions. Then weigh the advantages and disadvantages of each alternative. What are the costs, benefits, and consequences? What are the obstacles, and how can they be handled? Most important, what solution best serves your goals and those of your organization? Here's where your creativity is especially important.

5. Choose and implement the best alternative. Select an alternative and put it into action. Then monitor the results of implementing your plan. The freight company may decide to give its unhappy customers one month's free delivery service to make up for the lost packages and downtime. Be sure to continue monitoring and adjusting the solution to ensure its effectiveness over time.

Career Track Application

Try out the above process on a campus problem. Select one of the following for class discussion: limited campus parking, long lines at registration, restricted course offerings, or poor food service. Apply the critical-thinking plan to arrive at a solution.

In the academic skills area, which provides the basic foundation for getting, keeping, and progressing on a job and for achieving the best results, Canadian employers need a person who can **communicate, think, and learn.**[13] Although employers have long known the importance of communication, current workplace trends make it even more critical. As companies downsize and decentralize, teams are increasingly used. Team members must be able to work together to identify problems, analyze alternatives, and recommend solutions. They must be able to "sell" or communicate their ideas to others.[14]

FIGURE 1.1 ■ Classified Ads Seeking Knowledge Workers with Good Communication Skills

C-8 THE DAILY NEWS   Tuesday, March 26, 1996

ASSISTANT FACILITY MANAGER

ERA Enterprises, a manufacturer of medical devices, offers outstanding opportunity. Assistant facility manager helps in the security, safety, and maintenance of the manufacturing facility. Must have **excellent communication skills.**

FINANCIAL/REAL ESTATE PORTFOLIO ANALYST

You will review and analyze commercial/multi-family real property operating statements, rent rolls, loan agreements, and appraisals. Tasks include evaluating and writing detailed analyses of loans, developing and maintaining PC and mainframe data base, and analyzing economic and market data. Position demands **strong written communication skills. Writing sample required.**

ACCOUNT MANAGER

International   business

MARKETING ADMINISTRATIVE ASSISTANT

A leader in mass storage technology is seeking an adm. asst. to support the marketing team located at our corporate offices. Must be self-starter with secretarial skills including proficiency in PCs. **Must have excellent language skills and be able to communicate well with the public.** Please send résumé.

ACCOUNTING ANALYST

Major entertainment company seeks highly motivated accounting analyst to perform general ledger, statement, property, advertising, and other functions. Ideal candidate must have **strong oral and writing skills** to make presentations to all levels of management. Excellent benefits.

OFFICE PRODUCTS MARKETING

Looking for someone to help us sell our marketing concepts to businesses throughout the

ADMINISTRATIVE PERSONNEL ASSISTANT

Grow with our expanding cruise consultant business! Must be organized, personable, and well trained in WordPerfect and Lotus. **Communication skills a must! Will be tested.** AA degree in office technology preferred.

MANAGEMENT TRAINEE

One of Canada's leading companies is accepting résumés for trainees. Qualified candidates must have a bachelor's degree, **excellent writing and communication skills,** an ability to interface effectively with all levels of management and a diverse work staff, and leadership qualities.

INTERNATIONAL MARKETING COORDINATOR

Global computer electronics manufacturer seeks individual with marketing management training. The position requires **solid oral and written skills**

SALES M

Leader in direct sa in management. Earning opportuni $50,000 after tr and benefits.

MANAGEME PROG

We need 3 individuals for ou trainee program. hiring and trainin personnel, invento control, advertis marketing of new developing new s Retail experience not necessary. to train you if yo Rapid advancem agement, where sales managers $45,000+.

ACCOUNTING S

Mulit-faceted com company paid sharing, 401K a **2 year colleg must!!**

Even in technical fields communication skills are demanded. The chief executives of large public accounting firms put communication at the head of their list of three general skills needed to be successful in public accounting.[15] Moreover, as North American businesses continue to expand into global markets and as the national workforce becomes more diverse, you will need special sensitivity in communicating with people from different cultures.

As you advance in your career, communication becomes even more important. Probably the number one requirement for promotion to management is the ability to communicate. Corporate president Ben Ordover explains how he makes executive choices: "Many people climbing the corporate ladder are very good. When faced with a hard choice between candidates, I use writing ability as the deciding factor. Sometimes a candidate's writing is the only skill that separates him or her from the competition."[16] As individuals ascend the career ladder, oral and written communication skills become more important than their technical ability. That's because managers spend most of their time communicating—supervising, delegating, evaluating, clarifying, and interacting.

Even though writing on the job is an important skill, myths and misconceptions about it persist, as discussed in the following Career Skills box.

Employees with good communication skills tend to climb the career ladder faster than those lacking such skills.

FIVE COMMON MYTHS ABOUT WRITING ON THE JOB

A myth is an unfounded belief or a misconception. You may have seen movies or heard friends talk about some occupations, leading you to accept without scrutiny certain myths about writing on the job. These myths may affect the way you prepare for your career. Here are five common myths about writing and the facts that refute them.

MYTH. Because I'm in a technical field, I'll work with numbers, not words.
Fact. In truth, 90 percent of all business transactions involve written correspondence.[17] Conducting business in any field—even in technical and specialized areas like computing, accounting, engineering, marketing, hotel management, and so forth—involves some writing. A study of professional, technical, and managerial workers found that they spent 23 percent of their time writing—more than one full day a week![18] Moreover, with promotions, writing tasks will increase.

MYTH. My secretary will clean up my writing.
Fact. In today's world of tightened budgets, most businesspeople probably won't have a secretary. Although upper-level managers still have secretaries or assistants who may type their messages, many executives now write their own memos and letters on their computers because it's faster and more efficient. For those who do have administrative help, it's wise to remember that even the most highly skilled secretary cannot remedy fundamental problems in organization, emphasis, and tone.

MYTH. Technical writers do most of the real writing on the job.
Fact. Some companies employ technical writers to prepare manuals, documentation, and public documents like annual reports. Rarely, however, do these specialists write everyday messages (internal reports, letters, memos) for employees. Instead, sales representatives, programmers, accountants, engineers, technicians, and other professionals must rely on their own abilities to communicate their ideas.

MYTH. Computers can fix any of my writing mistakes.
Fact. Today's style, grammar, and spell checkers are wonderful aids to business writers. They can highlight selected problems and occasionally suggest revisions. What they can't do, though, is write the document and ensure its total accuracy. Spell checkers, for example, cannot distinguish between confusing words such as *their/there/they're* or *principal/principle*. Other checkers can't find or correct most errors of grammar, punctuation, style, tone, or organization. Only trained writers can do that.

MYTH. I can use form letters for most messages.
Fact. It is true that books and computer programs can provide dozens of ready-made letters or pattern paragraphs for which businesspeople merely fill in the blanks. When these letters are suitable and well written, they can be useful timesavers. Often, however, such letters are poorly written and ill-suited for specific situations. Most messages demand that writers do their own thinking.

Career Track Application

Interview a specialist in your field. What kinds of messages does she or he write? How often? After promotions, do these specialists have different writing tasks?

The Role of Communication

The mortar that holds together organizations—and the entire knowledge society—is communication. Without effective communication, information could not be collected, processed, or exchanged; words and data would remain isolated facts. For example, when Microsoft Corporation begins developing a new software product, such as its highly successful Excel or Office programs, it first collects information. Using questionnaires, interviews, and surveys, Microsoft studies the needs and difficulties of end users. What tasks are personal computer users performing that could be handled more easily or efficiently?

Performing a job well and being promoted depend greatly on your communication skills—your ability to explain ideas, lead meetings, convince customers, persuade management, and write clearly. Today's jobs focus increasingly on generating, processing, and exchanging information.

Data collection is an important first step. But all the data collected are useless until analyzed and communicated to designers, programmers, and project managers. Only when the words and data are translated into meaningful knowledge and are understood by decision-makers do they become valuable to Microsoft and to the economy. Communication is a central factor in the emerging knowledge society and a major consideration for anyone entering today's workforce.

The Process of Communication and Its Barriers

Just what is communication? For our purposes communication is the *transmission of information and meaning from one individual or group to another.* The crucial element in this definition is meaning. Communication has as its central objective the transmission of meaning. The process of communication is successful only when the receiver understands an idea as the sender intended it. Both parties must agree not only on the information transmitted but also on the *meaning* of that information. This entire book has one objective: to teach you to transmit meaning along with information. How does an idea travel from one person to another? Despite what you may have seen in science fiction movies, we can't just glance at another person and transfer meaning directly from mind to mind. We engage in an intricate process of communication that generally has five steps, discussed here and depicted in Figure 1.2.

The object of communication is the transmission of meaning from sender to receiver.

Sender has idea. The process of communication begins when the person with whom the message originates—*the sender*—has an idea. The form of the idea will be influenced by complex factors surrounding the sender: mood, frame of reference, background, culture, and physical makeup, as well as the context of the situation and many other factors. The way you greet people on campus, for example, depends a lot on how you feel, whom you are addressing (a classmate,

FIGURE 1.2 ■ The Communication Process

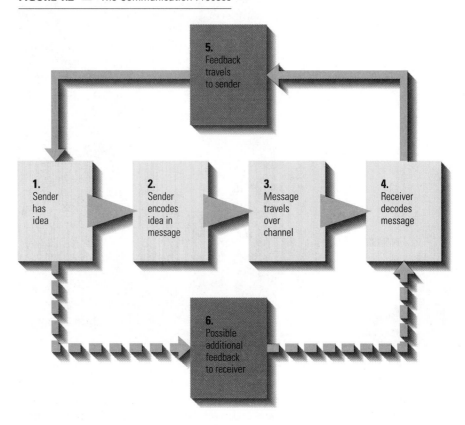

The communication process has five steps: idea formation, message encoding, message transmission, message decoding, and feedback.

a professor, or a campus worker), and what your culture has trained you to say ("How are you?" "How ya' doing?" or "Good morning").

The form of the idea, whether a simple greeting or a complex idea, is shaped by assumptions based on the sender's experiences. A manager sending a message to employees assumes they will be receptive, while direct-mail advertisers assume that receivers will only glance at their message. The ability to predict accurately how a message will affect its receiver and skill in adapting that message to its receiver are really the key factors in successful communication.

Encoding means converting an idea into words or gestures to convey meaning.

Sender encodes idea in message. The next step in the communication process involves *encoding*, converting the idea into words or gestures that will convey meaning. A major problem in communicating any message verbally is that words may have different meanings for different people. When misunderstandings result from missed meanings, it's called *bypassing*. You'll learn more about this communication obstacle shortly.

Recognizing how easy it is to be misunderstood, skilled communicators choose familiar words with concrete meanings on which both senders and receivers agree. In selecting proper symbols, senders must be alert to the receiver's communication skills, attitudes, background, experiences, and culture: How will the selected words affect the receiver? For example, a Dr. Pepper cola promotion failed miserably in Great Britain because American managers had not done their homework. They had to change their "I'm a Pepper" slogan after learning that *pepper* is British slang for *prostitute*.[19] Because the sender initiates a communication transaction, he or she has full responsibility for its success or failure. Choosing appropriate words or symbols is the first step.

Message travels over channel. The medium over which the message is physically transmitted is the *channel*. Messages may be delivered by computer, telephone, letter, memorandum, report, announcement, picture, spoken word, fax, or through some other channel. Because communication channels deliver both verbal and nonverbal messages, senders must choose the channel and shape the message carefully. A company may use its annual report, for example, as a channel to deliver many messages to its stockholders. The verbal message lies in the report's financial and organizational news. Nonverbal messages, though, are conveyed by the report's appearance (glitzy versus bland), layout (ample white space versus tightly packed columns of print), and tone (conversational versus formal).

Channels are the media— computer, telephone, letter, and so on—that transmit messages.

Anything that interrupts the transmission of a message in the communication process is called *noise*. Channel noise ranges from static that disrupts a telephone conversation to typographical errors in a letter that damage the credibility of the sender. Channel noise might even include the annoyance a receiver feels when the sender chooses an improper medium for sending a message, such as announcing a loan rejection by postcard. You'll learn more about choosing the proper channel or form for a message shortly, as well as ways of preventing noise from interfering with communication.

Receiver decodes message. The individual for whom the message is intended is the *receiver*. Translating the message from its symbol form into meaning involves *decoding*. Only when the receiver understands the meaning intended by the sender—that is, successfully decodes the message—does communication take place. Such success, however, is difficult to achieve because no two people share the same life experiences and because many barriers can disrupt the process.

Decoding can be disrupted internally by the receiver's lack of attention to or bias against the sender. It can be disrupted externally by loud sounds or illegible words. Decoding can also be sidetracked by semantic obstacles, such as misunderstood words or emotional reactions to certain terms. A memo that refers to all the women in an office as "girls," for example, may disturb its receivers so much that they fail to comprehend the total message.

Feedback travels to sender. The verbal and nonverbal responses of the receiver create *feedback*, a vital part of the communication process. Feedback helps the sender know that the message was received and understood. If as a receiver you hear the message "How are you?", your feedback might consist of words ("I'm fine") or body language (a smile or a wave of the hand). Although the receiver may respond with additional feedback to the sender (thus creating a new act of communication), we'll concentrate here on the initial message flowing to the receiver and the resulting feedback.

Feedback helps the sender know the message was received and understood.

Senders can encourage feedback by asking questions such as *Am I making myself clear?* and *Is there anything you don't understand?* Senders can further improve feedback by timing the delivery appropriately and by providing only as much information as the receiver can handle. Receivers can improve the process by paraphrasing the sender's message with comments like *Let me try to explain that in my own words* or *My understanding of your comment is ...*

The best feedback is descriptive rather than evaluative. For example, here's a descriptive response: *I understand you want to launch a chocolate chip cookie business.* Here's an evaluative response: *Your business ideas are always weird.* An evaluative response is judgmental and doesn't tell the sender if the receiver actually understood the message.

■ Barriers to Interpersonal Communication

The communication process is successful only when the receiver understands the message as intended by the sender. It sounds quite simple. Yet it's not. How many times have you thought that you delivered a clear message, only to learn later that your intentions were totally misunderstood?

Most messages that we send reach their destinations, but many are only partially understood. You can improve your chances of communicating successfully by learning to recognize the barriers that are known to disrupt the process. These barriers occur at any stage in the process, from the sender's initial development of the message to the receiver's feedback. The most significant communication misunderstandings result from problems in these areas: bypassing, frame of reference, lack of language and listening skills, emotional interference, and physical distractions.

Bypassing. In the business world and in our personal lives, we depend almost totally on words to exchange ideas. Each of us attaches a little bundle of meanings to every word, and these meanings are not always similar. Bypassing happens when people miss each other with their meanings.[20] Let's say your boss asks you to "help" with a large customer mailing. When you arrive to do your share, you learn that you are expected to do the whole mailing yourself. You and your boss attached different meanings to the word *help.* Bypassing can lead to major miscommunication because people assume that meanings are contained in words. Actually, meanings are in people. For communication to be successful, the receiver and sender must attach the same symbolic meanings to their words.

Frame of reference. Everything you see and feel in the world is translated through your individual frame of reference. This frame is formed by a combination of your experiences, education, culture, expectations, attitudes, personality, and many other elements. Because your frame of reference is unique, you will naturally perceive events differently from someone else. Since buying Woolco Canada in February 1994, Wal-Mart has had to change the corporate culture of over 16 000 employees and apply a retail philosophy that was new to its Canadian managers. Wal-Mart wanted to convince Canadians that it was not the bully that critics had described, so it quickly tried to reassure the Canadian consumer by using Canadian suppliers and Canadian advertisers.[21] This strategy was an attempt to overlap frames of reference to ensure communication would be positive. Wise business communicators, whether dealing with global or local audiences, strive to prevent communication failure by being alert to both their own frames of reference and those of others.

Lack of language skill. No matter how extraordinary the idea, it won't be understood or fully appreciated unless the communicators involved have good language skills. Each individual needs an adequate vocabulary, a command of basic punctuation and grammar, and skill in written and oral expression. Today's knowledge workers require especially fine-tuned skills because our economy increasingly revolves around the exchange of language-based information.

Barriers to successful communication include bypassing, differing frames of reference, lack of language or listening skills, emotional interference, and physical distractions.

Miscommunication often results when the sender's frame of reference differs markedly from the receiver's.

Lack of listening skill. Although most of us think we know how to listen, in reality many of us are poor listeners. Have you ever "faked" listening—made it appear you were paying attention when your mind was wandering elsewhere? Nearly everyone has. This inattention to oral messages often prevents us from hearing them clearly and thus responding properly.

Emotional interference. Communication suffers when emotions cloud the mind. Shaping an intelligent message is difficult when you're feeling joy, fear, resentment, hostility, sadness, or some other strong emotion. It's especially hard to concentrate when anger muddies your ability to reason. When angry, senders and receivers drop those cooperative roles and become adversaries, so that the communication process deteriorates into name-calling or other counterproductive behaviour.[22] To reduce the influence of emotions as a communication barrier, both senders and receivers should focus on the content of the message and try to remain objective.

Physical distractions. Faulty acoustics, noisy surroundings, or a poor telephone connection are physical distractions that may disrupt oral communication. Likewise, sloppy appearance, poor printing, careless formatting, and typographical errors can disrupt written messages.

Overcoming Barriers to Interpersonal Communication

The road to successful communication might appear to be filled with insurmountable obstacles. Effective communicators, however, have learned to overcome the barriers. Throughout this book you'll be taught countless techniques for becoming a successful communicator. Here are some suggestions for conquering barriers that disrupt interpersonal communication.

Realizing that the communication process is imperfect. Half the battle in communicating successfully is recognizing that the entire process is sensitive and susceptible to breakdown. Like a defensive driver who anticipates problems on the road, a good communicator anticipates problems in encoding, transmitting, and decoding a message. Just knowing what can go wrong helps you prepare strategies to reduce misunderstandings.

Adapting your message to the receiver. Successful communicators focus on the receiver's environment and frame of reference. They ask themselves questions such as, How is that person likely to react to my message? Does the receiver know as much about the subject as I do? What language level does that person understand? The better you are at anticipating the answers and viewing the message through the receiver's frame of reference, the more successful your communication will be.

Improving your language and listening skills. Misunderstandings are less likely if you arrange your ideas logically and use words precisely. Mark Twain was right when he said, "The difference between the right word and the almost right word is the difference between lightning and a lightning bug." But communicating is more than expressing yourself well. A large part of successful communication is listening. Peter Drucker observes that "too many [executives]

> To overcome barriers, communicators must recognize communication's imperfections, adapt their message to receivers, improve language and listening skills, question preconceptions, and plan for feedback.

> Using words precisely and listening carefully help reduce miscommunication.

think they are wonderful with people because they talk well. They don't realize that being wonderful with people means *listening* well."[23]

Questioning your preconceptions. Successful communicators continually examine their assumptions, biases, and prejudices. The more you pay attention to subtleties and know "where you're coming from" when you encode and decode messages, the better you'll communicate. Employees of the City of Toronto recognized these subtleties when they realized that the characters used to spell Mayor Barbara Hall's name in Chinese meant to "pull a fence." Understanding that Asians might refer to the Mayor as the "fence puller," a contest was created to produce a strong sounding, positive name. The choice *Haw Parc Lai*—in which the first character means prosperity, the second, amber (a jewel symbolizing femininity), and the third, diligence and perseverance—is represented as follows.[24]

Similarly, in Richmond, British Columbia, Mayor Greg Halsey-Brandt's business card reads *Ho Sai Bun* ("knowledge of" or "keeper of" the universe) in Cantonese.[25]

Planning for feedback. Finally, effective communicators create an environment for useful feedback. In oral communication this means asking questions such as "Do you understand?" and "What questions do you have?" as well as encouraging listeners to repeat instructions or paraphrase ideas. For a listener it means providing feedback that describes rather than evaluates. And in written communication it means asking questions and providing access: *Do you have my telephone number in case you have questions?* or *Please jot your answers down on my letter and return it in the enclosed envelope.*

■ Functions and Forms of Organizational Communication

Within organizations the process of communication is even more sensitive. Potential problems are created whenever individuals interact. Further complicating the process are barriers created by the atmosphere and management levels in an organization. Some barriers are beyond your control, while others are not. Understanding the functions, forms, and flow of organizational communication will help you surmount its barriers.

Functions

On the job you'll communicate internally and externally. Internally, you'll be exchanging ideas with superiors, co-workers, and subordinates. When these messages must be written, you'll probably choose E-mail or a printed memorandum, such as the Canadian Airlines memo shown in Figure 1.3. When you are communicating externally with customers, suppliers, government, and the public, you will generally send letters on company stationery, such as Canadian's letter also shown in Figure 1.3. Specifically, you'll be communicating to:

Organizational communication—both internal and external—has three basic functions: to inform, to persuade, and to promote goodwill.

Internal Functions

- Issue and clarify procedures and policies

- Inform management of progress

- Persuade employees or management to make changes or improvements

- Coordinate activities and provide assistance

- Evaluate, compliment, reward, and discipline employees

- Get to know someone

External Functions

- Answer inquiries about products or services

- Persuade customers to buy products or services

- Clarify supplier's specifications and quality requirements

- Issue credit and collect bills

- Respond to regulatory agencies

- Promote a favourable image of the organization

In all these tasks employees and managers use a number of communication skills: reading, listening, speaking, and writing. As a student, you have already begun to develop these skills. If, however, you're like most business undergraduates, you realize that you need to improve these skills to the proficiency level required for success in today's competitive job market. This book and this course will give you practical advice on how to do that.

Now, look back over the preceding lists of internal and external functions of communication in organizations. Although there appear to be a large number of diverse business communication functions, they can be summarized in three simple categories, as Figure 1.4 shows: (1) to inform, (2) to persuade, or (3) to promote goodwill.

Forms

Communication is needed in many organizational functions, both internal and external. The forms of that communication may be oral or, more often, written.

Organizational communication may be oral (two-way) or written (one-way).

In small businesses much communication can be oral, often face-to-face. As organizations grow in complexity and number of members, however, more messages must be written. When Stephen Jobs and Steve Wozniak launched the enormously successful Apple Computer company in a garage, for example, they could talk to each other about their production ideas and marketing plans. But as the company ballooned into a computer colossus employing thousands, their forms of communication had to change. They were forced to use more impersonal means of exchanging information, such as memos, reports, bulletins, and newsletters. Their business also required them to keep written records for legal purposes. Although they didn't lose face-to-face contact totally, they could no longer run their business with oral communication only.

FIGURE 1.3 ■ Internal and External Forms of Communication

Memo   Canadi▸n

DATE: August 9, 1996

TO: Bob Markum

FROM: Tim Smith   *TS*

SUBJECT: NEWS RELEASE ABOUT CALGARY CREW BASE

Enclosed is a draft of the news release announcing the Calgary crew base.
Please look it over and make any changes you like. We've tried to keep it short
and to the point. Captain Bill Baker has agreed to do the media conference
late Tuesday morning since your schedule is so tight.

Because *Info Canadian* is close to its deadline and would like to run a brief
story on the announcement, I ll need your response by August 12. Thanks for
your help.

Memorandums typically deliver written messages within organizations. They use a standard format and are concise and direct.

Canadi▸n

EXECUTIVE OFFICE

March 4, 1996

Ms. Christie Bonner
23 Dunkirk Drive
Hamilton, ON L8K 4W9

Dear Ms. Bonner:

For frequent international business travellers like you, Canadian Airlines is
pleased to introduce Club Empress, our enhanced international business class.

Beginning October 16, you will be able to experience the exceptional features
of our sleeper-style seat, which include extra armrest padding, electronic controls
for improved leg and lumbar support, and a headrest with forward tilt and
fully adjustable side wings for comfort and privacy when sleeping. In addition,
you will have your choice of six video and eight audio channels complete with
multi-lingual programming. Please find enclosed a copy of our Club Empress
brochure and more information about our new service.

We look forward to continuing to serve you well on your next flight to Hong Kong.

Sincerely,

Richard Peter

Richard Peter
Corporate Communications

enc

Canadian Airlines International Ltd.
Suite 2800, 700 - 2nd Street S.W., Calgary, Alberta, Canada T2P 2W2 Telephone (403) 294-2000

Letters on company stationery are written to outsiders. Notice how this one builds a solid relationship between Canadian Airlines and a satisfied customer.

FIGURE 1.4 ■ The Functions of Business Communication

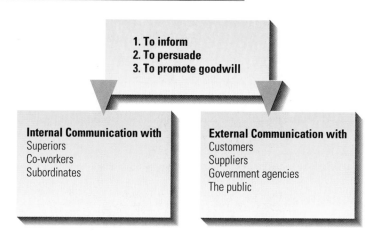

Oral communication. Probably the best way to transmit information meaningfully is orally. This communication form has many advantages. For one thing, it minimizes misunderstandings because the communicators can immediately ask questions to clarify uncertainties. For another, it enables communicators to see each other's facial expressions and hear voice inflections, further improving communication. Oral communication is also an efficient way to develop consensus when many people must be consulted. Finally, most of us enjoy face-to-face communication because it's easy and natural and promotes friendships.

> **Oral communication minimizes misunderstandings, provides immediate feedback, permits consensus, and promotes friendships.**

The main disadvantages of oral communication are that it produces no written record, sometimes wastes time, and may be inconvenient. When people meet face-to-face or speak on the telephone, someone's work has to be interrupted. And how many of us can limit a conversation to just business? Nevertheless, oral communication has many interpersonal and organizational uses, summarized in Figure 1.5.

Written communication. Written communication is impersonal in the sense that the two people cannot see or hear each other and cannot provide immediate feedback. Most forms of business communication—including announcements, memos, E-mail, faxes, letters, newsletters, reports, proposals, and manuals—fall into this category.

> **Written communication provides a permanent record, permits careful organization, is convenient and economical, and can be easily distributed.**

Organizations rely on written communication for many reasons. It provides a permanent record, a necessity in these times of increasing litigation and extensive government regulation. Writing out an idea instead of delivering it orally enables you to develop an organized, well-considered message. Written documents are also convenient. They can be composed and read when the schedules of both communicators permit, and they can be reviewed if necessary.

Written messages have drawbacks, of course. They require careful preparation and regard for their effect on the audience. Words spoken in conversation may soon be forgotten, but words committed to hard or soft copy become a public record—and sometimes an embarrassing one. Former IBM chairman John Akers, for example, must have had second thoughts about his E-mail memo blasting managers for complacency and product defects. When leaked to

FIGURE 1.5 ■ Forms of Organizational Communication

Oral, Two-way Communication	Written, One-way Communication
Form	**Form**
Phone call	Announcement
Conversation	Memo, E-mail, fax
Interview	Letter
Meeting	Report, proposal
Conference	Newsletter
Advantages	**Advantages**
Immediate feedback	Permanent record
Nonverbal clues	Convenience
Warm feeling	Economy
Forceful impact	Careful message
Multiple input	Easy distribution

the press, the memo shook up the financial world and damaged IBM's image and morale.

Another drawback to written messages is that they are more difficult to prepare. They demand good writing ability, and that ability is not inborn. The good news is that writing can be learned. Because at least 90 percent of all business transactions involve written correspondence,[26] and because writing is so important to your business success, you will be receiving special instruction in becoming a good writer.

In many organizations E-mail is rapidly replacing printed memos. Messages are transmitted almost instantaneously within the company or across the world. Mario Juarez at Microsoft admits that he has a love/hate relationship with his E-mail. He's thankful that he can be in touch with almost anyone in the company immediately. The disadvantage, though, is that he receives over 100 messages every day, resulting in what he calls "absolute information overload." An example of one of his E-mail messages appears in Figure 1.6. You'll learn more about E-mail and techniques for using it in Chapter 7.

In selecting a communication form, consider audience, organization, need for documentation, need for feedback, and level of formality needed.

Selection of form. To choose the best communication form, ask yourself several questions:

- *Does this message require a written record?* If so, use E-mail or a memo to send an interoffice message. Use a letter to communicate with a customer or other individual outside the organization. Write a report if considerable data are involved.

- *Do I need immediate feedback or multiple input?* Telephone calls, E-mail, or personal visits provide the fastest responses when immediate feedback is required. Group meetings and conferences are excellent for distributing information. They also work well when brainstorming for ideas and for building group consensus.

- *Does this message require careful organization and supporting documentation?* Complicated data or intricate procedures should be communicated in the form of long memos or reports, accompanied by visual aids.

FIGURE 1.6 ■ Sample E-mail Message

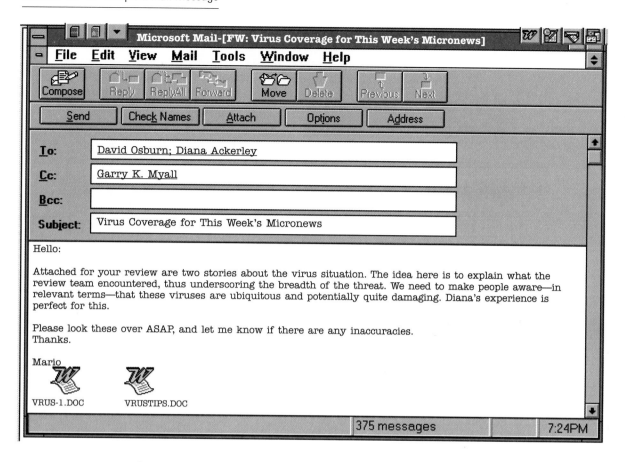

- *How quickly does the message need to be delivered?* Urgent news often requires oral transmission. More routine messages can be sent in memos or letters.

- *How large and how far away is the audience?* A supervisor announcing a lunch-time fitness seminar to three employees in the same room could tell them personally. The same message aimed at 300 employees in four departments would require a less personal form of communication, such as E-mail, a memo, or a newsletter announcement.

- *How easily will my audience accept this message?* If management wants to convince employees that a new health care plan is better than the current plan, it may elect to present this message in small group sessions led by a compelling speaker. Persuasion and selling are most effective with face-to-face communication.

- *Do I need to show empathy, friendliness, or other feelings?* Face-to-face conversations, of course, allow communicators to express the most feeling—in giving both positive and negative news. When delivering bad news, such as criticizing or firing employees, many managers believe that the news should be delivered in person. When praising or giving a pat on the back, they feel that a written message shows thoughtfulness.

FIGURE 1.7 ■ Formal Communication Channels

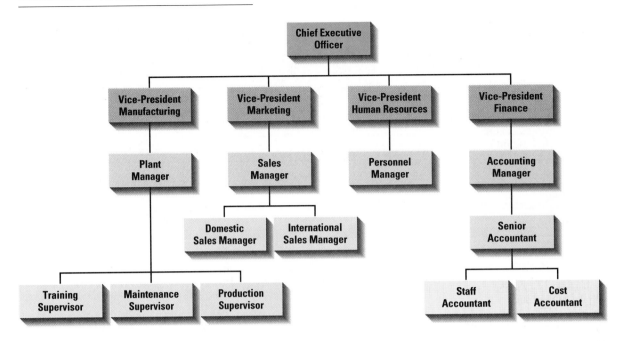

- *Does this message need the appearance of formality?* Some documents, such as proposals, contracts, and bylaws, gain credibility by looking formal. Disciplinary fact-finding and grievance-processing require formal documents. Sometimes, routine messages, such as ones granting credit or acknowledging orders for products, become more effective when conveyed in a formal, personally written letter rather than an informal postcard or an all-purpose form letter.

■ Flow of Organizational Communication

Organizational communication may flow through formal or informal channels.

Selecting the best form of communication demands some understanding of how messages and information flow through organizations. There are both formal and informal communication channels. Dynamic, robust organizations like Microsoft Corporation use both kinds of channels to encourage an open communication environment. A free exchange of information helps organizations solve problems, cut costs, serve the public better, and take full advantage of today's knowledge workers.

Formal channels. Formal channels of communication generally follow an organization's hierarchy of command, as shown in Figure 1.7. Information about policies and procedures originates with executives and flows down through managers to supervisors and finally to lower-level employees. Many corporations have official communication policies that encourage regular open communication, suggest means for achieving it, and spell out responsibilities. Whether an organization has developed such a communication policy or not, official information among workers typically flows through formal channels in three directions: downward, upward, and horizontally.

Downward flow. Information flowing downward generally moves from decision-makers, including the CEO and managers, through the chain of command to the workers. This information includes job plans, policies, instructions, and procedures. Managers also provide feedback about employee performance and instil a sense of mission to achieve the organization's goals. One problem in downward communication is distortion resulting from long lines of communication. If, for example, the CEO in Figure 1.7 wanted to change an accounting procedure, she or he would probably not send a memo directly to the staff or cost accountants who would implement the change. Instead, the CEO would relay the idea through proper formal channels—from the vice-president for finance, to the accounting manager, to the senior accountant, and so on—until the message reached the affected employees. Obviously, the longer the lines of communication, the greater the chance that a message will be distorted. Indeed, a study of over 100 businesses where messages were transmitted through five levels of management revealed that only 20 percent of a given message reached its target audience.[27] Many of today's companies have "re-engineered" themselves into smaller operating units and work teams. Thus, long lines of communication and layers of management are unnecessary.

Upward flow. Information flowing upward provides feedback from nonmanagement employees to management. Subordinate employees describe their progress in completing tasks, report roadblocks encountered, and suggest methods for improving efficiency. Channels for upward communication include memos, reports, departmental meetings, and suggestion systems. Ideally, the heaviest flow of information should be upward with information being fed steadily to decision-makers who can react and adjust quickly.

Horizontal flow. Lateral channels transmit information horizontally among workers at the same level, such as between the training supervisor and maintenance supervisor in Figure 1.7. These channels enable individuals to coordinate tasks, share information, solve problems, and resolve conflicts. Horizontal communication takes place through personal contact, E-mail, memos, and meetings. However, most organizations have few established regular channels for the horizontal exchange of information.

Informal channels. Not all the information in an organization passes through formal channels; often, it travels through informal channels called the *grapevine*. These channels are based on social relationships in which individuals talk about work when they are having lunch, jogging, golfing, or riding the elevators. Alert managers find the grapevine an excellent source of information about employee morale and problems. Employees using the grapevine also consider it valuable for two reasons: (1) they can get information without having to admit formally that they need it, and (2) they can think out loud about their problems, thus increasing their self-confidence and problem-solving ability.[28]

Researchers studying communication flow within organizations have revealed some unexpected facts about the grapevine. For one thing they have discovered that the grapevine can be a primary source of information for members of an organization. Some studies suggest that as much as two-thirds of an employee's information comes through informal channels.[29]

Lunching outside the office means a chance to sit in the sun and perhaps exchange news. Information transmitted among employees over informal communication channels travels quickly but may be incomplete. Studies show that workers prefer to learn company news from official, formal channels rather than through the grapevine.

Noncontroversial information transmitted over the grapevine can be surprisingly accurate.

Another unanticipated finding is that the grapevine is accurate. Because almost all the information transmitted over the grapevine is oral, you'd expect it to be riddled with mistakes and distortions. Surprisingly, though, many researchers have found that, for noncontroversial company information transmitted over the grapevine, 75 to 90 percent of the details of messages were accurate.[30] Moreover, news travelling over the grapevine is transmitted quickly: one specialist found that it was the fastest channel for sending messages to employees.[31] News of a position opening up in a department, for example, often reaches other workers long before an official announcement travels down through formal channels.

■ Barriers to Organizational Communication

Both formal and informal communication in most organizations is less than perfect. Before we examine ways to improve it, let's pinpoint six specific barriers to organizational communication.

Barriers to organizational communication include a closed communication climate, a top-heavy hierarchy, filtering, lack of trust, rivalry, and power and status issues.

Closed communication climate. An organization can enhance or inhibit communication by the environment it creates. In a closed climate, employees receive little organizational news. They don't know what's expected of them, and they feel that no one cares about them or listens to them. In the worst of such organizations, information is hoarded by top management, as if informing subordinates would weaken the control of management. Such a climate acts as a powerful barrier to communication. In an open communication climate, like that at Microsoft, management values its employees and appreciates their need for organizational information. Hence, Microsoft publishes regular employee newsletters, keeping employees informed of organizational goings-on. Moreover, Bill Gates has established an environment encouraging feedback especially through E-mail. Because they feel free to communicate upward with a sense of influence, employees are part of the decision-making process.

Top-heavy organizational structure. Long lines of communication result when an organization has a top-heavy, multilevel structure. Because messages travelling upward or downward must pass through many managerial levels, the result is often distortion, delays in delivery, and hostility between senders and receivers. Each layer of management creates a roadblock to efficient communication. Assume, for example, that Emma in Customer Service has a great idea for improving the company's product-return procedures. She may never suggest that idea if she knows that she must first submit it to her supervisor, who must then go through four more levels of management before the suggestion reaches a person who has the power to act on it.

Filtering. *Filtering* refers to the process of shaping, shortening, or lengthening messages as they travel through the communication network. Everyone who processes a message views it selectively through his or her own unique frame of reference. As a result, messages are *levelled* (some details are lost), *condensed* (facts are simplified), *sharpened* (selected details are highlighted), *assimilated* (confusions are clarified and interpreted), and *embellished* (details are added).[32] Filtering is most prevalent in organizations with long communication chains.

> **Filtering can cause distortion when messages are levelled, condensed, sharpened, assimilated, or embellished.**

Lack of trust. Employees who trust their managers are likely to communicate openly. Employees cease trusting managers if they feel they are being tricked, manipulated, criticized, or treated impersonally. Of course, establishing trust is a reciprocal process: managers who trust their employees will receive trust in return and will believe that subordinates have the desire and ability to perform their jobs responsibly. This kind of trust goes a long way toward reducing communication barriers.

Rivalry. Employees competing for recognition and advancement may misrepresent or conceal information from one another and from management. They are reluctant to reveal information because they fear it might benefit a fellow employee at their expense. Thus, instead of speaking truthfully, rivals put a spin or twist on facts in an effort to protect their own interests and turf. James might, for example, discount, criticize, or misrepresent Sue's proposal to expedite customer orders. Although her plan has merit, he fears she may beat him out for the next promotion.

Unethical behaviour resulting from rivalry can create barriers that distort the communication process. The Ethics box on page 26 contains suggestions for dealing with ethical dilemmas.

Power and status. The very fact that one person (the boss) has power in an organization while all others (the subordinates) lack that power constitutes a potential roadblock to open communication. Many bosses are afraid to reveal difficulties, losses, or other conditions that make them look weak. At the same time subordinates avoid disclosing information about lack of progress, frustrations, or disagreements among workers. They may even colour their reports to convey the appearance of achievement.

Surmounting Organizational Barriers

Facing stiff global competition, many organizations now recognize that improved internal communication is a key to better employee performance and increased productivity. As *Fortune* magazine reports, "Internal communications

FOUR ETHICAL GUIDELINES BUSINESS COMMUNICATORS SHOULD KNOW

Pressures on people and on organizations today can create dilemmas that require, in addition to communication skills, an ability to make ethical decisions. Often, the dilemmas have no clear-cut right or wrong answers.

Assume that Carolyn Song and you are competing for a promotion to regional manager in Surrey, B.C. In the past year Carolyn has been quite successful at her work. Although you acknowledge that Carolyn is doing a good job, you have been with the company longer and believe you deserve the position. Moreover, you feel threatened by her; and frankly, you don't like her. This promotion is important to you not only professionally but personally: your elderly parents live in the Surrey area, and you want to be close to help them out.

One day you happen to meet an old friend who has known Carolyn for some time. Over a cup of coffee you learn that Carolyn never graduated from the University of British Columbia, as stated on her résumé. In fact, she never attended university at all.

What should you do? Say nothing and, in effect, allow Carolyn to be rewarded for lying? Head straight to the vice president and expose the truth—which might, at the same time, conveniently eliminate a rival? Each action has possible consequences that make the decision difficult. Frequently, say ethicists, the "right" action is the one you can live with. But how do you arrive at that decision? Here are four simple guidelines that can help any business communicator make ethical choices:

- **Visualize the desired outcome.** What would you like to see happen as a result of resolving this issue? Will your choice produce the goal you seek?

- **Weigh the interests of all stakeholders.** Who will be affected by your choice? Consider the consequences for you and your fellow employees, your boss, the organization, your family, and the community. What effect will it have on Carolyn? Can you live with the consequences? Whose interests are most important?

- **Take the public-scrutiny test.** How would you feel about revealing your choice to your colleagues, friends, or family?

- **Balance your professional and personal goals.** Consider each choice and its effect on your career. Also consider its personal effects. Is there a choice that reconciles your professional goals with your personal values?

Career Track Application

Determine three or four actions you could take regarding Carolyn's dark secret. Then, evaluate each choice according to the four guidelines here. Be prepared to discuss your final choice and the reasoning behind it in class. Additional ethical guidelines will be presented in Chapter 3.

—talk back and forth within the organization, up and down the hierarchy—may well be more important to a company's success than external communications." Free-flowing information in an organization enables management "to identify and attack problems fast, say, when customer service representatives first get an earful about some quality glitch, or sales[people] in the field encounter a new competitor."[33] Open lines of communication also create an atmosphere of trust and employee goodwill. Here are specific ways in which organizations can reduce barriers to communication.

Encouraging an open environment for interaction and feedback. The climate an organization cultivates greatly influences communication. At Microsoft small groups of employees are invited to talk with managers. At Chrysler, Lee Iacocca used to hold "town hall" meetings for 175 randomly selected employees. "I talk for five minutes, and then they get an hour and a half to knock my head in," he said.[34] Agropur CEO Claude Menard oversees 1700 staff and 24 production sites in Quebec and Ontario. As it is a cooperative, communication with members is essential. Menard meets with groups of employees to plan organizational strategy and pass on information.[35] Sheelagh Whittaker, president of EDS Canada, recognizes the value of a sense of humour in the business world. Her merriment, which can cause sombre boardroom members to chuckle, is what she calls her "highly developed sense of the audacious." The effect is an atmosphere where a great deal of work gets done.[36] Irwin Toy has a unique and successful way to encourage interaction and feedback: it meets with a special group of shareholders—children—three or four times a year to collect their opinions. The children attend a "junior shareholders" meeting and then get a chance to play with toys and rate them. The plan successfully blends the interests of the junior shareholders with the interests of the company.[37]

Flattening the organizational structure. Businesses today are streamlining their operations and eliminating layers of unnecessary management, thus shortening lines of communication. Toy-maker Mattel transformed itself from an "out-of-control money loser" into a record-breaking money-maker by taking the advice of its employees and cutting six layers from its organizational hierarchy.[38] "One of the most effective ways of building responsiveness into organizations is to eliminate layers of management," says Andrew S. Grove, CEO of computer chip-maker Intel Corporation. "With fewer levels," he continues, "information flows more naturally and problems get solved faster."[39] In addition, because messages travel shorter distances, there is less distortion.

Promoting horizontal communication. Horizontal communication builds bonds among employees, boosts morale, decreases turnover, and enriches the organization through exchange of ideas. At Lucasfilms, producers of the *Star Wars* trilogy and other films, managers felt that there was too little horizontal communication among editors, cinematographers, and artists. They opened the channels by forming softball teams limited to one member from any one department. This forced individuals from different departments to start talking to one another.[40]

Establishing rumour-control centres. It's been estimated that at least 33 million fresh rumours circulate daily in American industries.[41] Many large organizations use telephone or voice mail rumour-control systems to deal with inaccurate or injurious rumours. Employees can inquire anonymously about rumours at a central office. If the truth is known, callers learn immediately; if facts must be verified, employees can call back later to hear updates.

Providing ample information through formal channels. Studies show that most employees would rather receive company news through formal channels than by the grapevine.[42] The grapevine becomes less important in organizations where employees are regularly informed of company news. If employees receive a steady flow of information through meetings, newsletters, and announcements, unofficial channels carry only personal tidbits, such as who's dating whom. Recognizing the power of internal communication in today's competitive markets, increasing numbers of managers are talking candidly with their employees, encouraging them to contribute ideas. Enlightened executives are using E-mail, videos, and satellite hookups to disseminate news of the organization.

Figure 1.8 summarizes two groups of obstacles that can sabotage interpersonal and organizational communication efforts.

> **Barriers to organizational communication are greatly reduced when managers seek employee feedback.**

> **Reducing layers of management shortens lines of communication.**

> **Horizontal communication improves morale and enriches an organization.**

> **Employees prefer to learn of organization news through official, formal channels.**

FIGURE 1.8 ■ Barriers to the Communication Process

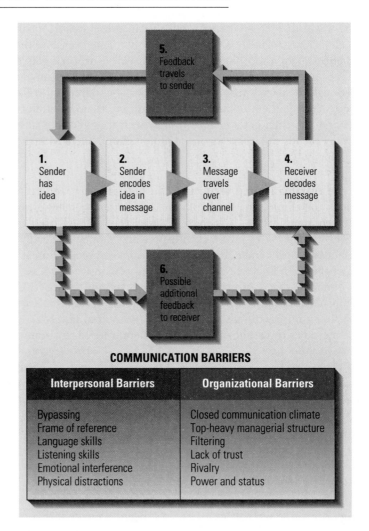

COMMUNICATION BARRIERS

Interpersonal Barriers	Organizational Barriers
Bypassing	Closed communication climate
Frame of reference	Top-heavy managerial structure
Language skills	Filtering
Listening skills	Lack of trust
Emotional interference	Rivalry
Physical distractions	Power and status

Strengthening Your Communication Skills

Communication skills—reading, speaking, listening, writing—can be learned.

You've just taken a brief look at the process of communication, its barriers, and its operation within organizations. This overview is the first step in strengthening your communication skills—your ability to read, listen, speak, and write. In addition to helping you feel confident in your personal life, these abilities are exceptionally important in your professional life. Whether you get the job you seek and the promotions you deserve depend on many factors, some of which you can't control. But one thing that you do control is how well you communicate. John Bryan, a respected CEO, recognized this when he said that communication skills are "about 99 percent developed." They are not inborn. Bryan contends that "the ability to construct a succinct memo, one that concentrates on the right issues, and the ability to make a presentation to an audience—these are skills that can be taught to almost anyone."[43]

Communication skills can certainly be learned. This book and this course will help you become a better communicator by studying techniques, observing models, and practising. Practice, of course, is most valuable when accompanied by appropriate feedback. You need someone like your instructor to comment on your work.

We've designed this book to provide you with the principles, process, models, and practice you need to become a successful business communicator and knowledge worker in today's new world of work.

▪ Summary of Learning Goals

1. **Explain the importance of communication skills for knowledge workers in the new world of work.** As businesses continue to downsize and decentralize, many are giving their employees more access to information and expecting them to participate in decision-making. Much of the world of work now revolves around generating, processing, and exchanging information. Knowledge workers in this new work environment must have excellent communication skills to ensure their own success and that of their organization.

2. **Describe the process of communication.** The sender encodes (chooses) words or symbols to express an idea. The message is sent verbally through a channel (such as a letter, E-mail, or a telephone call) or is expressed nonverbally, perhaps with gestures or body language. "Noise"—such as loud sounds, misspelled words, or other distractions—may interfere with the transmission. The receiver decodes (interprets) the message and attempts to make sense of it. The receiver responds with feedback, informing the sender of the effectiveness of the message. The goal of communication is the transmission of meaning so that a receiver understands a message as intended by the sender.

3. **Discuss barriers to interpersonal communication.** *Bypassing* causes miscommunication because people have different meanings for the words they use. One's *frame of reference* creates a filter through which all ideas are screened, sometimes causing distortion and lack of objectivity. *Weak language skills* as well as *poor listening skills* impair communication efforts. *Emotional interference*—joy, fear, anger, and so forth—hampers the sending and receiving of messages. *Physical distractions*—noisy surroundings, faulty acoustics, and so forth—can disrupt oral communication.

4. **Identify methods of overcoming barriers to interpersonal communication.** You can reduce or overcome many barriers to interpersonal communication if you (a) realize that the communication process is imperfect, (b) adapt your message to the receiver, (c) improve your language and listening skills, (d) question your preconceptions, and (e) plan for feedback.

5. **Analyze the purposes and forms of organizational communication.** The internal purposes of communication include issuing and clarifying procedures and policies, informing management of progress, persuading others to make changes or improvements, coordinating activities and giving assistance, interacting with employees, and getting to know people. The external purposes of communication include answering inquiries about products or services, persuading customers to buy products or services, clarifying suppliers' specifications and quality requirements, issuing credit, collecting bills, responding to regulatory agencies, and promoting a positive image of the organization. Probably the best form of communication is face-to-face discussion. More common, though, is written or electronic communication.

6. **Discuss the flow of organizational communication.** Formal channels of communication generally follow an organization's hierarchy of command. Downward flow carries policies, procedures, and directives from management to employees. Upward flow provides feedback to management. Horizontal flow transmits information among workers at the same level. Informal channels of communication, such as the grapevine, deliver unofficial news—both personal and organizational—among friends and co-workers.

7. **Describe barriers to organizational communication.** A *closed communication climate* prevents the free flow of information between management and subordinates. *Top-heavy organization* inhibits communication because messages must flow through many levels of management. *Filtering* causes distortion as receivers screen messages through their own perceptions. *Lack of trust* makes communication impossible. *Rivalry* and competition for recognition may cause people to distort or conceal essential information. *Power and status* can interfere with clear communication when, for example, the boss avoids admitting poor judgment or when employees are silent about circumstances that reflect poorly on them.

8. **Name methods of surmounting barriers to organizational communication.** Many barriers to effective communication can be overcome if an organization (a) encourages an open environment for interaction and feedback among all employees, (b) flattens the organizational structure by removing some levels of management, (c) promotes horizontal communication so that employees know what other employees are doing, (d) establishes rumour-control mechanisms to keep employees fully informed, and (e) provides ample organizational information directly from management to employees.

CHAPTER REVIEW

1. What positive effect has corporate "delayering," downsizing, and decentralizing had on many employees today? (Goal 1)

2. What are knowledge workers? Why are they hired? (Goal 1)

3. Define *communication,* and explain its most critical factor. (Goal 2)

4. Describe five steps in the process of communication. (Goal 2)

5. How can senders encourage and receivers provide effective feedback? (Goal 2)

6. List six barriers to interpersonal communication. Be prepared to discuss each. (Goal 3)

7. Name five things that you could do to reduce barriers in your communication. (Goal 4)

8. What are the three main purposes of organizational communication? (Goal 5)

9. Name five common myths about business writing. (Goal 5)

10. What are the advantages of oral communication? (Goal 5)

11. What are the advantages of written communication? (Goal 5)

12. What are the chief differences between formal and informal channels of organizational communication? (Goal 6)

13. In an organization what kinds of information flow downward? (Goal 6)

14. List six organizational barriers to communication. Be prepared to discuss each. (Goal 7)

15. List five means of overcoming barriers to organizational communication. (Goal 8)

DISCUSSION

1. Comment on the complaint of some companies that the more information provided to their employees, the more the employees want. (Goals 7, 8)

2. Recall a time when you had a problem as a result of poor communication. Analyze the causes and possible remedies for the problem. (Goal 2)

3. Research shows that the grapevine often carries accurate information. Why, then, is it considered unreliable? (Goal 6)

4. Describe the communication climate in an organization to which you belonged or for which you worked. (Goals 6, 7, 8)

5. **Ethical Issue:** What would you do if you heard through the grapevine that a fellow manager with whom you were competing for a promotion was suspected of falsifying an efficiency report so that his department's record looked better than it really was?

ACTIVITIES

1.1 Communication Assessment: How Do You Stack Up? (Goal 1)

You know more about yourself than anyone else does. That makes you the best person to assess your present communication skills. Take an honest look at your current skills and rank them using the following chart. How well you communicate will be an important factor in your future career—particularly if you are promoted into management. For each skill, circle the number from 1 (indicating low ability) to 5 (indicating high ability) that best describes your assessment of yourself.

Writing Skills	Low				High
1. Possess basic spelling, grammar, and punctuation skills	1	2	3	4	5
2. Am familiar with proper formats for business memos, letters, and reports	1	2	3	4	5
3. Can analyze a writing problem and quickly outline a plan for solving it	1	2	3	4	5
4. Can organize data coherently and logically	1	2	3	4	5
5. Can evaluate a document to determine its probable success	1	2	3	4	5
Reading Skills					
1. Am familiar with specialized vocabulary in my field as well as general vocabulary	1	2	3	4	5
2. Can concentrate despite distractions	1	2	3	4	5
3. Am willing to look up definitions whenever necessary	1	2	3	4	5
4. Can move from recreational to serious reading	1	2	3	4	5
5. Can read and comprehend college- and university-level material	1	2	3	4	5

Speaking Skills	**Low**				**High**
1. Feel at ease when talking to friends	1	2	3	4	5
2. Feel at ease speaking before a group of people	1	2	3	4	5
3. Can adapt my presentation to the audience	1	2	3	4	5
4. Am confident that I am pronouncing and using words correctly	1	2	3	4	5
5. Sense that I have credibility when I make a presentation	1	2	3	4	5

Listening Skills					
1. Spend at least half the time listening during conversations	1	2	3	4	5
2. Am able to concentrate on a speaker's words despite distractions	1	2	3	4	5
3. Can summarize a speaker's ideas and anticipate what's coming during pauses	1	2	3	4	5
4. Provide feedback, like nodding, paraphrasing, and asking questions	1	2	3	4	5
5. Listen with the expectation of gaining new ideas and information	1	2	3	4	5

Now analyze your scores. Where are you strongest? Weakest? How do you think outsiders would rate you on these skills and traits? Are you satisfied with your present skills? The first step to improvement is recognition of a need. Put a check mark next to the five traits you feel you should begin working on immediately.

1.2   Memo (Goal 1)

Write a memo of introduction to your instructor. Use this format:

TO:	Title, Instructor's name	DATE: Present
FROM:	Your name	
SUBJECT:	INTRODUCTION AND COMMUNICATION ASSESSMENT	

Begin your memo by describing your major and your entry-level and long-term employment goals. What communication skills do you think will be required of you when you reach your ultimate career position? Discuss your present strengths and weaknesses. Begin your final paragraph with "In addition to attending school, I like to ..." Describe some activities you enjoy.

1.3   Want Ads (Goal 1)

Conduct your own survey of advertisements for jobs in your field. Consult the weekend edition of a large newspaper. How many of the ads mention communication skills? What job tasks do the advertisements describe? How many of them require communication skills? What conclusions would you draw? Clip several ads that seem especially interesting or promising and bring them to class for discussion.

1.4   Information Flow (Goal 6)

Consider an organization to which you belong or a business where you've worked. How did members learn what was going on in the organization? What kind of information flowed through formal channels? What were those channels? What kind of information was delivered through informal channels? Was the grapevine as accurate as official channels? How could the flow of information be improved?

1.5   Communication Process (Goal 2)

Review the communication process and its barriers as described in the text. Now imagine that you are the boss in an organization where you've worked and you wish to announce a new policy aimed at improving customer service. Examine the entire communication process from sender to feedback. How will the message be encoded? What assumptions must you make about your audience? What channel is best? How can you encourage feedback? What noise may interfere with transmission? What barriers should you expect? How can you overcome them? Your instructor may ask you to write a memo describing your answers to these questions.

1.6 Communication Forms (Goal 5)

What is the best form for delivering information in the following situations? You may suggest a personal letter, memo, company newsletter, telephone call, face-to-face conversation, or some other form of communication. Be ready to discuss your reasons.

a. Informing many groups that your company cannot allow them to tour your bottling plant this summer because of remodelling

b. Asking your boss for permission to attend a two-day seminar to improve your job skills

c. Launching a major company campaign to encourage employees to submit more ideas for improving the way they do their jobs

d. Informing the winners of Employee-of-the-Month awards

e. Checking the references of a job candidate

f. Comparing the cost of purchasing diskettes from three local vendors

1.7 Document Analysis: Barriers to Communication (Goals 3, 7)

The following memo was actually written in a large business organization. Comment on its effectiveness, tone, and potential barriers to communication.

TO: All Departmental Personnel

SUBJECT: FRIDAY P.M. CLEAN-UP

Every Friday afternoon starting at 3 p.m. there is suppose to be a departmental clean-up. This practice will commence this Friday and continue until otherwise specified.

All CC162 employees will partake in this endeavour. This means not only cleaning his own area, but contributing to the cleaning of the complete department.

Thank you for your cooperation.

1.8 Communication Barriers (Goals 3, 8)

For each of the following situations, what interpersonal and/or organizational barriers might the message senders anticipate? How could the senders overcome these barriers?

a. During a recession an executive with an MBA from Queen's University must write to all employees persuading them to agree to temporary wage cuts.

b. An accountant wishes to explain to the marketing department why it must report monthly sales figures differently.

c. An administrative assistant has been asked to organize and publicize a departmental surprise party for the boss.

d. You try to summarize an instructor's lecture for a friend who was absent.

e. You are in charge of writing the company's annual report, which will be read by stockholders, suppliers, customers, management, and others.

1.9 Feedback (Goals 2, 6)

One of the most difficult tasks in communication is finding out if you were understood. What advice could you give a manager regarding feedback? Your instructor may ask you to write a one-page essay explaining your ideas.

1.10 Communication Failures (Goals 2, 3, 4)

Communication is not successful unless the receiver understands the message as the sender meant it. Analyze the following examples of communication failures. What went wrong?

a. A supervisor issued the following announcement: "Effective immediately the charge for copying services in Repro will be raised ½ to 2 cents each." Receivers scratched their heads.

b. The pilot of a military airplane about to land decided that the runway was too short. He shouted to his engineer, "Takeoff power!" The engineer turned off the engines; the plane crashed.

c. The following statements actually appeared in letters of application for an advertised job opening. One applicant wrote, "Enclosed is my résumé in response to Saturday's *Calgary Herald*." Another wrote, "Enclosed is my résumé in response to my search for an editorial/creative position." Still another wrote, "My experience in the production of newsletters, magazines, directories, and on-line data bases puts me head and shoulders above the crowd of applicants you have no doubtedly been inundated with."

d. The following sign in English appeared in an Austrian hotel that catered to skiers: "Not to perambulate the corridors in the hours of repose in the boots of ascension."

CLUE REVIEW 1

Each chapter includes an exercise based on Appendix A, "Competent Language Usage Essentials (CLUE)." This appendix is a business communicator's condensed guide to language usage, covering 50 of the most used, and abused, language elements. It also includes a list of 150 frequently misspelled words and a short summary review of some confusing words. The following exercise is packed with errors based on concepts and spelling words from the appendix. If you are rusty on these language essentials, spend some time studying the guidelines and examples in Appendix A. Then, test your skills with the chapter CLUE exercises. You will find the corrections for these exercises after Appendix D. Remember, these exercises contain only usage and spelling words from Appendix A.

On a separate sheet, edit the following sentences to correct faults in grammar, punctuation, spelling, and word use.

1. After he checked many statements our Accountant found the error in colume 2 of the balance sheet.

2. Because Mr. Lockwoods business owned considerable property. We were serprised by it's lack of liquid assets.

3. The mortgage company checked all property titles separatly, however it found no discrepancies.

4. When Ms. Khan finished the audit she wrote 3 letters. To appraise the owners of her findings.

5. Just between you and I whom do you think could have ordered all this stationary.

6. Assets and liabilities is what the 4 buyers want to see, consequently we are preparing this years statements.

7. Next spring my brother and myself plan to enroll in the following courses marketing english and history.

8. Dan felt that he had done good on the exam but he wants to do even better when it's given again next Fall.

9. Our records show that your end of the month balance was ninety-six dollars and 30 cents.

10. When the principle in the account grows to large we must make annual withdrawals.

Expanding Communication Power

L E A R N I N G   G O A L S

After studying this chapter, you should be able to

1 Explain the listening process and name four elements of good listening.

2 Name a three-step process as well as 10 specific techniques that improve listening effectiveness.

3 Discuss how meaning is created from nonverbal messages.

4 Apply specific techniques that enhance nonverbal communication skills.

5 Explain the importance of intercultural sensitivity and clarify pivotal North American cultural values.

6 Describe three key attitudes that help overcome cultural barriers.

7 Employ 10 specific procedures for adapting messages to intercultural audiences.

Bank of Montreal

When she first came to work at the Bank of Montreal in the mortgage department, Johanne Totta took her ability to communicate for granted. Of course, she was glad to be able to speak, listen, and negotiate well, but the graduate of McGill University's commerce program had no idea that it would shape her entire career. These days, communication describes the 38-year-old's full-time job—whether it be arbitrating a dispute between employees or speaking at an international conference.

As one of Canada's largest banks, which handles billions of dollars and employs some 37 000 people, the Bank of Montreal is first and foremost a service-oriented business. Its staff, from front-line bank tellers to loan officers, is its most important resource. When the bank realized that it was not making the most of its employees, it identified four areas that needed improvement—the advancement of women, of people with disabilities, of natives, and of visible minorities—then chose Johanne to head the project. "The people who had worked with me gave me very favourable reviews for my communication skills, particularly listening. That, combined with the fact that I had spent some time implementing policy, was the reason I was chosen for this position."

> *"Body language is one of the most important elements of communicating.... When you are sitting across a table from someone, it is almost as important as what they are saying."*

Now Johanne heads the program responsible for workplace equity. This requires extensive internal communication to understand the needs of the bank's employees, as well as external communication to share some of the ideas they have developed.

"Things have changed a great deal at the bank," she says. "Communication wasn't considered terribly important when I was hired—today it is recognized as essential. Now, as part of the interview process the bank uses Behavioural Focus Interviews which put the interviewee in a hypothetical situation that allows the bank to judge his or her skill in speaking, listening, and negotiating. We're placing a lot of emphasis on communicating now." Body language is also crucial in determining how well a new employee will communicate with customers. "Body language is one of the most important elements of communicating," Johanne explains. "When you are sitting across a table from someone, it is almost as important as what they are saying."

Johanne divides the kind of communicating required of her into three categories—external, internal, and individual—and has strategies for each. "On an individual level, I try to put myself in the other person's shoes, to listen through their ears. One thing I always do is treat each employee exactly the same, regardless of his or her status. Everyone brings a unique perspective to the table. By listening with an open mind to each, I can absorb all the complementary ideas and not miss anything."

Since her internal communication is necessarily two-way (she relies on the comments and responses of her co-workers to help her develop programs), Johanne's strategy is to determine what the employee wants. Hearing people out is crucial, she says. "I'll hear of an issue or dispute and go down to find out what it is all about: 95 percent of the time the solution is simply to talk it through. Sometimes the misunderstanding involves a cultural barrier and they may not even know it."

If she is dealing with people from a culture that is unfamiliar to her, Johanne tries to seek out information about the culture beforehand. One of the easiest things to do, she says, is call a friend or acquaintance of the cultural background with whom she feels comfortable enough to "ask stupid questions." And most important, she advises respect. "It's not a question of saying, 'I am dealing with Asians, I'll pick up a book on Asian culture.' It's the nuances that matter." For example, employees at the Bank of Montreal's Quebec offices address their superiors as "Monsieur" or "Madame." However, in less formal Toronto, bosses are called by their first names. Knowing that difference is the first step in accepting it, she explains.

Externally, Johanne's strategy is to understand her audience. Whether it is with customers or in a conference hall, she tailors her message with the audience's perspective in mind. "We make a real effort to understand the community we serve. Our customer base is diverse, and it helps us to know how we are perceived in the community. There is a link between understanding different cultures, actually employing people from those cultures, and creating good business opportunities."

Since she is often called upon to give speeches and lectures, Johanne's approach is to decide what message she wants to deliver, and then choose the clearest means of doing so. "I adapt my speeches to my audience. If I am speaking to a group of students, my delivery will be different from the same speech given to a board of trade. I find out who my audience is, and if necessary do a little background research, and adjust my delivery. The central message stays the same, but the references will change."

That skill was tested when the Canadian government sent Johanne overseas to help set the agenda for the United Nations Fourth World Conference on Women in Beijing. With an audience from around the world and very little time to prepare, Johanne could not do the kind of research she likes to do. Instead, she had to think on her feet; by paying close attention to the speeches before hers, she was able to incorporate some of their ideas and actually change the structure and direction of the debate. She was able to make a real contribution by concentrating on what was being said ... and *not* said.[1] ▪

Bank of Montreal's successful service-oriented approach is based on a willingness to get to know the different cultures that make up its diverse employee and customer base. By listening carefully and responding to its customers, the Bank of Montreal has been able to create good business opportunities.

Strengthening Listening Skills

Listening is a key personal and career skill.

Listening is one of the first requirements mentioned when employers describe crucial employment skills. Such skills open the door to promotion and career success. Effective listening powers require training and discipline. The good news, though, is that these skills and attitudes can be learned. By becoming a better listener, you may well be tapping into one of your greatest sources of success in your career and personal life.[2] This chapter discusses the listening process, barriers to effective listening, and suggestions for improving your ability to listen.

In Chapter 1 we examined the communication process primarily from the point of view of the sender, focusing on the importance of creating meaning in messages. Now we'll concentrate on the receiving end of communication, examining how to interpret meaning through verbal and nonverbal cues. In addition, this chapter describes how the already delicate process of communication becomes even more complex when we communicate with people from diverse backgrounds and cultures.

Most workers spend 30 to 45 percent of their communication time listening;[3] executives, however, devote 60 to 70 percent of this time to listening.[4] A new CEO at Apple Computer learned about some of his employees from the titles on their business cards. One card said "Hardware Wizard"; another announced "Software Evangelist"; still another proclaimed "Product Champion." After settling into his job, the new CEO decided that his title should reflect how he spent most of his time—"Chief Listener."[5]

Although executives and workers devote the bulk of their communication time to listening, research suggests that they're not very good at it. In fact, most of us are poor listeners. Some estimates suggest that only half the oral messages heard in a day are completely understood.[6] Experts say that we listen at only 25 percent efficiency. In other words, *we ignore, forget, distort, or misunderstand 75 percent of everything we hear.*

Reasons for inefficient listening include lack of training, competing sounds and stimuli, and the slowness of speech.

Such listening inefficiency may result from several factors. Lack of training is one significant reason. Few schools give as much emphasis to listening as to reading, speaking, and writing. In addition, our listening skills may be less than perfect because of the large number of competing sounds and stimuli in our lives that interfere with our concentration. Finally, we are inefficient listeners because of the slowness of speech. While most speakers talk at about 150 words per minute, listeners can process oral communication at over 400 words per minute. This lag time causes daydreaming, which in turn reduces listening efficiency.

Examining the process of listening, as well as its barriers, may shed some light on ways to improve your listening efficiency and retention.

The Listening Process and Its Barriers

Listening takes place in four stages, discussed here and illustrated in Figure 2.1. Like communication, listening can be obstructed by barriers, which may be grouped into two categories: mental and physical.

Perception. The listening process begins when you hear sounds and concentrate on them. Stop reading for a moment and become conscious of the sounds around you: do you notice the hum of an electrical appliance, background sounds from a TV program, the muffled noise of traffic, or the murmur of

FIGURE 2.1 ■ The Listening Process and Its Barriers

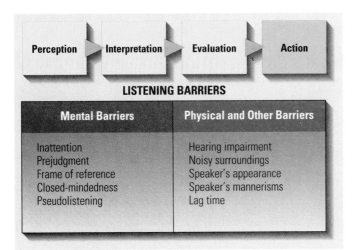

distant voices? Until you tuned in to them, these sounds went unnoticed. The conscious act of listening begins when you observe the sounds around you and choose which ones you want to hear. You tune in when (1) you sense that the message is important, (2) you are interested in the topic, or (3) you are in the mood to listen.

Perception is reduced by impaired hearing, noisy surroundings, inattention, and pseudolistening. Pseudolistening occurs when listeners pretend to be listening, but their minds are wandering.

Interpretation. Once you have turned your attention to a sound or message, you begin to interpret, or decode, it. As described in Chapter 1, interpretation of a message is coloured by your cultural, educational, and social frame of reference. The meanings you attach to the speaker's words are filtered through your expectations and all your life experiences. Thus your interpretation of the speaker's meaning may be quite different from what the speaker intended because your frame of reference is different.

Good listeners can improve their comprehension of messages by asking clarifying questions such as "Let me see if I am understanding you clearly" and by recapping what's been said.

Evaluation. After interpreting the meaning of a message, you analyze its merit and draw conclusions. To do this, you attempt to separate fact from opinion. Good listeners try to be objective; they avoid prejudging the message. In research with college students, one researcher determined that closed-mindedness and opinionated attitudes functioned as major barriers to listening. Certain students were not good listeners because their prejudices prevented them from opening up to a speaker's ideas.[7] The appearance and mannerisms of the speaker can also affect a listener's evaluation of a message. A juror, for example, might jump to the conclusion that an accused man is guilty because of his fierce expression or his substandard English. Thus, to evaluate a message accurately and objectively, you must (1) consider all the information, (2) be aware of your own biases, and (3) avoid jumping to conclusions.

The four stages in the listening process are perception, interpretation, evaluation, and action.

Evaluation involves separating fact from opinion and judging messages objectively.

Action. A response to a message may involve storing the message in memory for future use, reacting physically (with a frown, a smile, a laugh), or supplying feedback to the speaker. Listener feedback is essential because it helps clarify the message so that it can be decoded accurately. Feedback also helps the speaker to find out if the message is getting through clearly. In one-to-one conversation, of course, no clear distinction exists between the roles of listener and speaker—you give or receive feedback as your role alternates.

The Elements of Good Listening

Good listening means maintaining a positive attitude, being open to new ideas, getting involved in the listening process, and working to retain information.

A large part of the process of becoming a good listener is the ability to recognize and correct poor habits, such as those discussed in the following Career Skills box. Good listeners acknowledge their faults and resolve to correct them, a considerable task for most of us. You won't become a perfect listener overnight, but you can certainly begin the process by working on the elements of good listening dynamics, such as a positive attitude, involvement, and retention.

Positive attitude. Good listeners expect to learn something. In a sense they're listening selfishly. They're thinking, "What's in this for me? What can I learn that may help me?" They are willing to make the mental effort to listen hard because of the potential rewards. For example, students listen closely to lectures to earn higher grades; employees listen carefully to instructions from supervisors so that they can do their jobs better and earn promotions; company representatives listen attentively to their customers to discover how to keep their business. The first step to good listening is to acknowledge that listening is a valuable information-gathering activity.

Openness. Listening effectively requires an openness to new ideas. Good listeners are aware of feelings, attitudes, and prejudices that might block alternative views. In communicating with people from other cultures, good listeners try to look beyond their own narrow cultural values. They're tolerant and patient. Instead of tuning out with thoughts like "That's not the way we would do it where I come from" or "What a stupid idea," good listeners continue listening. Moreover, they are not distracted by a speaker's emotional words, unconventional appearance, or eccentric habits of speech. Considerable mental effort is required to concentrate on the message despite verbal and nonverbal "noise" in the communication process.

Involvement. Good listeners get involved in the listening process. They show commitment to the speaker nonverbally with steady eye contact, an alert body, and undivided attention. They refrain from distracting activities—fidgeting, playing with a pen or key, shifting in the chair, or trying to finish other work while listening. Good listeners also politely ask clarifying questions that do not attack the speaker. Instead of saying "But I don't understand how you could say that," a good listener says "Please help me understand by explaining more about ..."

Retention. An important aspect of listening is retaining what is said. One way to increase retention, particularly of complex data, is to separate the central idea, key points, and details. Sometimes the speaker's points are easy to recognize; other times, the listener must supply the organization. Another way to improve retention is paraphrasing, which involves silently rephrasing and

NINE POOR LISTENING HABITS THAT CAN SIDETRACK YOUR CAREER

Listening is a vital business skill, yet most of us have such underdeveloped listening skills that we fail to retain 75 percent of what we hear. The following poor habits cost businesses millions of dollars in mistakes and lost productivity. They can also retard your own career advancement if you are unable to recognize and correct them. How many of these apply to you?

- **Reacting to the speaker's appearance and speech mannerisms.** It's easy to be distracted by a speaker's looks, attire, age, or mannerisms. Poor listeners refuse to make the effort to overcome personal biases that block objective reception.

- **Failing to control distractions.** Some listeners yield easily to external and internal distractions. They fail to control or block out surrounding noises, or they fail to resist thoughts that interfere with their concentration.

- **Listening to evaluate rather than to understand.** Too often we listen only to determine if the speaker's ideas fit our frame of reference and beliefs. Listening for immediate evaluation interferes with hearing and understanding the speaker's ideas.

- **Daydreaming and pretending to listen.** We all know how to fix our gaze and look intently at the speaker while hearing nothing being said. This pseudolistening is one of the most serious of the bad listening habits.

- **Assuming the speaker wants input or advice.** Some listeners feel compelled to interrupt a speaker with comments like "Well, here's what I think about it" or "What you ought to do is ... " Unless the speaker requests it, keep your advice to yourself.

- **Avoiding listening to anything difficult.** Many listeners prefer light, recreational listening. They automatically tune out serious topics. In doing so, they deprive themselves of the opportunity to learn something new and to develop listening techniques for coping with complex issues.

- **Waiting to jump in and grab the limelight.** Too many listeners are uncomfortable in the role; they much prefer to be speaking. The result? They fail to concentrate on what's being said, but instead are mentally preparing their next comments to be interjected at the first pause.

- **Pretending to understand.** Fear of appearing stupid, impolite, or uninformed may cause us to nod in agreement when we don't really understand. Equally bad is presuming we already know what the speaker means, perhaps because we are familiar with the topic. In either case always ask clarifying questions to ensure that you understand.

- **Listening for facts only.** Failing to observe nonverbal cues can be crucial in one-to-one conversations. Poor listeners fail to pick up on voice intonation, eye movement, and body language. These cues help skilful listeners detect subtle meanings.

Career Track Application

During the next week complete two activities aimed at improving your listening skills. First, conduct a reality check. Ask your closest friends and family to evaluate your listening skill. And be grateful for their honest feedback! Second, evaluate your conversational style using the "50/50" rule. Do you listen 50 percent of the time?

---

summarizing a message in your own words. Effective listeners do this during lag time—the pause that naturally occurs when the listener is waiting for the speaker's next idea. A final technique for improving retention is selective note-taking. Good listeners jot down key points, especially if they know they will be responsible for the information later.

Improving Your Listening Effectiveness

Positive attitude, involvement, openness, and retention are key factors that influence effective listening, but people who want to improve their listening skills usually need pointers or specific techniques. The following checklist provides tips to help you become a better listener. To put these tips to work for you, try following this three-step plan:

- **Step 1: Identify your personal bad listening habits.** Do you pseudo-listen? Do you tune out difficult topics? Are you more eager to refute than to learn?

- **Step 2: Select techniques to begin working on immediately.** Choose at least two suggestions from the checklist that you feel you could put to work as soon as possible.

- **Step 3: Create opportunities for practice.** During your next classroom lecture or meeting, write at the top of your notepad, "Today I'm here to listen and learn." Then concentrate on doing just that.

Checklist for Improving Listening

✓ **Stop talking.** Accept the role of listener by concentrating on the speaker's words, not on what your response will be.

✓ **Work hard at listening.** Become actively involved, and expect to learn something.

✓ **Block out competing thoughts.** Concentrate on the message, and don't allow yourself to daydream during lag time.

✓ **Control the listening environment.** Turn off the TV, close the windows, and move to a quiet place. Tell the speaker when you cannot hear.

✓ **Keep an open mind.** Know your biases and try to correct for them. Be tolerant of speakers who have disabilities or an unusual appearance.

✓ **Provide verbal and nonverbal feedback.** Encourage the speaker with comments like "Yes," "I see," "Okay," and "Uh huh," and ask polite questions. Look alert by leaning forward.

✓ **Paraphrase the speaker's ideas.** Silently repeat the message in your own words, sort out the main points, and identify supporting details. In conversation sum up the main points to confirm what was said.

✓ **Take selective notes.** If you are hearing instructions or important data, record the major points; then, verify your notes with the speaker.

✓ **Listen between the lines.** Observe nonverbal cues, and interpret the feelings of the speaker: What is really being said?

✓ **Capitalize on lag time.** Use spare moments to organize, review, anticipate, challenge, and weigh the evidence.

FIGURE 2.2 ■ Elements in Message Meaning

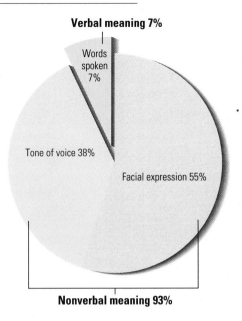

Verbal meaning 7%

Words spoken 7%

Tone of voice 38%

Facial expression 55%

Nonverbal meaning 93%

■ Creating Meaning from Nonverbal Messages

Understanding messages often involves more than merely listening to the spoken words. Nonverbal clues, in fact, can speak louder than words. Eye contact, facial expression, body movements, space, time, distance, appearance—all these nonverbal clues influence the way the message is interpreted, or decoded, by the receiver. In studies of interpersonal communication, researchers have found that only 7 percent of the "attitudinal" meaning of a message comes from the words spoken. An astounding 93 percent of the meaning, as shown in Figure 2.2, results from nonverbal cues.[8] At the Bank of Montreal, potential employees are evaluated on their body language as well as their verbal responses.

Nonverbal cues can contain up to 93 percent of a message's meaning.

Nonverbal communication includes all unwritten and unspoken messages, both intentional and unintentional. These silent signals exert a strong influence on the receiver; yet interpreting them is by no means a science. Does a downward glance indicate modesty, embarrassment, or fatigue? Does a constant stare reflect coldness, insensitivity, or dullness?

Messages are especially difficult to decipher when the verbal and nonverbal codes contradict each other. How would you interpret the following?

The silent signals of nonverbal messages carry different meaning for various listeners.

- Kim assures the hostess that the eggplant moussaka is excellent but eats very little.

- Stewart protests that he's not really angry but slams the door when he leaves.

- Kyoko claims she's not nervous about the interview but perspires profusely.

The nonverbal messages in these situations speak more loudly than the words uttered. As numerous studies indicate, when verbal and nonverbal messages

FIGURE 2.3 ■ Body Language Cues

Defensiveness

Crossing arms, glancing side-ways, touching or rubbing nose, rubbing eyes, buttoning coat, drawing away

Nervousness

Clearing throat, making "whew" sound, whistling, smoking, pinching flesh, fidgeting, covering mouth, jiggling money or keys, tugging eyes, wringing hands

Cooperation

Leaning forward, opening hands, sitting on edge of chair, making hand-to-face gestures, unbuttoning coat

Power, Confidence

Making expansive movements, sitting upright, steepling hands, placing hands behind back or in coat pockets with thumbs out, acting affably, turning one's back, sitting in relaxed, almost sprawling position

Weakness, Insecurity

Making small movements, hunching over, pinching flesh, chewing pen, twiddling thumbs, biting fingernails, leaning forward with feet together on floor

Frustration

Taking short breaths, making "tsk" sound, wringing hands, clenching fists, pointing index finger, running fingers through hair, rubbing back of neck

When verbal and nonverbal messages clash, listeners tend to believe the nonverbal message.

conflict, receivers put more faith in the nonverbal cues. In one experiment speakers delivered a positive message but averted their eyes as they spoke. Listeners perceived the overall message to be negative. Moreover, listeners thought that averted eyes suggested lack of affection, superficiality, lack of trust, and nonreceptivity.[9]

Successful communicators recognize the power of nonverbal messages. Though it's unwise to attach arbitrary meanings to specific gestures or actions, some of the cues broadcast by body language are helpful in interpreting the general feelings and attitudes of the sender. For example, body language can suggest defensiveness, cooperation, nervousness, frustration, weakness, and power, as Figure 2.3 points out.

How the Eyes, Face, and Body Send Silent Messages

Listeners are understandably confused when a speaker's nonverbal cues contradict the verbal message. Let's look more closely at the powerful effect eye contact, facial expressions, posture, and gestures have on communication.

Eye contact. The eyes have been called the "windows to the soul." Even if communicators can't look directly into the soul, they consider the eyes to be the most accurate predictor of a speaker's true feelings and attitudes. Most of us cannot look another person straight in the eyes and lie. As a result, we tend to believe people who look directly at us. We have less confidence in—and actually distrust—those who cannot maintain eye contact. Sustained eye contact suggests trust and admiration; brief eye contact signifies fear or stress.

Good eye contact enables the speaker to determine if a receiver is paying attention, showing respect, responding favourably, or feeling distress. From the receiver's perspective good eye contact reveals the speaker's sincerity, confidence, and truthfulness. Since eye contact is a learned skill, however, you must be respectful of people who do not maintain it. You must also remember that nonverbal cues, including eye contact, have different meanings in various cultures. For instance, while North Americans believe direct eye contact is crucial, in many countries it is considered impolite to look directly at a speaker. Lowered eyes are a sign of respect.

Facial expression. The expression on a communicator's face can be almost as revealing of emotion as the eyes. Researchers estimate that the human face can display over 250 000 different expressions.[10]

Although a few people can control these expressions and maintain a poker face when they want to hide their feelings, most of us display our emotions openly. Raising or lowering the eyebrows, squinting, swallowing nervously, clenching the jaw, smiling broadly—these voluntary and involuntary facial expressions supplement or entirely replace verbal messages.

Posture and gestures. Glance again at Figure 2.3 to see how important posture, gestures, and other body movements are in communicating attitudes and impressions. An individual's general posture can convey anything from high status and self-confidence to shyness and submissiveness. Leaning toward a speaker suggests attraction and interest; pulling away or shrinking back denotes fear, distrust, anxiety, or disgust.

Similarly, simple gestures can communicate entire thoughts. However, gestures may have different meanings in different cultures and can get you into trouble unless you know the local customs. In North America, for example, forming the thumb and forefinger into a circle means everything's OK. In Germany and parts of South America the OK sign is an obscene reference. In England and Scotland tapping the nose says "You and I are in on the secret." In Wales it means "You're really nosy." In Holland pointing a finger at your forehead means "How clever!" In the rest of Europe the same gesture means "You're crazy" or "That's a crazy idea!"[11]

Tuning in on nonverbal messages requires an awareness of their existence and an appreciation of their importance. To take stock of how effective you are in nonverbal communication, ask a classmate to evaluate your use of eye contact, facial expressions, and body movements. Another way to analyze your nonverbal style is to videotape yourself making a presentation and study your performance. This way you can make sure your nonverbal cues send the same message as your words.

How Time, Space, and Territory Send Silent Messages

In addition to nonverbal messages transmitted by your body, three external elements convey information in the communication process: time, space, and distance.

Eye contact, facial expressions, and posture and gestures can all convey meaning.

Nonverbal messages often have different meanings in different cultures.

People convey meaning in
how they structure and
organize time and how
they order the space
around themselves.

Time. How we structure and use time tells observers about our personality and attitudes. For example, when June Harris, a banking executive, gives a visitor a prolonged interview, she signals her respect for, interest in, and approval of the visitor or the topic to be discussed. By sharing her valuable time, she sends a clear nonverbal message. Likewise, when David Ing arrives late for two meetings with a real estate agent, it could mean that the appointments are unimportant to David, that the agent has low status, that David is a self-centred person, or that he has little self-discipline. These are assumptions that typical North Americans might make. In other cultures and regions, though, punctuality is viewed differently. We'll look more closely at interpreting nonverbal cues from other cultures later in this chapter.

The way an office is
arranged can send nonver-
bal messages about the
openness of its occupant.

Space. How we order the space around us tells something about ourselves and our objectives. Whether the space is a bedroom, a room in residence, an office, or a department, people reveal themselves in the design and grouping of furniture within that space. Generally, the more formal the arrangement, the more formal and closed the communication environment. An executive who seats visitors in a row of chairs across from his desk sends a message of aloofness and desire for separation. An instructor who arranges chairs informally in a circle rather than in straight rows or a rectangular pattern conveys her desire for a more open, egalitarian exchange of ideas. A manager who creates an open office space with few partitions separating workers' desks seeks to encourage an unrestricted flow of communication and work among areas.

Territory. Each of us has certain areas that we feel are our own territory, whether it's a specific spot or just the space around us. Your father may have a favourite chair in which he is most comfortable, a cook might not tolerate intruders in his or her kitchen, and veteran employees may feel that certain work areas and tools belong to them.

We all maintain zones of privacy in which we feel comfortable. Figure 2.4 categorizes the four zones of social interaction among North Americans, as formulated by anthropologist Edward T. Hall. Notice that North Americans are a bit standoffish; only intimate friends and family may stand closer than a foot and a half. If someone violates that territory, North Americans feel uncomfortable and defensive and may even step back to re-establish their space. A story is told of Argentines who were forced to rope off a section of a low-railed balcony. Too many North Americans had accidentally backed off it while protecting their space as they talked to Argentine associates who enjoy close communication.[12] Backing off sends a nonverbal message of intrusion. The Japanese require even more personal space than North Americans. They also frown on public touching of any kind.[13] Because the distance required for comfortable social interaction is largely controlled by culture, North Americans must be careful not to apply their norms universally.

How Appearance Sends Silent Messages

The physical appearance of a business document, as well as the personal appearance of an individual, transmits immediate and important nonverbal messages.

Appearance of business documents. The way a letter, memo, or report looks can have either a positive or a negative effect on the receiver. Envelopes—through their postage, stationery, and printing—can suggest routine, important, or junk mail. Letters and reports can look neat, professional, well

FIGURE 2.4 ■ Four Space Zones for Social Interaction

Zone	Distance	Uses
Intimate	0 to 1½ feet	Reserved for members of the family and other loved ones.
Personal	1½ to 4 feet	For talking to friends privately. The outer limit enables you to keep someone at arm's length.
Social	4 to 12 feet	For acquaintances, fellow workers, and strangers. Close enough for eye contact yet far enough for comfort.
Public	12 feet and over	For use in the classroom and for speeches before groups. Nonverbal cues become important as aids to communication.

organized, and attractive—or just the opposite. Sloppy, hurriedly written documents convey negative nonverbal messages regarding both the content and the sender. In succeeding chapters you'll learn how to create documents that send positive nonverbal messages through their appearance, format, organization, readability, and correctness.

Appearance of people. The way you look—your clothing, grooming, and posture—telegraphs an instant nonverbal message about you. Based on what they see, viewers quickly draw conclusions about your status, credibility, personality, and potential. Because appearance is such a powerful force in business, some aspiring professionals are turning for help to image consultants (who charge up to $500 an hour!). As one human relations specialist observes, "If you don't look and act the part, you will probably be denied opportunities."[14]

What specific advice do image consultants give? Try to invest in conservative, professional-looking clothing and accessories; quality is much more important than quantity. Avoid flashy garments, clunky jewellery, garish makeup, and overpowering colognes, because, as one image consultant remarks, "they speak volumes without your ever saying a word."[15] Pay attention to good grooming, including a neat hairstyle, body cleanliness, polished shoes, and clean nails. Project confidence in your posture—both standing and sitting.

Nonverbal communication can outweigh words in the way it influences how others perceive us. You can harness the power of silent messages by reviewing the tips in the following checklist, paying special attention to the last two.

> Your appearance and the appearance of your documents convey verbal and nonverbal meanings.

> The cues we send nonverbally are probably more important than those we send verbally.

■ Checklist of Techniques for Improving Nonverbal Communication Skills

✓ **Establish and maintain eye contact.** Remember that in North America appropriate eye contact signals interest, attentiveness, strength, and credibility.

✓ **Use posture to show interest.** Encourage communication interaction by leaning forward, sitting or standing erect, and looking alert.

✓ **Reduce or eliminate physical barriers.** Move out from behind a desk or lectern; shorten lines of communication; arrange meeting chairs in a circle.

✓ **Improve your decoding skills.** Watch facial expressions and body language to understand the complete verbal and nonverbal message being communicated.

✓ **Probe for more information.** When you perceive nonverbal cues that contradict verbal meanings, politely seek additional clues (*I'm not sure I understand, Please tell me more about ...* , or *Do you mean that ...*).

✓ **Avoid assigning nonverbal meanings out of context.** Make nonverbal assessments only when you understand a situation or a culture.

✓ **Associate with people from diverse cultures.** Learn about other cultures to widen your knowledge and tolerance of intercultural nonverbal messages.

✓ **Appreciate the power of appearance.** Keep in mind that the appearance of your business documents, your business space, and yourself sends an immediate positive or negative message to the receiver.

✓ **Observe yourself on videotape.** Ensure that your verbal and nonverbal messages are in sync by taping and evaluating yourself making a presentation.

✓ **Enlist friends and family.** Ask them to monitor your conscious and unconscious movements and gestures to help you become a more effective communicator.

Developing Intercultural Sensitivity

Although we are not always accurate, we generally know how to interpret nonverbal cues (such as appearance, facial expression, and body language) from people who share our cultural upbringing. But the rules change when we communicate with people from other cultures. For example, think of how you show embarrassment—chances are you blush or lower your head. By contrast, when embarrassed, Japanese generally laugh or giggle, while Arabs stick out their tongues slightly.

Understanding the meaning of a message requires special sensitivity and skills when business communicators are from different cultures. Robin Sears, an executive recruiter based in Japan, says that the most foolish mistake foreigners make is "being too forward and too familiar, too quickly: 'Hey, how are ya? We've gotta do business together.' They're shouting and being very intimate and aggressive when they've never before met somebody." Sears goes on to say that Canadians shouldn't try to alter their behaviour artificially too much while doing business abroad because they won't really fit in anyway. The best approach is just to be as aware as possible of the subtleties that are going on.[16]

As world markets and economies become increasingly intertwined, Canadians at home and abroad will be doing business with more people from other countries. Moreover, our population and workforce are rapidly becoming more ethnically diverse. In your future work you may find that your employers, fellow workers, or clients are from other countries. You might even travel abroad for your employer or on your own. Learning more about the powerful

The emerging global economy will require business communicators to work with people from other countries and cultures.

effect that culture has on behaviour will help you minimize misunderstanding in your dealings with people from other cultures.

Comprehending Cultural Diversity and Pivotal North American Values

Every country or region within a country has a unique common heritage, joint experience, and shared learning that produce its culture. This background gives its members a complex system of cultural values, traits, morals, and customs. It teaches them how to behave; it conditions their reactions. Comparing your values with those in other cultures will broaden your world view and help you develop the proper attitude for successful intercultural communication.

A typical North American has habits and beliefs similar to those of other members of Western, technologically advanced societies. In our limited space it's impossible to cover fully the infinite facets of Western culture. But we can outline some crucial North American habits and values[17] and briefly contrast them with other cultural views. Remember, though, that these are generalizations, intended to help us form a broad perspective. They may not describe you or every member of other cultures.

While this section examines North American values, it is important to note that there are distinctions between Canadians and Americans. A recent poll conducted by The Strategic Counsel for *Maclean's* magazine found that Canadians are convinced there is such a thing as a unique national identity— even if they are unable to agree on what constitutes it. Allan Gregg, chairman of the counsel, believes that a strong majority of Canadians share similar attitudes in a manner that transcends region, language, sex, income, and age lines.

Victor Konrad, the executive director of the Fulbright Program for Education Exchange between Canada and the United States and a citizen of both countries, believes that Canadians are generally less impulsive, more reflective, and more trusting than Americans. He also believes that Canadians are far more tolerant of racial diversity and more interested in other cultures than are Americans.

Konrad's opinions were supported by the results of the *Maclean's* poll. When asked what makes Canadians—as individuals—distinct, most respondents chose a tendency toward nonviolence (30 percent) or a tolerance of others (29 percent). As a nation, they cited social programs (38 percent) and a nonviolent tradition (23 percent) as the two leading factors that make Canada distinct from the United States and other countries.[18]

Individualism. North Americans value individualism, an attitude of independence, and freedom from control. They think that initiative and self-assertion result in personal achievement. They believe in individual action and personal responsibility, and they desire a large degree of freedom in their lives.

Other cultures emphasize membership in organizations, groups, and teams; they encourage acceptance of group values, duties, and decisions. They tend to resist independence because it fosters competition and confrontation instead of consensus. In group-oriented cultures like that of Japan, for example, self-assertion and individual decision-making are discouraged. "The nail that sticks up gets pounded down" is a common Japanese saying.[19] Business decisions are often made by all who have competence in the matter under discussion. Similarly, in China managers also focus on the group rather than on the individual, preferring a "consultative" management style over an autocratic style.[20]

While North Americans value individualism and personal responsibility, other cultures emphasize group- and team-oriented values.

While North Americans
value informality and
straightforwardness, other
cultures may value tradi-
tion and ceremony.

Formality. North Americans place less emphasis on tradition, ceremony, and social rules than do people in some other cultures. They dress casually and are soon on a first-name basis with others. Their lack of formality is often characterized by directness. In business dealings they come to the point immediately; indirectness, they feel, wastes time, a valuable commodity.

This informality and directness may be confusing abroad. In Mexico, for example, a typical business meeting begins with handshakes, coffee, and an expansive conversation about the weather, sports, and other light topics. An invitation to "get down to business" might offend a Mexican executive.[21] In Japan signing documents and exchanging business cards are important rituals. In Europe first names are never used without invitation. In Arab, South American, and Asian cultures, a feeling of friendship and kinship must be established before business can be transacted.

North Americans tend to
be direct and to under-
stand words literally.

Communication style. North Americans value straightforwardness, are suspicious of evasiveness, and distrust people who might have a "hidden agenda" or who "play their cards too close to the chest."[22] They also tend to be uncomfortable with silence and impatient with delays. Some Asian businesspeople have learned that the longer they drag out negotiations, the more concessions impatient North Americans are likely to make.

North Americans also tend to use and understand words literally. Hispanics on the other hand, enjoy plays on words; and Arabs and South Americans sometimes speak with extravagant or poetic figures of speech that may be misinterpreted if taken literally. Nigerians prefer a quiet, clear form of expression; and Germans tend to be direct but understated.[23]

Change. In cultures shaped by Western religious values, change is a phenomenon that can be influenced and even controlled. Change is accepted and planned for.

In other cultures change is perceived as inevitable, the natural evolution of people and society. Thus, the future cannot be altered; it is predetermined. To devout Muslims, for example, planning for the future is sacrilegious because such plans might circumvent the will of Allah. Managers of an American electronics company sent to Iran to establish a telephone switching station were aware of this belief. As a result, they trained Iranian employees in extensive troubleshooting techniques so that equipment problems would not be attributed to Allah.[24]

North Americans may
place different values on
change and time orienta-
tion than do people in
other cultures.

Time orientation. North Americans consider time a precious commodity to be conserved. They correlate time with productivity, efficiency, and money. Keeping people waiting for business appointments wastes time and is also rude. In other cultures time may be considered as an unlimited and never-ending resource to be enjoyed. An American businessperson, for example, was kept waiting two hours past a scheduled appointment time in Latin America. She wasn't offended, though, because she was familiar with the culture's more relaxed concept of time.[25]

Although Asians are punctual, their need for deliberation and contemplation sometimes clashes with our desire for speedy decisions. They do not like to be rushed. A Japanese businessperson considering the purchase of North American appliances, for example, asked for five minutes to consider the salesperson's proposal. The potential buyer crossed his arms, sat back, and closed his eyes in concentration. A scant 18 seconds later, the American resumed his sales pitch to the obvious bewilderment of the Japanese customer.[26]

Overcoming Cultural Barriers

Being aware of your own culture and how it differs from others is an important first step in preventing intercultural misunderstanding. Avoiding ethnocentrism and stereotyping while developing tolerance further helps business communicators overcome cultural barriers.

Avoiding ethnocentrism. The belief in the superiority of one's own race is known as *ethnocentrism*, a natural attitude inherent in all cultures. If you were raised in Canada, the values described previously probably seem "right" to you, and you might wonder why the rest of the world doesn't function in the same sensible fashion. A Canadian businessperson in an Arab or Asian country might feel irritated at time spent over coffee or other social rituals before any "real" business is transacted. In these cultures, however, personal relationships must be established and nurtured before negotiations may proceed.

Ethnocentrism causes us to judge others by our own values. We expect others to behave as we would, and they expect us to behave as they would. Misunderstandings naturally result. A Canadian who wants to set a deadline for completion of negotiations is considered pushy by an Arab. That same Arab, who prefers a handshake to a written contract, is seen as naive and possibly untrustworthy by the North American. These ethnocentric reactions can be reduced through knowledge of other cultures and development of flexible, tolerant attitudes.

Consider the dilemma of the international consulting firm Burns & McCallister, described in the Cross Culture box on page 52. In refusing to send women to negotiate in certain countries, the company enraged some women's rights groups. But was Burns & McCallister actually respecting the cultures of those countries?

Developing tolerance. Working among people from different cultures demands tolerance and acceptance of diversity. Closed-minded people cannot look beyond their own ethnocentrism. But as global markets expand and as our own society becomes increasingly multiethnic, tolerance becomes especially significant. Some job descriptions now include statements such as "Must be able to interact with ethnically diverse personnel."

To improve tolerance, practise empathy. This means trying to see the world through another's eyes. It means being nonjudgmental, recognizing things as they are rather than as they "should be." It includes the ability to accept others' contributions in solving problems in a culturally appropriate manner. When Kal Kan Foods began courting the pets of Japan, for example, an Asian adviser suggested that the meat chunks in its Pedigree dog food be cut into perfect little squares. Why? Some Japanese pet owners feed their dogs piece by piece with chopsticks. Instead of insisting on what "should be" (feeding dogs chunky meat morsels), Kal Kan solved the problem by looking at it from another cultural point of view (providing neat small squares).[27]

In business transactions North Americans often assume that economic factors are the primary motivators of people. It's wise to remember, though, that strong cultural influences are also at work. Saving face, for example, is important in many parts of the world. Because North Americans value honesty and directness, they come right to the point. Mexicans and Asians, on the other

last class

Learning about other cultures and respecting other cultural values helps you avoid ethnocentrism.

Developing intercultural tolerance means practicing empathy, being nonjudgmental, and being patient.

CULTURAL AND ETHICAL DILEMMA FOR WOMEN MANAGERS

The international management consulting firm of Burns & McCallister finds itself in cultural hot water. The problem? It refuses to send female executives abroad to negotiate contracts in certain countries.

Despite this recent bad publicity, Burns & McCallister has previously earned a reputation as a liberal firm that encourages the employment of women. Over 50 percent of its partners are female, and both *Working Woman* and *Working Mother* magazines have ranked it among the top North American firms for women. It attracts women by offering exceptional benefits, such as flexible hours, family leave, home-based work, and part-time partner-track positions.

SILENT WOMEN. Why, then, does it send only male partners on certain assignments? In over 50 years of consulting, Burns & McCallister has learned that the cultures in certain countries do not allow women to be treated as they are in North America. In some countries, for example, women are not permitted to speak in a meeting of men. Although clerical help in these cultures might be female, contact with clients must be through male partners or account executives.

Japan, for example, has a two-track hiring system with women represented in only 3 percent of all professional positions. Other women in the workforce are uniformed office ladies who do the filing and serve tea. They are generally pressured to leave the workforce when they marry in their mid-twenties. A recruiting brochure for Dentsu, a large Japanese advertising firm, pictured the typical Dentsu "Working Girl" and described only her attractive physical characteristics.[28] In North America, such a sexist ad would infuriate women. But attitudes toward working women differ in other cultures.

COMPANY JUSTIFICATION. In defence of its ban on sending women to negotiate in certain cultures, the head of Burns & McCallister said: "Look, we're about as progressive a firm as you'll find. But the reality of international business is that if we try to use women, we don't get the job. It's not a policy on all foreign accounts. We've just identified certain cultures in which women will not be able to successfully land or work on accounts. This restriction does not interfere with their career track."

The National Organization for Women (NOW) argues that Burns & McCallister should apply North American standards through the world. Since women are not restricted here, they should not be restricted abroad. No special policy, especially one so discriminatory against women, should be instituted for cultures that vary from ours. Our culture treats women fairly, and other cultures should recognize and respect that treatment. Unless Burns & McCallister stands up for its principles, change can never be expected.

Career Track Application

Organize a debate or class discussion on these questions: On what grounds do you support or oppose the position of Burns & McCallister to prohibit women from negotiating contracts in certain cultures? Should North American businesses impose their cultural values abroad? Should Burns & McCallister sacrifice potential business to advance a high moral position? If the career advancement of women within the firm is not affected by the policy, should women care? Do you agree with NOW that change cannot occur unless Burns & McCallister takes a stand?

While Canadians value directness, people from other cultures may strive for harmony and face-saving.

hand, are more concerned with preserving social harmony and saving face. They are indirect and go to great lengths to avoid giving offence by saying no. The Japanese, in fact, have 16 different ways to avoid an outright no. The empathic listener recognizes the language of refusal and pushes no further.

Being tolerant also takes patience. If a foreigner is struggling to express an idea in English, we must avoid the temptation to finish the sentence and provide the word that we presume is wanted. When we put words in their mouths, our foreign friends often smile and agree out of politeness, but our words may in fact not express their thoughts. Thus, our impatience may prevent us from learning their true thoughts. Remaining silent is another means of exhibiting tolerance. Instead of filling every lapse in conversation, Canadians should recognize that in Asian countries people deliberately use periods of silence for reflection and contemplation.

Moving beyond stereotypes. Our impressions of other cultures sometimes cause us to form stereotypes about groups of people. A *stereotype* is an oversimplified behavioural pattern applied uncritically to groups. For example, the Swiss are hard-working, efficient, and neat; Germans are formal, reserved, and blunt; Canadians are polite, trusting, and tolerant; Asians are gracious, humble, and inscrutable. These attributes may or may not accurately describe cultural norms, but when applied to individual businesspeople, such stereotypes create misconceptions and cause misunderstandings. As a Canadian, are you polite, trusting, and tolerant? Perhaps, but you may resent being lumped into this category. When you meet and work with people from other cultures, remember that they, too, resent being stereotyped. Look beneath surface stereotypes and labels to discover individual personal qualities. Like Johanne Totta at the Bank of Montreal, it is important to put yourself in the other person's shoes and to listen through their ears.

Looking beyond stereotypes means seeing individual qualities.

Adapting Messages to Intercultural Audiences

Working successfully with people from other cultures requires a certain amount of sensitivity and adjustment. The following suggestions provide specific tips for minimizing oral and written miscommunication.

Suggestions for communicating orally. Although it's best to speak a foreign language fluently, many of us do not. Fortunately, global business transactions are often conducted in English, though those for whom it is a second language may not be very fluent. An executive with Ford-Europe said that North Americans abroad make a big mistake in thinking that people who speak English always understand what is being said. "Comprehension can be fairly superficial," he warns. The following suggestions may help you be understood better in English.

- **Learn foreign phrases.** Even if English is used, foreign nationals appreciate it when you learn greetings and a few phrases in their language. Practise the phrases phonetically so that you will be understood.

- **Use simple English.** Use simple words, and speak in short sentences (under 15 words). Eliminate puns, sports and political references, slang, jargon (special business terms), and any words that can't be translated.

- **Observe eye messages.** Be alert to a glazed expression or wandering eyes—these tell you the listener is lost.

- **Encourage accurate feedback.** Ask probing questions, and encourage the listener to paraphrase what you say. Don't assume that a yes, a nod, or a smile indicates comprehension.

- **Check frequently for comprehension.** Avoid waiting until you finish a long explanation to request feedback. Instead, make one point at a time, pausing to check for comprehension, and don't proceed to B until A has been grasped.

- **Speak slowly and enunciate clearly.** However, don't raise your voice. Also, overpunctuate with pauses and full stops, and always write numbers for all to see.

Presentations in an intercultural setting, especially to an audience that uses English infrequently, require tact. Wise speakers use simple language, speak slowly, watch for eye messages, and encourage frequent feedback.

- **Accept blame.** If a misunderstanding results, graciously accept the blame for not making your meaning clear.

- **Listen without interrupting.** Curb your inclination to finish sentences or to fill out ideas for the speaker. Keep in mind that North Americans abroad are often accused of listening too little and talking too much.

After conversations or oral negotiations, confirm the results and agreements with follow-up letters. For proposals and contracts, engage a translator to prepare copies in the local language. Roger Axtell, international behaviour expert, offers three other important pieces of advice: smile, smile, smile. He calls the smile the single most understood and most useful form of communication in either personal or business transactions.[29]

Suggestions for communicating in writing. Many of the suggestions for oral communication hold true for written documents as well. In addition, you may find it helpful to find out how documents are formatted and how letters are addressed and developed in the intended reader's country. We'll examine these topics further in later chapters.

Translate your message into the receiver's language if the document is important, if it will have many readers, or if you must be persuasive.

Engage a translator if (1) your document is important, (2) your document will be distributed to many readers, or (3) you must be persuasive. As one international executive says, "You can buy in English, but you have to sell in the other person's language."[30]

In writing documents some simple guidelines will help you communicate effectively. Use short sentences and short paragraphs (under five lines). Include relative pronouns *(that, which, who)* for clarity in introducing clauses. Stay away from contractions (especially ones like *Here's the problem*). Use precise, simple words *(end* instead of *terminate, use* instead of *implement)*. Avoid idioms *(once in a blue moon)*, slang *(my presentation really bombed)*, acronyms *(ASAP* for *as soon as possible)*, abbreviations *(DBA* for *doing business as)*, and jargon *(input, output, bottom line)*.

Numbers can cause real confusion in cross-cultural communication. As shown in Figure 2.5, problem areas include dates, time, currency, money, and phone numbers. Although this chart presents only five countries, you can see how much variation exists. What date would you understand from a British letter giving a deadline of 5/3/96? To at least some Canadians, that date is May 3, but in Britain it means March 5. For clarity in expressing months, therefore, it's wise to use words *(May 3, 1996)*. Experts also advise converting dollar figures into local currency.[31]

Making the effort to communicate with sensitivity across cultures pays big dividends. "Much of the world wants to like us," says businessman and international consultant Kevin Chambers. "When we take the time to learn about others, many will bend over backward to do business with us."[32] The following checklist summarizes suggestions for helping you improve your intercultural sensitivity.

◼ Checklist for Improving Intercultural Sensitivity

✓ **Study your own culture.** Learn about your customs, prejudices, and views and how they differ from those in other societies.

✓ **Curb ethnocentrism.** Avoid judging others by your personal views. Learn to recognize and tolerate other behaviour as normal, rather than as right or wrong.

✓ **Look beyond stereotypes.** Remember, individuals are often unlike their cultural stereotypes, so forget preconceptions and probe beneath the surface.

✓ **Use plain English.** Speak and write in short sentences using simple words and standard English. Eliminate puns, slang, jargon, acronyms, abbreviations, and any words that cannot be easily translated.

✓ **Encourage accurate feedback.** In conversations ask probing questions, and listen attentively without interrupting. Don't assume that a yes or a smile indicates assent or comprehension.

✓ **Hire a translator.** When negotiations or documents are important and one or both of the communicators lack fluency in the other's language, engage a professional interpreter or translator.

✓ **Adapt to local expectations.** Shape your writing to reflect the reader's document styles, if appropriate. Express currency in local figures. Write out months of the year for clarity.

FIGURE 2.5 ▦ Typical Treatment of Numbers

	North American	United Kingdom	France	Germany	Portugal
Dates	May 15, 1996 5/15/96	15th May 1996 15/5/96	15 mai 1996 15.05.96	15.Mai 1996 15.5.96	96.05.15
Time	10:32 p.m.	10:32 p.m.	22.32 22 h 32	22:45 Uhr 22.32	22H32m
Currency	$123.45	£123.45 GB£123.45	123F45 123,45 F	DM 123,45 123,45 DM	123$45 ESC 123.45
Large number	1,234,567.89	1,234,567.89	1.234.567,89	1.234.567,89	1.234.567,89
Phone numbers	(905) 555-1234	(081) 987 1234 0255 876543	(15) 61-87-34-02 (15) 61.87.34.02	(089) 2 61 39 12	056-244 33 056 45 45 45

▦ Summary of Learning Goals

1. **Explain the listening process and name four elements of good listening.** The listening process involves (a) perception of sounds, (b) interpretation of those sounds, (c) evaluation of meaning, and (d) action, which might include a physical response or storage of the message in memory for future use. Good listening demands a positive attitude, openness to new ideas, active involvement in the listening process, and retention of main ideas.

2. **Name a three-step process as well as 10 specific techniques that improve listening effectiveness.** Listeners can improve their effectiveness by (a) identifying personal bad listening habits, (b) selecting techniques to begin work on, and (c) creating opportunities for practice. Specifically, listeners can improve their effectiveness by talking less, blocking out competing thoughts, becoming actively involved, controlling the listening environment, maintaining an open mind, providing verbal and nonverbal feedback, paraphrasing the speaker's ideas, taking selective notes, listening between the lines, and capitalizing on lag time.

3. **Discuss how meaning is created from nonverbal messages.** Nonverbal messages are sent by our eyes, face, and body. For example, sustained eye contact indicates trust or admiration; brief eye contact may signify fear or stress. Expressions on a communicator's face can supplement or entirely replace verbal messages. Posture can indicate status, confidence, shyness, or submissiveness. Gestures also send nonverbal messages, many of which are culture dependent. Moreover, how a communicator uses time, space, and territory sends messages that require no words. Keeping a person waiting, for instance, may suggest an appointment is unimportant. The arrangement of office furniture may indicate an individual's management or communication style. Finally, the amount of space we need for social interaction can be another means of sending messages nonverbally.

4. **Apply specific techniques that enhance nonverbal communication skills.** Skilful communicators improve their nonverbal effectiveness by maintaining eye contact, looking alert, eliminating physical barriers that separate them from their listeners, and improving their comprehension of nonverbal signals. They also evaluate nonverbal messages only in context, seek feedback, associate with diverse people, recognize the power of

appearance, see themselves on videotape, and ask friends and family to monitor their body language.

5. **Explain the importance of intercultural sensitivity and clarify pivotal North American cultural values.** Intercultural sensitivity is increasingly important because Canadians at home and abroad are doing business with more people from other countries. It's also important because our population and workforce are rapidly becoming more ethnically diverse. Important North American values that influence our world view include (a) respect for individualism, independence, and self-assertion, (b) emphasis on informality and directness, (c) respect for material objects and business profits, (d) the belief that change can be controlled, and (e) the feeling that time is valuable and should be used carefully.

6. **Describe three key attitudes that help overcome cultural barriers.** Business communicators will be better able to overcome cultural barriers if they (a) avoid ethnocentrism, which causes us to judge others by our own cultural values, (b) develop tolerance and empathy in working with people from diverse cultures, and (c) look beneath surface stereotypes to discover each individual's personal qualities.

7. **Employ 10 specific procedures for adapting messages to intercultural audiences.** In writing to people in other countries, (a) observe their document formats and conventions, (b) hire a translator for important or persuasive messages, (c) use short words, sentences, and paragraphs, (d) convert dollar amounts to local currency, and (e) adopt a more formal, less conversational tone. In speaking English with individuals from other cultures, (a) try to use a few phrases in their language, (b) speak slowly, use short sentences, and choose simple English words, (c) watch for comprehension in a listener's eyes, (d) pause frequently and encourage feedback, and (e) accept blame for any misunderstanding that occurs.

CHAPTER REVIEW

1. What percentage of most workers' communication time is spent listening? Of executives? (Goal 1)

2. Define *lag time*. (Goal 1)

3. Describe the four elements in the listening process. (Goal 1)

4. Discuss five poor listening habits and how they can be overcome. (Goal 2)

5. Name three specific techniques you can use to help yourself remember what a speaker says. (Goal 2)

6. Define *nonverbal communication*. (Goal 3)

7. When verbal and nonverbal messages disagree, which message does the receiver consider more truthful? Give an example. (Goal 3)

8. How does good eye contact help a speaker or sender? How does it benefit a listener or receiver? (Goal 3)

9. How can you ensure that the nonverbal and verbal messages you send are in agreement? (Goal 4)

10. How does the appearance of a business document send nonverbal messages? (Goal 3)

11. Describe five major elements of North American culture. (Goal 5)

12. What is *ethnocentrism*? (Goal 6)

13. Describe five specific ways in which you can improve *oral* communication with a foreigner. (Goal 7)

14. Describe five specific ways in which you can improve *written* communication with a foreigner. (Goal 7)

15. What is a *stereotype*? Give original examples. (Goal 6)

DISCUSSION

1. Discuss how listening skills are important to employees, supervisors, and executives. Who should have the best listening skills? (Goal 1)

2. Comment on the idea that body language is a science with principles that can be interpreted accurately by specialists. (Goal 3)

3. **Ethical Issue:** In many countries government officials are not well paid, and "tips" (called "bribes" in North America) are a way of compensating them. If such payments are not considered wrong in those countries, should you pay them as a means of achieving your business goals?

ACTIVITIES

2.1 Bad Listening Habits (Goal 2)

Concentrate for three days on your listening habits in class and on the job. What bad habits do you detect? Be prepared to discuss five bad habits and specific ways you could improve your listening skills. Your instructor may ask you to report your analysis in a memo.

2.2 Listening and Retention (Goals 1, 2)

Listen to a 30-minute segment of TV news using your normal listening habits. When you finish, make a list of the main items you remember, recording names, places, and figures. A day later watch the same 30-minute segment but put to use the good-listening tips in this chapter, including taking selective notes. When the segment is completed, make a list of the main items you remember. Which experience provided more information? What made the most difference for you?

2.3 Silent Messages (Goals 3, 4)

Analyze the kind of silent messages you send your instructor, your classmates, and your employer. How do you send these messages? What do they mean? Be prepared to discuss them in small groups or in a memo to your instructor.

2.4 Body Language (Goals 3, 4)

What attitudes do the following gestures and movements suggest to you? Do these movements always mean the same thing? What part does context play in your interpretations?
   a. Whistling, wringing hands
   b. Bowed posture, twiddling thumbs
   c. Steepled hands, sprawling sitting position
   d. Running hand through hair
   e. Open hands, unbuttoned coat
   f. Wringing hands, tugging ears

2.5 Document Appearance (Goals 3, 4)

Select a business letter and envelope that you have received at home or work. Analyze their appearance and the nonverbal messages they send. Consider the amount of postage, method of delivery, correctness of address, kind of stationery, typeface(s), format, and neatness. What assumptions did you make when you saw the envelope? How about the letter itself?

2.6 Gender Differences (Goals 3, 4)

Many researchers in the field of nonverbal communication report that women are better at interpreting nonverbal signals than are men. Conduct a class survey. On a scale of 1 (low) to 5 (high), how would you rank men in general on their ability to interpret the meaning of eye, voice, face, and body signals? Then rank women in general. Tabulate the class votes. Why do you think sex differences exist in the decoding of nonverbal signals?

2.7 Canadian Culture (Goal 5)

Your pen pal, who has never been to Canada, asks you to describe how the people behave. Report to the class what you might say to your pen pal. Enlarge on the pivotal values of North American culture presented in this chapter. Include a discussion of distinctly Canadian values. Be prepared to write a letter if your instructor asks.

2.8 Negotiating Traps (Goals 5, 6)

Discuss the causes and implications of the following common mistakes made by North Americans in their negotiations with foreigners:

a. Assuming that a final agreement is set in stone

b. Lacking patience and insisting that matters progress more quickly than the pace preferred by the locals

c. Assuming an interpreter is always completely accurate

d. Ignoring or misunderstanding the significance of rank

2.9 Global Economy (Goals 5–7)

A Canadian businessman said, "It is an inescapable fact that the Canadian economy is becoming much more like the European and Asian economies, entirely tied to global trade." Read local newspapers for a week and peruse national news magazines (*Maclean's, Canadian Business* and so forth) for articles that support or refute this assertion. Report your findings orally or in a memo to your instructor. This topic could be expanded into a long report for Chapter 13.

2.10 Collaborative Intercultural Panel (Goals 5–7)

Find two or three students from other countries (possibly members of your class) who could report on differences between their cultures and Canadian culture. Ask student travellers to report on their experiences abroad. In addition to individualism, formality, communication style, change, and time, consider such topics as importance of family, gender roles, and attitudes toward education, clothing, leisure, and work. Conduct a panel discussion. (See Activity 14.6 in Chapter 14 for a list of possible topics.)

CLUE REVIEW 2

On a separate sheet correct faults in grammar, punctuation, spelling, and word use in the following sentences.

1. To avoid embarassing any employee the personnell manager and myself has decided to talk personal to each individual.

2. 3 assistants were sent on a search and destroy mission in a conscious effort to remove at least fifteen thousand old documents from the files.

3. Electronic mail, now used by ¾ of Canada's largest companys will transmit messages instantly.

4. An article entitled whats new with managers appeared in reader's digest which is read by 2 000 000 Canadians.

5. Your account is now sixty days overdue consequently we have only 1 alternative left.

6. The marketing managers itinerary listed the following three destinations montreal winnipeg victoria.

7. Each of the beautifully-printed books available at pickwick book company have been reduced to thirty dollars.

8. We recommend therefor that a committee study our mail procedures for a 3 week period and submit a report of it's findings.

9. Their going to visit there relatives in Fredericton, New Brunswick over the Victoria Day weekend.

10. The hotel can accommodate three hundred convention guests but it has parking facilities for only one hundred cars.

The Writing Process

Analyzing, Anticipating, and Adapting

LEARNING GOALS

After studying this chapter, you should be able to

1 Describe three basic elements that distinguish business writing from academic writing. Summarize the three phases of the 3 × 3 writing process.

2 Explain the importance of task analysis and audience anticipation in Phase 1 of the writing process.

3 Specify six writing techniques that help communicators adapt messages to their audiences.

4 Name five common ethical traps that business communicators must avoid.

5 List the goals of ethical business communication and describe important tools for doing the right thing.

6 Recognize language that may lead to lawsuits.

WIC Communications

For Western International Communications, the medium is the message. The broadcasting and communications firm is parent company for eleven radio and eight television stations across Canada, and its Westcom TV division has a burgeoning entertainment branch that coordinates investments on behalf of the television stations and works with writers, producers, and directors on coproductions for television series, movies, and feature films.

These days, the pace of advances in information technology is breathtaking. A company like WIC—which employs about 2000 and boasts 1994 revenues of more than $390 million—must keep abreast or ahead of the pack or get lost in the high-tech shuffle. When your business has such a broad communications mandate realized through a complex nationwide infrastructure, your overall corporate message had better be clear. WIC's message is designed, fine-tuned, and delivered from its corporate headquarters in downtown Vancouver.

As acting director of communications for WIC, a contract position, Angela Barker heads into the Vancouver office knowing her job may take her in many strategic turns on any given day. But her goal remains clear: to gather and assess a cross-section of corporate information and deliver the data in words that will be understood.

"One day," she says, "I might be writing a quarterly report that's going to be read by the investor community; another day the job at hand might be putting out the company newsletter, which is pretty informal compared to press releases and corporate report figures. Still, that newsletter will be read by employees at stations from Vancouver to Toronto, as well as members of the public who pick it up from a reception-room coffee table."

> *"My aim is always to get the facts geared to the particular audience of that publication, and my challenge in this job is to take whatever information must be delivered and make it really comprehensive and clear."*

Angela says while business communication and writing skills are honed from fairly basic abilities, they must be strengthened through experience and an understanding of the different demands and considerations of a varied readership.

"It's important to read a lot, be aware of different styles, and be sensitive as well as keep an open mind. It sounds easy, but it's not. When I'm tackling the company newsletter, I have to be diplomatic—a lot of different people in the company like to contribute, and the publication should reflect the personal input but still be a professional enough product that it can serve as a useful promotional and public relations tool for the company.

"My aim is always to get the facts geared to the particular audience of that publication, and my challenge in this job is to take whatever information must be delivered and make it really comprehensive and clear."

Angela believes her varied media background and broad interests continually pay off. After graduating from Carleton University with a degree in journalism, she went to work on a small-town newspaper as a reporter and photographer, then joined a national magazine as assistant editor, and ended up working for six years at the Global Television Network as a writer with some media-relations responsibilities.

From there it was off to the corporate head office of WIC, where she is responsible for finding out what the main message of the day is and determining the best format, tone, and style for delivering that information. Usually she starts this process by beginning at the end of the delivery line: by assessing the needs of her readers.

"I start there, with that basic need of the reader in mind; and since I often deal with investor relations, I write fairly straightforward press releases and quarterly reports. In these instances, it's not my job to be interpretive; I want to give the reader the numbers and let them come to their own conclusions."

When she's writing WIC quarterly reports, Angela usually seeks direction from the chief financial officer—gathering the right figures and verifying the tone and substance of the information to be covered in the publication. "I assess the needs of the audience, but I don't make any assumptions—facts and figures must be analyzed in the context of the whole industry and how it is faring. Sometimes less is more, when you want to be clear."

The ability to pare down complicated details and express them in simple, straightforward wording is an essential part of writing for Angela.

"Right now, for instance, I'm working on a pamphlet that's going to be read by a broad cross-section of people—shareholders, financial analysts, the media, as well as our customers. And the subject is complicated—advanced technology that's in the pipeline. So the challenge here is to keep this broad readership in mind, focus on what they really need to know, and convey things in such a way that everyone understands the essentials.

"In this instance, it helps if you can really grasp the technological concepts because the writing and researching task involves putting these concepts into terms that the ordinary person will understand. The overall tone is simple; I break the message down into pieces to see what is really being said."

The bottom line comes down to one simple rule of thumb, she says: "If the message isn't clear, if I don't get it myself, chances are the reader won't."[1] ■

Sending positive messages depends greatly on the communication technique used by the sender. At WIC, using direct language and paring down complicated details to essential concepts has proved to be a successful strategy for getting a message across to their audiences.

Approaching the Writing Process Systematically

Writing, like other goal-oriented activities, is easier when the writer follows a plan. Whether you're preparing quarterly reports like Angela Barker at WIC or preparing interoffice memos, reports, or oral presentations, the final product will be more effective and the act of producing it less stressful if you apply a systematic process.

The Basics of Business Writing

Business writing differs from other writing you may have done. Academic writing probably required you to explain your ideas, display your knowledge, and meet a specified word count. Business writing is as different from this kind of academic writing as night is from day. In the business world, you'll find that your writing needs to be:

- **Purposeful.** You will be writing to solve problems and convey information.

- **Economical.** You will try to present ideas clearly but concisely—verbiage is not rewarded in any type of writing.

- **Reader-oriented.** You will concentrate on looking at a problem from the reader's perspective instead of seeing it from your own.

These distinctions actually ease the writer's task. In writing most business documents, you won't be searching your imagination for creative topic ideas. Moreover, you won't be trying to dazzle readers with your extensive knowledge, powerful vocabulary, or graceful phrasing. The goal in business writing is to express rather than impress.

In many ways business writing is easier than creative writing, but it still requires hard work, especially from beginners. But by following a process, studying models, and practising the craft, nearly anyone can become a successful business writer. This book provides all three components: process, models, and practice. First, you'll focus on the process of writing.

The 3 × 3 Writing Process

This book divides the writing process into three distinct phases, as shown in Figure 3.1, with each phase further divided into three major activities. This 3 × 3 process provides you with a systematic plan for developing all your business communications—from simple memos and informational reports to corporate proposals and presentations.

The time spent on each phase varies with the deadline, purpose, and audience for the message. Let's consider how the 3 × 3 writing process might work in a typical business situation. Suppose you must write a letter to a department store buyer about a jeans order that your company cannot fill. The first phase prepares you to write and involves analyzing, anticipating, and adapting. In analyzing the situation, you decide to focus your letter on retaining the order. That can best be done by persuading the buyer to accept a different jeans model. You anticipate that the buyer will be disappointed that the original model is unavailable. What's more, she will probably be reluctant to switch to a different model. Thus, you must find ways to adapt your message to reduce her reluctance and persuade her to switch.

The second phase involves researching, organizing, and then composing the message. To collect facts for this letter, you would probably investigate the

FIGURE 3.1 ■ The 3 × 3 Writing Process

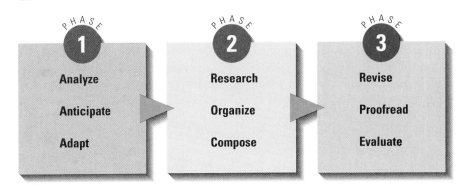

PHASE 1	PHASE 2	PHASE 3
Analyze	**Research**	**Revise**
Anticipate	**Organize**	**Proofread**
Adapt	**Compose**	**Evaluate**

buyer's past purchases. You would check to see what jeans you have in stock that she might accept as a substitute. You might do some brainstorming or consult your colleagues for their suggestions about how to keep this order. Then you would organize your information into a loose outline and decide on a plan for revealing your information most effectively. Equipped with a plan, you're ready to compose the first draft of the letter.

The third phase of the writing process involves revising, proofreading, and evaluating your letter. After writing the first draft, you'll revise the message for clarity, conciseness, tone, and readability. You'll proofread carefully to ensure correct spelling, grammar, punctuation, and layout. Finally, you'll evaluate the message to see if it accomplishes your goal.

Although our diagram of the writing process shows the three phases equally, the time you spend on each varies. One expert gives these rough estimates for scheduling a project: Phase 1: 25 percent worrying and planning, Phase 2: 25 percent writing, Phase 3: 45 percent revising and 5 percent proofreading. These are rough guides, yet you can see that good writers spend considerable time on Phase 3. Much depends, of course, on your project, its importance, and your familiarity with it. What's essential to remember, though, is that revising is a large part of writing.

This process may seem a bit complicated for the daily messages that many businesspeople write. Does this same process apply to memos and short letters? And how do collaborators and modern computer technologies affect the process?

Adapting the process. Although good writers proceed through each phase of the writing process, some steps may be compressed for short, routine messages. Brief, everyday documents enlist the 3 × 3 process, but many of the steps are performed quickly, without prolonged deliberation. For example, Phase 1 may take the form of a few moments of reflection. Phase 2 may consist of looking in the files quickly, jotting a few notes in the margin of the original document, and composing at your computer. Phase 3 may consist of reading a printout, running a spell check, and making a few changes. Longer, more involved documents—like persuasive memos, sales letters, management reports, proposals, and résumés—require more attention to all parts of the process.

One other point about the 3 × 3 writing process needs clarification. It may appear that you perform one step and progress to the next, always following the

The steps in the 3 × 3 writing process may be altered, compressed, and rearranged depending on the nature of the document and the experience of the writer.

same order. Most business writing, however, is not that rigid. Although writers perform the tasks described, the steps may be rearranged, abbreviated, or repeated. Some writers revise every sentence and paragraph as they go. Many find that new ideas occur to them after they've begun to write, causing them to back up, alter the organization, and rethink their plan. You should expect to follow the 3 × 3 process closely as you begin developing your business writing skill. With experience, though, you'll become like other good writers who alter, compress, and rearrange the steps as needed.

Collaborating with others. The composition process is changed when two or more people work together on a project. Collaborative composition may be necessary for (1) big tasks, (2) items with short deadlines, and (3) projects that require the expertise or consensus of many people.

Let's say four people are working on a committee report as a group. The group members may work together as they analyze and organize the data. Then one member composes the first draft and submits it to the others for suggestions. This revision and evaluation phase might be repeated several times before the final document is completed.

 Working with a computer. The composition process is further affected by today's computer tools. Software exists to help you generate ideas, conduct research electronically, and organize facts into outlines. In fact, all phases of the writing process—including keyboarding, revision, and collaboration—are simplified by word processing programs, discussed more fully in the accompanying Technology box.

Wonderful as these powerful technological tools are, however, they do not automatically produce effective letters and reports. They can neither organize data into concise and logical presentations nor shape ideas into persuasive arguments. Only a well-trained author can do that. Nevertheless, today's technology enhances every aspect of writing. Therefore, skill in using computers is essential for anyone whose job requires composition.

Phase 1: Preparing to Write

By following the 3 × 3 writing process, you can reduce anxiety, write more efficiently, and craft better messages.

Whether you're writing with a team, composing by yourself, or preparing an oral presentation, the product of your efforts can be improved by following the steps described in the 3 × 3 writing process. Not only are you more likely to get your message across, but you'll feel less anxious and your writing will progress more quickly. The remainder of this chapter concentrates on the first phase of composition: analyzing, anticipating, and adapting.

Analyzing the Task

In analyzing the composition task, you'll first need to identify the purpose of the message and select the best channel or form in which to deliver it.

Identifying your purpose. As you begin to compose a message, ask yourself two important questions: (1) Why am I sending this message? and (2) What do I hope to achieve? Your responses will determine how you organize and present your information.

SEVEN WAYS COMPUTER SOFTWARE CAN HELP YOU BECOME A BETTER BUSINESS WRITER AND COMMUNICATOR

Although computers and software programs cannot actually do the writing for you, they provide powerful tools that make the composition process easier and the results more professional. Here are seven ways your computer can help you be a better business communicator.

- **Fighting writer's block.** Because word processors enable ideas to flow almost effortlessly from your brain to a screen, you can expect fewer delays resulting from writer's block. You can compose rapidly, and you can experiment with structure and phrasing, later keeping and polishing your most promising thoughts. Many authors "sprint-write," recording unedited ideas quickly, to start the composition process and also to brainstorm for ideas on a project. Then they tag important ideas and use computer outlining programs to organize those ideas into logical sequences.

- **Collecting information electronically.** As a knowledge worker in an information economy, you will need to find information quickly. Much of the world's information is now accessible by computer. You can find the titles of books, magazine and newspaper articles, and government publications by using on-line services or CD-ROM (compact disks) that hold massive data collections. Through specialized information-retrieval services (such as *InfoGlobe Online*) you can have at your fingertips up-to-the-minute legal, scientific, scholarly, and business information. By subscribing to Rose Media, CRS Online, CompuServe, or Prodigy, you gain access to many electronic services including databases and special-interest forums. And the Internet, a loose collection of voluntarily linked global computer networks, is opening additional vast information treasures. You'll learn more about exciting, dynamic electronic resources in Chapter 11.

- **Outlining and organizing ideas.** Most high-end word processors include some form of "outliner," a feature that enables you to divide a topic into a hierarchical order with main and subpoints. Your computer keeps track of the levels of ideas automatically so that you can easily add, cut, or rearrange points in the outline. This feature is particularly handy when you're preparing a report or organizing a presentation. Some programs even enable you to transfer your outline directly to slide frames to be used as visual aids in a talk.

- **Improving correctness and precision.** Nearly all word processing programs today can catch and correct spelling and typographical errors. Poor spellers and weak typists universally bless their spell checkers for repeatedly saving them from humiliation. Still, writers must recognize that misused words (*affect/effect*) and confusing words (*its/it's*) will escape detection by the spell check. Other writing tools include grammar and style checkers. These programs make suggestions about word usage, readability, jargon, and various other writing problems. Thesaurus programs help you choose precise words that say exactly what you intend.

- **Adding graphics for emphasis.** Your letters, memos, and reports may be improved by the addition of graphs and artwork to clarify and illustrate data. You can import charts, diagrams, and illustrations created in database, spreadsheet, graphics, and draw-and-paint programs. Moreover, ready-made pictures, called "clip art," can be used to symbolize or illustrate ideas.

- **Designing and producing professional-looking documents and presentations.** Gone are the days when writers were forced to take their copy to printers or in-house art departments for professional effects. Most high-end word processing programs today include scalable fonts (for different type sizes and styles), italics, boldface, and other print features to aid you in producing professional-looking results. Moreover, today's presentation software enables you to incorporate colour, sound, pictures, and even movies into your talks before management or customers.

- **Using collaborative software for team writing.** Assume you are part of a group preparing a lengthy proposal to secure a government contract. You expect to write one segment of the proposal yourself and help revise parts written by others. Special word processing programs with commenting and strikeout features allow you to revise easily and to identify each team member's editing. These collaborative programs, called "groupware," also include decision-support tools to help groups generate, organize, and analyze ideas more efficiently than in traditional meetings.

Career Track Application

Individually or in teams, identify specific software programs that perform the tasks described here. Prepare a table naming each program, its major functions, and its advantages and disadvantages for business writers in your field.

Before writing a letter or preparing a presentation, think carefully about your audience. Visualizing the receiver and anticipating a reaction to your message help you determine the words to use, the amount of detail to include, the best method of organization, and many other important factors.

Most business communication has both primary purposes (to inform or persuade) and secondary purposes (to promote goodwill).

Your message may have primary and secondary purposes. For academic work your primary purpose may be merely to complete the assignment; secondary purposes might be to make yourself look good and to get a good grade. The primary purposes for sending business messages are usually to inform and to persuade. A secondary purpose is to promote goodwill; you (and your organization) want to look good in the eyes of your audience.

Most business messages do nothing more than inform—explain procedures, announce meetings, answer questions, and transmit findings. Some business messages, however, are meant to *persuade*—to sell products, convince managers, motivate employees, and win over customers.

Choosing an appropriate form or channel for a message often depends on the sensitivity of the message.

Selecting the form. After deciding the purpose of your message, you need to choose the most suitable form (communication channel). As you learned in Chapter 1, some information is most efficiently and effectively delivered in person. A phone call or a quick meeting could convey a message or solve a problem, thus saving the considerable cost of writing, producing, delivering, reading, and storing a business document. Written documents, of course, also have advantages. They are relatively cheap and easy to distribute to a large or distant audience, and they are usually worded more carefully than oral messages. Moreover, they provide a permanent record confirming specifications, decisions, dates, and so forth.

Anticipating the Audience

Visualizing the audience for a message helps you choose the most suitable words.

Some messages miss the mark. Consider the following letter sent to a 7-year-old boy who had written to a chocolate company asking for a Milky Bar pencil case. "Due to the overwhelming response this promotion has generated, we have unfortunately run out of stock temporarily. We are, therefore, holding your application pending stock replenishment."[2] The chocolate company's representative had no sense of audience; as a result, the language was totally inappropriate.

A good writer anticipates the audience for a message: What is the reader like? How will that reader react to the message? One technique is to visualize the

FIGURE 3.2 ■ Asking the Right Questions to Profile Your Audience

Primary Audience

Who is my primary reader or listener?

What is my personal and professional relationship with that person?

How much does that person know about the subject?

What do I know about that person's education, beliefs, culture, and attitudes?

Should I expect a neutral, positive, or negative response to my message?

Secondary Audience

Who might see this message after the primary audience?

How do these people differ from the primary audience?

reader when writing. By profiling your audience and shaping a message to respond to that profile, you are more likely to achieve your communication goals.

Profiling the audience. Visualizing your audience is a pivotal step in the writing process. The questions in Figure 3.2 will help you profile your audience. How much time you devote to answering these questions depends greatly on your message and its context. An analytical report that you compose for management or an oral presentation before a big group would, of course, demand considerable audience anticipation. On the other hand, a memo to a co-worker or a letter to a familiar supplier might require only a few moments of planning. No matter how short your message, though, spend some time thinking about the audience so that you can tailor your words to your readers or listeners. "The most often unasked question in business and professional communication," claims a writing expert, "is as simple as it is important: HAVE I THOUGHT ENOUGH ABOUT MY AUDIENCE?"[3]

Responding to the profile. Anticipating your audience helps you make decisions about shaping the message. You'll discover what kind of language is appropriate—whether you're free to use specialized technical terms, whether you should explain everything, and so on. You'll decide whether your tone should be formal or informal, and you'll select the most desirable channel. Imagining whether the receiver is likely to be neutral, positive, or negative will help you determine how to organize your message.

Another result of profiling your audience will be knowing whether a secondary audience is possible. If so, you'll provide more background information and be more specific in identifying items than would be necessary for the primary audience only. Analyzing the task and anticipating the audience assist you in adapting your message so that it will accomplish what you intend.

By profiling your audience before you write, you can choose the right tone, language, and channel.

Adapting to the Task and Audience

After analyzing your purpose and anticipating your audience, you must convey your purpose to that audience. Adaptation is the process of creating a message that suits your audience.

Ways to adapt to the audience include choosing the right words and tone, spotlighting reader benefits, cultivating a "you" attitude, and using sensitive, courteous language.

One important aspect of adaptation is tone. Conveyed largely by the words in a message, tone reflects how a receiver feels upon reading or hearing a message. For example, think how you would react to these statements:

You must return the form by 5 p.m.

Would you please return the form by 5 p.m.

The wording of the first message establishes an aggressive or negative tone—no one likes being told what to do. The second message is reworded in a friendlier, more positive manner. Poorly chosen words may sound demeaning, condescending, discourteous, pretentious, or demanding. Notice in Lise Andrews's customer response letter in Figure 3.3 the courteous and warm tone she achieves. Her letter responds to a customer's concern about the changing merchandise mix available in Tilley's catalogues. The customer also wanted to receive fewer catalogues. Lise's letter explains Tilley's expanded merchandise line and reassures the customer that Tilley has not abandoned its emphasis on classic styles.

Skilled communicators create a positive tone in their messages by using a number of adaptive techniques, some of which are unconscious. These include spotlighting receiver benefits, cultivating a *you* attitude, and avoiding gender, racial, age, and disability bias. Additional adaptive techniques include being courteous, using familiar words, and choosing precise words.

Empathic communicators envision the receiver and focus on benefits to that person.

Spotlighting receiver benefits. Focusing on the audience may sound like a modern idea, but Samuel Johnson, the British lexicographer and writer, recognized this fundamental idea over 200 years ago. In describing the purpose of writing, Johnson observed, "The only end of writing is to enable the reader better to enjoy life or better to endure it."[4] This wise advice can serve as a fundamental guide for today's business communicators. A communication consultant gives this solid advice to his business clients, "Always stress the benefit to the readers of whatever it is you're trying to get them to do. If you can show them how you're going to save *them* frustration or help them meet their goals, you have the makings of a powerful message."[5]

Adapting your message to the receiver's needs means putting yourself into that person's shoes. It's called empathy. Empathic senders think about how a receiver will decode a message. They try to give something to the receiver, solve the receiver's problems, save the receiver's money, or just understand the feelings and position of the person. Which of the following messages are more appealing to the receiver?

Sender-focused	**Receiver-focused**
To enable us to update our stockholder records, we ask that the enclosed card be returned.	So that you may promptly receive dividend cheques and information related to your shares, please return the enclosed card.
Our warranty becomes effective only when we receive an owner's registration.	Your warranty begins working for you as soon as you return your owner's registration.
We offer an audiocassette language course that we have complete faith in.	The sooner you order the audiocassette language program, the sooner the rewards will be yours.

FIGURE 3.3 ■ Successful Customer Response Letter

February 23, 1996

Mrs. Elaine Hough
2175 Edenwood Road
Brandon, MB R7A 6A9

Dear Mrs. Hough:

Your letter was a strong endorsement of our belief that we made the right choice when we devoted our company to comfort, ease of care, durability, and a smart appearance — and that it's still the right choice.

Opens response to inquiry by agreeing with customer

It's true we've made changes. In the past few years, with the markets soft and tastes changing, we reexamined our merchandise with a view to continuing to serve valued customers while introducing ourselves to new ones. We decided we want to give you more choices for more occasions.

Explains evolving merchandise line from company's and reader's view

Our commitment to the classics hasn't weakened, as I hope you'd agree, having seen recent catalogues. But we've defined "classic" more inclusively than in the past. We're using new fabrics, new colours, a more relaxed fit. There's more imagination in our product mix now, but the hats, pants, vests, jackets, and other basics for which you've relied on us are still here. You may not find each one in every catalogue, and you may notice the new products more than those you've seen before. The classics are still here, and the selection will be growing.

Emphasizes areas of agreement

Uses conversational language to convey warmth and sincerity

I've arranged to send you just the four catalogues a year you wanted. I hope you'll keep an eye out for them. I think that, more and more, you'll be able to come to us for the styles you want.

Concludes by giving customer what she wants and promoting future business

Sincerely,

Lise Andrews

Lise Andrews
Customer Service

Tilley Endurables Inc., 900 Don Mills Road, Don Mills, Ontario M3C 1V6 • Telephone (416) 441-6141 • Fax (416) 444-3860

The Human Resources Department requires that the enclosed questionnaire be completed immediately so that we can allocate our training resources funds.	You can be one of the first employees to sign up for the new career development program. Fill out the attached questionnaire and return it immediately.

Cultivating the "you" view. Notice how many of the previous receiver-focused messages included the word *you*. In concentrating on receiver benefits, skilled communicators naturally develop the "you" view. They emphasize second-person pronouns (*you, your*) instead of first-person pronouns (*I/we, us, our*). Whether your goal is to inform, persuade, or promote goodwill, the catchiest words you can use are *you* and *your*. Compare the following examples.

Effective communicators develop the "you" view— in a sincere, not manipulative or critical, tone.

"I/We" View	"You" View
I have scheduled your vacation to begin May 1.	You may begin your vacation May 1.
We have shipped your order by UPS, and we are sure it will arrive in time for the sales promotion January 15.	Your order will be delivered by UPS in time for your sales promotion January 15.
I'm asking all our employees to respond to the attached survey about working conditions.	Because your ideas count, please complete the attached survey about working conditions.

Avoid overusing "you" or including it when it suggests blame.

To see if you're really concentrating on the reader, try using the "empathy index." In one of your messages, count all the second-person references. Then, count all the first-person references. Your empathy index is low if the number of *I*'s and *we*'s outnumbers the *you*'s and *your*'s.

But the use of *you* is more than merely a numbers game. Second-person pronouns can be overused and misused. Readers appreciate genuine interest, but they resent obvious attempts at manipulation. Some sales messages, for example, are guilty of overkill when they include *you* dozens of times in a direct-mail promotion. Furthermore, the word *can* sometimes creates the wrong impression. Consider this statement: *You cannot return merchandise until you receive written approval. You* appears twice, but the reader feels singled out for criticism. In the following version the message is less personal: *Customers may return merchandise with written approval.* In short, avoid using *you* for general statements that suggest blame and could cause ill will.

Skilled communicators are able to convey sincerity, a particularly difficult feeling to achieve with words alone. These communicators send hidden messages that say to readers and customers "You are important, I hear you, and I'm honestly trying to please you."

Sensitive communicators avoid gender, racial or ethnic, and disability biases.

Using bias-free language. In adapting a message to its audience, be sure your language is tactful and bias-free. Few writers set out to be offensive. Sometimes, though, we all say things that we never thought might hurt someone. The real problem is that we don't *think* about the words that stereotype groups of people, such as *the boys in the mail room* or *the girls in the typing pool.* Be cautious about expressions that might be biased in terms of gender, race, ethnicity, age, and disability.[6]

Avoiding gender bias. You can defuse gender time bombs by replacing words that exclude or stereotype women (sometimes called sexist language) with neutral, inclusive expressions. In the following examples note how sexist terms and phrases were replaced with neutral ones.

Gender-biased	Improved
female doctor, woman lawyer, cleaning woman	doctor, lawyer, cleaner
waiter or waitress, authoress, stewardess	server, author, cabin attendant
mankind, man-hour, man-made	humanity, working hours, artificial
office girls	office workers
the doctor ... he	doctors ... they
the teacher ... she	teachers ... they
executives and their wives	executives and their spouses
foreman, flag-man, workman	lead worker, flagger, worker
businessman, salesman	businessperson, sales representative

Gender-biased	Improved
Every employee must have his picture taken.	Every employee must have a picture taken.
	All employees must have their pictures taken.
	Every employee must have his or her picture taken.
	You (or *one*) must have a picture taken.

Generally, you can avoid gender-biased language by leaving out the words *man* or *woman*, by using plural nouns and pronouns, or by changing to a gender-free word (*person* or *representative*).

Avoiding racial or ethnic bias. You need indicate racial or ethnic identification only if the context demands it.

Racially or Ethnically Biased	Improved
An Indian accountant was hired.	An accountant was hired.
James Lee, a native Canadian, applied.	James Lee applied.

Avoiding age bias. Again, specify age only if it is relevant, and avoid expressions that are demeaning or subjective.

Age-biased	Improved
The law applied to old people.	The law applied to people over 65.
Sally Kay, 55, was transferred.	Sally Kay was transferred.
spry old gentleman	man
little old lady	woman

Avoiding disability bias. Unless relevant, do not refer to an individual's disability. When necessary, use terms that do not stigmatize disabled individuals.

Disability-biased	Improved
afflicted with, suffering from, crippled by	has
defect, disease	condition
confined to a wheelchair	uses a wheelchair

These examples give you a quick look at a few problem expressions. The real key to bias-free communication, though, lies in your awareness and commitment. Always be on the lookout to be sure that your messages do not exclude, stereotype, or offend people.

Expressing yourself positively. Certain negative words create ill will because they appear to blame or accuse readers. For example, opening a letter to a customer with *You claim that* suggests that you don't believe the customer. Other loaded words that can get you into trouble are *complaint, criticism, defective, failed, mistake,* and *neglected.* Often the writer is unconscious of the effect of these words. Take a look at the Career Skills box on page 77 to see eight easy ways to make your readers and listeners angry. To avoid these angry reactions, restrict negative words and try to find positive ways to express ideas. You provide more options to the reader when you tell what can be done instead of what can't be done.

Negative	Positive
You failed to include your credit card number, so we can't mail your order.	We'll mail your order as soon as we receive your credit card number.
Your letter of May 2 claims that you returned a defective headset.	Your May 2 letter describes a headset you returned.
You cannot park in Lot H until April 1.	You may park in Lot H starting April 1.
You won't be sorry that ...	You will be happy that ...
The problem cannot be solved without the aid of top management.	With the aid of top management, the problem can be solved.

Being courteous. Maintaining a courteous tone involves not just guarding against rudeness but also avoiding words that sound demanding or preachy. Expressions like *you should*, *you must*, and *you have to* cause people to instinctively react with "Oh, yeah?" One remedy is to turn these demands into rhetorical questions that begin with *Will you please* ... Giving reasons for a request also softens the tone.

Less Courteous	More Courteous
You must complete this report before Friday.	Will you please complete the report by Friday.
You should organize paper recycling in this department.	Organizing paper recycling will reduce your office costs and help preserve the environment.

Even when you feel justified in displaying anger, remember that losing your temper or being sarcastic will seldom accomplish your goals as a business communicator—to inform, to persuade, and to create goodwill. When you are irritated, frustrated, or infuriated, keep cool and try to defuse the situation. Concentrate on the real problem. What must be done to solve it?

Even when you are justifiably angry, courteous language is the best way to achieve your objectives.

You May Be Thinking This	Better to Say This
This is the second time I've written. Can't you get anything right?	Please credit my account for $843. My latest statement shows that the error noted in my letter of June 2 has not been corrected.
Am I the only one who can read the operating manual?	Let's review the operating manual together so that you can get your documents to print correctly next time.
Hey, don't blame me! I'm not the promoter who took off with the funds.	Please accept our sincere apologies and two free tickets to our next event. Let me try to explain why we had to substitute performers.

The simpler the language, the better.

Simplifying your language. In adapting your message to your audience, whenever possible use short, familiar words that you think they will recognize. Don't, however, avoid a big word that (1) conveys your idea efficiently and (2) is appropriate for the audience. Your goal is to shun pompous and pretentious language. One communication expert advises writers to use "GO" words. If you mean *begin*, don't say *commence* or *initiate*. If you mean *give*, don't write *render*.[7] By substituting everyday, familiar words for unfamiliar ones, as shown here, you help your audience comprehend your ideas quickly.

EIGHT EASY WAYS TO MAKE READERS AND LISTENERS ANGRY

Communicators in all fields run the risk of angering receivers by using certain expressions that have hidden meanings. Here are techniques and expressions to avoid because they are guaranteed to offend your audience.

- **Call them stupid (even if done unintentionally):**

  If you had read the instruction booklet ...

  You are probably ignorant of the fact that ...

- **Suggest that they are lying (even if you don't say so directly):**

  You claim that you returned the item.

  According to you, the item stopped working.

- **Issue commands and orders:**

  You must comply with our regulations.

  We expect you to complete all portions of the form.

- **Confuse a person's name or gender:**

  Dear Ms. Lee: We understand, Mr. Lee, that ...

  Dear Phoung: As a lady of fine tastes, you ...

- **Imply that they are complainers:**

  You complain that ...

  We have received your complaint describing ...

- **Blame them:**

  Obviously you overlooked ...

  You forgot to...

  You neglected to ...

  You failed to ...

- **Write in a language that requires interpretation:**

  When your financial status ameliorates, your application will be given expeditious scrutiny.

  Because of current electronic compositional instrumentation, you need no longer fear exposure of your grammatical foibles.

- **Issue ultimatums:**

  This will be the last memo sent on this subject. Anyone dressing inappropriately faces immediate disciplinary action!

  Either comply with the regulations or face the consequences.

Career Track Application

Collect actual memos, letters, or other documents that illustrate unintentionally offensive language. Bring the documents for discussion and revision.

Unfamiliar	Familiar
commensurate	equal
interrogate	question
mandate	require
materialize	appear
remunerate	pay
terminate	end

At the same time, be selective in your use of jargon. Jargon describes technical or specialized terms within a field. These terms enable insiders to communicate complex ideas briefly, but to outsiders they mean nothing. Human resources professionals, for example, know precisely what's meant by "cafeteria plan" (a benefits option program), but most of us would be thinking about lunch. Geologists refer to *plate tectonics*, and physicians discuss *metastatic carcinomas*, but these terms mean little to most of us. Use specialized language only when the audience will understand it. And don't forget to consider secondary audiences: Will those potential readers understand any technical terms used?

Using precise, vigorous words. Strong verbs and concrete nouns give readers more information and keep them interested. Don't overlook the thesaurus (or the thesaurus program on your computer) for expanding your word choices and vocabulary. Whenever possible, use specific words as shown here.

Imprecise, Dull	More Precise
a gain in profits	a jump in profits
	a 23 percent hike in profits
it takes memory	it hogs memory
	it demands 2 MG of RAM
to think about	to identify, diagnose, analyze
	to probe, examine, inspect

By reviewing the tips in the following checklist, you can master the steps in preparing to write. As you review these tips, remember the three basics of preparing for the composition process: analyze, anticipate, and adapt.

▉ Checklist for Adapting a Message to Its Audience

✓ **Identify the message purpose.** Ask yourself why you are communicating and what you hope to achieve. Look for primary and secondary purposes.

✓ **Select the most suitable form.** Determine whether you need a permanent record or whether the message is too sensitive to put in writing.

✓ **Profile the audience.** Identify your relationship with the reader and your knowledge about that individual or group. Assess how much they know about the subject.

✓ **Focus on reader benefits.** Phrase your statements from the reader's viewpoint, not the writer's. Concentrate on the "you" view (*Your order will arrive*, *You can enjoy*, *Your ideas count*).

✓ **Avoid bias in gender and racial expressions.** Use bias-free words (*businessperson* instead of *businessman*, *working hours* instead of *man-hours*). Omit ethnic identification unless the context demands it.

✓ **Avoid bias in age and disability language.** Include age only if relevant. Avoid potentially demeaning expressions (*spry old gentleman*), and use terms that do not stigmatize people with disabilities (*he is disabled* instead of *he is a cripple* or *he has a handicap*).

✓ **Express ideas positively rather than negatively.** Instead of *Your order can't be shipped before June 1*, say *Your order can be shipped June 1*.

✓ **Use short, familiar words.** Use technical terms and big words only if they are appropriate for the audience (*end* not *terminate*, *required* not *mandatory*).

✓ **Search for precise, vigorous words.** Use a thesaurus if necessary to find strong verbs and concrete nouns (*announces* instead of *says*, *brokerage* instead of *business*).

Adapting to Ethical and Legal Responsibilities

The process of adaptation hits a sensitive nerve when we confront ethical and legal issues. Is a message honest? Is an action ethical? Will the message cause a lawsuit?

The 1990s have intensified interest in business ethics. Business leaders are speaking out more about ethics, and organizations and many postsecondary institutions are offering courses in ethics. Because of this increased interest in corporate ethics, assistance to companies is readily available. For example, organizations such as the Canadian Centre for Ethics and Corporate Policy have been established. In addition, many larger companies are making their codes of conduct public knowledge.[8] Some companies also use their codes of conduct for additional purposes. For example, Imperial Oil requires all its employees— 12 500 people—to read the code of ethics and sign a statement that they have read and understood it. At the Royal Bank, all employees receive a copy of the bank's code of conduct and are reminded of the code when performance appraisals are done.[9] It's obvious that many businesses recognize that ethical practices make good business sense. Ethical companies endure less litigation, less resentment, and less government regulation.[10] Equally important, ethical business managers and businesses "tend to be more trusted and better treated by employees, suppliers, stockholders, and consumers."[11] For individuals, ethical behaviour makes sense because once a reputation is tainted, trust can never be regained.

> Ethical conduct not only promotes social responsibility but also makes good business sense.

Just what is ethical behaviour? Ethics author Mary E. Guy defines it as "that behaviour which is the right thing to do, given the circumstances."[12] Ethical behaviour involves four principles: honesty, integrity, fairness, and concern for others. "These four principles are like the four legs of a stool," explains ethics authority Michael Josephson. "If even one leg is missing, the stool wobbles, and if two are missing, the stool falls. It's not enough to pride yourself on your honesty and integrity if you're not fair or caring."[13] Consider a manager who would never dream of behaving dishonestly on the job or off. Yet this same manager forces an important employee to choose between losing her job and staying home with a sick child. The manager's lack of caring and failure to consider the circumstances creates a shaky ethical position that would be difficult to justify.

Five Common Ethical Traps

In making ethical decisions, business communicators commonly face five traps that can make choosing the right decision more difficult.[14]

> Recognizing five ethical traps can help communicators avoid them.

The false necessity trap. Companies may act from the belief that they are doing what they must do. They convince themselves that they have no choice, when in fact it may be a matter of convenience, comfort, or cost. Consider the Ford Pinto example. In order to meet the challenge of competing in the smaller car market in the 1960s, Ford Motor Company sped up its production schedule to have its car ready. Internal memos had reported problems with the fuel tank. Nevertheless, Ford proceeded with production of the Pinto without remedying the problem. The justification was that the car met the required production standards.[15] Apparently, falling into the false necessity trap, Ford felt it had no choice but to continue with the production.

The doctrine-of-relative-filth trap. Unethical actions sometimes look good when compared with the worse behaviour of others. What's a little fudging on an expense account compared with the pleasure cruise the boss took and charged as a business trip? On Toronto's Bay Street many stockbrokers probably considered their minor deviations from ethical sales techniques to be insignificant, and therefore acceptable, when compared with the major crimes of the American junk-bond king Michael Milken and others.

The rationalization trap. In falling into the rationalization trap, people try to justify unethical actions by justifying them with excuses. Consider employees who "steal" time from their employers—taking long lunch and coffee breaks, claiming sick leave when not ill, and doing their own tasks on company time. It's easy to rationalize such actions: "I deserve an extra-long lunch break because I can't get all my shopping done on such a short lunch hour" or "I'll just write my class report at the office because the computer printer is much better than mine, and they aren't paying me what I'm worth anyway."

The self-deception trap. Applicants for jobs often fall into the self-deception trap. They are all too willing to inflate grade-point averages or exaggerate past accomplishments to impress prospective employers. One applicant, for example, claimed to have worked as a broker's assistant at a prestigious securities firm. A background check revealed that he had interviewed for the securities job but was never offered it.[16] Another applicant claimed that in his summer job he was "responsible for cross-corporate transferral of multidimensional client receivables." In other words, he moved boxes from sales to shipping. Self-deception can lead to unethical and possibly illegal behaviour.

The ends-justify-the-means trap. Taking unethical actions to achieve a desirable goal is a common trap. Consider a manager in the claims division of a large health insurance company who coerced clerical staff into working overtime without pay. The goal was the reduction of a backlog of unprocessed claims. The goal was worthy, but the means of reaching it was unethical.

Goals of Ethical Business Communication

Business communicators can minimize the danger of falling into ethical traps by setting specific ethical goals. Although the following goals hardly constitute a formal code of conduct, they will help business writers maintain a high ethical standard.

Telling the truth. Ethical business communicators do not intentionally make statements that are untrue or deceptive. We become aware of dishonesty in business when violators break laws, notably in advertising, packaging, and marketing. The Ontario Court's General Division, for example, ruled that Robin Hood's ads comparing its pie crusts to those of Maple Leaf were false and misleading and affected Maple Leaf's reputation. As a result of cases such as this, advertisers are warned that shading the truth is unacceptable.[17]

Half-truths, exaggerations, and deceptions constitute unethical communication. But conflicting loyalties sometimes blur the line between right and wrong for businesspeople. Let's say you helped the marketing director, who is both your boss and your friend, conduct consumer research about a new company product. When you see the final report, you are astonished at how the findings have been distorted to show a highly favourable product approval rating. You are torn between loyalty to your boss (and friend) and loyalty to the company. Tools for helping you solve such ethical dilemmas will be discussed shortly.

Labelling opinions. Sensitive communicators know the difference between facts and opinions. Facts are verifiable and often are quantifiable; opinions are beliefs held with confidence but without substantiation. It's a fact, for example, that women are starting new businesses twice as fast as men.[18] It's an opinion, though, that increasing numbers of women are abandoning the corporate employment arena to start these businesses. Such a statement can't be verified. Stating opinions as if they were facts is unethical.

Facts **are verifiable;** *opinions* **are beliefs held with conviction.**

Being objective. Ethical business communicators recognize their own biases and strive to keep them from distorting a message. Suppose you are asked to investigate microcomputers and write a report recommending a brand for your office. As you visit stores and watch computer demonstrations, you discover that an old high school friend is selling Brand X. Because you always liked this individual and have faith in his judgment, you may be inclined to tilt your recommendation in his direction. However, it's unethical to misrepresent the facts in your report or to put a spin on your arguments based on friendship. To be ethical, you could note in your report that you have known the person for 10 years and that you respect his opinion. In this way, you have disclosed your relationship as well as the reasons for your decision. Honest reporting means presenting the whole picture and relating all facts fairly.

Writing clearly. The ethical business communicator feels an obligation to write clearly so that the reader understands easily and quickly. Some companies write their policies, warranties, and contracts in "plain English," that is, in language comprehensible to average readers. Plain English means short sentences, simple words, and clear organization. Writers who intentionally obscure the meaning with long sentences and difficult words are being unethical.

"**Plain English" requires simple, understandable language in policies, contracts, warranties, and other documents.**

A thin line separates unethical composition from inefficient composition. Some might argue that writers who send wordy, imprecise messages requiring additional correspondence to clarify the meaning are acting unethically. However, the problem may be one of experience and skill rather than ethics. Although such messages waste the time of both senders and receivers, they are not unethical unless the intent is to deceive.

Giving credit. As you probably know, using the written ideas of others without credit is called *plagiarism*. Ethical communicators give credit for ideas by (1) referring to originators' names within the text, (2) using quotation marks, and (3) documenting sources with endnotes, footnotes, or internal references. (You'll learn how to do this in Chapter 13.) One student writer explained his reasons for plagiarizing material in his report by rationalizing, "But the encyclopedia said it so much better than I could!" This may be so, yet such an argument is no justification for appropriating the words of others. Quotation marks and footnotes could have saved the student. In school or on the job, stealing ideas or words from others is unethical and may even be illegal.

Talking with a co-worker whose advice you value can be an important tool in resolving ethical problems. When you are torn by conflicting loyalties or responsibilities, discuss your concerns with someone you trust.

Tools for Doing the Right Thing

Acting ethically means doing the right thing—given the situation.

In composing messages or engaging in other activities on the job, business communicators can't help being torn by conflicting loyalties. Do we tell the truth and risk our jobs? Do we show loyalty to friends even if it means bending the rules? Should we be tactful or totally honest? Is it our duty to make a profit or to be socially responsible? Acting ethically means doing the right thing *given the circumstances*. Each set of circumstances requires analyzing issues, evaluating choices, and acting responsibly.

Resolving ethical issues is never easy, but the task can be made less difficult if you know how to identify key issues. The following questions may be helpful.

- *Is the action you are considering legal?* No matter who asks you to do it nor how important you feel the result will be, avoid anything that is prohibited by law. Giving a kickback to a buyer for a large order is illegal, even if you suspect that others in your field do it and you know that without the kickback you will lose the sale.

Business communicators can help resolve ethical issues through self-examination.

- *How would you see the problem if you were on the opposite side?* Looking at all sides of an issue helps you gain perspective. Consider the issue of mandatory drug testing among employees. From management's viewpoint such testing could stop drug abuse, improve job performance, and lower health insurance premiums. From the employees' viewpoint mandatory testing reflects a lack of trust of employees and constitutes an invasion of privacy. By weighing both sides of the issue, you can arrive at a more equitable solution.

- *What are alternative solutions?* Consider all dimensions of other options. Would the alternative be more ethical? Under the circumstances, is the alternative feasible? Can an alternative solution be implemented with a minimum of disruption and with a high degree of probable success? In the situation involving your boss's distortion of consumer product research, you could go to the head of the company and tell what you know. A more tactful alternative, however, would be to approach your boss and ask if you misunderstood the report's findings or if an error might have been made.

- *Can you discuss the problem with someone whose advice you trust?* Suppose you feel ethically bound to report accurate information to a client—even though your boss has ordered you not to do so. Talking about your dilemma with a co-worker or with a colleague in your field might give you helpful insights and lead to possible alternatives.

- *How would you feel if your family, friends, employer, or co-workers learned of your action?* If the thought of revealing your action publicly produces cold sweats, your choice is probably not a wise one. Losing the faith of your friends or the confidence of your customers is not worth whatever short-term gains might be realized.

Perhaps the best advice in ethical matters is contained in the Golden Rule: Do unto others as you would have others do unto you. The ultimate solution to all ethics problems is treating others fairly and doing what is right to achieve what is good.

Language that avoids litigation. Ethics questions are perplexing because there are few written rules to guide us. Legal questions are equally confusing because, although laws exist, they are not always interpreted consistently. And in our current business environment, lawsuits abound, many of which centre on the use and abuse of language. You can protect yourself and stay out of court by knowing what's legal and by adapting your language accordingly. Be especially careful when communicating in the following four areas: investments, safety, marketing, and human resources. Because these information areas generate the most lawsuits, we must examine them more closely.[19]

<aside>Careful communicators should familiarize themselves with information in four information areas: investments, safety, marketing, and human resources.</aside>

Investment information. Writers describing the sale of stocks or financial services must follow specific laws written to protect investors. Any messages—including letters, newsletters, and pamphlets—must be free from misleading information, exaggerations, or half-truths. One American company inadvertently violated the law by declaring that it was "recession-proof." After going bankrupt, the company was sued by angry stockholders claiming that they had been deceived. Another company, Lotus Development Corporation, caused a flurry of lawsuits by withholding information that revealed problems in a new version of its 1-2-3 program. Stockholders sued, charging that managers had deliberately concealed the bad news, thus keeping stock prices artificially high. Experienced financial writers know that careless language and even poor timing may provoke litigation.

Safety information. Writers describing potentially dangerous products worry not only about being sued but also about protecting people from physical harm. Warnings must do more than suggest danger; they must also clearly tell people how to use the product safely and motivate them to do so. Clearly written safety messages avoid vague, abstract, and unfamiliar words. They include presentation techniques, such as headings and bullets—devices you'll learn more about in coming chapters.

<aside>Warnings on dangerous products must be written especially clearly.</aside>

Marketing information. Sales and marketing messages are illegal if they falsely advertise prices, performance capability, quality, or other product characteristics, or deceive the buyer in any way. A Western Canadian electronics

Sales and marketing
messages must not make
claims that can't or won't
be fulfilled or verified.

firm was convicted of bait-and-switch selling. This practice occurs when a company advertises a very low price on a product, but the customer has great difficulty getting the special price. Instead, the company attempts to sell the customer a similar but higher-priced product or offers a rain check that will not be honoured. This tactic for attracting customers is a form of deceptive marketing.[20] Furthermore, sellers of services must also be cautious about the language they use to describe what they will do. Letters, reports, and proposals that describe services to be performed are interpreted as contracts in court. Therefore, language must not promise more than intended. Here are some dangerous words (and recommended alternatives) that have created misunderstandings leading to lawsuits.[21]

Dangerous Word	Court Interpretation	Recommended Alternative
inspect	to examine critically; to investigate and test officially; to scrutinize	review study tour the facilities
determine	to come to a decision; to decide; to resolve	evaluate assess analyze
assure	to render safe; to make secure; to give confidence; to cause to feel certain	to facilitate; to provide further confidence; to enhance the reliability of

Human resources information. The vast number of lawsuits relating to employment makes this a treacherous area for business communicators. In evaluating employees in the workplace, avoid making unsubstantiated negative comments. It's also unwise to assess traits (*she is unreliable*) because they require subjective judgment. Concentrate instead on specific incidents (*in the last month she missed four work days and was late three times*). Fear of lawsuits causes some companies to stop providing letters of recommendation for former employees. To be safe, give recommendations only when the former employee authorizes the recommendation and when you can say something positive. Stick to job-related information.

Statements in employee handbooks also require careful wording, because the courts might rule that such statements are "implied contracts." Consider the following handbook remark: "We at Data Corporation show our appreciation for hard work and team spirit by rewarding everyone who performs well." This seemingly harmless statement could make it difficult to fire an employee because of the implied employment promise.[22]

In adapting messages to meet today's sensitive business environment, be sensitive to the rights of others and to your own rights. The key elements in this adaptation process are awareness of laws, sensitivity to interpretations, and careful use of language.

■ Summary of Learning Goals

1. Describe three basic elements that distinguish business writing from academic writing. Summarize the three phases of the 3 × 3 writing process. Business writing differs from creative writing in that it is purposeful, economical, and reader-oriented. Business writers seek to solve problems and convey information. Phase 1 of the writing process involves analyzing the message, anticipating the audience, and considering ways to adapt the message to the audience. Phase 2 involves researching the topic, organizing the material, and composing the message. Phase 3 involves revising, proofreading, and evaluating the message.

2. **Explain the importance of task analysis and audience anticipation in Phase 1 of the writing process.** An important part of preparation for writing is deciding your purpose and knowing what you hope to achieve. Your message may have a primary purpose (explaining company policy or selling a product) and a secondary purpose (promoting goodwill). Equally important is profiling your primary and secondary audiences so that you will know what adaptations to make.

3. **Specify six writing techniques that help communicators adapt messages to their audiences.** Skilled communicators strive to (a) spotlight reader benefits, (b) look at a message from the receiver's perspective (the "you" view), (c) use tactful language that avoids gender, racial, ethnic, and disability biases, (d) state ideas positively, (e) show courtesy, and (f) use short, familiar, and precise words.

4. **Name five common ethical traps that business communicators must avoid.** Five ethical pitfalls to avoid are (a) the false-necessity trap, in which people feel they have only one choice; (b) the doctrine-of-relative-filth trap, whereby unethical actions look acceptable when compared with worse behaviour of others; (c) the rationalization trap, in which people justify unethical actions with excuses; (d) the self-deception trap whereby people convince themselves that unethical behaviour is acceptable; and (e) the ends-justify-the-means trap, in which unethical methods are used to achieve a worthy goal.

5. **List the goals of ethical business communication and describe important tools for doing the right thing.** Ethical business communicators strive to (a) tell the truth, (b) label opinions so that they are not confused with facts, (c) be objective and avoid distorting a message, (d) write clearly and avoid obscure language, and (e) give credit when using the ideas of others. When you face a difficult decision, the following questions serve as valuable guides: (a) Is the action you are considering legal? (b) How would you see the problem if you were on the opposite side? (c) What are alternative solutions? (d) Can you discuss the problem with someone whose advice you trust? (e) How would you feel if your family, friends, employer, or co-workers learned of your action?

6. **Recognize language that may lead to lawsuits.** Actions and language in four information areas generate the most lawsuits: investments, safety, marketing, and human resources. In these areas writers must avoid misleading information, exaggerations, and half-truths. Safety information, including warnings, must clearly tell people how to use a product safely and persuade them to do so. In addition to being honest, marketing information must not promise more than intended. And communicators in human resources must use careful wording (particularly in employment recommendations and employee handbooks) to avoid lawsuits.

CHAPTER REVIEW

1. What are three ways in which business writing differs from other writing? (Goal 1)

2. Describe the components in each stage of the 3×3 writing process. (Goal 1)

3. Why should you "profile" your audience before composing a message? (Goal 2)

4. What is *empathy*, and how does it apply to business writing? (Goal 2)

5. Discuss the effects of first- and second-person pronouns. (Goal 2)

6. What unspoken message does a reader perceive from the words *You claim that ...* ? (Goal 1)

7. What is gender-biased language? Give examples. (Goal 3)

8. When should a writer include racial or ethnic identification, such as *Ellen Lee, an Asian, ...* ? (Goal 3)

9. What is jargon and when is it suitable for business writing? (Goal 3)

10. What's wrong with using words like *commence*, *mandate*, and *interrogate*? (Goal 3)

11. How would you describe *ethical behaviour*? (Goals 4, 5)

12. Discuss five traps that block ethical behaviour. (Goal 4)

13. When faced with a difficult ethical decision, what questions should you ask yourself? (Goal 5)

14. What four information areas generate the most lawsuits? (Goal 6)

15. How can business communicators protect themselves against lawsuits? (Goal 6)

DISCUSSION

1. How can the 3×3 writing process help the writer of a business report as well as the writer of an oral presentation? (Goals 1, 2)

2. Comment on the idea that the most important step in composition is in audience analysis. (Goal 2)

3. Discuss the following statement: "The English language is a landmine—it is filled with terms that are easily misinterpreted as derogatory and others that are blatantly insulting. ... Being fair and objective is not enough; employers must also appear to be so."[23] (Goal 3)

4. How are the rules of ethical behaviour that govern businesses different from those that govern your personal behaviour? (Goals 4, 5)

5. **Ethical Issue:** Suppose your superior asked you to change year-end financial data, and you knew that if you didn't, you might lose your job. What would you do if it were a small amount? A large amount?

ACTIVITIES

3.1 Document for Analysis (Goal 3)

Discuss the following memo, which is based on an actual document sent to employees. How could you apply what you learned in this chapter to improving this memo?

TO: All Employees Using HP 5000 Computers

It has recently come to my attention that a computer security problem exists within our organization. I understand that the problem is twofold in nature:

a. You have been sharing computer passwords.

b. You are using automatic log-on procedures.

Henceforth, you are prohibited from sharing passwords for security reasons that should be axiomatic. We also must forbid you to use automatic log-on files because they empower anyone to have access to our entire computer system and all company data.
Enclosed please find a form that you must sign and return to the aforementioned individual, indicating your acknowledgment of and acquiescence to the procedures described here. Any computer user whose signed form is not returned will have his personal password invalidated.

3.2 Analyzing Audiences (Goal 2)

Using the questions in Figure 3.2, write a brief analysis of the audience for each of the following communication tasks.

a. Your letter of application for a job advertised in your local newspaper. Your qualifications match the job description.

b. A memo to your boss persuading her to allow you to attend a computer class that will require you to leave work early two days a week for 10 weeks.

c. An unsolicited sales letter promoting life insurance to a targeted group of executives.

d. A letter from the municipal water department explaining that while the tap water may taste and smell bad, it poses no threats to health.

e. A letter from a credit card organization refusing credit to an applicant.

3.3   Ethics Survey (Goals 4, 5, 6)

How do your ethics compare with those of businesspeople across the country? Complete the following survey and then compare your responses with the results obtained from readers of *Business Month* magazine.[24] Be prepared to discuss your responses in class.

a. Corporate ethics should be as important a priority as profits.

❏ ❏ ❏ ❏ ❏
Strongly   Agree   Undecided   Disagree   Strongly
agree   disagree

b. In an overzealous attempt to help their companies, officials with two generic drug makers lied to the Department of Health and Welfare. Is this kind of dishonesty ever acceptable?

Yes, because _____

No, because _____

c. It's okay to bend the rules if your job is at stake.

❏ ❏ ❏ ❏
Always   Often   Occasionally   Never

d. How would you rank the following infractions, where 1 represents the most offensive and 5 the least offensive infraction?

_____ cheating on an expense report

_____ playing dirty tricks on a competitor

_____ taking credit for someone else's accomplishment

_____ paying bribes in a country where it's the accepted custom

_____ lying to protect a friend

e. Although he voted to deny shareholders a lucrative $200-a-share takeover offer, Time Inc.'s CEO entered into a different merger deal guaranteeing himself a 10-year contract for at least $14.6 million. Was this ethical?

❏ ❏ ❏
Yes   No   Don't know

3.4   Reader Benefits and "You" View (Goal 3)

Revise the following sentences to emphasize the reader's perspective and the "you" view.

a. Our safety policy forbids us to rent power equipment to anyone who cannot demonstrate proficiency in its use.

b. We take pride in announcing a new schedule of low-cost flights to Halifax.

c. So that we may bring our customer records up to date and eliminate the expense of duplicate mailings, we are asking you to complete the enclosed card.

d. Our 50 years of experience in direct-mail advertising will enable us to help you dazzle your customers.

e. I give my permission for you to attend the two-day workshop.

f. We're requesting all employees to complete the enclosed questionnaire so that we may develop a master schedule for summer vacations.

g. I think my background and my education match the description of the manager trainee position you advertised.

h. We are offering an in-house training program for employees who want to improve their writing skills.

i. We are pleased to announce an arrangement with IBM that allows us to offer discounted computers in the student bookstore.

j. We have approved your application for credit.

k. We are pleased to announce that we have selected you to join our trainee program.

l. Because we need to clear out all old model VCRs to make space for the new ones, we're offering savings up to 50 percent.

m. We will reimburse you for all travel expenses.

n. To enable us to continue our policy of selling name brands at discount prices, we cannot give cash refunds on returned merchandise.

o. We offer a free catalogue of computer and office supplies that saves money and shopping time for readers.

3.5   Language Bias (Goal 3)

Revise the following sentences to eliminate gender, racial, age, and disability stereotypes.

a. A skilled secretary proofreads her boss's documents and catches any errors he makes.

b. The award went to Jean Kim, a Korean-Canadian.

c. Because she is confined to a wheelchair, we look for restaurants without stairs.

d. Each worker has his assigned parking place.

e. Some theatres have special prices for old people.

f. How many man-hours will the project require?

g. James is afflicted with arthritis, but his crippling rarely interferes with his work.

h. Debbie Dubois, 24, was hired; and Tony Morris, 57, was promoted.

i. All conference participants and their wives are invited to the banquet.

j. Our company encourages the employment of handicapped people.

k. Representing the community are a businessman, a lady lawyer, and a female doctor.

l. A salesman would have to use all his skill to sell those condos.

m. Their child suffers from cerebral palsy.

n. Every homeowner should check his policy carefully.

o. We have an excellent Jamaican computer technician.

3.6 Positive Expression (Goal 3)

Revise the following statements to make them more positive.

a. We can't send you a catalogue until our next set is printed June 15.

b. In your letter you claim that you returned a defective headset.

c. Although you apparently failed to read the operator's manual, we are sending you a replacement blade for your food processor. Next time read page 18 carefully so that you will know how to attach this blade.

d. We can't process your application because you neglected to insert your social insurance number.

e. Construction cannot begin until the building plans are approved.

f. Because of a mistake in its address, your letter did not arrive until January 3.

g. In response to your complaint, we are investigating our agent's behaviour.

h. It is impossible to move forward without community support.

i. Customers are ineligible for the 10 percent discount unless they show their membership cards.

j. You won't be disappointed with your new credit card.

3.7 Courteous Expression (Goal 3)

Revise the following messages to show greater courtesy.

a. You must sign and return this form immediately.

b. This is the last time I'm writing to try to get you to record my January 6 payment of $500 to my account. Anyone who can read can see from the attached documents that I've tried to explain this to you before.

c. As manager of your department, you will have to get your employees to use the correct forms.

d. To the Staff: Can't anyone around here read instructions? The operating manual for our copy machine very clearly describes how to remove jammed paper on page 12. But I'm the only one who ever does it, and I've had it! No more copies will be made until you learn how to remove jammed paper.

e. If you had listened to our agent more carefully, you would know that your policy does not cover accidents outside Canada.

3.8 Familiar Words (Goal 3)

Revise the following sentences to avoid unfamiliar words.

a. Your remuneration for a day's work will be $50.

b. Pursuant to your invitation, we will interrogate our manager.

c. Recent laws mandate equal remuneration for men and women who perform equal tasks.

d. In a dialogue with the manager, I learned that you plan to terminate our agreement.

e. Did the steering problem materialize subsequent to our recall effort?

f. Once we ascertain how much it costs, we can initiate the project.

3.9 Precise Words (Goal 3)

From the words in parentheses, select the most precise, vigorous words.

a. Please try to *(contact, reach, telephone)* me as soon as you arrive.

b. He is *(engaged by, associated with, employed by)* the Dana Corporation.

c. We plan to *(acknowledge, publicize, applaud)* the work of exemplary employees.

d. The splendid report has *(a lot of, many, a warehouse of)* facts.

e. The board of directors thought the annual report was (*good, nice, helpful*).

For the following sentences provide more precise alternatives for the italicized words.

f. Management is (a) *looking* for a (b) *better way* to solve the problem.

g. The CEO (a) *said* that only (b) *the right kind* of applicants should apply.

h. After (a) *reading* the report, I decided it was (b) *bad*.

i. Marci said the movie was (a) *different* but her remarks weren't very (b) *clear* to us.

j. I'm (a) *going* to Grande Prairie tomorrow, and I plan to (b) *find out* the real problem.

k. Most (a) *people* don't have much (b) *feeling toward* brand names unless the brands are heavily promoted.

l. The (a) *news* made us feel particularly (b) *positive*.

3.10 Legal Language (Goal 6)

To avoid possible lawsuits, revise the italicized words in the following sentences taken from proposals.

a. We will *inspect* the building plans before construction begins.

b. Our goal is to *assure* completion of the project on schedule.

c. We will *determine* the amount of stress for each supporting column.

CLUE REVIEW 3

On a separate sheet rewrite the following sentences correcting the faults in grammar, punctuation, spelling, and word use.

1. If I was you I would schedule the conference for one of these cities Ottawa Kingston or Montreal.

2. The committees next meeting is scheduled for May fifth at three p.m., and should last about two hours.

3. Were not asking you to altar the figures, we are asking you to check there accuracy.

4. Will you please fax me a list of our independent contractors names and addresses?

5. The vacation calender fills up quick for the Summer months, therefore you should make your plans early.

6. After the inspector issues the waver we will be able to procede with the architects plan.

7. If we can't give out neccessary information what is the point in us answering the telephone.

8. Every new employee will receive their orientation packet, and be told about their parking priviledges.

9. About eighty-five percent of all new entrants into the workforce in the 1990s is expected to be: women, minorities and immigrants.

10. Our Vice President in the Human Resources Development Department asked the Manager and I to come to her office at three-thirty p.m.

Researching, Organizing, and Composing

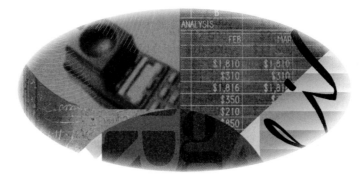

LEARNING GOALS

After studying this chapter, you should be able to

1 Contrast formal and informal methods for researching and generating ideas.

2 Specify how to organize data into lists and alphanumeric or decimal outlines.

3 Compare direct and indirect patterns for organizing ideas.

4 Discuss composing the first draft of a message, concentrating on techniques for creating forceful sentences.

5 Define a paragraph. Describe three classic plans and techniques for composing effective paragraphs.

6 Describe conditions that make team writing necessary. Discuss typical collaboration patterns.

7 List specific guidelines that make team efforts more productive and less stressful.

Seagull Pewter

It's not unusual for Harry Moore to spend a lot of his year sitting in different cars, in different cities across North America, with different business-suited sales representatives. Harry just lets them "talk and drive around the neighbourhoods they know best."

That simple assessment of one of his main responsibilities as director of sales and marketing for Seagull Pewterers & Silversmiths Ltd. tells a lot about the company.

Seagull Pewter (as the company is known) has earned a reputation as one of the best giftware design companies in North America and the acknowledged leader in sales of pewter giftware. The company is solely based in and operated from picturesque Pugwash, Nova Scotia.

"I concentrate, whether I'm talking to a sales rep or considering trade and marketing policy, on our ability to provide delivery on demand in a known, niche market. You can't do that if you don't do your research."

The impact this relatively small operation has had on the global giftware market is not unlike its impact upon the little community it inhabits. Seagull's workforce—comprising a collection of people who live in a 45-mile radius of Pugwash—design, manufacture, market, and sell all their goods from these company headquarters. That's 450 people doing $30 million in sales a year from a village of 700.

"It's a small place," Harry notes, "and that dynamic plays a significant part in one's life and how this company operates. Folks here get to be pretty tight."

That closeness is reflected in many ways—from how Harry handles his sales and marketing responsibilities to the design and delivery of the final product on store shelves across North America and around the world. "In Canada and the U.S. we have approximately 100 sales representatives on the road—the sales representatives manage the principal buyers, the people who own the showrooms and agencies and store suppliers.

"I spend two days with every representative we have, every year. We'll end up going out for supper maybe, then driving around—St. Louis, or Minneapolis, or whatever place it may be—looking at the lay of the land, talking about the nature of business in that particular area."

The point, says Harry, is to focus on individual buyers—and that means knowing the individual, distinctive markets in which they are found.

In Canada, it isn't so important to adapt to your regional tastes, he says. In the United States, on the other hand, you really have to know your regions; a few hundred miles and you can be talking a completely different language from the buyer's point of view. "And if we're not talking the same language, no one's buying—no matter how well designed your product is—and ours is among the very best."

In helping his sales reps to identify and appreciate the product niche that must be found, Harry says his sales strategy centres on building trust—trust in the quality of the product and the company's commitment to deliver the goods.

"To develop that kind of trust, credibility must be established. Part of the key to our marketing strategy is to establish ourselves as very different from larger companies. You can place an order with Seagull Pewter one day and get what you want the next. And when an order is placed, it's shipped right from here in Pugwash. We do direct shipping to France, Sweden, and mainland Europe, and now have a warehouse for distribution in Australia and Great Britain."

Harry says the key to sales is to analyze the audience and market demand and adapt to meet that need. That is one of the benefits of keeping the entire company under one roof, as it were. "That's why I spend the time with the sales representatives. It sounds a little crazy, I suppose, driving around, sometimes in the dark, looking at storefronts. But it's really the bottom line discussion of product that's important.

"I concentrate, whether I'm talking to a sales representative or considering trade and marketing policy, on our ability to provide delivery on demand in a known, niche market. You can't do that if you don't do your research."

Empathy for the salesperson on the street comes easy for the 39-year-old. For more than 20 years Harry has been "in the business"—working with small craft, jewellery and design companies in his home town of Pugwash.

In the 1960s the village was a booming crafts community; many Americans moved to the region and started their own fledgling businesses from this beautiful Maritime base. Harry worked with several companies and designers in the area; as the federal and provincial governments provided support to these tradespeople, Seagull Pewter evolved into a booming business and Harry took over the marketing duties—developing marketing programs, assisting the production people, and coordinating sales strategies. He studied business at Acadia University in Wolfville, Nova Scotia, but says his most valuable sales insights were learned from working firsthand with the craftspeople and sellers. "To a large degree, you learn by doing.

"The hardest part of this job is fitting it all together—coordinating sales strategies in places with diverse cultures. That's why sometimes the most important investment I can make is the time I spend with the sales folks. You can't look someone in the eye over the phone. It sounds like small stuff, but it all evens out and adds up."[1] ▪

Researching a customer base is key to sustaining and growing sales of a product or service. Getting to know a customer or finding a sales opportunity can take on many forms—from computerized information networks to Seagull Pewter's approach of familiarizing themselves with the "lay of the land" of the various regions they serve.

Researching Data and Generating Ideas

Before writing, conduct formal or informal research to collect or generate necessary information.

Business communicators like Harry Moore face daily challenges that require data collection, idea generation, and organization. These activities are part of the second phase of the writing process, which includes researching, generating ideas, and organizing.

No smart businessperson would begin writing a message before collecting all the needed information. We call this collection process "research," a rather formal-sounding term. For simple documents, though, the procedure can be quite informal. Research is necessary before you begin writing because the data you collect help shape the message. Discovering significant information after a message is half completed often means starting over and reorganizing. To avoid frustration and inaccurate messages, collect information that answers a primary question:

- *What does the receiver need to know about this topic?*

When the message involves action, search for answers to secondary questions:

- *What is the receiver to do?*

- *How is the receiver to do it?*

- *When must the receiver do it?*

- *What will happen if the receiver doesn't do it?*

Whenever your communication problem requires more information than you have in your head or at your fingertips, you must conduct research. This research may be formal or informal.

Formal Research Methods

Formal research may involve searching libraries and electronic databases or investigating primary sources (interviews, surveys, and experiments).

Long reports and complex business problems generally require some use of formal research methods. Let's say you are a market specialist for Coca-Cola, and your boss asks you to evaluate the impact of private-label or generic soft drinks. Or let's assume you must write a term paper for class. Both tasks require more data than you have in your head or at your fingertips. To conduct formal research, you could:

- **Search manually.** You'll find helpful background and supplementary information through manual searching of resources in public and school libraries. These traditional sources include periodical indexes for lists of newspaper, magazine, and journal articles, along with the card catalogue for books. Other manual sources are book indexes, encyclopedias, reference books, handbooks, dictionaries, directories, and almanacs.

- **Access electronically.** Like other facets of life, the research process has been changed considerably by the computer. Much of the printed material just described is now available on CD-ROM or from mainframe databases that can be accessed by computer. School and public libraries subscribe to retrieval services that permit you to access thousands of bibliographic or full-text databases.

- **Investigate primary sources.** To develop firsthand, primary information for a project, go directly to the source. For the Coca-Cola report, for example, you would find out what consumers really think by conducting interviews or surveys, by putting together questionnaires, or by organizing focus groups. Formal research includes scientific sampling methods that enable investigators to make accurate judgments and valid predictions.

- **Experiment scientifically.** Another source of primary data is experimentation. Instead of merely asking for the target audience's opinion, scientific researchers present choices with controlled variables. Assume, for example, that Coca-Cola wants to determine at what price and under what circumstances consumers would switch from Coca-Cola to a generic brand. The results of such experimentation would provide valuable data for managerial decision-making.

Because formal research techniques are particularly necessary for reports, you'll learn more about these techniques in Part 4.

Informal Research and Idea Generation

Most routine tasks—such as familiar memos, letters, and informational reports—require data that you can collect informally. For some projects, though, you rely more on your own ideas instead of—or in addition to—researching existing facts. Here are some techniques for collecting informal data and for generating ideas:

- **Look in the files.** Before asking others for help, see what you can find yourself. For many routine messages you can often find previous documents to help you with content and format.

- **Talk with your boss.** Get information from the individual making the assignment. What does that person know about the topic? What slant should be taken? What other sources would he or she suggest?

- **Interview the target audience.** Consider talking to people at whom the message is aimed. Often, they can provide clarifying information that tells you what they want to know and how you should shape your remarks.

- **Conduct an informal survey.** Gather unscientific but helpful information by questionnaires or telephone surveys. In preparing a memo report predicting the success of company van pools, for example, circulate a questionnaire asking for employee reactions.

- **Brainstorm for ideas.** Alone or with others, discuss ideas for the writing task at hand, and record at least a dozen ideas without judging them. Small groups are especially fruitful in brainstorming because people spark off ideas from one another.

- **Develop a cluster diagram.** Prepare a cluster diagram (discussed in the next section) to help you generate and organize ideas. Clustering allows your mind to open up and free-associate.

Researching Data and Generating Ideas on the Job

The following steps outline how to collect data and generate ideas for two projects—one simple and one complex.

Writing an informational memo. The first is an informational memo, shown in Figure 4.1, to all employees describing a photo contest sponsored by Liz Claiborne. For this memo the writer, Susanne Tully, began by brainstorming

FIGURE 4.1 ■ Informational Memo

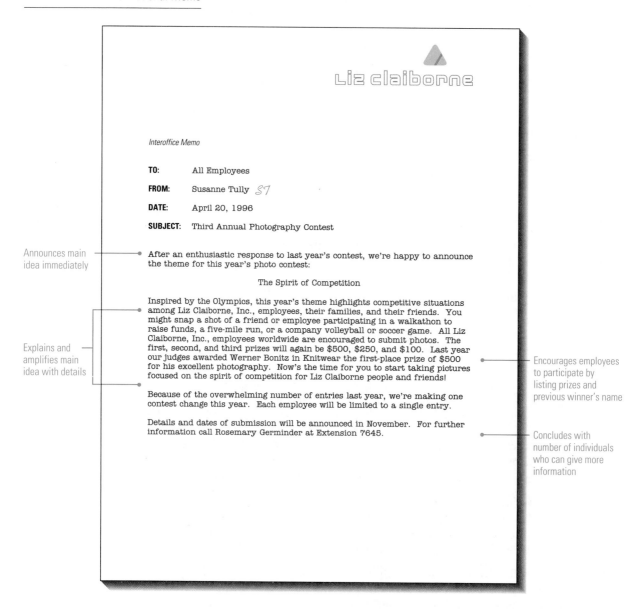

with her staff, other employees, and her boss to decide on a theme for the photo contest. After naming a theme, "The Spirit of Competition," inspired by the Olympics, she consulted the files to see who had won prizes in last year's contest. She also double-checked with management to ensure that the prize money—$500, $250, and $100—remained the same. Then she made the following quick scratch list outlining the points she wanted to cover in her memo.

Photo Contest Memo

1. Announce theme; give examples
2. Encourage all employees worldwide to participate
3. Review prizes; name last year's winner
4. Limit: one entry each
5. Details in November; call Rosemary for more info

Many business messages, like Susanne's finished memo, require only simple data collection and idea generation techniques.

Preparing a recruitment brochure. Susanne's second project, though, demanded both formal and informal research, along with considerable creativity. She needed to produce a recruitment brochure that explained career opportunities for students at Liz Claiborne. She had definite objectives for the brochure: it should be colourful, exciting, concise, lightweight (because she had to carry stacks of them to campuses!), and easily updated. Moreover, she wanted the brochure to promote Liz Claiborne, describing its progressive benefits, community involvement, career potential, and corporate values program (called "Priorities").

Some of her thoughts about this big project are shown in the cluster diagram in Figure 4.2. Cluster diagrams spark our creativity and encourage ideas to spill forth because the process is unrestricted. From the jumble of ideas in the initial cluster diagram, main categories—usually three to five—are extracted. At this point some people are ready to make an outline; others need further visualization, such as a set of subclusters, shown in Figure 4.3. Notice that four major categories (Purpose, Content, Development, and Form) were extracted from the initial diagram. These categories then became the hub of related ideas. This set of subclusters forms the basis for an outline, to be discussed shortly.

To collect data for this project, Susanne employed both formal and informal research methods. She studied recruiting brochures from other companies. She talked to students to ask what information they looked for in a brochure. She conducted more formal research among the numerous division presidents and executives in her company to learn what really went on in all the departments, such as Information Systems, Operations Management, Production, and Design. She also had to learn the specific educational and personality requirements for careers in those areas. Working with an outside consultant, she prepared a questionnaire, which was used in personal interviews with company executives. The interviews included some open-ended questions, such as "How did you start with the company?" It also contained more specific questions about the number of employees in their departments, intended career paths, educational requirements, personality traits desired, and so forth. Organizing the mass of data collected was the next task.

> Cluster diagrams help generate ideas and reveal relationships between ideas.

Organizing Data

The process of organization may begin before you collect data, as it did for Susanne Tully, or occur simultaneously with data collection. For complex projects, organization may be ongoing. Regardless of when organization occurs, its primary goals are grouping and patterning. Well-organized messages group similar items together; ideas follow a sequence that helps the reader understand relationships and accept the writer's views. Unorganized messages proceed freeform, jumping from one thought to another. Such messages fail to emphasize important points. Puzzled readers can't see how the pieces fit together, and they become frustrated and irritated. Many communication experts regard poor organization as the greatest failing of business writers.

This section introduces two simple techniques that can help you organize data: the scratch list and the outline. (Chapter 12 presents additional advice for

> Well-organized messages group similar ideas together so that readers can see relationships and follow arguments.

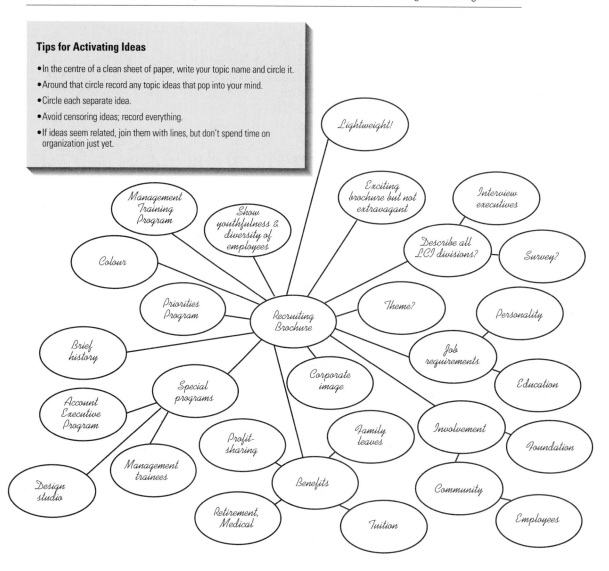

Tips for Activating Ideas

- In the centre of a clean sheet of paper, write your topic name and circle it.
- Around that circle record any topic ideas that pop into your mind.
- Circle each separate idea.
- Avoid censoring ideas; record everything.
- If ideas seem related, join them with lines, but don't spend time on organization just yet.

organizing data in reports.) This section also covers two common patterns for arranging business messages—direct and indirect.

Listing and Outlining

In developing simple messages, some writers make a quick scratch list of the topics they wish to cover, as Susanne Tully did for her memo in Figure 4.1. Writers often jot this scratch list in the margin of the letter or memo to which they are responding—and the majority of business messages are written in response to other documents. These writers can then dictate or compose a message at their computers directly from the scratch list.

Most writers, though, need to organize their ideas—especially if the project is complex—into a hierarchy, such as an outline. Figure 4.4 shows two outline

FIGURE 4.3 ■ Organizing Ideas from Cluster Diagram into Subclusters

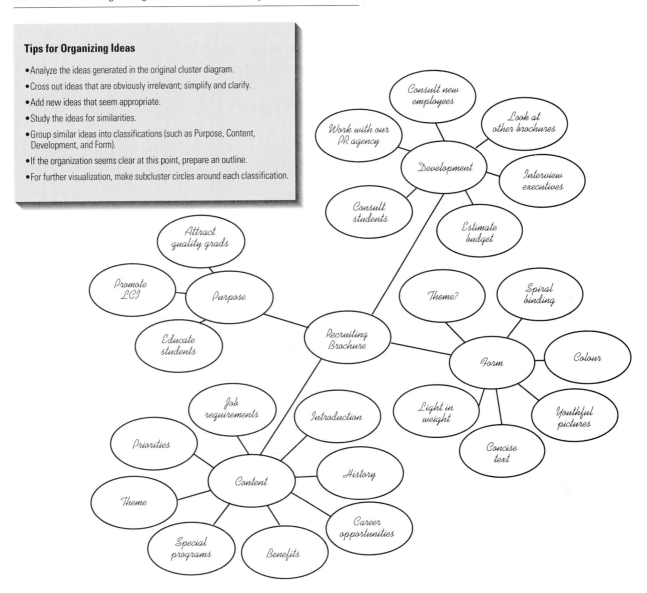

Tips for Organizing Ideas

- Analyze the ideas generated in the original cluster diagram.
- Cross out ideas that are obviously irrelevant; simplify and clarify.
- Add new ideas that seem appropriate.
- Study the ideas for similarities.
- Group similar ideas into classifications (such as Purpose, Content, Development, and Form).
- If the organization seems clear at this point, prepare an outline.
- For further visualization, make subcluster circles around each classification.

formats: alphanumeric and decimal. The familiar alphanumeric format uses roman numerals, letters, and numbers to show major and minor ideas. The decimal format, which takes a little getting used to, has the advantage of showing how every item at every level relates to the whole. Both outlining formats force you to focus on the topic, identify major ideas, and support those ideas with details, illustrations, or evidence. Many computer outlining programs now on the market make the mechanics of the process simple.

The hardest part of outlining is grouping ideas into components or categories—ideally three to five in number. If you have more than five components, look for ways to combine smaller segments into broader topics. The example following Figure 4.4 shows how a portion of the Liz Claiborne brochure subcluster (Figure 4.3) can be organized into an alphanumeric outline.

Alphanumeric outlines show major and minor ideas; decimal outlines show how ideas relate to one another.

FIGURE 4.4 ■ Two Outlining Formats

Tips for Making Outlines

- Define the main topic (purpose of message) in the title

- Divide the main topic into major components or classifications (preferably three to five). If necessary, combine small components into one larger category.

- Break the components into subpoints.

- Don't put a single item under a major component; if you have only one subpoint, integrate it with the main item above it or reorganize.

- Strive to make each component exclusive (no overlapping).

- Use details, illustrations, and evidence to support subpoints.

Format for Alphanumeric Outline

Title: Major Idea, Purpose

```
I. First major component
   A. First subpoint
      1. Detail, illustration, evidence
      2. Detail, illustration, evidence
   B. Second subpoint
      1.
      2.
II. Second major component
   A. First subpoint
      1.
      2.
   B. Second subpoint
      1.
      2.
III. Third major component
   A.
      1.
      2.
   B.
      1.
      2.
```

(This method is simple and familiar.)

Format for Decimal Outline

Title: Major Idea, Purpose

```
1.0 First major component
   1.1 First subpoint
      1.1.1 Detail, illustration, evidence
      1.1.2 Detail, illustration, evidence
   1.2 Second subpoint
      1.2.1
      1.2.2
2.0 Second major component
   2.1 First subpoint
      2.1.1
      2.1.2
   2.2 Second subpoint
      2.2.1
      2.2.2
3.0 Third major component
   3.1
      3.1.1
      3.1.2
   3.2
      3.2.1
      3.2.2
```

(This method relates every item to the overall outline.)

```
I. Introduction
   A. Brief history of Liz Claiborne
      1. Founding, Fortune 500 status
      2. Product lines
   B. Corporate environment
      1. System of values: "Priorities"
      2. Team spirit; corporate image
II. Career opportunities
   A. Operations management
      1. Traffic
      2. International trade and corporate customs
      3. Distribution
   B. Accounting and finance
      1. General accounting
      2. Internal audit
      3. Treasury and risk management
   C. Special opportunities
      1. Management training program
      2. Account executive sales training program
      3. Design studio
```

In organizing this Liz Claiborne recruitment brochure, Susanne Tully and her staff achieved coherence and readability by converting each topic from the outline into a consistent, reader-centred heading. Notice the emphasis on "you," an important lesson for every business communicator to learn.

Notice that each major category is divided into at least two subcategories, which in turn are fleshed out with examples, details, statistics, case histories, and other data. In moving from major point to subpoint, you are progressing from large abstract concepts to small concrete ideas. And each subpoint could be further subdivided with more specific illustrations if you desired. You can determine the appropriate amount of detail by considering what your audience (primary and secondary) already knows about the topic and how much persuading you must do.

How you group ideas into components depends on your topic and your channel of communication. The finished Liz Claiborne recruitment brochure, shown above, required careful editing so that each component would fit into the page layout. Business documents, on the other hand, do not have rigid page constraints and usually contain typical components arranged in traditional patterns, as shown in Figure 4.5.

The topic and the communication channel determine how ideas are grouped into components.

Thus far, you've seen how to collect information, generate ideas, and prepare an outline. How you order the information in your outline, though, depends on what pattern or strategy you choose.

Organizing Ideas into Patterns

Two organizational patterns provide plans of action for typical business messages: the direct pattern and the indirect pattern. The primary difference between the two patterns is where the main idea is placed. In the direct pattern the main idea comes first, followed by details, explanation, or evidence. In the indirect pattern the main idea follows the details, explanation, and evidence. The pattern you select is determined by how you expect the audience to react to the message, as shown in Figure 4.6.

FIGURE 4.5 ■ Typical Major Components in Business Outlines

Letter of Memo	Procedure	Informational Report	Analytical Report	Proposal
I. Opening	I. Step 1	I. Introduction	I. Introduction/Problem	I. Introduction
II. Body	II. Step 2	II. Facts	II. Facts/Findings	II. Proposed solution
III. Close	III. Step 3	III. Summary	III. Conclusions	III. Staffing
	IV. Step 4		IV. Recommendations (if requested)	IV. Schedule, cost
				V. Authorization

Business messages typically follow either the direct pattern, with the main idea first, or the indirect pattern, with the main idea following explanation and evidence.

The direct pattern for receptive audiences. In preparing to write any message, you need to anticipate the audience's reaction to your ideas and frame your message accordingly. When you expect the reader to be pleased, mildly interested, or at worst neutral, use the direct pattern. That is, put your main point—the purpose of your message—in the first or second sentence. Notice how long it takes the sender to get to the main idea of this message:

> As you know, the Management Council has been considering the possibility of starting an internship program for students here at LaserPro. Such a program might attract better-qualified prospective job candidates than our present system. It would enable us to begin training students and would also help develop a sense of loyalty toward LaserPro before those students finish their education. But such a program would require considerable research and promotion before it could be implemented. We have, therefore, voted to begin a pilot program starting next fall.

To open more directly, this message would read, *The Management Council has voted to begin an internship pilot program starting next fall*, with explanation and details following. This direct method, also called *frontloading*, has at least three advantages:

- **Saves the reader's time.** Many of today's businesspeople can devote only a few moments to each message. Messages that take too long to get to the point may lose their readers along the way.

- **Sets a proper frame of mind.** Learning the purpose up front helps the reader put the subsequent details and explanations in perspective. Without a clear opening, the reader may be thinking, "Why am I being told this?"

Frontloading saves the reader time, establishes the proper frame of mind, and prevents frustration.

- **Prevents frustration.** Readers forced to struggle through verbiage before reaching the main idea become frustrated with and resentful toward the writer. Poorly organized messages create a negative impression of the writer.

This frontloading technique works best with audiences that are likely to be receptive to or at least not disagree with what you have to say. Typical business messages that follow the direct pattern include routine requests and responses, orders and acknowledgements, nonsensitive memos, and informational reports. All these messages have one element in common: *none has a sensitive subject that will upset the reader.*

The indirect pattern for unreceptive audiences. When you expect the audience to be uninterested, unwilling, displeased, or perhaps even hostile, the indirect pattern is more appropriate. In this pattern don't reveal the main idea

FIGURE 4.6 ■ Audience Response Determines Pattern of Organization

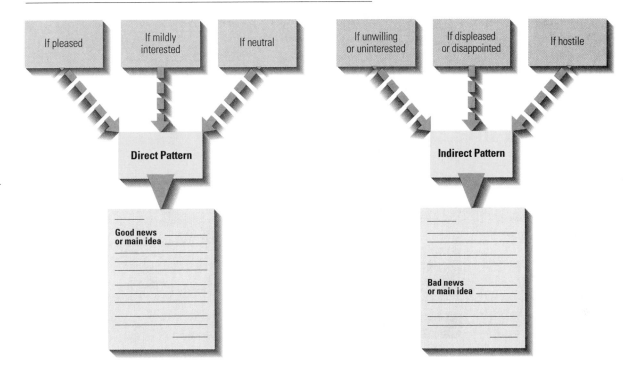

until after you have offered explanation and evidence. This approach works well with three kinds of messages: (1) bad news, (2) ideas that require persuasion, and (3) sensitive news, especially when being transmitted to superiors. The indirect pattern has these benefits:

- **Respects the feelings of the audience.** Bad news is always painful, but the trauma can be lessened when the receiver is prepared for it.

- **Ensures a fair hearing.** Messages that may upset the reader are more likely to be read when the main idea is delayed. Beginning immediately with a piece of bad news or a persuasive request, for example, may cause the receiver to read no further.

- **Minimizes the negative reaction.** A reader's overall reaction to a negative message is generally improved if the news is delivered gently.

Typical business messages that could be developed indirectly include letters and memos that refuse requests, deny claims, and disapprove credit. Persuasive requests, sales letters, sensitive messages, and some reports also benefit from the indirect strategy. You'll learn more about how to use the indirect pattern in Chapters 8 and 9. The indirect strategy causes some communicators concern because it seems devious. For further discussion of this issue, see the Ethics box on page 105.

In summary, business messages may be organized directly, with the main idea first, or indirectly, with the main idea delayed. Although these two patterns cover many communication problems, they should be considered neither universal nor inviolate. Every business transaction is distinct. Some messages are mixed: part good news, part bad; part goodwill, part persuasion. In later chapters you'll practise applying the direct and indirect patterns in typical situ-

The indirect pattern is appropriate when the audience may be uninterested in, displeased by, or hostile to the message.

Chapter 4
Researching, Organizing,
and Composing

Skilled communicators save their time (and that of their readers!) by organizing their ideas into logical patterns before sitting down at the computer to write. Deciding where to place the main idea and grouping similar thoughts together are important prewriting tasks.

ations. Then you'll have the skills and confidence to evaluate communication problems and vary these patterns depending on the goals you wish to achieve.

▇ Composing the First Draft

When composing the first draft, write quickly and save revision for later.

Once you've researched your topic, organized the data, and selected a pattern of organization, you're ready to begin composing. Communicators who haven't completed the preparatory work often suffer from writer's block and sit staring at a piece of paper or at the computer screen. It's difficult to get started without organized ideas and a plan. Composition is also easier if you have a quiet environment in which to concentrate. Businesspeople with messages to compose set aside a given time and allow no calls, visitors, or other interruptions. This is a good technique for students as well.

As you begin composing, keep in mind that you are writing the first draft, not the final copy. Experts advise that you write quickly, getting your thoughts down now and refining them in later versions.[2] This method works especially well for those composing on a computer because it's simple to make changes at any point of the composition process. If you are handwriting the first draft, double-space, so that you have room for changes.

Creating Forceful Sentences

As you create your first draft, you'll be working at the sentence level of composition. Although you've used sentences all your life, you may be unaware of how they can be shaped and arranged to express your ideas most forcefully. First, let's review some basic sentence elements.

ETHICS AND COMMUNICATOR MOTIVATION

You may worry that the indirect organization strategy is unethical since a writer deliberately delays the main idea. But let's put that strategy into context. Assume that you are writing a letter denying credit to a customer. Instead of bluntly announcing the denial, you begin by explaining the reasons necessitating the denial. Then you present the bad news. By delaying bad news, you soften the blow somewhat, as well as ensure that your reasoning will be read while a receiver is still receptive. Your motives are not to deceive the reader or to hide the news; instead, your goal is to be a compassionate, yet effective communicator.

The key to ethical communication lies in the motives of the sender. Unethical communicators *intend to deceive.* The following are selected news items for you to consider. Although you can't read the minds of those involved, examine these cases and think about the ethics of the communicators. Is it ethical communication? Did they intend to deceive or not?

- Victoria's Secret offers free $10 gift certificates. However, when customers try to cash the certificates, they find they are required to make a minimum purchase of $50 worth of merchandise.[3]

- An advertisement (by Comb Authorized Liquidators) lists IBM PS/2 computers (IBM Quality! IBM Durability! IBM Reliability!) at a remarkably low price of $698. The advertisement describes a colour monitor, enhanced keyboard, expansion slots, and hard drive, along with many other features. Buried in the text is this statement: "Factory renewed by IBM."[4] In other words, the machines are used.

- TV and print advertisements proclaim Volvo's durability when a monster truck named "Bear Foot" roars across the tops of parked cars, flattening every one except a Volvo 240. However, the Volvo used in the car-crushing exhibition in Austin, Texas, is actually reinforced with steel to withstand being run over. Moreover, although the ads re-create a Vermont truck rally, they do not identify the action as a dramatization.[5]

- Advertisements for the Discover credit card assert that it does not charge interest on cash advances. It does, however, charge stiff transaction fees.[6]

- Trans World Airlines advertises a $149 round-trip fare to Puerto Rico, but barely mentions requirements for a hotel stay or car rental.[7]

Career Track Application

Assume that one of your tasks for a national chain of copy stores is writing advertisements. One national ad on which you work shouts in huge letters, "SAME-DAY DELIVERY." You know, however, that such service is available only when customers bring in their copy before 10 a.m. What would you do?

Complete sentences have subjects and verbs and make sense.

SUBJECT VERB   SUBJECT   VERB
This report is clear and concise. Our employees write many reports.

Clauses and phrases, the key building blocks of sentences, are related groups of words. Clauses have subjects and verbs; phrases do not.

PHRASE   PHRASE
The CEO of that organization sent a letter to our staff.

PHRASE   PHRASE
By reading carefully, we learned about the merger.

CLAUSE   CLAUSE
Because she writes well, Tracy answers most customer letters.

CLAUSE | CLAUSE

If we accumulate too many letters, | we assign other writers.

Clauses may be divided into two groups: independent and dependent. Independent clauses can stand alone; thus, every grammatically complete sentence contains at least one independent clause. Dependent clauses depend for their meaning on independent clauses; they cannot stand alone. In the two preceding examples the clauses beginning with *If* and *Because* are dependent. Dependent clauses are often introduced by words like *if*, *when*, *because*, and *as*.

INDEPENDENT CLAUSE

Tracy is a customer service representative.

DEPENDENT CLAUSE | INDEPENDENT CLAUSE

When Tracy writes to customers, | she uses simple language.

By learning to distinguish phrases, independent clauses, and dependent clauses, you'll be able to punctuate sentences correctly and avoid three basic sentence faults: the fragment, the run-on sentence, and the comma splice. In Appendix A, we examine these writing problems in greater detail. For now, however, let's look at some ways to make your sentences more readable and forceful.

Using short sentences. Because your goal is to communicate clearly, you're better off limiting your sentences to about 20 words or fewer. The American Press Institute reports that readers' comprehension drops off markedly as sentences become longer.[8] Thus, in crafting your sentences, keep the following correspondences between sentence length and comprehension in mind:

Sentence Length	Comprehension Rate
8 words	100%
15 words	90%
19 words	80%
28 words	50%

Instead of stringing together clauses with *and*, *but*, and *however*, break some of those complex sentences into separate segments. Business readers want to grasp ideas immediately. They can do that best when thoughts are separated into short sentences. On the other hand, too many monotonous short sentences will sound childish and may bore or even annoy the reader. Strive for a balance between longer sentences and shorter ones. Your computer software can probably point out long sentences and give you an average sentence length.

Emphasizing important ideas. You can stress prominent ideas in three ways. The first is to place an important idea at the beginning of a sentence. Notice how this sentence obscures the date of the meeting by burying it: *All production and administrative personnel will meet May 23, at which time we will announce a new plan of salary incentives.* To emphasize the date, start the sentence with it: *On May 23 all personnel will meet ...* A secondary position of importance is the end of a sentence: *All personnel will meet to discuss salary incentives on May 23.* Remember this guideline when composing paragraphs as well; put the main idea at the start and then follow up with supporting material.

A second way to emphasize an important idea is to be sure that it acts as the subject in a sentence. Notice the difference between the sentences *Michelle wrote the environmental report* and *The environmental report was written by Michelle.* Michelle receives the emphasis in the first version; the report receives it in the second.

A third way to emphasize an idea is to place it in a short sentence. Important ideas can get lost when enveloped by numerous competing words. How quickly can you grasp the important idea in this sentence? *This announcement is to inform all employees and guests that the hotel's restaurant will be closed Thanksgiving Day, although we do plan to resume restaurant services Tuesday at 7 a.m.* To give impact to the main idea, present it in a short sentence: *The hotel's restaurant will be closed Thanksgiving Day.* Then, provide explanations and details.

Using the active voice. In the active voice the subject performs the action: *Brandon selected new computers.* In the passive voice the subject receives the action: *New computers were selected by Brandon.* Passive-voice sentences de-emphasize the performer of the action. The performer is in a phrase (*by Brandon*) or is totally absent: (*New computers were selected*). If you suspect that a verb is passive but you're not sure, try the "by whom?" test: *New computers were selected [by whom?].* If you can fill in the performer of the action, the sentence is probably passive.

Active-voice sentences are forceful and easy to understand.

What difference does it make if the verb is active or passive? Active-voice sentences are more direct because they reveal the performer immediately: they're easier to understand, more forceful, and shorter. Most business writing should be in the active voice.

Using the passive voice selectively. Although we prefer active verbs in business writing, passive verbs are useful in certain instances. For example, when the performer is unknown or insignificant, use the passive voice: *Drug tests are given to all applicants.* Who performs the drug tests is unimportant. You can also use the passive voice to tactfully deflect attention away from the people involved: *Three totals were calculated incorrectly.* Notice that this sentence stresses the problem while concealing the person who committed the error.

Passive-voice sentences are useful for tact and to direct attention to actions instead of people.

Avoiding dangling phrases. Verbal phrases must be immediately followed by the words they can logically describe or modify. When such phrases dangle without a clearly modified term, they confuse—and sometimes amuse—readers, as in these examples:

Dangling Modifier	Improved
Belching steam and hissing dangerously, the driver cautiously examined the overheated radiator. *(This sentence says the driver is belching steam and hissing dangerously.)*	Belching steam and hissing dangerously, the overheated radiator was examined cautiously by the driver.
Locked safely in the office vault, only the vice-president had access to the corporate securities. *(Is the vice-president locked in the vault?)*	Locked safely in the office vault, the corporate securities were accessible only to the vice-president.

Try this trick for detecting and remedying dangling modifiers. Ask the question Who? or What? after any introductory verbal phrase. The words immediately following any verbal phrase should tell the reader *who* or *what* is performing the action. Try the Who? test on the previous danglers.

Another form of misplaced modifier is a phrase separated from the word(s) it describes. The solution is simply to move the misplaced phrase closer to the words it modifies.

Misplaced Modifier

The busy personnel director interviewed only candidates who had excellent computer skills in the morning. *(This sentence says the candidate's computer skills were effective only before lunch.)*

Improved

In the morning the busy personnel director interviewed only candidates who had excellent computer skills.

Drafting Effective Paragraphs

Effective paragraphs have one topic, link ideas to build coherence, and use transitional devices to enhance coherence.

From composing sentences, we progress to paragraphs. A paragraph is one or more sentences designated as a separate thought group. To avoid muddled and meaningless paragraphs, writers must recognize basic paragraph elements, conventional sentence patterns, and ways to organize sentences into one of three classic paragraph patterns. They must also be able to polish their paragraphs by linking sentences and using transitional expressions.

Discussing one topic. Well-constructed paragraphs discuss only one topic. They reveal the primary idea in a main sentence that usually, but not always, appears first. Other ideas, connected logically with transitional expressions (verbal road signs), support or illustrate that idea.

Organizing sentences into paragraphs. Paragraphs are usually composed of three kinds of sentences:[9]

- **Main sentence:** expresses the primary idea of the paragraph.

- **Supporting sentence:** illustrates, explains, or strengthens the primary idea.

- **Limiting sentence:** opposes the primary idea by suggesting a negative or contrasting thought; it may precede or follow the main sentence.

These sentences may be arranged in three classic paragraph plans: direct, pivoting, and indirect.

The direct paragraph pattern is appropriate when defining, classifying, illustrating, or describing.

Using the direct paragraph plan. Paragraphs arranged in the direct plan begin with the main sentence, followed by supporting sentences. Most business messages use this paragraph plan because it clarifies the subject immediately. This plan is useful whenever you must define (a new product or procedure), classify (parts of a whole), illustrate (an idea), or describe (a process). Simply start with the main sentence; then strengthen and amplify that idea with supporting ideas, as shown here:

Main Sentence
Supporting
Sentences

A social audit is a report on the social performance of a company. Such a report may be conducted by the company itself or by outsiders who evaluate the company's efforts to produce safe products, engage in socially responsible activities, and protect the environment. Many companies publish the results of their social audits in their annual reports. VanCity, Canada's biggest institution of its kind, includes in its annual report a "social accounting" page providing information ranging from financial assistance to daycares, to having "an ethical screen on investments." Noranda is an example of another company that provides a separate annual environmental report.[10]

You can alter the direct plan by adding a limiting sentence if necessary. Be sure, though, that you follow up with sentences that return to the main idea and support it, as shown here:

Main Sentence	Flexible work scheduling could immediately increase productivity and enhance employee satisfaction in our entire organization.
Limiting Sentence	Such scheduling, however, is impossible for all employees. Managers would be required to maintain their regular hours. For
Supporting Sentences	many other employees, though, flexible scheduling permits extra time to manage family responsibilities. Feeling less stress, employees are able to focus their attention better at work; hence, they become more relaxed and more productive.

Using the pivoting paragraph plan. Paragraphs arranged in the pivoting plan start with a limiting sentence that offers a contrasting or negative idea before delivering the main sentence. Notice in the following example how two limiting sentences about drawbacks to foreign service careers open the paragraph; only then do the main and supporting sentences describing rewards in foreign service appear. The pivoting plan is especially effective for comparing and contrasting ideas. In using the pivoting plan, be sure you emphasize the turn in direction with an obvious *but* or *however*.

The pivoting paragraph pattern is appropriate when comparing and contrasting.

Limiting Sentences	Military careers are certainly not for everyone. Many overseas posts are in remote countries where there are harsh climates, health hazards, security risks, and other discomforts.
Main Sentence	However, careers in the military service offer special rewards for the special people who qualify. Military employees enjoy the pride and satisfaction of representing their country abroad. They
Supporting Sentences	relish frequent travel, enrich their cultural and social experiences in living abroad, and enjoy action-oriented work.

Using the indirect paragraph plan. Paragraphs arranged in the indirect plan start with the supporting sentences and conclude with the main sentence. This useful plan enables you to build a rationale, a foundation of reasons, before hitting the audience with a big idea—possibly one that is bad news. It enables you to explain your reasons and then in the final sentence draw a conclusion from them. Notice in the following example that the supporting sentences describe a scenario of computer use leading up to a new procedure that some readers may resent. The indirect plan works well for describing causes followed by an effect.

The indirect paragraph pattern is appropriate when delivering bad news.

Supporting Sentences	Since 1986 we have actively supported the use of personal computers by sales reps. We now have over 1,000 computer users, and the number continues to grow. As a result of this dramatic growth, our expenses for software programming, testing, and duplication have become a major item in our budget. Last year we spent over $150,000 to deliver personal computer
Main Sentence	software to the field. As a result of escalating expenses, we've decided to standardize two elements in our computer use: Microsoft Windows and laptop machines.

You'll learn more techniques for implementing these plans when you write letters, memos, and reports in subsequent chapters.

Linking ideas to build coherence. Paragraphs are coherent when ideas are linked, that is, when one idea leads logically to the next. Well-written paragraphs take the reader through a number of steps. When the author skips from Step 1 to Step 3 and forgets Step 2, the reader is lost. You can use several techniques to keep the reader in step with your ideas.

> **Coherent paragraphs link ideas by sustaining the main idea, using pronouns, dovetailing sentences, and using transitional expressions.**

Sustaining the key idea. This involves simply repeating a key expression or using a similar one. For example:

> Our philosophy holds that every customer is really a *guest*. All new employees to our theme parks are trained to treat *guests* as *VIPs*. These *VIPs* are never told what they can or cannot do.

Notice how the repetition of *guest* and *VIP* connects ideas.

Using pronouns. Familiar pronouns, such as *we*, *they*, *he*, *she*, and *it*, help build continuity, as do demonstrative pronouns like *this*, *that*, *these*, and *those*. These words confirm that something under discussion is still being discussed. For example:

> All new park employees receive a two-week orientation. *They* learn that every staffer has a vital role in preparing for the show. *This* training includes how to maintain enthusiasm.

Be careful with *this*, *that*, *these*, and *those*, however. These words usually need a noun with them to make their meaning absolutely clear. In the last example notice how confusing this becomes if the word *training* is omitted.

Dovetailing sentences. Sentences are "dovetailed" when an idea at the end of one connects with an idea at the beginning of the next. For example:

> New hosts and hostesses learn about the theme park and its *facilities*. These *facilities* include telephones, food services, washrooms, and attractions, as well as the location of *offices*. Knowledge of administrative *offices* and internal workings of the company, such as who's who in administration, ensures that staffers will be able to *serve guests* fully. *Serving guests*, of course, is our No. 1 priority.

Dovetailing of sentences is especially helpful with dense, difficult topics. However, this technique should not be overused.

Using transitional expressions to build coherence. Transitional expressions are another excellent device for achieving paragraph coherence. These words, some of which are shown in Figure 4.7, act as verbal road signs to readers and listeners. Transitional expressions enable the receiver to anticipate what's coming, to reduce uncertainty, and to speed up comprehension. They signal that a train of thought is moving forward, being developed, possibly detouring, or ending. Transitions are especially helpful in persuasive writing.

> **Transitional expressions help readers anticipate what's coming, reduce uncertainty, and speed up comprehension.**

As Figure 4.7 shows, transitions can add and strengthen, show cause and effect, indicate time or order, contradict, clarify, and contrast ideas. Thus, you must be careful to select the best transition for your purpose. Look back at the examples of direct, pivoted, and indirect paragraphs to see how transitional expressions and other devices build paragraph coherence. Remember that coherence in communication rarely happens spontaneously; it requires effort and skill.

FIGURE 4.7 ■ Transitional Expressions to Build Coherence

To Add or Strengthen	To Show Time or Order	To Clarify	To Show Cause and Effect	To Contradict	To Contrast
additionally	after	for example	accordingly	actually	as opposed to
again	before	for instance	as a result	but	at the same time
also	earlier	I mean	consequently	however	by contrast
besides	finally	in other words	for this reason	in fact	conversely
likewise	first	that is	so	instead	on the contrary
moreover	meanwhile	this means	therefore	rather	on the other hand
further	next	thus	thus	still	
furthermore	now	to put it another	under the circum-	though	
	previously	way	stances	yet	
	then				

Composing short paragraphs. Although no rule regulates the length of paragraphs, business writers recognize the value of short paragraphs. Paragraphs with fewer than eight lines look inviting and readable, whereas long, solid hunks of print appear formidable. If a topic can't be covered in fewer than ten printed lines (not sentences), consider breaking it up into smaller segments.

The following checklist summarizes the key points of writing a first draft.

Paragraphs with fewer than ten lines are attractive and readable.

■ Checklist for Composing Sentences and Paragraphs

For Effective Sentences

✓ **Use short sentences.** Keep in mind that sentences with fewer than 20 words are easier to read. Use longer sentences occasionally, but rely on short sentences.

✓ **Emphasize important ideas.** Place main ideas at the beginning of short sentences for emphasis.

✓ **Apply active and passive verbs carefully.** Use active verbs (*She wrote the letter* instead of *The letter was written by her*) most frequently; they immediately identify the doer. Use passive verbs to be tactful, to emphasize an action, or to conceal the performer.

✓ **Eliminate misplaced modifiers.** Be sure that introductory verbal phrases are followed by the words that can logically modify them. To check the placement of modifiers, ask Who? or What? after such phrases.

For Effective Paragraphs

✓ **Develop one idea.** Use main, supporting, and limiting sentences to develop a single idea within each paragraph.

✓ **Use the direct plan.** Start most paragraphs with the main sentence followed by supporting sentences. This direct plan is useful in defining, classifying, illustrating, and describing.

✓ **Use the pivoting plan.** To compare and contrast ideas, start with a limiting sentence; then, present the main sentence followed by supporting sentences.

✓ **Use the indirect plan.** To explain reasons or causes first, start with supporting sentences. Build to the conclusion with the main sentence at the end of the paragraph.

✓ **Build coherence by linking sentences.** Hold ideas together by repeating key words, using pronouns, and dovetailing sentences (beginning one sentence with an idea from the end of the previous sentence).

✓ **Provide road signs with transitional expressions.** Use verbal signals to help the audience know where the idea is going. Words like *moreover*, *accordingly*, *as a result*, and *thus* function as idea pointers.

✓ **Limit paragraph length.** Remember that paragraphs with fewer than eight printed lines look inviting. Consider breaking up longer paragraphs if necessary.

■ Working in Teams

Business professionals increasingly work in teams that require collaborative writing.

From what you've learned thus far you might think that writing is a solitary task—and it generally is. But not always. Nine out of ten business professionals report that they sometimes collaborate or work as part of a team to create documents.[11] Some business writers say that one fifth of all the writing they do is produced with a group.[12]

As discussed in Chapter 1, today's businesses are searching for ways to reduce costs and improve productivity. Many are turning to work teams. Thus, business communicators can increasingly expect to be part of collaborative efforts.

Susanne Tully collaborated with graphics specialists, public relations experts, and editors in producing the Liz Claiborne recruitment brochure. This big project was more than she could handle alone and also required expertise that she lacked.

Group writing is necessary when a task is too large or complex for one individual to complete, when a deadline is near, when a task requires varied viewpoints and expertise, and when agreement is needed from many people.

Collaborative efforts may fall into many patterns. Regardless of the pattern, though, the project can take less effort and be more successful if the group follows some of the guidelines presented in the next section.

Collaboration Patterns

Whether you collaborate voluntarily (seeking advice and differing perspective) or involuntarily (through necessity or by assignment), your on-the-job team efforts fall into one of four patterns.

One author writing for someone else's approval. Subordinates often draft documents for the signature of their busy superiors. For example, your boss might ask you to draft a memo to all supervisors describing how to use a new computer program for preparing work schedules. Your boss talks to you about what to include, you write a draft, the boss reads and revises it, and you complete the final memo.

One author writing for a group. Suppose you're part of a task force named by the CEO to iron out a bonus plan for the sales force. Your group meets several times, then they ask you, the best writer in the group, to write the final report. You prepare a draft that the entire group discusses and edits. Then you compose the final version for all members to sign.

Many authors preparing individual segments of the document. Some documents require the input of many individuals. Assume that the president wants a report analyzing the effects of centralized customer service. Managers from several divisions—Sales, Customer Relations, and Human Resources— write segments of the report describing how centralization would affect them. Then the segments are joined together into one document. This method can result in a poor product unless one skilled individual has authority to edit the final report to achieve consistency.

Many authors preparing the entire document. This collaboration pattern is the least efficient because all contributors must work together through some or all of the writing stages: analyzing, adapting, organizing, composing, revising, and evaluating. Such a combined effort, though, can produce a consistent, timely, and valuable document. Let's assume your organization has a short time in which to produce a proposal for a contract that means survival for the entire company. You and your co-authors work together for three straight days, hammering out every sentence. A variation on this pattern finds the team members gathering to analyze goals and organize the topic. Then they disperse to compose their individual segments, returning to work together in preparing the final version and revising it.

Team Writing

When you work in teams, you generally have considerable control over how the project is organized and completed. If you've been part of any team efforts before, you know that such projects can be frustrating, particularly when some team members don't carry their weight or when conflict breaks out. Team projects, though, can be harmonious and productive when members establish ground rules at the outset and adhere to guidelines such as the following.

Preparing to work together. Before you discuss the project, talk about how your group will function.

- Limit the size of your team, if possible, to three or four members. Larger groups have more difficulties. An odd number is usually preferable so that ties in voting are avoided.
- Name a meeting leader (to plan and conduct meetings), a recorder (to keep a record of group decisions), and an evaluator (to determine if the group is on target and meeting its goals).

- Decide whether your team will be governed by consensus (everyone must agree) or by majority rule.

- Compare schedules of team members, and set up the best meeting times. Plan to meet often. Avoid other responsibilities during meetings.

- Discuss the value of conflict. By bringing conflict into the open and encouraging confrontation, your team can prevent personal resentment and group dysfunction. Confrontation can actually create better final documents by promoting new ideas and avoiding "group think."

- Discuss how you will deal with team members who are not pulling their share of the load.

Planning the document. Once you've established group rules, you're ready to discuss the project and resulting document. Be sure to keep a record of the following decisions your team makes.

- Establish the document's specific purpose and identify the main issues involved.

- Decide on the final form of the document. What parts will it have?

- Discuss the audience(s) for the document and what appeal would help it achieve its purpose.

- Develop a work plan. Assign jobs. Set deadlines.

- Decide how the final document will be written: everyone working separately on assigned portions, one person writing the first draft, the entire group writing the complete document together, or some other method.

Collecting information. The following suggestions help teams gather accurate information.

- Brainstorm for ideas; consider cluster diagramming.

- Decide who will be responsible for gathering what information.

- Establish deadlines for collecting information.

- Discuss ways to ensure the accuracy of the information collected.

Organizing, writing, and revising. As the project progresses, your team may wish to modify some of its earlier decisions.

- Review the proposed organization of your final document, and adjust if necessary.

- Write the first draft. If separate team members are writing segments, they should use the same word processing program to facilitate combining files.

- Meet to discuss and revise the draft(s).

- If everyone is working on a different part, appoint one person (probably the best writer) to coordinate all the parts, striving for consistent style and format.

Editing and evaluating. Before the document is submitted, complete these steps.

- Give one person responsibility for finding and correcting grammatical and mechanical errors.

- Meet as a group to evaluate the final document. Does it fulfil its purpose and meet the needs of the audience?

Successful group documents emerge from thoughtful preparation, clear definition of contributors' roles, commitment to a group-approved plan, and willingness to take responsibility for the final document.

Summary of Learning Goals

1. **Contrast formal and informal methods for researching and generating ideas.** Formal research for long reports and complex problems may involve searching library data manually or electronically, as well as conducting interviews, surveys, focus groups, and experiments. Informal research for routine tasks may include looking in company files, talking with your boss, interviewing the target audience, conducting informal surveys, brainstorming for ideas, and cluster diagramming.

2. **Specify how to organize data into lists and alphanumeric or decimal outlines.** One method for organizing data in simple messages is to list the main topics to be discussed. Organizing more complex messages usually requires an outline. To prepare an outline, divide the main topic into three to five major components. Break the components into subpoints consisting of details, illustrations, and evidence. For an alphanumeric outline arrange items using roman numerals (I, II), capital letters (A, B), and numbers (1, 2). For a decimal outline show the ordering of ideas with decimals (1, 1.1, 1.1.1).

3. **Compare direct and indirect patterns for organizing ideas.** The direct pattern places the main idea first. This pattern is useful when audiences will be pleased, mildly interested, or neutral. It saves the reader's time, sets the proper frame of mind, and prevents reader frustration. The indirect pattern places the main idea after explanations. This pattern is useful for audiences that will be unwilling, displeased, or hostile. It respects the feelings of the audience, encourages a fair hearing, and minimizes negative reactions.

4. **Discuss composing the first draft of a message, concentrating on techniques for creating forceful sentences.** Compose the first draft of a message in a quiet place where you won't be interrupted. Compose quickly, preferably at a computer. Plan to revise. As you compose, remember that sentences are most forceful when they are short (under 20 words). A main idea may be emphasized by making it the subject of the sentence, placing it first, and removing competing ideas. Forceful sentences use active verbs, although passive verbs may be necessary for tact or de-emphasis. Forceful sentences avoid dangling phrases.

5. **Define a paragraph. Describe three classic paragraph plans and techniques for composing effective paragraphs.** A paragraph consists of one or more sentences designated as a separate thought group. Typical paragraphs follow one of three plans. Direct paragraphs (main sentence followed by supporting sentences) are useful for defining, classifying, illus-

trating, and describing. Pivoting paragraphs (limiting sentence, main sentence, supporting sentences) are useful for comparing and contrasting. Indirect paragraphs (supporting sentences followed by main sentence) build a rationale and foundation of ideas before presenting the main idea. Paragraphs may be improved through the use of coherence techniques and transitional expressions.

6. **Describe conditions that make team writing necessary. Discuss typical collaboration patterns.** Collaborating is necessary when (a) one person cannot do the task alone, (b) a deadline is near, (c) a task requires varied viewpoints and expertise, and (d) agreement is needed from many people. Typical collaboration patterns consist of (a) one author writing for someone else's approval, (b) one author writing for a group, (c) many authors writing individual segments of the document, or (d) many authors writing the entire document—the least efficient method.

7. **List specific guidelines that make team efforts more productive and less stressful.** Team efforts will be more successful if the team is limited to three or four members. Teams should name a meeting leader, a recorder, and an evaluator, and they should decide on rule by majority or consensus. Meetings should be arranged at convenient times. Members should discuss how to deal with conflict and with members who do not do their share. In planning the final document, the team must establish its purpose, main issues, and format. Members must develop a work plan, assign jobs, and set deadlines. They should brainstorm for ideas and decide who will collect what information. The final document should be written and revised by one or more people or by the entire group, as determined at the outset. One person should be responsible for finding and correcting errors. The entire group should meet to decide if the document fulfils its purpose.

CHAPTER REVIEW

1. How does a writer "brainstorm"? (Goal 1)

2. What is a cluster diagram, and when might it be useful? (Goal 1)

3. Describe an alphanumeric outline. (Goal 2)

4. Distinguish between the direct and indirect patterns of organization for typical business messages. (Goal 3)

5. Why should most messages be "frontloaded"? (Goal 3)

6. List some business messages that *should be* frontloaded and some that should *not* be frontloaded. (Goal 3)

7. Why should writers plan for revision? How can they do it? (Goal 4)

8. Distinguish an independent clause from a dependent clause. Give examples. (Goal 4)

9. Name three ways to emphasize important ideas in sentences. (Goal 4)

10. Distinguish between active-voice sentences and passive-voice sentences. Give examples. (Goal 4)

11. Describe three kinds of sentences used to develop ideas in paragraphs. (Goal 5)

12. Describe three paragraph plans. Identify the uses for each. (Goal 5)

13. What is coherence, and how is it achieved? (Goal 5)

14. Describe four patterns in which collaborative writing might occur in the workplace. (Goal 6)

15. Name at least seven important guidelines or work rules that members of a collaborative writing effort should agree on before beginning to work together. (Goal 7)

DISCUSSION

1. Why is cluster diagramming considered an *intuitive* process while outlining is considered an *analytical* process? (Goal 1)

2. Why is audience analysis so important in choosing the direct or indirect pattern of organization for a business message? (Goal 2)

3. In what ways do you imagine that writing on the job differs from the writing you do in your academic studies? Consider process as well as product. (Goals 1, 6)

4. What are the ethics of collaborative writing? How ethical is it for a subordinate to compose a document that a superior will sign? Is it ethical for one person to do most of the writing on a project that a team will take credit for? (Goal 6)

5. **Ethical Issue:** Discuss the ethics of the indirect pattern of organization. Is it manipulative to delay presentation of the main idea in a message?

ACTIVITIES

4.1 Document for Analysis (Goals 3, 4, 5)

First, read the following memo to see if you can understand what the writer requests from all Western Division employees. Then discuss why this memo is so hard to read. How long are the sentences? How many passive-voice constructions can you find? How effective is the paragraphing? Can you spot four dangling modifiers? In the next activity you'll improve the organization of this message.

To: All Western Division Employees

[1]Personal computers and all the software to support these computers are appearing on many desks of Western Division employees. [2]After giving the matter considerable attention, it has been determined by the Systems Development Department (SDD) that more control should be exerted in coordinating the purchase of hardware and software to improve compatibility throughout the division

so that a library of resources may be developed. [3]Therefore, a plan has been developed by SDD that should be followed in making all future equipment selections and purchases. [4]To make the best possible choice, SDD should be contacted as you begin your search because questions about personal computers, word processors, hardware, and software can be answered by our knowledgeable staff, who can also provide you with invaluable assistance in making the best choice for your needs at the best possible cost.

[5]After your computer and its software arrive, all your future software purchases should be channelled through SDD. [6]To actually make your initial purchase, a written proposal and a purchase request form must be presented to SDD for approval. [7]A need for the purchase must be established; benefits that you expect to derive resulting from its purchase must be analyzed and presented, and an itemized statement of all costs must be submitted. [8]By following these new procedures, coordinated purchasing benefits will be realized by all employees. [9]I may be reached at x466 if you have any questions.

4.2 Organizing Data (Goal 2)

Use either a cluster diagram or an outline to organize the garbled message in Activity 4.1. Beyond the opening and closing of the message, what are the three main points the writer is trying to make? Should this message use the direct pattern or the indirect pattern? Your instructor may ask you to (1) discuss how this entire message could be revised or (2) actually rewrite it.

4.3 Collaborative Brainstorming (Goals 1, 6)

In teams of four or five, analyze a problem on your campus such as the following: unavailable classes, unrealistic degree/diploma requirements, lack of field-placement programs, poor parking facilities, inadequate registration process, lack of diversity among students on campus, and so forth. Use brainstorming techniques to generate ideas that clarify the problem and explore its solutions. Each team member should prepare a cluster diagram to record the ideas generated. Either individually or as a team, organize the ideas into an outline with three to five main points and numerous subpoints. Assume that your ideas will become part of a letter to be sent to an appropriate campus official or to your campus newspaper discussing the problem and your solution.

4.4 Individual Brainstorming (Goals 1, 2)

Analyze a problem that exists where you work or go to school, such as long lines at the copy or fax machines, overuse of express mail services, understaffing during peak hours, poor scheduling of employees, inferior or inflexible benefit package, outdated office or other equipment, or one of the campus problems discussed in Activity 4.3. Choose a problem about which you have some knowledge. Assume your boss or department chair wants you to submit a short report analyzing the problem. Draw a cluster diagram to develop ideas. Then, organize the ideas into an outline with three to five main points and numerous subpoints.

4.5   Outlining (Goal 2)

The following topics will be part of a report that a consultant is submitting to a group of investors who requested information about starting a new radio station in Regina, Saskatchewan. Arrange the topics into a coherent alphanumeric outline. Clue: the items are already in the right order.

Problem: determining program format for new radio station CFSD-FM

Background: current radio formats available to listeners in Fredericton

Background: demographics of target area (population, age, sex, income)

Survey results: music preferences

Survey finds that top two favourites are easy listening and soft rock

Next two favourites are country and rock

Other kinds of music mentioned in survey: classical, jazz

Survey results: newscast preferences

News emphasis: respondents prefer primarily national news but with some local items

Respondents say yes to news but only short, hourly newscasts

Analysis of findings: discussion of all findings in greater detail

Recommendations: hybrid format combining easy listening and soft rock

Recommendations: news in 3- to 5-minute newscasts hourly; cover national news but include local flavour

We recommend starting new station immediately.

4.6   Collaborative Letter (Goals 6, 7)

Divide into teams of three to five people who have similar majors. Work together to compose an inquiry letter requesting information from someone in your field. Include questions about technical and general courses to take, possible starting salaries, good companies to apply to, technical skills required, necessary interpersonal skills, computer tools currently used, and tips for getting started in the field. Although this is a small project, your team can work more harmoniously if you follow appropriate guidelines from this chapter. For example, appoint a meeting leader, recorder, and evaluator.

Your instructor may vary this project by asking teams to compose group letters to campus administrators discussing problems on campus; to newspaper editors commenting on news items or editorials; or to local, provincial, or federal elected officials discussing policies that you support or oppose.

EXERCISES

4.7   Sentence Elements (Goal 4)

In the following sentences underscore and identify dependent clauses (DC), independent clauses (IC), and phrases (P). Circle subjects and verbs in clauses.

a. To attract customers and make money, Arthur Quickert opened his own Milky Way Castle.

b. Although the castle and surrounding theme park have been designed for entertainment, Reid's Dairy offers high-quality dairy products processed farm-fresh daily.

c. Through hard work and excellent business sense, the Quickert family is also involved in chains of Reid's Milky Way stores.

d. When customers shop, they are also met by a Disney-style castle, milk bottle collection, and a petting zoo.

e. To ensure customer satisfaction, all Reid holdings maintain high standards of product excellence and personal service that are crucial to success.

4.8   Length of Sentence (Goal 4)

Break the following sentences into shorter sentences. Use appropriate transitional expressions.

a. If firms have a substantial investment in original research or development of new products, they should consider protecting those products with patents, although all patents eventually expire and what were once trade secrets can become common knowledge in the industry.

b. As soon as consumers recognize a name associated with a product or service, that name is entitled to legal protection as a trademark; in fact, consumers may even create a trademark where none existed or create a second trademark by using a nickname as a source indicator, such as the name "Coke," which was legally protected even before it had ever been used by the company.

c. Although no magic formula exists for picking a good trademark name, firms should avoid picking the first name that pops into someone's head; moreover, they should be aware that unique and arbitrary marks are best, while descriptive terms such as "car" or "TV repair" are useless, and surnames and geographic names are weak because they lack distinction and exclusivity.

4.9 Active and Passive Voice (Goal 4)

In the following sentences convert passive-voice verbs to active-voice verbs. Add subjects if necessary. Be prepared to discuss which sentence version is more effective.

a. A decision to concentrate on customer service was made by the board.

b. First, the product line was examined to determine if it met customers' needs.

c. In the past, products had been built to the company's internal expectations of market needs.

d. When it was realized that changes were in order, a new product line was designed.

e. After just-in-time inventory procedures were introduced, our inventories were cut in half.

f. Our company was recently named "Vendor of the Year" by Texas Instruments.

Now convert active-voice verbs to passive-voice verbs, and be prepared to discuss which version is more effective.

g. We cannot authorize repair of your VCR since you have allowed the warranty period to expire.

h. I cannot give you a cash refund for merchandise that you purchased over 60 days ago.

i. Valley Golf Course does not accept players who are not members or members' guests.

j. You must submit all reports by Friday at 5 p.m.

k. Joan added the two columns instead of subtracting them, thus producing the incorrect total.

4.10 Misplaced Modifiers (Goal 4)

Remedy any dangling or misplaced modifiers in the following sentences. Add subjects as needed, but retain the introductory phrases. Mark "C" if correct.

a. To stay in touch with customers, telephone contacts were encouraged among all sales reps.

b. By making sales reps a part of product design, a great deal of money was saved.

c. Addressing a large audience for the first time, my knees shook and my voice wobbled.

d. To receive a bachelor's degree, complete 120 units of study. *(Tricky!)*

e. Noxious fumes made the office workers sick coming from the storage tanks of a nearby paint manufacturer.

f. Using available evidence, it becomes apparent that the court has been deceived by the witness.

g. Having found the misplaced report, the search was ended.

h. The parliamentary candidate announced his intentions to run for office in his home town of Blue Bell, Saskatchewan.

i. Although T-Mart is a self-service department store, every effort is made to give customers personalized, patient service. *(Tricky!)*

j. Ignoring the warning prompt on the screen, the computer was turned off resulting in the loss of data.

4.11 Transitional Expressions (Goal 5)

Add transitional expressions to the following sentences to improve the flow of ideas (coherence).

a. Computer style checkers rank somewhere between artificial intelligence and artificial ignorance. They are like clever children: smart but not wise. Business writers should be fully aware of the limitations and the usefulness of style checkers.

b. Our computerized file includes all customer data. It provides space for name, address, and other vital information. It has an area for comments, a feature that comes in handy and helps us keep our records up-to-date.

c. No one likes to turn out poor products. We began highlighting recurring problems. Employees make a special effort to be more careful in doing their work right the first time. It doesn't have to be returned to them for corrections.

d. In-depth employment interviews may be structured or unstructured. Structured interviews have little flexibility. All candidates are asked the same questions in the same order. Unstructured interviews allow a free-flowing conversation. Topics are prepared for discussion by the interviewer.

e. Fringe benefits consist of life, health, and dental insurance. Some fringe benefits might include paid vacations and sick pay. Other fringe benefits include holidays, funeral leave, and emergency leave. Paid lunch, rest periods, tuition reimbursement, and child care are also sometimes provided.

f. Service was less than perfect for many months. We lacked certain intangibles. We didn't have the customer-specific data that we needed. We made the mistake of removing all localized, person-to-person coverage. We are returning to decentralized customer contacts.

4.12 Paragraph Organization (Goal 5)

The following poorly written paragraphs follow the indirect plan. Find the main sentence in each paragraph. Then revise each paragraph so that it is organized directly. Improve coherence by using the techniques described in this chapter.

a. Many of our customers limp through their business despite problems with their disk drives, printers, and peripherals. We cannot service their disk drives, printers, and peripherals. These customers are unable to go without this equipment long enough for the repair. We've learned that there are two times when we can get to that equipment. We can do our repairs in the middle of the night or on Sunday. All of our staff of technicians now work every Sunday. Please authorize additional budget for my department to hire technicians for night and weekend service hours.

b. Air express is one of the ways SturdyBilt power mowers and chain saws may be delivered. Air express promises two-day delivery but at a considerable cost. The cheapest method is for retailers to pick up shipments themselves at our nearest distribution centre.

We have distribution centres in Regina, Winnipeg, and Thunder Bay. Another option involves having our trucks deliver the shipment from our distribution centre to the retailer's door—for an additional fee. These are the options SturdyBilt provides for the retailers purchasing our products.

CLUE REVIEW 4

Edit the following sentences to correct faults in grammar, punctuation, spelling, and word use.

1. Although, we formally used a neighbourhood printer for all our print jobs we are now saving almost five hundred dollars a month by using desktop publishing.

2. Powerful softwear however cannot garantee a good final product.

3. To develop a better sense of design we collected desireable samples from: books, magazines, brochures, and newsletters.

4. We noticed that, poorly-designed projects often was filled with cluttered layouts, incompatible typefaces, and to many typefaces.

5. Our layout design are usually formal but occassionally we use an informal layout design which is shown in figure six.

6. We ussually prefer a black and white design; because colour printing is much more costly.

7. Expensive colour printing jobs are sent to foreign countries such as china italy and japan.

8. Jeffreys article which he entitled "The Shaping of a corporate image" was excepted for publication in "the journal of communication."

9. Every employee will persenally recieve a copy of his Performance Evaluation which the President said will be the principle basis for promotion.

10. We will print three hundred and fifty copies of the newsletter, to be sent to whomever is currently listed in our database.

Revising, Proofreading, and Evaluating

LEARNING GOALS

After studying this chapter, you should be able to

1 Identify revision techniques that make a document clear, conversational, and concise.

2 Describe revision tactics that make a document vigorous and direct.

3 Discuss revision strategies that improve readability.

4 List problem areas that good proofreaders examine carefully.

5 Compare the proofreading of routine and complex documents.

6 Evaluate a message to judge its success.

Maclean's Magazine

Within a year of landing a job at "Canada's weekly newsmagazine," *Maclean's*, Joe Chidley made a copy-editing error he will never forget. Proofreading the editorial (which appears at the front of the magazine), he made a late change to the end of the column that meant a correction had to be pasted in place. During the correction process, the last word of the editorial disappeared—something Joe should have caught, but didn't. The word that got dropped was "all," and since the *Maclean's* editor's signature appears below the editorial, the version that appeared in millions of copies read: "And that is the most disturbing fact of" followed by the editor's name.

Although it is humorous now, at the time Joe was certain the mistake would cost him his job. It didn't, and he has since become an associate editor at *Maclean's*—a job that includes both writing and editing.

> *"Just get to the point, write what you mean. That doesn't mean you can't have or use a wide vocabulary, just that you choose the word that works best."*

Although he holds a master's degree in English from the University of Western Ontario, Joe had no experience in magazine writing or proofreading when he started at *Maclean's* in 1989. Short deadlines were his first hurdle ("Whether you are writing, editing, or proofreading, part of the process is getting used to a really hectic pace"), followed by the change in gears from academic writing to professional journalism. "Writing for a magazine like *Maclean's*, addressing more than 2 million people each week, you have to cast a wider net when it comes to diction and what you demand from an article. Because we are a weekly magazine, you don't have time to ponder every word."

Every story is different, but Joe has developed a basic strategy for writing that can be broken down into three parts: the "lead," or first paragraph; the "tail," or last paragraph; and the body of the text. "First, I isolate a piece of the story with a direct or compelling impact—this will be my lead. This is the part that says 'Read on,'" says Joe, who points out that "if you lose them in the first 15 lines of a story, you've lost them for good." His second step is to think about how he will close the story—"what sort of impression will I leave with the reader?" Then he fills in the middle, making sure to cover the main points. "Much like a university essay," he says, "a magazine story will have an introductory paragraph summarizing your position, a body that describes it in detail, and a conclusion." Of course, a magazine story also has to be entertaining.

The style of writing is different as well, in part because of the constraints of space—which is where editing comes in. For Joe, that almost always involves cutting for length.

QUEBEC'S REFERENDUM FEVER

CANADA'S WEEKLY NEWSMAGAZINE   SEPTEMBER 25, 1995 $2.95

Maclean's

ALTERNATIVE MEDICINE

Healers Or Quacks?

THE CONTROVERSY OVER UNCONVENTIONAL TREATMENTS

"Usually I spend 100 words 'clearing my throat,' before I get to what the story is actually about. When it is time to send the story on to an editor, I will go back to the beginning and cut out that section." His editing is a two-step process: a first edit for the obvious things, such as spelling and grammar, and a second for more complex issues, such as poor transitions between paragraphs or unclear passages.

From the first stage of a story to the last, it is important to be sure that what is written is factual. "Much of a writer's time is spent checking facts," says Joe. "As I am writing, I will be spending a fair amount of time doing research—going through my notes or doing additional checking."

Whenever possible, he leaves himself a breather between writing the story and giving it a first edit. Even when time is tight, he advises that "if you've got 10 minutes, take 10 minutes." Since most writers "fall in love" with what they have written, that time will give the writer some perspective, so he or she can see the story objectively.

As well as making sure the story flows well, Joe tries to avoid common pitfalls, such as using too many adjectives or writing in sentence fragments. He also stays away from clutter. "Don't write 'utilize' when you mean 'use,' or 'lengthy' when you mean 'long.' Just get to the point; write what you mean. That doesn't mean you can't have or use a wide vocabulary, just that you choose the word that works best." Some of the rules of grammar can be broken, he says, if the change will add something to the story. " I wouldn't want to read a whole article written in sentence fragments," he explains, "but used judiciously they're fantastic." The important thing is conveying your meaning in the best way possible. Of course, that is not always as easy as it sounds, and the very act of writing can sometimes be difficult.

"Every writer knows how it feels to run into a wall," Joe says. "What I do when that happens is decide, 'If I were sitting with someone, how would I tell this story?' I aspire to write the way I speak—in a conversational style." Although there are no hard and fast rules for good writing, Joe advises that, apart from remembering your audience, the best way to learn to write well is "Read, read read. If you read good books, writing well and using good grammar become second nature."[1] ■

As a national newsmagazine, *Maclean's* must cover all current events across Canada and provide the most up-to-date coverage for publication. Joe Chidley's ability to research, write, edit, and revise quickly is essential to help meet tight deadlines. To hone these skills, Joe recommends reading, reading, reading!

Revising Messages

Because few writers can produce copy on the first attempt, revision is an important step in the writing process.

This chapter focuses on the final phase in the 3 × 3 writing process: revising, proofreading, and evaluating. Revising means improving the content and sentence structure of your message. Proofreading involves correcting grammar, spelling, punctuation, format, and mechanics. Evaluating is the process of analyzing whether your message achieved its purpose. Although the composition process differs for different people and situations, this final phase should occupy a significant share of the total time you spend on a message. As you learned earlier, some experts recommend devoting about half the total composition time to revising and proofreading.[2]

Rarely is the first or even second version of a message satisfactory. One authority says, "Only the amateur expects writing perfection on the first try."[3] The revision stage is your chance to make sure your message really says what you mean. Many professional writers, like Joe Chidley at *Maclean's* magazine, compose the first draft quickly without worrying about language, precision, or correctness. Then they revise and polish extensively. Other writers, however, prefer to revise as they go—particularly for shorter business documents.

Important messages—like those you send to customers or superiors or turn in to instructors for grades—deserve careful revision and proofreading. When you finish a first draft, plan for a cooling-off period. Put the document aside and return to it after a break, preferably after 24 hours or longer.

Whether you revise immediately or after a break, you'll want to examine your message critically. You should be especially concerned with ways to improve its clarity, conciseness, vigour, and readability.

Clarity: Keeping It Clear

One of the first revision tasks is assessing the clarity of your message. A clear message is one that is understood immediately. To achieve clarity, resist the urge to show off or be fancy. Remember, too, that you're not trying to impress a teacher or professor. In fact, the essential difference between academic writing and business writing is that business writing is more straightforward and clear. It is not meant to show how much you know. Put simply, the goal of business writing is to *express*, not *impress*. This involves two simple rules: (1) keep it simple and (2) keep it conversational.

To achieve clarity, remember to KISS—Keep It Short and Simple!

Applying the KISS formula. Why do some communicators fail to craft simple, direct messages? For several reasons:

- Untrained executives and professionals worry that plain messages don't sound important.

- Subordinates fear that plain talk won't impress the boss.

- Unskilled writers create foggy messages because they've not learned how to communicate clearly.

Whatever the cause, you can eliminate the fog by applying the familiar KISS formula: *Keep It Short and Simple!* One way to achieve clear writing is to use active-voice sentences that avoid negative, indirect, and pompous language.

Indirect	**Improved**
Employees have not been made sufficiently aware of the potentially adverse consequences involved regarding these chemicals.	Warn your employees about these chemicals.
To be sure of obtaining optimal results, it is essential that you give your employees the implements that are necessary for completion of the job.	To get the best results, give employees the tools they need to do the job.

Keeping It Conversational

Clarity is further enhanced by language that sounds like conversation. This doesn't mean that your letters and memos should be chatty or familiar. Rather, you should strive to sound professional, yet not artificial or formal. This means avoiding legal terminology, technical words, and third-person constructions (*the undersigned, the writer*). It also means sounding friendly and warm, just as you do in conversation. Thus, you may include occasional contractions (*can't, doesn't*) and first-person pronouns (*I/we*) in all but the most formal business reports. To decide if your writing is conversational, try the kitchen test. If it wouldn't sound natural in your kitchen, it probably needs revision. Note how the following formal sentences were revised to pass the kitchen test.

To achieve a conversational tone, sound professional but not stilted.

Formal	**Conversational**
As per your verbal instruction, steps will be undertaken immediately to investigate your billing problem.	At your suggestion I'm investigating your billing immediately.
Our organization would like to inform you that your account has been credited in the aforementioned sum.	We're crediting your account for $78.

Keeping It Concise

Another revision task is making certain that a message makes its point in the fewest possible words. One of the shortest and most effective business letters ever written contained only 19 words. Composed by business tycoon Cornelius Vanderbilt, the following masterpiece in brevity was sent to a pair of business associates who tried to swindle him while he vacationed in Europe:

Main points are easier to understand in concise messages.

> Gentlemen:
>> You have undertaken to cheat me. I won't sue you, for the law is too slow. I'll ruin you.
>
>> Yours truly,
>>
>> Cornelius Vanderbilt

Messages without flabby phrases and redundancies are easier to comprehend and more forceful because main points stand out, as Vanderbilt's letter proves. Efficient messages also save the reader valuable time.

Concise writing begins with clear thinking. A famous Hollywood producer once said, "If you can't write your idea on the back of my calling card, you don't have a clear idea." Similarly, Procter & Gamble, the giant household products manufacturer, for years required all memos to be limited to one page. The president returned long messages, urging writers to "boil it down to something I

Concise messages are the
product of clear thinking
and a solid grasp of the
material.

can grasp." Conciseness indicates clear thinking and total control over the material.

But concise writing is not easy. As one expert copyeditor observes, "Trim sentences, like trim bodies, usually require far more effort than flabby ones."[4] To turn out slim sentences and lean messages, you do not have to be brusque, rude, or simple-minded. Instead, you must take time in the revision stage to trim the fat. And before you can do that, you must learn to recognize it. Finding and excising wordiness involves (1) removing opening fillers, (2) eliminating redundancies, (3) reducing compound prepositions, and (4) purging empty words.

Removing opening fillers. Openers like *The purpose of this letter is to inform you that ...* fill in sentences but generally add no meaning. These fillers reveal writers spinning their wheels until deciding where the sentence is going. Train yourself to question this kind of construction.

Eliminating redundancies. Expressions that repeat meaning or include unnecessary words are redundant. To say *important essentials* is like saying "essential essentials" because *important* carries the same meaning as *essential*. Excessive adjectives, adverbs, and phrases often create redundancies. The following list represents a tiny segment of the large number of redundancies appearing in business writing today. What word in each expression creates the redundancy?

Redundancies to Avoid

advance warning	exactly identical	perfectly clear
alter or change	few in number	personal opinion
assemble together	free and clear	potential opportunity
basic fundamentals	grateful thanks	positively certain
collect together	great majority	proposed plan
consensus of opinion	integral part	serious interest
contributing factor	last and final	refer back
dollar amount	midway between	true facts
each and every	new changes	very unique
end result	past history	visible to the eye

Reducing wordiness. Many wordy phrases can be expressed in single words. In the following examples the shorter forms say the same thing much more efficiently.

Wordy Expression	Shorter Substitute
as to whether	whether
at a later date	later
at this point in time	now
at such time, at which time	when
by means of, in accordance with	by
despite the fact that	although
due to the fact that, inasmuch as, in view of the fact that	because

for the amount of	for
in advance of, prior to	before
subsequent to	after
the manner in which	how
until such time as	until

Purging empty words. Familiar phrases roll off the tongue easily, but many contain expendable parts. Be alert to these empty words: *case, degree, the fact that, factor, instance, nature,* and *quality.* Notice how much better the following sentences sound when the empty words are removed:

In the case of *Maclean's*, the magazine improved its readability.

Because of the degree of active participation by our sales reps, profits soared.

We are aware of the fact that many managers need assistance.

Except for the instance of Mazda, Japanese imports sagged.

She chose a career in a field that was analytical in nature. (Or, she chose a career in an analytical field.)

Student writing in that class is excellent in quality.

Also avoid saying the obvious. In the following examples notice how many unnecessary words can be omitted:

When it arrived, I cashed your cheque immediately. (Announcing the cheque's arrival is unnecessary. That fact is assumed in its cashing.)

We need printer cartidges; therefore, please send me two dozen laser cartridges. (The first clause is obvious.)

This is to inform you that the meeting will start at 2 p.m. (Avoid unnecessary lead-ins.)

Finally, look carefully at clauses beginning with *that, which,* and *who.* They can often be shortened without loss of clarity. Search for phrases, such as *it appears that,* that can be reduced to a single adjective or adverb, such as *apparently.*

successful
Changing the name of a ∧ company that is successful is always risky.

final
Our ∧ proposal, which was slightly altered in its final form, won approval.

weekly
We plan to reschedule ∧ meetings on a weekly basis.

◼ Revising for Vigour and Directness

Much business writing has been criticized as lifeless, cautious, and "really, really boring."[5] This boredom is caused not so much by the content as by wordiness and dull, trite expressions. An Ottawa consulting firm, Prosebusters, was hired to rewrite a 100-page document at a cost of $10 500. The educational document, *The Common Curriculum*, was packed with so much technical jargon it was described as "virtually impossible to understand."[6] You've already studied

Much business writing is plagued by wordiness and triteness.

A new emphasis on readability in business contracts, policies, and other documents has sent researchers and writers back to the books. Instead of producing documents written in legalese, many companies are now emphasizing comprehensibility and plain English.

ways to improve clarity and conciseness. You can also reduce wordiness and improve vigour by (1) kicking the noun habit and (2) dumping trite business phrases.

Kicking the Noun Habit

Overusing noun phrases lengthens sentences, saps verbs, and muddies the message.

Some writers become addicted to nouns, needlessly using abstract nouns *(we make a recommendation of* instead of *we recommend)*. This bad habit increases sentence length, drains verb strength, slows the reader, and muddies the thought. Notice how efficient, clean, and forceful the verbs below sound compared with their noun phrase counterparts.

Wordy Noun Phrase	Verb
conduct a discussion of	discuss
create a reduction in	reduce
engage in the preparation of	prepare
give consideration to	consider
is dependent on	depends
make an assumption of	assume
make a discovery of	discover
perform an analysis of	analyze
reach a conclusion about	conclude
take action on	act

Dumping Trite Business Phrases

To sound "businesslike," many writers repeat the same stale expressions that other writers have used over the years. Your writing will sound fresher and more vigorous if you eliminate these phrases or find more original ways to convey the idea.

Trite Phrase	Improved Version
as per your request	as you request
pursuant to your request	at your request
enclosed please find	enclosed is
every effort will be made	we'll try
in accordance with your wishes	as you wish
in receipt of	have received
please do not hesitate to	please
thank you in advance	thank you
under separate cover	separately
with reference to	about

Revising for Readability

To help receivers anticipate and comprehend ideas quickly, two special writing techniques are helpful: (1) parallelism, which involves balanced writing, and (2) highlighting, which makes important points more visible. And to ensure that your document is readable, consider applying the Fog Index, a readability measure outlined later in this chapter.

Comprehension can be enhanced through parallelism and graphic highlighting.

Developing Parallelism

As you revise, be certain that you express similar ideas in balanced or parallel construction. For example, the phrase *clearly, concisely, and correctly* is parallel because all the words end in *-ly*. To express the list as *clearly, concisely, and with correctness* is jarring because the last item is not what the receiver expects. Instead of an adverb, the series ends with a noun. To achieve parallelism, match nouns with nouns, verbs with verbs, phrases with phrases, and clauses with clauses. Avoid mixing active-voice verbs with passive-voice verbs.

Parallelism means matching nouns with nouns, verbs with verbs, phrases with phrases, and so on.

Nonparallel	Improved
The policy affected all vendors, suppliers, and those involved with consulting.	The policy affected all vendors, suppliers, and consultants. (*Series matches nouns.*)
Good managers analyze a problem, collect data, and alternatives are evaluated.	Good managers analyze a problem, collect data, and evaluate alternatives. (*Series matches verb forms.*)

Be alert to a list or series of items; the use of *and* or *or* should signal you to check for balanced construction. When elements cannot be balanced fluently, consider revising to subordinate or separate the items.

Nonparallel	**Improved**
Foreign service employees must be able to communicate rapidly, concisely, and be flexible in handling diverse responsibilities.	Foreign service employees must be able to communicate rapidly and concisely; they must also be flexible in handling diverse responsibilities.

Applying Graphic Highlighting

Graphic devices such as lists, bullets, headings, and white space spotlight important ideas.

One of the best ways to improve comprehension is through graphic highlighting techniques. Spotlight important items by setting them off with

- Letters, like (a), (b), and (c), within the text
- Numerals, like 1, 2, and 3, listed vertically
- Bullets—black squares, raised periods, or other figures
- Headings
- Capital letters, underscores, boldface, and italics

Ideas formerly buried within sentences or paragraphs stand out when targeted with one of these techniques. Readers not only understand your message more rapidly and easily but also consider you efficient and well organized. In the two sentences following, notice how highlighting with letters makes the three items more visible and forceful. Numerals are also appropriate, particularly to indicate numbered groups or a sequence.

Original	**Highlighted**
Nordstrom attracts upscale customers by featuring quality fashions, personalized service, and a generous return policy.	Nordstrom attracts upscale customers by featuring (a) quality fashions, (b) personal service, and (c) a generous return policy.

Lists offset from the text and introduced with bullets have a strong visual impact.

If you have the space and wish to create even greater visual impact, you can list items vertically and use bullets. Capitalize the word at the beginning of each line. Don't add end punctuation unless the statements are complete sentences. In the following items notice how each one begins with an *-ing* verb. Parallel construction is very important whenever you itemize ideas.

Several factors contribute to our successful service program:
- Setting and broadcasting goals for the organization
- Instilling an understanding of what quality service means
- Conducting customer surveys

Headings help writers to organize information and enable readers to absorb important ideas.

Headings benefit both the writer and the reader. They force the writer to organize carefully so that similar data are grouped together. And they help the reader separate major ideas from details. Moreover, headings enable a busy reader to skim familiar or less important information. They also provide a quick preview or review. Although headings appear more often in reports, they are equally helpful in complex letters and memos. Here, they informally summarize items within a message:

Our staff is developing a policy that eliminates as many barriers as possible to an international assignment for dual-career couples. Thus far, the policy has these unique conditions.

Dislocation allowance. The dislocated spouse receives a one-time payment of 33 percent of the last three months' gross taxable income up to $10,000.

APPLYING THE FOG INDEX TO DETERMINE READABILITY

One way to calculate the readability of a document is by applying the Gunning Fog Index. Here's how you can figure it manually for the business letter shown here. (This same calculation can be performed by many computer software programs.)

- **Step 1: Select the passage.** Choose a continuous passage of between 100 and 130 words.

- **Step 2: Count the total words.** Count numbers, dates, and abbreviations as separate words. Our business letter sample has 110 words.

- **Step 3: Count the sentences.** Count all independent clauses separately. For example, *He applied, and he was hired* counts as two sentences. Our sample has seven sentences, marked with superscript numbers.

- **Step 4: Find the average sentence length.** Divide the total number of words by the number of sentences (110 ÷ 7 = 16 words).

- **Step 5: Count the number of long words.** A word is long if it has three or more syllables. Exclude (a) capitalized words, (b) compound words formed from short words (*nevertheless*), and (c) verbs made into three syllables by the addition of *-ed* or *-es (located, finances)*. In our sample the long words are underlined.

- **Step 6: Find the percentage of long words.** Divide the number of long words by the number of total words (10 ÷ 110 = .09 or 9 percent).

- **Step 7: Add the results.** Add the average sentence length (16) and the percentage of long words (9). The result is 25.

- **Step 8: Multiply.** Multiply by 0.4 (25 x 0.4 = 10). The reading level of this letter is 10.

Dear Mrs. Lawrence:

[1]Yes, I can meet with you Thursday, April, 3, at 10 a.m. to discuss <u>possible</u> ways to finance the purchase of a new home in Montreal, QC. [2]Before we meet, though, you might like to <u>consider</u> two <u>possible</u> plans.

[3]The first plan finances your purchase with a swing loan, which has a fixed <u>interest</u> rate for a short <u>period</u> of time. [4]A second plan requires you to <u>refinance</u> your present <u>residence</u>. [5]We have located five programs from three <u>different institutions</u> that would do this. [6]Enclosed is a <u>summary</u> of these five plans.

[7]I look forward to seeing you Thursday to find a way for you to own a home in Montreal.

Sincerely,

The reading level of this short letter is 10, indicating appropriate writing for a business message. Your goal should be to keep your writing between the levels of 8 and 12. Two factors that most influence reading level are sentence length and word length.

Career Track Application

Compare the reading levels of several publications. Calculate the Fog Index for short passages from two of your college textbooks, your local newspaper, a business document (letter, memo, report), and an insurance policy. Discuss in class the appropriateness of the reading levels for each document.

Premove visit. Spouses may receive a loss-of-earnings payment up to $4000 to cover any premove visit to the foreign assignment.

Language and other training. While on assignment, the spouse may be reimbursed for language training and any schooling that advances the spouse's career.

To highlight individual words, use capital letters, underlining, bold type, or italics. Be careful with these techniques, though, because they SHOUT at the reader. Consider how the reader will react.

The following chapters supply additional ideas for grouping and spotlighting data. Although highlighting techniques can improve comprehension, they can also clutter a message if overdone. Many of these techniques also require more space, so use them judiciously.

Too much graphic highlighting can clutter a document and reduce comprehension.

Baseball players, notes playwright Neil Simon, get only three swings at a pitch and then they're out. In rewriting, however, "you get almost as many swings as you want and you know, sooner or later, you'll hit the ball." Although it takes real effort, revision allows the writer to work out the rough spots so that every message can score a hit.

Readability formulas like the Fog Index are based on word and sentence lengths.

Measuring readability. Experts have developed methods for measuring how easy, or difficult, a message is to read. Probably the best known is Robert Gunning's Fog Index, which measures long words and sentence length to determine readability. Many commercial word processing packages have an embedded readability program that can help the writer create documents at the right level for the reader. The Career Skills box on page 131 shows you how to apply eight steps in figuring the Fog Index for a piece of writing, such as the sample business letter shown.

Our calculation indicates that this sample letter is written at a reading grade level of 10. The foggier a message, the higher its reading level. Magazines and newspapers that strive for wide readership keep their readability between levels 8 and 12. By occasionally calculating the Fog Index of your writing, you can ensure that you stay within the 8–12 range. Remember that long sentences and long words—those over two syllables—make your writing foggy.

Readability formulas, however, don't always tell the full story. Although they provide a rough estimate, those based solely on word and sentence counts fail to measure meaningfulness. Even short words (like *skew*, *onus*, and *wane*) can cause trouble if readers don't recognize them. More important than length are a word's familiarity and meaningfulness to the reader. In Chapter 3 you learned to adapt your writing to the audience by selecting familiar words. Other techniques that can improve readability include well-organized paragraphs, transitions to connect ideas, headings, and lists.

The task of revision, summarized in the following checklist, is hard work. It demands objectivity and a willingness to cut, cut, cut. Though painful, the process is also gratifying. It's a great feeling when you realize your finished message is clear, concise, and readable.

Checklist for Revising Messages

✓ **Keep the message simple.** Express ideas directly. Don't show off or use fancy language.

✓ **Be conversational.** Include occasional contractions (*hasn't, don't*) and first-person pronouns (*I/we*). Use natural-sounding language.

✓ **Avoid opening fillers.** Omit sentence fillers like *The purpose of this letter is.*

✓ **Shun redundancies.** Eliminate words that repeat meanings, such as *mutual cooperation.* Watch for repetitious adjectives, adverbs, and phrases.

✓ **Tighten your writing.** Check phrases involving *case, degree, the fact that, factor,* and other words that unnecessarily increase wordiness. Avoid saying the obvious.

✓ **Don't use abstract nouns in place of verbs.** Keep your writing vigorous by avoiding the noun habit (*analyze,* not *make an analysis of*).

✓ **Avoid trite phrases.** Keep your writing fresh, direct, and contemporary by skipping such expressions as *enclosed please find* and *pursuant to your request.*

✓ **Strive for parallelism.** Help receivers anticipate and comprehend your message by using balanced writing (*planning, drafting,* and *constructing* not *planning, drafting,* and *construction*).

✓ **Highlight important ideas.** Use graphic techniques such as letters, numerals, bullets, headings, capital letters, underlining, boldface, or italics to spotlight ideas and organization.

✓ **Test readability.** Check your writing occasionally to identify its reading level. Remember that short, familiar words and short sentences help readers comprehend.

Proofreading for the Finishing Touch

Once you have the message in its final form, it's time to proofread it. Don't proofread earlier because you may waste time checking items that are eventually changed or omitted.

Proofreading before a document is completed is generally a waste of time.

What to Watch For in Proofreading

Careful proofreaders check for problems in these areas:

- **Spelling**. Now's the time to consult the dictionary. Is *recommend* spelled with one or two *c*'s? Do you mean *affect* or *effect*? Use your computer spell

checker, but don't rely on it totally. See the following Technology box to learn more about the benefits and hazards of computer spell checkers.

- **Grammar.** Locate sentence subjects; do their verbs agree with them? Do pronouns agree with their antecedents? Review the CLUE principles in Appendix A if necessary.

- **Punctuation.** Make sure that introductory clauses are followed by commas. In compound sentences put commas before coordinating conjunctions (*and, or, but, nor*). Double-check your use of semicolons and colons.

- **Names and numbers.** Compare all names and numbers with their sources because inaccuracies are not immediately visible. Especially verify the spelling of the names of individuals receiving the message. Most of us immediately dislike someone who misspells our name.

- **Format.** Be sure that your document looks balanced on the page. Compare its parts and format with those of standard documents shown in Appendix B. If you indent paragraphs, be certain that all are indented.

How to Proofread Routine Documents

Most routine documents require a light proofreading. You may be working with a handwritten or a printed copy or on your computer screen. If you wish to print a copy, make it a rough draft (don't print it on letterhead stationery). In time you may be able to produce a "first-time-final" message, but beginning writers seldom do.

SPELL CHECKERS ARE WONDERFUL, BUT ...

Nearly all high-end word processing programs now include spell checkers. Also called dictionaries, these programs compare your typed words with those in the computer's memory and mark all discrepancies.

Spell checkers find a great many—but not all—word use and spelling errors. One study of college writing found that 75 percent of the students' spelling and usage errors would have been found by spelling software.[10] Doubtless, students are thankful for such assistance! But the flip side of the story is that 25 percent of the errors were not found. How this might happen is illustrated by the following poem:

> I have a spell checker
> That came with my PC.
> It plainly marks four my review
> Mistakes I cannot sea.
> I've run this poem threw it,
> I'm sure your pleased too no.
> Its letter perfect in it's weigh—
> My checker tolled me sew.[11]

The lesson to be learned here is that you can't rely totally on any spell checker. Misused words will not be highlighted because the spell checker doesn't know what meaning you have in mind. That's why you're wise to print out every message and proofread it word by word. Proofreading is the only way you can detect keyboarding errors like *they* for *the* or *prepared* for *prepare*. Double-check confusing duos like *than/then*, *personal/personnel*, and *principle/principal*.

Career Track Application

Run a paper from this or another class through a spell checker. Then have a friend or classmate proofread it to see what the computer missed.

For handwritten or printed messages, read the entire document. Watch for all of the items just described. Use standard proofreading marks, shown in Figure 5.1, to indicate changes.

For computer messages you can read the document on the screen, preferably in WYSIWYG mode (what you see is what you get). Use the down arrow to reveal one line at a time, thus focusing your attention at the bottom of the screen. A safer proofreading method, however, is reading from a printed copy. You're more likely to find errors and to observe the tone.

For both routine and complex documents, it's best to proofread from a printed copy, not on a computer screen.

How to Proofread Complex Documents

Long, complex, or important documents demand more careful proofreading using the following techniques:

Complex documents should be proofread at least twice.

- Print a copy, preferably double-spaced, and set it aside for at least a day. You'll be more alert after a breather.

- Allow adequate time to proofread carefully. A common excuse for sloppy proofreading is lack of time.

- Be prepared to find errors. One student confessed, "I can find other people's errors, but I can't seem to find my own." Psychologically, we don't *expect* to find errors, and we don't *want* to find them. Overcome this

FIGURE 5.1 ■ Proofreader's Marks

✐	Delete	∧	Insert
≡	Capitalize	#∧	Insert space
/lc	Lowercase (don't capitalize)	∧	Insert punctuation
∩	Transpose	⊙	Insert period
⌒	Close up	¶	Start paragraph

Marked Copy

This is to inform you that beginning september 1 the doors leading to the Westside of the building will have alarms. Because of the fact that these exits also function as fire exits they can not actually be locked consequently we are instaling alarms. Please utilize the east side exists to avoid setting off the ear-piercing alarms.

obstacle by anticipating errors and congratulating, not criticizing, yourself each time you find one.

- Read the message at least twice—once for word meanings and once for grammar/mechanics. For very long documents (book chapters and long articles or reports), read a third time to verify consistency in formatting.

- Reduce your reading speed. Concentrate on individual words rather than ideas.

- For documents that must be perfect, have someone read the message aloud. Spell names and difficult words, note capitalization, and read punctuation.

- Use standard proofreading marks, shown in Figure 5.1, to indicate changes.

Joe Chidley suggests "taking a breather" before you proofread. Even when time is tight, he advises, "if you've got 10 minutes, take 10 minutes."

You may want to try a computer program that analyzes certain aspects of your writing style. These style checkers identify such writing characteristics as use of the passive voice, trite phrases, split infinitives, and wordy expressions, as well as readability level. Some can even find selected grammar errors. At this point, however, these software programs are probably most useful when an instructor is available to interpret and discuss the recommendations. For more discussion of grammar and style checkers, see the Technology box that follows.

Computer programs can help analyze writing, calculate readability, and locate some grammar errors.

GRAMMAR AND STYLE CHECKERS: GOOD AND BAD NEWS

Like most of us, you probably welcome any aid that improves your writing. Leading word processing programs—WordPerfect for Windows, Microsoft Word for Windows, and Microsoft Word for the Macintosh—now have built-in grammar and style checkers that are almost as easy to use as spell checkers. That's the good news.

The bad news is that they may be limited in the accuracy of "errors" they detect. Analyzing written material is complicated, and most grammar and style checkers tend to offer inappropriate suggestions along with useful advice. Moreover, no grammar and style checker is currently able to evaluate the quality of a person's writing. Despite these drawbacks, though, many writers find them useful.

Just how do they operate? Generally, you keyboard or make a selection from the word processing menu to begin the checking program. As the checker flags each "problem," you read the suggestions and decide whether to revise. On the right are sample suggestions made by three leading grammar and style checker programs. Notice that the decision to revise is still up to the writer.

Checkers can flag certain sentence fragments, passive-verb constructions, wordy phrases, unfamiliar words, and clichés. They can also calculate readability level, average sentence and paragraph length, and number of difficult words. Such programs are especially good at mechanical tasks. But don't rely on them to solve all your writing problems. They aren't that sophisticated.

Most leading grammar and style checkers recognize documents created in a number of word processing programs for Macintosh, DOS, and Windows environments. They compare your writing to a set of "rules" and then flag errors that do not follow the rules. Many programs also allow you to customize the rules to your writing needs (business, technical, journalistic, fiction, and so forth).

As you can see from our examples, grammar and style checks don't correct anything. They merely make suggestions. Although such checkers are useful for pinpointing elements that may need revision, only *you* can be the final authority on how your document should be written.

Sentence	Checker Suggestion
Grammatik	
John was responsible for implementation of the program.	Try using a form of "carry out," set up," "use," or "tool."
Although management anticipates changes.	"Although" can't begin an independent clause.
RightWriter	
Vancouver is only 2085 miles away as the crow flies.	Reconsider the use of the cliché "as the crow flies."
Although management anticipates changes.	Consider replacing "anticipates" with the correct form of the simpler "expect." Is this a complete sentence? If so, is a comma missing?
Correct Grammar	
An error was found in the report.	This verb group [was found] may be in the passive voice.
This idea is first and foremost in our minds.	Wordy. Consider "first," "foremost," or "primarily" instead.

Career Track Application

Use a word processing program with a built-in grammar and style checker in preparing letters and memos for this class. Analyze the suggestions made by the checker. Revise your documents using your judgment about what changes improve message effectiveness.

Evaluating the Product

As part of applying finishing touches, take a moment to evaluate your writing. How successful will this message be? Does it say what you want it to? Will it achieve your purpose? How will you know if it succeeds?

As you learned in Chapter 1, the best way to judge the success of your communication is through feedback. Thus, you should always encourage the

FIGURE 5.2 ■ The Complete 3 × 3 Writing Process

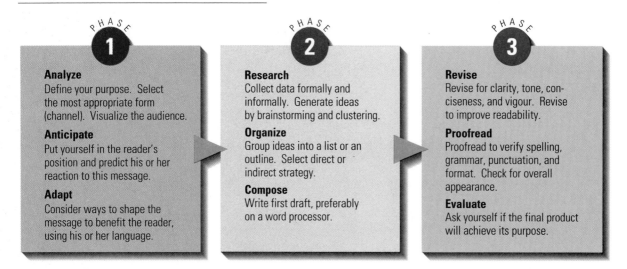

PHASE 1

Analyze
Define your purpose. Select the most appropriate form (channel). Visualize the audience.

Anticipate
Put yourself in the reader's position and predict his or her reaction to this message.

Adapt
Consider ways to shape the message to benefit the reader, using his or her language.

PHASE 2

Research
Collect data formally and informally. Generate ideas by brainstorming and clustering.

Organize
Group ideas into a list or an outline. Select direct or indirect strategy.

Compose
Write first draft, preferably on a word processor.

PHASE 3

Revise
Revise for clarity, tone, conciseness, and vigour. Revise to improve readability.

Proofread
Proofread to verify spelling, grammar, punctuation, and format. Check for overall appearance.

Evaluate
Ask yourself if the final product will achieve its purpose.

A good way to evaluate messages is through feedback

receiver to respond to your message. This feedback will tell you how to modify future efforts to improve your communication technique.

Your instructor will also be evaluating some of your writing. Although any criticism is painful, try not to be defensive. Look on these comments as valuable advice tailored to your specific writing weaknesses—and strengths. Many businesses today spend hundreds of dollars per employee bringing in communication consultants to improve writing. You're getting the same training in this course. Take advantage of this chance—one of the few you may have—to improve your skills. The best way to improve is through instruction, practice, and evaluation.

In this class you have all three elements: instruction in the writing process (summarized in Figure 5.2), practice materials, and someone willing to guide and evaluate your efforts. Because it's almost impossible to improve alone, grab this chance. Multimillionaire Malcolm Forbes, founder of *Forbes* magazine, wisely observed, "The best place to learn to write is in school. If you're still there, pick your teachers' brains!"[12]

■ Summary of Learning Goals

1. **Identify revision techniques that make a document clear, conversational, and concise.** Clear documents use active-voice sentences and simple words and avoid negative expressions. Clarity is further enhanced by language that sounds like conversation, including occasional contractions and first-person pronouns (*I/we*). Conciseness can be achieved by excluding opening fillers (*There are*), redundancies (*basic essentials*), and compound prepositions (*by means of*).

2. **Describe revision tactics that make a document vigorous and direct.** Writers can achieve vigour in messages by revising wordy phrases that needlessly convert verbs into nouns. For example, instead of *we conducted a discussion of*, write *we discussed*. To make writing more direct, good writers replace trite business phrases, such as *please do not hesitate to* with *please*.

3. **Discuss revision strategies that improve readability.** One technique that improves readability is the use of balanced constructions *(parallelism)*. For example, *collecting, analyzing, and illustrating data* is balanced and easy to read. *Collecting data that must be analyzed and illustrated* is more difficult to read because it is unbalanced. Parallelism involves matching nouns with nouns, verbs with verbs, phrases with phrases, and clauses with clauses. Another technique that improves readability is graphic highlighting. It incorporates devices such as lettered items, numerals, bullets, headings, capital letters, underlining, italics, and boldface print to highlight and order ideas. A readability scale, such as the Fog Index, is helpful in measuring how easy or difficult a document is to read.

4. **List problem areas that good proofreaders examine carefully.** Proofreaders must be especially alert to these problem areas: spelling, grammar, punctuation, names, numbers, and layout.

5. **Compare the proofreading of routine and complex documents.** Routine documents may be proofread immediately after completion. They may be read line by line on the computer screen or, better yet, from a printed draft copy. More complex documents, however, should, be proofread after a breather. To do a good job, you must allow adequate time, reduce your reading speed, and read the document at least three times—for word meanings, for grammar and mechanics, and for formatting.

6. **Evaluate a message to judge its success.** Encourage feedback from the receiver so that you can determine whether your communication achieved its goal. Welcome advice from your instructor on how to improve your writing skills. Both techniques help you evaluate the success of a message.

CHAPTER REVIEW

1. Approximately how much of the total composition time should be spent revising, proofreading, and evaluating? (Goal 1)

2. What is the KISS method? What three ways can it apply to business writing? (Goal 1)

3. What is a redundancy? Give an example. Why should writers avoid redundancies? (Goal 1)

4. Why should communicators avoid openings such as *there is*? (Goal 1)

5. What shorter forms could be substituted for the expressions *by means of, despite the fact that*, and *at this point in time*? (Goal 1)

6. Why should a writer avoid the opening *This memo is to inform you that our next committee meeting is Friday*? (Goal 1)

7. Why should a writer avoid an expression like *We hope you will give consideration to our proposal*? (Goal 2)

8. What's wrong with businesslike expressions such as *enclosed please find* and *as per your request*? (Goal 2)

9. Discuss five ways to highlight important ideas. (Goal 3)

10. What two characteristics raise the Fog Index of written matter? (Goal 3)

11. What is parallelism, and how can it be achieved? (Goal 3)

12. Name five specific items to check in proofreading. Be ready to discuss methods you find useful in spotting these errors. (Goal 4)

13. In proofreading, what major psychological problem do you face in finding errors? How can you overcome this barrier? (Goal 4)

14. List four or more techniques for proofreading complex documents. (Goal 4)

15. How can you overcome defensiveness when your writing is criticized constructively? (Goal 5)

DISCUSSION

1. Why is it difficult to recommend a specific process that all writers can follow in composition? (Goal 1)

2. Discuss this statement by writing expert William Zinsser: "Plain talk will not be easily achieved in corporate America. Too much vanity is on the line." (Goals 1, 2)

3. To be conversational, should you write exactly as you talk? Support your opinion. (Goal 1)

4. Why should the proofreading of routine documents differ from that of complex documents? (Goals 4, 5)

5. **Ethical Issue:** What advice would you give in this ethical dilemma? Lisa is serving as interim editor of the company newsletter. She receives an article written by the company president describing, in abstract and pompous language, the company's goals for the coming year. Lisa thinks the article will need considerable revising to make it readable. Attached to the president's article are complimentary comments by two of the company vice presidents. What action should Lisa take?

ACTIVITIES

5.1 Document for Analysis (Goals 1–3)

Revise the following memo to improve its clarity, conciseness, vigour, and readability. How many wordy constructions can you spot?

To: All Management

This memo is addressed to all members of management to advise you that once a year we like to remind management of our policy in relation to the matter of business attire. In this policy there is a recommendation that all employees should wear clothing that promotes a businesslike atmosphere and meets requirements of safety.

Employees who work in offices and who, as part of their jobs, meet the public and other outsiders should dress in a professional manner, including coat, tie, suit, dress, and so forth. In areas of industrial applications, supervisors may prohibit loose clothing (shirttails, ties, cuffs) that could become entangled in machinery that moves.

Where it is necessary, footwear should provide protection against heavy objects or sharp edges at the level of the floor. In the manufacturing and warehousing areas, prohibited footwear includes the following: shoes that are open toe, sandals, shoes made of canvas or nylon, tennis shoes, spiked heels, and heels higher than 1½ inches.

Each and every manager has the responsibility for the determination of suitable business attire, and employees should be informed of what is required.

5.2 Document for Analysis (Goals 4, 5)

Use proofreading marks to show corrections needed in the following letter. Check spelling, typos, grammar, punctuation, names and numbers, and layout.

Dear Ms. Willis,

We appreciate you interest in employe leasing through Dominion Staff Network. Our programs and our service has proved to be powerful management tools for business owners, like you.

Our seventeen year history, Ms. Williams, provide the local service and national strength neccesary to offer the best employee leasing programs available, we save business owners time, and money, employee hassles and employer liability.

Your employees' will receive health care benifits, retirement plan choices and a national credit union. As a small business owner you can eliminate personel administration. Which involves alot of goverment paperwork today.

Whether you have one or 1,000 employees and offer no benefits to a full-benefits package employee leasing will get you back to the basics of running your business more profitably. I will call you to arrange a time to meet, and talk about your specific needs.

Cordially,

5.3 Computing Fog Index (Goals 3,4,5)

As an in-class project or for homework, do the following: (1) Compute the Fog Index for the following letter. (2) Then revise the letter using proofreading marks. Reduce its length and improve its readability by eliminating redundancies, wordiness, and trite expressions. Use simple, clear words. Shorten sentences. (3) Prepare a clean copy of the revised letter. (4) Finally, calculate the Fog Index for your revision.

Dear Mr. Sato:

Pursuant to your request, the undersigned is transmitting to you herewith the attached materials and documents with regard to the improvement of security in your business. To ensure the improvement of your after-hours security, you should initially make a decision with regard to exactly what you contemplate must have protection. You are, in all probability, apprehensive not only about your electronic equipment and paraphernalia but also about your company records, information, and data.

Inasmuch as we feel you will want to obtain protection for both your equipment and data, we will make suggestions for taking a number of judicious steps to inhibit crime. First and foremost, we recommend that you install defensive lighting. A consultant for lighting, currently on our staff, can design both outside and inside lighting, which brings me to my second point. Exhibit security signs, due to the fact that nonprofessional thieves are often as not deterred by posted signs on windows and doors. As my last and final recommendation, you should install space alarms, which are sensors that look down over the areas that are to receive protection, and activate bells or additional lights, thus scaring off intruders.

After reading the enclosed materials, please call me to further discuss the protection of your business.

Sincerely,

5.4 Interview (Goals 1–5)

To learn more about on-the-job writing, interview someone—preferably in your field of study. Ask questions like these: *What kind of writing do you do? What kind of planning do you do before writing? Where do you get information? Do you brainstorm? Make lists? Do you compose with pen and paper, a computer, or a dictating machine? How long does it take you to compose a routine one- or two-page memo or letter? Do you revise? How often? Do you have a preferred method for proofreading? When you have questions about grammar and mechanics, what or whom do you consult? Does anyone read your drafts and make suggestions? Can you describe your entire composition process? Do you ever work with others to produce a document? How does this process work? What makes writing easier or harder for you? Have your writing methods and skills changed since you left school?* Your instructor may ask you to present your findings orally or in a written report.

EXERCISES

5.5 Clarity (Goal 1)

Revise the following sentences to make them direct, simple, and conversational.

a. It has been determined by the staff that our process of cheque verification for customers must be simplified.

b. A request that we are making to managers is that they not spend all their time in their departments and instead visit other departments one hour a month.

c. It is the personal opinion of this writer that when deadlines have the characteristics of negotiation, they are no longer effective.

d. Our organization is honoured to have the pleasure of extending a welcome to you as a new customer.

e. Please be advised that it is our intention to make every effort to deliver your order by the date of your request, April 1.

f. Enclosed herewith are the report and brochures to which you refer in your esteemed letter of the 12th.

g. It has been established that the incontestable key to the future success of this organization is a deep and firm commitment to quality.

h. It is our suggestion that you do not attempt to move forward until you seek and obtain approval of the plan from the department head prior to beginning the project.

i. Experience has indicated that employees who have had the opportunity to attend training sessions benefit most greatly when those sessions are not overly long.

j. If doubt is entertained regarding an optimal solution to the problem of acquiring new equipment, may I suggest that we refer the problem to a committee.

5.6 Conciseness (Goal 1)

Suggest shorter forms for the following expressions.

a. for the purpose of

b. in reference to

c. in regard to

d. without further delay

e. on a yearly basis

f. in the event that

g. a report for which you have no use

h. an accountant who took great care

i. arranged according to the alphabet

j. a program that is designed to save money

5.7 Conciseness (Goal 1)

Revise and shorten the following sentences.

a. There are four reasons that explain the sudden sales spurt for our product.

b. As per your suggestion, we will not attempt to make alterations or changes in the blueprints at this point in time.

c. It is perfectly clear that meetings held on a weekly basis are most effective.

d. Despite the fact that the bill seemed erroneous, we sent a cheque in the amount of $150.

e. We have received your letter, and we are pleased to send the pamphlets you request.

f. All accounts that are overdue must be sent a last and final notice before January 1.

g. There are numerous benefits that can result from a good program that focuses on customer service.

h. Because of the degree of active employee participation, we are of the opinion that the stock bonus plan will be successful.

i. At this point in time in the program, I wish to extend my grateful thanks to all the support staff who helped make this occasion possible.

j. There is a short questionnaire enclosed that is designed to help us take action on the proposed environment plan.

k. In accordance with your wishes, we are sending you under separate cover two contract forms.

l. Although the sales returns for July are high in number, experience has indicated that this is not an unusual condition for summer.

m. This is to inform you that quality should be our first and foremost goal.

n. It is important to give consideration to the fact that people do change.

o. For each and every single customer who complains, there are 10 to 15 other ones out there who are not bothering to speak up about their dissatisfaction or unhappiness.

p. Our consultants can assist you in answering questions which you have about carpet care.

q. It is our expectation that we will see increases in sales when the reps learn the new system.

r. Those who function as suppliers may not have a full understanding of the problem.

s. Except in the instance of Fat-Burger, most fast-food chains are aware of the fact that many consumers want choices on the menu that are healthful.

t. Two weeks in advance of its planned date of release, the announcement regarding our relocation was leaked to the press.

u. This is just to let you know that applications will be accepted at a later date for employees who are at the entry level.

v. Did he give you any indication as to whether he was coming?

w. There are many words that can be eliminated through revision that is carefully done.

5.8 Vigour (Goal 2)

Revise the following sentences to reduce the number of abstract nouns, trite expressions, and other wordiness.

a. We must make the assumption that you wish to be transferred.

b. Please give consideration to our latest proposal, despite the fact that it comes into conflict with the original plan.

c. The committee reached the conclusion that a great majority of students had a preference for mail-in registration.

d. Please conduct an investigation of employee turnover in that department for the period of June through August.

e. After we engage in the preparation of a report, our recommendations will be presented in their final form before the Executive Committee.

f. There are three members of our staff who are making every effort to locate your lost order.

g. Whether or not we make a continuation of the sales campaign is dependent upon its success in the city of Toronto.

h. If you need further assistance, please do not hesitate to call me at 889–1901.

i. Please forward any bills in connection with the construction, in accordance with our agreement, to the address of my lawyer.

j. We are in receipt of your cheque in the dollar amount of $200.

5.9 Parallelism (Goal 2)

Revise the following sentences to improve parallelism. If elements cannot be balanced fluently, use appropriate subordination.

a. Critics argue that Canadian business is too concerned with machinery, capital, and operations that result in profitability.

b. Ensuring equal opportunities, the removal of barriers, and elimination of age discrimination are our goals.

c. Mr. Nadeau reads all incoming mail, and its distribution is made by him to all appropriate responders.

d. Last year Ms. Thompson wrote letters and was giving speeches to promote investment in her business.

e. Because of its air-conditioning and since it is light and attractive, I prefer this office.

f. For this position we assess oral and written communication skills, how well individuals solve problems, whether they can lead others, and we're also interested in interpersonal skills, such as cultural awareness and sensitivity.

5.10 Highlighting (Goal 3)

Revise the following statements using highlighting techniques. Improve parallel construction and reduce wordiness if necessary.

a. Use a vertical list with numbers.

The Small Business Administration provides a variety of ways in which it aids small businesses. These services include loans (both private and government), helping out with the procurement of government contracts, and the provision of management training and consulting.

b. Use letters within the sentence.

The major benefits our organization offers include annual leave and sick leave, insurance for group life and medical expenses, and a private retirement fund.

c. Use a vertical list with bullets.

Our lawyer made a recommendation that we take several steps to avoid litigation in regard to sexual harassment. The first step we should take involves establishing an unequivocal written statement prohibiting sexual harassment within our organization. The second thing we should do is make sure training sessions are held for supervisors regarding a proper work environment. Finally, some kind of procedure for employees to lodge complaints is necessary. This procedure should include investigation of complaints.

5.11 Proofreading (Goals 4–5)

Use proofreading marks to correct the spelling, grammar, punctuation, capitalization, and other errors in the following sentences.

a. To be elligible for this job, you must: (1) Be a Canadian citizen, (2) Be able to pass a through back ground investigation, and (3) Be available for world wide assignment.

b. Some businesses view "quality" as a focus of the organization rather then a atribute of there goods or services.

c. Its easy to get caught up in internal problems, and to overlook customers needs.

d. Incidently we expect both the ceo and the president to make speechs.

e. This is to inform you that wordiness destroys clarity therefore learn to cut the fat from your writing.

f. A clothing outlet opened at lakeland plaza in June, however business is slow.

CLUE REVIEW 5

Edit the following sentences to correct faults in grammar, punctuation, spelling, and usage.

1. Business documents must be written clear to insure that readers comprehend the message quick.

2. We expect Mayor Wilson to visit the premier in an attempt to increase the cities share of Provincial funding.

3. The caller could have been him but we don't know for sure. Since he didn't leave his name.

4. The survey was sited in an article entitled "Whats new in softwear, however I can't locate it now.

5. All three of our companys auditors—Jim Lucus, Doreen Stein, and Brad Kirby—critisized there accounting procedures.

6. Anyone of the auditors are authorized to procede with an independant action, however, only a member of the management counsel can alter policy.

7. Because our printer has been broke everyday this week; were looking at new models.

8. Have you all ready ordered the following? a dictionary a reference manual and a style book.

9. In the morning Mrs Williams ordinarilly opens the office, in the evening Mr Williams usualy closes it.

10. When you travel in england and ireland I advice you to charge purchases to your visa credit card.

Letters and Memos

Direct Letters

L E A R N I N G   G O A L S

After studying this chapter, you should be able to

1 List three characteristics of good letters, and describe the direct pattern for organizing letters.

2 Write letters requesting information and action.

3 Compose letters placing orders.

4 Prepare letters making claims.

5 Write letters complying with requests.

6 Compose letters acknowledging customer orders.

7 Prepare letters granting claims and making adjustments.

8 Modify international letters to accommodate other cultures.

Tilley Endurables

Writing good letters is an art. Tilley Endurables has shown that a few well-crafted paragraphs can also form the cornerstone of a $20-million-a-year business.

The Toronto maker of "travel/adventure clothing" has made letters from satisfied customers an advertising vehicle all its own. "There is no more powerful advertising message than testimonials," says David Kappele, marketing director for Tilley Endurables. The company's unique ads—complete with photo of the customer-cum-copywriter—which run nationally in *The Globe and Mail* have helped transform the company from a tiny basement mail-order business into a multimillion-dollar-a-year retailer with five Canadian stores and a sales and distribution network spanning seven countries.

Much of this growth comes as the result of hard work and foresight on the part of the founder and president, Alex Tilley. An avid sailor, Tilley started his business in 1980 when he designed a safari-style hat that was both fashionable and functional (it blocked the sun but did not fly off while he tacked across Lake Ontario). Reviews of the hat were good, and Tilley asked that satisfied customers take a moment to commit their comments to paper. The testimonials quickly became a marketing tool extraordinaire for Tilley, who added other practical garments to his clothes line and incorporated the company in 1984.

The feedback was appreciated and valuable, but communication is a two-way street. Enter Lise Andrews. The fiftysomething graduate of Toronto's Eastern High School of Commerce returned to the workforce after a 25-year hiatus to become assistant to the president at Tilley Endurables. She landed the job after answering a newspaper ad that called for an organized person with flair—but not before her first interview for the job (by phone) had ended with a tough lesson in communications. "The president said, 'Well, you haven't told me anything very interesting. Call me back if you can think of anything.' That was like throwing down a challenge," says Lise, who promptly called back and detailed the years she'd spent abroad and the resulting knowledge she could bring to the company's head office. Her message came through loud and clear, and she landed the part-time job.

As the company has grown, so have her duties and her hours on the payroll. Now a full-time employee (she suggests that a lot of people entering today's workforce will begin as part-timers), Lise spends the bulk of her day replying to the 100 or so customers that write to Tilley Endurables each week. These people usually tell tales that reinforce the company's claim of producing long-lasting, easy-wear clothing, including shorts, hats and

> *"My goal is to treat the customers with fairness, to please them, and to give them confidence in our company."*

trousers. But occasionally a letter bears bad tidings, and then the one-woman front line has to mollify the customer.

Tackling such a hefty mailbag also demands good organization, says Lise, who ranks the letters, then gives her immediate attention to the ones that contain an article of clothing being returned. But whether it's a question of durability or a query about a new line of clothing, all letters must be answered—quickly. "If I write a letter to someone, I expect a reply pretty soon," she says.

More than just a good filing system is needed. Composing a good letter demands patience ("The public will try your patience beyond belief sometimes") and a willingness to spend the time gathering the information needed to reply to a customer's question or comment. Says Lise: "If I don't know the answer to a question, I track it down, and then let the customer know right away."

When it comes to composing each return letter (the majority of which are hand-written), she tackles the salient points in way that is "not too wordy" and often light-hearted. "It's absolutely mandatory to have a sense of humour when dealing with the public in any way," insists Lise, who describes her style as both off-the-cuff and short and sweet. Catchy phrases aside, structure and grammar are the keystones of any written composition. However, owing to the volume of mail Tilley Endurables receives, proofreading each response would take far too much time; operating as a one-woman show, Lise doesn't have anyone looking over her shoulder. It makes sense, she says, because "if someone had to proofread everything I did I wouldn't be worth my salt."

Letter writing does, however, demand great attention to detail and a clear understanding of one's audience, which is why Lise encourages aspiring communications professionals to get a solid grounding in grammar, composition, and "anything to do with English usage." This will help them to draft tight, well-organized letters that have a clear beginning, middle, and end. This ability to use pen and paper to communicate effectively with customers allows the writer to project the best possible image of the company he or she represents. "It's always important to put your best foot forward," says Lise, who sees this objective as paramount. "My goal is to treat the customers with fairness, to please them, and to give them confidence in our company."

In the process of answering customers' inquiries, Lise proves that although the art of letter writing has been pronounced dead many times during the Information Age, it is alive and well wherever people give correspondence the close attention it deserves.[1] ■

Letters to customers and customer testimonials are key channels of communication at Tilley Endurables. By focusing on direct and clear communication about their quality products and services, Tilley Endurables gets their message across to existing and potential customers.

Strategies for Direct Letters

Letters are a primary channel of communication for delivering messages *outside* an organization. In this book we'll divide letters into four groups: (a) direct letters communicating straightforward requests and replies (Chapter 6), (b) negative letters delivering refusals and bad news (Chapter 8), (c) persuasive letters containing sales and other messages (Chapter 9), and (d) special letters conveying goodwill and special messages (Chapter 10).

This chapter concentrates on direct, straightforward letters through which we conduct everyday business with outsiders. Such letters go to suppliers, government agencies, other businesses, and, most important, to customers. At Tilley Endurables and most other organizations, letters to customers receive a high priority because these messages encourage product feedback, project a favourable image of the company, and promote future business.

Publisher Malcolm Forbes understood the power of business letters when he said, "A good business letter can get you a job interview, get you off the hook, or get you money. It's totally asinine to blow your chances of getting *whatever* you want—with a business letter that turns people off instead of turning them on."[2] This chapter teaches you what turns readers on. You'll study the characteristics of good letters, techniques for organizing direct requests and responses, and ways to apply the 3 × 3 writing process. You'll also learn how to write six specific kinds of direct letters.

Characteristics of Good Letters

Although direct letters deliver straightforward facts, they don't have to sound and look dull or mechanical. At least three characteristics distinguish good business letters: clear content, a tone of goodwill, and correct form.

Clear content. A clearly written letter separates ideas into paragraphs, uses short sentences and paragraphs, and guides the reader through the ideas with transitional expressions. Moreover, a clear letter uses familiar words and active-voice verbs. In other words, it incorporates all the writing techniques you studied in Chapters 3, 4, and 5.

One business observer estimated that "more than one-third of business letters do nothing more than seek clarification of earlier correspondence."[3] A clear letter answers all the reader's questions or comments so that no further correspondence is necessary. Most effective business writers double-check all letters before sending them out to be certain that every point mentioned by the writer has been covered.

A tone of goodwill. Good letters, however, have to do more than deliver clear messages; they also must build goodwill. Goodwill is a positive feeling the reader has toward an individual or an organization. By analyzing your audience and adapting your message to the reader, you can ensure that your letters establish an overall tone of goodwill.

To achieve goodwill, look for ways to present the message from the reader's perspective. In other words, emphasize the "you" point of view and point out benefits to the reader. In addition, be sensitive to words that might suggest gender, ethnic, age, or disability bias. Finally, frame your ideas positively because they will sound more pleasing and will give more information than negative constructions. And, of course, always be courteous.

FIGURE 6.1 ■ Business Letter Formatting

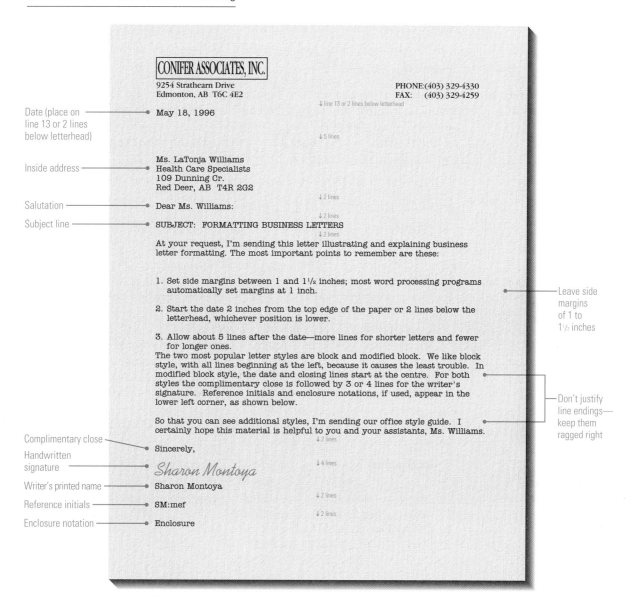

Date (place on line 13 or 2 lines below letterhead)

Inside address

Salutation

Subject line

Complimentary close

Handwritten signature

Writer's printed name

Reference initials

Enclosure notation

Leave side margins of 1 to 1½ inches

Don't justify line endings— keep them ragged right

CONIFER ASSOCIATES, INC.
9254 Strathearn Drive
Edmonton, AB T6C 4E2

PHONE:(403) 329-4330
FAX: (403) 329-4259

↓ line 13 or 2 lines below letterhead

May 18, 1996

↓ 5 lines

Ms. LaTonja Williams
Health Care Specialists
109 Dunning Cr.
Red Deer, AB T4R 2G2

↓ 2 lines

Dear Ms. Williams:

↓ 2 lines

SUBJECT: FORMATTING BUSINESS LETTERS

↓ 2 lines

At your request, I'm sending this letter illustrating and explaining business letter formatting. The most important points to remember are these:

1. Set side margins between 1 and 1½ inches; most word processing programs automatically set margins at 1 inch.

2. Start the date 2 inches from the top edge of the paper or 2 lines below the letterhead, whichever position is lower.

3. Allow about 5 lines after the date—more lines for shorter letters and fewer for longer ones.

The two most popular letter styles are block and modified block. We like block style, with all lines beginning at the left, because it causes the least trouble. In modified block style, the date and closing lines start at the centre. For both styles the complimentary close is followed by 3 or 4 lines for the writer's signature. Reference initials and enclosure notations, if used, appear in the lower left corner, as shown below.

So that you can see additional styles, I'm sending our office style guide. I certainly hope this material is helpful to you and your assistants, Ms. Williams.

↓ 2 lines

Sincerely,

↓ 4 lines

Sharon Montoya

Sharon Montoya

↓ 2 lines

SM:mef

↓ 2 lines

Enclosure

Correct form. A business letter conveys silent messages beyond that of its printed words. The letter's appearance and format reflect the writer's carefulness and experience. A short letter bunched at the top of a sheet of paper, for example, looks as if it was prepared in a hurry or by an amateur.

For your letters to make a good impression, you need to select an appropriate format. The block style shown in Figure 6.1 is a popular format. Other letter formats are illustrated later in this chapter and shown in Appendix B. In the block style the parts of your letter—date, inside address, body, and so on—are set flush left on the page. Also, the letter is centred on the page and framed by white space. Most letters will have margins of 1 to 1½ inches.

Finally, be sure to use ragged-right margins; that is, don't allow your word processor to justify the right margin and make all lines end evenly. Unjustified

Appropriate letter formats send silent but positive messages.

margins improve readability, say experts, by providing visual stops and by making it easier to tell where the next line begins. Study Figure 6.1 for more tips on making your letters look professional.

Using the Direct Pattern for Letters

Most business messages are direct requests or direct responses.

The everyday transactions of a business consist mainly of direct requests and responses. Because you expect the reader's response to be positive or neutral, you won't need special techniques to be convincing, to soften bad news, or to be tactful. Thus, in composing direct letters, you can organize your message, as shown in Figure 6.2, into three parts:

- **Opening:** a statement that announces the purpose immediately

- **Body:** details that explain the purpose

- **Closing:** a request for action or a courteous conclusion

Everyday business messages "front-load" by presenting the main idea or purpose immediately.

Front-loading in the opening. You should begin everyday messages in a straightforward manner by "front-loading" the main idea. State immediately why you are writing so that the reader can anticipate and comprehend what follows. Remember, every time a reader begins a message, he or she is thinking, "Why was this sent to me, and what am I to do?"

Some writers make the mistake of organizing a message in the same sequence in which they thought through the problem: they review the background, discuss the reasons for action, and then request an action. Most business letters, though, are better written "backwards." Don't get bogged down in introductory material, justifications, or old-fashioned "business" language; instead, reveal your purpose immediately. Compare these indirect and direct openers:

Indirect Opening

Our company is experiencing difficulty in retaining employees. We also need help in screening job applicants. Our current testing program is unsatisfactory. I understand that you offer employee testing materials, and I have a number of questions to ask.

Direct Opening

Please answer the following questions about your personnel-testing materials.

Most simple requests can open immediately with a statement of purpose. Occasionally, however, complex requests may require a sentence or two of explanation or background before the purpose is revealed. What you want to avoid, though, is delaying the purpose of the letter beyond the first paragraph.

The body explains the purpose for writing, perhaps using graphic devices to highlight important ideas.

Explaining in the body. After a direct opening that tells the reader why you are writing, present details that explain your request or response. This is where your planning pays off, allowing you to structure the information for maximum clarity and readability. Here you should consider using some graphic devices to highlight the details: a numbered or bulleted list, headings, columns, or boldface or italic type.

If you have considerable information, you'll want to develop each idea in a separate paragraph with transitions to connect them. The important thing to remember is to keep similar ideas together. The biggest problem in business writing is poor organization, and the body of a letter is where that failure becomes apparent.

FIGURE 6.2 ■ Three-Part Direct Pattern for Requests and Responses

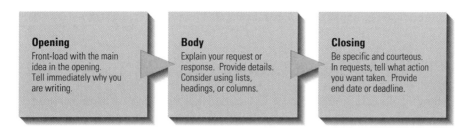

Opening
Front-load with the main idea in the opening. Tell immediately why you are writing.

Body
Explain your request or response. Provide details. Consider using lists, headings, or columns.

Closing
Be specific and courteous. In requests, tell what action you want taken. Provide end date or deadline.

Being specific and courteous in the closing. In the last paragraph of direct letters, readers look for action information: schedules, deadlines, activities to be completed. Thus, at this point, you should specify what you want the reader to do. If appropriate, include an end date—a date for completion of the action. If possible, give reasons for establishing the deadline. Research shows that people want to know why they should do something—even if the reasons seem obvious. Moreover, people want to be treated courteously (*Please answer these questions before April 1, when we must make a final decision*), not bossed around (*Send this information immediately*).

The closing courteously specifies what the receiver is to do.

Applying the 3 × 3 Writing Process to Direct Letters

Although direct letters may be short and straightforward, they benefit from attention to composition. "If you force yourself to think through what you want to say and to whom you want to say it," observes a communication consultant in *Business Week*, "the writing task becomes infinitely easier."[4] Here's a quick review of the 3 × 3 writing process to help you think through its application to direct letters.

Before writing direct letters, make yourself analyze your purpose and anticipate the response.

Analysis, anticipation, and adaptation. Before writing, spend a few moments analyzing your task and audience. Your goals here are (1) determining your purpose, (2) anticipating the reaction of your audience, and (3) visualizing the audience. Too often, letter writers aren't sure of their purpose when they start writing. According to British author Matthew Arnold, you must "have something to say and say it as clearly as you can."[5]

Research, organization, and composition. Collect information and make a list of the points you wish to cover. For short messages, such as an answer to a customer's inquiry, jot down notes on the document you are answering. For longer documents that require formal research, use a cluster diagram or the outlining techniques discussed in Chapter 4. When business letters carry information that won't upset the receiver, you can organize them in the direct manner described earlier. And be sure to plan for revision—a writer can seldom turn out an excellent message on the first attempt. For easier revision, keyboard your message on a computer.

Revision, proofreading, and evaluation. When you finish the first draft, revise for clarity. The receiver should not have to read the message twice to grasp its meaning. Proofread for correctness. Check for mistakes and inconsistencies in punctuation, typos, misspelled words, or other mechanical problems.

Always take time to run your spelling checker if you have one. Finally, evaluate your product. Before any letter leaves your desk, reread it and put yourself in the shoes of the reader: "How would I feel if I were receiving it?"

Direct Request Letters

Many of your business request letters will fall into one of three categories: (1) asking for information or action, (2) placing orders for products, or (3) making a claim requiring an adjustment when something has gone wrong. In this section you'll learn how to write good letters for each of these circumstances. Before you write any letter, though, consider its costs in terms of your time (and workload). Whenever possible, don't write! Instead of asking for information, could you find it yourself? Would a telephone call or a brief visit to a co-worker solve the problem quickly? If not, use the direct pattern to present your request efficiently.

Requesting Information and Action

A direct letter may open with a question or a polite request.

The majority of your business letters will request information or action. Suppose you have questions about a payroll-accounting service your company is considering, or you need to ask a customer to supply missing data from an order. For these direct messages put the main idea first. If your request involves several questions, you could open with a polite request, such as *Will you please answer the following questions about your payroll service.* Note that although this request sounds like a question, it's actually a disguised command. Since you expect an action rather than a reply, punctuate this polite command with a period instead of a question mark.

In the letter body explain your purpose and provide details. If you have questions, express them in parallel form. To elicit the most information, pose open-ended questions (*What computer lock-down device can you recommend?*) instead of yes-or-no questions (*Do you carry computer lock-down devices?*). If you are asking someone to do something, be sure your tone is polite and undemanding. Remember that your written words cannot be softened by a smile. When possible, focus on benefits to the reader (*To ensure that you receive the exact sweater you want, send us your choice of colour*).

In the closing tell the reader courteously what is to be done. If a date is important, set an end date and explain why. Many request letters end simply with *Thank you*, forcing the reader to review the contents to determine what is expected and when. You can save the reader time by spelling out the action to be taken. Avoid other overused endings such as *Thank you for your cooperation* (trite), *Thank you in advance for ...* (presumptuous), and *If you have any questions, do not hesitate to call me* (suggests that you didn't make yourself clear).

Direct request letters maintain a courteous tone, spell out what needs to be done, and focus on reader benefits.

It's always appropriate to show appreciation, but try to do so in a fresh and efficient manner. For example, you could hook your thanks to the end date (*Thanks for returning the questionnaire before May 5, when we will begin tabulation*). You might connect your appreciation to a statement developing reader benefits (*We are grateful for the information you will provide because it will help us serve you better*). Or you could describe briefly how the information will help you (*I genuinely appreciate this information that will enable me to ... *). When possible, make it easy for the reader to comply with your request (*Note your answers on this sheet and return it in the postage-paid envelope*). Customers appreciate a toll-free number so that they can respond without having to write a letter.

Let's now analyze the first draft of a direct request letter written by office manager Melanie Marshall. She wants information about computer security devices, but the first version of her letter is confusing and inefficient. Melanie makes a common mistake: writing a message "backwards." Notice that her letter starts with the problem, telling the story from the writer's perspective, not the reader's.

Dear Ms. Ivorson:

Our insurance rates will be increased soon if we don't instal security devices on our computer equipment. We have considered some local suppliers, but none had exactly what we wanted.

Starts with background information and explanation instead of request.

We need a device that can be used to secure separate computer components at a workstation including a computer, keyboard, and monitor. We currently own 18 computers, keyboards, and monitors, along with six printers.

Fails to organize information into logical order.

We wonder if professionals are needed to instal your security devices. We're also interested in whether the devices can be easily removed when we need to move equipment around. We are, of course, very interested in prices and quantity discounts, if you offer them.

Confuses reader by jumping around among many topics. Fails to ask specific questions.

Thank you for your attention to this matter.

Ends with a cliché. Fails to reveal what to do and when to do it.

Melanie's second version, shown in Figure 6.3, begins more directly. The opening sentence introduces the purpose immediately so that the reader quickly knows why the letter was sent. Melanie then provides background information. Most important, she organizes all her requests into specific questions, which are sure to bring a better result than her previous diffuse request. Study the 3 × 3 writing process in Figure 6.3 to see the plan Melanie followed in improving her letter.

Placing Orders

You may occasionally need to write a letter that orders supplies, merchandise, or services. Generally, such purchases are made by telephoning an order desk or by filling out a catalogue form and faxing or mailing it to the vendor. Sometimes, however, you may not have a telephone number or an order form but only an address. To order items by letter, supply the same information that an order blank would require. In the opening let the reader know immediately that this is a purchase authorization and not merely an information inquiry. Instead of *I saw a number of interesting items in your catalogue*, begin directly with order language such as *Please send me by Purolator the following items from your fall merchandise catalogue*.

Letters placing orders specify items or services, quantities, dates, prices, and payment method.

If you're ordering many items, list them vertically in the body of your letter. Include as much specific data as possible: quantity, order number, complete description, unit price, and total price. Show the total amount, and figure the tax and shipping costs if possible. The more information you provide, the less likely that a mistake will be made.

In the closing tell how you plan to pay for the merchandise. Enclose a cheque, provide a credit card number, or ask to be billed. Many business organizations have credit agreements with their regular suppliers that enable them to send goods without prior payment. In addition to payment information, tell when the merchandise should be sent and express your appreciation. The letter on page 157 requesting personnel cards and envelopes for a human resources department illustrates the order letter pattern.

FIGURE 6.3 ■ Direct Request Letter

The Three Phases of the Writing Process

1

Analyze
The purpose of this letter is to gain specific data about devices to lock down computer equipment.

Anticipate
The audience is expected to be a busy but receptive customer service representative.

Adapt
Because the reader will probably react positively to this inquiry, the direct pattern is best.

2

Research
Determine how much equipment must be locked down and what questions must be answered.

Organize
Open by asking the reader to answer questions about security devices. In the body provide details and arrange any questions logically. Close by courteously providing a specific deadline.

Compose
Draft the first copy on a computer.

3

Revise
Improve the clarity by grouping similar ideas together. Improve readability by listing and numbering questions. Eliminate wordiness.

Proofread
Look for typos and spelling errors. Check punctuation and placement. Indent the second line of all listed items for a clean look.

Evaluate
Is this message attractive and easily comprehended?

---

inner **Circle** graphics

32 Hershey Road, Dartmouth, NS B2Y 2H5

(902) 488·3310 phone (902) 488·3319 fax

February 3, 1996

Ms. Sue Ivorson, Customer Service
Micro Supplies and Software
P.O. Box 862
Montreal, QC G5B 2G6

Dear Ms. Ivorson:

Please provide information and recommendations regarding security equipment to prevent the theft of office computers, keyboards, monitors, and printers. — Introduces purpose immediately

Our office now has 18 computer work stations and 6 printers that we must secure to desks or counters. Answers to the following questions will help us select the best devices for our purpose. — Explains need for information

1. What device would you recommend that can secure a work station consisting of a computer, monitor, and keyboard?

2. What expertise and equipment are required to instal and remove the security device?

3. How much is each device? Do you offer quantity discounts, and if so, how much?

— Groups open-ended questions into list for quick comprehension and best feedback

Because our insurance rates will be increased if this equipment is not secured before April 1, we would appreciate your response by February 15. — Courteously provides end date and reason

Sincerely,

Melanie Marshall

Melanie Marshall
Office Manager

Ladies and Gentlemen:

Please send by Priority Post the following items from your summer catalogue.

250	No. OG–18 Payroll greeting cards	$102.50
250	No. OG–22 Payroll card envelopes	21.95
100	No. OM–01 Performance greeting cards	80.00
	Subtotal	$204.45
	GST at 7%	14.31
	PST at 8%	16.36
	Shipping	24.00
	Total	$259.12

We would appreciate receiving these cards immediately since we are beginning an employee recognition program February 12. Enclosed is our cheque for $259.12. If additional changes are necessary, please bill my company.

Order letter opens directly with authorization for purchase, method of delivery, and catalogue number.

Uses orderly columns to make quantity, catalogue number, description, and price stand out.

Calculates totals to prevent possible mistakes.

Expresses appreciation and tells when items are expected. Identifies method of payment.

Making Claims

In business many things can go wrong—promised shipments are late, warranted goods fail, or service is disappointing. When you as a customer must write to identify or correct a wrong, the letter is called a "claim." Simple claims are those to which you expect the receiver to agree readily.

Most businesses today honestly want to satisfy their customers. The 1990s have been called the decade of quality—in both products and service. To compete globally and to pump up local markets, North American industry is particularly sold on the idea of improving service.[6] Like Tilley Endurables, many organizations are increasingly aware of the importance of listening to consumers. Since it costs three times as much to win a new customer as it does to retain a current one, businesses especially want to hear what their customers have to say. And they know that customers are perceptive. As one computer executive says, "Quite frankly, customers are actually wrong only about 2 percent of the time."[7]

Because you can expect a positive response when you have a legitimate claim or complaint, you should open a claim letter with a clear statement of the problem or with the action you want the receiver to take. You might expect a replacement, a refund, a new order, credit to your account, correction of a billing error, free repairs, free inspection, or cancellation of an order. When the remedy is obvious, state it immediately (*Please send us 24 Royal hot-air popcorn poppers to replace the 24 hot-oil poppers sent in error with our order shipped January 4*). When the remedy is less obvious, you might ask for a change in policy or procedure or simply for an explanation (*Because three of our employees with confirmed reservations were refused rooms September 16 in your hotel, would you please clarify your policy regarding reservations and late arrivals*).

In the body of a claim letter, explain the problem and justify your request. Provide the necessary details so that the difficulty can be corrected without further correspondence. Avoid becoming angry or trying to fix blame. Bear in mind that the person reading your letter is seldom responsible for the problem. Instead, state the facts logically, objectively, and unemotionally; let the reader decide on the causes. Include copies of all pertinent documents such as invoices,

Claims letters open with a clear statement of the problem, support the claim with specifics, and close with a statement of goodwill.

Providing details without getting angry improves the effectiveness of a claim letter.

sales slips, catalogue descriptions, and repair records. When service is involved, give names of individuals spoken to and dates of calls. Assume that a company honestly wants to please its customers—because most do. When an alternative remedy exists, spell it out (*If you are unable to send 24 Royal hot-air popcorn poppers immediately, please credit our account now and notify us when they become available*).

Conclude a claim letter with a courteous statement that promotes goodwill and expresses a desire for continued relations. If appropriate, include an end date (*We realize that mistakes in ordering and shipping sometimes occur. Because we've enjoyed your prompt service in the past, we hope that you will be able to send us the hot-air poppers by January 15*).

Written claims submitted promptly are taken more seriously than delayed ones.

Finally, in making claims, act promptly. Delaying claims makes them appear less important. Delayed claims are also more difficult to verify. By taking the time to put your claim in writing, you indicate your seriousness. A written claim starts a record of the problem should later action be necessary, so keep a copy of your letter.

Figure 6.4 shows a first draft of a hostile claim that vents the writer's anger but accomplishes little else. Its tone is belligerent, and it assumes that the company mischarged the customer intentionally. Furthermore, it fails to tell the reader how to remedy the problem. The revision tempers the tone, describes the problem objectively, provides facts and figures, and, most important, specifies exactly what the customer wants done.

To sum up, use the direct pattern with the main idea first when you expect little resistance to letters making requests. The following checklist reviews the direct strategy for orders, and adjustments, and requests for information or action.

■ Checklist for Writing Direct Requests

Information or Action Request Letters

✓ **Open by stating the main idea.** To elicit information, ask a question or issue a polite command (*Will you please answer the following questions ...*).

✓ **Explain and justify the request.** In seeking information use open-ended questions structured in parallel form.

✓ **Request action in the closing.** Express appreciation, and set an end date if appropriate. Avoid clichés (*Thank you for your cooperation*).

Order Letters

✓ **Open by authorizing the purchase.** Use order language (*Please send me ...*), designate the delivery method, and state your information source (such as a catalogue, advertisement, or magazine article).

✓ **List items in the body.** Include quantity, order number, description, unit price, extension, GST, provincial sales tax if applicable, shipping, and total costs.

✓ **Close with the payment data.** Tell how you are paying and when you expect delivery. Express appreciation.

FIGURE 6.4 ■ Direct Claim Letter

First Draft

Dear Good Vibes:

You call yourselves Good Vibes, but all I'm getting from your service is bad vibes! I'm furious that you have your salespeople slip in unwanted service warranties to boost your sales. — Sounds angry

When I bought my Panatronic VCR from Good Vibes, Inc., in August, I specifically told the salesperson that I did NOT want a three-year service warranty. But there it is on my VISA statement this month! You people have obviously billed me for a service I did not authorize. I refuse to pay this charge. — Jumps to conclusions / Forgets that mistakes happen

How can you hope to stay in business with such fraudulent practices? I was expecting to return this month and look at CD players, but you can be sure I'll find an honest dealer this time. — Fails to suggest solution

Sincerely,

Revision

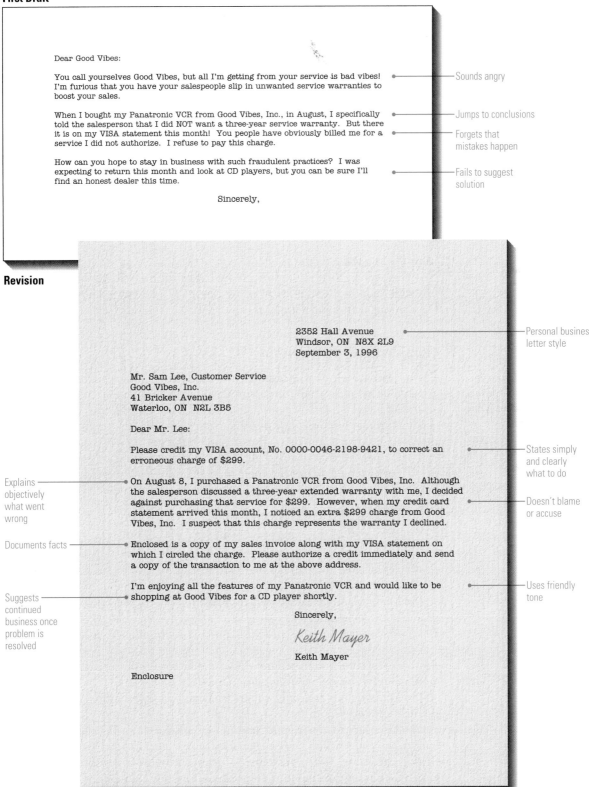

2352 Hall Avenue
Windsor, ON N8X 2L9
September 3, 1996
— Personal business letter style

Mr. Sam Lee, Customer Service
Good Vibes, Inc.
41 Bricker Avenue
Waterloo, ON N2L 3B5

Dear Mr. Lee:

Please credit my VISA account, No. 0000-0046-2198-9421, to correct an erroneous charge of $299. — States simply and clearly what to do

Explains objectively what went wrong — On August 8, I purchased a Panatronic VCR from Good Vibes, Inc. Although the salesperson discussed a three-year extended warranty with me, I decided against purchasing that service for $299. However, when my credit card statement arrived this month, I noticed an extra $299 charge from Good Vibes, Inc. I suspect that this charge represents the warranty I declined. — Doesn't blame or accuse

Documents facts — Enclosed is a copy of my sales invoice along with my VISA statement on which I circled the charge. Please authorize a credit immediately and send a copy of the transaction to me at the above address.

Suggests continued business once problem is resolved — I'm enjoying all the features of my Panatronic VCR and would like to be shopping at Good Vibes for a CD player shortly. — Uses friendly tone

Sincerely,

Keith Mayer

Keith Mayer

Enclosure

Claim Letters

✓ **Begin with the purpose.** Present a clear statement of the problem or the action requested—such as a refund, replacement, credit, explanation, or correction of error.

✓ **Explain objectively.** In the body tell the specifics of the claim. Provide copies of necessary documents.

✓ **End by requesting action.** Include an end date if important. Add a pleasant, forward-looking statement. Keep a copy of the letter.

▮ Direct Reply Letters

When you can respond favourably to requests, use the direct pattern.

Occasionally, you will receive requests for information or action. In these cases your first task is deciding whether to comply. If the decision is favourable, your letter should let the reader know immediately by using the direct pattern and front-loading the good news.

This section focuses on direct reply letters in three situations: (1) complying with requests for information or action, (2) acknowledging orders, and (3) granting claims and adjustments.

Complying with Requests

Letters responding to requests may open with a subject line to identify the topic immediately.

Often, your messages will respond favourably to requests for information or action. A customer wants information about a product. A supplier asks to arrange a meeting. Another business inquires about one of your procedures or about a former employee. In complying with such requests, you'll want to apply the same direct pattern you used in making requests.

The opening of a direct reply letter might contain a subject line, which helps the reader recognize the topic immediately. Usually appearing two lines below the salutation, the subject line refers in abbreviated form to previous correspondence and/or summarizes a message (*Subject: Your Letter of August 5 about Award Programs*). It often omits articles (*a, an, the*), is not a complete sentence, and does not end with a period. Knowledgeable business communicators use a subject line to refer to earlier correspondence so that in the first sentence, the most emphatic spot in a letter, they are free to emphasize the main idea.

In the first sentence deliver the information the reader wants. Avoid wordy, drawn-out openings such as *I have before me your letter of August 5, in which you request information about ...* More forceful and more efficient is an opener that answers the inquiry (*Here is the information you wanted about ...*). When agreeing to a request for action, announce the good news promptly (*Yes, I will be happy to speak to your business communication class on the topic of ...*).

In the body of your reply, supply explanations and additional information. Because a letter written on company stationery is considered a legally binding contract, be sure to check your facts and figures carefully. If a policy or procedure needs authorization, seek approval from a supervisor or executive before writing the letter. When answering a group of questions or providing many facts and figures, arrange the information logically and make it readable by using lists, tables, headings, boldface, italics, or other graphic devices.

Before answering nonroutine requests, you may need to confer with co-workers and superiors to decide how to respond. Once you decide to comply with a request, announce the good news directly in the first sentence of your reply. In letters to customers you may provide extra information about products and services.

When customers or prospective customers inquire about products or services, your response should do more than merely supply answers. You'll also want to promote your organization and products. Often, companies have particular products and services they want to spotlight. Thus, when a customer writes about one product, provide helpful information that satisfies the inquiry, but consider using the opportunity to introduce another product as well. Be sure to present the promotional material with attention to the "you" view and to reader benefits (*You can use our standardized tests to free yourself from time-consuming employment screening*). You'll learn more about special techniques for developing sales and persuasive messages in Chapter 9.

Responding to customer inquiries gives you a good opportunity to promote your business.

In concluding, make sure you are cordial and personal. Refer to the information provided or to its use (*I hope this information about our experiences helps you solve your problems with disk storage*). If further action is required, describe the procedure and help the reader with specifics (*The Ministry of Consumer Affairs publishes a number of helpful booklets. Its address is ... *).

In replying to a customer's request for information, the writer in Figure 6.5 begins with a subject line that immediately identifies the topic and refers to previous correspondence. He uses the first sentence to present the most important information. Then he itemizes his list of responses to the customer's questions. If he had written these responses in paragraph form, they would have been less emphatic and more difficult to read. He goes on to describe and promote the product, being careful to show how it would benefit the customer. And he concludes by referring specifically to pages in an enclosed pamphlet and providing a number for the customer's response.

FIGURE 6.5 ■ Customer Reply Letter

The Three Phases of the Writing Process

1

Analyze
The purpose of this letter is to provide helpful information and to promote company products.

Anticipate
The reader is the intelligent owner of a small business who needs help with personnel administration.

Adapt
Because the reader requested this data, she will be receptive to the letter. Use the direct pattern.

2

Research
Gather facts to answer the business owner's questions. Consult brochures and pamphlets.

Organize
Prepare a scratch outline. Plan for a fast, direct opening. Use bulleted answers to the business owner's three questions.

Compose
Write the first draft on computer. Strive for short sentences and paragraphs.

3

Revise
Eliminate jargon and wordiness. Look for ways to explain how the product fits the reader's needs. Revise for "you" view.

Proofread
Double-check the form of numbers (July 12, page 6, 8 to 5 Pacific time).

Evaluate
Does this letter answer the customer's questions and encourage an order?

Office Headquarters, Inc.
777 Raymer Road, Kelowna, BC V1W 1H7

July 15, 1996

Ms. Jessica White
White-Rather Enterprises
220 Telford Court
Leduc, AB T9E 5M6

Dear Ms. White:

SUBJECT: YOUR JULY 12 INQUIRY ABOUT PERSONNEL RECORD-KEEPING SYSTEM
— *Identifies previous correspondence and subject*

Yes, we do offer a personnel record-keeping system specially designed for small businesses. I'm happy to answer your three questions about this system.
— *Puts most important information first*

1. Our Personnel Manager system provides standard employee application forms that meet current government regulations.

2. The system includes an interviewer's guide for structured employee interviews, as well as a scripted format for checking references by telephone.

3. Yes, you can update your employees' records easily without the need for computer programs, hardware, or training.
— *Lists answers to sender's questions in order asked*
— *Emphasizes "you" view*

Our Personnel Manager system was specially designed to provide you with expert forms for interviewing, verifying references, recording attendance, evaluating performance, and tracking the status of your employees. We even provide you with step-by-step instructions and suggested procedures. You can treat your employees as if you had a professional human resources specialist on your staff.
— *Links sales promotion to reader benefits*

On page 6 of the enclosed pamphlet you can read about our Personnel Manager system. To receive samples of these items or to ask questions about their use, just call 1-800-354-5500. Our specialists are eager to help you weekdays from 8 to 5 Pacific time.
— *Helps reader find information by citing pages*
— *Makes it easy to respond*

Sincerely,

Mark E. Austin

Mark E. Austin
Senior Marketing Representative

Enclosure

FIGURE 6.6 ■ Direct Reply from Toronto Raptors

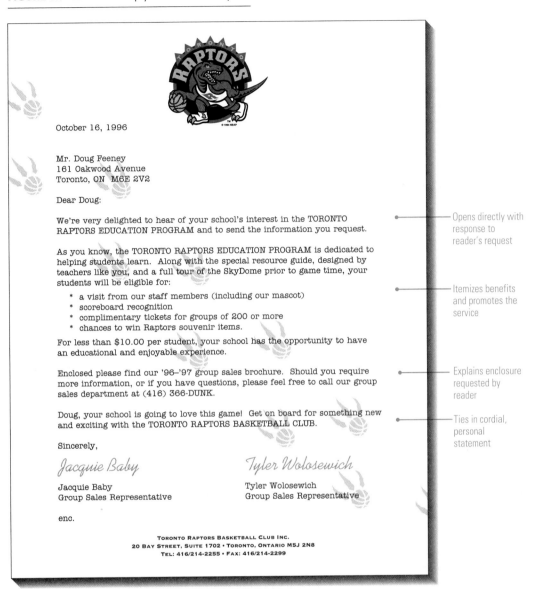

October 16, 1996

Mr. Doug Feeney
161 Oakwood Avenue
Toronto, ON M6E 2V2

Dear Doug:

We're very delighted to hear of your school's interest in the TORONTO RAPTORS EDUCATION PROGRAM and to send the information you request. — *Opens directly with response to reader's request*

As you know, the TORONTO RAPTORS EDUCATION PROGRAM is dedicated to helping students learn. Along with the special resource guide, designed by teachers like you, and a full tour of the SkyDome prior to game time, your students will be eligible for: — *Itemizes benefits and promotes the service*

* a visit from our staff members (including our mascot)
* scoreboard recognition
* complimentary tickets for groups of 200 or more
* chances to win Raptors souvenir items.

For less than $10.00 per student, your school has the opportunity to have an educational and enjoyable experience.

Enclosed please find our '96–'97 group sales brochure. Should you require more information, or if you have questions, please feel free to call our group sales department at (416) 366-DUNK. — *Explains enclosure requested by reader*

Doug, your school is going to love this game! Get on board for something new and exciting with the TORONTO RAPTORS BASKETBALL CLUB. — *Ties in cordial, personal statement*

Sincerely,

Jacquie Baby

Jacquie Baby
Group Sales Representative

Tyler Wolosewich

Tyler Wolosewich
Group Sales Representative

enc.

TORONTO RAPTORS BASKETBALL CLUB INC.
20 BAY STREET, SUITE 1702 • TORONTO, ONTARIO M5J 2N8
TEL: 416/214-2255 • FAX: 416/214-2299

A direct reply letter written by Jacquie Baby and Tyler Wolosewich, shown in Figure 6.6, responds to a request from a high-school teacher and Raptors fan. The writers announce the letter's purpose immediately and also establish rapport with the reader by highlighting the educational value of this offer. The body of the letter includes a bulleted list and an explanation of the information being provided. Notice how the writers use this opportunity to promote business by enclosing a sales brochure and an easy-to-remember phone number. The cordial, personalized closing concludes a direct reply letter that is sure to build goodwill and promote future business while delivering the information sought.

The direct pattern is also appropriate for messages that are mostly good news but may have some negative elements. For example, a return policy has time limits; an air fare may contain holiday restrictions; a speaker can come but not at the time requested; an appliance can be repaired but not replaced. When the message is mixed, emphasize the good news by presenting it first (*Yes, I would be delighted to address your marketing class on the topic of ...*). Then, explain why a problem exists (*My schedule for the week of October 10 takes me to Calgary and Edmonton, where I am ...*). Present the bad news in the middle (*Although I cannot meet with your class at that time, perhaps we can schedule a date during the week of ...*). End the message cordially by returning to the good news (*Thanks for the invitation. I'm looking forward to arranging a date in October when I can talk with your students about careers in marketing*).

Your goal is to present the negative news clearly without letting it become the focus of the message. Thus, you want to spend more time talking about the good news. And by placing the bad news in the middle of the letter, you de-emphasize it. You'll learn other techniques for presenting bad news in Chapter 8.

Acknowledging Customer Orders

Companies that are able to ship all of a customer's order usually acknowledge the order by sending a printed card. These cards confirm the items ordered and tell when the shipment will be sent. In the following instances, though, it pays to send personal letters

- When the order is large

- When the order is from a first-time or an infrequent customer

- When the order has irregularities, such as back-ordered items, delivery delays, or missing items

In these special cases you can use a letter to build goodwill, promote your products, and cement a friendly relationship.

Your order reply letter should begin with the information the customer most wants: when and how the delivery will be made. Don't waste the reader's time with an obvious statement such as *We have received your order of December 1*. Even the seemingly courteous expression *Thank you for your recent order* doesn't tell readers what they are most eager to learn. To show appreciation, you might couple your statement of thanks with information about delivery, such as *Thanks for your December 1 order, which was sent by Federal Express on December 4 and should arrive by December 6*. To emphasize the "you" view, consider this opening: *Your computer paper and printer ribbons were sent by FedEx, and you should be receiving them by December 4, two days ahead of your deadline.*

In the body of the letter, discuss details of the order, including any irregularities. If an item is unavailable, must be sent from another location, or is back-ordered, discuss this negative news as positively as possible (*Although the ribbon cartridges for your printer must be sent from our Brandon warehouse, you should receive them within two weeks*). The middle of the letter is also a suitable place for promoting new products or for presenting resale information. *Resale* is a marketing technique that reassures customers that their choices were good ones by emphasizing a product's best features, popularity, economy, and usefulness. A resale statement such as *The ribbons you have selected are the best we make* confirms the customer's discrimination and good judgment. Whereas resale information emphasizes a product that the customer has already selected, *sales promotion* focuses on additional products the customer may want. Both kinds of information are most effective when customers see how they can benefit from the products.

In the conclusion you'll want to make a personalized statement that shows reader benefits, expresses appreciation, offers further help, or conveys the expectation of continued good relations. For example: *Thanks for your order, Mr. Waters. If you have any questions about installing the ribbon cartridges or ordering other office supplies, give our experts a call at 1-800-555-3241.*

In the following case a bicycle helmet manufacturer could have acknowledged an order merely by sending a printed card or a form letter. Instead, this smart manufacturer seized the opportunity to welcome a new customer, resell the products already ordered, and promote a new line. Notice how the letter defuses the bad news that part of the order will be delayed.

Dear Ms. Brown:

In less than one week, your sporting goods store will have your order of ProTec bicycle helmets for adults. These adult helmets were shipped by UPS on October 12.

> Reveals when and how shipment will arrive.

Because the youth helmets you ordered have become very popular as holiday gift items, we are temporarily out of stock. We expect a shipment by October 17 and will send them to you immediately. You won't be billed, of course, until they are sent.

> Presents bad news in positive manner. Explains why item is delayed. Maintains "you" view.

As a new customer, you may be interested to know that the ProTec bike helmets you ordered are tops in the field. They received the highest rating by *Consumer Reports* in tests comparing 15 of the best-known models. Because of their impact protection and the strength of their straps and buckles, they will provide your customers with what is probably the safest bike helmet made today.

> Builds customer's confidence in product with resale information. Creates bond with reader by offering special information for the new customer.

With proposed provincial legislation making bike helmets mandatory, many adults will now require helmets. However, there is still a lot of resistance. Why? Some of your customers have probably told you that helmets are uncomfortable and look "nerdy." However, a new generation of helmets has done away with hard-shell designs. Your customers will marvel at the new thin, semi-rigid-shell helmets made by Race Team. They're light, safe, and incredibly colourful. Enclosed is literature describing the all-new Race Team fashion helmets, now offered at low introductory prices.

> Recognizes weakness in market and ties it in with promotion of new product. Takes advantage of this customer's already identified interest in bike helmets to cultivate desire for new bike helmet.

We genuinely appreciate your order for ProTec helmets. To add the customer-pleasing fashion line of Race Team helmets to your inventory or to ask questions about your current order, just call 1–800–310–BIKE.

> Closes with thanks and offers of help. Promotes future business.

Granting Claims and Making Adjustments

Even the best-run and best-loved businesses occasionally receive claims or complaints from consumers. Most businesses grant claims and make adjustments promptly—they replace merchandise, refund money, extend discounts, send coupons, and repair goods. Businesses make favourable adjustments to legitimate claims for two reasons. First, consumers are protected by law for recovery of damages. Consumer protection is a joint effort of both federal and provincial legislation.[8] Second, and more obviously, most organizations genuinely want to please their customers and maintain their goodwill to encourage repeat business.

> **Businesses generally respond favourably to claims because of legal constraints and the desire to maintain customer goodwill.**

Wise business organizations recognize customer complaints as an important source of feedback. These organizations listen carefully to the reasons for dissatisfaction and then jump at the chance to remedy the problem.

A 1993 public opinion poll of 1000 Canadian consumers by Market Vision found that almost half the respondents had boycotted a company at some time for a variety of reasons. The most common reasons were bad service, poor-quality products, or environmentally unsound actions.[9] Other research reveals that

Smart companies know their customers' needs and concerns. The Body Shop serves the needs of its environmentally responsible customers by living by the motto "Reduce, Reuse, Recycle." More than 45 of The Body Shop products can be refilled, and a discount is given to those customers who take advantage of the offer.

less than one customer in twenty with a major problem will complain. Customers give the following reasons for not complaining:

It's not worth the trouble.

I don't know to whom to complain.

Nothing will be done anyway.

I don't want to be victimized.

Furthermore, of the customers who do complain, up to 80 percent are dissatisfied with the way their complaint was handled.[10]

Therefore, it is important to welcome complaints from customers as a way of ensuring repeat business and loyal customers. The Strategic Planning Institute found that companies that are seen by customers as offering good service achieve a 12 percent return on sales, compared with a 1 percent return on sales for companies that do not offer good service.[11]

Favourable responses to customer claims follow the direct pattern; unfavourable responses follow the indirect.

In responding to customer claims, you must first decide whether to grant the claim or not. Unless the claim is obviously fraudulent or represents an excessive sum, you'll probably grant it. When you say yes, your adjustment letter will be good news to the reader, so you'll want to use the direct pattern. When your response is no, the indirect pattern is appropriate. Chapter 8 discusses the indirect pattern for conveying negative news.

You'll have three goals in adjustment letters:

- Rectifying the wrong, if one exists

- Regaining the confidence of the customer

- Promoting further business

The opening of a positive adjustment letter should approve the customer's claim immediately. Notice how quickly the following openers announce the good news:

The enclosed $250 refund cheque demonstrates our desire to satisfy our customers and earn their confidence.

You will be receiving shortly a new Techtronic cordless telephone to replace the one that shattered when dropped recently.

Please take your Sanyo cassette tape deck to A–1 Appliance Service, 220 Orange Street, Saskatoon, where it will be repaired at no cost to you.

You're right! We agree that the warranty on your Diamond Standard Model UC600 dishwasher should be extended for six months.

Opening sentences to positive adjustment letters tell the good news quickly.

In making an adjustment, avoid sounding resentful or grudging. Once you decide to grant a claim, do so willingly. Remember that a primary goal in adjustments is future business. Statements that sound reluctant (*Although we generally refuse to extend warranties, we're willing to make an exception in this case*) may cause greater dissatisfaction than no response at all.

Adjustment letters seek to right wrongs, regain customer confidence, and promote further business.

In the body of an adjustment letter, your goal is to win back the confidence of the customer. You can do this by explaining what caused the problem (if you know) or by describing the measures you are taking to avoid recurrences of the problem, such as in the following:

In preparing our products, we take special care to see that they are wholesome and free of foreign matter. Approved spraying procedures are used in the field to control insects when necessary during the growing season. Our processing plants use screens, air curtains, ultraviolet lights, and other devices to exclude insects. Moreover, we inspect and clean every product to ensure that insects are not present.

Notice that this explanation does not admit error. Many companies sidestep the issue of responsibility because they feel that such an admission damages their credibility or might even encourage legal liability. Others admit errors indirectly (*Oversights may sometimes occur*) or even directly (*Once in a while a product that is less than perfect goes out*). The emphasis, however, should be on explaining how diligently you work to avoid disappointing your customers.

Another sticky issue is whether to apologize. Studies of adjustment letters received by consumers show that a majority of the letters contained apologies, either in the opening or in the closing.[12] Many business writing experts, however, advise against apologies, contending that they are counterproductive and merely remind the customer of the unpleasantness related to the claim. If you do apologize, do it early and briefly. Do not apologize if you are not to blame or if the error is minor. Since you are agreeing to the claim, your focus should be on how you are complying with the request.

Concentrate on how you are complying with the request, not on apologizing.

The language of adjustment letters must be particularly sensitive, since customers are already upset. Here are some don'ts:

- Don't use negative words (*trouble, regret, misunderstanding, fault, error, inconvenience, you claim*).

- Don't blame customers—even when they may be at fault.

- Don't blame individuals or departments within your organization; it's unprofessional.

- Don't make unrealistic promises; you can't guarantee that the situation will never recur.

To regain the confidence of your reader, consider including resale information. Describe a product's features and any special applications that might appeal to the reader. Promote a new product if it seems appropriate.

To close an adjustment letter, assume that the problem has been resolved and that future business will continue. You might express appreciation that the reader wrote, extend thanks for past business, refer to your desire to be of service, or mention a new product. Here are a variety of effective adjustment letter closings for various purposes:

> You were most helpful in informing us of this situation and permitting us to correct it. We appreciate your thoughtfulness in writing to us.

> Thanks for writing. Your satisfaction is important to us.

> We hope that this refund cheque convinces you that service to our customers is our No. 1 priority. Our goal is to earn your confidence and continue to justify that confidence with quality products and excellent service.

> Your cordless telephone will come in handy when you're playing and working outside this summer. For additional summer enjoyment take a look at the portable CD player on page 37 of the enclosed catalogue. We value your business and look forward to your future orders.

The tone of an adjustment letter should suggest that the writer is on the customer's side.

The adjustment letter in Figure 6.7 offers to replace dead rose bushes. It's very possible that the plants died because of a mistake by the customer, but the letter doesn't say so. Notice, too, how resale and sales promotion information is introduced without seeming pushy. Most important, the tone of the letter suggests that the company is on the customer's side and wants to do what is right.

Although the direct pattern works for many requests and replies, it obviously won't work for every situation. With more practice and experience, you'll be able to alter the pattern and apply the writing process to other communication problems. The following checklist summarizes the process of writing direct replies.

▓ Checklist for Writing Direct Replies

Complying with Requests

✓ **Use a subject line.** Identify previous correspondence and the topic of this letter.

✓ **Open directly.** In the first sentence deliver the information the reader wants (*Yes, I can meet with your class* or *Here is the information you requested*). If the message is mixed, present the best news first.

✓ **In the body provide explanations and additional information.** Arrange this information logically, perhaps using a list, headings, or columns. For prospective customers build your company image and promote your products.

✓ **End with a cordial, personalized statement.** If further action is required, tell the reader how to proceed and give helpful details.

FIGURE 6.7 ■ Adjustment Letter

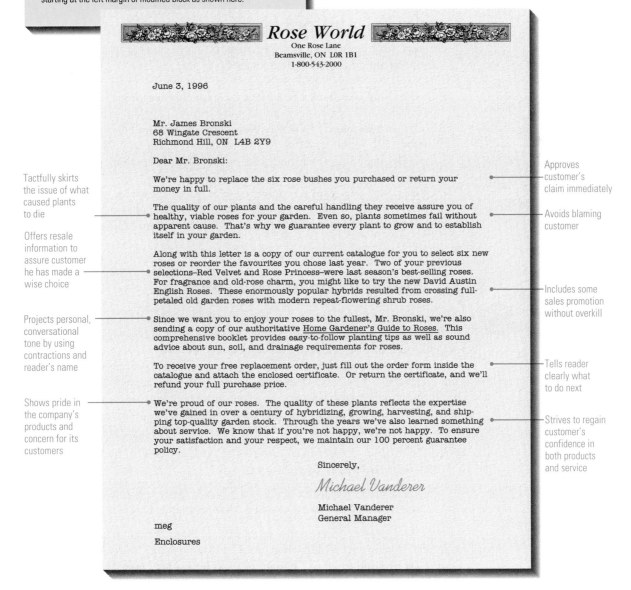

Tips for Letter Formatting

- Single-space business letters. Double-space between paragraphs.
- Place the date on line 13 or 2 lines below the letterhead.
- Set margins so that letter looks centred on the page.
- Leave three blank lines for the handwritten signature.
- Use a colon after the salutation and a comma after the complimentary close.
- Be consistent in letter format. For example, use full block with all lines starting at the left margin or modified block as shown here.

Rose World
One Rose Lane
Beamsville, ON L0R 1B1
1-800-543-2000

June 3, 1996

Mr. James Bronski
68 Wingate Crescent
Richmond Hill, ON L4B 2Y9

Dear Mr. Bronski:

We're happy to replace the six rose bushes you purchased or return your money in full.

The quality of our plants and the careful handling they receive assure you of healthy, viable roses for your garden. Even so, plants sometimes fail without apparent cause. That's why we guarantee every plant to grow and to establish itself in your garden.

Along with this letter is a copy of our current catalogue for you to select six new roses or reorder the favourites you chose last year. Two of your previous selections—Red Velvet and Rose Princess—were last season's best-selling roses. For fragrance and old-rose charm, you might like to try the new David Austin English Roses. These enormously popular hybrids resulted from crossing full-petaled old garden roses with modern repeat-flowering shrub roses.

Since we want you to enjoy your roses to the fullest, Mr. Bronski, we're also sending a copy of our authoritative Home Gardener's Guide to Roses. This comprehensive booklet provides easy-to-follow planting tips as well as sound advice about sun, soil, and drainage requirements for roses.

To receive your free replacement order, just fill out the order form inside the catalogue and attach the enclosed certificate. Or return the certificate, and we'll refund your full purchase price.

We're proud of our roses. The quality of these plants reflects the expertise we've gained in over a century of hybridizing, growing, harvesting, and shipping top-quality garden stock. Through the years we've also learned something about service. We know that if you're not happy, we're not happy. To ensure your satisfaction and your respect, we maintain our 100 percent guarantee policy.

Sincerely,

Michael Vanderer

Michael Vanderer
General Manager

meg

Enclosures

Tactfully skirts the issue of what caused plants to die

Offers resale information to assure customer he has made a wise choice

Projects personal, conversational tone by using contractions and reader's name

Shows pride in the company's products and concern for its customers

Approves customer's claim immediately

Avoids blaming customer

Includes some sales promotion without overkill

Tells reader clearly what to do next

Strives to regain customer's confidence in both products and service

Acknowledging Customer Orders

✓ **Open with delivery information.** Tell when and how delivery will be made.

✓ **In the body give details of the order.** Discuss any irregularities, such as delays or back-ordered items. Use resale information to reassure customers of their wise choices. Consider sales promotion to highlight other products.

✓ **Close positively.** Show appreciation, offer help, and/or anticipate future orders.

Granting Claims and Adjustments

✓ **Open with approval.** Comply with the customer's claim immediately. Avoid sounding grudging or reluctant.

✓ **In the body win back the customer's confidence.** Explain the cause of the problem or describe your ongoing efforts to avoid such difficulties. Focus on your efforts to satisfy customers rather than admitting blame or apologizing. Avoid negative words, accusations, and unrealistic promises. Consider including resale and sales promotion information.

✓ **Close positively.** Express appreciation to the customer for writing, extend thanks for past business, anticipate continued orders, refer to your desire to be of service, and/or mention a new product if it seems appropriate.

Writing International Letters

The letter-writing suggestions you've just studied work well for correspondence in this country and the United States. You may wish, however, to modify the organization, format, and tone of letters going abroad.

North American businesspeople appreciate efficiency, straightforwardness, and conciseness in letters. Moreover, North American business letters tend to be informal and conversational. Foreign correspondents, however, may look upon such directness and informality as inappropriate, insensitive, and abrasive. Letters in Japan, for example, may begin with deference, humility, and references to nature:

> Allow us to open with all reverence to you:
>
> The season for cherry blossoms is here with us and everybody is beginning to feel refreshed. We sincerely congratulate you on becoming more prosperous in your business.[13]

Letters in Germany commonly start with a long, formal lead-in, such as *Referring to your kind inquiry from the 31st of the month, we take the liberty to remind you with this letter* ...[14] Italian business letters may refer to the receiver's family and children. And French correspondents would consider it rude to begin a letter with a request before it is explained. French letters typically include an ending with this phrase (or a variation of it): *I wish to assure you, [insert reader's most formal title], of my most respectful wishes [followed by the writer's title and signature].*[15] Foreign letters are also more likely to include passive-voice

ETHICS

GREED IS OUT; ETHICS AND MISSION STATEMENTS ARE IN (OR ARE THEY?)

As businesses emerged from the profit-oriented 1980s, values and social responsibilities were being emphasized in corporate mission statements. Greed was out; ethics were in. Scrambling to do the right thing, businesses and their employees became actively engaged in activities that contributed to their communities. Many businesses also re-evaluated their product lines and investments to enhance quality of life and the environment.

To spell out their goals, companies increasingly developed codes of ethics and mission statements like the one shown here. Such statements were not easily written because they required consensus and commitment.

Not everyone, however, agreed with the trend toward the strong social stances of some public corporations. Respected economist Milton Friedman, a Nobel laureate, contended, "Few trends could so thoroughly undermine the very foundations of our free society as the acceptance by corporate officials of a social responsibility other than to make as much money for their stockholders as possible."[16]

Robert D. Haas, chairman of the board and CEO of Levi Strauss & Co., expressed another viewpoint about mission statements when speaking before the Conference Board of New York City in May 1994: "Our compliance-based program sent a disturbing message to our people—WE DON'T RESPECT YOUR INTELLIGENCE OR TRUST YOU!"[17]

Career Track Application

Analyze the Seagull Pewter mission statement in terms of applying it. If you were an employee at Seagull Pewter, how would the mission statement affect your actions if you worked in production, marketing, or accounting? As an employee, would such a detailed document insult you? Do you see any contradictions in the statement that might force compromises for the company and its employees? Investigate other ways in which companies are addressing these important issues.

SEAGULL PEWTER

MISSION STATEMENT

We at Seagull are a creative, innovative team, committed to working together in the following areas to further our vision of being the best gift-ware company in the world.

BUSINESS We believe that business is a primary vehicle for transformation on our planet. We recognize that business has a social and ethical responsibility to contribute to the creation of a peaceful, healthy world. We advocate business practices that enhance the relationship between commercial activity and social good. Our decisions reflect a healthy balance between:

1. The generation of wealth
2. The offering of quality goods and services in a timely and innovative manner
3. Our social mission

PRODUCT We are committed to designing, producing, and marketing gifts of lasting quality that reflect man's creative ability and that touch and inspire the human spirit.

SERVICE We are aware that success derives from service to and partnership with our employees, customers and suppliers. These partnerships must reflect our integrity and a commitment to the well-being of all.

FINANCES We regard money as a vital resource and are responsible to see that it is earned and spent effectively and wisely in all areas.

TEAMWORK We believe in teamwork in a workplace that encourages continuous personal and professional improvement in an atmosphere of trust, fair play and fun.

ENVIRONMENT We recognize that as part of the global environment we are responsible to see that our natural world is sustained in a manner that supports the quality of life for all living things.

PEOPLE As global citizens we express our caring for people in the workplace, community, and in the world. We believe that a small group of people can make a measurable difference in building a better world.

EDUCATION We believe in educational and training opportunities that enable individuals to acquire the skill, knowledge and experience needed to make responsible decisions in the workplace and in society.

SURROUNDINGS We are committed to maintaining clean, safe and orderly surroundings that reflect our pride in our work.

FUTURE We believe that our future is limited only by our imagination and we appreciate the wonder of life.

constructions (*your letter has been received*), exaggerated courtesy (*great pleasure, esteemed favour*), and obvious flattery (*your eminent firm*).[18]

Foreign letters may also use different formatting techniques. Whereas North American business letters are typewritten and single-spaced, in other countries they may be handwritten and either single- or double-spaced. Address arrangements vary as well, as shown in the following:

German	**Japanese**
Herr [title, Mr., on first line]	Ms. Atsuko Takagi [title, name]
Dieter Woerner [name]	5–12 Koyo-cho 4 chome [street, house number]
Fritz-Kalle-Strasse 4 [street, house number]	Higashinada-ku [city]
6200 Wiesbaden [postal district, city]	Tokyo 194 [prefecture, postal district]
Germany [country]	Japan [country]

Dates and numbers can be particularly confusing, as shown here:

North American	**Some European Countries**
June 3, 1996	3rd of June 1996
6/3/96	3.6.96
$5,320.00 *or* $5320.00	$5,320,00

To be safe, spell out the names of months instead of using figures. Verify sums of money and identify the currency unit. Before sending a letter abroad, review the section "Developing Intercultural Sensitivity" in Chapter 2.

Because the placement and arrangement of letter addresses and closing lines vary greatly, you should always research local preferences before writing. For important letters going abroad, it's also wise to have someone familiar with local customs read and revise the message. A graduate student learned this lesson when she wrote a letter, in French, to a Paris museum asking for permission to do research. She received no response. Before writing a second time, she took the letter to her French tutor. "No, no, mademoiselle! It will never do! It must be more respectful. You must be very careful of individuals' titles. Let me show you!" The second letter won the desired permission.

◼ Summary of Learning Goals

1. **List three characteristics of good letters, and describe the direct pattern for organizing letters.** Good letters are characterized by clear content, a tone of goodwill, and correct form. Letters carrying positive or neutral messages should be organized directly. That means introducing the main idea (the purpose for writing) immediately in the opening. The body of the letter explains and gives details. Letters that make requests close by telling what action is desired and establishing a deadline (end date) for that action.

2. **Write letters requesting information and action.** The opening immediately states the purpose of the letter, perhaps asking a question. The body explains and justifies the request. The closing tells the reader courteously what to do and shows appreciation.

3. **Compose letters placing orders.** The opening introduces the order and authorizes a purchase (*Please send me the following items ...*). The body lists the desired items including quantity, order number, description, unit price, and total price. The closing describes the method of payment, tells when the merchandise should be sent, and expresses appreciation.

4. **Prepare letters making claims.** The opening describes the problem clearly or tells what action is to be taken. The body explains and justifies the request without anger or emotion. The closing, which might include an end date, contains a pleasant statement that expresses a desire for continued relations.

5. **Write letters complying with requests.** A subject line identifies previous correspondence, while the opening immediately delivers the good news. The body explains and provides additional information. The closing is cordial and personalized.

6. **Compose letters acknowledging customer orders.** The opening tells when and how the delivery will be made. The body discusses details of the order, including any irregularities. It may include resale or sales promotion information. The closing includes a personalized statement that demonstrates reader benefits, appreciation, helpfulness, and/or expectation of continued good relations.

7. **Prepare letters granting claims and making adjustments.** The opening immediately grants the claim without sounding grudging. To regain the confidence of the customer, the body may explain what went wrong and how the problem will be rectified. However, it may avoid accepting responsibility for any problems. The closing expresses appreciation, extends thanks for past business, refers to a desire to be of service, and/or mentions a new product.

8. **Modify international letters to accommodate other cultures.** Letters being sent abroad in some cultures, should probably use a less direct organizational pattern and be more formal in tone. They should also be adapted to the letter formats used in that country.

CHAPTER REVIEW

1. What is *goodwill*? Briefly describe five ways to develop goodwill in a letter. (Goal 1)

2. Why is it best to write most business letters "backwards"? (Goal 1)

3. What kind of questions elicit the most information? Give an example. (Goal 2)

4. Why is the direct letter strategy appropriate for most business messages? (Goal 2)

5. For order letters what information goes in the opening? In the body? In the closing? (Goal 3)

6. What is a *claim*? (Goal 4)

7. Why are most companies today particularly interested in listening to customers? (Goal 4)

8. In complying with requests, why is it especially important to be sure all the facts are correct in letters written on company stationery? (Goal 5)

9. When customers or prospective customers inquire about products or services, what kind of information should be provided? (Goal 6)

10. When should companies send personal letters to acknowledge customer orders? (Goal 6)

11. Distinguish between *resale* and *sales promotion* information. (Goal 6)

12. Why do smart companies welcome complaints? (Goal 7)

13. What are a writer's three goals for adjustment letters? (Goal 7)

14. Name four things to avoid in adjustment letters. (Goal 7)

15. What three elements of business letters going abroad might be modified? (Goal 8)

DISCUSSION

1. What's wrong with using the indirect pattern for writing routine requests and replies? If in the end the reader understands the message, why make a big fuss over the organization? (Goal 1)

2. Is it insensitive to include resale or sales promotion information in an adjustment letter? (Goal 6)

3. Why is it important to regain the confidence of a customer in an adjustment letter? How can it be done? (Goal 7)

4. How are North American business letters different from those written in other countries? Why do you suppose this is so? (Goal 8)

5. **Ethical Issue:** Let's say you've drafted a letter to a customer in which you apologize for the way the customer's account was fouled up by the accounting department. You show the letter to your boss, and she instructs you to remove the apology. It admits responsibility, she says, and the company cannot allow itself to be held liable. You're not a lawyer, but you can't see the harm in a simple apology. What should you do? Refer to the section "Tools for Doing the Right Thing" in Chapter 3 to review the five questions you might ask yourself in trying to do the right thing.

EXERCISES

6.1 Direct Openings (Goals 1–7)

Revise the following openings so that they are more direct.

a. Pursuant to your letter of June 3, I am writing in regard to your inquiry about sliding mirror doors. We produce a variety of styles and finishes, all with heavy-duty tracking systems and shatter-resistant safety mirrors.

b. Please allow me to introduce myself. I am Lisa Caruso, and I am writing to inquire about the mountain bike that I saw on the cover of your magazine, *Mountain Bike Action*, in April. This bike interests me, and I'd like to know what kind it is and where I can find out more about it.

c. Because I've lost your order blank, I have to write this letter. I hope that it's all right to place an order this way. I am interested in ordering a number of things from your summer catalogue, which I still have although the order blank is missing.

d. Your letter of March 21 has been referred to my desk for response. In your letter you inquire about the mountain bike featured on the cover of our magazine in April. That particular bike is a Series 70 Paramount and is manufactured by Schwinn.

e. I am pleased to receive your inquiry regarding the possibility of my acting as a speaker at the final semester meeting of your business management club on May 21. The topic of personnel interviewing interests me and is one on which I think I could impart helpful information to your members. Therefore, I am responding in the affirmative to your kind invitation.

f. Thank you for your recent order of November 2. We are sure you will enjoy the letterhead stationery that you ordered from our summer catalogue. Your order is currently being processed and should leave our printing facility in Montreal early next week. We use UPS for all deliveries in southern Ontario. Because you ordered stationery with engraving, it cannot be shipped until December 4. You should not expect it before December 9.

g. We have just received your letter of December 13 regarding the unfortunate troubles you are having with your Hitachi videocassette recorder. In your letter you ask if you may send the VCR to us for inspection. Although we normally handle all service requests through our local dealers, in your circumstance we are willing to take a look at your unit here at our St. Catharines plant. Therefore, please send it to us so that we may determine what's wrong.

6.2 Subject Lines (Goals 1–7)

Write efficient subject lines for each of the messages in Exercise 6.1. Add dates and other information if necessary.

6.3 Letter Formatting (Goal 1)

On a sheet of paper draw two rectangles about 4 inches wide and 6 inches high. Within these rectangles show where the following parts of letters go: letterhead, dateline, inside address, salutation, body, complimentary close, signature, and writer's name. Use lines to show how much space each part would occupy. Illustrate two different letter styles, such as block and personal business style. Be prepared to discuss your drawings. Consult Appendix B for format guidelines.

6.4 Document for Analysis: Letter Requesting Information (Goal 2)

Analyze the following letter. List its weaknesses. If your instructor directs, revise the letter.

> Dear Sir:
>
> Because we are one of the largest banking systems in the country, we receive hundreds of résumés from job candidates every day. We need help in sorting and ranking candidates by categories, such as job classification, education, work history, skill, and experience.
>
> Recently, I was reading *Personnel* magazine, and the March issue has a story about your new software program called Resumix. It sounds fascinating and may be the answer to our problem. We would like more information about this program, which is supposed to read and sort résumés.
>
> In addition to learning if the program can sort candidates into the categories mentioned earlier, I'm wondering if the program can read all the different type fonts and formats that candidates use on their résumés. Another important consideration for us is training and trouble-shooting. If we need help with the program, would you supply it?
>
> Thank you for your cooperation.
>
> Sincerely,

6.5 Document for Analysis: Claim Request (Goal 4)

Analyze the following letter. List its weaknesses. If your instructor directs, revise the letter.

> Gentlemen:
>
> I don't think I should be charged twice for a flight I took only once! When I made my reservation to fly from Victoria to Los Angeles, I didn't know my father would get sick and require hospitalization on September 19. As a result, I could not make the trip on September 20 as I had originally planned.
>
> I finally did make the trip on September 30. But WestAir charged me $169 again! Your booking agent refused to look at the letter from my father's doctor describing the hospitalization. She said I had to write to headquarters. I still have my tickets from the September 20 flight, so you know I didn't use them. My travel agent says that I'm entitled to a refund. So why did I have to pay twice?

I'm all for deregulation of the airline industry, but what happened to compassion and integrity?

> Angrily yours,

6.6 Document for Analysis: Favourable Adjustment Letter (Goal 7)

Analyze the following letter. List its weaknesses. If your instructor directs, revise the letter.

> Dear Mrs. Winston:
>
> Thank you for your letter of May 18 in which you complain that you are receiving two issues of *Popular Electronics* each month.
>
> We have checked into the matter and ascertained that the misunderstanding resulted when you placed an order under the name of Mrs. Wendy Winston. You claim that this new subscription was made as part of your daughter's magazine fund-raising program at her school. You must be aware that the entire circulation operation of a large magazine is computerized. Obviously, a computer cannot distinguish between your current subscription for Mrs. H. C. Winston and a new one for another name.
>
> But we think we've straightened the problem out. We're extending your subscription for 14 months. That's a bonus of two issues to make up for the double ones you've received. However, we can't prevent you from receiving one or two more double issues.
>
> Sincerely,

PROBLEMS

6.7 Request Letter: Tell Me More (Goal 2)

Select an advertisement from a newspaper or magazine that describes a product or service that interests you. Write a letter that asks for information not provided in the ad, such as price, availability, warranty, service, or restrictions. Ask at least four significant questions. Attach a copy of the ad to your letter.

6.8 Request Letter: June Move (Goal 2)

Write to a real estate agent in a distant city. Assume that you have a family of four and will be changing jobs in June. Ask the agent about houses or apartments in your price range. Inquire about availability, taxes, and desirable locales. Describe your needs. Provide enough information to ensure that you'll receive a useful response. You plan to visit the agent and look at listings in April.

6.9 Request Letter: Assist from Dormans (Goal 2)

Assume that you are Brian Keppler, personnel manager, Commercial Bank of Manitoba. Your bank employs over 8000 workers in Western Canada. At your Winnipeg location you hire about 100 people each year and you process internal transfers for another 100. Processing all those applications has become increasingly burdensome. At a recent professional meeting you met Lawrence V. Moore, manager of placement at Dorman Manufacturing Company. He told you briefly about a computer system he had developed that enabled him to make the entire personnel task more manageable. He indicated that he would be happy to tell you more about his system if you would write him at 2380 Westside Drive, Vancouver, BC V6P 1W8. Ask Mr. Moore to describe how his system allows candidates to be ranked on a variety of requirements (such as experience, skills, and education). You wonder about weighing job requirements. For example, if certain skills are much more important than experience, how does his system handle this? You're very concerned about legislation requiring fair and equal treatment of all candidates. You understand that his system promotes such consistency, but you wonder how. When candidates are interviewed, how does his system allow them to be ranked, especially on such subjective traits as communication skills and ability to work in a team? Ask for any other information you think would be helpful.[19]

6.10 Request Letter: Be Your Own Boss (Goal 2)

Your rich uncle has just agreed to provide financial backing for you to start your own business. Fortunately, you recently read an article about the hottest small business franchises, complete with addresses for more information. Write to one of the following: Gift Baskets International, VIP Event Planning, Silk Plant City, Auto Detailing Specialists, Canadiana Bed and Breakfast Inns, Mobile Disk Jockeys, Wertz Self-Service Storage, I-Don't-Believe-It's-Yogurt, Yummy Donut Shops, BigMouth (voice-mail services), Videotaping Pros, Smyth Secretarial/Word Processing Services, PIP Printing, or Starmaker Image Consultants. Request information about start-up costs, equipment requirements, training, advertising support, potential customers, profit sharing, and growth potential. Your questions will be determined by the kind of franchise you select. Provide an appropriate address.

6.11 Order Letter: Dracula in London (Goal 3)

In your local newspaper (supply name and date) you see an advertisement listing close-out prices on hundreds of computer games. The prices are so good you decide to place an order—either for yourself or for gifts. Because no order blank or toll-free telephone number is supplied, you write a letter to Discount Computer Sales, 22050 Ontario Street, Lennoxville, QC J1M 1Z7 ordering the following games: Dracula in London (No. RVGA4.3) for $10.95; Duke Nukem (No. TVGA2.3) for $12.95; Myst (No. EVGA4.2) for $10.95; and SIM City 2000 (No. WVGA3.2) for $12.95. Applicable sales taxes will be added. The shipping cost is $6.50 for UPS or $11.50 for Federal Express. Figure the total and include it in your order.

6.12 Order Letter: AV Supplies (Goal 3)

As audiovisual supervisor for TechData Ltd., write a letter ordering the following supplies from Nordstrum Suppliers, 627 Nordstrum Road, Antigonish, NS B2G 1C0. You need 20 Kodak slide trays (No. A41–7829) at $13.78 each; 1000 foil-back slide labels (No. A41–1632) at $10.76 for 1000; and 1 double-decker slide file (No. A41–5492) at $24.55. You saw these items advertised in the September issue of *Visuals* magazine. Because you need these items for an immediate project, ask for two-day Priority Post delivery service at a cost of $16. Request that the invoice be sent to Rita Kemp, Purchasing Department, TechData, Inc., 701 Queen Street, Antigonish, NS B2G 3A4.

6.13 Claim Letter: Windows that Won't Stretch (Goal 4)

Assume you are Linda Jurado, owner of Linda's Interiors. Recently you completed a kitchen remodelling that required double-glazed, made-to-order oak windows. You ordered them from Bella Windows, 200 Main Street, Mississauga, ON L5B 3X3. When they arrived, your carpenter gave you the bad news: the windows were cut ⅝ inch too small—instead of 47⅞ inches, they were only 47¼ inches wide. In his words, "No way can I stretch those windows to fit these openings!" You waited three weeks for these windows, and your clients wanted them installed immediately. To please them, you had your carpenter rebuild the opening, but he charged you an extra $214 for his labour. You feel that Bella Windows should reimburse you for this amount since it was their error. In fact, you actually saved them a bundle of money by not returning the windows. Write a claim letter that requests a payment to you. Enclose a copy of your original order showing your measurements and your carpenter's bill. Perhaps you should also include a copy of Bella's invoice. You are a good customer of Bella, having used their quality windows on many other jobs. You're confident that they will grant this claim.

6.14 Claim Letter: Mouldy Grout Is Missing (Goal 4)

You're mad! You purchased two $35 tickets to a concert featuring King Fisher and his Mouldy Grout band at Five Flags Lake Point Park. When you arrived for the concert May 25, neither King nor the Grout appeared. Three decidedly not-ready-for-prime-time groups filled in. You had been looking forward to this concert for seven weeks. You're angry and disappointed and feel that you've been taken. After the concert started, you stayed through two acts to see if the talent might improve. It didn't. It seems to you that you remember seeing newspaper advertisements publicizing the Mouldy Grout performance as recently as the day of the concert. As you left the Five Flags parking lot, you saw a small poster describing a change in the talent for the evening's concert.

Two weeks later you're still angry. You decide to write to Five Flags Lake Point Park, P.O. Box 4300, Dartmouth, NS B2Z 5B2 requesting a refund of the purchase price for two $35 tickets.

6.15 Claim Letter: The Real Thing (Goal 4)

Think of a product or service that has disappointed you. Write a claim letter requesting a refund, replacement, explanation, or whatever seems reasonable. Generally, such letters are addressed to customer service departments. For food product claims you should include bar-code identification from the package, if possible. Your instructor may ask you to actually mail this letter. Remember that smart companies want to know what their customers think, especially if a product could be improved. When you receive a response, share it with your class.

6.16 Collaborative Request Response: McDonald's Goes Green (Goal 5)

Karen Capatosto, director of Customer Service for McDonald's Corporation, has received a letter from an environmentalist wanting to know what McDonald's is doing to reduce the huge amounts of waste products that its restaurants generate. This inquiry argues that these wastes not only deplete world resources but also clog our already overburdened landfills.

Karen thinks that this is a good opportunity for her student interns to sharpen their reasoning and writing skills on the job. She asks you and the other interns to draft a response to the inquiry telling how McDonald's is cleaning up its act. Here are some of the facts that Karen supplies to your group.

Actually, McDonald's has been quite active in its environmental efforts. Working with the Environmental Defense Fund, McDonald's has initiated a series of 42 resolutions that are cutting by more than 80 percent the huge waste stream from its 12 000 restaurants. McDonald's efforts meant making changes in packaging, increasing its recycling campaign, trying more composting, and retraining employees. McDonald's was one of the food industry leaders to abandon the polystyrene "clamshell" box for hamburgers and sandwiches. Formerly using an average of 20 pounds of polystyrene a day per restaurant, McDonald's now uses only 10 percent of that figure.

McDonald's suppliers have been asked to use corrugated boxes that contain at least 35 percent recycled content. Moreover, suppliers will be asked to make regular reports to McDonald's that measure their progress in reaching new waste-reduction goals. Other environmental efforts include testing a starch-based material in consumer cutlery to replace plastic forks, knives, and spoons. Many restaurants have also begun trial composting of eggshells, coffee grounds, and food scraps. McDonald's is also starting a nationwide program for recycling corrugated boxes. In addition, the company is testing reusable salad lids and shipping pallets, pump-style bulk dispensers for condiments, and refillable coffee mugs.

McDonald's has retrained its restaurant crews to give waste reduction equal weight with other priorities, such as quickness, cleanliness, and quality service. The company is trying to reduce the waste both behind the counter (which accounts for 80 percent of the total waste) and over the counter. Although this letter draft should be addressed to Bruce W. Quinn, 1762 Evergreen Road, Waterloo, ON N2A 3G6, it may be used for other customer inquiries as well.[20]

6.17 Response Letter: You Can Account on Us (Goal 5)

Assume that you are Marsha Morrison, manager of Account-on-Us, an agency that supplies temporary and permanent accounting and bookkeeping personnel. Respond to the letter of Diane Morantz, Morantz Investment Properties, 120 Wentworth Road, Hamilton, ON L9B 2F5, who inquired about your service. Ms. Morantz wants to find a full-charge bookkeeper, and she sent a description of the job she has available. She asked several questions, the first of which related to your fee. Tell her that the fee is based on the annual salary—you charge 1 percent per thousand of the annual salary. Enclose your fee schedule so that she can see what you're talking about. Her next question dealt with the candidate's qualifications. Assure Ms. Morantz that you test all applicants for accounting knowledge and that you contact all previous employers. Her last question concerned a guarantee. You offer a 30-day guarantee. If during the first 30 days of employment, the employee does not perform satisfactorily, you will find a replacement or refund the fee on a prorated basis, depending on the number of days worked.

Since you specialize in accounting and bookkeeping personnel, you attract qualified candidates. Nevertheless, you administer rigorous theory and applications tests; then you select only the top performers. Seldom does any employer exercise your 30-day guarantee. Your service can take the trouble out of hiring new employees since you do all the testing, screening, and reference checking. You have a file of satisfied local employers who have used your service. Tell her that you will call her next week (give specific date) to discuss background information on potential candidates. Along with your fee schedule, send Ms. Morantz your booklet entitled "How to Help a New Employee Get Off to a Good Start." Refer her to pages 4–5 where she can read 10 tips for improving an employee's first week on the job.

6.18   Response Letter: Answering Real Customers (Goal 5)

In a job you currently hold or one you've had in the past, consider the kinds of inquiries that customers, suppliers, or other outsiders typically make. What information do they want? Prepare a response letter using information with which you are familiar. Include answers to at least three significant questions. How can you develop reader benefits? What resale or sales promotion information can you use? Use the title of the person who would normally be answering these inquiries.

6.19   Order Response: Dusky Blue Is Worth Waiting For (Goal 6)

Acknowledge the September 16 order of the Concoran Company, 127 Beamer Road, Sault Ste. Marie, ON P6B 2V8. You are sending them three Micron microfiche readers by Interprovincial Express; they should arrive in two weeks (give expected date). However, the five 10-drawer microform file cases in the order must be special-ordered because of the dusky blue colour selected. These file cases will be shipped from Hamilton. Manufacturing takes three weeks and shipping will require another two weeks. Encourage the Concoran people to consider your acid-free microfiche envelopes (for temporary storage of microfiche records). You also have a special rate on microfiche file folder guides. These have DuPont Mylar tabs; a package of 50 has been reduced from $31.99 to $25.99. The file cases they ordered are your best high-grade steel, and the baked enamel finish—no matter which of the 15 fashion colours they order—is extremely durable, withstanding heavy-duty

office use. If Concoran wants the file cases a little faster, it should call your Traffic Department at (800) 689–2120 to discuss ways to expedite shipping.

6.20   Order Response: Drying Wet Heads at MillionHairs (Goal 6)

Send a letter to MillionHairs Salon, 2605 Pinebloom Drive, Charlottetown, PEI C1A 4P3 acknowledging its February 4 order for hair dryers. Tell MillionHairs that you are shipping ten Turbo pistol-grip styling dryers by UPS with arrival expected about February 9. You won't, however, be able to send immediately the new Euro Air Diffusers they ordered. This device has unique styling "fingers" that lift and separate curly, permed, or fine hair to bring out natural texture. Because salons are snapping them up, you have run out. You expect a new supply in two weeks, and you will ship then, if that's all right with MillionHairs. To sell to their customers, MillionHairs might be interested in your Neon Combo pack, which includes a brightly coloured fanny pack that holds their hair essentials while they are biking or at the beach. It includes a 1250-watt dryer, a ¾-inch curling iron, a spiral curling iron, and a hairbrush—all colour-coordinated in neon green or pink. This take-along hair care product makes a great gift.

6.21   Adjustment Letter: Tearful Inquiry (Goal 7)

As Rod Fournier, manager, Consumer Affairs, Grant Laboratories, respond to the letter you received from Tina Gambrell, 2860 Clarkson Avenue, St. John's, Nfld., A1C 5S7. Ms. Gambrell said that she has used Opti-Tears before without incident. A recent purchase, however, hurt her eyes and caused painful tears when she used it to lubricate her contact lenses. She returned her bottle of Opti-Tears and wants you to test it. Because Grant Laboratories welcomes letters from customers, you appreciate Ms. Gambrell's inquiry. You are, naturally, very concerned when your customers experience eye discomfort in using your products. Let her know that Opti-Tears particularly appreciates her efforts in returning the bottle so that its laboratories can analyze the product for conformity to specifications. Opti-Tears continually evaluates its products, and the results of this analysis will provide useful information. Promise her that you'll send her results of the analysis when they become available. Send her several free bottles of Adapettes Especially for Sensitive Eyes. This product contains a special ophthalmic lubricating solution that is formulated without preservatives. People who have reacted to other products have had no problems with Adapettes.

6.22 Adjustment Letter: We'll Have to Eat This One (Goal 7)

As Thomas T. Thompson, vice-president, Customer Operations, Bella Windows, respond to Linda Jurado, owner of Linda's Interiors, 230 Barnes Street, Oakville, ON L6H 2B7 (Problem 6.13). She asks for reimbursement of $214 for the extra amount she paid to have her oak windows installed. You check the invoice and the order and discover that your company did indeed cut the windows the wrong size. Now you must decide what to do. You can send her the money, but you'd rather give her a credit toward her next order—to encourage her repeat business. Give her a choice. Would she prefer a cheque for $214 or a credit of $350 toward her next order?

Tell her how Bella Windows prides itself on its quality-control procedures. All orders are verified when they are received, cut to order by expert wood artisans in the factory, and inspected before being shipped. Inform her that the mistake was certainly yours, though, and you realize that you need to redouble your efforts in scrutinizing custom orders. As the factory manager Leo said after seeing her letter and the original order, "She's right. Don't know what went wrong, but we'll have to eat this one." Leo was surprised—and thankful—that she kept the windows.

Remind her of your comprehensive line of traditional and European-style kitchen and bath cabinetry. Your cabinets come in hardwoods such as oak, cherry, hickory, and maple; you offer up to six finishes. You now manufacture high-tech laminate cabinets as well. Enclose a copy of your booklet, "Functional and Elegant Cabinets from Bella." You think she'll like the section on planning a social kitchen.

6.23 Adjustment Letter: Red Roses for a Blue Customer (Goal 7)

Assume you are Barbara L. Hunt, vice-president, Customer Service, Atlantic Trust, 1340 Old Trenton Road, Lethbridge, AB T1K 3M4. An irate bank customer—Michelle A. Marrinan, 340 Gateway Drive, Lethbridge, AB T3K 8J7—calls to say that your bank humiliated her by bouncing six of her cheques. Ms. Marrinan had deposited $11 500 to her account on December 1 and began writing cheques on that deposit about four days later. Every one of them bounced, and she's furious. You look into the problem and find that the cheque she deposited was drawn on a California bank. For its protection Atlantic has a policy prohibiting withdrawals from a large deposit until the deposit cheque has cleared the bank on which it was drawn. In this case it took 11 days for Ms. Marrinan's deposit to clear. Generally, it takes only five to seven days. You don't know why this cheque took so long.

Your tellers are trained to tell a customer making a large deposit that the amount will not be credited to the account until it clears its maker bank. Your teller apparently slipped up in warning Ms. Marrinan. You can understand why she is so angry. Not only did all those cheques bounce, damaging her reputation, but the people to whom she wrote the cheques also had to pay processing fees to their banks. Ms. Marrinan wants Atlantic to write letters of apology to each person who received one of the cheques explaining why the cheque bounced. She also wants you to pay any processing fees involved.

You think this situation points up a real need to change your company's policy. For all future large deposits, you want a company official to place a telephone call immediately to the issuing bank to verify the cheque. This should reduce the "hold" time on deposits. In the meantime, you wish to do everything possible to placate Ms. Marrinan, a valued customer. You decide to write her at once, agreeing that Atlantic will send letters of explanation to her six payees. Atlantic will also pay all processing fees caused by the cheques that bounced. But more than that, you are sending her a dozen red roses to let her know that Atlantic cares about its customers.[21]

6.24 International Inquiry: Coming to Canada (Goal 8)

Assume that you are Jane Tozak, assistant registrar, at the college or university you attend (or one with which you are familiar). You have been asked to respond to an inquiry from Ms. Harui Yamaguchi. She wants to come to Canada to study. She seeks information about an educational program at your institution (select the program in which you are enrolled or another). She also wants to know the tuition costs for international students and whether your institution has any special groups for international students. Write a supportive and informative letter to Ms. Harui Yamaguchi, 3–13 Tsukiji 5–chome (street, house number), Chuo-ku (city), Tokyo 104 (prefecture, postal district), Japan. Her letter was in English and she included a self-addressed envelope, but you can tell that she's not fluent in the language. In a separate memo to your instructor, describe how you adapted your message to this reader.

6.25 International Inquiry: Info to Germany (Goal 8)

You are Denise Moore, customer service representative for an organization where you have worked or one with which you are familiar. Write a letter to Wolfgang Schleuter, Steinberg 21 (street address), 5840 Dortmund (district and city), Germany. Mr. Schleuter wants information about one of your products or services. He's considering buying it or distributing it in his country. His inquiry was in English, but you guess he's not expert at the language. In a separate memo to your instructor, describe how you adapted your message to this reader.

CLUE REVIEW 6

Edit the following sentences to correct faults in grammar, punctuation, spelling, and word use.

1. The extrordinary increase in sales is related to us placing the staff on a commission basis and the increase also effected our stock value.

2. She acts as if she was the only person who ever received a complement about their business writting.

3. Karen is interested in working for the department of foreign affairs. Since she is hopping to travel.

4. Major Hawkins whom I think will be elected has all ready served three consecative terms as a member of the oshawa city counsel.

5. After Mr. Freeman and him returned from lunch the customer's were handled more quick.

6. Our new employees cafeteria, which opened six months ago has a salad bar that everyone definitly likes.

7. On Tuesday Ms Adams can see you at two p.m., on Wednesday she has a full skedule.

8. His determination courage and sincerity could not be denied however his methods were often questioned.

9. After you have checked the matter farther report to the CEO and I.

10. Mr. Thomson and her advised me not to dessert my employer at this time. Although they were quite sympathetic to my personel problems.

Direct Memos

1 Discuss the characteristics of successful memos.

2 Adapt the writing process to memos.

3 Describe the organization of memos.

4 Distinguish between standard and electronic memos.

5 Explain smart E-mail practices that can make communicators more effective and prevent embarrassment.

6 Write information and procedure memos.

7 Write request and reply memos.

8 Write confirmation memos.

Moosehead Breweries

"This is like a marketing boot camp," says Susan O'Brien, assistant brand manager in the International Marketing division at Moosehead Breweries Ltd. in Saint John, New Brunswick. "Because not many people can tell the difference in taste between brands of beer, you are really working with image."

The beer business may be tough, but O'Brien was not conscripted into her position. "I love this job," says the 22-year-old, who, after working as a co-op student at Canada's largest independent brewery, was asked to stay on during the school year as a part-time employee. This led to an offer of full-time employment in April of 1995—a month before she graduated from the commerce program at Dalhousie University in Halifax. O'Brien got her degree but missed a few classes in the home stretch.

Among her duties, O'Brien is responsible for keeping the lines of communication open between the brewery and their overseas agents in places as far-flung as the United Kingdom, the Republic of Ireland, Norway, Finland, Hong Kong, and Australia. For this she uses letters, telephone calls, and faxes; she prefers faxes because of the speed of the transmission and the need to "leave a paper trail" documenting changes and the reasoning that went into a recommendation.

> *"[A memo has] to be brief because executives reading it will most likely only be able to give it 10 or 15 minutes. Often you have to sell a thousand-hour project in a very short time."*

"I liaise with Moosehead agents in countries around the world— it's quite a thing to have to develop a relationship over the phone or fax with someone ... but I do. We talk every day and discuss a broad range of issues—everything from packaging concepts to government regulations to political problems that affect the brewery."

This kind of rapport is based on understanding exactly whom you are communicating with, says O'Brien. "There are so many time zones and so many different cultural ideas of what is appropriate or professional business writing. The daily memo you might write to Finland is definitely not the one you would write to Japan. The most important thing I do is observe the receiver's information and adapt my writing style to that situation—and always act professionally.

"One agent always opens with some funny informal comment," she says, whereas correspondence from Japan tends to be straightforward and to the point. "In Japan it's a case of 'This is my business. This is what I'm doing.'"

"Each person is different and each situation is different, but basically the business part is the same."

Internally O'Brien regularly sends memos to Moosehead executives, "letting them know what's going on in each country, analyzing the product, and letting them know if sales are up in one country and why." For this she has developed a style all her own.

"We have some standards on how letters and recommendations within the company are to be written, but it's not dictated absolutely how you should write them. There's a typical memo heading, followed by a statement explaining the recommendations and the bottom-line, core benefit to the company, whether it's the financial contribution or image enhancement. The next step is the background to the project—for instance, I might say, 'We've been in the Pacific Rim for years and it's time to move on to another country. We're at that stage.' Then I would move on to the financial rationale, and then conclude with four or five reasons that form the basis for the recommendations—for instance, incremental volume or perhaps it's the next step in our four-year plan. These reasons are meant to really drive home why I want to do it."

As for the length, O'Brien says brevity is best; she does not write a memo longer than a page and a half. "It's got to be brief because executives reading it will most likely only be able to give it 10 or 15 minutes. Often you have to sell a thousand-hour project in a very short time."

The feedback she gets on her memos is almost as important as the words she puts on the page. It is at this stage O'Brien gets to reel in the reader. "The memos usually bring to mind a number of other questions that an executive will ask you. If it's a well-thought-out document you can answer these."

Sounding more like a wily veteran than a recent graduate, she explains, "Basically you pique the reader's interest enough that he or she is willing to ask another question and get excited about a project or recommendation too. It's sort of like feeding someone slowly— you don't want the reader to think, 'Oh, it's too much to take in.' You grab their attention, then you can give them more."

Much of her experience has come on the job, but O'Brien has made her own breaks. "When I began, I made a point of updating my boss once a week on everything I was doing that was relevant." How did she do this? In a memo, of course. "I put 'Highlights' and then went into detail on each country. And if I had a problem, I always offered a solution. Whether it was right or wrong didn't matter, as long as a solution was included. You are not just saying, 'We have a problem. What do we do about it?' This problem-solving approach not only reduces work for everyone else, but also has earned O'Brien respect and new responsibilities.

She warns that this style may not be universally acceptable; corporate communications differ from place to place. Her advice: "If your company is into sitting down and chatting, then do that; if they're into writing three- or four-page memos then discussing things after that, do it that way. You have to be flexible."[1] ■

Communicating with Moosehead Brewery agents around the world means not only knowing their different styles of communication but also making sure they clearly understand the point of the correspondence. The daily memos that Susan O'Brien writes to international agents must be structured to convey the essential information taking into account the appropriate cultural nuances.

Writing Direct Memos

In most organizations today, employees spend more time writing memos, computer mail messages, and other internal notes than writing to individuals outside the business.[2] U.S. executives devote as much as 22 percent of their time to reading and writing memos.[3]

Newly hired employees also make extensive use of internal communication. A study of recent graduates recruited by Fortune 500 companies found that the most-used forms of communications—including both internal and external messages—were memoranda and computer networks.[4]

Developing skill in writing internal messages brings you two important benefits. First, well-written documents are likely to achieve their goals. Second, such documents enhance your image within the organization. Competent, professional writers are noticed and rewarded; most often, they are the ones promoted to management.

This chapter concentrates on direct memos. These straightforward messages open with the main idea first because their topics are not sensitive and require little persuasion. You'll study the characteristics, writing process, organization, and forms for preparing procedure, information, request, reply, and confirmation memos.

Characteristics of Successful Memos

Because memos are standard forms of communication in most organizations, they may become your most common type of business communication. These indispensable messages inform employees, request data, supply responses, confirm decisions, and give directions. Good memos generally share certain characteristics.

TO, FROM, DATE, SUBJECT headings. Memos contain guide-word headings, often printed on special interoffice memo stationery, as shown in Figure 7.1. The guide words help readers immediately identify the date, origin, destination, and purpose of a message. You'll learn more about the form of memos shortly.

Single topic. Good memos generally discuss only one topic. Limiting the topic helps the receiver act on the subject and file it correctly. A memo writer, for example, who discusses a computer printer problem and also requests permission to attend a conference runs the risk of 50 percent failure. The reader may respond to the printer problem but forget about the conference request.

Conversational tone. The tone of interoffice memos is expected to be conversational because the communicators are usually familiar with one another. This means using occasional contractions (*I'm, you'll*), ordinary words, and first-person pronouns (*I, we*). Beware, however, of overusing *I*. Many organizations today want individuals who can work as part of a team. One experienced advertising executive recalls the first memo he put together for his boss. "I thought it was 'the end' in terms of creative problem solving. I eagerly awaited his reaction. When the memo arrived back on my desk, it had no comment and only three corrections. They were small, but I still feel their impact today. In three places I used the word 'I.' In each case, he crossed out the 'I' and wrote in 'We.' It was my first and most important lesson in teamwork."[5]

FIGURE 7.1 ■ Interoffice Memo Formatting

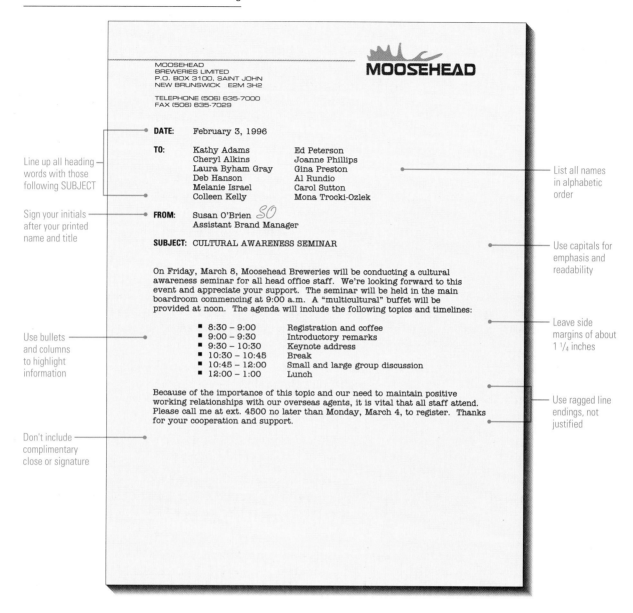

Conciseness. As functional forms of communication, routine memos contain only what's necessary to convey meaning and be courteous. Often, they require less background explanation and less attention to goodwill efforts than do letters to outsiders. Be particularly alert to eliminating wordiness. Avoid long lead-ins (*I am writing this memo to inform you that*), wordy phrases (*because of the fact that*), and pompous polysyllabic words (*utilize, parameter*).

Graphic highlighting. To make important ideas stand out and to improve readability, memo writers make liberal use of graphic highlighting techniques. The content of many informational, procedural, and confirmation memos lends itself to numbered or bulleted items, headings, tables, and other techniques you studied in Chapter 5.

Effective memos contain guide-word headings, focus on a single topic, are concise and conversational, and use graphic highlighting.

Writing Process for Memos

Memo writing requires careful preparation and follows the 3 × 3 writing process.

Like letters and other messages, good memos require careful preparation. Although they often seem routine, it's wise to remember that they may travel farther than you expect. Consider the market researcher in Toronto, new to her job and eager to please her boss, who was asked to report on the progress of her project. Off the top of her head, she prepared a quick summary of her work and delivered her handwritten memo to her boss. Later that week the vice president of Marketing asked her boss how the project was progressing and was given the market researcher's hurried memo. The resulting poor impression was difficult for the new employee to overcome.

Careful writing takes time—especially at first. By following a systematic plan and practising, however, you can speed up your efforts and greatly improve the product. Bear in mind, moreover, that the effort you make to improve your communication skills can pay big dividends. Frequently, your speaking and writing abilities determine how much influence you'll have in your organization. Like other writing tasks, memo writing follows the familiar three-phase writing process.

Analyzing the purpose of a message helps determine whether a permanent record is required.

Analysis, anticipation, and adaptation. In Phase 1 you'll need to spend some time analyzing your task before writing. It's amazing how many of us are ready to put our pens or computers into gear before engaging our minds. Ask yourself three important questions:

- *Do I really need to write this memo?* A phone call or a quick visit to a nearby co-worker might solve the problem—and save the time and expense of a written message. On the other hand, as Susan O'Brien says, some memos are needed as a permanent record.

- *Why am I writing?* Know why you are writing and what you hope to achieve. This will help you recognize what the important points are and where to place them.

- *How will the reader react?* Visualize the reader and the effect your message will have. Consider ways to shape the message to benefit the reader.

Research, organization, and composition. In Phase 2 you'll want to check the files, gather documentation, and prepare your message. Make an outline of the points you wish to cover. For short messages you can jot down notes on the document you are answering. Be sure to prepare for revision because excellence is rarely achieved on the first attempt. Remember that a computer makes writing and especially rewriting much easier.

Revision, proofreading, and evaluation. In Phase 3, careful and conscientious writers revise their messages, proofread the final copy, and make an effort to evaluate the success of their communication.

- **Revise for clarity.** Viewed from the receiver's perspective, are the ideas clear? Do they need more explanation? If the memo is passed on to others, will they need further explanation? Consider having a colleague critique your message.

- **Proofread for correctness.** Are the sentences complete and punctuated properly? Are there any typos or misspelled words? Remember to run your spelling checker and to proofread your printout before sending it.

The writing process for memos—as for all documents—begins with analysis. Do you really need to send this message? A phone call might save the time and expense of a written message. But when you must deliver clear instructions or make a lasting record, plan to write. The time executives spend writing, revising, and reading memos can add up to one full month a year.

- **Plan for feedback.** How will you know if this message is successful? You can improve feedback by making it easy for the receiver to respond, with comments such as *Just initial your approval on this memo, return it to me, and I'll get started immediately.*

Organization of Memos

Direct memos—those that deliver good news or routine information—generally contain four parts: (1) a subject line that summarizes the message, (2) an opening that reveals the main idea immediately, (3) a body that explains and justifies the main idea, and (4) an action closing.

Direct memos contain a subject line, an opener stating the main idea, a body with explanation and justification, and an action closing.

Subject line. In letters a subject line is optional; in memos it is mandatory. The subject line should summarize the central idea. It provides quick identification for the reader and for filing. As you learned in Chapter 6, the subject line is usually written in an abbreviated style, often without articles (*a, an, the*). It need not be a complete sentence, and it does not end with a period. It should be concise but provide enough information to be clear, as shown here:

SUBJECT: Staff Meeting May 3, 9 a.m., Room 10 (rather than simply *Meeting*)

SUBJECT: Proposal for Spring Marketing Plan (rather than *Proposal*)

SUBJECT: Instructions for Operating New Copy Machine (rather than *Copy Machine*)

Opening. Most internal communication covers nonsensitive information that can be handled in a straightforward manner. "The memos that grab me tell right away what the writer has in mind," says corporate executive Doris Margonine.[6] Begin by frontloading; that is, reveal the main idea immediately. Even though the purpose of the memo is summarized in the subject line, that purpose should be restated—and amplified—in the first sentence. Some readers skip the subject line and plunge right into the first sentence. Notice how the following indirect memo openers can be improved by frontloading.

Most direct memos convey nonsensitive information and thus frontload the main idea in the opening.

Indirect Opening	**Direct Opening**
For the past six months the Human Resources Development Department has been considering changes in our employees' benefit plan.	Please review the following proposal regarding employees' benefits, and let me know by May 20 if you approve these changes.
As you may know, employees in Document Production have been complaining about tired eyes as a result of the overhead fluorescent lighting in their centre.	If you agree, I'll order six high-intensity task desk lamps at $189 each for use in the Document Production Centre.

Body. The body of a memo provides more information about the reason for writing. It explains and discusses the subject logically. Arrange your data for easy comprehension by using numbered lists, headings, tables, and other graphic highlighting techniques. Compare the following versions of the same message. Observe how the graphic devices of columns, headings, and white space make the main points easy to comprehend.

Hard-to-Read Paragraph Version

Effective immediately are the following air travel guidelines. Between now and December 31, only account executives may take company-approved trips. These individuals will be allowed to take a maximum of two trips, and they are to travel economy or budget class only.

Improved Version with Graphic Highlighting

Effective immediately are the following air travel guidelines:

- Who may travel: Account executives only
- How many trips: A maximum of two trips
- By when: Between now and December 31
- Air class: Economy or budget class only

Closing. Memos generally end with (1) action information, dates, or deadlines; (2) a summary of the message; or (3) a closing thought. Here again the value of thinking the message through before actually writing it becomes apparent. This is where readers look for deadlines and action language. An effective memo closing might be *Please submit your report by June 15 so that we can have your data before our July planning session.*

In more complex memos a summary of main points may be an appropriate closing. If no action request is made and a closing summary is unnecessary, you might end with a simple concluding thought (*I'm glad to answer your questions* or *This sounds like a useful project*). Although you needn't close memos with good-will statements such as those found in letters to customers or clients, some closing thought is often necessary to prevent a feeling of abruptness. Closings can show gratitude or encourage feedback with remarks such as *I sincerely appreciate your cooperation* or *What are your ideas on this proposal?* Other closings look forward to what's next, such as *How would you like to proceed?* As in routine letters, avoid trite expressions. Overused endings such as *Please let me know if I may be of further assistance* sound mechanical and insincere.

Putting it all together. Now let's put it all together. The following memo is the first draft of a message Steven Wu, Mail Services supervisor, wrote to his supervisor. Although it contains solid information, the message is so wordy and poorly organized that the reader will have trouble grasping its significance.

MEMO TO: Andrea Kanarek

This memo is in response to your recent inquiry about mail costs. Your message of April 30 said that you wanted a brief explanation of what is being done in Mail Services to cut back on overall costs. I can tell you that I've been doing many things to cut costs.

For one thing, I'm trying very hard to locate duplicate names and addresses inadvertently included in our mailing lists. This problem is particularly difficult when we merge multiple mailing lists. Another thing I'm doing relates to envelope size. Departments that use envelopes larger than 6⅛ by 11½ are costing us a lot of money, which they do not realize. Therefore, I am making a proposal to all departments to limit envelope size.

Finally, I'm looking into the possibility of presorting some of our first- and third-class mail. Mailings that are presorted are charged less.

Repeats information the reader already knows. Fails to open with information the reader wants.

Fails to help reader see the three main points. Overuses "I." Uses wordy expressions, such as "making a proposal" instead of *proposing*.

Fails to provide any form of conclusion.

Steven's revised message appears in Figure 7.2. To improve readability, he used bullets and boldfaced headings that emphasize the three actions he's taking to cut costs in his department. Notice, too, that he developed a more conversational tone and de-emphasized "I" in his second version. Compare the revision with Steven's first draft. Which memo will make a better impression on his boss?

Forms of Memos

Memos in today's offices may appear in two forms: (1) hard-copy standard memos (printed on paper) or (2) electronic mail (E-mail) memos (sent over computer networks). Although many larger companies are rapidly installing E-mail networks, smaller organizations still rely on standard memos printed and distributed on paper. In 1994 the Computer and Telecommunications Services Division of the Management Board Secretariat estimated that approximately 28 000 government employees were using some form of E-mail system.[7]

Memos may be transmitted by hard-copy or E-mail.

Standard Memos

Most memos printed on paper begin with TO, FROM, DATE, and SUBJECT. Some organizations provide stationery with these printed guide words (see Figure 7.1). Aligning the text that follows the guide words, however, can be difficult on today's computers and printers. Employees using computers may prefer to skip the printed memo stationery and type in the guide words themselves, as Steven Wu did in his memo in Figure 7.2. You can simplify the process by storing a master form to be recalled any time you begin a memo.

Master formats stored in word processors are useful in standard memos.

The position of the date varies; it could appear first, in the middle, or after the subject line. Some memos, especially in large organizations, include additional guide words, such as *Routing*, *Department*, *Floor*, or *Reference File*. When memos are addressed to groups of people, their names may be listed under the word *Distribution* in the heading or in the lower left corner.

Unlike business letters, memos are usually unsigned. Instead, writers initial the *FROM* line. Close friends may add salutations *(Dear Jan)* and signatures to personalize their memos, but generally memos do not include these items. For additional information about formatting memos, consult Appendix B.

FIGURE 7.2 ■ Information Memo

The Three Phases of the Writing Process

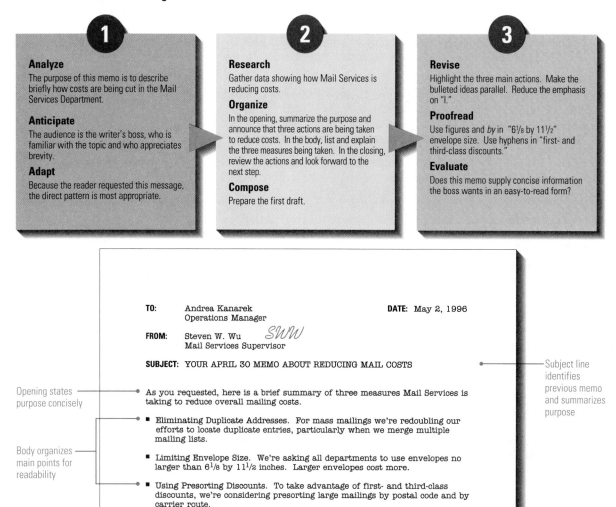

1

Analyze
The purpose of this memo is to describe briefly how costs are being cut in the Mail Services Department.

Anticipate
The audience is the writer's boss, who is familiar with the topic and who appreciates brevity.

Adapt
Because the reader requested this message, the direct pattern is most appropriate.

2

Research
Gather data showing how Mail Services is reducing costs.

Organize
In the opening, summarize the purpose and announce that three actions are being taken to reduce costs. In the body, list and explain the three measures being taken. In the closing, review the actions and look forward to the next step.

Compose
Prepare the first draft.

3

Revise
Highlight the three main actions. Make the bulleted ideas parallel. Reduce the emphasis on "I."

Proofread
Use figures and *by* in "6^1/$_8$ by 11^1/$_2$" envelope size. Use hyphens in "first- and third-class discounts."

Evaluate
Does this memo supply concise information the boss wants in an easy-to-read form?

TO: Andrea Kanarek Operations Manager	**DATE:** May 2, 1996
FROM: Steven W. Wu *SWW* Mail Services Supervisor	

SUBJECT: YOUR APRIL 30 MEMO ABOUT REDUCING MAIL COSTS

Subject line identifies previous memo and summarizes purpose

Opening states purpose concisely

As you requested, here is a brief summary of three measures Mail Services is taking to reduce overall mailing costs.

Body organizes main points for readability

■ Eliminating Duplicate Addresses. For mass mailings we're redoubling our efforts to locate duplicate entries, particularly when we merge multiple mailing lists.

■ Limiting Envelope Size. We're asking all departments to use envelopes no larger than 6^1/$_8$ by 11^1/2 inches. Larger envelopes cost more.

■ Using Presorting Discounts. To take advantage of first- and third-class discounts, we're considering presorting large mailings by postal code and by carrier route.

These are cost-reduction steps we've taken thus far. If you'd like more detailed information, I'd be happy to talk with you about our efforts or to prepare a more formal report.

Closing summarizes and looks forward to next action

Electronic Mail Memos

Instead of sending memos printed on paper, increasing numbers of business-people are communicating by electronic mail (E-mail). E-mail requires computers, modems, and software. Messages travel electronically over networks connected by telephone lines and satellites. Almost instantly, a keyboarded memo travels to another computer—whether on the next desk or halfway around the world. The message remains stored in the receiver's mailbox until accessed. Then the receiver may edit, store, delete, print, or forward the message—and all without paper.

North America's larger business organizations are rapidly embracing communication by E-mail (called "messaging" as in "Why don't you 'message'

FIGURE 7.3 ■ Sample E-mail Message

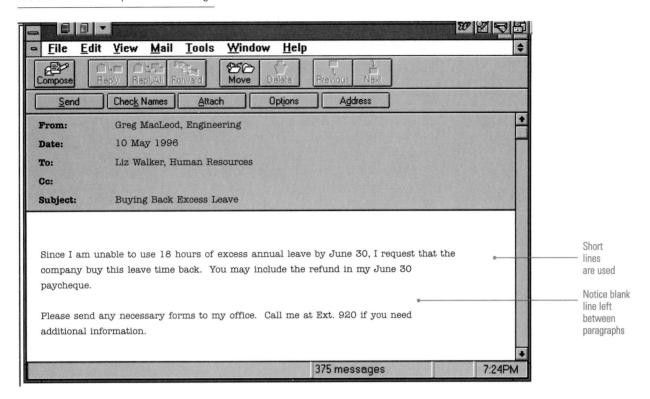

From:	Greg MacLeod, Engineering
Date:	10 May 1996
To:	Liz Walker, Human Resources
Cc:	
Subject:	Buying Back Excess Leave

Since I am unable to use 18 hours of excess annual leave by June 30, I request that the company buy this leave time back. You may include the refund in my June 30 paycheque.

Please send any necessary forms to my office. Call me at Ext. 920 if you need additional information.

Short lines are used

Notice blank line left between paragraphs

375 messages   7:24PM

me?"). In fact, the growth of E-mail has outpaced that of telephones when they first appeared. Millions of messages are now sent electronically. But some users have legitimate complaints about "brain dumping" and information overload. Although the benefits of E-mail far outweigh its disadvantages, organizations can take measures to make E-mail more efficient and less burdensome, as discussed in the Technology box on page 193.

Currently, E-mail is most effective in delivering simple messages, such as that shown in Figure 7.3. Complex information should probably be sent by hard copy. Although E-mail messages are usually short, they require the same planning and care as conventional communication.

Early users were encouraged to "ignore stylistic and grammatical considerations." They thought that "words on the fly," as E-mail messages were considered, required little editing or proofing. Correspondents used emoticoms (like sideways happy faces) to express their emotions. And some E-mail today is still "quick and dirty." But as the medium matures, messages are becoming more proper and more professional. Today, the average E-mail message may remain in the company's computer system for up to five years. And in some instances the only impression a person has of the E-mail writer is from a transmitted message. That's why it's important to take the time to organize your thoughts, compose carefully, and be concerned with correct grammar, spelling, and punctuation. Because of the increase of E-mail use, the Information and Privacy

Use E-mail to deliver simple messages and hard-copy for more complex messages.

Commissioner of Ontario published a report entitled *Privacy Protection Principles for Electronic Mail Systems*. The report covers principles that should be considered when implementing corporate E-mail. Organizations are being encouraged "to create an explicit policy which addresses the privacy of E-mail users."[8]

Smart E-mail Practices

Simplicity and economy are especially important in E-mail messages. The small size of computer monitors makes short sentences and small paragraphs most readable. Writers will therefore want to curb any tendencies toward wordiness. But they should also avoid excessive informality. One researcher found that E-mail writers used "much more emotional language than when they communicated in other ways, up to and including language used in locker rooms."[9]

Smart E-mail business communicators are also learning its dangers. They know that their messages can travel (intentionally or unintentionally) long distances. A quickly drafted note may end up in the boss's mailbox or be forwarded to an adversary's box. Making matters worse, recent events in the United States have shown that computers—like elephants and spurned lovers—never forget.[10] Even erased messages can remain on disk drives, as Colonel Oliver North and his accusers learned during the Iran-Contra hearings. In another highly publicized case, comments made by the police over an internal E-mail system were recovered and became evidence in the Rodney King beating case in Los Angeles. "It's as if people put their brains on hold when they write E-mail," said one expert. "It's a substitute for a phone call, and that's the danger."[11]

Despite its dangers and limitations, E-mail is definitely here to stay. Here are some pointers to help you use it safely and effectively.

- **Think first!** Because E-mail is far from private, do not send sensitive, confidential, inflammatory, or potentially embarrassing messages. E-mail is not like a telephone call. It creates a permanent record; even deleting it does not always remove it permanently from company records.

- **Upload your message.** For all but the briefest messages, compose in a word processing program and upload to the E-mail network. Many E-mail text editors are primitive; therefore, you'll be able to compose and revise more easily with your familiar word processing program.

- **Provide a descriptive subject line.** Nearly all E-mail systems include a prompt for a subject. This subject often determines *whether* a message will be read and *when* it will be read. Thus, you'll want to make subject lines compelling, accurate, and informative. For example, instead of *Meeting*, try *Attend Urgent Budget-Slashing Meeting*.

- **Remember the reader's monitor.** Because some monitors have a limited capacity, don't rely on word wrap. Keep your lines under 80 characters (under 60 characters if your message may be forwarded), and use the enter key whenever you want to end a line. Write short paragraphs, preceding each with a blank line. Moreover, avoid boldface and italics if you have any doubt that the receiver can accommodate them.

- **Care about correctness.** Initially, senders and receivers of E-mail tended to be casual about spelling, grammar, and punctuation. Today, though, E-mail is becoming a mainstream channel of communication. It's wise to remember that people are still judged by their writing, whether electronic

E-MAIL: BRAIN DUMP OR COMMUNICATION ENHANCER?

Once viewed as the panacea for paper-clogged offices, E-mail is fast becoming a brain dump, complain many users. Because of its remarkable advantages, electronic mail rapidly revolutionized business communication in the 1990s. Even its greatest critics would not dispute that E-mail:[12]

- Reduces telephone tag, shrinks telephone bills, and improves response times.

- Eliminates time-zone barriers, enabling users to send and receive messages 24 hours a day, 365 days a year.

- Shortens the cycle of written communication because messages need not be rekeyed.

- Encourages open communication and flattens corporate hierarchies.

- Speeds decision-making, reduces telephone interruptions, and facilitates meeting planning.

- Enhances workday flexibility by allowing people to work at home or at remote locations.

So what's the beef? Users now complain of information overload. They're receiving too much E-mail! It's not unusual for managers to receive 50 to 150 messages daily, all demanding reading and response. Computer systems are increasingly clogged with hundreds of unsorted electronic messages, some important and many not so important. E-mail is so convenient that people use it for everything. One manager griped, "It's a brain dump. I think 50 percent of E-mail is a complete waste of time to the person who receives it."[13]

Just a flick of a key distributes a message to an entire organization. As a result, many E-mail users are overwhelmed by the rapid accumulation of messages. One Fortune 500 manager had a system in which each mailbox held 458 messages. After one was full, the manager would open a second mailbox, which also quickly filled up. Eventually, the company called in consultants to teach its managers how to keep up with the volume of mail and to dispose of messages they had acted on.

Here are some of the suggestions given by consultants to organizations striving to help users control their glut of E-mail:[14]

- Designate an E-mail team to develop procedures for getting the most out of the system.

- Pre-program function keys to capture time-saving keystrokes such as calendar reminders and delete functions.

- Create electronic files for messages that must be saved.

- Organize electronic subject folders for quick retrieval of filed messages.

- Name a common folder or electronic bulletin board where senders can route reports and memos meant for general distribution.

- Recommend that a busy manager give his or her computer access codes to a trained assistant to screen unwanted messages.

- Set up formal training for everyone using an organization's E-mail system.

Properly managed, E-mail can enhance communication and boost productivity. The trick, though, is in the managing.

Career Track Application

Conduct a class discussion about the use and abuse of E-mail. Who is using E-mail at home or on the job? What kind of messages are sent? What do users like about E-mail? What complaints do they have? Is E-mail appropriate for personal messages on the job? Is it safe for transmitting confidential information? Should company guidelines for use of E-mail be established?

or paperbased. Some business people have been passed over for promotions as a result of sloppy E-mail messages. And some E-mail memos never intended for mass distribution have been downloaded into print and distributed through entire organizations. Correctness still counts.

- **Practise E-mail etiquette.** Don't read printed E-mail messages waiting to be picked up from a printer. They are considered confidential. To avoid possible embarrassment, always ask for permission before forwarding someone else's E-mail message.

Planning for the arrival of special guests includes the exchange of many procedure and information memos within the host organization. Communication about unusual events, as well as everyday business, can be carried out by sending E-mail messages or traditional hard-copy memos.

- **Protect against E-mail break-ins.** Don't give your password to anyone (except perhaps a trusted assistant who sorts your messages). Change your password frequently. Beware of anyone claiming by phone or E-mail to be a technician or administrator working on the system.

Writers of memos, both electronic and hard-copy, run other risks. For advice on specific pitfalls to avoid in crafting memos, see the Career Skills box on page 196.

Kinds of Memos

Although many different kinds of memos are written to conduct the operations of any organization, their functions can generally be grouped into three categories: (1) procedure and information memos, (2) request and reply memos, and (3) confirmation memos.

Procedure and Information Memos

Procedure and information memos usually flow downward and convey clear information about daily operations.

Most internal memos describe procedures and distribute information. These messages typically flow downward from management to employees and relate to the daily operation of an organization. These nonsensitive messages follow the overall memo plan: clear subject line, direct opening, explanation, and closing. They have one primary function: to convey your idea so clearly that no further explanation (return memo, telephone call, or personal visit) is necessary.

In writing information and procedure memos, be careful of the tone. Today's managers seek employee participation and cooperation, but they can't achieve that rapport if they sound like dictators or autocrats. Avoid making accusations and fixing blame. Rather, explain changes, give reasons, and suggest benefits to the reader. Assume that employees want to contribute to the success of the organization and to their own achievements. Remember, too, that saying something negatively *(Don't park in Lot A)* is generally less helpful than saying it positively *(Park only in Lot B until Lot A is repaired)*.

The following procedure memo about large printing bills is disappointing both in content and tone.

MEMO TO: Staff Members

Lately, very large expenditures for printing jobs have been submitted, particularly bills being paid to PrintMasters. These bills are suspiciously large and can no longer be honoured without careful scrutiny.

Henceforth, all employees may not send out printing jobs without prior written notice. Using PrintMasters as our sole source must stop. Therefore, authorization is now required for all printing. Two copies of any printing order must be submitted to Kelly before any job is commenced. Please see Kelly if you have any questions.

Thank you for your cooperation.

The following improved version of this memo delivers essentially the same message. It reflects, however, a more cooperative tone and illustrates clear thinking and expression.

MEMO TO: Staff

To improve budget planning and to control costs, please follow the new procedures listed below in submitting future requests for outside printing jobs.

In our business, of course, printing is a necessary expenditure. However, our bills seem very high lately, particularly those from PrintMasters. The following procedures should help protect us from being overcharged:

1. Determine your exact printing specifications for a particular job.

2. Secure two estimates for the job.

3. Submit the written estimates to Kelly.

4. Place the order after receiving approval.

These new procedures will result in more competitive pricing and perhaps may even provide you with new creative printing options.

The preceding procedure memo applies a direct strategy in telling how to complete a task. Information memos also use that straightforward approach in supplying details about organization activities, services, and actions. The following memo describes four child-care options. Notice how the information was designed for maximum visual impact and readability. Imagine how it would have looked if it had been presented in one or two big paragraphs.

MEMO TO: Staff

Members of your employee council have met with representatives from management to consider the following four options for providing child care.

1. *On-site day-care centres.* This option accommodates employees' children on the premises. Weekly rates would be competitive with local commercial day-care facilities. This option is the most costly but is worth pursuing, particularly if local facilities are deficient.

2. *Off-site centres in conjunction with other local employers.* We are looking into the possibility of developing central facilities to be shared with nearby firms.

3. *Neighbourhood child-care centres.* We would contract with local centres to buy open slots for employees' children, perhaps at a discount.

AVOIDING SIX CARDINAL SINS IN WRITING MEMOS

Used carefully, memos deliver vital information and serve valuable functions within organizations. Used incorrectly, they only create problems and reduce productivity. Here are six cardinal sins you'll want to avoid in composing memos on the job:

- **Using an open memo—known as a shotgun or blister memo—to criticize a person or a department.** Shooting it out in a memo can trigger feuds that hurt even those not directly targeted. In the end the initial gunner may be the individual who gets shot down. If you are angry or emotional when writing, don't send the message immediately. Set it aside. After a cooling-off period, you'll probably see the situation differently. When delivering criticism, try to do it in person.

- **Distributing a memo universally.** Resist the urge to send your memo—no matter how artistically crafted—to the entire staff for their edification and enjoyment. Address only the individuals directly involved. If a message requires no reply, put Information Only at the top or near the subject line.

- **Expecting confidential memos to remain a secret.** Don't write anything that you couldn't say publicly. When your memo (or E-mail) leaves your computer, it's no longer under your control. And marking a document

"Personal" or "Confidential" may actually attract attention. Remember that sensitive topics should be discussed in person.

- **Requiring readers to locate previous correspondence.** It's inconsiderate and inefficient to ask readers to locate documents that may be filed or difficult to find. Help readers by attaching copies of relevant reference materials or by providing brief summaries.

- **Forgetting to make it easy for readers to respond.** You can save your readers' time (and your organization's money) by encouraging them to jot a response down on your memo and return it. Be sure to indicate exactly what information or action you expect.

- **Copying your predecessor's style.** Unless your predecessor was an exceptionally fine writer, you're probably better off developing a writing style that fits your personality. Remember that today's writing is warmer and less formal than the style of messages in the past.

Career Track Application

Collect and analyze memos from your work, your college or university, and your friends. Do any seem to commit the sins described here? Throughout your course collect memos and other internal documents for class discussion.

---

4. *Sick-child services.* This plan would provide employees with alternatives to missing work when their children are sick. We are investigating sick-child programs at local hospitals and services that send workers to employees' homes to look after sick children.

Ends with forward-looking statement. No action required.

As soon as we gather more information about these options, we will pass it along to you.

Request and Reply Memos

Request and reply memos follow the direct pattern in seeking or providing information.

In requesting routine information or action within an organization, the direct approach works best. Generally, this means asking for information or making the request without first providing elaborate explanations and justifications. Remember that readers are usually thinking, "Why me? Why am I receiving this?" Readers can understand the explanation better once they know the request.

If you are seeking answers to questions, you have two options for opening the memo: (1) Ask the most important question first, followed by an explanation and then the other questions. (2) Use a polite command, such as *Please answer the following questions regarding ...*

In the body of the memo, you can explain and justify your request or reply. When many questions must be asked, list them, being careful to phrase them similarly. Be courteous and friendly. In the closing include an end date (with a reason, if possible) to promote a quick response. For simple requests some writers encourage their readers to jot down their responses directly on the request memo. This practice saves everyone time.

The following request memo seeks information from managers about the use of temporary office workers. It begins with a polite command followed by numbered questions. Notice that the writer develops reader's benefits by describing how the data collected will be used to help the reader. Notice, too, the effort to promote the feeling that the writer is part of a team working together with employees to achieve their common goals.

MEMO TO: Department Managers

Please answer the questions below about the use of temporary help in your department.

> *Opens with polite command. Explains the purpose concisely.*

With your ideas we plan to develop a policy that will help us improve the process of budgeting, selecting, and hiring temporaries.

1. What is the average number of temporary office workers you employ each month?

2. What is the average length of a temporary worker's assignment in your department?

3. What specific job skills are you generally seeking in your temporaries?

4. What temporary agencies are you now using?

> *Lists parallel questions for easy reading and comprehension.*

Just write your answers on this sheet, and return it to me before January 20. By the end of the month, we plan to have an improved policy that will help you fill your temporary employment needs as efficiently as possible.

> *Includes end date, along with reason; makes it easy for reader to respond.*

In replying to simple requests that require no file copies, you can simply write your remarks on the original memo and return it. For more complex answers, use the direct approach outlined earlier.

Writers sometimes fall into bad habits in answering memos. Here are some trite and long-winded openers that are best avoided:

In response to your message of the 15th ... *(States the obvious.)*

Thank you for your memo of the 15th in which you ... *(Suggests the writer can think of nothing more original.)*

I have before me your memo of the 15th in which you ... *(Unnecessarily identifies the location of the previous message.)*

Pursuant to your request of the 15th ... *(Sounds old-fashioned.)*

This is to inform you that ... *(Delays getting to the point.)*

Please refer to your memo of ... *(Asks reader to search for original document. Always supply a copy if necessary or summarize its points.)*

Instead of falling into the trap of using one of the preceding shopworn openings, start directly by responding to the writer's request. If you agree to the request, show your cheerful compliance immediately. Consider these good-news openers:

Yes, I will be glad to ... *(Sends message of approval by opening with "Yes.")*

Here are answers to the questions you asked about ... *(Sounds straightforward, businesslike, and professional.)*

You're right in seeking advice about ... *(Opens with two words that every reader enjoys seeing and hearing.)*

We are happy to assist you in ... *(Shows writer's helpful nature and goodwill.)*

The information you requested is shown on the attached ... *(Gets right to the point.)*

After a direct and empathic opener, give the information requested in a logical and coherent order. If you're answering a number of questions, arrange your answers in the order of the questions. In the favourable reply shown in Figure 7.4, information describing dates, speakers, and topics is listed in columns with headings. Although it requires more space than the paragraph format, this arrangement vastly improves readability and comprehension.

In providing additional data, use familiar words, short sentences, short paragraphs, and active-voice verbs. When alternatives exist, make them clear. Consider using graphic highlighting techniques, as shown in Figure 7.4 for both the speakers' schedules and the two program choices offered further along in the memo. Imagine how much more effort would be required to read and understand the memo without the speaker list or the numbered choices.

If further action is required, be specific in spelling it out. What may be crystal clear to you (because you have been thinking about the problem) is not always immediately apparent to a reader with limited time and interest. Figure 7.4 not only illustrates a readable, well-organized reply memo, it also reviews formatting tips.

Confirmation Memos

Confirmation memos—also called to-file reports or incident reports—record oral decisions, directives, and discussions. They create a concise, permanent record that could be important in the future. Because people may forget, alter, or retract oral commitments, it's wise to establish a written record of significant happenings. Such records are unnecessary, of course, for minor events. The confirmation memo shown in Figure 7.5 reviews the significant points of a sales agreement discussed in a telephone conversation. When you write a memo to confirm an oral agreement, remember these tips:

- Include names and titles of individuals involved.

- Itemize major issues or points concisely.

- Request feedback regarding unclear or inaccurate points.

Another type of confirmation memo simply verifies receipt of materials or a change of schedule. It is brief and often kept on file to explain your role in a project. For example, suppose you are coordinating an interdepartmental budget report. Marie Nadeau from Human Resources calls to let you know that her part of the report will be a week late. To confirm, you would send Marie the following one-sentence memo: *This memo verifies our telephone conversation of November 5 in which you said that your part of the budget report will be submitted November 14 instead of November 7.* Notice that the tone is objective, not accusatory. However, if you are later questioned about why your project is running late (and you probably will be), you'll have a record of the explanation. In fact, you should probably give your superior a copy so that he or she can intervene if necessary.

FIGURE 7.4 ■ Reply Memo

Tips for Memo Formatting

• Set one tab to line up all entries evenly after SUBJECT.

• Leave two blank lines between SUBJECT line and first line of memo text.

• Single-space all but the shortest memos. Double-space between paragraphs.

• For memos printed on plain paper, leave a top margin of 2 inches for full-page memos and 1 inch for half-page memos.

• Use 1¼-inch side margins.

• If a memo requires two pages, use a second-page heading that includes the addressee's name, page number, and date.

• Write your initials by hand after your typed name.

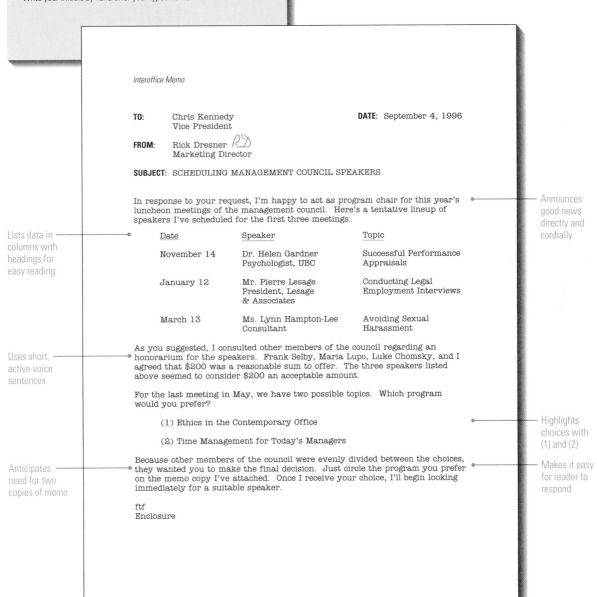

Interoffice Memo

TO: Chris Kennedy   **DATE:** September 4, 1996
           Vice President

FROM: Rick Dresner *RD*
           Marketing Director

SUBJECT: SCHEDULING MANAGEMENT COUNCIL SPEAKERS

In response to your request, I'm happy to act as program chair for this year's luncheon meetings of the management council. Here's a tentative lineup of speakers I've scheduled for the first three meetings.

Date	Speaker	Topic
November 14	Dr. Helen Gardner Psychologist, UBC	Successful Performance Appraisals
January 12	Mr. Pierre Lesage President, Lesage & Associates	Conducting Legal Employment Interviews
March 13	Ms. Lynn Hampton-Lee Consultant	Avoiding Sexual Harassment

As you suggested, I consulted other members of the council regarding an honorarium for the speakers. Frank Selby, Maria Lupo, Luke Chomsky, and I agreed that $200 was a reasonable sum to offer. The three speakers listed above seemed to consider $200 an acceptable amount.

For the last meeting in May, we have two possible topics. Which program would you prefer?

    (1) Ethics in the Contemporary Office

    (2) Time Management for Today's Managers

Because other members of the council were evenly divided between the choices, they wanted you to make the final decision. Just circle the program you prefer on the memo copy I've attached. Once I receive your choice, I'll begin looking immediately for a suitable speaker.

ftf
Enclosure

Announces good news directly and cordially

Lists data in columns with headings for easy reading

Uses short, active-voice sentences

Highlights choices with (1) and (2)

Anticipates need for two copies of memo

Makes it easy for reader to respond

FIGURE 7.5 ■ Confirmation Memo

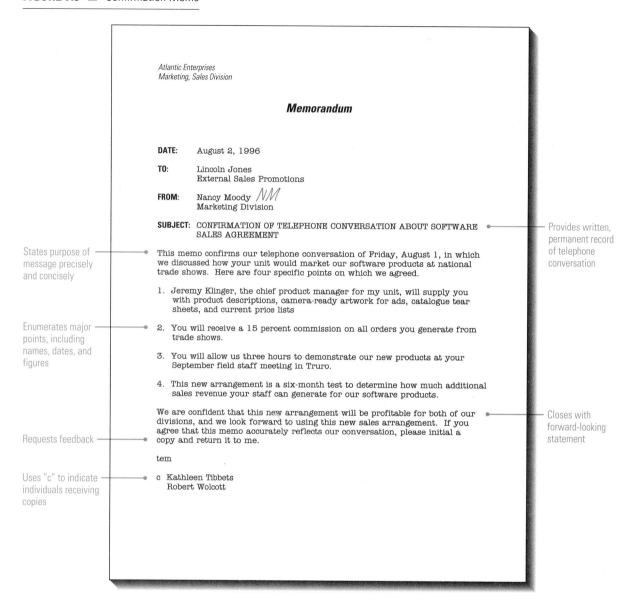

Atlantic Enterprises
Marketing, Sales Division

Memorandum

DATE: August 2, 1996

TO: Lincoln Jones
External Sales Promotions

FROM: Nancy Moody *NM*
Marketing Division

SUBJECT: CONFIRMATION OF TELEPHONE CONVERSATION ABOUT SOFTWARE SALES AGREEMENT

Provides written, permanent record of telephone conversation

States purpose of message precisely and concisely

This memo confirms our telephone conversation of Friday, August 1, in which we discussed how your unit would market our software products at national trade shows. Here are four specific points on which we agreed.

Enumerates major points, including names, dates, and figures

1. Jeremy Klinger, the chief product manager for my unit, will supply you with product descriptions, camera-ready artwork for ads, catalogue tear sheets, and current price lists
2. You will receive a 15 percent commission on all orders you generate from trade shows.
3. You will allow us three hours to demonstrate our new products at your September field staff meeting in Truro.
4. This new arrangement is a six-month test to determine how much additional sales revenue your staff can generate for our software products.

Closes with forward-looking statement

Requests feedback

We are confident that this new arrangement will be profitable for both of our divisions, and we look forward to using this new sales arrangement. If you agree that this memo accurately reflects our conversation, please initial a copy and return it to me.

tem

Uses "c" to indicate individuals receiving copies

c Kathleen Tibbets
Robert Wolcott

Confirmation memos can save employees from being misunderstood or blamed unfairly.

Some critics complain that too many "cover-your-tail" memos are written, thus creating excessive and unnecessary paperwork.[15] However, legitimate memos that confirm and clarify events have saved many thoughtful workers from being misunderstood or blamed unfairly.

Though sometimes taken lightly, office memos, like other business documents, should be written carefully. Once they leave the author's hands, they are essentially published. They can't be retrieved, corrected, or revised. Review the following checklist for tips in writing memos that accomplish what you intend.

■ Checklist for Writing Direct Memos

Subject Line

✓ **Summarize the central idea.** Make the subject line read like a newspaper headline—brief but clear.

✓ **Use an abbreviated style.** Omit articles (*a*, *an*, *the*), and do not try to make the subject line a complete sentence. Omit an ending period.

Opening

✓ **State the purpose for writing.** Include the same information that's in the subject line, but expand it.

✓ **Ask questions immediately.** If you are requesting information, begin with the most important question or use a polite command (*Please answer the following questions about …*).

✓ **Supply information directly.** If responding to a request, give the reader the requested information immediately in the opening. Explain later.

Body

✓ **Explain details.** Arrange information logically. For complex topics use separate paragraphs developed coherently.

✓ **Enhance readability.** Use short sentences, short paragraphs, and parallel construction for similar ideas.

✓ **Supply graphic highlighting.** Provide bulleted and/or numbered lists, tables, or other graphic devices to improve comprehension.

✓ **Be cautious.** Remember that memos, like other documents, often travel far beyond their intended audiences.

Closing

✓ **Request action.** If appropriate, state specifically what you want the reader to do. Include a deadline, with reasons, if possible.

✓ **Summarize the memo or provide a closing thought.** For long memos provide a summary of the important points. If neither an action request nor a summary is necessary, end with a closing thought.

✓ **Avoid clichéd endings.** Use fresher remarks than overused expressions such as *If you have additional questions, please do not hesitate to call* or *Thank you for your cooperation.*

Summary of Learning Goals

1. **Discuss the characteristics of successful memos.** Successful memos begin with TO, FROM, SUBJECT, and DATE, and they generally cover just one topic. They are written conversationally and concisely. Their content often can be highlighted with numbered or bulleted lists, headings, and tables.

2. **Adapt the writing process to memos.** Before writing, decide if you really must write. If you must, analyze your purpose and audience. Collect information, prepare an outline, and compose the first draft on a computer. Revise for clarity and correctness. Encourage feedback from the reader.

3. **Describe the organization of memos.** The subject line summarizes the central idea, while the opening repeats that idea and amplifies it. The body explains and provides more information. The closing includes (a) action information, dates, and deadlines, (b) a summary of the memo, and/or (c) a closing thought.

4. **Distinguish between standard and electronic memos.** Standard memos are printed on paper and circulated in the interoffice mail. Electronic memos are keyboarded on computers and transmitted electronically to computer mailboxes, where they may be printed, edited, stored, deleted, or forwarded.

5. **Explain smart E-mail practices that can make communicators more effective and prevent embarrassment.** Careful E-mail users do not transmit sensitive, confidential, inflammatory, or potentially embarrassing messages. They compose a message on a word processing program and then upload it to the E-mail network. Each message receives a descriptive subject line. To accommodate small-screen monitors, the lines and paragraphs should be kept short. Spelling, grammar, and usage should be correct. Careful E-mail users don't read printed messages waiting to be picked up from a printer, and they do not forward messages without permission. Finally, they protect against break-ins by keeping their passwords confidential.

6. **Write information and procedure memos.** Memos delivering information or outlining procedures follow the direct memo plan with the main idea stated immediately. Ideas must be explained so clearly that no further explanation is necessary. The tone of the memo should encourage cooperation.

7. **Write request and reply memos.** Memos requesting action or information open with a specific request, followed by details. Memos that reply to requests open with the information the reader most wants to know. The body contains details, and the closing may summarize the important points or look forward to a subsequent event or action.

8. **Write confirmation memos.** Sometimes called "to-file reports" or "incident reports," confirmation memos create a permanent record of oral decisions, directives, and discussions. They should include names and titles of involved individuals, major issues discussed, and a request for approval of the receiver.

CHAPTER REVIEW

1. Name five characteristics of successful memos. (Goal 1)

2. What is graphic highlighting, and why is it particularly useful in memos? (Goal 1)

3. Briefly describe the writing process for memos. (Goal 2)

4. What three questions should you ask yourself before writing a business memo? (Goal 2)

5. How is the subject line different from the first sentence of a memo? (Goal 3)

6. Name three ways to close a memo. (Goal 3)

7. How is a standard memo different from an E-mail memo? (Goal 4)

8. What are some of the dangers for users of E-mail? (Goals 4, 5)

9. What advice would you give a first-time E-mail user? (Goal 5)

10. What tone should managers avoid in writing procedure or information memos? (Goal 6)

11. Why should writers of information memos strive to express ideas positively instead of negatively? (Goal 6)

12. Should a request memo open immediately with the request or with an explanation? Why? (Goal 7)

13. What's wrong with a memo opener such as *This is to inform you that...?* (Goal 7)

14. What is a confirmation memo? What other names could it be given? (Goal 8)

15. What three elements should most confirmation memos include? (Goal 8)

DISCUSSION

1. What is the general organizational plan for writing interoffice memos? What are the advantages and disadvantages of using such a plan? (Goals 1, 2)

2. What factors would help you decide whether to write a memo, make a telephone call, or deliver a message in person? (Goals 1, 2)

3. How do memos differ from letters? Consider characteristics such as format, tone, content, and style. (Goals 1, 2, 3)

4. Discuss the ramifications of the following statement: Once a memo or any other document leaves your hands, you have essentially published it. (Goals 2–8)

5. **Ethical Issue:** Should managers have the right to monitor the E-mail messages of employees? Why or why not? What if employees are warned that E-mail could be monitored? If a company sets up an E-mail policy, should only in-house transmissions be monitored? Only outside transmissions?

EXERCISES

7.1 Memo Openers (Goals 1–3)

Revise the following memo openers so that they are more direct.

a. At the meeting of the management council last Thursday, you mentioned a very interesting study that you conducted last year. It reported data regarding employee turnover, and you said that it revealed some intriguing findings. Please send me a copy of your study.

b. I appreciate your asking me for my ideas on quality circles. You know how firmly I believe in them; they could very well be a solution to our longstanding production problems. I've worked out six suggestions that I will describe below.

c. I have before me your memo of the 16th in which you request permission to attend the Desktop Publishing Seminar sponsored by Presentation Planners. As I understand it, this is a two-day seminar scheduled for February 25 and 26. Your reasons for attending were well stated and convincing. You have my permission to attend.

d. As you are aware, the document specialists in your department have been unhappy about their chairs and their inability to adjust the back height. The chairs are uncomfortable and cause back fatigue. As a result, I looked into the possibility of purchasing new adjustable chairs that I think will be just right for these employees. I've ordered new chairs for all employees; they should be arriving in about three weeks.

7.2 Subject Lines

Write effective subject lines for the memos in Exercises 7.1. (Goals 1–3)

7.3 Graphic Highlighting Techniques

Revise the following sets of information so that each is concise and readable. Include an introductory statement or a title before presenting the data in bulleted or numbered lists.

a. When you prepare your departmental budget this year, we want to try something different. We want to use more consistent categories than we've had in the past, so we've added three groups. All requests for personnel (and that includes hourly as well as permanent employees) should now go in one place. Supplies should now be listed as a distinct category, instead of including them under separate projects. Equipment will be handled like supplies, as a new category.

b. Our employee leasing program has proven to be an efficient management tool for business owners because we take care of everything. Our program will handle your payroll preparation. Moreover, benefits for employees are covered. We also know what a chore calculating worker's compensation premiums can be, so we do that for you. And we make all the necessary provincial and federal reports that are required today.

c. We are concerned about your safety in using our automated teller machines (ATMs) at night, so we think you should consider the following tips. Users of ATMs are encouraged to look around—especially at night—before using the service. If you notice anything suspicious, the use of another ATM is recommended. Or you could come back later. Another suggestion that we give our customers involves counting your cash. Be sure that the cash you receive is put away quickly. Don't count it as soon as you get it. It's better to check it in the safety of your car or at home. Also, why not take a friend with you if you must use an ATM at night? We also suggest that you park in a well-lighted area as close to the actual location of the ATM as possible.

7.4 Document for Analysis: Procedure Memo (Goal 6)

Analyze the following memo. List its weaknesses. If your instructor directs, revise the memo.

TO: Field Supervisors
FROM: Estelle McMillan, Senior Supervisor
SUBJECT: Lack of Communication

I shouldn't have to tell you how much we depend on our community volunteers. Without them, many of our programs would fail.

It has come to my attention that field supervisors are not working as effectively with community volunteers as they could be. At a recent field conference, which turned out to be excellent, I picked up a few pointers that I think could prevent us from making any more careless errors in announcing events or in working with our volunteers.

One thing we can do is pay more attention to our flyers and event forms. If they are checked more thoroughly before they are sent out, we may be less likely to leave out vital information—such as the location of one recent event (we received dozens of telephone calls on that boner!). Another thing we must do is make sure that those event announcements go out at least six weeks before the occasion. At the field conference, I also picked up another idea. Other supervisors noted that Girl Guide jargon (such as "Service Unit," "SUM," and "TOS Sale") is not always comprehensible to everyone. We should guard against using such jargon with our volunteers, because chances are that they won't understand it. Another thing we should do: Wake up and show our volunteers how much we appreciate them. They should be praised and recognized for their contributions.

By the way, all trip reports must be turned in by the last Friday in the month if you expect reimbursement.

If you have any questions or suggestions about working with volunteers, please do not hesitate to call me.

7.5 Document for Analysis: Request Memo (Goal 7)

Analyze the following memo. List its weaknesses. If your instructor directs, revise it.

TO: All Employees   DATE: Current
SUBJECT: Elizabeth Risutto, Human Resources
FROM: NEW HOLIDAY PLAN

In the past we've offered all employees 11 holidays (starting with New Year's Day in January and proceeding through Christmas Day the following December). Other companies offer similar holiday schedules.

In addition, we've given all employees one floating holiday. As you know, we've chosen that day by a company-wide vote. As a result, all employees had the same day off. Now, however, management is considering a new plan that we feel would be better. This new plan involves a floating holiday that each individual employee may decide for herself or himself. We've given it considerable thought and decided that such a plan could definitely work. We would allow each employee to choose a day that he or she wants. Of course, we would have to issue certain restrictions. Selections would have to be subject to our staffing needs within individual departments. For example, if everyone wanted the same day, we could not allow everyone to take it. In that case, we would allow the employee with the most seniority to have the day off.

Before we institute the new plan, though, we wanted to see what employees thought about this. Is it better to continue our current company-wide uniform floating holiday? Or should we try an individual floating holiday? Please let us know what you think as soon as possible.

PROBLEMS

7.6 Information Memo: Excellence in Georgia (Goal 6)

After a depressing year of bad news and poor profits, Georgia Power was eager to find ways to improve employee morale. Its president, Bill Dahlberg, dreamed up an award program he calls "Everybody Has a Customer." This program would encourage employees to recognize fellow employees for outstanding effort and excellent achievement on the job.

You think that the award should be a certificate, with room for a picture of the winner. You arrange for Polaroid cameras to be purchased and distributed to all locations. When an employee wishes to make an award, the awarder fills out the certificate and takes two pictures. For maximum visibility you think that one certificate should go to the winner and another should be posted in the central entrance hall—on an employee bulletin board of honour. The program is to begin April 1. To make this program successful, you need to enlist the support of all managers. They, in turn, should inform and encourage employees to participate.

As vice-president of Human Resources Development, write a memo to all managers describing the program and asking for their help. Tell them to discuss the program with their employees and distribute flyers you've had prepared. Encourage them to make comments and suggestions.[16]

7.7 Collaborative Information Memo: Holiday Partying (Goal 6)

You feel that your department should have a Christmas or holiday party this year. After considerable urging, your boss finally agrees to allow one, so long as you and the other employees plan the event and share the costs with the company. You consult most of the people in your department and find that they'd like a Christmas dinner party at a local restaurant. In teams of four or five, work out details, such as date and time, type of dress, costs, guests, exchange of gifts, and entertainment. Then write a memo to your boss, Brian Lockwood, describing your plans and

asking his permission to proceed. Be sure to make it easy for him to read and respond to your memo.

7.8 Procedure Memo: Ticket-Free Parking (Goal 6)

Assume that you are Tran Crozier, director of the Human Resources Division of IBM at Markham, Ontario. Both day- and swing-shift employees need to be reminded of the parking guidelines. Day-shift employees must park in Lots A and B in their assigned spaces. If they have not registered their cars and received their white stickers, the cars will be ticketed.

Day-shift employees are forbidden to park at the curb. Swing-shift employees may park at the curb before 3:30 p.m. Moreover, after 3:30 p.m. swing-shift employees may park in any empty space—except those marked Tandem, Handicapped, Van Pool, Car Pool, or Management. Day-shift employees may lend their spaces to other employees if they know they will not be using the space.

One serious problem is lack of registration (as evidenced by white stickers). Registration is done by Employee Relations. Any car without a sticker will be ticketed. To encourage registration, Employee Relations will be in the cafeteria May 12 and 13 from 11:30 a.m. to 1:30 p.m. and from 3 p.m. to 5 p.m. to take applications and issue white parking stickers.

Write a memo to employees that reviews the parking guidelines and encourages them to get their cars registered. Use itemization techniques and strive for a tone that fosters a sense of cooperation rather than resentment.

7.9 Procedure Memo: Hot Calls in August (Goal 6)

Play the part of Sally Chernoff, division sales manager of DataCom Electronics. The company's long-distance telephone bills have been skyrocketing. Sales reps use the telephone to make "hot" calls—to close deals or to persuade hard-sells. However, Paul Wilson, vice-president of Sales, is not sure that the cost of these calls is worth the return. He suggested sharply reducing or even eliminating all long-distance calls made by sales reps, but you want to collect information first. You propose a plan.

For the month of August, all sales reps are to place their long-distance calls through the company operator (rather than dialling direct). They are to keep a log of all calls, including the date, time, city, and reason for the call. In September you'd like them to give you that telephone log. Then you can analyze the data and perhaps solve this telephone budget crisis. Privately, you hope that the cumbersome procedure will, by itself, decrease the number of calls.

Write a memo to all sales reps describing this procedure. Attach a telephone log. Include reader benefits and itemization techniques.

7.10 Request Memo: Visiting Computers (Goal 7)

Revise the following poorly expressed memo.

TO: Keisha Wilson   DATE: Current
FROM: Douglas Rockland
SUBJECT: Computer Visit

    Please refer to my memo of May 20 in which I raised the possibility of a visitation to be made by you to Berkshire Furniture Company. As I discussed in my memo, my friend Jim Ling is president at Berkshire; and he was telling me how his new multiuser computer system was solving some of the same problems that we have. I've arranged for you to tour their organization Thursday, June 4, at 1 p.m.

    I am interested in a number of things, which we can talk about in my office Monday, June 8 at 10 a.m. after you return from your tour. One problem is connection of terminals from their factory to their order department. How do they do it? Another question I have relates to their accounting department and executive offices. Are these areas on the same computing system? The last thing I want you to be sure to find out about is how this computer system tracks shipments to customers.

    Thank you for your cooperation.

7.11 Reply Memo: Rescheduling Interviews (Goal 7)

Your boss, Fred Knox, had scheduled three appointments to interview applicants for an accounting position. All these appointments were for Friday, October 7. However, he now must travel to Halifax on that weekend. He asks you to reschedule all the appointments for one week later. He also wants a brief summary of the background of each candidate.

You call each person and arrange these times. Paul Scheffel, who has been an accountant for 15 years with Bechtel Corporation, agreed to come at 10:30 a.m. Mark Cunningham, who is a CA and a consultant to many companies, will come at 11:30. Geraldine Simpson, who has a B.A. degree and eight years of experience in payroll accounting, will come at 9:30 a.m. You're wondering if Mr. Knox forgot to include Don Stastry, operations personnel officer, in these interviews. Mr. Stastry usually is part of the selection process.

Write a memo to Mr. Knox including all the vital information he needs.

7.12 Confirmation Memo: Dream Vacation (Goal 8)

Play the role of Jack Otnar. You had a vacation planned for September 2 through 16. But yesterday your wife suggested delaying the vacation for several weeks so that you could drive through Quebec when the fall colours are most beautiful. She said it would be the vacation of her dreams, and you agree. Perhaps you could change your vacation dates. Alas, you remember that you're scheduled to attend the Hampshire marketing exhibit September 29–30. But maybe Melanie Grasso would fill in for you and make the presentation of the company's newest product, JuiceMate. You see your boss, Mas Watanabe, in the hall and decide to ask if you can change your vacation to September 28 through October 12. To your surprise, he agrees to the new dates. He also assures you that he will ask Melanie to make the presentation—and encourage her to give a special demonstration to the Dana Corporation, which you believe should be targeted.

Back in your office, you begin to worry. What if Mas forgets about your conversation? You can't afford to take that chance. Write a confirmation memo that summarizes the necessary facts—and also conveys your gratitude.

CLUE REVIEW 7

Edit the following sentences to correct all language faults, including grammar, punctuation, spelling, and word use.

1. Mr. Krikorian always tries however to wear a tie and shirt that has complimentary colours.

2. The house of commons committee on trade and commerce are holding hearings in twenty-one city's.

3. Consumer buying and spending for the past 5 years, is being studied by a Federal team of analysts.

4. Because we recommend that students bring there own supplies; the total expense for the trip should be a miner amount.

5. Wasnt it Mr Cohen not Ms Lyons who asked for a tuition waver.

6. As soon as we can verify the figures either my sales manager or myself will call you, nevertheless, you must continue to disperse payroll funds.

7. Our human resources department which was formerally in room 35 has moved it's offices to room 5.

8. We have arranged interviews on the following dates, Wednesday at 330 pm thrusday at 1030 am and Friday at 415 pm.

9. The bay news our local newspaper featured as its principle article a story entitled, Smarter E-Mail is here.

10. Every one on the payroll, which includes all dispatchers and supervisers were cautioned to maintain careful records everyday.

Negative News

LEARNING GOALS

After studying this chapter, you should be able to

1 Describe the goals of business communicators when delivering bad news.

2 Identify the causes of legal problems in business writing.

3 Explain the components of a bad-news message.

4 Compare the direct and indirect patterns for breaking bad news. List situations when the direct pattern is more effective.

5 Identify routine requests and describe a strategy for refusing such requests.

6 Describe a strategy for sending bad news to customers while retaining their goodwill.

7 Explain the best strategy for managing negative organization news.

Pepsi-Cola

"It's amazing how a soft drink can become so much a part of people's lives that they feel passionate about it," says Cathy Dial, manager of Consumer Relations at Pepsi-Cola.

Cathy deals with many passionate consumers every day at Pepsi-Cola headquarters in Somers, New York. Her office employs 23 representatives who answer at least 1000 telephone calls and 100 letters every day. The majority of these calls and letters are inquiries about promotions or products, and she can reply with positive information. But sometimes she has to deliver disappointing news or refuse a request.

"The refillable bottle is a really passionate issue for some consumers," says Cathy. "The entire beverage industry has moved away from returnable glass bottles because they are cumbersome, heavy, and expensive. Nonrefillable bottles or cans are lighter, safer, and cheaper. And there's little market for used glass beverage bottles today. What's more, we've learned over the years that the majority of the public likes the convenience of nonrefillable bottles or cans. Yet, we still receive letters saying, 'Pepsi just doesn't taste the same in the cans or in plastic bottles; I want my bottle back!' " Cathy's job is to tell why such a request is impossible for Pepsi-Cola to grant.

"Any consumer who took the time to call or write us represents many more who did not bother to let us know that something is wrong. And people who take the time to call or write are usually our most loyal customers."

Consumers also become passionate when Pepsi-Cola phases out an item. "We have to explain to consumers," says Cathy, "that it's not economically feasible for us to make a tiny batch of one product and maintain an inventory. There are just too many products and too little shelf space."

Other inquiries are from customers who think they have won a prize in a promotion. In one contest a few years ago, the word "Van" appeared under a Pepsi bottle cap. Many people saw the word and called or wrote to claim their car. "Actually," explains Cathy, "'Van' meant that consumers were entitled to a 10 percent discount at Van's Shoes. In a situation like this, our job is to explain carefully the rules of the promotion to the consumer and thank them for participating.

"Sometimes people complain about our sponsorship of TV shows that have celebrities or messages that they don't like or agree with. Because Pepsi-Cola aims for a wholesome,

family-oriented image, we listen carefully to any comments from consumers."

Cathy's office also receives passionate letters asking Pepsi-Cola to contribute money to a charity, to contribute soft drinks for an event, to send employees to participate in events, and to sponsor programs. Pepsi-Cola's employees give generously of their own time, and the company also is a frequent contributor to the United Way, the American Cancer Society, many scholarship funds, and other causes. But it cannot grant every request it receives. In saying no, Cathy tries to explain why the request can't be granted, and she is very careful about the tone of her words.

Targeting teens and young adults, Pepsi launched a Mountain Dew promotion with the tagline "Get Vertical," featuring high-adventure sports. Part of the promotion involved "Vertical Bucks," which consumers used to win prizes. Many more consumers participated than expected, and delays in the delivery of prizes had to be explained. Delivering disappointing news while retaining goodwill requires tact, empathy, and good communication skills.

Generally, when Cathy must deliver disappointing news to consumers, she begins by expressing appreciation. "Any consumer who took the time to call or write us represents many more who did not bother to let us know that something is wrong. And people who take the time to call or write us are usually our most loyal customers. We appreciate their comments, and we channel that information to our internal partners within the company, such as our buyers, public relations people, marketing managers, quality control experts, and senior management."

After expressing appreciation, Cathy usually explains what went wrong or offers reasons to justify a refusal. In some cases, she is able to offer alternatives to soften the bad news. "In one promotion," confesses Cathy, "we underestimated customer response and ran out of gift merchandise. As an alternative, we offered substitute merchandise."

She closes negative-news letters by expressing appreciation again. If the inquiry is about a product, Cathy encourages customers to give Pepsi-Cola another try and encloses coupons for free products.

"Our primary goal," says Cathy, "is to listen with empathy. Consumers want to know that their requests or comments are taken seriously."[1] ▪

Strategies for Breaking Bad News

The sting of bad news can be reduced by giving reasons and communicating sensitively.

Breaking bad news is a fact of business life for Cathy Dial and for most other communicators. Because bad news disappoints, irritates, and sometimes even angers the receiver, such messages must be written carefully. As Cathy suggests, disappointment can be reduced if (1) the reader knows the reasons for the rejection and (2) the bad news is revealed with sensitivity. You've probably heard people say, "It wasn't so much the bad news that I resented. It was the way I was told!"

This chapter concentrates on how to use the indirect pattern in delivering negative messages. You'll apply that pattern to messages that refuse routine requests, deliver bad news to customers, and deal with negative organization news. But you'll also learn to recognize four instances when the direct pattern may be preferable in announcing bad news.

Goals in Communicating Bad News

In communicating bad news, the main goals are to get the receiver to accept it, maintain goodwill, and avoid legal liability.

As a business communicator who must deliver bad news, you have many goals. First, you want to make the reader understand and *accept* the bad news. The indirect pattern helps achieve these objectives. Second, you want to promote and maintain a good image of yourself and your organization. This goal is especially challenging since you are delivering bad news. Third, you want to make the message so clear that additional correspondence is unnecessary. Finally, you want to avoid creating legal liability or responsibility.

These are ambitious goals, and we don't always achieve them all. The patterns you're about to learn, however, provide the beginning communicator with strategies and tactics that many writers have found successful in conveying disappointing news sensitively and safely. With experience, you'll be able to vary these patterns and adapt them to your organization's specific writing tasks.

Using the Indirect Pattern to Prepare the Reader

The indirect pattern softens the impact of bad news by giving reasons and explanations first.

Revealing bad news indirectly shows sensitivity to your reader. Whereas good news can be revealed quickly, bad news must be broken gradually. By preparing the reader, you soften the impact. A blunt announcement of disappointing news might cause the receiver to stop reading and toss the message aside. The indirect strategy enables you to keep the reader's attention until you have been able to explain the reasons for the bad news. The indirect plan consists of four parts, as shown in Figure 8.1:

- **Buffer**—a neutral or positive opening that does not reveal the bad news
- **Reasons**—an explanation of the causes for the bad news before disclosing it
- **Bad news**—a clear but understated announcement of the bad news that may include an alternative or compromise
- **Close**—a personalized, forward-looking, pleasant statement

Avoiding Three Causes of Legal Problems

Before we examine the components of a bad-news message, let's look more closely at how you can avoid exposing yourself and your employer to legal liability in writing negative messages. Although we can't always anticipate the consequences of our words, we should be alert to three causes of legal difficul-

FIGURE 8.1 ■ Four-Part Indirect Pattern for Bad News

Buffer

Open with a neutral or positive statement that does not reveal the bad news.

Reasons

Explain causes of the bad news before disclosing it.

Bad News

Reveal bad news without emphasizing it. Provide alternative or compromise, if possible.

Closing

End with a personalized, forward-looking, pleasant statement. Avoid referring to bad news or apologizing.

ties: (1) abusive language, (2) careless language, and (3) the "good-guy syndrome."

Abusive language. Calling people names (such as "deadbeat," "crook," or "quack") can get you into trouble. *Defamation*, the legal term for injury to reputation is divided into two categories: libel and slander. Libel covers statements that are printed, written, filmed, or recorded in a permanent record. Slander covers oral statements only.

To be actionable (likely to result in a lawsuit), the remarks must (1) be made in public and (2) cause harm. There is a difference between libel law in Canada and in the United States. In the States, the plaintiff "must prove that the statement was made with the intent to cause harm or with a reckless disregard for the truth."[2] Since Canadian courts have not accepted this rule, it is easier to sue for libel in Canada than in the United States.

In a new wrinkle, you may now be prosecuted if you transmit a harassing or libellous message by E-mail on a computer bulletin board. Such electronic transmission is considered to be "published." Moreover, a company may incur liability for messages sent through its computer system by employees. That's why the Eastman Kodak Company does not allow its employees to post Internet messages using the Kodak return address. Other firms are adding a "not speaking for the company" disclaimer to private messages transmitted over networks.[3]

Obviously, competent communicators avoid making unproved charges and letting their emotions prompt abusive language—in print or electronically.

Careless language. As the marketplace becomes increasingly litigious, we must be certain that our words communicate only what we intend. Take the American case of the factory worker injured on the job. Company documents contained a seemingly harmless letter sent to a group regarding a plant tour. These words appeared in the letter: "Although we are honored at your interest in our company, we cannot give your group a tour of the plant operations as it would be too noisy and dangerous." In this case, the court ruled in favour of the worker inferring from the letter that working conditions were indeed hazardous.[4] Although a legal case would not result in Canada in such an instance because of provincial workers' compensation plans, companies must still be aware of such careless wording. The letter writer did not intend to convey the impression of dangerous working conditions, but the court accepted that interpretation.

> Abusive language becomes legally actionable when it is false, harmful to a person's good name, and "published."

This case points up two important cautions. First, be careful in making statements that are potentially damaging or that could be misinterpreted. Be wary of explanations that convey more information than you intend. Second, be careful about what documents you save. Lawyers may demand, in pursuing a lawsuit, all company files pertaining to a case. Even documents marked "Confidential" or "Personal" may be used.

Remember, too, that files deleted from a computer disk can easily be restored by an expert. Thus, an incriminating note or document drawn up on a computer can be recovered even after it has been "erased."

The good-guy syndrome. Most of us hate to have to reveal bad news—that is, to be the bad guy. To make ourselves look better, to make the reader feel better, and to maintain good relations, we are tempted to make statements that are legally dangerous. Consider the case of a law firm interviewing job candidates. One of the firm's partners was asked to inform a candidate that she was not selected. The partner's letter said, "Although you were by far the most qualified candidate we interviewed, unfortunately, we have decided we do not have a position for a person of your talents at this time." To show that he personally had no reservations about this candidate and to bolster the candidate, the partner offered his own opinion. But he differed from the majority of the recruiting committee. When the rejected interviewee learned later that the law firm had hired two male lawyers, she sued, charging sexual discrimination. The court found in favour of the rejected candidate, agreeing that a reasonable inference could be made from the partner's letter that she was the "most qualified candidate."[5] Since The Canadian Human Rights Act prohibits discrimination in employment, such a case might also have a similar ruling.

There are two important lessons here. First, business communicators act as agents of their organizations. Their words, decisions, and opinions are assumed to represent those of the organization. So, if you want to communicate your personal feelings or opinions, use plain paper (rather than company letterhead) and sign your name without your title or affiliation. Second, volunteering extra information can lead to trouble. Thus, avoid supplying information that could be misused, and avoid making promises that can't be kept. Don't admit or imply responsibility for conditions that caused damage or injury. Even apologies (*We're sorry that a faulty bottle cap caused damage to your carpet*) may suggest liability.

In Chapter 3 we discussed four information areas that generate the most lawsuits: investments, safety, marketing, and human resources. In this chapter we'll make specific suggestions for avoiding legal liability in writing responses to claim letters, credit letters, and personnel documents. You may find that in the most critical areas (such as collection letters or hiring and firing messages) your organization provides language guidelines and form letters approved by legal counsel. As the business environment becomes more perilous, we must be not only sensitive to the reader but also keenly aware of risks to ourselves and to the organizations we represent.

Components of a Bad-News Message

Legal issues aside, let's move on to the main topic of this chapter—how to deliver a bad-news message using the indirect pattern. The message will have four parts, as shown in Figure 8.2: buffer, reasons, bad news, and closing.

FIGURE 8.2 ■ Delivering Bad News Sensitively

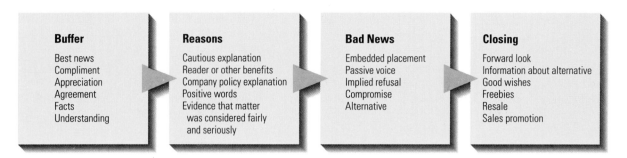

Buffering the opening. A buffer is a device to reduce shock or pain. To buffer the pain of bad news, begin with a neutral or positive statement that makes the reader continue reading. The buffer should be relevant and concise and provide a natural transition to the explanation that follows. The individual situation, of course, will help determine what you should put in the buffer. Here are some possibilities for opening bad-news messages.

Best news. Start with the part of the message that represents the best news. For example, in a memo that announces a new service along with a cutback in mail room hours, you might write, *To ensure that your correspondence goes out with the last pickup, we're starting a new messenger pickup service at 2:30 p.m. daily beginning June 1.*

Compliment. Praise the receiver's accomplishments, organization, or efforts. But do so with honesty and sincerity. For instance, in a letter declining an invitation to speak, you could write, *The Thalians have my sincere admiration for their fund-raising projects on behalf of hungry children. I am honoured that you asked me to speak Friday, November 5.*

Appreciation. Convey thanks to the reader—for doing business, for sending something, for expressing their confidence in your organization, for expressing feelings, or simply for providing feedback. Suppose you had to draft a letter that refuses employment. You could say, *I appreciated learning about your qualifications and the professional secretaries program at Valley College in our interview last Friday.* Avoid thanking the reader, however, for something you are about to refuse.

Agreement. Make a relevant statement with which both reader and receiver can agree. A letter that rejects a loan application might read, *We both realize how much the export business has been affected by the relative strength of the dollar in the past two years.*

Facts. Provide objective information that introduces the bad news. For example, in a memo announcing cutbacks in the hours of the employees' cafeteria, you might say, *During the past five years the number of employees eating breakfast in our cafeteria has dropped from 32 percent to 12 percent.*

Understanding. Show that you care about the reader. Notice how in this letter to customers announcing a product defect, the writer expresses concern: *We know that you expect superior performance from all the office products you order from*

> To reduce negative feelings, use a buffer opening for sensitive bad-news messages.

> Openers can buffer the bad news with compliments, appreciation, agreement, relevant facts, and understanding.

Quill. That's why we're writing personally about the Exell printer ribbons you recently ordered.

Good buffers avoid revealing the bad news immediately. Moreover, they do not convey a false impression that good news follows. Additionally, they provide a natural transition to the next bad-news letter component—the reasons.

Bad-news messages should explain reasons before stating the negative news.

Presenting the reasons. The most important part of a bad-news letter is the section that explains why a negative decision is necessary. As part of your planning before writing, you analyzed the problem and decided to refuse a request for specific reasons. Before disclosing the bad news that may upset the reader, try to explain those reasons.

Being cautious in explaining. If the reasons are not confidential and if they will not create legal liability, you can be specific: *Growers supplied us with a limited number of patio roses, and our demand this year was twice that of last year.* In refusing a speaking engagement, tell why the date is impossible: *On January 17 we have a board of directors meeting that I must attend.* Don't, however, make unrealistic or dangerous statements in an effort to be the "good guy."

Citing reader or other benefits if plausible. Readers are more open to bad news if it helps them. In refusing a customer's request for free hemming of skirts and slacks, one clothing company wrote: "We tested our ability to hem skirts a few months ago. This process proved to be very time-consuming. We have decided not to offer this service because the additional cost would have increased the selling price of our skirts substantially, and we did not want to impose that cost on all our customers."[6] Readers also accept bad news better if they recognize that someone or something else benefits, such as other workers or the environment: *Although we would like to consider your application, we prefer to fill managerial positions from within.* Avoid trying to show reader benefits, though, if they appear insincere: *To improve our service to you, we're increasing our brokerage fees.*

Explaining company policy. Readers resent blanket policy statements prohibiting something: *Company policy prevents us from making cash refunds* or *Contract bids may be accepted from local companies only* or *Company policy requires us to promote from within.* Instead of hiding behind company policy, gently explain why the policy makes sense: *We prefer to promote from within because it rewards the loyalty of our employees. In addition, we've found that people familiar with our organization make the quickest contribution to our team effort.* By offering explanations, you demonstrate that you care about your readers and are treating them as important individuals.

Choosing positive words. As you learned in Chapter 3, the words you use affect a reader's response. Remember that the objective of the indirect pattern is to hold the reader's attention until you've had a chance to explain the reasons justifying the bad news. To keep the reader in a receptive mood, avoid expressions that might cause the reader to tune out. Be sensitive to negative words like *claim, error, failure, fault, impossible, mistaken, misunderstand, never, regret, unwilling, unfortunately,* and *violate.*

Showing that the matter was treated seriously and fairly. In explaining reasons, demonstrate to the reader that you take the matter seriously, have investigated carefully, and are making an unbiased decision. As Cathy Dial at Pepsi-Cola points out, "Consumers are more accepting of disappointing news when they feel that their requests have been heard and that they have been treated fairly." Avoid passing the buck or blaming others within your organization. Such unprofessional behaviour makes the reader lose faith in you and your company.

Cushioning the bad news. Although you can't prevent the disappointment that bad news brings, you can reduce the pain somewhat by breaking the news sensitively. Be especially considerate when the reader will suffer personally from the bad news. A number of thoughtful techniques can cushion the blow.

Positioning the bad news strategically. Instead of spotlighting it, sandwich the bad news between other sentences, perhaps among your reasons. Don't let the refusal begin or end a paragraph—the reader's eye will linger on these high-visibility spots. Another technique that reduces shock is putting a painful idea in a subordinate clause: *Although another candidate was hired, we appreciate your interest in our organization and wish you success in your job search.* Subordinate clauses often begin with words like *although, as, because, if,* and *since.*

Using the passive voice. Passive-voice verbs enable you to depersonalize an action. Whereas the doer of the action has to be named when the verb is in the active voice *(We don't give cash refunds)*, with the passive voice the doer of the action can be omitted, thus highlighting the action *(Cash refunds are not given because …).* Use the passive voice for the bad news.

Accentuating the positive. As you learned in Chapter 3, messages are far more effective when you describe what you can do instead of what you can't do. Rather than *We will no longer allow credit card purchases,* try a more positive appeal: *We are now selling gasoline at discount cash prices.*

Implying the refusal. It's sometimes possible to avoid a direct statement of refusal. Often, your reasons and explanations leave no doubt that a request has been denied. Explicit refusals may be unnecessary and at times cruel. In this refusal to contribute to a charity, for example, the writer never actually says no: *Because we will soon be moving into new offices in Glendale, all our funds are earmarked for moving and furnishings. We hope that next year we'll be able to support your worthwhile charity.* The danger of an implied refusal, of course, is that it is so subtle that the reader misses it. Be certain that you make the bad news clear, thus preventing the need for further correspondence.

Suggesting a compromise or an alternative. A refusal is not so depressing—for the sender or the receiver—if a suitable compromise, substitute, or alternative is available. In denying permission to a class to visit a historical private residence, for instance, this writer softens the bad news by proposing an alternative: *Although private tours of the grounds are not given, we do open the house and its gardens for one charitable event in the fall.*

You can further reduce the impact of the bad news by not dwelling on it. Present it briefly (or imply it), and move on to your closing.

Closing pleasantly. After explaining the bad news sensitively, close the message with a pleasant statement that promotes goodwill. The closing should be personalized and may include a forward look, an alternative, good wishes, freebies, resale information, or an off-the-subject remark.

> Techniques for cushioning bad news include positioning it strategically, using the passive voice, implying the refusal, and suggesting alternatives or compromises.

Forward look. Anticipate future relations or business. A letter that refuses a contract proposal might read: *Thanks for your bid. We look forward to working with your talented staff when future projects demand your special expertise.*

Alternative. If an alternative exists, end your letter with follow-through advice. For example, in a letter rejecting a customer's demand for replacement of land-scaping plants, you might say: *I will be happy to give you a free inspection and consultation. Please call 746–8112 to arrange a date for my visit.*

Good wishes. A letter rejecting a job candidate might read: *We appreciate your interest in our company, and we extend to you our best wishes in your search to find the perfect match between your skills and job requirements.*

Freebies. When customers complain—primarily about food products or small consumer items—companies often send coupons, samples, or gifts to restore confidence and to promote future business. In response to a customer's complaint about a frozen dinner, you could write, *Your loyalty and your concern about our frozen entrees are genuinely appreciated. Because we want you to continue enjoying our healthful and convenient dinners, we're enclosing a coupon that you can use at your local store for your next Green Valley entree.*

Resale or sales promotion. When the bad news is not devastating or personal, references to resale information or promotion may be appropriate: *The computer workstations you ordered are unusually popular because of their stain-, heat-, and scratch-resistant finishes. To help you locate hard-to-find accessories for these workstations, we're enclosing our latest catalogue, in which you'll find surge suppressors, multiple outlet strips, security devices, and PC tool kits.*

Avoid endings that sound canned, insincere, inappropriate, or self-serving or that invite further correspondence (*If you have any questions, do not hesitate ...*). Don't refer to the bad news, and in general don't apologize. Apologies tend to be counterproductive; they undermine your decision and may unwittingly suggest legal responsibility. To review these suggestions for delivering bad news sensitively, take another look at Figure 8.2.

When to Use the Direct Pattern

Most bad-news letters are best organized indirectly, beginning with a buffer and reasons. The direct pattern, with the bad news first, may be more effective, though, in situations like the following:

- **When the receiver may overlook the bad news.** With the crush of mail today, many readers skim their messages, looking only at the opening. If they don't find substantive material, they may discard the message. Rate increases, changes in service, new policy requirements—these critical messages may require boldness to ensure attention.

- **When organization policy suggests directness.** Some companies expect all internal messages and announcements—even bad news—to be straightforward and presented without frills.

- **When the receiver prefers directness.** Busy managers may prefer directness. Such shorter messages enable the reader to get into the proper frame of mind immediately. If you suspect that the reader prefers that the facts be presented straightaway, use the direct pattern.

- **When firmness is necessary.** Messages that must demonstrate determination and strength should not use delaying techniques. For example, the last in a series of collection letters that seek payment of overdue accounts may require a direct opener.

Applying the 3 × 3 Writing Process

Thinking through the entire process is especially important in bad-news letters. Not only do you want the receiver to understand and accept the message, but you want to be careful that your words say only what you intend. Thus, you'll want to apply the familiar 3 × 3 writing process to bad-news letters.

The 3 × 3 writing process is especially important in crafting bad-news messages because of the potential consequences of poorly written messages.

Analysis, anticipation, and adaptation. In Phase 1 you need to analyze the bad news so that you can anticipate its effect on the receiver. If the disappointment will be mild, announce it directly. If the bad news is serious or personal, consider techniques to reduce the pain. Adapt your words to protect the receiver's ego. Instead of *You neglected to change the oil, causing severe damage to the engine,* switch to the passive voice: *The oil wasn't changed, and as a result there was severe damage to the engine.* Choose words that show you respect the reader as a responsible, valuable person.

Research, organization, and composition. In Phase 2 you can gather information and brainstorm for ideas. Jot down all the reasons you have that explain the bad news. If you had four or five reasons for your negative decision, concentrate on the strongest and safest ones. Avoid presenting any weak reasons; readers may seize on them to reject the entire message. After selecting your best reasons, outline the four parts of the bad-news pattern: buffer, reasons, bad news, closing. Flesh out each section as you compose your first draft.

Revision, proofreading, and evaluation. In Phase 3 you're ready to switch positions and put yourself into the receiver's shoes. Have you looked at the problem from the receiver's perspective? Is your message too blunt? Too subtle? Does the message make the refusal, denial, or bad-news announcement clear? Prepare the final version, and proofread for format, punctuation, and correctness.

Refusing Routine Requests

Every business communicator will occasionally have to say no to a request. Depending on how you think the receiver will react to your refusal, you can use the direct or the indirect pattern. If you have any doubt, use the indirect pattern.

Rejecting Requests for Favours, Money, Information, and Action

Most of us prefer to be let down gently when we're being refused something we want. That's why the reasons-before-refusal pattern works well when you must turn down requests for favours, money, information, action, and so forth.

The reasons-before-refusal pattern works well when turning down requests for favours, money, information, or action.

Let's say you must refuse a request from Mark Stevenson, one of your managers, who wants permission to attend a conference. You can't let him go because the timing is bad; he must be present at budget-planning meetings scheduled for the same two weeks. Normally, you'd try to discuss this with Mark in person. But he's been travelling among branch offices recently, and you haven't been able to catch him in. Your first inclination might be to send a quick memo, as shown below, and "tell it like it is."

MEMO TO: Mark Stevenson

We can't allow you to attend the conference in September, Mark. Perhaps you didn't know that budget-planning meetings are scheduled for that month.

Your expertise is needed here to help keep our telecommunications network on schedule. Without you, the entire system—which is shaky at best—might fall apart. I'm sorry to have to refuse your request to attend the conference. I know this is small thanks for the fine work you have done for us. Please accept my apologies.

In the spring I'm sure your work schedule will be lighter, and we can release you to attend a conference at any time.

In revising, you realize that this message is going to hurt and that it has some possible danger areas. Moreover, you see that this memo misses a chance to give Mark some positive feedback.

An improved version of the memo, shown in Figure 8.3, starts with a buffer that delivers honest praise ("pleased with your leadership" and "your genuine professional commitment"). By the way, don't be stingy with compliments; they cost you nothing. As a philosopher once observed, "We don't live by bread alone. We need buttering up once in a while." The buffer also includes the date of the meeting, used strategically to connect the reasons that follow. You will recall from Chapter 4 that repetition of a key idea is an effective transitional device to provide smooth flow between components of a message.

The middle paragraph provides reasons for the refusal. Notice that they focus on positive elements: Mark is the specialist; the company relies on his expertise; and everyone will benefit if he passes up the conference. In this section it becomes obvious that the request will be refused. The writer is not forced to say, "No, you may not attend." Although the refusal is implied, the reader gets the message.

The closing suggests a qualified alternative ("If our work loads permit, we'll try to send you then"). It also ends positively with gratitude for Mark's contributions to the organization and with another compliment ("You're a valuable player"). Notice that the improved version emphasizes explanations and praise rather than refusals and apologies.

The success of this message depends on attention to the entire writing process, not just on using a buffer or scattering a few compliments throughout. Review the components of the 3 × 3 writing process and how they relate to request refusals by studying the boxes at the top of Figure 8.3.

Just as managers must refuse proposals from employees, they must also reject requests for contributions of money, time, equipment, or other support. Requests for contributions to charity are common. Cathy Dial's office at Pepsi-Cola receives hundreds of such requests annually—from the public as well as from Pepsi-Cola employees. Although the causes may be worthy, resources are always limited. If you were often required to write refusals, you might prepare a form letter, changing a few variables as needed. See the accompanying Technology box to learn how you can personalize form letters by using word processing software. As you read the following letter, think about how it could be adapted, using word processing equipment, to serve other charity requests.

Dear Ms. Brown:

We appreciate your letter describing the good work your Tri-Valley chapter of the National Reye's Syndrome Foundation is doing in preventing and treating this serious affliction. Your organization is to be commended for its significant achievements resulting from the efforts of dedicated members.

Supporting the good work of your organization and others, although unrelated to our business, is a luxury we have enjoyed in past years. Because of sales declines and organizational downsizing, we're forced to take a much harder look at funding requests that we receive this year. We must focus our charitable contributions on areas that directly relate to our business.

We're hopeful that the worst days are behind us and that we'll be able to renew our support for worthwhile projects like yours next year.

Opens with acknowledgment of inquiry and praise for the writer. Doesn't say yes or no.

Repeats the key ideas of "good work." Explains that a decline in sales requires a cutback in gifts. Reveals refusal gently without actually stating it.

Closes graciously by looking forward to next year.

Declining Invitations

When we must decline an invitation to speak or attend a program, we generally try to provide a response that says more than "I can't" or "I don't want to." Unless the reasons are confidential or business secrets, try to explain them. Because responses to invitations are often taken personally, make a special effort to soften the refusal. In the following letter, an accountant must say no to the invitation of a friend's son to speak before the young man's college business club. The refusal is embedded in a long paragraph and de-emphasized in a subordinate clause ("Although I must decline your invitation"). The reader naturally concentrates on the main clause that follows. In this case that main clause contains an alternative that draws attention away from the refusal.

Notice, too, that this refusal does not offer apologies. The writer has done nothing for which to be sorry. Moreover, an apology emphasizes the pain of the refusal and casts a cloud over the message. Try to keep the tone of a refusal cheerful and positive. This refusal starts with conviviality and compliments.

Dear William:

I'm delighted to hear of your leadership position in your campus business honourary club. Your father must be proud, indeed, of your educational and extracurricular achievements.

You honour me by asking me to speak to your group in the spring about codes of ethics in the accounting field. Because our firm has not yet adopted such a code, we have been investigating the codes developed by other accounting firms. I am decidedly not an expert in this area, but I have met others who are. Although your invitation must be declined, I would like to recommend Juliana Pinkney, who is a member of the ethics subcommittee of the Institute of Internal Auditors. Ms. Pinkney is a CA who often addresses groups on the subject of ethics in accounting. I spoke with her about your club, and she said she would be happy to consider your invitation.

It's good to learn that you are guiding your organization toward such constructive and timely program topics. Please call Ms. Pinkney at (416) 389–2210 if you would like to arrange for her to address your club.

Letters declining invitations give explanations and suggest alternatives but do not offer apologies.

Opens cordially with buffer statement praising reader's accomplishments.

Explains the writer's ignorance on the topic of ethics. Lessens the impact of the refusal by placing it in a subordinate clause ("Although your invitation must be declined") using the passive voice. Concentrates attention on the alternative.

Ends positively with compliments and assistance for arranging the substitute speaker.

Although the direct refusal in this letter is softened by a subordinate clause, perhaps the refusal could have been avoided altogether. Notice how the following statement implies the refusal: *I'm certainly not an expert in this area, but I have met others who are. May I recommend Juliana Pinkney... .* If no alternative is available, refer to something positive about the situation: *Although I'm not an expert, I commend your organization for selecting this topic.*

PERSONALIZING
FORM LETTERS

If you had to send the same information to 200 or more customers, would you write a personal letter to each? Probably not! Responding to identical requests can be tedious, expensive, and time-consuming. That's why many businesses turn to form letters for messages like these: announcing upcoming sales, responding to requests for product information, and updating customers' accounts.

But your letters don't have to sound or look as if a computer wrote them. Word processing programs can help you personalize those messages so that the receivers feel they are being treated as individuals. Here's how the process works.

First, create a form letter, inserting codes or "field names" at each point where information will vary. Next, make a list of "variable" information, such as the customer's name and address, item ordered, balance due, or due date. These two documents (files) are then merged to create a personalized letter for each individual. It's usually wise to minimize the variable information within the body of your message to keep the merging operation as simple as possible.

Form Letter

Current Date

[Title] [First name] [Last name]

[Street]

[City], [Province] [Postal Code]

Dear [Title] [Last name]:

Thanks for your recent order from our fall catalogue.

One item that you requested, [Item], has proved to be very popular this season. Occasionally, we are able to appeal to our manufacturers to make more of a popular item. In this instance, though, our pleas went unanswered.

More than anything, we want to please customers like you, [Title] [Last name]. We pledge to do better with your future orders.

Sincerely,

Cindy Scott

List of Variable Information

[Title] Mr.

[First name] Drew

[Last name] Jamison

[Street] 7700 Glover Road

[City] Langley

[Province] BC

[Postal Code] V3A 4P9

[Item] No. 8765 Ivory Pullover

Final Letter

Current Date

Mr. Drew Jamison
7700 Glover Road
Langley, BC V3A 4P9

Dear Mr. Jamison:

Thanks for your recent order from our fall catalogue.

One item that you requested, No. 8765 Ivory Pullover, has proved to be very popular this season. Occasionally, we are able to appeal to our manufacturers to make more of a popular item. In this instance, though, our pleas went unanswered.

More than anything, we want to please customers like you, Mr. Jamison. We pledge to do better with your future orders.

Sincerely,

Cindy Scott

Career Track Assignment

Bring in a business letter that could be adapted as a form letter. Using it as a guide, prepare a rough draft of the same message indicating the exact locations of all necessary variables. Then ask someone from your class or your campus computer centre to demonstrate how this letter would be set up and merged.

FIGURE 8.3 ■ Refusing a Request

The Three Phases of the Writing Process

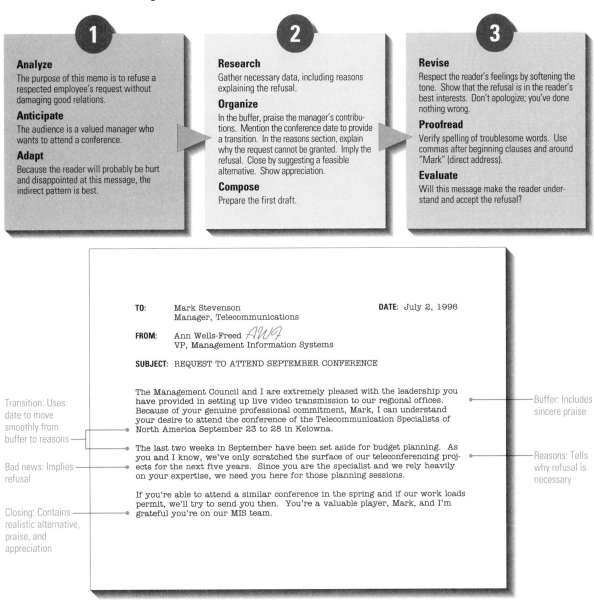

1

Analyze
The purpose of this memo is to refuse a respected employee's request without damaging good relations.

Anticipate
The audience is a valued manager who wants to attend a conference.

Adapt
Because the reader will probably be hurt and disappointed at this message, the indirect pattern is best.

2

Research
Gather necessary data, including reasons explaining the refusal.

Organize
In the buffer, praise the manager's contributions. Mention the conference date to provide a transition. In the reasons section, explain why the request cannot be granted. Imply the refusal. Close by suggesting a feasible alternative. Show appreciation.

Compose
Prepare the first draft.

3

Revise
Respect the reader's feelings by softening the tone. Show that the refusal is in the reader's best interests. Don't apologize; you've done nothing wrong.

Proofread
Verify spelling of troublesome words. Use commas after beginning clauses and around "Mark" (direct address).

Evaluate
Will this message make the reader understand and accept the refusal?

TO: Mark Stevenson   DATE: July 2, 1996
           Manager, Telecommunications

FROM: Ann Wells-Freed *AWF*
           VP, Management Information Systems

SUBJECT: REQUEST TO ATTEND SEPTEMBER CONFERENCE

The Management Council and I are extremely pleased with the leadership you have provided in setting up live video transmission to our regional offices. Because of your genuine professional commitment, Mark, I can understand your desire to attend the conference of the Telecommunication Specialists of North America September 23 to 28 in Kelowna.

The last two weeks in September have been set aside for budget planning. As you and I know, we've only scratched the surface of our teleconferencing projects for the next five years. Since you are the specialist and we rely heavily on your expertise, we need you here for those planning sessions.

If you're able to attend a similar conference in the spring and if our work loads permit, we'll try to send you then. You're a valuable player, Mark, and I'm grateful you're on our MIS team.

Transition: Uses date to move smoothly from buffer to reasons

Bad news: Implies refusal

Closing: Contains realistic alternative, praise, and appreciation

Buffer: Includes sincere praise

Reasons: Tells why refusal is necessary

The following checklist reviews the steps in composing a letter refusing a routine request.

Checklist for Refusing Routine Requests

✓ **Open indirectly with a buffer.** Pay a compliment to the reader, show appreciation for something done, or mention some mutual understanding. Avoid raising false hopes or thanking the reader for something you will refuse.

Problems with customer orders can sometimes be resolved by telephone. Large companies, though, more often rely on written messages. If the message contains any good news, begin with that. For messages that are primarily disappointing, use the indirect method, beginning with a buffer and an explanation.

✓ **Provide reasons**. In the body explain why the request must be denied—without revealing the refusal. Avoid negativity (*unfortunately, unwilling*, and *impossible*) and potentially damaging statements. Show how your decision benefits the reader or others, if possible.

✓ **Soften the bad news**. Reduce the impact of bad news by using (1) a subordinate clause, (2) the passive voice, (3) a long sentence, or (4) a long paragraph. Consider implying the refusal, but be certain it is clear. Suggest an alternative, if a suitable one exists.

✓ **Close pleasantly**. Supply more information about an alternative, look forward to future relations, or offer good wishes and compliments. Avoid referring to the refusal, and do not apologize if you've done nothing wrong.

▓ Sending Bad News to Customers

Messages with bad news for customers follow the same pattern as other negative messages. Letters to customers, though, differ in one important way: they usually include resale or sales promotion emphasis. Bad-news messages to customers typically handle problems with orders, denial of claims, or credit refusals.

Handling Problems with Orders

In handling problems with orders, the indirect pattern is suitable unless the message has some good-news elements.

Not all orders can be filled as received. Suppliers may be able to send only part of an order or none at all. Substitutions may be necessary, or the delivery may be delayed. The supplier may suspect that all or part of the order is a mistake; the customer may actually want something else. In writing to customers about problem orders, it's generally wise to use the direct pattern if the message has some good-news elements. But when the message is disappointing, the indirect pattern is better.

Let's say you represent Patelle Toys, and you're scrambling for business in a slow year. A big customer, Child Land, calls in August and asks you to hold a block of your best-selling dolls. Like most vendors you require a deposit on large orders. September rolls around, and you still haven't received any money from Child Land. You must now write a tactful letter asking for the deposit—or else you will release the dolls to other buyers.[7] The problem, of course, is delivering the bad news without losing the customer's order and goodwill. Another challenge is making sure the reader understands the bad news. Do you think the resale and sales promotion emphases in the following letter dilute or obscure the bad news?

Dear Mr. Jones:

We appreciate your interest in our Wendy Walkalong dolls. We've been holding a block of 500 of these top-selling dolls for you since August.

As we approach the holidays, the demand for all our dolls—including Wendy Walkalong—is increasing. Toy stores from St. John's to Victoria are asking us to ship these dolls. One reason the Wendy Walkalong is moving out of our warehouses so quickly is its low unit price, which makes it an economical gift and a fast mover in an otherwise slow market. As soon as we receive your deposit of $4000, we'll have this popular item on its way to your stores. Without a deposit by September 20, though, we must release this block to other retailers. Use the enclosed envelope to send us your cheque immediately. You can begin showing the hit doll Wendy Walkalong in your stores by November 1.

Please glance through the enclosed catalogue for other toys to stock this season. Many retailers have told us that Baby Thumbelina, a moderately priced cuddle doll (shown on page 23), is walking right off their shelves. We look forward to your cheque as well as to continuing to serve all your toy needs.

Includes appreciation and resale while establishing the facts.
Reasons justify the coming bad news. Instead of focusing on the writer's needs (*we have a full warehouse and we need your deposit*), the reasons concentrate on motivating the reader. After the reasons, the bad news is clearly spelled out.

Closing uses sales promotion in suggesting another product. It also looks ahead to more business.

Denying Claims

Customers occasionally want something they're not entitled to or that you can't grant. They may misunderstand warranties or make unreasonable demands. Because these customers are often unhappy with a product or service, they are emotionally involved. Letters that say no to emotionally involved receivers will probably be your most difficult communication task. As publisher Malcolm Forbes observed, "To be agreeable while disagreeing—that's an art."[8]

Fortunately, the reasons-before-refusal plan helps you be empathic and artful in breaking bad news. Obviously, in denial letters you'll need to adopt the proper tone. Don't blame customers, even if they are at fault. Avoid "you" statements that sound preachy (*You would have known that cash refunds are impossible if you had read your contract*). Use neutral, objective language to explain why the claim must be refused. Consider offering resale information to rebuild the customer's confidence in your products or organization.

In Figure 8.4 the writer denies a customer's claim for the difference between the price the customer paid for speakers and the price he saw advertised locally (which would have resulted in a cash refund of $151). While the catalogue service does match any advertised lower price, the price-matching policy applies only to exact models. This claim must be rejected because the advertisement the customer submitted showed a different, older model.

The letter to Matthew Tyson opens with a buffer that agrees with a statement in the customer's letter. It repeats the key idea of product confidence as a transition to the second paragraph. Next comes an explanation of the price-matching policy. The writer does not assume that the customer is trying to pull a fast one. Nor does he suggest that the customer didn't read or understand the price-matching policy. The safest path is a neutral explanation of the policy along with precise distinctions between the customer's speakers and the older ones. The writer also gets a chance to resell the customer's speakers and

In denying claims, the reasons-before-refusal pattern sets an emphatic tone and buffers the bad news.

FIGURE 8.4 ■ Denying a Claim

Combines agreement with resale

Explains price-matching policy and how reader's purchase is different from lower-priced model

Without actually saying no, shows why reader's claim can't be honoured

Builds reader's confidence in wisdom of purchase

Avoids apologizing; looks forward to future business

---

c·e·l·e·s·t·i·a·l
c a t a l o g u e   s a l e s
479 Pleasant Street, Truro, NS B2N 5J9 · phone (902) 456-2100 · fax (902) 455-3260

February 19, 1996

Mr. Matthew R. Tyson
177 Beech Avenue
Toronto, ON M4E 3K4

Dear Mr. Tyson:

You're right, Mr. Tyson. We do take pride in selling the finest products at rock-bottom prices. The Boze speakers you purchased last month are premier concert hall speakers. They're the only ones we present in our catalogue because they're the best.

We have such confidence in our products and prices that we offer the price-matching policy you mention in your letter of February 15. That policy guarantees a refund of the price difference if you see one of your purchases offered at a lower price for 30 days after your purchase. To qualify for that refund, customers are asked to send us an advertisement or verifiable proof of the product price and model. As our catalogue states, this price-matching policy applies only to exact models with Canadian warranties.

Our Boze AM-5 II speakers sell for $749. You sent us a local advertisement showing a price of $598 for Boze speakers. This advertisement, however, describes an earlier version, the Boze AM-4 model. The AM-5 speakers you received have a wider dynamic range and smoother frequency response than the AM-4 model. Naturally, the improved model you purchased costs a little more than the older AM-4 model that the local advertisement describes. Your speakers have a new three-chamber bass module that virtually eliminates harmonic distortion. Finally, your speakers are 20 percent more compact than the AM-4 model.

You bought the finest compact speakers on the market, Mr. Tyson. If you haven't installed them yet, you may be interested in ceiling mounts, shown in the enclosed catalogue on page 48. We value your business and invite your continued comparison shopping.

Sincerely yours,

Rick Thalman

Rick K. Thalman
Customer Service

mmt
Enclosure

Buffer

Reasons

Implied refusal

Positive closing

---

demonstrate what a quality product they are. By the end of the third paragraph, it's evident to the reader that his claim is unjustified.

Refusing Credit

Goals when refusing credit include maintaining customer goodwill and avoiding actionable language.

As much as companies want business, they can extend credit only when payment is likely to follow. Credit applications, from individuals or from businesses, are generally approved or disapproved on the basis of the applicant's credit history. This record is supplied by a credit-reporting agency, such as Equifax. After reviewing the applicant's record, a credit manager applies the organization's guidelines and approves or disapproves the application.

If you must deny credit to prospective customers, you have four goals in conveying the refusal:

Bad news is easier to break when you can do it in person and when you have facts and reasons to justify it. The challenge to writers is to explain the facts, while at the same time showing empathy and sincerity. In sending bad news to customers, try to show them that they are respected and that their patronage is prized.

- Avoiding language that causes hard feelings
- Retaining customers on a cash basis
- Preparing for possible future credit—without raising false expectations
- Avoiding disclosing information that could cause a lawsuit

Because credit applicants are likely to continue to do business with an organization even if they are denied credit, you'll want to do everything possible to encourage that patronage. Thus, keep the refusal respectful, sensitive, and cheerful. To avoid possible litigation, some organizations give no explanation of the reasons for the refusal. Instead, they give the name of the credit-reporting agency and suggest that inquiries be directed to it. Here's a credit refusal letter that uses a buffer but does not explain the reasons for the denial. Notice how the warm tone reassures the reader that she is respected and that her patronage is valued. The letter implies that her current credit status is temporary, but it does not raise false hopes by promising future credit.

Dear Ms. Margolis:

We genuinely appreciate your application of January 12 for a Fashion Express credit account.

After receiving a report of your current credit record from Equifax Information Services, we find that credit cannot be extended at this time. To learn more about your record, you may call an Equifax credit counsellor at (905) 356–0922. We've arranged for you to take advantage of this service for 60 days from the date of this letter at no charge to you.

Thanks, Ms. Margolis, for the confidence you've shown in Fashion Express. We invite you to continue shopping at our stores, and we look forward to your reapplication in the future.

Buffer identifies application and shows appreciation for it.

Long sentence and passive voice deemphasize bad news. To prevent possible litigation offers no reasons for denial.

Closes cordially and looks forward to continued patronage.

Some businesses do explain their reasons for credit denials (*Credit cannot be granted because your firm's current and long-term credit obligations are nearly twice as great as your firm's total assets*). They may also offer alternatives, such as deferred billing or cash discounts. When the letter denies a credit application that accompanies an order, the message may contain resale information. The writer tries to convert the order from credit to cash.

Whatever form the bad-news letter takes, it's a good idea to have the message reviewed by legal counsel because of the litigation landmines awaiting unwary communicators in this area. The following checklist contains tips on how to write effective bad-news letters.

Checklist for Delivering Bad News to Customers

✓ **Begin indirectly**. Express appreciation (but don't thank the reader for something you're about to refuse), show agreement on some point, review facts, or show understanding.

✓ **Provide reasons**. Except in credit denials, justify the bad news with objective reasons. Use resale if appropriate to restore the customer's confidence. Avoid blaming the customer or hiding behind company policy. Look for reader benefits.

✓ **Present the bad news**. State the bad news objectively or imply it. Although resale or sales promotion is appropriate in order letters, it may offend in claim or credit refusals.

✓ **Close pleasantly**. Suggest an alternative, look forward to future business, offer best wishes, refer to gifts, or use resale sensitively. Don't apologize, and don't mention the bad news.

Managing Negative Organization News

A tactful tone and a reasons-first approach help preserve friendly relations with customers. These same techniques are useful when delivering bad news to employees and when rejecting job applicants.

Announcing Bad News to Employees

Internal bad-news memos should use the indirect pattern to convey news that adversely affects employees.

Bad news within organizations might involve declining profits, lost contracts, harmful lawsuits, public relations controversies, and changes in policy. Whether you use a direct or an indirect pattern in delivering that news depends primarily on the anticipated reaction of the receiver. When bad news affects employees personally—such as cutbacks in pay, reduction of benefits, or relocation plans—you can generally lessen its impact and promote better relations by explaining the reasons before revealing the bad news.

The first version of the following memo, which announces a substantial increase in the cost of employee health care benefits, suffers from many problems.

MEMO TO: Staff

Beginning January 1 your payment for health care benefits will require 10 percent payment for medical costs.

Hits readers with bad news without any preparation.

Every year health care costs go up. Although we considered dropping other benefits, Midland decided that the best plan was to keep the present comprehensive package. Unfortunately, we can't do that unless we pass along some of the extra cost to you. Last year the company was forced to absorb the total increase in health care premiums. However, such a plan this year is inadvisable.

Offers no explanation of why health care costs are rising. Action sounds arbitrary. Fails to take credit for absorbing previous increases.

We did everything possible to avoid the sharp increase in costs to you this year. A rate schedule describing the increases in payments for your family and dependants is enclosed.

Sounds defensive; fails to provide reasons.

The improved version of this bad-news memo, shown in Figure 8.5, uses the indirect pattern. Notice that it opens with a relevant, upbeat buffer regarding health care—but says nothing about increasing costs. For a smooth transition, the second paragraph begins with a key idea from the opening ("comprehensive package"). The reasons section discusses rising costs with explanations and figures. The bad news ("you will be paying 10 percent toward major medical costs") is presented clearly but embedded within the paragraph. Throughout, the writer strives to show the fairness of the company's position. The ending, which does not refer to the bad news or apologize, emphasizes how much the company is paying and what a wise investment it is. Notice that the entire memo demonstrates a gentler approach than that shown in the first draft. Of prime importance in breaking bad news to employees is clear, convincing reasons that explain the decision.

Most organizations involved in a crisis (serious performance problems, major relocation, massive layoffs, management shakeup, or public controversy) prefer to communicate the news openly to employees, customers, and stockholders. Instead of letting rumours distort the truth, they explain the organization's side of the story honestly and early. Morale can be destroyed when employees learn of major events affecting their jobs through the grapevine or from news accounts—rather than from management. For example, Exxon's poor handling of the *Valdez* oil spill—including delaying release of information and downplaying the environmental damage—harmed employee morale, angered stockholders, and lost the company thousands of customers.

Organizations can sustain employee morale by communicating bad news openly and honestly.

Saying No to Job Applicants

Being refused a job is one of life's major rejections. The blow is intensified by tactless letters (*Unfortunately, you were not among the candidates selected for* ...). You can reduce the receiver's disappointment somewhat by using the indirect pattern—with one important variation. In the reasons section it's wise to be vague in explaining why the candidate was not selected. First, giving concrete reasons may be painful to the receiver (*Your grade point average of 2.7 was low compared with those of other candidates*). Second, and more important, providing extra information may prove fatal in a lawsuit. Hiring and firing decisions generate considerable litigation today. To avoid charges of discrimination or wrongful actions, legal advisers warn organizations to keep employment rejection letters general, simple, and short.

Letters that deny applications for employment should be courteous and tactful but free of specifics that could trigger lawsuits.

The following job refusal letter is tactful but intentionally vague. It implies that the applicant's qualifications don't match those needed for the position, but the letter doesn't reveal anything specific.

FIGURE 8.5 ■ Announcing Bad News to Employees

The Three Phases of the Writing Process

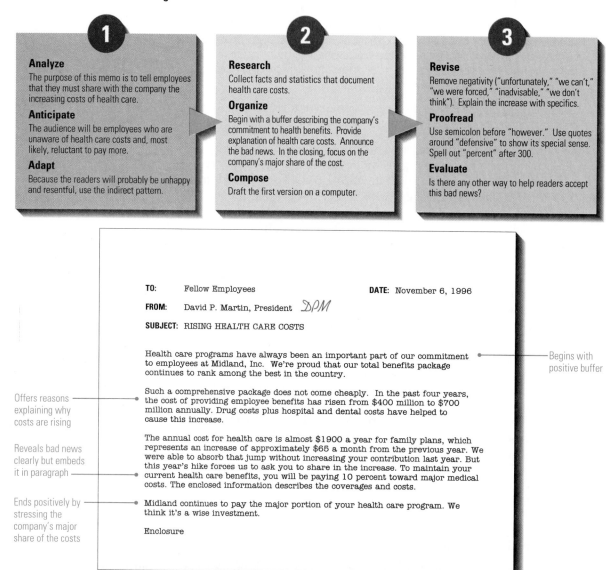

1

Analyze
The purpose of this memo is to tell employees that they must share with the company the increasing costs of health care.

Anticipate
The audience will be employees who are unaware of health care costs and, most likely, reluctant to pay more.

Adapt
Because the readers will probably be unhappy and resentful, use the indirect pattern.

2

Research
Collect facts and statistics that document health care costs.

Organize
Begin with a buffer describing the company's commitment to health benefits. Provide explanation of health care costs. Announce the bad news. In the closing, focus on the company's major share of the cost.

Compose
Draft the first version on a computer.

3

Revise
Remove negativity ("unfortunately," "we can't," "we were forced," "inadvisable," "we don't think"). Explain the increase with specifics.

Proofread
Use semicolon before "however." Use quotes around "defensive" to show its special sense. Spell out "percent" after 300.

Evaluate
Is there any other way to help readers accept this bad news?

TO: Fellow Employees   **DATE:** November 6, 1996

FROM: David P. Martin, President *DPM*

SUBJECT: RISING HEALTH CARE COSTS

Health care programs have always been an important part of our commitment to employees at Midland, Inc. We're proud that our total benefits package continues to rank among the best in the country.
— Begins with positive buffer

Offers reasons explaining why costs are rising —
Such a comprehensive package does not come cheaply. In the past four years, the cost of providing employee benefits has risen from $400 million to $700 million annually. Drug costs plus hospital and dental costs have helped to cause this increase.

Reveals bad news clearly but embeds it in paragraph —
The annual cost for health care is almost $1900 a year for family plans, which represents an increase of approximately $65 a month from the previous year. We were able to absorb that jump without increasing your contribution last year. But this year's hike forces us to ask you to share in the increase. To maintain your current health care benefits, you will be paying 10 percent toward major medical costs. The enclosed information describes the coverages and costs.

Ends positively by stressing the company's major share of the costs —
Midland continues to pay the major portion of your health care program. We think it's a wise investment.

Enclosure

Dear Mr. Danson:

Shows appreciation. Doesn't indicate good or bad news.

Thanks for letting us review your résumé submitted for our advertised management trainee opening.

To prevent possible lawsuits, gives no explanation. Places bad news in a dependent clause.

We received a number of impressive résumés for this opening. Although another candidate was selected, your interest in our organization is appreciated. So that you may continue your search for a position at another organization, we are writing to you immediately.

Ends with best wishes.

We wish you every success in finding a position that exactly fits your qualifications.

The following checklist gives tips on how to communicate bad news within an organization.

PRESENTING BAD NEWS IN OTHER CULTURES

To minimize disappointment, North Americans generally prefer to present negative messages indirectly. Other cultures may treat bad news differently.

In Germany, for example, business communicators occasionally use buffers but tend to present bad news directly. In Latin countries the question is not how to organize negative messages but whether to present them at all. It's considered disrespectful and impolite to report bad news to one's superiors. Thus, reluctant employees may fail to report accurately any negative message to their bosses.

In Asian cultures harmony and peace are sought in all relationships. Disrupting the harmony with bad news is avoided. Saying no is particularly difficult, even in situations where we would expect no hard feelings to result. Notice how evasive, polite, and charming a Beijing newspaper is in rejecting an article submitted by a British journalist:

We have read your manuscript with boundless delight. If we were to publish your paper, it would be impossible for us to publish any work of a lower standard. And as it is unthinkable that, in the next thousand years, we shall see its equal, we are, to our regret, compelled to return your divine composition, and beg you a thousand times to overlook our short sight and timidity.

To prevent discord, Japanese communicators use a number of techniques to indicate no—without being forced to say it. In conversation they may respond with silence or with a counter question, such as "Why do you ask?" They may change the subject or tell a white lie to save face for themselves and for the questioner. Sometimes the answer sounds like a qualified yes: "I will do my best, but if I cannot, I hope you will understand," "Yes, but ... ," or "yes" followed by an apology. All these responses should be recognized as no. In Thailand the negativism represented by a refusal is completely alien; the word *no* does not exist.

In many cultures negative news is offered with such subtleness or in such a positive light that it may be overlooked or misunderstood by literal-minded North Americans. To understand what's really being said, we must look beyond an individual's actual words, considering the communication style, culture, and situation as well.

Career Track Application

Interview fellow students or work colleagues who are from other cultures. How is negative news handled? How would typical individuals refuse a request for a favour, for example? How would a business refuse credit to customers? Is directness practised? Report your findings to the class.

Checklist for Managing Negative Organization News

✓ **Start with a relevant, cheerful buffer.** Open with a small bit of good news, praise, appreciation, agreement, understanding, or a discussion of facts leading to the reasons section.

✓ **Discuss reasons.** Except in job refusal letters, explain what caused the decision necessitating the bad news. Use objective, nonjudgmental, and nondiscriminatory language. Show empathy and fairness.

✓ **Reveal the bad news.** Make the bad news clear but don't accentuate it. Avoid negative language.

✓ **Close harmoniously.** End on a positive, friendly note. For job refusals, extend good wishes.

You've now studied the indirect method for revealing bad news and analyzed many examples of messages applying this method. As you observed, business writers generally try to soften the blow; however, they do eventually reveal the bad news. No effort is made to ignore it totally. In other cultures bad news may be more difficult to reveal. The Cross Culture box on page 229 gives insights into how negative messages are treated abroad.

■ Summary of Learning Goals

1. **Describe the goals of business communicators when delivering bad news.** Good communicators strive to (a) make the reader understand and accept the bad news, (b) promote and maintain a good image of themselves and their organizations, (c) make the message so clear that additional correspondence is unnecessary, and (d) avoid creating legal liability or responsibility.

2. **Identify the causes of legal problems in business writing.** Abusive language is libelous and actionable when it (1) is made in public, and (2) causes harm. Even careless language (saying, for instance, that a manufacturing plant is "dangerous") can result in litigation. Moreover, any messages written on company stationery represent that company and can be legally binding.

3. **Explain the components of a bad-news message.** Begin with a buffer, such as a compliment, appreciation, a point of agreement, objective information, understanding, or some part of the message that contains good news. Then explain the reasons that necessitate the bad news, trying to cite benefits to the reader or others. Choose positive words, and clarify company policy if necessary. Announce the bad news strategically, mentioning a compromise or alternative if possible. Close pleasantly with a forward-looking good-will statement.

4. **Compare the direct and indirect patterns for breaking bad news. List situations when the direct pattern is more effective.** Messages written directly begin by announcing the bad news immediately. Indirect messages, on the other hand, begin with a buffer, offer an explanation, and then disclose the bad news. The direct pattern is most effective when (a) the receiver may overlook the bad news, (b) organization policy suggests directness, (c) the receiver prefers directness, or (d) firmness is necessary.

5. **Identify routine requests and describe a strategy for refusing such requests.** Routine requests ask for favours, money, information, action, and other items. When the answer will be disappointing, use the reasons-before-refusal pattern. Open with a buffer, give reasons, announce the refusal sensitively, suggest possible alternatives, and end with a positive, forwardlooking comment.

6. **Describe a strategy for sending bad news to customers while retaining their goodwill.** In addition to using the indirect pattern, consider including resale information (reassuring the customer that he or she has made a wise choice) or sales promotion (pushing a new product). Be especially careful of the tone of words used. Strive for neutral, objective language, and avoid blaming the customer.

7. **Explain the best strategy for managing negative organization news.** When breaking bad news to employees, use the indirect pattern but be sure to include clear, convincing reasons that explain a decision. In refusing job applicants, however, keep letters short, general, and tactful.

CHAPTER REVIEW

1. Discuss four goals of a business communicator who must deliver bad news. (Goal 1)

2. How can business documents in an organization's files become part of a lawsuit? (Goal 2)

3. Describe the four parts of the indirect message pattern. (Goal 3)

4. Why should a writer give reasons before revealing bad news? (Goal 3)

5. Name four or more ways to de-emphasize bad news when it is presented. (Goal 3)

6. What is the most important difference between direct and indirect letters? (Goal 4)

7. Name four times when the direct pattern should be used for bad news. (Goal 4)

8. Name four kinds of routine requests that businesses must frequently refuse. (Goal 5)

9. Why should you be especially careful in cushioning the refusal to an invitation? (Goal 5)

10. What is the main difference between bad-news messages for customers and those for other people? (Goal 6)

11. List four goals a writer seeks to achieve in writing messages that deny credit to prospective customers. (Goal 6)

12. Why should a writer be somewhat vague in the reasons portion of a letter rejecting a job applicant? (Goal 7)

13. When organizations must reveal a crisis (such as the Exxon *Valdez* disaster), how should they communicate the news to employees, customers, stockholders, and the public? (Goal 7)

14. What techniques might a Japanese businessperson use to avoid saying no? (Goal 7)

15. To avoid possible litigation in a letter refusing credit, what technique can be used in explaining reasons for the denial? (Goal 6)

DISCUSSION

1. Under what circumstances would form letters be appropriate for delivering bad news? (Goal 5)

2. Discuss the contention that all letters addressed to customers or prospective customers should contain resale or sales promotion information. (Goal 6)

3. Consider times when you have been aware that others have used the indirect pattern in writing or speaking to you. How did you react? (Goals 1, 3)

4. Discuss the ethics and legality of using company stationery to write personal letters. (Goal 2)

5. **Ethical Issue:** In considering negative organization news, should companies immediately reveal grave illnesses of executives? Or should executives be entitled to keep their health a private matter? Does it matter if the company is public or private? (Goals 3, 7)

EXERCISES

8.1 Organizational Patterns (Goal 3–7)

Which organizational pattern would you use for the following messages: direct or indirect?

a. A letter refusing a request by a charitable organization to use your office equipment on the weekend.

b. A memo from the manager denying an employee's request for special parking privileges. The employee works closely with the manager on many projects.

c. An announcement to employees that a fitness specialist has cancelled a scheduled lunchtime talk and cannot reschedule.

d. A letter from a bank refusing to fund a company's overseas expansion plan.

e. A form letter from an insurance company announcing new policy requirements that many policyholders may resent. If policyholders do not indicate the plan they prefer, they may lose their insurance coverage.

f. A letter from an amusement park refusing the request of a customer who was unhappy with a substitute concert performer.

g. The last in a series of letters from a collection agency demanding payment of a long-overdue account. The next step will be to hire a lawyer.

h. A letter from a computer company refusing to authorize repair of a customer's computer on which the warranty expired six months ago.

i. A memo from an executive refusing a manager's plan to economize by purchasing reconditioned copiers. The executive and the manager both appreciate efficient, straightforward messages.

j. A letter informing a customer that the majority of the customer's recent order will not be available for six weeks.

8.2   Passive-Voice Verbs (Goal 3)

Revise the following sentences to present the bad news with passive-voice verbs.

a. We will no longer be accepting credit cards for purchases.

b. No one is allowed to park in the yellow zone.

c. Our technicians cannot service your VCR.

d. We are unable to grant your request for a loan.

8.3   Subordinating Bad News (Goal 3)

Revise the following sentences to position the bad news in a subordinate clause. (Hint: Consider beginning the clause with *Although*.) Use passive-voice verbs for the bad news.

a. We cannot refund your purchase price, but we are sending you two coupons toward your next purchase.

b. We appreciate your interest in our organization. Unfortunately, we are unable to extend an employment offer to you at this time.

c. It is impossible for us to ship your complete order at this time. However, we are able to send the four oak desks now; you should receive them within five days.

8.4   Implying Bad News (Goal 3)

Revise the following statements to *imply* the bad news. Use passive-voice verbs and subordinate clauses to further de-emphasize the bad news.

a. I already have an engagement in my appointment calendar for the date you mention. Therefore, I am unable to speak to your group. However, I would like to recommend another speaker who might be able to address your organization.

b. Because of the holiday period, all our billboard space was used this month. Therefore, we are sorry to say that we could not give your charitable group free display space. However, next month, after the holidays, we hope to display your message as we promised.

c. We cannot send you a price list nor can we sell our equipment directly to customers. Our policy is to sell only through dealers, and your dealer is Stereo City, located on Yonge Street in Toronto.

8.5   Evaluating Bad-News Statements (Goal 3)

Discuss the strengths or weaknesses of the following bad-news statements.

a. It's impossible for us to ship your order before May 1.

b. Frankly, we like your résumé, but we were hoping to hire someone a little younger who might be able to stay with us longer.

c. I'm thoroughly disgusted with this entire case, and I will never do business with shyster lawyers like you again.

d. We can assure you that on any return visit to our hotels you will not be treated so poorly.

e. We must deny your credit application because your record shows a history of late payments, nonpayment, and irregular employment.

f. *(In a confidential company memo:)* I cannot recommend that we promote this young lady into any position where she will meet the public. Her colourful facial decoration, as part of her religion, may offend our customers.

8.6   Document Analysis: Refusal of a Favour Request (Goals 1, 3, 4, 6)

Analyze the following letter. List its weaknesses. If your instructor directs, revise it.

Dear Mr. Singh:

Unfortunately, we cannot allow you to apply the lease payments you've been making for the past 10 months toward the purchase of your Sako 600 copier.

Company policy does not allow such conversion. Have you ever wondered why we can offer such low leasing and purchase prices? Obviously, we couldn't stay in business long if we agreed to proposals such as yours.

You've had the Sako 600 copier for 10 months now, Mr. Singh, and you say you like its versatility and reliability. Perhaps we could interest you in another Sako model—one that's more within your price range. Do give us a call.

8.7 Document Analysis: Negative News for Customers (Goals 1, 3, 4, 6)

Analyze the following letter. List its weaknesses. If your instructor directs, revise it.

Dear Charge Customers:

This letter is being sent to you to announce the termination of in-house charge accounts at Golden West Print and Frame Shop. We are truly sorry that we can no longer offer this service.

Because some customers abused the privilege, we must eliminate local charge accounts. We regret that we must take this action, but we found that carrying our own credit had become quite costly. To continue the service would have meant raising our prices. As a small but growing business, we decided it was more logical to drop the in-house charges. As a result, we are forced to begin accepting bank credit cards, including VISA and MasterCard.

Please accept our apologies in trimming our services somewhat. We hope to see you soon when we can show you our new collection of museum-quality gilded wood frames.

8.8 Document Analysis: Saying No to a Job Applicant (Goals 1, 2, 3, 7)

Analyze the following letter. List its weaknesses. If your instructor directs, revise it.

Dear Mr. Franklin:

Ms. Sievers and I wish to thank you for the pleasure of allowing us to interview you last Thursday. We were delighted to learn about your superb academic record, and we also appreciated your attentiveness in listening to our description of the operations of the Maxwell Corporation.

However, we had many well-qualified applicants who were interested in the advertised position of human resources assistant. As you may have guessed, we were particularly eager to find a minority individual who could help us fill out our Employment Equity goals. Although you do not belong to one of the designated groups, we enjoyed talking with you. We hired a woman graduate of Ryerson Polytechnic University who had most of the qualities we sought.

Although we realize that the job market is difficult at this time, you have our heartfelt wishes for good luck in finding precisely what you are looking for.

PROBLEMS

8.9 Request Refusal: The Answer Is No (Goals 5, 6)

In an organization to which you belong or one where you have worked, identify a request that must be refused in writing. Do customers or organizations solicit contributions of money, time, products, or equipment? Do customers request actions that can't be taken? Do officers or members of a student organization want favours or actions that can't be granted? Must the organization refuse to participate in some event? Write a tactful letter refusing the request.

8.10 Request Refusal: Ascending Sales Stars (Goal 5)

Gerry Ronzonni, a magazine editor, asks your organization, Panatronics International, for confidential information about the salaries and commissions of your top sales representatives. The magazine, *Marketing Monthly*, plans to spotlight young sales professionals "whose stars are ascending." You've got some great young superstars, as well as many excellent mature sales representatives. Frankly, the publicity would be great. You would agree in a minute except that (1) you don't want to be forced to pick favourites among your sales reps and (2) you can't reveal private salary information. Every sales rep operates under an individual salary contract. During salary negotiations several years ago, an agreement was reached in which both sales staff members and management agreed to keep the terms of these individual contracts confidential. Perhaps the editor would be satisfied with a list that ranks your top sales reps for the past five years. You could also send a fact sheet describing your top reps. You notice that three of the current top sales reps are under the age of 35. Write a refusal that retains the goodwill of *Marketing Monthly*, 1326 Henderson Avenue, Calgary AB T3Z 1X5.

8.11 Invitation Refusal: A Dog of a Company (Goal 5)

Your boss, John A. Berman, CEO, International Paper Co., has just been voted Paper Industry Man of the Year by the American Paperwork Association. To receive the award, though, he has to agree to present the keynote address to the association at its February 18 meeting in Boston. It's impossible for him to attend since he'll be in Japan scouting for new paper company acquisitions. Mr. Berman is determined that IP should become less dependent on U.S. markets. He's particularly interested in expanding into specialty paper items, such as photographic papers. In fact, his wise acquisitions and aggressive management style explain why he's being singled out for this award. As one company director said, "Berman has taken a company that was a dog in the industry and made it into the best." Although Mr. Berman would like to attend, he cannot. He wants you, his assistant, to write to the American Paperwork Association refusing the invitation. It's unlikely, but if the APA could reschedule the meeting for March, Mr. Berman could attend. He's unavailable in April and May. For Mr. Berman's signature prepare a draft of the refusal letter addressed to Roberta A. Wexler, Executive Secretary, American Paperwork Association, 3981 Rosslyn Road, Arlington, VA 22209.[9]

8.12   Request Refusal: Mountain Bike Race Regrets (Goals 5, 6)

As president of CycleTech, you must refuse a request from the North American Biking Association. This group wants your company to become a major sponsor of the first annual Durango World Mountain Bike Championship—to the tune of $25 000! This is one tune you can't dance to. The stakes are just too high. You applaud the NABA for encouraging families to participate in the sport of mountain biking. The NABA was also instrumental in opening up ski resorts to mountain bikers during the summer. Actually, you'd like to support the Durango World Mountain Bike Championship. There's no doubt that such races increase interest in mountain biking and ridership. You have sponsored some bike races in the past, but for small amounts—usually under $500—which paid for trophies. But the NABA wants to offer large cash prizes and pay the expenses of big-name champions to enter.

You are a small Kamloops, BC, company, and all your current profits are being ploughed into research to compete with the Japanese imports. You're very proud of your newly introduced brake pads and trigger-action shift levers. But these kinds of engineering breakthroughs are costly. You don't have the big bucks the NABA wants. You wouldn't mind taking an ad in their program or contributing $500 toward trophies. But that's the limit. Write a refusal to Joe W. Breeze, North American Biking Association, 1720 Waterloo St., Vancouver, BC V6R 3G2.

8.13   Request Refusal: Fragrance from Local Botanicals (Goal 6)

Your home fragrance company, Aromatix, is riding a wave of popularity and explosive growth. Specializing in natural potpourris using only botanicals (dried flowers, leaves, pods, seeds, and other plant parts), you have become an industry leader. One of your projected markets is fragrant bath products—and perhaps perfume in the more distant future.

The manager of your Cambridge, Ontario, production plant, Annette Buchanan, has written a memo to you asking if she can make a four-week trip to Europe and Asia in April. Specifically, she wants to visit India (for bakuli pods), Pakistan (for red rosebuds), Bulgaria (for sloe berries), and France (for lavender flowers and other exotic dried flora). As an aside, she also mentioned visiting Hampton Farms, Manchester, Ohio, which cultivates scented geraniums used in various fragrances.

You must refuse the European and Asian part of Annette's request for many reasons. You don't want her to be gone for four weeks in April, when your staff will be brainstorming ideas for new package designs. In addition, the trip would set a bad precedent. You've turned down the requests of other managers for European and Asian trips because, frankly, you don't think the benefits outweigh the considerable expense of travel abroad. Your company is pleased with the work of local nationals acting on your behalf. These representatives have been able to supply quality botanicals from overseas at reasonable prices. You feel that Canadians are at a disadvantage in negotiations because they don't speak the necessary languages.

You would, however, like Annette to inspect the scented geraniums in Ohio. Oils from these plants are essential in making naturally scented shower gels and body lotions. With the proliferation of elegant bath shops, these products could become hot items soon. You know Annette will be disappointed, and you hope she won't take this rejection personally. She's one of those rare managers who can combine management skills with creativity. You'd hate to lose her. She's made the Cambridge warehouse and distribution centre a marvel of efficiency, computerizing the inventory so that you can locate and replenish items automatically. Moreover, it was Annette who came up with "microwave potpourri," one of the most successful new ideas in the industry. Popping a potpourri mix in the microwave causes its aromas to be released without the need for messy candles or awkward light bulbs. Her creativity is needed at the April design meetings. Therefore, as Jane Burke, Aromatix president (with headquarters in Montreal), write a memo to Annette Buchanan, operations manager, refusing the major part of her request.

8.14   Claim Denial: Virus Infects Invaders (Goal 6)

As Monty McAdams, director of marketing for Quixell, a software game manufacturer, you must respond to an angry customer, Donald V. Cruz. Mr. Cruz has reason to be upset. Your Galaxy Invaders program carried a computer virus, unbeknownst to you at the time of distribution, that has infected his computer.

As soon as you learned about the virus two months ago, you stopped production and traced its source to a certain step in manufacturing. Your company, Quixell, doesn't know how the virus infected the manufacturing process; but you've corrected the problem, and your disks are now clean. Fortunately, only a small number of contaminated programs were distributed. Some of the buyers have written to you, and you've been responding to each complaint individually.

Computer viruses are programs written to perform malicious tasks. They attach themselves secretly to data files and are then copied either by diskette or by a computer network. The particular virus contaminating your Galaxy Invaders program is called "Stoned III."[10] First reported in Europe just six months ago, it represents a new class of "stealth" viruses. They mask their location and are extremely difficult to detect. Quixell already has extensive virus-detection defences, but this new virus slipped by. Quixell has just licensed special digital-signature software that will make it difficult for future viruses to spread undetected. But the new technology doesn't solve the current problem.

You doubt that your customers will sue over the virus. Courts in the past have generally found that if a company has been reasonably prudent in its production process, that company is not liable for damage caused by a third person (the individual who planted the virus). Nevertheless, you feel an obligation to do whatever is possible—within reason—to rectify the damage caused. Mr. Cruz wants Quixell to pay for a computer virus specialist to clean up his hard disk and restore it to its previous uncontaminated state. Such a solution is out of the question. It's much too expensive. Moreover, you can't be sure that his computer doesn't have problems that have nothing to do with the Invaders virus.

You are doing what other software manufacturers have done when faced with viruses—offering a clean disk and advice. You feel that Quixell is exceptional among software companies. Because of your vigilance and concern for product quality, you've never had a virus contaminate any of your 350 products—before Stoned III. You acted immediately to correct the problem, and you're trying to do the right thing now in helping the few customers who were affected. You have assigned a specialist on your staff, Roxanne Sawicky, to answer specific questions from affected customers. Her number is (416) 831–6690.

Write to Donald V. Cruz, 2360 Red River Road, Winnipeg, MB R2C 1M8 denying his request. Tell him that you're rushing him a clean copy of Galaxy Invaders. To remove the virus and clean up his hard disk, he should use the Integrity Anti-Virus program. It has special routines that will detect, remove, and prevent more than 400 viruses, including Stoned III. He can purchase this program by calling Integrity's toll-free number (1–800–555–4690).

8.15 Bad News for a Customer: The StairClimber or the LifeStep? (Goal 6)

You are delighted to receive a large order from Susan Sweetman, Beaches Fitness Centre, 2396 Queen Street E., Toronto, ON M4E 1H4. This order consists of two Lifecycle Trainers (at $1295 each), four Pro Abdominal Boards (at $295 each), three Tunturi Muscle Trainers (at $749 each), and three Dual-Action StairClimbers (at $1545 each).

You could ship immediately except for one problem. The Dual-Action StairClimber is intended for home use, not for gym or club use. Customers like it because they say it's more like scaling a mountain than climbing a flight of stairs. With each step, users exercise their arms to pull or push themselves up. And its special cylinders absorb shock so that no harmful running impact results. However, this model is not what you would recommend for gym use. You feel Ms. Sweetman should order your premier stairclimber, the LifeStep (at $2 395 each). This unit has sturdier construction and is meant for heavy use. Its sophisticated electronics provide a selection of customer-pleasing programs that challenge muscles progressively with a choice of workouts. It also quickly multiplies workout gains with computer-controlled interval training. Electronic monitors inform users of step height, calories burned, elapsed time, upcoming levels, and adherence to fitness goals. For gym use the LifeStep is clearly better than the StairClimber. The bad news is that the LifeStep is considerably more expensive.

You get no response when you try to telephone Ms. Sweetman to discuss the problem. Should you ship what you can, or hold the entire order until you learn whether she wants the StairClimber or the LifeStep? Or perhaps you should substitute the LifeStep and send only two of them. Decide what to do and write a letter to Ms. Sweetman.

8.16 Customer Bad News: College Bookstore Housecleaning (Goal 6)

As the customer service manager of Randall House Publishing, you must refuse most of a shipment of books returned from the Mackenzie College Bookstore. Your policy is to provide a 100 percent return on books provided the books are returned prepaid in *new, unmarked*, and *resaleable* condition. The return must be within 12 months of the original invoice date. Old editions of books must be returned within 90 days of your announcement that you will no longer be printing that edition. These conditions are published and sent with every order of books shipped.

The return shipment from the Mackenzie College Bookstore looks as if someone was housecleaning and decided to return all unsold books to you. Fourteen books are not your titles; return them. You could have accepted the 22 copies of Donner's *Introduction to Marketing*—if they were not imprinted with "Mackenzie College Bookstore," the price, and return instructions on the inside cover. The 31 copies of Hefferman's *College Writing Handbook* are second editions. Since you've been selling the third edition for 14 months, you can't accept them. Five copies of Quigley's *Business Law* appear to be water-damaged; they're unsaleable. From the whole mess it looks as if you'll be able to give them credit for 25 copies of Miller's *The Promotable Woman* (wholesale price $31). However, since Mackenzie sent no invoice information, you'll have to tack on a 15 percent service charge to cover the effort involved in locating the order in your records.

Write a letter to Richard M. Quong, Manager, Mackenzie College Bookstore, Peterborough, ON K9H 5Z4, that retains his goodwill. Mackenzie has been a valued customer in the past. They've placed orders on time and paid on time. Tell Mr. Quong what is being returned and how much credit you are allowing. From the credit total, deduct $12.50 for return shipping costs.

8.17   Customer Claim Denial: Telling Time under Water (Goal 6)

As customer service representative Patricia Garrison, you receive the following letter from a customer:

Dear Rayco Watch Company:

I'm sending back my Windsurfer V-2 watch. I received this watch as a gift for my birthday June 3, and I've been wearing it surfing and scuba diving for the past two weeks. I love all its features, but now it's stopped working. I thought this watch was supposed to be waterproof! My parents said it cost $96.20. Please refund this amount.

Jerry Golden.

The service department says the watch is water-damaged. Your technicians remind you that this watch is water-resistant—not waterproof. Apparently it's undergone prolonged submersion. Mr. Golden admits that he's worn it scuba diving. You must refuse the claim. The Windsurfer V-2 is a fine watch, but it's meant for sailing and windsurfing, not for diving. As your advertisement says, "Wear the watch built for bad weather and good times." It contains many fine features for sailing enthusiasts: a rotating compass-points bezel for setting your course, dual time, tachymeter, stopwatch, calendar, alarm, microlight, and ventilated rubber band with wind conversion chart. But it's not intended for underwater wear.

For that purpose you would recommend one of your SportDiver models. Each of these is constructed with a rugged resin case and has a scratch-resistant plastic crystal that is guaranteed to maintain water resistance up to 150 feet. Tell Mr. Golden that you can't refund the full price, but you will give him 30 percent off the purchase price of a SportDiver model. Send him a current catalogue and let him select one. Make it easy for him to respond. Write to Jerry Golden, 2390 Silver Creek Drive, Windsor, ON N8N 4W2.

8.18   Claim Denial: A Mess with Mouldy Grout (Goal 6)

Assume you are Deborah Pool Dixon, manager, Promotions and Advertising, Five Flags Lake Point Park. You are upset by the letter you received from Jennifer Sledgeman, who complained that she was "taken" by Five Flags when you had to substitute performers for King Fisher and the Mouldy Grout band concert (see Problem 6.14). Explain to her that the concert was planned by an independent promoter. Your only obligation was to provide the theatre facility and advertising. Three days before the event, the promoter left town, taking with him all advance payments from financial backers. As it turned out, many of the artists he had promised to deliver were not even planning to attend.

Left with a pretty messy situation, you decided on Thursday to go ahead with a modified version of the event since you had been advertising it and many would come expecting some kind of talent. At that time you changed your radio advertising to say that for reasons beyond your control, King Fisher and the Mouldy Grout band would not be appearing. You described the new talent and posted signs at the entrance and in the parking lot announcing the change. Contrary to Ms. Sledgeman's claim, no newspaper advertising featuring Fisher and Moldy Grout appeared on the day of the concert (at least you did not pay for any to appear that day). Somehow she must have missed your corrective radio advertising and signs at the entrance. You feel you made a genuine effort to announce the changed program. In your opinion most people who attended the concert thought that Five Flags had done everything possible to salvage a rather unfortunate situation.

Ms. Sledgeman wants a cash refund of $70 (two tickets at $35 each). Five Flags has a no-money-back policy on concerts after the event takes place. If Ms. Sledgeman had come to the box office before the event started, you could have returned her money. But she stayed to see the concert. She claims that she didn't know anything about the talent change until after the event was well under way. This sounds unlikely, but you don't quarrel with customers. Nevertheless, you can't give her her money back. You already took a loss on this event. But you can give two complimentary passes to Five Flags Lake Point Park. Perhaps if Ms. Sledgeman and a friend return as guests under happier circumstances, they will look on Five Flags more positively.

8.19 Credit Refusal: No Job, No Loan (Goal 6)

As Peter Quinette, credit manager, Auto City, you must refuse the credit application of Mark E. Victor, 340 Sugar Grove Avenue, Apt. 2–B, Brandon, MB R3J 7F3. His credit application shows that he has no current employment. Although his credit history from the Columbus Data Service looks reasonably good, without employment you can't grant him credit for a car loan. One of the few rigid guidelines that Auto City maintains in credit applications is that the applicant must have a steady source of income, and Auto City's policy is to make this clear to applicants. After Mark finds work, he could reapply. An alternative is co-signing. If he finds a suitable co-signer, you might be able to make the loan. To do this, he needs to talk to you personally. Write to Mark telling him why you can't make the loan.

8.20 Credit Refusal: Waiting for the Boom Boxes (Goal 6)

As Tyler Meadows, sales manager, Dominion Sound Labs, you are delighted to land a sizable order for your new Panatronic CD boom boxes. This great little four-speaker sound system comes loaded with features, including 32-track memory CD and disc-to-tape dubbing.

The purchase order is from High Point Electronics, a retail distributor in Regina, Saskatchewan. You send the order on to Tiffany Smythe, your credit manager, for approval of the credit application attached. To your disappointment, Tiffany tells you that High Point doesn't qualify for credit. Specifically, Equifax reports that High Point has current and long-term credit obligations that are nearly twice as great as its total assets. Such a dismal financial picture means that it would be too risky to grant credit.

You decide to write to High Point with the bad news and an alternative. Suggest that High Point order a smaller number of the boom boxes. If it pays cash, it can receive a 2 percent discount. After High Point has sold these fast-moving units, it can place another cash order through your toll-free order number. With your fast delivery system, its inventory will never be depleted. High Point can get the units it wants now and can replace its inventory almost overnight.

Credit Manager Smythe tells you that your company generally reveals the name of your reporting service. You also give a general reason (such as *Your credit obligations are nearly twice as great as your assets*) in explaining why an application has been refused. Write a credit refusal to E.A. Familian, High Point Electronics, 1586 Albert Avenue, Regina, SK S4V 6W3.

8.21 Collaborative Memo: Bad News for Employees (Goal 7)

As one of the managers at Atlantic Health Services, you have been asked to meet with other managers to hammer out the details of a smoking policy. Last year's partial smoking ban is about to be revised. The Administrative Council, with the concurrence of the Executive Office, has agreed that, effective January 1, all workstations and offices should be smoke-free. What you must decide is whether rest rooms, elevator areas, lobbies, hallways, stairwells, and cafeterias should also be smoke-free.

As an insurer and a provider of health care services, Atlantic is concerned with the wellbeing of its employees, their families, and its clients. It feels a responsibility to provide the most healthful work environment possible. Increasing evidence suggests that secondary smoke is harmful to nonsmokers. Many workplaces are now completely smoke-free.

In small student groups discuss how extensive the smoking ban should be. Then write a memo that announces the smoking policy to employees. You might add that Human Resources is investigating smoking cessation programs and the possibility of providing discounts for employees. When more information is available, you'll distribute it. Prepare a memo for Human Resources to send to all employees explaining your smoking policy decision.

8.22 Bad News to Employees: Putting Off New Frames (Goal 7)

As Martha Petroff, manager of Human Resources for Laseronics, write a memo to all employees announcing changes in their vision care benefits and procedures. The message will contain a little good news and substantial bad news.

In the past employees could have eye examinations, along with new lenses and frames, once every 12 months. However, before employees could request eye examinations, they had to mail in a request and then wait for a benefit form to be sent. Then they filled out the benefit form and submitted it to Vision Service Program, the vision care provider. Eventually, members received authorization for eye care. You know how slow and irritating this procedure has been to employees. Now, VSP has a new method for requesting vision care. Employees may call a toll-free number, 1–800–346–2200, to obtain the benefit form. That's good news. Employees may also continue using the request form, if they choose.

The bad news is that, effective January 1, coverage for new frames will be changed from once every 12 months to once every 24 months (counting from the last date members received new frames). The frequency of eye examinations and lenses will remain the same (every 12 months). This reduction in benefits is necessitated by sharply increasing overall costs of vision care and by concessions made by the employees' union. The union opted for reduced vision care benefits instead of charging employees a fee to maintain the previous levels of care.

8.23 Saying No to a Job Applicant: See Us When You Have a Degree (Goal 7)

As Andrea Resnik, human resources vice-president at Annapolis Valley Enterprises, you must write to Cheryl Ann Fontana telling her that she was not selected for the position of administrative assistant. Cheryl Ann was one of the finalists for the advertised opening, but you decided to hire Richard Herringshaw because he knew Lotus, WordPerfect, and Word. He seemed to be more knowledgeable about computers than Cheryl Ann. On her résumé Cheryl had said that she was familiar with computing, but during the interview she revealed that she had taken only beginning courses. Moreover, Richard had finished a B.A. degree, whereas Cheryl Ann was still working on hers. When Cheryl completes more advanced courses and finishes her degree, you might be able to offer her something.

CLUE REVIEW 8

Edit the following sentences to correct all language faults, including mistakes in grammar, punctuation, spelling, and usage.

1. Your advertisement in the June second edition of the Montreal Gazette, caught my attention; because my training and experience matches your requirements.

2. Undoubtlessly the bank is closed at this hour but it's ATM will enable you to recieve the cash you need.

3. A flow chart detailing all sales' procedures in 4 divisions were prepared by our Vice President.

4. The computer and printer was working good yesterday, and appeared to be alright this morning; when I used it for my report.

5. If I was you I would be more concerned with long term not short term returns on the invested capitol.

6. We make a conscience effort by the way to find highly-qualified individuals with up to date computer skills.

7. If your résumé had came earlier I could have showed it to Mr. Sutton and she before your interview.

8. Deborahs report summary is more easier to read then David because she used consistant headings and efficient writing techniques.

9. At McDonald's we ordered 4 big macs 3 orders of french fries, and 5 coca-colas for lunch.

10. Because the budget cuts will severely effect all programs the faculty have unanimously opposed it.

Persuasive and Sales Messages

LEARNING GOALS

After studying this chapter, you should be able to

1 Apply the 3 × 3 writing process to persuasive messages.

2 Explain the components of a persuasive message.

3 Deliver a persuasive yet ethical argument.

4 Request favours and action effectively.

5 Write convincing persuasive messages within organizations.

6 Request adjustments and make claims successfully.

7 Compose successful sales messages.

IWK Children's Hospital Foundation

Every year for more than a decade, television viewers have been tuning into the telethons produced for the Children's Miracle Network, an international organization with more than 160 member hospitals in Canada and the United States. Established in 1983 to help children by actively supporting improved health care, the CMN raises more than $100 million a year.

Every year one of those telethons is produced at the Halifax studios of the CBC, for the Izaak Walton Killam Hospital for Children. The hospital is considered one of Canada's best, caring for more than 75 000 children annually. Its 24-hour televised fundraising telethon is also one of the best; the IWK has consistently placed in the top five hospitals in total dollars raised.

Behind that success are members of the IWK Children's Hospital Foundation, set up in 1987 to operate separately from the institution as its fundraising arm. Thousands of volunteers and donors have contributed to the IWK telethon over the years; in 1994 more than $3.2 million was raised, bringing the telethon's fundraising total to more than $26 million.

The research and organizational effort behind this event, and the publications, press releases, and promotional material that advertise it are monumental. It's a big job—one that Elizabeth Clarke took over in the fall of 1990 as telethon coordinator.

As a professional fundraiser, Elizabeth has to translate the needs of the institution into publications and campaigns that appeal to corporate and private sponsors, the media, and the public, and find innovative ways to raise capital in a very competitive market. "It's organizational work, primarily, that is done in traditional ways—developing a variety of programs, looking at annual appeals, organizing mailing campaigns as well as the telethon," Elizabeth says.

"I focus first on the research, which I approach from the point of view of a sponsor or donor, so that I can then organize promotional material and orchestrate mailing campaigns and events that allow us to reach out to the community. But I make sure that, whatever the specific campaign or strategy, we always speak to the mission of the hospital and maintain the integrity of the institution.

"That requires tailoring each effort in two ways—to appeal to the needs of the individual sponsor or donor and, at the same time, to reflect the principles and demands inherent in a carefully thought-out mission statement. It's always a balance, no matter what written or management work must be addressed on a given day."

> *"You have to sell the project you're working on, and to do that you first have to be a critical thinker, able to assess needs and strip down the essence of the job at hand as much as possible."*

Elizabeth puts to daily use all the tools she gained on her academic and professional path. She graduated from what is now Ryerson Polytechnic University in Toronto and went immediately to work for the National Film Board of Canada. Working in the marketing department, she handled the promotion of a variety of documentary films produced by the NFB—writing press releases, coordinating event management, and identifying markets, institutions, and organizations that might be interested in the films.

When she left the NFB, she accepted a job in Halifax that required equally strong skills in research, organization, and writing—director of the Atlantic Film Festival. "It was a completely different job, but all the same problems applied. But it was certainly my biggest organizational challenge in terms of maintaining my focus and streamlining my efforts to hit the market. In any of these jobs you have to sell the project you're working on, and to do that you first have to be a critical thinker, able to assess needs, and strip down the essence of the job at hand as much as possible.

"It doesn't matter if you're writing a speech or a film festival program, you have to know what you're talking about and what they want to hear—and give it to them clearly. You can't do that unless you've done the legwork, know what you want to say, have as many details and as much information at hand as possible, and then produce publications and events that 'talk' to each audience.

"The telethon is different from the film festival in its overall goals; the sole purpose of our 24-hour television event is to raise money, and that requires large amounts of research, time spent communicating with new donors and existing donor corporations and with community groups and organizations.

"It's incredibly competitive—it's a challenge to design pamphlets, event, and promotional materials that will attract people to your cause. We're competing with the United Way, the Red Cross, the Canadian Cancer Society, and the Children's Wish Foundation. Talk about competition! They're all good causes, and you can only carve out your niche if you've done solid research first."

The telethon has a fundraising guide that reflects the mission of the hospital and outlines the institution's exact needs. "It clearly explains why and how we are trying to raise a specific amount of money to cover special equipment. It's a successful fundraising tool because it gives a clear indication of what the hospital needs in order to deliver the best service possible. People are most likely to understand and respond to a need or request when it's been clearly explained.

"You have to be very analytical. And before you undertake any task, whether it's producing a brochure or producing a television fundraising show, set out what you want to achieve, identify what you need to accomplish in the particular task, then organize your notes and your job in a very logical way."[1] ▪

Before being able to persuade prospective donors to donate funds during an IWK telethon, the goals of the fundraiser must be clearly communicated. If potential donors understand how the funds raised will be used to benefit a specific project, they will be more likely to respond to the request.

Strategies for Making Persuasive Requests

The ability to persuade is one of life's important skills. Persuading means using argument or discussion to change a person's beliefs or actions. At IWK Children's Hospital, Elizabeth Clarke uses many persuasive techniques to appeal to corporate and private sponsors. Doubtless you've used persuasion at home, at school, and on the job to convert others to your views or to motivate them to do what you want. The outcome of such efforts depends largely on the reasonableness of your request and the ability to present your argument. Business requests and sales messages work the same way.

When you think that your listener or reader is inclined to agree with your request, you can start directly with the main idea. But when the receiver is likely to resist, don't reveal the purpose too quickly. Like bad news, ideas that require persuasion benefit from preparation.

Assume you want a new, powerful office computer that is compatible with your home computer and other data sources. In a memo to your boss, Laura, who is likely to resist this request because of budget constraints, you wisely decide not to open with a direct request. Instead, you gain her attention and move to logical reasons supporting your request. This indirect pattern is effective when you must persuade people to grant you favours, accept your recommendations, make adjustments in your favour, or grant your claims.

The success of most sales messages rests on knowing your product well, developing credibility, and hooking your request to benefits for the receiver. In persuasive messages other than sales, you need to know precisely what you want the receiver to think or do. You also need to anticipate what appeals to make or "buttons to push" to motivate action. Achieving these goals in written messages requires special attention to the initial steps in the writing process.

Applying the 3 × 3 Writing Process to Persuasive Messages

Persuasion means changing people's views, and that's a difficult task. Pulling it off demands planning and perception. The 3 × 3 writing process provides you with a helpful structure for laying a foundation for persuasion. Of particular importance here are (1) analyzing the purpose, (2) adapting to the audience, (3) collecting information, and (4) organizing the message.

Analyzing the purpose. The purpose of a persuasive message is to convert the receiver to your ideas or to motivate action. A message without a clear purpose is doomed. Not only must you know what your purpose is and what response you want, but you must know these things when you start writing. Too often, ineffective communicators reach the end of a message before discovering exactly what they want the receiver to do. Then they must start over, giving the request a different emphasis. Because your purpose establishes the strategy of the message, decide first what it is.

Let's return to your memo requesting a new computer. What exactly do you want your boss to do? Do you expect Laura to (1) meet with you so that you can show her how much computer time is lost with incompatible data, (2) purchase Brand X computer for you now, or (3) include your computer request in the department's five-year equipment forecast? By deciding at the beginning what your purpose is, you can shape the message to point toward it. This planning effort saves considerable rewriting time and produces the most successful persuasive messages.

"A picture is worth a thousand words." This is particularly true when you are trying to relay information to an audience who may not have the time or interest in rationale but are interested in the bottom line. In this presentation, the sender captures her audience's attention with a stimulating visual.

Adapting to the audience. While you're considering the purpose of a persuasive message, you also need to concentrate on the receiver. How can you adapt your request to that individual so that your message is heard? Zorba the Greek wisely observed, "You can knock forever on a deaf man's door." A persuasive message is equally futile—unless it meets the needs of its audience. In a broad sense, you'll be seeking to show how your request helps the receiver achieve some of life's major goals or fulfil key needs: money, power, comfort, confidence, importance, friends, peace of mind, and recognition, to name a few.

On a more practical level, you want to show how your request solves a problem, achieves a personal or work objective, or just makes life easier for your audience. In your request for a new computer, for example, you could appeal to your boss's expressed desire for greater productivity. If you were asking for a four-day work schedule, you could cite the need for improved efficiency and better employee morale.

To adapt your request to the receiver, consider these questions that the receiver will very likely be asking himself or herself.[2]

> Why should I?   Says who?
> Who cares?   So what?
> What's in it for me?   What's in it for you?

Adapting to your audience means being ready to answer these questions. It means learning about the audience and analyzing why they might resist your proposal. It means searching for ways to connect your purpose with their needs. If completed before you begin writing, such analysis goes a long way toward overcoming resistance and achieving your goal. The Career Skills box on page 246 presents additional strategies that can make you a successful persuader.

Researching and organizing ideas. Once you've analyzed the audience and considered how to adapt your message to their needs, you're ready to collect data and organize them. You might brainstorm and make cluster diagrams to get a rough outline. For your computer request, if your strategy was to show that a

Effective persuasive messages focus on the needs or goals of the audience.

new computer would increase your productivity, you would gather data to show how much time and effort could be saved with the new machine. To overcome resistance to cost, you would need information about prices. To ensure getting exactly the machine you want, you would document models and features.

The next step is to organize your data. Suppose you have already decided that your request will meet with resistance. Thus, you decide not to open directly with your request. Instead, you use the four-part indirect pattern, listed below and shown graphically in Figure 9.1:

- Gain attention

- Build interest

- Reduce resistance

- Motivate action

The indirect pattern discussed and illustrated here suggests a specific plan for making persuasive requests.

Blending the Components of a Persuasive Message

Although the indirect pattern appears to contain four separate steps, successful persuasive messages actually blend these steps into a seamless whole. Moreover, the sequence of the components may change depending on the situation and the emphasis. Regardless of where they are placed, the key elements in persuasive requests are (1) gaining the audience's attention, (2) convincing them that your proposal is worthy, (3) overcoming resistance, and (4) motivating action.

Gaining attention. To grab the reader's attention, the opening statement in a persuasive request should be brief, relevant, and engaging. When only mild persuasion is necessary, the opener can be low-key and factual. If, however, your request is substantial and you expect strong resistance, the opening should be thoughtful and provocative. The following examples suggest possibilities.

- **Description of problem.** In a recommendation to hire temporary employees: *Last month legal division staff members were forced to work 120 overtime hours, costing us $6000 and causing considerable employee ill will.* With this opener you've presented a capsule of the problem your proposal will help solve.

- **Unexpected statement.** In a memo to encourage employees to attend an optional sensitivity seminar: *Men and women draw the line at decidedly different places in defining what constitutes sexual harassment.* Note how this opener gets readers thinking immediately.

- **Benefit for reader.** In a proposal offering writing workshops to an organization: *For every letter or memo your employees can avoid writing, your organization saves $78.50.* Companies are always looking for ways to cut costs, and this opener promises significant savings.

- **Compliment.** In a letter inviting a business executive to speak: *Because our members admire your success and value your managerial expertise, they want you to be our speaker.* In offering praise or compliments, however, be careful to avoid obvious flattery.

- **Related fact.** In a memo encouraging employees to start car-pooling: *A car pool is defined as two or more persons who travel to work in one car at least once a*

FIGURE 9.1 ■ Four-Part Indirect Pattern for Persuasion

Gain Attention
Open with brief, relevant, and engaging statement that does not reveal the request immediately.

Build Interest
Retain attention and convince the reader that request is reasonable. Generally, present strongest benefit before making request.

Reduce Resistance
Anticipate reader's objections and offer counterarguments. Picture benefits from the reader's view.

Motivate Action
Encourage reader to act by coupling strongest benefit with easy, clear method of responding.

week. An interesting, relevant, and perhaps unknown fact sets the scene for the interest-building section that follows.

- **Stimulating question.** In a plea for funds to support environmental causes: *What do Madonna, the Sequoia redwood tree, and the spotted owl have in common?* Readers will be curious to find the answer to this intriguing question.

Building interest. After capturing attention, a persuasive request must retain that attention and convince the audience that the request is reasonable. To justify your request, be prepared to invest in a few paragraphs of explanation. Persuasive requests are likely to be longer than direct requests because the audience must be convinced rather than simply instructed. You can build interest and conviction through the use of the following:

- Facts, statistics
- Expert opinion
- Direct benefits
- Examples
- Specific details
- Indirect benefits

Showing how your request can benefit the audience directly or indirectly is a key factor in persuasion. If you were asking alumni to contribute money to a college foundation, for example, you might promote *direct benefits*, such as listing the donor's name in the alumni magazine or sending a sweatshirt with the college logo. Another direct benefit is a tax write-off for the contribution. An *indirect benefit* comes from feeling good about helping the college and knowing that students will benefit from the gift. Nearly all charities rely in large part on indirect benefits—the selflessness of givers—to promote their causes.

Reducing resistance. One of the biggest mistakes in persuasive requests is the failure to anticipate and offset audience resistance. How will the receiver object to your request? In brainstorming for clues, try *What if?* scenarios. Let's say you are trying to convince management that the employees' cafeteria should switch from paper and plastic plates and cups to ceramic. What if they say the change is too expensive? What if they argue that they are careful recyclers of paper and plastic? What if they contend that ceramic dishes would increase the cost of cafeteria labour and energy tremendously? What if they protest that ceramic is less hygienic? For each of these *What if?* scenarios, you need a counterargument.

> The body of a persuasive request may require several paragraphs to build interest and reduce resistance.

> Persuasive requests reduce resistance by addressing *What if?* questions and establishing credibility.

SEVEN RULES EVERY PERSUADER SHOULD KNOW

Successful businesspeople create persuasive memos, letters, reports, and presentations that get the results they want. Yet their approaches are all different. Some persuaders are gentle, leading readers by the hand to the targeted recommendation. Others are brisk and authoritative. Some are objective, examining both sides of an issue like a judge deciding a difficult case. Some move slowly and carefully toward a proposal, while others erupt like a volcano in their eagerness to announce a recommendation. No single all-purpose strategy works for every persuasive situation because of the immense number of variables involved. You wouldn't, for example, use the same techniques in asking for a raise from a stern supervisor as you would use in persuading a close friend to see a movie of your choice. Different situations and different goals require different techniques. The following seven rules suggest various strategies—depending on your individual need.

- **Consider whether your views will create problems for your audience.** A student engineer submitted a report recommending a simple change at a waste-treatment facility. His recommendation would save $200 000 a year, but the report met with a cool reception. Why? His supervisors would have to explain to management why they had allowed a waste of $200 000 a year! If your views make trouble for the audience, think of ways to include the receivers in your recommendation if possible. Whatever your strategy, be tactful and empathic.

- **Don't offer new ideas, directives, or recommendations for change until your audience is prepared for them.** Receivers are threatened by anything that upsets their values or interests. The greater the change you suggest, the more slowly you should proceed. For example, if your boss is enthusiastic about a new marketing scheme (which would cost $50 000 to develop), naturally you will go slowly in shooting it down. If, on the other hand, your boss had little personal investment in the scheme, you could be more direct in your attack.

- **Choose a strategy that supports your credibility.** If you have great credibility with your audience, you can proceed directly. If not, you might want to establish that credibility first. *Given* credibility results from position or reputation, such as that of the boss of an organization or highly regarded scientist. *Acquired* credibility is earned. To acquire credibility, successful persuaders often identify themselves, early in the message, with the goals and interests of the audience (*As a small business owner myself ...*). Another way to acquire credibility is to mention evidence or ideas that support the audience's existing views (*We agree that small business owners need more government assistance*). Finally, you can acquire credibility by citing authorities who rate highly with your audience (*Richard Love, recently named Small Businessperson of the Year, supports this proposal*).

Unless you anticipate resistance, you give the receiver an easy opportunity to dismiss your request. Countering this resistance is important, but you must do it with finesse (*Although ceramic dishes cost more at first, they actually save money over time*). You can minimize objections by presenting your counterarguments in sentences that emphasize benefits: *Ceramic dishes may require a little more effort in cleaning, but they bring warmth and graciousness to meals. Most important, they help save the environment by requiring fewer resources and eliminating waste.* However, don't spend too much time on counterarguments, thus making them overly important. Finally, avoid bringing up objections that may never have occurred to the receiver in the first place.

Another factor that reduces resistance is credibility. Receivers are less resistant if your request is reasonable and if you are believable. When the receiver does not know you, you may have to establish your expertise, refer to your credentials, or demonstrate your competence. Even when you are known, you may have to establish your knowledge in a given area. To establish your credibility in making a computer request to your boss, for example, you could

- **If your audience disagrees with your ideas or is uncertain about them, present both sides of the argument.** You might think that you would be most successful by revealing only one side of an issue— your side, of course. But persuasion doesn't work that way. You'll be more successful—particularly if the audience is unfriendly or uncertain— by disclosing all sides of the argument. This approach suggests that you are objective. It also helps the receiver remember your view by showing the pros and cons in relation to one another. Thus, if you want to convince the owners of a real estate firm that an expensive new lock box system is a wise investment, be truthful about any shortcomings, weaknesses, and limitations.

- **Win respect by making your opinion or recommendation clear.** Although you should be truthful in presenting both sides of an argument, don't be shy about supporting your conclusions or final proposals. You will, naturally, have definite views and should persuade your audience to accept them. The two-sided strategy is a means to an end, but it does not mean compromising your argument. One executive criticized reports from his managers because they presented much data and concluded, in effect, with "Here is what I found out and maybe we should do this or maybe we should do that." Be decisive and make specific recommendations.

- **Place your strongest points strategically.** Some experts argue that if your audience is deeply interested in your subject, you can afford to begin with your weakest points. Because of its commitment, the audience will stay with you until you reach the strongest points at the end. For an unmotivated audience, begin with your strongest points to get them interested. Other experts feel that a supportive audience should receive the main ideas or recommendations immediately, to avoid wasting time. Whichever position you choose, don't bury your recommendation, strongest facts, or main ideas in the middle of your argument.

- **Don't count on changing attitudes by offering information alone.** "If customers knew the truth about our costs, they would not object to our prices," some companies reason. Well, don't bet on it. Companies have pumped huge sums into advertising and public relations campaigns that provided facts alone. Such efforts often fail because teaching something new (that is, increasing the knowledge of the audience) is rarely an effective way to change attitudes. Researchers have found that presentations of facts alone may strengthen opinions—but primarily for people who already agree with the persuader. The added information reassures them and gives them ammunition for defending themselves in discussions with others.

Career Track Application

Consider a career-oriented problem in a current or past job: Customer service must be improved, workers need better training, inventory procedures are inefficient, equipment is outdated, work scheduling is arbitrary, and so forth. Devise a plan to solve that problem. How could the preceding rules help you persuade a decisionmaker to adopt your plan? In a memo to your instructor or in a class discussion, outline the problem and your plan for rectifying it. Describe your persuasive strategy.

---

describe visits to five showrooms where you tried 18 different models before deciding on the best one for your purposes.

Motivating action. After gaining attention, building interest, and reducing resistance, you'll want to inspire the receiver to act. This is where your planning pays dividends. Knowing exactly what action you want *before* you start to write enables you to point your arguments toward this important final paragraph. Here you will make your recommendation as specifically and confidently as possible—without seeming pushy. A proposal from one manager to another might conclude with *So that we can begin using the employment assessment tests by May 1, please initial a copy of this memo and return it to me immediately.* In making a request, don't sound apologetic (*I'm sorry to have to ask you this, but ...*), and don't supply excuses (*If you can spare the time, ...*). Compare the following closings for a persuasive memo recommending training seminars in communication skills.

Persuasive requests motivate action by specifying exactly what should be done.

FIGURE 9.2 ■ Techniques to Overcome Resistance

Gaining Attention	**Building Interest**	**Reducing Resistance**	**Motivating Action**
Summary of problem	Facts, figures	Anticipate objections	Describe specific request
Unexpected statement	Expert opinion	Offer counterarguments	Sound confident
Reader benefit	Examples	Play *What if?* scenarios	Make action easy to take
Compliment	Specific details	Establish credibility	Don't apologize
Related fact	Direct benefits	Demonstrate competence	Don't provide excuses
Stimulating question	Indirect benefits	Show value of proposal	Repeat main benefit

Too General

We are certain we can develop a series of training sessions that will improve the communication skills of your employees.

Too Timid

If you agree that our training proposal has merit, perhaps we could begin the series in June.

Too Pushy

Because we're convinced that you will want to begin improving the skills of your employees immediately, we've scheduled your series to begin in June.

Effective

May we work with you in improving the communication skills of your employees? Please call me at 439–2201 by May 1 to give your approval so that training sessions may start in June, as we discussed.

Note how the last opening suggests a specific and easy-to-follow action.

Figure 9.2 summarizes techniques to overcome resistance and compose successful persuasive messages.

Being Persuasive but Ethical

Business communicators may be tempted to make their persuasion even more forceful by fudging on the facts, exaggerating a point, omitting something crucial, or providing deceptive emphasis. Consider the case of a manager who sought to persuade employees to accept a change in insurance benefits. His memo emphasized a small advantage (easier handling of claims) but de-emphasized a large reduction in total coverage. Some readers missed the main point—as the manager intended. Others recognized the deception, however, and before long the manager's credibility was lost. A persuader is effective only when he or she is believable. If receivers suspect that they are being manipulated or misled, or if they find any part of the argument untruthful, the total argument fails.

Persuasion becomes unethical when facts are distorted, overlooked, or manipulated with an intent to deceive. Of course, persuaders naturally want to put forth their strongest case. But that argument must be based on truth, objectivity, and fairness.

In prompting ethical and truthful persuasion, two factors act as powerful motivators. The first is the desire to preserve your reputation and credibility. Once lost, a good name is difficult to regain. An equally important force prompting ethical behaviour, though, is your opinion of yourself.

Ethical business communicators maintain credibility and respect by being honest, fair, and objective.

Writing Successful Persuasive Requests

Persuading someone to change a belief or to perform an action when that individual is reluctant takes planning and skill—and sometimes a little luck. When the request is in writing, rather than face to face, the task is even more difficult. The four-part indirect pattern, though, can help you shape effective persuasive appeals that (1) request favours and action, (2) persuade within organizations, and (3) request adjustments and make claims.

The indirect pattern is appropriate when requesting favours and action, persuading within organizations, and requesting adjustments or making claims.

Requesting Favours and Actions

Persuading someone to do something that largely benefits you is not easy. Fortunately, many individuals and companies are willing to grant requests for time, money, information, special privileges, and cooperation. They grant these favours for a variety of reasons. They may just happen to be interested in your project, or they may see goodwill potential for themselves. Often, though, they comply because they see that others will benefit from the request. Professionals sometimes feel obligated to contribute their time or expertise to "pay their dues."

Requests for favours such as time, money, special privileges, or cooperation, usually focus on indirect benefits to the reader.

You may find that you have few direct benefits to offer in your persuasion. Instead, you'll be focusing on indirect benefits, as the writer does in Figure 9.3. In asking a manager to speak before a marketing meeting, the writer has little to offer as a direct benefit other than a $300 honorarium. But indirectly, the writer offers enticements such as an enthusiastic audience and a chance to help other companies solve overseas marketing problems. This persuasive request appeals primarily to the reader's desire to serve his profession—although a receptive audience and an opportunity to talk about one's successes have a certain appeal to the ego as well. Together, these appeals—professional, egoistic, monetary—make a persuasive argument rich and effective.

As another example, consider the following persuasive message, which asks a company to take part in a survey requesting salary data—usually a touchy subject. Few organizations are willing to reveal how much they pay their employees. Yet this request may succeed because of the explanation provided and the benefit offered (free salary survey data).

Dear Ms. Masi:

Has your company ever lost a valued employee to another organization that offered 20 percent more in salary for the same position? Have you ever added a unique job title but had no idea what compensation the position demanded?

Gains attention with two short questions that suggest problems the reader knows.

To remain competitive in hiring and to retain qualified workers, companies rely on survey data showing current salaries. My organization collects such data, and we need your help. Would you be willing to complete the enclosed questionnaire so that we can supply companies like yours with accurate salary data?

Discusses a benefit that leads directly to the frank request for help. Notice that the request is coupled with a reader's benefit.

Your information, of course, will be treated confidentially. The questionnaire takes but a few moments to complete, and it can provide substantial dividends for professional organizations that need comparative salary data.

Anticipates and counters resistance to confidentiality and time/effort objections.

To show our gratitude for your participation, we'll send you comprehensive salary surveys for your industry and your metropolitan area. Not only will you find basic salaries, you'll also learn about bonus and incentive plans, special pay differentials, expense reimbursements, perquisites such as a company car and credit card, and special payments like beeper pay.

Offers free salary data as a direct benefit. Describes the benefit in detailed to strengthen its appeal.

Comparative salary data are impossible to provide without the support of professionals like you. Please complete the questionnaire and return it in the prepaid envelope before November 1, our fall deadline. You'll know how much your employees earn compared with others in your industry.

Appeals to professionalism. Motivates action with a deadline and a final benefit that relates to the opening questions.

FIGURE 9.3 ■ Persuasive Favour Request

The Three Phases of the Writing Process

1

Analyze
The purpose of this letter is to persuade the reader to speak at a dinner meeting.

Anticipate
Although the reader is busy, he may respond to appeals to his ego (describing his successes before an appreciative audience) and to his professionalism.

Adapt
Because the reader will be uninterested at first and require persuasion, use the indirect pattern.

2

Research
Study the receiver's interests and find ways to relate this request to the reader's interests.

Organize
Gain attention by opening with praise or a stimulating remark. Build interest with explanations and facts. Show how compliance benefits the reader and others. Reduce resistance by providing ideas for the dinner talk. Motivate action by making it easy.

Compose
Prepare first draft on a computer.

3

Revise
Revise to show direct and indirect benefits more clearly.

Proofread
Use quotes around "R" to reflect their usage. In the fourth paragraph, use a semicolon in the compound sentence. Start all lines at the left for block-style letter.

Evaluate
Will this letter convince the reader to accept the invitation?

Hamilton–Wentworth
North American Marketing Association
484 Mountain Park Drive
Hamilton, ON L8V 4X2

January 28, 1996

Mr. Elliott P. Tarkanian
Marketing Manager
Toys "R" Us, Inc.
2777 Langstaff Avenue
Thornhill, ON L3J 3M8

Dear Mr. Tarkanian:

One company is legendary for marketing North American products successfully in Japan.

That company, of course, is Toys "R" Us. The triumph of your thriving toy store in Amimachi, Japan, has given other North American marketers hope. But this success story has also raised numerous questions. Specifically, how did Toys "R" Us circumvent local trade restrictions? How did you solve the complex distribution system? And how did you negotiate with all the levels of Japanese bureaucracy?

The members of the Hamilton–Wentworth chapter of the North American Marketing Association asked me to invite you to speak at our March 19 dinner meeting on the topic of "How Toys 'R' Us Unlocked the Door to Japanese Trade." By describing your winning effort, Mr. Tarkanian, you can help launch other North American companies who face the same quagmire of Japanese restrictions and red tape that your organization overcame. Although we can offer you only a small honorarium of $300, we can assure you of a big audience of enthusiastic marketing professionals eager to hear your war story.

Our relaxed group doesn't expect a formal address; they are most interested in what steps Toys "R" Us took to open its Japanese toy outlet. To make your talk easy to organize, I've enclosed a list of questions our members submitted. Most talks are about 45 minutes long.

Can we count on you to join us for dinner at 7 p.m. March 19 at the Fisherman's Inn in Hamilton? Just call me at (905) 860-4320 by February 15 to make arrangements.

Sincerely,

Timothy W. Ellison

Timothy W. Ellison
Program Chair, AMA

TWE:grw
Enclosure

Annotations (left): Piques reader's curiosity; Notes indirect benefit; Notes direct benefit; Offsets reluctance by making the talk informal and easy to organize; Makes acceptance as simple as a telephone call

Annotations (right): Gains attention; Builds interest; Reduces resistance; Motivates action

FIGURE 9.4 ■ Persuasive Action Request

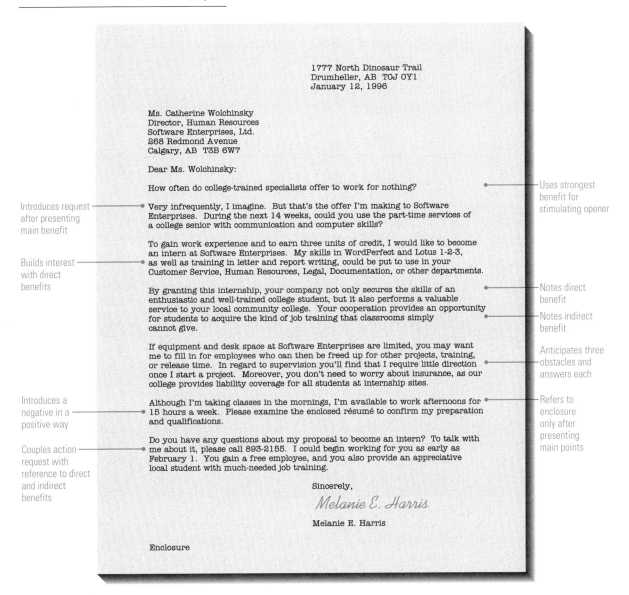

The annotations on the letter read:

Introduces request after presenting main benefit

Builds interest with direct benefits

Introduces a negative in a positive way

Couples action request with reference to direct and indirect benefits

Uses strongest benefit for stimulating opener

Notes direct benefit

Notes indirect benefit

Anticipates three obstacles and answers each

Refers to enclosure only after presenting main points

The letter text:

1777 North Dinosaur Trail
Drumheller, AB T0J 0Y1
January 12, 1996

Ms. Catherine Wolchinsky
Director, Human Resources
Software Enterprises, Ltd.
268 Redmond Avenue
Calgary, AB T3B 6W7

Dear Ms. Wolchinsky:

How often do college-trained specialists offer to work for nothing?

Very infrequently, I imagine. But that's the offer I'm making to Software Enterprises. During the next 14 weeks, could you use the part-time services of a college senior with communication and computer skills?

To gain work experience and to earn three units of credit, I would like to become an intern at Software Enterprises. My skills in WordPerfect and Lotus 1-2-3, as well as training in letter and report writing, could be put to use in your Customer Service, Human Resources, Legal, Documentation, or other departments.

By granting this internship, your company not only secures the skills of an enthusiastic and well-trained college student, but it also performs a valuable service to your local community college. Your cooperation provides an opportunity for students to acquire the kind of job training that classrooms simply cannot give.

If equipment and desk space at Software Enterprises are limited, you may want me to fill in for employees who can then be freed up for other projects, training, or release time. In regard to supervision you'll find that I require little direction once I start a project. Moreover, you don't need to worry about insurance, as our college provides liability coverage for all students at internship sites.

Although I'm taking classes in the mornings, I'm available to work afternoons for 15 hours a week. Please examine the enclosed résumé to confirm my preparation and qualifications.

Do you have any questions about my proposal to become an intern? To talk with me about it, please call 893-2155. I could begin working for you as early as February 1. You gain a free employee, and you also provide an appreciative local student with much-needed job training.

Sincerely,

Melanie E. Harris

Melanie E. Harris

Enclosure

Notice that the last paragraph gives details about how to comply with the request. It also takes advantage of an "emphasis spot" (the end of a letter) to include a final benefit reminder echoing the opening questions.

An offer to work as an intern, at no cost to a company, would seem to require little persuasion. Actually, though, companies hesitate to participate in internship programs because student interns require supervision, desk space, and equipment. They also pose an insurance liability.

In Figure 9.4 college student Melanie Harris seeks to persuade Software Enterprises to accept her as an intern. In the analysis process before writing, Melanie thought long and hard about what benefits she could offer the reader and how she could present them strategically. She decided that the offer of a trained college student's free labour was her strongest benefit. Thus, she opens with it, as well as mentioning the same benefit in the body of the letter and in the closing. After opening with the main benefit to the audience, she introduces the actual request ("Could you use the part-time services of a college senior ... ?").

In the interest section, Melanie tells why she is making the request and describes its value in terms of direct and indirect benefits. Notice how she transforms obstacles (lack of equipment or desk space) into helpful suggestions about how her services would free up other staff members to perform more important tasks. She delays mentioning a negative (being able to work only 15 hours a week and only in the afternoon) until after building interest and reducing resistance. And she closes confidently and motivates action with reference to both direct and indirect benefits.

Persuading Within Organizations

Internal persuasive memos present honest arguments detailing specific reader benefits.

Instructions or directives moving downward from superiors to subordinates usually require little persuasion. Employees expect to be told how to perform their jobs. These messages (such as information about procedures, equipment, or customer service) follow the direct pattern, with the purpose immediately stated. However, employees are sometimes asked to perform in a capacity outside their work roles or to accept changes that are not in their best interests (pay cuts, job transfers, or reduced benefits). In these instances, a persuasive memo using the indirect pattern may be most effective.

The goal is not to manipulate employees or to seduce them with trickery. Rather, the goal is to present a strong but *honest* argument, emphasizing points that are important to the receiver. In business, honesty is not just the best policy—it's the *only* policy. Especially within your own organization, people see right through puffery and misrepresentation. For this reason, the indirect pattern is effective only when supported by accurate, honest evidence.

Evidence also is critical when subordinates submit recommendations to their bosses. "The key to making a request of a superior," advises communication consultant Patricia Buhler, "is to know your needs and have documentation [facts, figures, evidence]." Another important factor is moderation. "Going in and asking for the world [right] off the cuff is most likely going to elicit a negative response," she adds.[3]

The following draft of a request for a second copy machine fails to present convincing evidence of the need. Although the request is reasonable, the argument lacks credibility because of its high-pressure tactics and lack of proof.

Begins poorly by reminding reader of negative past feelings.

Sounds high-pressured and poorly conceived.

Presents persuasive arguments illogically. Fails to tell exactly how much money could be saved.

Doesn't suggest specific action for reader to take

TO: Mike Sherman, Vice-President
FROM: Sheila Montgomery, Marketing
SUBJECT: COPIERS

Although you've opposed copier purchases in the past, I think I've found a great deal on a copier that's just too good to pass up—if we act before May 1.

Copy City has reconditioned copiers that they are practically giving away. If we move fast, they will provide many free incentives—like a free copier stand, free starter supplies, free delivery, and free installation.

We must find a way to reduce copier costs in my department. At the present time we are making a total of 10 000 copies a month by sending secretaries or sales reps to Copy Quick, where we spend 5 cents a page and waste a lot of time. We're making at least eight trips a week, adding up to a considerable expense in travel time and copy costs.

Please give this matter your immediate attention and get back to me as soon as possible. We don't want to miss this great deal!

The preceding memo will probably fail to achieve its purpose. Although the revised version in Figure 9.5 is longer, it's far more effective. Remember that a persuasive message will usually take more space than a direct message because proving a case requires evidence. Notice that the subject line in Figure 9.5 tells the purpose of the memo without disclosing the actual request. By delaying the request until she's had a chance to describe the problem and discuss a solution, the writer prevents the reader from rejecting the request prematurely.

The strength of this revision, though, is in the clear presentation of comparison figures showing how much money can be saved by purchasing a re-manufactured copier. Although the organization pattern is not obvious, the revised memo begins with an attention-getter (frank description of problem), builds interest (with easily read facts and figures), describes the benefits, and reduces resistance. Notice that the conclusion tells what action is to be taken, makes it easy to respond, and repeats the main benefit to motivate action.

Requesting Adjustments and Making Claims

Persuasive adjustment letters make claims about damaged products, mistaken billing, inaccurate shipments, warranty problems, return policies, insurance mix-ups, faulty merchandise, and so on. Generally, the direct pattern is best for requesting adjustments (see Chapter 6). But if a past request has been refused or ignored or if you expect reluctance, then the indirect pattern is appropriate.

In a sense, an adjustment letter is a complaint letter. Someone is complaining about something that went wrong. Some complaint letters just vent the writer's anger; the writer is mad and wants to tell someone about it. But if the goal is to change something (and why bother to write except to motivate change?), then persuasion is necessary. Effective adjustment letters make a reasonable claim, present a logical case with clear facts, and adopt a moderate tone. Anger and emotion are not effective persuaders.

You'll want to open an adjustment letter with some sincere praise, an objective statement of the problem, a point of agreement, or a quick review of what you have done to resolve the problem. Then you can explain precisely what happened or why your claim is legitimate. Don't provide a blow-by-blow chronology of details; just hit the highlights. Be sure to enclose copies of relevant invoices, shipping orders, warranties, and payments. And close with a clear statement of what you want done: refund, replacement, credit to your account, or other action. Be sure to think through the possibilities and make your request reasonable.

The tone of the letter is important. You should never suggest that the receiver intentionally deceived you or intentionally created the problem. Rather, appeal to the receiver's sense of responsibility and pride in its good name. Calmly express your disappointment in view of your high expectations of the product and of the company. Expressing your feelings, without rancour, is often your strongest appeal.

Brent Barry's letter, shown in Figure 9.6, follows the persuasive pattern as he seeks to return three answering machines. Notice that he uses simplified letter style (skipping the salutation and complimentary close) because he doesn't have a person's name to use in addressing the letter. Note also his positive opening; his calm, well-documented claims; and his request for specific action.

The following checklist reviews the pointers for helping you make persuasive requests of all kinds.

Effective adjustment letters make reasonable claims backed by solid evidence.

Adjustment requests should adopt a moderate tone, appeal to the receiver's sense of responsibility, and specify needed actions.

FIGURE 9.5 ■ Persuasive Memo

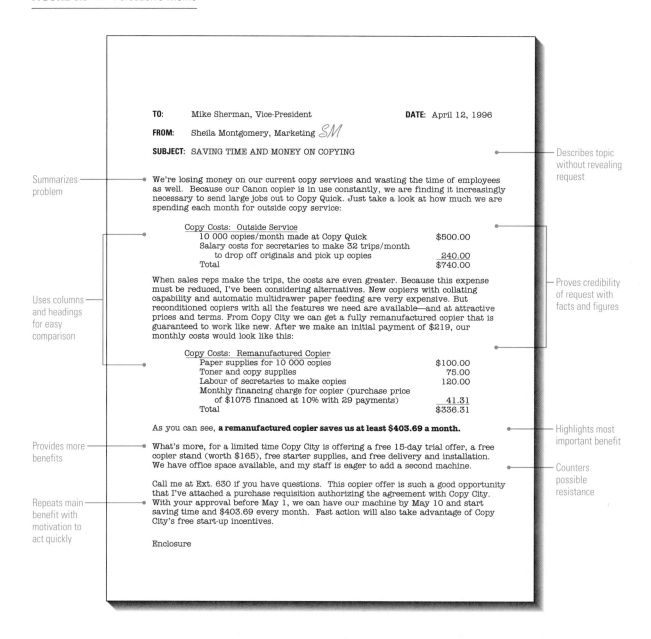

Describes topic without revealing request

Summarizes problem

Uses columns and headings for easy comparison

Proves credibility of request with facts and figures

Provides more benefits

Highlights most important benefit

Counters possible resistance

Repeats main benefit with motivation to act quickly

TO: Mike Sherman, Vice-President   DATE: April 12, 1996

FROM: Sheila Montgomery, Marketing *SM*

SUBJECT: SAVING TIME AND MONEY ON COPYING

We're losing money on our current copy services and wasting the time of employees as well. Because our Canon copier is in use constantly, we are finding it increasingly necessary to send large jobs out to Copy Quick. Just take a look at how much we are spending each month for outside copy service:

Copy Costs: Outside Service
10 000 copies/month made at Copy Quick $500.00
Salary costs for secretaries to make 32 trips/month
   to drop off originals and pick up copies   240.00
Total $740.00

When sales reps make the trips, the costs are even greater. Because this expense must be reduced, I've been considering alternatives. New copiers with collating capability and automatic multidrawer paper feeding are very expensive. But reconditioned copiers with all the features we need are available—and at attractive prices and terms. From Copy City we can get a fully remanufactured copier that is guaranteed to work like new. After we make an initial payment of $219, our monthly costs would look like this:

Copy Costs: Remanufactured Copier
Paper supplies for 10 000 copies $100.00
Toner and copy supplies   75.00
Labour of secretaries to make copies   120.00
Monthly financing charge for copier (purchase price
   of $1075 financed at 10% with 29 payments)   41.31
Total $336.31

As you can see, **a remanufactured copier saves us at least $403.69 a month.**

What's more, for a limited time Copy City is offering a free 15-day trial offer, a free copier stand (worth $165), free starter supplies, and free delivery and installation. We have office space available, and my staff is eager to add a second machine.

Call me at Ext. 630 if you have questions. This copier offer is such a good opportunity that I've attached a purchase requisition authorizing the agreement with Copy City. With your approval before May 1, we can have our machine by May 10 and start saving time and $403.69 every month. Fast action will also take advantage of Copy City's free start-up incentives.

Enclosure

■ Checklist for Making Persuasive Requests

✓ **Gain attention.** In requesting favours, begin with a compliment, statement of agreement, unexpected fact, stimulating question, benefit to reader, summary of problem, or candid plea for help. For claims also consider opening with a review of what you have done to solve the problem.

✓ **Build interest.** Prove the accuracy and merit of your request with solid evidence, including facts, figures, expert opinion, examples, and details. Suggest direct and indirect benefits for the receiver. Avoid sounding overbearing, angry, or emotional.

FIGURE 9.6 ■ Request for Adjustment

Tips for Requesting Adjustments

- Begin with a compliment, point of agreement, statement of the problem, or brief review of action you have taken to resolve the problem.
- Provide identifying data.
- Prove that your claim is valid; explain why the receiver is responsible.
- Enclose document copies supporting your claim.
- Appeal to the receiver's fairness, ethical and legal responsibilities, and desire for customer satisfaction.
- Describe your feelings and your disappointment.
- Avoid sounding angry, emotional, or irrational.
- Close by telling exactly what you want done.

CHAMPLAIN AUTOMOTIVES
141 Rue Champlain, Gatineau, QC J8T 3H9 (819) 690-3500

November 21, 1996

Customer Service
Raytronic Electronics
57 Émile Simard Avenue
Edmundston, NB E3V 3N9

SUBJECT: CODE-A-PHONE MODEL 100S

Your Code-A-Phone Model KXTXAT answering unit came well recommended. We liked our neighbour's unit so well that we purchased three for different departments in our business.

After the three units were unpacked and installed, we discovered a problem. Apparently our office fluorescent lighting interferes with the electronics in these units. When the lights are on, every telephone call is interrupted by heavy static. When the lights are off, the static disappears.

We can't replace the fluorescent lights, so we tried to return the Code-A-Phones to the place of purchase (Office Mart, 479 Pleasent Street, Truro, NS B2N 3J9). A salesperson inspected the units and said they could not be returned since they were not defective and they had been used.

Because the descriptive literature and instructions for the Code-A-Phones say nothing about avoiding use in rooms with fluorescent lighting, we expected no trouble. We were quite disappointed that this well-engineered unit—with its time/date stamp, room monitor, and auto-dial features—failed to perform as we hoped it would.

If you have a model with similar features that would work in our offices, give me a call. Otherwise, please authorize the return of these units and refund the purchase price of $419.85 (see enclosed invoice). We're confident that a manufacturer with your reputation for excellent products and service will want to resolve this matter quickly.

Brent W. Barry

BRENT W. BARRY, PRESIDENT

BWB:ett
Enclosure

Begins with compliment

Describes problem calmly

Suggests responsibility

Stresses disappointment

Tells what action to take

Uses simplified letter style when name of receiver is unknown

Appeals to company's desire to preserve good reputation

✓ **Reduce resistance.** Anticipate what factors will be obstacles to the receiver; offer counterarguments. Demonstrate your credibility by being knowledgeable. In requesting favours or making recommendations, show how the receiver or others will benefit. In making claims, appeal to the receiver's sense of fairness and desire for good will. Express your disappointment.

✓ **Motivate action.** Confidently ask for specific action. For favours include an end date (if appropriate) and try to repeat an important benefit for the reader.

Planning and Composing Sales Messages

Direct-mail marketing, a rapidly growing multibillion-dollar industry, involves the sale of goods and services through letters, catalogues, brochures, and other messages delivered by mail. Professionals who specialize in direct-mail services have made a science of analyzing a market, developing an effective mailing list, studying the product, planning a sophisticated campaign aimed at a target audience, and motivating the reader to act. You've probably received many direct-mail packages, often called junk mail. These packages usually contain a sales letter, a brochure, a price list, illustrations of the product, testimonials, and other persuasive appeals.

We're most concerned here with the sales letter: its strategy, organization, and evidence. Because sales letters are generally written by specialists, you may never write one on the job. Why, then, learn how to write a sales letter? In many ways, every letter we create is a form of sales letter. We sell our ideas, our organizations, and ourselves. Learning the techniques of sales writing will help you be more successful in any communication that requires persuasion and promotion. Furthermore, you'll recognize sales strategies, thus enabling you to become a more perceptive consumer of ideas, products, and services.

Applying the 3 × 3 Writing Process to Sales Messages

Successful sales messages require research on the product or service offered and analysis of the purpose for writing.

Marketing professionals analyze every aspect of a sales message because consumers reject most direct-mail offers. Like the experts, you'll want to pay close attention to the preparatory steps of analysis and adaptation before writing the actual message.

Analyzing the product and purpose. Before writing a sales letter, you should study the product carefully. What can you learn about its design, construction, raw materials, and manufacturing process? About its ease of use, efficiency, durability, and applications? Be sure to consider warranties, service, price, and special appeals. At the same time, evaluate the competition so that you can compare your product's strengths with the competitor's weaknesses.

Now you're ready to identify your central selling points. One very effective marketing campaign centres totally on price: "If you paid full price, you didn't buy it at Crown Books." Another campaign emphasizes service with a testimonial: "When we went looking for copiers, service was our number one concern ... and Pitney Bowes was our number one choice." Analyzing your product and the competition helps you determine what to emphasize in your sales letter.

Another important decision in the preparatory stage involves the specific purpose of your letter. Do you want the reader to call for a free video and brochure? Fill out an order form? See a demonstration? Send a credit card authorization? Before you write the first word of your message, know what features of the product you will emphasize and what response you want.

Adapting to the audience. Blanket mailings sent "cold" to occupants produce low responses—typically only 2 percent. That means that 98 percent of us usually toss direct-mail sales letters directly into the garbage. But the response rate can be increased dramatically by targeting the audience through selected mailing lists. These lists can be purchased or compiled. Let's say you're selling fitness equipment. A good mailing list might come from subscribers to fitness or exercise magazines. By directing your message to a selected group, you can make certain assumptions about the receivers. You would expect similar interests, needs, and demographics (age, income, and other characteristics). With this knowledge you can adapt the sales letter to a specific audience.

Crafting a Winning Sales Message

Your sales message may promote a product, a service, an idea, or yourself. In each case the most effective messages will (1) gain attention, (2) build interest, (3) reduce resistance, and (4) motivate action.

Gaining attention. One of the most critical elements of a sales letter is its opening paragraph. This opener should be short (one to five lines), honest, relevant, and stimulating. Marketing pros have found that eye-catching typographical arrangements or provocative messages, like the following, can catch a reader's attention:

Openers for sales messages should be brief, honest, relevant, and provocative.

- **Offer:** *A free trip to Hawaii is just the beginning!*

- **Promise:** *Now you can raise your sales income by 50 percent or even more with the proven techniques found in ...*

- **Question:** *Do you yearn for an honest, fulfilling relationship?*

- **Quotation or proverb:** *Necessity is the mother of invention.*

- **Product feature:** *At last—a collection of personnel forms that help you both hire and manage employees, while complying with government regulations.*

- **Testimonial:** *"It is wonderful to see such a well written and informative piece of work" ... (Thomas J. Bata, chairman Bata Ltd., about* Secrets of Power Presentations*)*

- **Startling statement:** *Let the poor and hungry feed themselves! For just $100 they can.*

- **Personalized action setting:** *It's 4:30 p.m. and you've got to make a decision. You need everybody's opinion, no matter where they are. Before you pick up your phone to call them one at a time, call Bell Canada and ask for the Teleforum™ (teleconferencing) operator.*

Other openings calculated to capture attention might include a solution to a problem, an anecdote, a personalized statement using the receiver's name, or a relevant current event.

Building interest. In this phase of your sales message, you should describe clearly the product or service. In simple language emphasize the central selling points that you discovered during your prewriting analysis. Those selling points can be developed using rational or emotional appeals.

Rational appeals are associated with reason and intellect. They translate selling points into references to making or saving money, increasing efficiency, or making the best use of resources. In general, rational appeals are appropriate when a product is expensive, long-lasting, or important to health, security, and financial success. Emotional appeals relate to status, ego, and sensual feelings. Appealing to the emotions is sometimes effective when a product is inexpensive, short-lived, or nonessential. Many clever sales messages, however, combine emotional and rational strategies for a dual appeal. Consider these examples:

Rational Appeal

You can buy the things you need and want, pay household bills, pay off higher-cost loans and credit cards—as soon as you're approved and your Credit-Line account is opened.

Emotional Appeal

Leave the urban bustle behind and escape to sun-soaked Bermuda! All you need is your bathing suit, a little suntan lotion, and your Credit-Line card to recharge your batteries with an injection of sun and surf.

Dual Appeal

New Credit-Line cardholders are immediately eligible for a $100 travel certificate and additional discounts at fun-filled resorts. Save up to 40 percent while lying on a beach in picturesque, sun-soaked Bermuda, the year-round resort island.

A physical description of your product is not enough, however. Zig Ziglar, described as America's greatest salesperson, points out that no matter how well you know your product, no one is persuaded by cold, hard facts alone. In the end, he contends, "People buy because of the product benefits."[4] Your job is to translate those cold facts into warm feelings and reader benefits. Let's say a sales letter promotes a hand cream made with aloe and cocoa butter extracts, along with vitamin A. Those facts become, "Nature's hand helpers—including soothing aloe and cocoa extracts, along with firming vitamin A—form invisible gloves that protect your dry, rough skin against the hardships of work, harsh detergents, and constant environmental assaults."

Reducing resistance. Marketing professionals use a number of techniques to overcome resistance and build desire. When price is an obstacle, consider these suggestions:

- Delay mentioning the price until after you've created a desire for the product.

- Show the price in small units, such as the price per issue of a magazine.

- Demonstrate how the reader saves money by, for instance, subscribing for two or three years.

- Compare your prices with those of a competitor.

Techniques for reducing resistance include testimonials, guarantees, warranties, samples, and performance polls.

In addition, you need to anticipate other objections and questions the receiver may have. When possible, translate these objections into selling points *(If you've never ordered software by mail, let us send you our demonstration disks at no charge)*.

Other techniques to overcome resistance and prove the credibility of the product include the following:

- **Testimonials:** *"I learned so much in your language courses that I began to dream in French."—Holly Franker, Woodstock, Ontario.*

- **Names of satisfied users** (with their written permission, of course): *Enclosed is a partial list of private pilots who enthusiastically subscribe to our service.*

- **Money-back guarantee or warranty:** *We offer the longest warranties in the business—all parts and on-site service for two years!*

- **Free trial or sample:** *We're so confident that you'll like our software that we want you to try it absolutely free.*

- **Performance tests, polls, or awards:** *Last year our computer won customer satisfaction polls in Canada, the U.S., Germany, and France.*

Motivating action. All the effort put into a sales message is lost if the reader fails to act. To make it easy for readers to act, you can provide a reply card, a stamped and preaddressed envelope, a toll-free telephone number, or a promise of a follow-up call. Because readers often need an extra push, consider including additional motivators, such as the following:

Techniques for motivating action include offering a gift or incentive, limiting an offer, and guaranteeing satisfaction.

- **Offer a gift:** *You'll receive a free calculator with your first order.*

- **Promise an incentive:** *With every new, paid subscription, we'll plant a tree in one of Canada's national parks.*

- **Limit the offer:** *Only the first 100 customers receive free cheques.*

- **Set a deadline:** *You must act before June 1 to get these low prices.*

- **Guarantee satisfaction:** *We'll return your full payment if you're not entirely satisfied—no questions asked.*

The final paragraph of the sales letter carries the punch line. This is where you tell readers what you want done and give them reasons for doing it. Most sales letters also include postscripts because they make irresistible reading. Even readers who might skim over or bypass paragraphs are drawn to a P.S. Therefore, use a postscript to reveal your strongest motivator, to add a special inducement for a quick response, or to re-emphasize a central selling point.

Figure 9.7 summarizes useful techniques for developing the four components of successful sales letters.

Putting it all together. Direct marketing in Canada generates over $7 billion annually in business, and the average consumer spends $170 a year on goods sold through direct marketing.[5] This figure represents only about one-third of what Americans spend; therefore, there could be tremendous growth potential of this type of marketing in Canada.[6] Sales letters are a preferred marketing medium because they can be personalized, directed to target audiences, and filled with a more complete message than other advertising media. But direct mail is expensive. That's why the total sales message is crafted so painstakingly.

Let's examine a sales letter, shown in Figure 9.8, addressed to a target group of small-business owners. To sell the new magazine *Small Business Monthly*, the letter incorporates all four components of an effective persuasive message. Notice that the personalized action-setting opener places the reader in a familiar situation (getting into an elevator) and draws an analogy between failing to reach the top floor and failing to achieve a business goal. The writer develops a rational central selling point (a magazine that provides valuable information for a growing small business) and repeats this selling point in all the components of the letter. Notice, too, how a testimonial from a small-business executive lends

Because direct mail is an expensive way to advertise, messages should present complete information in a personalized tone for a specific audience.

FIGURE 9.7 ■ Techniques for Successful Sales Letters

Gain Attention	**Build Interest**	**Reduce Resistance**	**Motivate Action**
Free offer	Rational appeals	Testimonials	Gift
Promise	Emotional appeals	Satisfied users	Incentive
Question	Dual appeals	Guarantee	Limited offer
Quotation	Product description	Warranty	Deadline
Proverb	Reader benefits	Free trial	Guarantee
Product feature	Cold facts mixed with	Sample	Repetition of
Testimonial	warm feelings	Performance tests	selling feature
Startling statement		Polls, awards	
Action setting			

support to the sales message, and how the closing pushes for action. Since the price of the magazine is not a selling feature, it's mentioned only on the reply card. This sales letter saves its strongest motivator—a free booklet—for the high-impact P.S. line.

Let's look at one more example. The following letter sells an "Employee Attendance Log," a system of cards that helps employers keep track of their employees' attendance. Because a sample is included, the letter doesn't require much physical description of the product. Instead, it concentrates on what the attendance log can do for a business. Remember that the most powerful appeals in business are to making and saving money. In this case, the employee attendance system saves managers and organizations money by spotlighting unauthorized absenteeism, a threat to productivity and profits.

Dear Business Manager:

Opens with provocative question.

How much is unauthorized absenteeism costing your company?

Builds interest by showing the reader how this product can save money and improve productivity.

If you're like most managers, the answer to that question is "Too much!" Now you can start saving your company money and boost productivity by tracking and controlling employee absenteeism. Our exclusive Employee Attendance Log system gives you a proven program for documenting absenteeism.

Describes product features by telling how they can help the reader. Accentuates central selling point.

Each Employee Attendance Log card displays a one-year calendar with plenty of space for entries. An easy-to-use code documents the reason for every absence. This graphic calendar format instantly alerts you to employees who are chronically tardy or absent—so that you can correct abusive trends before they strain productivity or profits.

Reduces resistance by providing sample. Suggests additional uses.

Please examine the enclosed Employee Attendance Log card sample. See for yourself how simple and effective this system really is. It's also a useful tool for performance appraisals.

Closes by repeating main sales point and telling how to respond quickly.

To start tracking and controlling your employees' attendance immediately, just place your mailing label on the enclosed card and drop it in the mail. For even faster action, call us toll free at 1–800–369–5590 or fax your order to 1–613–444–9301.

Sincerely,

Uses P.S. to announce a strong motivator, a 20 percent savings.

P.S. Place your order before January 31, and you save 20 percent! New prices go into effect February 1.

Whether you actually write sales letters on the job or merely receive them, you'll better understand their organization and appeals by reviewing this chapter and the tips in the following checklist.

FIGURE 9.8 ■ Sales Letter

The Three Phases of the Writing Process

1

Analyze
The purpose of this letter is to persuade the reader to return the reply card and subscribe to *Small Business Monthly*.

Anticipate
The targeted audience consists of small-business owners. The central selling point is providing practical business data that will help their businesses grow.

Adapt
Because readers will be reluctant and disbelieving, use the indirect pattern.

2

Research
Gather facts to promote your product, including testimonials.

Organize
Gain attention by opening with a personalized action picture. Build interest with an analogy and a description of magazine features. Use a testimonial to reduce resistance. Motivate action with a free booklet and an easy-reply card.

Compose
Prepare first draft for pilot study.

3

Revise
Use short paragraphs to make reading seem easy. Break long sentences into shorter ones. Replace words like *malfunction* with *glitch*.

Proofread
Indent long quotations on the left and right sides. Italicize or underscore titles of publications. Hyphenate *hard-headed* and *first-of-its-kind*.

Evaluate
Monitor the response rate to this letter to assess its effectiveness.

---

small business monthly
160 Duncan Mills Road, Toronto, ON M3B 1Z5

April 15, 1996

Mr. Keith Hall
160 Davidson Avenue North
Listowel, ON N4W 3A2

Dear Mr. Hall:

Puts reader into action setting → You walk into the elevator and push the button for the top floor. The elevator glides upwards. You step back and relax. ← *Gains attention*

But the elevator never reaches the top. A glitch in its electronics prevents it from processing the information it needs to take you to your destination.

Suggests analogy → Do you see a similarity between your growing company and this elevator? You're aiming for the top, but a lack of information halts your progress. Now you can put your company into gear and propel it toward success with a new publication—*Small Business Monthly*.

Emphasizes central selling point → This first-of-its-kind magazine brings you marketing tips, hard-headed business pointers, opportunities, and inspiration. This is the kind of savvy information you need today to be where you want to go tomorrow. One executive wrote: ← *Builds interest*

Uses testimonial for credibility →
> As president of a small manufacturing company, I read several top business publications, but I get my "bread and butter" from *Small Business Monthly*. I'm not interested in a lot of "pie in the sky" and theory. I find practical problems and how to solve them in *SBM*.
> —Mitchell M. Perry, Oshawa, Ontario
← *Reduces resistance*

Mr. Perry's words are the best recommendation I can offer you to try *SBM*. In less time than you might spend on an average business lunch, you learn the latest in management, operations, finance, taxes, business law, compensation, and advertising.

Repeats central sales pitch in last sentence → To evaluate *Small Business Monthly* without cost or obligation, let me send you a free issue. Just initial and return the enclosed card to start receiving a wealth of practical information that could keep your company travelling upward to its goal. ← *Motivates action*

Cordially,

Richard Roberts

Richard Roberts
Vice President, Circulation

Spotlights free offer in P.S. to prompt immediate reply → P.S. Act before May 15 and I'll send you our valuable booklet *Managing for Success*, revealing more than 100 secrets for helping small businesses grow.

Checklist for Writing Sales Letters

✓**Gain attention.** Offer something valuable, promise the reader a result, pose a stimulating question, describe a product feature, present a testimonial, make a startling statement, or show the reader in an action setting. Other attention-getters are a solution to a problem, an anecdote, a statement using the receiver's name, and a relevant current event.

✓**Build interest.** Describe what the product can do for the reader: save or make money, reduce effort, improve health, produce pleasure, boost status. Connect cold facts with warm feelings and needs.

✓**Reduce resistance.** Counter reluctance with testimonials, money-back guarantees, attractive warranties, trial offers, or free samples. Build credibility with results of performance tests, polls, or awards. If price is not a selling feature, describe it in small units (only 99 cents an issue), show it as savings, or tell how it compares favourably with the competition.

✓**Motivate action.** Close with repetition of the central selling point and clear instructions for an easy action to be taken. Prompt the reader to act immediately with a gift, incentive, limited offer, deadline, and/or guarantee of satisfaction. Put the strongest motivator in a postscript.

Summary of Learning Goals

1. **Apply the 3 × 3 writing process to persuasive messages.** The first step in writing a persuasive message is to analyze the audience and your purpose. The writer must know exactly what he or she wants the receiver to do or think. The second step involves thinking of ways to adapt the message to the audience. It is particularly important to express the request so that it may benefit the reader. Next, the writer must collect facts and ideas and organize them into a suitable strategy. An indirect strategy is probably best if the audience will resist the request.

2. **Explain the components of a persuasive message.** The most effective persuasive messages gain attention by opening with a problem, unexpected statement, reader benefit, compliment, related fact, stimulating question, or similar device. They build interest with facts, expert opinions, examples, details, and additional reader benefits. They reduce resistance by anticipating objections and presenting counterarguments. They conclude by motivating a specific action and making it easy for the reader to respond.

3. **Deliver a persuasive yet ethical argument.** A communicator's reputation and self-esteem suffer if his or her messages are unethical. Thus, skilled communicators avoid distortion, exaggeration, and deception when making persuasive arguments.

4. **Request favours and action effectively.** When writing to ask for a favour, the indirect pattern is best. Such requests should emphasize, if possible, direct and indirect benefits to the reader. Appeals to professionalism are a useful technique. Writers can counter any anticipated resistance with explanations and motivate action in the closing.

5. **Write convincing persuasive messages within organizations.** In writing internal messages that require persuasion, the indirect pattern is appropriate. These messages might begin with a frank discussion of a problem.

They build interest by emphasizing points that are important to the readers. They support the request with accurate, honest evidence.

6. **Request adjustments and make claims successfully.** When writing about damaged products, mistaken billing, or other claims, the indirect pattern is appropriate. These messages might begin with a sincere compliment or an objective statement of the problem. They explain concisely why a claim is legitimate. Copies of relevant documents should be enclosed. The message should conclude with a clear statement of the action to be taken.

7. **Compose successful sales messages.** Before writing a sales message, it's necessary to analyze the product and purpose carefully. The letter begins with an attention-getting statement that is short, honest, relevant, and stimulating. It builds interest by describing the product or service clearly in simple language, incorporating appropriate appeals. Testimonials, a money-back guarantee, a free trial, or some other device can reduce resistance. A gift, incentive, deadline, or other device can motivate action.

CHAPTER REVIEW

1. List the four steps in the indirect pattern for persuasive messages. (Goals 1, 2)

2. List six or more techniques for opening a persuasive request for a favour. (Goal 2)

3. List techniques for building interest in a persuasive request for a favour. (Goal 2)

4. Describe ways to reduce resistance in persuasive requests. (Goal 2)

5. How should a persuasive request end? (Goal 2)

6. When does persuasion become unethical? (Goal 3)

7. What are the differences between direct and indirect reader benefits? Give an original example of each (other than those described). (Goals 2, 4)

8. When would persuasion be necessary in messages moving downward in organizations? (Goal 5)

9. Why are persuasive messages usually longer than direct messages? (Goals 1, 2, 4, 5)

10. When is it necessary to use the indirect pattern in requesting adjustments or making claims? (Goal 6)

11. What is direct-mail marketing? (Goal 7)

12. What percentage of response can be expected from an untargeted direct-mail campaign? (Goal 7)

13. Name eight or more ways to attract attention in opening a sales message. (Goal 7)

14. How do rational appeals differ from emotional appeals? Give an original example of each. (Goal 7)

15. Name five or more ways to motivate action in closing a sales message. (Goal 7)

DISCUSSION

1. Compare and contrast persuasive requests for action and sales letters. (Goals 4, 7)

2. Discuss some of the underlying motivations that prompt people to agree to requests that do not directly benefit themselves or their organizations. (Goals 2, 4, 7)

3. In view of the burden that "junk" mail places on society (depleted landfills, declining timber supplies, overburdened postal system), how can "junk" mail be justified? (Goal 7)

4. Why is it important to know your needs and have documentation when you make requests of superiors? (Goal 5)

5. **Ethical Issue:** Give examples of and discuss direct-mail sales messages that you consider unethical.

EXERCISES

9.1 Document for Analysis: Weak Persuasive Memo (Goal 4)

Analyze the following document. List its weaknesses. If your instructor directs, revise it.

TO: Jay S. Jacobs, VP, Human Resources

Sue Simmons and I, along with other Intercontinental employees, have been eager to return to school, but we can't afford the costs of tuition and books.

Many of us were forced to go to work before we could complete our degrees. We know that the continuing education divisions of some institutions offer good courses that we could take at night. Sue and I—and we think many other employees as well—would like to enrol for these courses. Would Intercontinental be interested in helping us with a tuition-reimbursement program?

We've heard about other local companies (General Motors, Bell, Hydro, and others) that offer reimbursement for fees and books when employees complete approved courses with a C or higher. Sue and I have collected information, including a newspaper clipping that we're enclosing. Surveys show that tuition-reimbursement programs help improve employee morale and loyalty. They also result in higher productivity because employees develop improved skills.

We'd like a chance to talk over this worthwhile employee program with you at your convenience.

9.2 Document for Analysis: Adjustment Request (Goal 4)

Analyze the following document. List its weaknesses. If your instructor directs, revise it.

Gentlemen:

Three months ago we purchased four of your CopyMaster Model S–5 photocopiers, and we've had nothing but trouble ever since.

Your salesperson, Kevin Woo, assured us that the S–5 could easily handle our volume of 3 000 copies a day. This seemed strange since the sales brochure said that the S–5 was meant for 500 copies a day. But we believed Mr. Woo. Big mistake! Our four S–5 copiers are down constantly; we can't go on like this. Because they're still under warranty, they eventually get repaired. But we're losing considerable business in downtime.

Your Mr. Woo has been less than helpful, so I telephoned the district manager, Keith Sumner. I suggested that we trade in our S–5 copiers (which we got for $2 500 each) on two S-55 models (at $13 500 each). However, Mr. Sumner said he would have to charge 50 percent depreciation on our S–5 copiers. What a rip-off! I think that 20 percent depreciation is more reasonable since we've had the machines only three months. Mr. Sumner said he would get back to me, and I haven't heard from him since.

I'm writing your headquarters because I have no faith in either Mr. Woo or Mr. Sumner, and I need action on these machines. If you understood anything about business, you would see what a sweet deal I'm offering you. I'm willing to stick with your company and purchase your most expensive model—but I can't take a 30 percent loss on the S–5 copiers. The S–5 copiers are relatively new; you should be able to sell them with no trouble. And think of all the money you'll save by not having your repair technicians making constant trips to service our S–5 copiers! Please let me hear from you immediately.

9.3 Sales Letter Analysis (Goal 7)

Select a one- or two-page sales letter that you or a friend has received. Study the letter and then answer these questions:

a. What techniques capture the reader's attention?

b. Is the opening effective? Explain.

c. What are the central selling points?

d. Does the letter use rational, emotional, or a combination of appeals? Explain.

e. What reader benefits are suggested?

f. How does the letter build interest in the product or service?

g. How is price handled?

h. How does the letter anticipate reader resistance and offer counterarguments?

i. What action is the reader to take? How is the action made easy?

j. What motivators spur the reader to act quickly?

PROBLEMS

9.4 Persuasive Favour Request: Inviting a Winner (Goal 4)

As program chair of Women in Business, a national group of businesswomen, you must persuade Joann R. Schulz to be the speaker at your annual conference April 14 in Edmonton. Ms. Schulz was recently named Small Business Person of the Year by the president of the United States. She is the first woman to receive the award in the 27-year history of the U.S. Small Business Administration.

After her 44-year-old husband died of a heart attack, Ms. Schulz threw herself into their fledgling company and eventually transformed it from a small research company into an international manufacturer of devices for treatment of eye problems. Under her leadership, her St. Petersburg, Florida, company grew from 3 to 75 employees in six years and now sells more than $5 million worth of artificial lenses in 22 countries.

In overcoming adversity, Ms. Schulz has remarked, "We have an old saying in my family that if you break eggs, you make an omelet." You're certain that she would be an excellent speaker. SBA administrator Patricia Saiki said about Schulz, "Her firm's dramatic growth is evidence of her determination and can-do spirit that exemplify the best of American entrepreneurship." Central to Ms. Schulz's business and personal success is her outlook, says Paul Getting of the St. Petersburg Area Chamber of Commerce: "She radiates positive thoughts and vibrations."

Although you can offer Ms. Schulz only $1 000, you have heard that she is eager to encourage female entrepreneurs. You feel she might be receptive to your invitation. Write to Ms. Joann R. Schulz, President, NBR Industries, 3450 West 16 Street, St. Petersburg, FL 33201.[7]

9.5 Collaborative Persuasive Action Request: Selling Your School (Goals 4, 7)

Working in small groups, prepare a letter to be sent to all high school students in your area. The long-range goal is to persuade them to enrol at your school; the short-range goal is to get them to attend an open house. Point out specific benefits that high school students would enjoy by enrolling. Describe such things as small classes, useful courses, stimulating instructors, well-equipped facilities, a supportive environment, low fees, financial aid, or other features. Encourage them to attend the open house—name a date and describe its attractions. If the students can't attend the open house, suggest that they drop by the Admissions Office for information and an enrolment application.

9.6 Persuasive Action Request: Celebrity Auction (Goals 4, 7)

As treasurer of the Associated Students' Organization, you must find ways to raise money for your institution's pledge to aid the United Way's battle against adult illiteracy in your community. The ASO is planning the usual bake sales, car washes, and recycling fundraising efforts. But you have a brilliant idea for an additional funding source: a celebrity raffle. At a spring ASO rally, items or services from local and other celebrities could be auctioned. The ASO approves your idea and asks you to begin by writing a letter persuading your institution president to donate one hour of tutoring in a subject he or she chooses.

If you have higher aspirations, write to a celebrity (of your choice), who as an undergraduate attended your college or university. Persuade the star to donate an item that could be auctioned at your ASO rally. The campaign against adult illiteracy has targeted an estimated 10 000 people in your community who cannot read or write.

9.7 Persuasive Memo: Convincing the Boss (Goal 5)

In your own work or organization experience, identify a situation where persuasion is necessary. Should a procedure be altered to improve performance? Would a new or different piece of equipment help you perform your work more efficiently? Do you want to work other hours or perform other tasks? Do you deserve a promotion? Could customers be better served by changing something? Do you have a suggestion to improve profitability?

Once you have identified a situation, write a persuasive memo to your boss or organizational head. Use actual names and facts. Employ the concepts and techniques in this chapter to convince your boss that your idea should prevail. Include direct and indirect appeals, anticipate and counter objections, and emphasize reader benefits. End with a specific action to be taken.

9.8 Persuasive Memo: Overusing Overnight Shipments (Goal 6)

As office manager of Cupertino Software, write a memo persuading technicians, engineers, programmers, and other employees to reduce the number of overnight or second-day mail shipments. Your courier and other shipping bills have been sky high, and you suspect that staff members are overusing these services.

Encourage employees to send messages by fax. Sending a fax costs only about 35 cents a page to most long-distance areas and nothing to local areas. There's a whopping difference between 35 cents and $10 for courier service! Whenever possible, staff members should obtain the courier account number of the recipient and use it for charging the shipment. If staff members plan ahead and allow enough time, they can use UPS ground service, which takes three to five days.

Ask the staff to consider whether the recipient is really going to use the message as soon as it arrives. Does it justify an overnight shipment? You'd like to reduce overnight delivery services voluntarily by 50 percent over the next two months. Unless a sizable reduction occurs, the CEO is threatening severe restrictions in the future. Address the memo to all employees.

9.9 Persuasive Memo: Fitness Pays (Goal 6)

You can't believe your eyes. In *The Financial Post* you see an article describing how General Electric saves up to $1 million a year in health insurance costs for employees who joined a fitness centre at the company's aircraft engine headquarters in Cincinnati. This is just the kind of ammunition you need to support your argument for a fitness program and centre at your company, Westinghouse Enterprises. As fitness programs manager in the Human Resources Division, you suggested a fitness centre in a long memo you wrote last year. Nothing much resulted.

Now you will write again, using this material to persuade Norton P. O'Dell, president, that such a program could pay for itself in time. The article states that for two years GE compared the health care costs of 800 fitness centre members and 2700 non members of the same age, sex, and work classification. In the six months before the members-to-be joined the health club, their medical costs averaged 35 percent higher than those of nonmembers. But in the year after they joined, the fitness centre's members saw their annual health costs plunge 38 percent to $757. The health care costs of nonmembers jumped 21 percent to $841. Moreover, GE executives estimate that the company has gained 762 workdays from shorter hospital stays by fitness centre members.[8]

In your memo to President O'Dell, attach a copy of last year's memo giving the specifics of the proposed fitness program. This year, focus your argument on health care savings and increased number of employee workdays.

9.10 Persuasive Memo: Travel Time and Meetings (Goal 5)

The following memo (the names have been changed) was actually sent. Can you improve it? Expect the staff to be somewhat resistant because they've never had meeting restrictions before.

DATE: March 13, 1994
TO: All Managers and Employees
FROM: Mark Mendelsohn, CEO
Subject: Scheduling Meetings

Please be reminded that travel in the greater Toronto area is time-consuming. In the future we're asking that you set up meetings that

1. Are of critical importance
2. Consider travel time for the participants
3. Consider phone conferences in lieu of face-to-face meetings
4. Meetings should be at the location where most of the participants work and at the most opportune travel times

We all have our war stories. A recent one is that a certain manager was asked to attend a one-hour meeting in Guelph. This required one hour travel in advance of the meeting, one hour for the meeting, and two and a half hours of travel through Toronto afterward. This meeting was scheduled for 4 p.m. Total time consumed by the manager for the one-hour meeting was four and a half hours.

Thank you for your consideration.

9.11 Persuasive Memo: Software Switch (Goal 5)

As a word processing specialist, you're fed up with PFR-Write, a low-level word processing program used in your department. It lacks many functions that could improve your efficiency, such as merging, character string location, headers and footers, and macros. You want your department to switch to [name a program of your choice, such as WordPerfect, Word, Works, or WordStar]. Your manager, Holly Bogdassian, has been considering changing to a new program but hasn't made much progress. Two major obstacles are the need to train employees and to convert current files to a new software program. Write a memo that persuades her to switch to your favourite word processing program.

9.12 Persuasive Memo: Supreme Credit Card (Goal 5)

The following memo was actually sent (the names have been changed) to cashiers in a retail store to persuade them to promote the store's own credit card. Write an improved version.

TO: All Cashiers
FROM: Ramona Heiser, Manager

Don't forget, every Visa and MasterCharge card user that comes through your check-out counter is wasting money! It is your duty (as well as your job responsibility) to explain this to them and to persuade them to convert to our Supreme card.

Red pens are to be used to circle Visa and Master fees and this is going to be monitored by the supervisory staff, as well as by security for they check every receipt that leaves the building. Those that fail to circle will be reported to me and to the supervisory staff and corrective action will be taken. If you need a red pen, ask a supervisor. When you close down to go home, leave the red pen in your drawer for the next cashier. We need to boost our Supreme sales higher in order to meet company standards and you are a vital part in helping us attain this.

I need all of you to sign at the bottom stating you have read and understand the policy. Thank you.

9.13   Request for Adjustment: Second Effort (Goal 6)

As Jerry Golden (Problem 8.17), you were unsuccessful in persuading the Rayco Watch Company to replace your Windsurfer V–2 watch, which stopped working after you wore it scuba diving. Since writing your first letter, you've taken a course in business communication and learned to be more persuasive. Rayco offered you 30 percent off on a new SportDiver watch. But the SportDiver costs $199.99, and you don't want to spend that much for a waterproof watch. You would prefer that Rayco replace your Windsurfer V–2 (which cost $96.20). You feel that Rayco is obligated to give you a new watch because of its misleading advertising. Nowhere does it specifically prohibit underwater wear. How is a consumer to know that the Windsurfer V–2 is not waterproof? Actually, you've given up scuba diving and won't be wearing the watch in the water again. You were most disappointed when the V–2 stopped working. Its many features pleased you; you want another V–2. Address your follow-up letter requesting a replacement of the Windsurfer V–2 to Jacquelyn Palmer, Customer Service Manager, Rayco Watch Company, 135 Queen Street W., Saint John, NB E2M 2C5

9.14   Request for Adjustment: Angry over Printer (Goal 6)

As Becky W. Ellson, owner of a secretarial service, you are most unhappy with a printer you recently purchased. The salesperson promised that the Jetson Multiwriter II could produce proportional spacing at near letter quality. The printer does produce 10- and 12-pitch spacing, but not proportional spacing. You particularly need proportional spacing for preparing client grant proposals. After reading the manual carefully, you find no reference to proportional spacing. You decide to consult a friend who is a programmer; she says that this printer is incapable of producing proportional printing. You are very angry because the product has been misrepresented and because you have wasted enormous amounts of time and energy trying to make it work. You decide to control your anger and write to the manufacturer explaining your complaint without being too harsh. You want a full refund or a replacement printer that will generate proportional spacing with your IBM-compatible computer and your WordPerfect software program. Include your salesperson's name and a copy of the invoice. Write to Jetson, Inc., Office Products Division, 719 Acadia Drive, S.E., Calgary, AB T2J OC2

9.15   Sales Letter: Promoting Your Product or Service (Goal 7)

Identify a situation in your current job or a previous one in which a sales letter is (or was) needed. Using suggestions from this chapter, write an appropriate sales letter that promotes a product or service. Use actual names, information, and examples. If you have no work experience, imagine a business you'd like to start: word processing, student typing, pet grooming, car detailing, tutoring, specialty knitting, balloon decorating, delivery service, child care, gardening, lawn care, or something else. Write a letter selling your product or service to be distributed to your prospective customers. Be sure to tell them how to respond.

CLUE REVIEW 9

Edit the following sentences to correct faults in grammar, punctuation, spelling, and word use.

1. 2 loans made to consumer products corporation must be repaid within 90 days. Or the owners will be in default.

2. One loan was for property apprised at forty thousand dollars, the other was for property estimated to be worth ten thousand dollars.

3. Our Senior Marketing Director and the sales manager are quite knowledgable about communications hardware, therefore they are traveling to the Computer show in north bay.

4. We congratulate you on winning the award, and hope that you will continue to experience similer success, in the future.

5. Mr. Salazar left three million dollars to be divided among 4 heirs; one of whom is a successful manufacture.

6. If the CEO and him had behaved more professional the chances of a practicle settlement would be considerably greater.

7. Just inside the entrance, is the desk of the receptionist and a complete directory of all departments'.

8. Every new employee must receive their permit to park in lot 5-A or there car will be sited.

9. When we open our office in Montreal we will need at least 3 people whom are fluent in french and english.

10. Most company can boost profits almost one hundred percent by retaining just 5% more of there permenant customers.

Goodwill and Special Messages

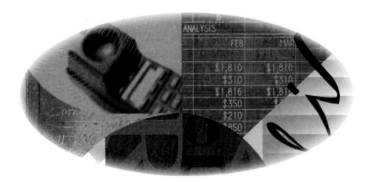

LEARNING GOALS

After studying this chapter, you should be able to

1 Identify essential characteristics of messages that deliver thanks, praise, or sympathy.

2 Discuss specific points to cover in expressing thanks, recognition, and sympathy.

3 Specify guidelines that a careful writer follows in writing employment recommendations.

4 Explain the purposes of employee performance appraisals.

5 List important topics to be covered in employee warnings.

6 Explain how to write clear operational instructions and announcements.

7 Describe the basic elements included in effective news releases.

Canadian Airlines

Whatever you know about Canadian Airlines, the services it provides, its public message and its corporate style, has a lot to do with Richard Peter.

A writer-researcher at the airline's national headquarters in Calgary, Richard is one of the people responsible for handling the company's profile in Canada and throughout the world. As part of Canadian's corporate communications department, Richard knows better than most how competitive the global transportation market has become and how important it is to maintain an accurate, well-defined corporate image and public record.

How he got that job is a lesson in itself—a lesson in initiative. "We had a great speaker address our public relations class at Mount Saint Vincent University [in Halifax] who was from Canadian, and I sent him a résumé—basically, I was hired right out of class. From the time he spoke to us, to the time I started work at Canadian ... was a one-month interval. Thirty days in total!"

Richard was a class or two short of graduation when he got the call from Canadian Airlines. (He already had a political science degree and was keen on putting his skills to work.)

"I had also completed a work co-op program through Mount Saint Vincent; I can't emphasize enough how valuable that is, especially for business students. It teaches you how to talk the same language as a potential employer, and gain firsthand experience about their business needs and about market demands. That's a terrific plus."

The airline, which has 16 000 employees, maintains its corporate headquarters in Calgary; its largest domestic hub is in Toronto. With destinations in 18 countries on 5 continents, Canadian also operates more flights between Canada and Asia than any other airline.

The diversity of its employees, coupled with a broad geographic market, makes daily internal and external communication a challenge. "An airline is a high-visibility company, and hardly a day goes by that the media don't want to know something specific. We're constantly being analyzed on some level," says Richard. "There are any number of issues that the media, and therefore our public, are curious about: from fares or smoking policies, to our menus or air quality. You name it, we'll have a question about it—and all those questions require responses."

In terms of handling external communications, the media are a major factor—as is government. "Although we're fairly deregulated domestically, there's still a lot of government jurisdiction that comes into play in major bilateral agreements with other companies. Our customers are a huge focus of our external communications effort, naturally, and we

> *"If we raise a particular issue in a publication that draws lots of strong response, we address that issue in InfoToday—we invite, accept, and apply in-house feedback. And we use it to help position ourselves."*

communicate with them generally through the media. So we have to be able to respond to the wide range of issues quickly and completely."

Differentiating and disseminating external and internal information are an important part of Richard's job—a job made all the more essential by the fact that Canadian employees are also shareholders in the company. "We want employees to know information about their company as fast as possible and as early as possible. One of our publications, a daily news bulletin called InfoToday, is regularly broadcast and tackles every topic: new initiatives regarding customers, updates on finances, all kinds of topics. It's distributed through electronic mail, available on reservations computers throughout our global network and accessible on a toll-free number, with special updates as required."

Recognizing the goodwill value of maintaining an open-access policy to corporate news, Canadian asks its employees for feedback through communications links like InfoToday. "If we raise a particular issue in a publication that draws lots of strong response, we address that issue in InfoToday—we invite, accept, and apply in-house feedback. And we use it to help position ourselves."

Some feedback has been very clear: employees want the hard statistics on how well their investment is doing. "We've learned we have to concentrate on issues and impacts on cost and revenue; that's what employees, as shareholders, want to know. And, especially when that hard news is good news, we make sure it's displayed pretty prominently."

Spreading the good word and goodwill in a company with 16 000 employees can require creativity as well as corporate initiative. Canadian Airlines president's awards are given annually to reward superior service among employees. As well, anyone in the organization can respond to a co-worker's effort to help them in their work by sending them a "recognition-gram"—an in-house telegram; Richard says a lot of recipients like to post their recognition-grams on their walls as a public reminder of a thoughtful gesture.

When you are a conduit for information, be it an internal memo regarding a job well done or a press release about new plane routes, there are basic, practical rules Richard applies. "The essential task of the writer is to communicate information clearly. And that requires a good knowledge of grammar and punctuation. Whether it's marketing information, financial data, it doesn't matter—my job is to translate that information into the client's language—and one way to evaluate how clearly you've communicated is to see how well you've been understood."

How well Canadian's communications people have done their job has been documented: a survey conducted every two years by Angus Reid asks Canadian journalists how well this country's top 25 companies did at communicating. In the most recent survey, in 1993, Canadian Airlines ranked number one.[1] ■

Developing employee involvement and commitment depends greatly on special efforts by the organization. Every successful organization, like Canadian Airlines, uses goodwill and special messages to improve employee morale and to forge strong ties with its customers.

Goodwill Messages

The work of Richard Peter at Canadian Airlines revolves around developing goodwill for his company and writing special messages not ordinarily considered to be "business communication." Because these kinds of messages may play an important role in your personal success as well as that of your organization, this chapter provides many examples and writing tips. In addition to goodwill messages, you'll learn about letters of recommendation, performance appraisals, warnings, news releases, instructions, and announcements. These special messages follow no particular pattern. Each document is different, but the overall writing process you've learned, plus the specific tips provided here, will help you develop each document successfully.

Messages of thanks, recognition, and sympathy fulfil deep human needs.

Goodwill letters and memos express good wishes, warm feelings, and sincere thoughts to friends, customers, and employees. These messages can be among the most important that you write. Although such messages are not really necessary to make an organization run, they satisfy profound human needs. We all need to be accepted, remembered, consoled, appreciated, and valued. And goodwill messages fulfil these desires. Moreover, as many companies know, such messages give you a competitive edge by establishing a positive organizational image and building solid employee loyalty. Goodwill messages include those that convey thanks, recognition, and sympathy.

Suggestions for Writing Goodwill Messages

Written goodwill messages—instead of phone calls or cards—provide a record that can be savoured and treasured.

Goodwill messages seem to intimidate many communicators. Finding the right words to express feelings is thought to be more difficult than writing ordinary business documents. Writers tend to procrastinate when it comes to goodwill messages, or else they send a ready-made card or pick up the telephone. Remember, though, that the personal sentiments of the sender are always more expressive and more meaningful to readers than are printed cards or oral messages. Taking the time to write attaches more importance to our good wishes. A note also is a record that can be reread, savoured, and treasured.

In expressing thanks, recognition, or sympathy, you should always do so promptly. These messages are easier to write when the situation is fresh in your mind. They also mean more to the recipient. And don't forget that a prompt thank-you note carries the hidden message that you care and that you consider the event to be important.

The best goodwill messages—whether thanks, congratulations, praise, or sympathy—concentrate on the five Ss. These goodwill messages are:

- **Selfless.** Be sure to focus the message solely on the receiver—not the sender. Don't talk about yourself; avoid such comments as *I remember when I was promoted.*

- **Specific.** Personalize the message by mentioning specific incidents or characteristics of the receiver. Telling a colleague *Great speech* is much less effective than *Great story about McDonald's marketing in Moscow.* Take care to verify names and other facts.

- **Sincere.** Let your words show genuine feelings. Rehearse in your mind how you would express the message to the receiver orally. Then transform that conversational language to your written message. Avoid pretentious, formal, or flowery language *(It gives me great pleasure to extend felicitations on the occasion of your twentieth anniversary with our firm).*

- **Spontaneous.** Keep the message fresh and enthusiastic. Avoid canned phrases *(Congratulations on your promotion, Thank you for the ... , Good luck in the future)*. Strive for directness and naturalness, not creative brilliance.

- **Short.** Although goodwill messages can be as long as needed, try to accomplish your purpose in only a few sentences. What's most important is remembering a person; such caring does not require documentation or wordiness. Special stationery or note cards are often used for brief messages.

Thanks

When someone has done you a favour or when an action merits praise, you need to extend thanks or show appreciation. Letters of appreciation may be written to customers for their orders, to hosts and hostesses for their hospitality, to individuals for kindnesses performed, or to colleagues for jobs well done.

Because the receiver will be pleased to hear from you, you can open directly with the purpose of your message. The letter in Figure 10.1 thanks a speaker who addressed a group of marketing professionals. Although such thank-you notes can be quite short, this one is a little longer because the writer wants to lend importance to the receiver's efforts. Notice that every sentence refers to the receiver and offers enthusiastic praise. And, by using the receiver's name along with contractions and positive words, the writer makes the letter sound warm and conversational.

Goodwill messages within organizations may not seem like business writing. Canadian Airlines and many other organizations today, however, feel that employee recognition is an important factor in reaching corporate goals. Appreciating and respecting employees go a long way toward maintaining employee morale. Satisfied workers mean higher productivity, better relations with customers, and increased staff loyalty.

Some organizations use special stationery or company greeting cards to convey good wishes. These cards carry imprinted messages like the following:

Keep up the good work!

It's a pleasure ... to work with someone as special as you.

Congratulations ... on your accomplishment.

Vacations are special ... just like you; enjoy yours!

Hang in there.

Inside these cards the writer pens a few personal comments. One company created special "Credit Cards" on which managers write spontaneous positive comments recognizing the efforts of employees.[2] Canadian-owned and operated W.K. Buckley Limited believes in the importance of employee incentives. All levels in the company are given service bonuses as well as discretionary bonuses. And a small goodwill tradition is to give everyone a birthday card with $20 inside.[3]

When your goodwill thoughts on the job require a more formal message than a card, you can use company letterhead stationery for letters to outsiders and memo forms or special notepaper for colleagues. The following messages provide models for expressing thanks for a gift, for a favour, and for hospitality.

FIGURE 10.1 ■ Thank-you Letter for a Favour

The Three Phases of the Writing Process

1

Analyze
The purpose is to express appreciation to a business executive for presenting a talk before professionals.

Anticipate
The reader will be more interested in personalized comments than in general statements showing gratitude.

Adapt
Because the reader will be pleased, use the direct pattern.

2

Research
Consult notes taken during the talk.

Organize
Open directly by giving the reason for writing. Express enthusiastic and sincere thanks. In the body provide specifics. Refer to facts and highlights in the talk. Supply sufficient detail to support your sincere compliments. Conclude with appreciation. Be warm and friendly.

Compose
Write the first draft.

3

Revise
Revise for tone and warmth. Use the reader's name. Include concrete detail but do it concisely. Avoid sounding gushy or phony.

Proofread
Check the spelling of the receiver's name; verify facts. Check the spelling of *gratitude*, *patience*, *advice*, *persistence*, and *grateful*.

Evaluate
Does this letter convey sincere thanks?

Hamilton–Wentworth Chapter
North American Marketing Association
484 Mountain Park Drive
Hamilton, ON L8V 4X2

March 20, 1996

Mr. Elliott P. Tarkanian
Marketing Manager
Toys "R" Us, Inc.
2777 Langstaff Avenue
Thornhill, ON L3T 3M8

Dear Elliott:

You have our sincere gratitude for providing the Hamilton–Wentworth chapter of the NAMA with one of the best presentations our group has ever heard.
— Tells purpose and delivers praise

Your description of the battle Toys "R" Us waged to begin marketing products in Japan was a genuine eye-opener for many of us. Nine years of preparation establishing connections and securing permissions seems an eternity, but obviously such persistence and patience pays off. We now understand better the need to learn local customs and nurture relationships when dealing in Japan.
— Personalizes the message by using specifics rather than generalities

In addition to your good advice, we particularly enjoyed your sense of humour and jokes—as you must have recognized from the uproarious laughter. What a great routine you do on faulty translations!
— Spotlights the reader's talents

We're grateful, Elliott, for the entertaining and instructive evening you provided our marketing professionals. Thanks!
— Concludes with compliments and thanks

Cordially,

Timothy W. Ellison

Timothy W. Ellison
Program Chair, NAMA

TWE:grw

People like to have their accomplishments and special events recognized by employers, co-workers, and friends. Whether done formally at a banquet or informally in a note, the recognition builds goodwill and self-esteem. Caring people send letters, notes, and memos to recognize achievements, awards, and special events in the lives of others.

To Express Thanks for a Gift

Thanks, Laura, to you and the other members of the department for honouring me with the elegant Waterford crystal vase at the party celebrating my twentieth anniversary with the company.

The height and shape of the vase are perfect to hold roses and other bouquets from my garden. Each time I fill it, I'll remember your thoughtfulness in choosing this lovely gift for me.

(1) Identifies the gift, (2) tells why you appreciate it, and (3) explains how you will use it.

To Send Thanks for a Favour

I sincerely appreciate your filling in for me last week when I was too ill to attend the planning committee meeting for the spring exhibition.

Without your participation much of my preparatory work would have been lost. It's comforting to know that competent and generous individuals like you are part of our team, Mark. Moreover, it's my very good fortune to be able to count you as a friend. I'm grateful to you.

Describes what the favour means to you. Avoids gushing (*How can I ever thank you enough!*) and doesn't overdo the superlatives (*You are positively the most wonderful human being alive!*).

To Extend Thanks for Hospitality

Jeffrey and I want you to know how much we enjoyed the dinner party for our department that you hosted Saturday evening. Your charming home and warm hospitality, along with the lovely dinner and sinfully delicious chocolate dessert, combined to create a truly memorable evening.

Most of all, though, we appreciate your kindness in cultivating togetherness in our department. Thanks, Jennifer, for being such a special person.

Offers praise for the (1) fine food, (2) charming surroundings, (3) warm hospitality, (4) excellent host and hostess, and (5) good company. Includes details to personalize the thoughts.

Recognition

Recognition means paying attention to accomplishments and significant events in the lives of friends, customers, and fellow workers. Caring individuals send letters, notes, or memos to congratulate individuals who have received honours, awards, and promotions. Thoughtful people also remember births, engagements, marriages, and other important events. On the job, considerate managers praise extraordinary effort, welcome new staff members, and honour retirees.

In Figure 10.2 the president of a company recognizes and congratulates an employee who recently received an award. The important elements in giving recognition are timeliness (writing while the event is still current) and personalizing the message (including specific details).

The following messages provide recognition to a new employee and to a friend who was promoted.

To Greet a New Employee

Welcome to the Marketing Department. We're pleased, Jason, to have you join our family of product specialists.

Please remember that Jerry and I—along with all the members of the department—are eager to explain our procedures and to make you feel at home. Once you get your feet on the ground, we'd like to introduce you to Charlie's, our favourite lunch-time restaurant. I'll call you to arrange a date next week.

We sincerely look forward to getting to know you and working with you.

To Recognize a Promotion

Congratulations, Lisa, on your recent promotion to the position of director of marketing in the Hertz car sales division! I'm delighted to learn of this well-deserved advancement. Your success, of course, was predictable, given your enthusiasm, sincerity, and perseverance. Best wishes for the continuation of a winning career.

Response

Should you respond when you receive a congratulatory note or a written pat on the back? By all means! These messages are attempts to connect personally; they are efforts to reach out, to form professional and/or personal bonds. Failing to respond to notes of congratulations and most other goodwill messages is like failing to say "You're welcome" when someone says "Thank you."[4] Responding to such messages is simply the right thing to do. Do avoid, though, minimizing your achievements with comments that suggest you don't really deserve the praise or that the sender is exaggerating your good qualities.

To Answer a Congratulatory Note

Thanks for your kind words regarding my award, and thanks, too, for sending me the newspaper clipping. I truly appreciate your thoughtfulness and best wishes.

To Respond to a Pat on the Back

Your note about my work made me feel good. I'm grateful for your thoughtfulness.

Sympathy

Most of us can bear misfortune and grief more easily when we know that others care. Notes expressing sympathy, though, are probably more difficult to write than any other kind of message. Commercial "In sympathy" cards make the task easier—but they are far less meaningful. Grieving friends want to know what you think—not what Hallmark's card writers believe. To help you get started, you can always glance through cards expressing sympathy. They will supply ideas about the kinds of thoughts you might wish to convey in your own words. In writing a sympathy note, (1) refer to the death or misfortune sensitively, using words that show you understand what a crushing blow it is, (2) in the case of a death, praise the deceased in a personal way, (3) offer assistance without going into excessive detail, and (4) end on a reassuring, forward-looking note.

FIGURE 10.2 ■ Recognition Memo

Tips for Giving Recognition

- Send your congratulations promptly. Don't procrastinate until the moment has passed.
- Get the facts (and spelling) right in identifying the event.
- Tell why the event deserves special recognition.
- Give reasons to explain why you are pleased at the news.
- Focus your praise and compliments on the reader.
- Attach a clipping of any published account if available.

InterOffice Correspondence

DATACOM GENERAL, INC.
Office of the President

To: Terri Rae Young
           Accounting Department

From: Jane Mangrum, President   *JM*

Date: February 12, 1996

Subject: CONGRATULATIONS ON YOUR AWARD!

We just learned that you were named Volunteer of the Year by the Charlottetown chapter of the Muscular Dystrophy Foundation, and we are very proud! On behalf of the management and your fellow employees at DataCom, please accept our heartfelt congratulations.

Receiving this recognition is a great honour. It symbolizes your humanitarian concerns and your willingness to contribute your time and considerable talent to help others who are less fortunate. We are very pleased for you, Terri Rae, and admire your efforts.

Enclosed is a clipping from The Guardian and Patriot describing your honour.

JM:rpy

Enclosure

Opens directly by naming reason for recognition

Concentrates on virtues of reader

Shows thoughtfulness by including clipping

Sympathy messages may be typed, although handwriting seems more personal. In either case, use notepaper or personal stationery.

To Express Condolences

It is with deep sorrow, Dolores, that we learned of the death of your husband. Harold's kind nature and friendly spirit endeared him to all who knew him. He will be missed.

Although words seem empty in expressing our grief, we want you to know that your friends at DataCom extend their profound sympathy to you. If we may help you or lighten your load in any way, you have but to call.

We know that the treasured memories of your many happy years together, along with the support of your family and many friends, will provide strength and comfort in the months ahead.

Mentions the loss tactfully and recognizes good qualities of the deceased.
Assures receiver of your concern. Offers assistance.

Concludes on positive, reassuring note.

Checklist for Writing Goodwill Messages

General Guidelines: The Five *S*s

✓ **Be selfless.** Discuss the receiver, not the sender.

✓ **Be specific.** Instead of general statements *(You did a good job)*, include specific details *(Your marketing strategy targeting key customers proved to be outstanding)*.

✓ **Be sincere.** Show your honest feelings with conversational, unpretentious language *(We're all very proud of your award)*.

✓ **Be spontaneous.** Strive to make the message natural, fresh, and direct. Avoid canned phrases *(If I may be of service, please do not hesitate ...)*.

✓ **Keep the message short.** Remember that, although they may be as long as needed, most goodwill messages are fairly short.

Giving Thanks

✓ **Cover three points in gift thank-yous.** (1) Identify the gift, (2) tell why you appreciate it, and (3) explain how you will use it.

✓ **Be sincere in sending thanks for a favour.** Tell what the favour means to you. Avoid superlatives and gushiness. Maintain credibility with sincere, simple statements.

✓ **Offer praise in expressing thanks for hospitality.** Compliment, as appropriate, the (1) fine food, (2) charming surroundings, (3) warm hospitality, (4) excellent host and hostess, and (5) good company.

Showing Recognition

✓ **Write promptly.** Don't procrastinate in recognizing accomplishments and significant events in the lives of friends, customers, and fellow workers.

✓ **Personalize the message.** Include specific details, anecdotes, and meaningful tidbits that show your thoughtfulness and feelings. Verify all facts and spellings.

Answering Congratulatory Messages

✓ **Respond to congratulations.** Send a brief note expressing your appreciation. Tell how good the message made you feel.

✓ **Accept praise gracefully.** Don't make belittling comments *(I'm not really all that good!)* to reduce awkwardness or embarrassment.

Extending Sympathy

✓ **Refer to the loss or tragedy directly but sensitively.** In the first sentence mention the loss and your personal reaction.

- ✓ **For deaths, praise the deceased.** Describe positive personal characteristics *(Howard was a forceful but caring leader)*.

- ✓ **Offer assistance.** Suggest your availability, especially if you can do something specific.

- ✓ **End on a reassuring, positive note.** Perhaps refer to the strength the receiver finds in friends, family, colleagues, or religion.

Special Business Messages

In addition to writing goodwill messages, you will probably be called on, in your business career, to compose various special messages. Particularly when you become a manager, you'll be writing letters of recommendation, performance appraisals, and, possibly, employee warnings. You may also have to compose operational instructions, news releases, and announcements. Even if these assignments seem distant to you now, you'll find them interesting to analyze. Although our advice is presented from a manager's perspective, it will be equally interesting to employees. For example, when your performance as an employee is being appraised, just what is the manager looking for or trying to accomplish?

Like goodwill messages these special messages follow no particular pattern. Each document is different, but the overall writing process you've learned, plus the specific tips provided here, will help you develop these messages successfully.

Letters of Recommendation

Letters of recommendation evaluate individuals. Although recommendations may be written to nominate people for awards and for membership in organizations, they are usually written by employers to appraise the performance of employees. The central concern in these messages is honesty. Thus, you must avoid puffing up the candidate's qualifications or distorting them to cover up weaknesses or to destroy the person's chances. Ethically and legally, we have a duty to the candidate as well as to other employers to describe that person truthfully and objectively.

Letters of recommendation present honest, objective evaluations of individuals and help match candidates to jobs.

We don't, however, have to endorse everyone who asks. Since recommendations are generally voluntary, we can—and should—resist writing a letter for people we can't truthfully support. Ask them to find other recommenders who know them better.

Some business people argue that recommendations are useless because they're always positive. Despite the general avoidance of negatives, well-written recommendations do help match candidates with jobs. Hiring companies learn more about a candidate's skills and potential, thus enabling them to place the candidate properly.

Legal and ethical issues. Regardless of the helpfulness of recommendations, a number of companies today, fearing lawsuits, prohibit their managers from recommending ex-employees. Instead, when these companies are asked about former employees, they provide only the essentials, such as date of employment and position held. Employers are gun-shy because former employees have

For legal and ethical reasons, a letter of recommendation should be written only for someone whom the writer truly supports.

sued—and won—charging defamation of character. Letters of recommendation carrying negative statements can damage reputations, thus preventing former employees from gaining employment.

Although companies may be reluctant to provide recommendation letters, they may not have a choice. This intensifies their difficulties. In the case of fired or terminated employees, employers may be required to provide a letter of reference to help the employee get another job, as ruled in an Ontario court decision. Here is a case in point. An Ontario accountant with extensive experience was terminated from his job as a corporate controller for a computer technology and software company. The company informed him that he would be given a positive letter of reference and they would make some telephone calls to help him obtain another job. However, neither of these things was done. Ten months later, after spending more than $4000 and sending out 200 resumes, the accountant found another job. However, he sued his former employer, claiming that the lack of a reference letter had increased the difficulty of the search.

The judge ruled that normally three months' pay would be appropriate, but since a depressed economy plus the lack of a letter of reference increased the difficulty of getting a job, he added two months. The plaintiff was awarded more than $26 000 plus legal costs and interest. Greg Roberts, the lawyer representing the employee, noted that this decision means that "if you [the employer] do anything to prevent a fired employee from getting a job, the notice period will be lengthened."[5]

Because they may face legal action, many Canadian companies are becoming more reluctant to write reference letters for departing employees.

Despite such rulings, Canadian companies are becoming more reluctant to write reference letters for employees who quit or are fired for fear of legal action. For quite some time, General Motors of Canada has had a policy of not providing references even though it requests references for people it hires. A 1990 U.S. survey found that 80 percent of employer respondents wanted references for job candidates; however only 6 percent were willing to provide references for former employees.[6]

The credibility of the references is also another issue. In a recent survey, executives responded that they thought only 55 percent of references were honest. The number one reason cited for providing less than totally honest responses was "fear of lawsuits." Max Messmer, chairman of Accountemps stated, "The fear of defamation suits has made it increasingly difficult to get references to speak frankly about anything more than a candidate's employment dates and salary."[7]

Good letters of recommendation provide confidential, truthful, and specific job-related information.

Most businesspeople, however, recognize that letters of reference serve a valuable purpose. Yet, they are cautious in writing them. Here are six guidelines that a careful writer can follow in writing recommendations:

- **Respond only to written requests.** Moreover, don't volunteer information, particularly if it's negative.

- **State that your remarks are confidential.** While such a statement does not prevent lawsuits, it is evidence of the writer's intentions.

- **Provide only job-related information.** Avoid commenting on behaviour or activities away from the job.

- **Avoid vague or ambiguous statements.** Keep in mind that imprecise, poorly explained remarks (*She left the job suddenly*) may be made innocently but could be interpreted quite differently.

- **Supply specific evidence for any negatives.** Support any damaging information with verifiable facts.

Part III
Letters and Memos

280

- **Stick to the truth.** Avoid making any doubtful statements. Truth is always a valid defence against libel or slander.

How to write a recommendation. Recommendations often have three parts: opening, body, and conclusion. In the opening of an employment recommendation, you should give the name of the candidate and the position sought, if it is known. State that your remarks are confidential, and suggest that you are writing at the request of the applicant. Describe your relationship with the candidate, as shown here:

> Ms. Cindy Rosales, whom your organization is considering for the position of media trainer, requested that I submit confidential information on her behalf. Ms. Rosales worked under my supervision for the past two years in our Video Training Centre.

Letters that recommend individuals for awards may open with more supportive statements, such as *I'm very pleased to nominate Robert Walsh for the Employee-of-the-Month award. For the past 16 months, Mr. Walsh served as staff accountant in my division. During that time he distinguished himself by ...*

The body of an employment recommendation should describe the applicant's job performance and potential. Employers are particularly interested in such traits as communication skills, organizational skills, people skills, ability to work with a team, ability to work independently, honesty, dependability, ambition, loyalty, and initiative. In describing these traits, be sure to back them up with evidence. One of the biggest weaknesses in letters of recommendation is that writers tend to make broad, general statements[8] *(He was careful and accurate* versus *He completed eight financial statements monthly with about 99 percent accuracy)*. Employers prefer definite, task-related descriptions:

> As a training development specialist, Ms. Rosales demonstrated superior organizational and interpersonal skills. She started as a Specialist I, writing scripts for interactive video modules. After six months she was promoted to team leader. In that role she supervised five employees who wrote, produced, evaluated, revised, and installed 14 computer/videodisk training courses over a period of 18 months.

Be especially careful to support any negative comments with verification (not *He was slower than other customer service reps* but *He answered 25 calls an hour, while most service reps average 40 calls an hour)*. In reporting deficiencies, be sure to describe behaviour *(Her last two reports were late and had to be rewritten by her supervisor)* rather than evaluate it *(She is unreliable and her reports are careless)*.

In the final paragraph of a recommendation, you should offer an overall evaluation. Say how you would rank this person in relation to others in similar positions. Many managers add a statement indicating whether they would rehire the applicant, given the chance. If you are strongly supportive, summarize the candidate's best qualities. In the closing you might also offer to answer questions by telephone. Such a statement, though, could suggest that the candidate has weak skills and that you will make damaging statements orally but not in print. Here's how our sample letter might close:

> Ms. Rosales is one of the most productive employees I have supervised. I would rank her in the top 10 percent of all the media specialists with whom I have worked. Were she to return to Regina, we would be pleased to rehire her. If you need additional information, call me at (613) 440–3019.

General letters of recommendation, written when the candidate has no specific position in mind, often begin with the salutation TO PROSPECTIVE EMPLOYERS. More specific recommendations, to support applications to

The body of a letter of recommendation should describe the candidate's job performance and potential in specific terms.

The opening establishes the reason for writing and the relationship of the writer.

A good recommendation describes general qualities ("organizational and interpersonal skills") backed up by specific evidence that illustrates those qualities.

The closing of a recommendation presents an overall ranking and may provide an offer to supply more information by telephone.

known positions, address an individual. When the addressee's name is unknown, consider using the simplified letter format, shown in Figure 10.3, which avoids a salutation.

Figure 10.3 illustrates the entire writing process for preparing an employment letter of recommendation. After naming the applicant and the position sought, the letter describes the applicant's present duties. Instead of merely naming positive qualities (*personable*, *superior people skills*, *works well with a team*, *creativity*, and *initiative*), these attributes are demonstrated with specific examples and details.

Performance Appraisals

Many companies today review the performance of employees annually, semi-annually, or quarterly. These appraisals have several purposes:

- Encouraging employees to share in setting performance goals.

- Identifying employees' performance strengths and weaknesses.

- Determining whether employees are attaining their performance goals.

- Establishing an action plan for improving performance before the next evaluation.

- Providing management with a basis for determining salaries, promotions, and assignments.

Generally, the appraisal process begins when a manager and an employee sit down to develop the job description, standards, and objectives for the next review period. Then the manager observes the employee throughout the review period and prepares a written report evaluating the employee's performance. In a personal conference the manager and employee discuss the performance appraisal. Although appraisal practices and forms vary widely, most companies agree on one point. The primary focus should be on employee goal-setting and self-development. The manager encourages the employee to outline his or her personal plans for self-development.

Notice in Figure 10.4 that the evaluator spends more time on strengths than on weaknesses. In fact, most appraisals tend to be positive. When you must report negative performance, make sure you are objective, nonjudgmental, and nondiscriminatory. Avoid observations suggesting that decisions were affected by an employee's age, gender, race, or disability. To be most helpful and least actionable, stick to facts that can be verified.

Dangerous	More Objective
Jane didn't get much done in the mornings because of her partying at night. She also had an arrogant attitude that caused considerable friction within the department.	Jane was late on an average of three mornings a week. She would not accept morning calls from customers. Moreover, three co-workers (see incident reports dated 3/15, 5/29, and 6/2) reported that her attitude made it difficult for them to work with her.

Performance appraisals are often prepared on forms like the one shown in Figure 10.4. For companies without forms, though, managers may write memos describing the strengths and weaknesses of an employee's performance. These memo reports might include headings such as *Quality of Work*, *Quantity of Work*, *Human Relations*, *Progress*, and *Personal Development Goals*.

Performance appraisals help boost productivity, improve employee skills, identify future goals, and determine salaries, promotions, and duties.

Useful performance appraisals focus on employee goal-setting and self-development.

FIGURE 10.3 ■ Employment Recommendation Letter

The Three Phases of the Writing Process

1

Analyze
The purpose of this letter is to describe and evaluate the job performance of a former employee seeking a recommendation.

Anticipate
The reader wants information to help make a hiring decision.

Adapt
Because the reader will be interested and receptive, open directly with the purpose.

2

Research
Gather information about the candidate and the job sought.

Organize
Open by identifying the candidate, the position, and your relationship. State that your remarks are confidential and requested. In the body describe the candidate's job and accomplishments. Close by providing an overall evaluation.

Compose
Write the first draft.

3

Revise
Revise vague statements that might be misinterpreted. Remove any unsupported negative comments.

Proofread
Use commas after introductory clauses and in series. Use simplified letter style because the receiver's name is unknown.

Evaluate
Is this letter objective, truthful, and accurate? Is it fair to the candidate and to other candidates?

Good Samaritan Hospital
701 Queen Street
Saskatoon, SK S7K 0M7

February 21, 1996

Vice-President, Human Resources
Healthcare Enterprises
475 Topsoil Road
St. John's, Newfoundland A1E 2C6

RECOMMENDATION OF LANCE W. OLIVER

At the request of Lance W. Oliver, I submit this confidential information in support of his application for the position of assistant director in your Human Resources Department. Mr. Oliver served under my supervision as assistant director of Guest Relations at Good Samaritan Hospital for the past three years.

Mentions confidentiality of message

Tells relationship to writer

Identifies applicant and position

Mr. Oliver was in charge of many customer service programs for our 770-bed hospital. A large part of his job involved monitoring and improving patient satisfaction. Because of his personable nature and superior people skills, he got along well with fellow employees, patients, and physicians. His personnel record includes a number of citations for exemplary service.

Supports general qualities with specific details

Mr. Oliver works well with a team, as evidenced by his participation on the steering committee to develop our "Service First Every Day" program. His most significant contributions to our hospital, though, came as a result of his own creativity and initiative. He developed and implemented a patient hotline to hear complaints and resolve problems immediately. This enormously successful telephone service helped us improve our patient satisfaction rating from 7.2 last year to 8.4 this year. That's the highest rating in our history, and Mr. Oliver deserves a great deal of the credit.

Describes and interprets accomplishments

We're sorry to lose Mr. Oliver, but we recognize his desire to advance his career. I am confident that his resourcefulness, intelligence, and enthusiasm will make him successful in your organization. I recommend him without reservation.

Summarizes main points and offers evaluation

Mary E. O'Rourke

MARY E. O'ROURKE, DIRECTOR, GUEST RELATIONS

MEO:rtd

FIGURE 10.4 ■ Employee Performance Appraisal

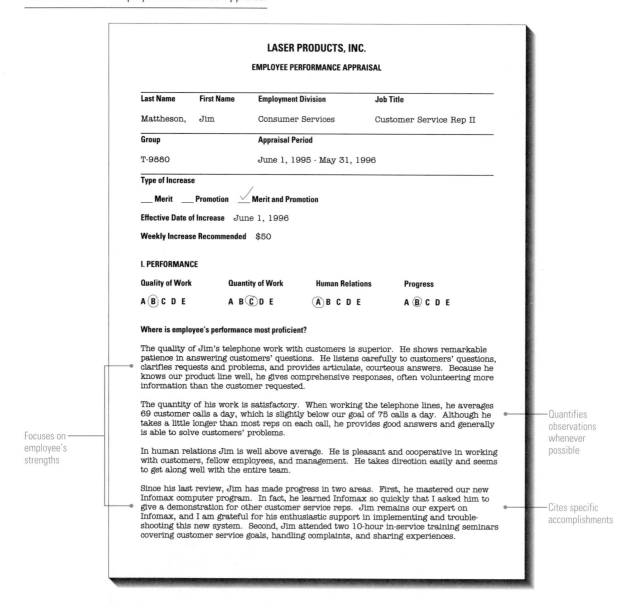

Focuses on employee's strengths

Quantifies observations whenever possible

Cites specific accomplishments

Warnings

Warnings specify problems with performance or job-related behaviour in firm yet sympathetic terms.

Managers must occasionally give employees written warnings that document problems in performance or work-related behaviour.[9] Warnings are generally written at the time of the problem and are placed in an employee's personnel file. Causes for warnings include habitual tardiness or absenteeism, insubordination, low productivity, sexual harassment, or serious violations of company policy. Like performance appraisals, warnings may be prepared on printed forms or written as memos. Here are tips for writing warnings:

- Describe the time, place, and details of the infraction or problem.

Where does employee's performance need improvement?

When he switches to administrative work, which accounts for 25 percent of his assignment, Jim's performance falters somewhat. In working with correspondence, product mailings, and follow-ups, he has difficulty expressing his ideas in writing. Proofreaders return about half of his letters with errors in spelling, grammar, and punctuation. Other customer service reps average a correction return rate of only 5 percent. Because he must rewrite so many of his documents, his productivity in this area is low.

— Reports negatives with objective, nonjudgmental language

List employee's performance development goals and plans for the next evaluation period.

1. Jim will participate in an in-service training course in basic language skills.
2. He will also enroll in an evening college class in business writing.
3. Jim will reduce his correspondence correction return rate from 50 percent to 5 percent or less.
4. He will concentrate on increasing his customer-calls rate to reach the goal of 75 calls a day.

— Establishes quantifiable goals

Overall Performance Rating (circle one).

A - Outstanding. Consistently exceeds job requirements. Sets example for others.
B - Excellent. Consistently meets job requirements and often exceeds them.
(C)- Good. Consistently meets job requirements.
D - Acceptable. Meets most job requirements but occasionally needs assistance.
E - Unsatisfactory. Well below job requirements. Immediate attention needed.

II. ATTENDANCE AND PUNCTUALITY

Is attendance and/or punctuality a problem to the extent that this increase is reduced or deferred?   No

Expected date of next performance evaluation   June 1, 1997

Signature of Evaluator _Craig C. Binsky_   **Date** _6/1/96_
Signature of Employee _Jim Mattheson_   **Date** _6/1/96_

- Explain why the company objects to the behaviour or what the effects of the problem are.

- Document details of prior occurrences of the problem.

- Itemize the steps necessary for the employee to correct the problem; include a schedule and deadline.

- Specify the action that management will take if the problem is not corrected.

- Say when management will review the employee's progress.

The following warning memo projects a tone of firmness, yet shows some warmth and concern for the employee in the last sentence.

TO:	Marilyn O'Riley
FROM:	John Pearson, Manager
DATE:	January 30, 1996
SUBJECT:	Attendance and Productivity Warning

Over the past year, Marilyn, your attendance has been irregular, affecting your job performance and productivity.

For the six-month period of January to June of last year, you had nine unauthorized absences and were late 16 times. From July to the end of the year you missed another 10 days and were late 14 times, according to our personnel records.

Other customer service representatives have complained that they must carry a heavier load of calls and correspondence when you are missing. Morale in your department is declining, and some reps are asking if an additional person can be hired to handle the workload.

At your performance review conferences June 4, 1995, and again January 5, 1996, you promised that your attendance would improve as soon as you settled temporary personal problems. I have not seen any change in your punctuality or attendance.

To remain with our organization, Marilyn, you must have no unauthorized absence or tardiness in the next three-month period. On April 30, I will review with you your attendance record and productivity. If they are unsatisfactory, we must release you and hire a new employee for your position. I sincerely hope you'll be able to stay with us, Marilyn.

Written warnings may also result from charges of sexual harassment. To be sure you understand what this term means and how casual comments might be misunderstood, read the following Ethics box explaining sexual harassment.

Operational Instructions

Business writers must occasionally explain how to perform an operation, such as filling out an expense report or ordering office supplies. The important thing to remember in writing instructions is that they must be so clear that readers know exactly what to do without asking questions.

To write good instructions, you'll want to divide the task into three segments: (1) planning to write, which involves practising and observing the process, (2) describing the process, which includes the actual writing, and (3) following up, which means testing, evaluating, and revising the instructions.

Planning to Write Instructions

- **Learn about the process yourself.** Become familiar with the process. Try it repeatedly. Talk to experts.

- **Examine a parts list.** If you're describing a machine, use the exact wording your reader will see on the equipment.

- **Consider your audience.** Ask yourself, how much do they already know about the procedure? How sophisticated is their level of language?

SEXUAL HARASSMENT: REDUCING THE RISKS

In today's sexually sensitive workplace, both men and women are becoming more aware of their words and actions. Women are learning that innocent gestures like brushing back their hair or making nervous movements, like crossing and uncrossing their legs, can be misinterpreted as being provocative.

And "a lot of good-hearted men are realizing that their old behaviour isn't appropriate any more," says Julian Fast, author of *Subtexts: Making Body Language Work in the Workplace.* Pats, hugs, and neck rubs are out. And a man shouldn't shake a woman's hand for more than a few seconds. In fact, any touching by men or women should be light, brief, and in a neutral zone: the elbow or shoulder. Touching superiors of either sex is always taboo.

Men and women are becoming more sensitive because of litigation surrounding sexual harassment. Just what constitutes harassment? Eight of the provincial human rights acts in Canada specifically prohibit sexual harassment, but the wording of the specific prohibitions varies. However, it is generally understood that sexual harassment consists of unwelcome sexual advances, requests for sexual favours, and other verbal or physical conduct of a sexual nature when

- Submission to such conduct is made either explicitly or implicitly a term or condition of employment.

- Submission to or rejection of such conduct by an individual is used as a basis for employment decisions affecting that person or third parties.

- Such conduct has the purpose of unreasonably interfering with an individual's work performance or creating an intimidating, hostile, or offensive working environment.

The most notable case of alleged sexual harassment came in the American Senate confirmation hearings for Supreme Court Justice Clarence Thomas. Lawyer and law professor Anita Hill, a former colleague of Judge Thomas's, testified that Thomas's sexual jokes and discussions of pornographic films at the office constituted sexual harassment.

Even a well-intended compliment can be misconstrued. Suppose you say to a colleague, "That dress (or shirt) looks nice on your body." Although you may have intended it as a compliment to the person's fitness as well as to her or his taste in clothes, it could be taken as a sexual comment.

Remember, too, that men and women interpret behaviour differently. A man may think a touch on the hand is innocent. But a woman may view it as a prelude to a sexual advance.

Career Track Application

Conduct research to learn about sexual harassment policies currently being adopted by business organizations. Why are companies developing such polices? What do such policies usually include? Report your findings in a memo or in a class presentation.

Describing the Process

- **Begin with a clear title.** Remember that the title should suggest the purpose of the instructions (not *Fax Machine* but *Operating Instructions for Fax Machine*).

- **Provide a short explanation.** Justify the reason for providing the instructions. You may wish to relate the instructions to a broader goal.

- **Divide the process into parts.** Separate the operation into major parts if necessary (*Reception of Fax Messages* and *Transmission of Fax Messages*). Further divide the process into smaller units for step-by-step instruction.

Effective operational instructions break the process into parts, number steps chronologically, include cautions and warnings, and incorporate necessary visuals.

- **Number the steps chronologically.** Begin with the logical starting point in the process and number each step.

- **Use active-voice verbs in the form of a command.** Instead of *The paper should be installed*, say *Install the paper*.

- **Use verbs rather than abstract nouns.** Instead of *Make an adjustment to the document guide*, say *Adjust the document guide*.

- **Strive for parallel construction.** Try to express all the steps in the same grammatical way. Look back over the steps in this process description. Notice how each sentence after the bullet is expressed similarly.

- **Include cautions and warnings.** If necessary, alert users to possible damage to equipment or injury to themselves if the instructions are not followed.

- **Supply visuals if appropriate.** Keep in mind that complex tasks may require pictures, graphs, or diagrams to clarify the process.

Following Up

After writing operational instructions, you should review, revise, and test.

- **Review and revise.** Study the steps you have written and revise as needed. Decide whether you have provided the appropriate amount of detail.

- **Test the instructions.** Have someone else test the process to see if the instructions are operational.[10]

Compare the following two versions of brief instructions for writing a résumé. Notice how much more quickly you can understand the second version because every item is a command starting with an active verb.

Poor Instructions	Good Instructions with Command Language
1. Make a decision on a career goal.	1. Decide on a career goal.
2. Then your background must be analyzed.	2. Analyze your background.
3. Next make a description of your education.	3. Describe your education.
4. You should list your work experience.	4. List your work experience.

Now look at the instructions for operating a photocopier in Figure 10.5. Although these directions apply to all the suggestions just listed, the real test occurs when readers try to follow the instructions. That's why it's a good idea to try out operational instructions on typical users before submitting the final version.

News Releases

Effective news releases feature an attention-getting opener, place key information up front, appeal to the target audience, and maintain visual interest.

News (or press) releases announce information about your company to the media: new products, new managers, new facilities, participation in community projects, awards given or received, joint ventures, donations, or seminars and demonstrations. Naturally, you hope that this news will be published and provide good publicity for your company. However, this kind of largely self-serving information is not always appealing to magazine and newspaper editors or to TV producers. To get them to read beyond the first sentence, try these suggestions:

FIGURE 10.5 ■ Operational Instructions

Tips for Writing Instructions

- Know the process thoroughly.
- Write a clear title.
- Explain the purpose of the instructions.
- Separate the process into major segments.
- Number the steps.
- Start each step with a verb.
- Express all steps in the same form.
- Include warnings and visuals if appropriate.
- Test instructions on typical users.

HOW TO OPERATE THE CANON XL20 PHOTOCOPY MACHINE ● — Begins with clear title

The Canon XL20 copy machine located in the Reprographics Department on the second floor may be used by any employee making work-related copies. If everyone follows these instructions and uses the machine carefully, we can reduce service costs and also experience less downtime.

Explains why these instructions are important

Loading Paper ●

1. Remove Paper Tray 1 by pulling backward firmly.

2. Select about 250 sheets of $8^1/_2$ x 11-inch xerographic paper and align the edges.

3. Insert the paper in the tray. Place paper edges under the retaining clips.

4. Return the paper tray to its drawer.

Numbers items in chronological order for systematic use

— Divides process into two segments for quick reference

Making Copies ●

1. Press power switch to On. Wait for flashing ready indicator to become solid.

2. Place the original facing down on the copyboard glass. Centre the copy.

3. Set the number of copies to be made by pressing the plus or minus key.

4. Press the Start key.

Starts each step with active verb in form of command

FIGURE 10.6 ■ News Release

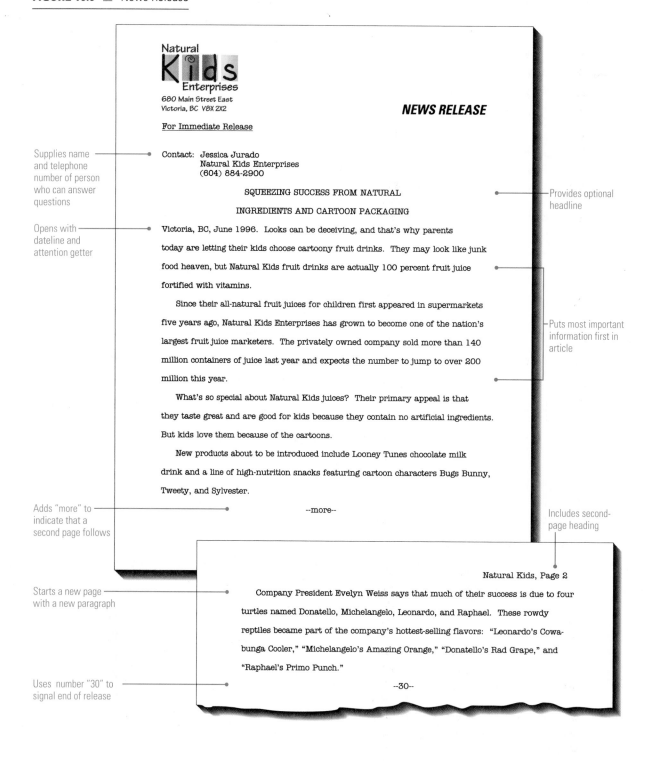

Supplies name and telephone number of person who can answer questions

Opens with dateline and attention getter

Adds "more" to indicate that a second page follows

Starts a new page with a new paragraph

Uses number "30" to signal end of release

Provides optional headline

Puts most important information first in article

Includes second-page heading

Natural **Kids** Enterprises
680 Main Street East
Victoria, BC V8X 2X2

NEWS RELEASE

For Immediate Release

Contact: Jessica Jurado
Natural Kids Enterprises
(604) 884-2900

SQUEEZING SUCCESS FROM NATURAL

INGREDIENTS AND CARTOON PACKAGING

Victoria, BC, June 1996. Looks can be deceiving, and that's why parents today are letting their kids choose cartoony fruit drinks. They may look like junk food heaven, but Natural Kids fruit drinks are actually 100 percent fruit juice fortified with vitamins.

Since their all-natural fruit juices for children first appeared in supermarkets five years ago, Natural Kids Enterprises has grown to become one of the nation's largest fruit juice marketers. The privately owned company sold more than 140 million containers of juice last year and expects the number to jump to over 200 million this year.

What's so special about Natural Kids juices? Their primary appeal is that they taste great and are good for kids because they contain no artificial ingredients. But kids love them because of the cartoons.

New products about to be introduced include Looney Tunes chocolate milk drink and a line of high-nutrition snacks featuring cartoon characters Bugs Bunny, Tweety, and Sylvester.

--more--

Natural Kids, Page 2

Company President Evelyn Weiss says that much of their success is due to four turtles named Donatello, Michelangelo, Leonardo, and Raphael. These rowdy reptiles became part of the company's hottest-selling flavors: "Leonardo's Cowabunga Cooler," "Michelangelo's Amazing Orange," "Donatello's Rad Grape," and "Raphael's Primo Punch."

--30--

- Open with an attention-getting lead, or summary of the important facts.

- Include answers to the five Ws and one H (who, what, when, where, why, and how) in the article—but not all in the first sentence!

- Appeal to the audience of the target media. Emphasize reader benefits written in the style of the focus publication or newscast.

- Present the most important information early, followed by supporting information. Don't put your best ideas last because they may be chopped off or ignored.

- Make the release visually appealing. Limit the text to one or two double-spaced pages with attractive formatting.

- Look and sound credible—no typos, no imaginative spelling or punctuation, no factual errors.

The most important ingredient of a press release, of course, is news. Articles that merely plug products end up in the circular file. The news release in Figure 10.6 emphasizes the most newsworthy aspects of an announcement introducing nutritious drinks and snacks for children.

Announcements

Publicity for public events within business organizations usually takes the form of announcements. Formal announcements may be sent to printers for professional composition and typesetting. Today, though, individuals are likely to design and write their own notices on computers. Such messages may announce a speaker, a company training program, the new location of a department, or some special event. Announcements may appear alone or within other messages, such as memos or letters.

Like news releases, announcements should include answers to the five Ws: who, what, where, when, and why. To make them more readable and attractive, you might wish to centre each line as shown here.

GRAND OPENING
Monday, August 1
Media Production Services
Now located in Room 202, South Wing
Photocopying, collating, brochures, binding, and other services

Like news releases, formal announcements include answers to the five Ws: who, what, where, when, why.

Summary of Learning Goals

1. **Identify essential characteristics of messages that deliver thanks, praise, or sympathy.** Such messages should be selfless, specific, sincere, spontaneous, and short.

2. **Discuss specific points to cover in expressing thanks, recognition, and sympathy.** Gift thank-yous should identify the gift, say why you appreciate it, and explain how you will use it. Thank-yous for favours should say, without gushing, what they mean to you. Messages expressing recognition should be timely, include details of the accomplishment, and use natural language. In the case of death, expressions of sympathy should mention the loss tactfully, recognize good qualities in the deceased, offer assistance and conclude on a positive reassuring note.

3. **Specify guidelines that a careful writer follows in writing employment recommendations.** To avoid litigation, writers of recommendations should write only in response to specific written requests, state that the remarks are confidential, provide only job-related information, avoid vague and ambiguous statements, supply specific evidence for any negative statements, and include only truthful statements.

4. **Explain the purposes of employee performance appraisals.** Performance appraisals are conducted to (1) encourage employees to share in setting goals, (2) identify an employee's performance strengths and weaknesses, (3) determine whether employees are attaining their goals, (4) establish an action plan for improving before the next evaluation, and (5) provide management with a basis for determining salaries, promotions, and assignments.

5. **List important topics to include in employee warnings.** Employee warnings should (1) describe the time, place, and details of the infraction or problem, (2) explain why the company objects to the behaviour, (3) document details of prior occurrences of the problem, (4) list the steps necessary to correct the problem, (5) specify the action that will be taken if the problem is not corrected, and (6) say when the employee's progress will next be reviewed.

6. **Explain how to write clear operational instructions and announcements.** Clear instructions start with a clear title, explain the process in parts, number the steps chronologically, use active verbs in the form of commands. Strive for parallel construction, include cautions and warnings, and supply visuals if appropriate. Good announcements include answers to the five Ws: who, what, where, when, and why.

7. **Describe the basic elements included in effective news releases.** Good news releases (1) open with an attention-getting lead or summary of the important facts, (2) answer the questions who, what, when, where, why, and how, (3) appeal to the audience of the target media, (4) present the most important information early, (5) make the release visually appealing, and (6) look and sound credible.

CHAPTER REVIEW

1. What human needs do goodwill messages satisfy? (Goal 1)

2. List the five Ss of goodwill messages. Be prepared to explain them. (Goal 1)

3. What three topics should you include in a gift thank-you? (Goal 2)

4. What four topics are usually covered in a hospitality thank-you? (Goal 2)

5. What are the two most important elements in extending recognition? (Goal 2)

6. List four topics often included in a message expressing sympathy to a friend who has lost a loved one. (Goal 2)

7. Why are employers fearful of writing recommendations for former employees? (Goal 3)

8. List six guidelines that careful recommenders follow to avoid lawsuits. (Goal 3)

9. What should be discussed in the opening of a letter of recommendation? (Goal 3)

10. What should be included in the body of a recommendation? (Goal 3)

11. What goes in the conclusion of a recommendation? (Goal 3)

12. What is the primary focus of a performance appraisal? (Goal 4)

13. List six or more important items that should be included in a written warning. (Goal 5)

14. How should you prepare for writing a set of operational instructions? (Goal 6)

15. Name three or more topics that an organization might feature in a press release. (Goal 7)

DISCUSSION

1. Why are many writers reluctant to compose messages that deliver thanks, sympathy, or congratulations? (Goals 1, 2)

2. Why are written messages more meaningful than commercial cards or telephone calls? (Goals 1, 2)

3. Should you refuse to write a recommendation for someone you can't recommend? Defend your answer. (Goal 3)

4. Why are companies increasingly requiring regular employee performance appraisals? (Goal 4)

5. **Ethical Issue:** Should businesses be obligated to write letters of recommendation evaluating the performance of former employees?

EXERCISES

10.1 Document for Analysis: Thank-you Letter (Goals 1, 2)

Analyze the following poor letter. Discuss its weaknesses. If your instructor directs, revise it. Add details.

Dear Ms. Palko:

Thanks for the guided tour of the Communications Services Centre at Microtech, Inc. Everyone in our

business communications class liked it. You must have spent a long time getting ready for us. We thought it was great! Everyone said how much they liked it. Especially the teleconferencing demo. Most of us had no idea how it worked. We also liked the electronic mail and voice mail systems. Thanks again.

10.2 Document for Analysis: Letter of Recommendation (Goal 3)

Analyze the following poor letter. Discuss its weaknesses. If your instructor directs, revise it, adding needed information.

To Whom It May Concern:

I am happy to be able to recommend Mr. Quentin Ross. In his work for us, he was a good technician. He was responsible, creative, industrious, and always cooperative. Once in a while he was late, but we understood why.

If we may be of further service, please call on us.

PROBLEMS

10.3 Thanks for a Gift: Thoughtful Boss (Goals 1, 2)

On your birthday your boss gives you an unexpected gift (such as a wallet, key case, fountain pen, or something similar). Write a thank-you note expressing your gratitude.

10.4 Thanks for a Favour: You're Special! (Goals 1, 2)

Express your appreciation to a fellow worker at your place of employment for performing a special favour for you: teaching you a procedure, showing you how to operate a piece of equipment, filling in during an emergency, helping you with a project, or just for offering encouragement and support when you needed it. If you are not employed, select an instructor or friend to thank for some special act.

10.5 Thanks for a Favour: Got the Job! (Goals 1, 2)

After completing your degree/diploma, you have taken a job in your field. One of your instructors was especially helpful to you when you were a student. This instructor also wrote an effective letter of recommendation that helped you obtain your job. Write a letter thanking your instructor.

10.6 Collaborative Thanks for a Favour: The Perfect Résumé (Goals 1, 2)

Your business communication class was fortunate to have Thomas Fallo, author of *The Perfect Résumé* speak to you about preparing résumés for today's competitive job market. Mr. Fallo provided the class with excellent tips for targeting jobs and defining an applicant's strengths. He showed an old-fashioned "tombstone" résumé and explained how to make today's résumés more persuasive. His special advice for college students and women re-entering the job market made a great deal of sense. You know that he did not come to plug his book; but when he left, most class members wanted to head straight for a bookstore to buy it. His talk was a big hit. Your professor asks the class to break into small groups so that each can draft a thank-you letter. Address the letter to Mr. Thomas Fallo, 50 Finlayson Drive, Yellowknife, NT X1A 3J5.

10.7   Thanks for the Hospitality: Holiday Entertaining (Goals 1, 2)

Write a thank-you letter to your boss (supervisor, manager, vice-president, president, or chief executive officer) or to the head of an organization to which you belong. Assume that you and other members of your staff or organization were entertained at an elegant dinner during the winter holiday season. Include specific details that will make your letter personal and sincere.

10.8   Recognition: Congratulations! (Goals 1, 2)

Write a note of congratulations to a co-worker or friend in recognition of a special accomplishment: promotion, award, election to an office or special group, achievement of a goal, or some other significant event.

10.9   Recognition: Top Prof (Goals 1, 2)

After graduation you learn from a story in an alumni publication that one of your favourite professors was named Professor of the Month. Write a letter expressing your good wishes.

10.10   Recognition: Old Friend, New Job (Goals 1, 2)

A friend of yours in Moncton was just named marketing manager for Codex (they sell modems, telecommunications components, and networking systems). You've known her (or him) since childhood, but you had lost touch in the last five years. You saw your friend's picture and the accompanying story about the new position in your home-town paper. Write your old friend a letter of recognition—and send the clipping.

10.11   Sympathy: To a Spouse (Goals 1, 2)

Imagine that a co-worker was killed in a car accident. Write a letter of sympathy to his or her spouse.

10.12   Responding to Good Wishes: Saying Thank You (Goals 1, 2)

Write a short note thanking a friend who sent you good wishes when you recently completed your degree/diploma.

10.13   Letter of Recommendation: Technical Editor (Goal 3)

As Taylor Watson, director, Documentation Division, write a letter recommending Derek R. Roth. Derek has been a technical editor in your division for four years. He's applying for a position of document administrator in the Research Department of Signal Labs (at a salary you can't match). You've always liked Derek; and it's easy to recommend him, much as you hate to see him go. Derek ranks among the top 10 percent of all the editors you've known. Under your supervision Derek generally worked with engineers in revising their reports. His job was to improve expression, revise poor organization, develop internal consistency, and correct grammatical errors—without antagonizing the report writer. He succeeded very well both in editing reports and in getting along with the engineers—no easy task considering how defensive the engineers could become when their writing was being revised ("attacked" is the word they used). But Derek's professional manner, his sincere and serious tone, and his obvious expertise elicited respect and willing cooperation from even the most reluctant engineers. They could see how much he was improving the quality of their reports.

Derek's language skills are superior. Because of his excellent general and technical vocabulary, you often assigned him to work with the engineers who had the weakest writing skills. He's also a meticulous proofreader. The documents he produces have about the lowest error rate of any technical writer in your department.

In addition to working with written text, he's had experience in artwork from graphics to drafting. Your department uses Ventura desktop publishing software. Although Derek is not the best keyboarder with Ventura, he knows the system well enough to be able to produce quality design features. He's reliable, works well under pressure, and meets deadlines. Address the recommendation to Ms. Darcy Adams-Johnson, Director, Human Resources, Signal Labs, 410 Macdonald Avenue, Ottawa, ON K2H 1B6

10.14   Letter of Recommendation: For Yourself (Goal 3)

You've decided it's time to move on from your current job to a new position (select a realistic job for which you could apply). Step outside yourself for a moment; imagine that you are now your current supervisor. As supervisor write a letter of recommendation that describes your current duties and evaluates your accomplishments. Send this letter to Mr. Sam W. Engel, Vice-President, Human Resources (name a company and add an address).

10.15 Performance Appraisal: Rating a Senior Secretary (Goal 4)

As office manager for Rodeo Realty, you have to evaluate the six-month performance of Margaret Olson, senior secretary. Margaret prepares correspondence, reports, and announcements for six sales associates. She's a very fast keyboarder (over 80 words a minute), but sometimes her fingers fly too fast. She makes typos, especially in figure amounts, that are sometimes costly. Everyone likes Margaret, but all sales associates have learned to proofread her work very carefully. Two months ago your office sent out a new property listing that should have been for $1 200 000; Margaret omitted one of the zeros, causing a great deal of confusion.

Her sunny disposition makes Margaret popular among customers and staff. She has an excellent attendance record, having taken only one day of sick leave in the past year. Her output is outstanding; Margaret completes more work than any of your previous secretaries. When she uses the spell checker on her computer, her work has fewer typos. It seems, though, that she doesn't always use it. Margaret is reliable, conscientious, and eager to please. Her attitude is excellent.

When she started over a year ago, she knew little about the real estate business. She attended training seminars and learned real estate jargon and procedures quickly. You would be totally satisfied with her performance if she were more accurate. Perhaps her eyes could be causing some of the problem; she's complained of eye fatigue and irritation from her contacts.

Write a performance report on Margaret, focusing on two sections of comments (see Figure 10.4): (1) Where is employee's performance most proficient? and (2) Where does employee's performance need improvement?

10.16 Performance Appraisal: Rating Yourself (Goal 4)

Study the employee performance appraisal form shown in Figure 10.4. Imagine you are your own boss. In a job that you now hold or one you've had before, evaluate your own performance. Prepare two sections of the report: (1) Where is employee's performance most proficient? and (2) Where does employee's performance need improvement? Describe your job duties and rate your performance. Be honest!

10.17 Warning: Sleeping on the Job (Goal 5)

As supervisor of Shipping and Receiving, write an employee warning memo to Richmond U. White. Rich is a shipping clerk who works a swing shift (from 4 p.m. to midnight). He was discovered sleeping on the job January 5 at 11 p.m. Sleeping on the job is a serious violation of company rules. Since he is the only clerk in the receiving area, one of his tasks is to guard the warehouse. In addition, he has paperwork to do during his shift. In a previous performance review, his shift reports were noted as being "sketchy" and sometimes late. If he is found sleeping on the job again, he will be suspended or dismissed on the spot (you decide which). You would hate to see this happen since Rich has been with the company for five years.

10.18 Instructions: Guide to New Employees (Goal 6)

Your boss asks you to write instructions for operating a piece of equipment (such as a fax machine, copier, camera, or printer) or to describe a procedure (such as how to fill out expense reports). Your instructions will guide new employees. Use a real situation if possible. Include your instructions in a memo to your boss.

10.19 Collaborative Instructions: Registration Help (Goal 6)

The director of admissions at your institution asks a group of student workers to help him revise the admission and registration instructions. He's heard complaints that the present instructions are unclear. Find these instructions in your class schedule or catalogue. Write an improved version, including a title.

10.20 Instructions: Faxing It (Goal 6)

The following instructions came with a new imported fax machine, the TurboFax 3200. Everyone in your office is eager to use the machine, but they can't understand the instructions. Write improved instructions that include a reminder that this machine is intended for office work only.

For Transmission. Document is facing down for loading. Document guides adjusted to document width. Operator is inserting the leading butt of document into feeding slot. [With sheets of two or more pages, leading edges are forming a slope as the operator lightly inserts them into feeding position; bottom sheet is proceeding first.] Operator is then picking up telephone handset. With continuous dial tone, dialling other fax number. Other fax's answering tone signals. Operator is pressing START key. When start lamp twinkles on-off, operator is hanging up handset.

10.21 Announcement: Personnel Party (Goal 6)

Prepare an announcement for a flyer. The Personnel Department is honouring and welcoming its new director, Mary K. Nakovey, at an open house, 2 June, from 2 to 4 p.m., in its offices on the second floor. Encourage employees to drop by to greet Mary and their other friends in Personnel at this open house. Arrange the information in a centred format.

10.22 Collaborative News Release: Attention Student Writers (Goal 6)

As part of a team of student interns at Academic Software, you have been asked to write a press release describing a new product. Your press release will be sent to student newspapers; the content should be aimed at college students. Dr. Janet Adams, a former professor of communications, founded Academic Software 10 years ago because she realized that "computers could help students with their writing problems." With the aid of programmers, Dr. Adams developed a student style checker called EditWriter. It helps writers eliminate problems such as wordiness, poor usage, punctuation errors, and inappropriate gender-based language. The program actually helps both students and experienced writers improve their composition styles—but your current pitch is toward students.

EditWriter has many features. It covers over 16 000 common writing problems in 40 categories. It's menu-driven, fast, and easy to use. It comes with a 130-page manual that offers samples of incorrect and proper usage and mechanics. Best of all for students, it runs on low-end IBM computer systems; it requires only 256 KB of RAM and a monochrome monitor. Its output prints on nearly all printers.

Originally designed for writing courses, EditWriter is especially adaptable for use in the classroom and in writing labs. Work sessions can be tailored to the level or interests of a particular class or an individual student. For students only, a half-price introductory offer of $45 is available. The program will be stocked at most college and university bookstores.

10.23 News Release: Heirloom Jeans (Goal 7)

As Jeff Spiegel, public relations specialist, prepare a press release for Hamilton newspapers and TV and radio stations. Your company, Dollars for Denim (27 Richmond Street, St. Catharines, ON L2V 3G5), buys used denim clothing. The market for old Levi Strauss jeans (preferably pre-1970) is booming in Japan. An authentic pair of 1950 Levi Strauss 501 jeans might fetch $2000 in a Tokyo boutique. Apparently, the Japanese are obsessed with Western fash-

ions, particularly the cowboy look. "They seem to have a longing for things from the Wild West," says Hideyuki Kawamura, manager of Delaware, a Tokyo specialty store.

At first, you collected old jeans quietly, so that you could keep the prices low. But as the demand grew, you had to go public. You're now willing to pay $50 to $200 for high-quality old jeans (1970–1985). Boys' sizes are particularly prized among Japanese men, who tend to be smaller than North American men.

How can you tell really old Levis? Outside copper rivets held on the pockets in the 1930s. The rivets were moved inside in the late 1930s to 1960s. A real-leather patch marked 501 jeans in the 1950s.

You're looking for denim jeans or jackets without holes or stains. Although you dream of pre-1970s jeans, you are happy with even 5- and 10-year-old denim. Tokyo's collectors don't seem to care. As you've told reporters, "We'll buy denim anywhere. I've even bought jackets from people's backs as they're walking down the street."[11]

10.24 News Release: It's New! (Goal 7)

In a company where you now work or for an organization you belong to, identify a product or service that could be publicized. Consider writing a press release announcing a new course at your college or university, a new president, new equipment, or a campaign to raise funds. Write an announcement for your local newspaper.

CLUE REVIEW 10

Edit the following sentences to correct faults in grammar, punctuation, spelling, and word use.

1. North American exports has increased by seventy-six percent in the past five years; and the trade deficit has fell to it's lowest level since 1974.

2. After years of downsizing and restructuring Canada has now become one of the worlds most competitive producers in many industry's.

3. However many companies products still sell better at home then abroad; because these companys lack overseas experience.

4. Company's like Amway, discovered that there unique door to door selling method was very successful in japan.

5. The ministry of industry and technology asked Mr. Sato and I to describe the marketing of: aircraft, high-tech products, and biomedical technology.

6. Some of the products most likely to succeed abroad are: blue jeans, coke, home appliances and prepared foods.

7. As North American companys learn to accomodate global tastes they will be expanding into vast new markets in china, south america and europe.

8. The seminar emphasising exporting will cost three hundred dollars; which seems expensive for a newly-formed company.

9. The manager thinks that you attending the three day seminar is a good idea, however we must still check your work calender.

10. Exports from small companies has increased; thereby effecting this countrys trade balance positively.

Report Planning and Research

L E A R N I N G   G O A L S

After studying this chapter, you should be able to

1 Describe nine typical business reports.

2 Distinguish between informational and analytical reports.

3 Identify four report formats.

4 Apply the writing process to reports.

5 Conduct research by locating secondary data.

6 Generate primary data for research projects.

7 Describe three formats for documenting sources.

DMR Group Inc.

There is a saying in the consulting business: "Get it once, and get it right." For Peter Le Piane these words ring especially true.

As a programmer-analyst with the Montreal consulting firm DMR Group, Inc., Peter spends anywhere between "a few days and a few weeks" in meetings with clients gathering information which is in turn used to compile a report that determines whether or not a client could benefit from DMR's expertise in the information technology field. A publicly traded company with revenues of $267 million (1993) and more than 2500 employees around the world, DMR specializes in management issues specifically related to information technology.

> *"Typically you can't give a really good answer on the spot, so this is where the report comes in."*

The first step in providing these services involves research at a client's site, for which DMR uses its unique and proprietary "methodology" ("our special sauce," says Peter) to assess each company's needs. The goal is to offer a solution that increases competitiveness, productivity, and profitability. These solutions usually involve the installing and setting up of computer systems, including hardware and software—but they could be as simple as reorganizing the way a company operates from day to day.

As a DMR consultant, Peter, 26, is responsible for gathering a broad range of technical information from client sites. This requires intensive meetings that often test his communications skills. "You have to be a decent facilitator in these meetings. ... You can't sit there and expect these people to have three-hour meetings with you four or five different times. You have to be able to ask the right questions and make sure you're asking all of them." Perhaps the most important of these questions is, 'How do you want this system to work?' "

But asking the right questions is only half the job; it is equally important to draft a tight, accurate report. "Typically you can't give a really good answer on the spot, so this is where the report comes in."

On the basis of this document, a company will decide whether or not to proceed with the consulting services offered. "It's what the client has to sign off on—it's your Go/No-go decision point," says Peter, who is charged with sending clearly written messages to clients, many of whom know little about information technology. This requires a writing style far different from the style he used in university.

Peter is a graduate of the computer science program at the University of Waterloo, in Ontario. It was there, during his five years in the co-op education system, that he acquired

valuable on-the-job training (students must take part in six work placements, each lasting four months) as well as the basic skills needed to write reports. "The thing that really teaches you how to act in a business environment is the work terms and the fact that you have to produce reports at the end of these jobs."

But these undergraduate papers were long (about 7000 words each) and heavy on computer jargon—a far cry from the writing he does at DMR. Says Peter: "Waterloo taught me what a business report is, but the reports I wrote there were very technical. The ones I do now have to explain actual business processes. It's a very different type of writing; the only similarity is the format."

How Peter gets his raw data is also much different. "The only information gathering I had to do at university involved sitting down in a library; now the only information gathering I do involves sitting down in front of a bunch of users in a meeting room." The information collected for these preliminary reports is done by a two- or three-member team of DMR consultants ("You don't want to throw too many people at a client") who mould a report into something that covers technical issues as well as such issues as the cost and size involved in making company-wide changes.

"You try to keep things short and get them done as fast as you can," says Peter. Regardless, a typical preliminary report from DMR runs 80 pages. To offset the heft of the document and simplify the more technical aspects of their findings, DMR often uses diagrams. "A picture is worth a thousand words," remarks Peter. In the preliminary analysis, however, he stays away from technology and explains the process of what happens now, and *will* happen with the new system. "It's the first step a client takes toward understanding what's going on, so this type of report has to be written at that level," he says.

"Other companies fail to understand what the user wants, and it ends up costing them fifty times more to fix things rather than get it right the first time. You might spend $10 000 to do one of these preliminary analysis reports, which may seem like a lot of money for an 80-page document, but it's probably going to end up saving a client $200 000."

After the preliminary report is researched and written, it's up to the client to decide if they want to proceed and have DMR install a new information technology system. If at this stage the client cannot get a handle on what is needed and what DMR has to offer, Peter knows whom to blame. "If you've really misguided the client and not given them an accurate picture, it's your own fault. It means you haven't asked the right questions and you didn't see the right people."[1] ■

If a client decides to invest thousands of dollars to have DMR instal a new information technology system, the client wants to be sure the new system will suit its specific needs. A well-written preliminary analysis that clearly explains the processes of the new system—and avoids technological jargon—has an excellent chance of winning the client's trust and approval.

Clarifying and Classifying Reports

Reports are a fact of life in North American business. Although your career may not centre on research and report writing, as does that of Peter Le Piane, you'll undoubtedly be called on to write reports at some time. North American values and attitudes seem to prompt us to write reports. We analyze the pros and cons of problems, studying alternatives and assessing facts, figures, and details. We pride ourselves on being practical and logical; we solve problems by applying scientific procedures. For this kind of analysis, we need systematic information. And we often present this information in the form of reports.

This chapter examines categories, functions, organization formats, and writing styles of reports. It also introduces the report-writing process and discusses methods of collecting and documenting data.

Effective business reports solve problems and answer questions systematically.

Because of their abundance and diversity, business reports are difficult to define. They may range from informal half-page trip reports to formal 200-page financial forecasts. Reports may be presented orally in front of a group or electronically on a computer screen. Some reports appear as words on paper in the form of memos and letters. Others, such as tax reports or profit-and-loss statements, consist primarily of numerical data. Some seek to provide information only; others aim to analyze and make recommendations. Although reports vary greatly in length, content, form, and formality, they all have one common purpose: *Business reports are systematic attempts to answer questions and solve problems.*

Typical Business Reports

In searching for answers and solving problems, organizations prepare thousands of different kinds of reports for managers, employees, customers, and the government. Many of these reports can be grouped into nine categories, briefly described below. Chapters 13 and 14 present "how-to" information and models for writing these reports.

Periodic, situational, investigative, and compliance reports often present data without interpretation.

Periodic operating reports. The most common reports in many organizations are written at regular intervals to monitor operations. These operating reports—like weekly activity reports from sales reps—answer questions about what employees are doing and how effectively the organization is achieving its mission. They monitor and control operations, including production, sales, shipping, and customer service.

Situational reports. Unlike periodic reports, situational reports describe non-recurring activities. This broad category includes trip, conference, and seminar reports, as well as progress reports for unusual activities, such as sponsoring a mountain-bike riding competition. Since situational reports describe one-time events, the writer generally has no ready models to follow. Thus, these reports are usually more difficult, but also more creative, than periodic reports.

Investigative and informational reports. Reports that examine situations or problems and supply facts—with little in the way of interpretation or recommendations—are investigative. Assume, for example, that your boss asked you to research Revenue Canada's position on the hiring of independent contractors. You would collect and organize facts into a logical, informational report. Now assume that your boss also wanted you to analyze the status of the independent contractors working for your organization and make recommendations about retaining them. Your report would become more analytical and would be classified differently.

Compliance reports. Prompted by the government, compliance reports answer such questions as "How much profit did your organization earn and what taxes do you owe?" These reports comply with laws and regulations that protect employees, investors, and customers. Such reports respond to government agencies like Revenue Canada, Employment and Immigration Canada, and Health and Welfare Canada. A securities prospectus is a compliance report that answers questions from potential stockholders regarding company performance and finances.

Justification and recommendation reports. When managers and employees must justify or recommend something (like purchases, changes in operations, new programs, or personnel), they write justification or recommendation reports. These analytical reports usually travel upward to management, where the recommendations are approved or refused. In analyzing alternatives, interpreting findings, and making recommendations, these reports become important tools for managers in solving problems and making decisions.

Justification and recommendation, yardstick, and feasibility reports analyze alternatives, interpret findings, and often make recommendations.

Yardstick reports. When a problem has two or more solutions, a helpful way to evaluate the alternatives is to establish consistent criteria—a yardstick—by which to measure the alternatives. For example, let's say that a company must decide whether to (1) continue using its outdated mainframe computers, (2) purchase networked personal computers, or (3) hire an outside agency to handle some of its computing needs. A yardstick report assesses the alternatives by applying the same criteria to each, such as cost, service, security, and reliability. Each alternative is measured against the criteria to find the best option.

Feasibility reports. Feasibility reports use analysis to predict whether projects or alternatives are practical or advisable. They answer questions such as "Should we open a branch office in Thunder Bay?" Feasibility reports examine the benefits and problems connected with the project, as well as its costs and schedule for implementation. The emphasis is on whether to proceed with the venture.

Research studies. Business organizations sometimes commission research studies that examine problems thoroughly and scientifically. Researchers analyze a problem, suggest ways to solve it (called *hypotheses*), collect data about each possible solution, analyze those data, draw conclusions, and, if requested, make recommendations. The emphasis in these studies is on conducting objective research and interpreting the findings. For example, Peter Le Piane is responsible for gathering technical information from client sites to provide solutions that increase competitiveness, productivity, and profitability.

Research studies examine problems thoroughly and scientifically, while proposals offer to solve problems.

Proposals. As attempts to secure new business, proposals offer to solve problems, investigate ideas, or sell products and services. They are organized to answer the receiver's questions regarding the offer and its budget, schedule, and staffing. Another form of proposal is the business plan, a report that seeks to persuade investors to fund a new company.

Functions of Reports

Most of the reports just described can be placed in two broad categories: informational reports and analytical reports.

Informational reports. Reports that present information without analysis or recommendations are primarily informational. Although the writers collect and organize facts, they are not expected to analyze the facts for their readers. A trip report describing an employee's visit to a trade show, for example, simply presents information. Other reports that present information without analysis involve routine operations, compliance with regulations, and company policies and procedures.

Analytical reports. Reports that provide data, analyses, and conclusions are analytical. If requested, the writer also supplies recommendations. Analytical reports may attempt to persuade readers to act or to change their beliefs. Assume you're writing a feasibility report that compares several possible locations for a video rental shop. After analyzing and discussing alternatives, you might recommend one site, thus attempting to persuade your readers to accept this choice.

Direct and Indirect Patterns

Like letters and memos, reports may be organized directly or indirectly. The pattern of development of a report is determined by the reader's expectations and the content of the report, as illustrated in Figure 11.1. In long reports, such as corporate annual reports, some parts may be organized directly and others indirectly.

Direct pattern. When the purpose for writing is presented close to the beginning, the organizational pattern is direct. Informational reports, such as the letter report shown in Figure 11.2, are usually arranged directly. They open with an introduction, followed by the facts and a summary. In Figure 11.2 the writer explains a legal services plan. The report letter begins with an introduction. Then it presents the facts, which are divided into three subtopics identified by descriptive headings. The letter ends with a summary and a complimentary close.

Analytical reports may also be organized directly, especially when the readers are supportive or are familiar with the topic. Many busy executives prefer this pattern because it gives them the results of the report immediately. They don't have to spend time wading through the facts, findings, discussion, and analyses to get to the two items they are most interested in—conclusions and recommendations. Figure 11.3 illustrates such an arrangement. This analytical memo report describes the environmental hazards of a property that a real estate firm has just listed. The firm is familiar with the investigation and eager to find out the recommendations. Therefore, the memo is organized directly.

You should be aware, though, that unless readers are familiar with the topic, they may find the direct pattern confusing. Many readers prefer the indirect pattern because it seems logical and mirrors the way we solve problems.

Indirect pattern. When the conclusions and recommendations, if requested, appear at the end of the report, the organizational pattern is indirect. Such reports usually begin with an introduction or description of the problem,

FIGURE 11.1 ■ Audience Analysis and Report Organization

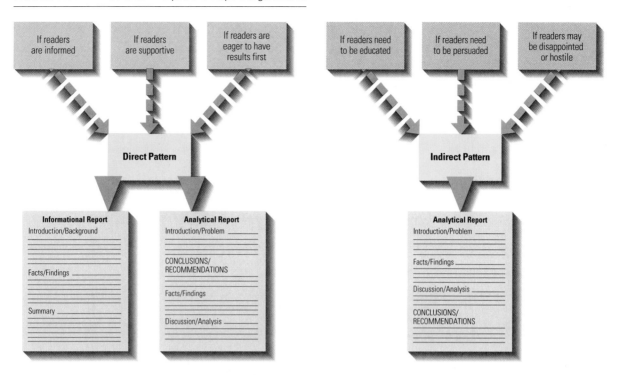

followed by facts and interpretation from the writer. They end with conclusions and recommendations. This pattern is helpful when readers are unfamiliar with the problem. It's also useful when readers must be persuaded or when they may be disappointed in or hostile toward the report's findings. The writer is more likely to retain the reader's interest by first explaining, justifying, and analyzing the facts and then making recommendations. This pattern also seems most rational to readers because it follows the normal thought process: problem, alternatives (facts), solution.

Figure 11.4 shows a portion of an analytical report organized indirectly. Note how readers are introduced, in a background discussion, to the problem of vehicle emissions and smog. Then facts (research findings and proposed solutions to the problem) are presented and analyzed. Finally, the report concludes with recommendations suggesting solutions to the problem.

The indirect pattern is appropriate for analytical reports that seek to persuade or that convey bad news.

Formats of Reports

The format of a report is governed by its length, topic, audience, and purpose. After considering these elements, you'll probably choose from among the following four formats:

A report's format depends on its length, audience, topic, and purpose.

- **Letter format.** Use letter format for short (say, 10 or fewer pages) informal reports addressed outside an organization. Printed on office stationery, a letter report contains a date, inside address, salutation, and complimentary close, as shown in Figure 11.2. Although they may contain information similar to that found in correspondence, letter reports usually are longer and show more careful organization than most letters. They also include headings.

FIGURE 11.2 ■ Informational Report—Letter Format

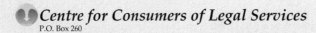

Centre for Consumers of Legal Services
P.O. Box 260
Kitchener, ON N2K 2V5

Uses letterhead stationery for an informal report addressed to an outsider

September 7, 1996

Ms. Lisa Burgess, Secretary
Westwood Homeowners
85 Westwood Drive
Guelph, ON N1H 6Y7

Dear Ms. Burgess:

As executive director of the Centre for Consumers of Legal Services, I'm pleased to send you this information describing how your homeowners' association can sponsor a legal services plan for its members. After an introduction with background information, this report will discuss three steps necessary for your group to start its plan.

Presents introduction and facts without analysis or recommendations

Introduction

A legal services plan promotes preventive law by letting members talk to lawyers whenever problems arise. Prompt legal advice often averts or prevents expensive litigation. Because groups can supply a flow of business to the plan's lawyers, groups can negotiate free consultation, follow-up, and discounts.

Two kinds of plans are commonly available. The first, a free plan, offers free legal consultation along with discounts for services when the participating groups are sufficiently large to generate business for the plan's lawyers. These plans actually act as a substitute for advertising for the lawyers. The second common type is the prepaid plan. Prepaid plans provide more benefits, but members must pay annual fees, usually of $200 or more a year.

Since you inquired about a free plan for your homeowners' association, the following information describes how to set up such a program.

Arranges facts of report into sections with descriptive headings

Determine the Benefits Your Group Needs

The first step in establishing a free legal services plan is to meet with the members of your group to decide what benefits they want. Typical benefits include the following:

Free consultation. Members may consult a participating lawyer—by phone or in the lawyer's office—to discuss any matter. The number of consultations is unlimited, provided each is about a separate matter. Consultations are generally limited to 30 minutes, but they include substantive analysis and advice.

Emphasizes benefits in paragraph headings with boldface type

Free document review. Important papers—such as leases, insurance policies, and instalment sales contracts—may be reviewed with legal counsel. Members may ask questions and receive an explanation of terms.

Discount on additional services. For more complex matters, participating lawyers will charge members 75 percent of the lawyer's normal fee. However, some organizations choose to charge a flat fee for commonly needed services.

Select the Lawyers for Your Plan

Groups with geographically concentrated memberships have an advantage in forming legal plans. These groups can limit the number of participating lawyers and yet provide adequate service. Generally, smaller panels of lawyers are advantageous.

Assemble a list of candidates, inviting them to apply. The best way to compare prices is to have candidates submit their fees. Your group can then compare fee schedules and select the lowest bidder, if price is important. Arrange to interview the lawyers in their offices.

After selecting a lawyer or a panel, sign a contract. The contract should include the reason for the plan, what the lawyer agrees to do, what the group agrees to do, how each side can end the contract, and the signatures of both parties. You may also wish to include references to malpractice insurance, assurance that the group will not interfere with the lawyer-client relationship, an evaluation form, a grievance procedure, and responsibility for government filings.

Publicize the Plan to Your Members

Members won't use a plan if they don't know about it, and a plan will not be successful if it is unused. Publicity must be vocal and continual. Announce it in newsletters, meetings, bulletin boards, and flyers.

Persistence is the key. All too frequently, leaders of an organization assume that a single announcement is all that's needed. They expect members to see the value of the plan and remember that it's available. Most organization members, though, are not as involved as the leadership. Therefore, it takes more publicity than the leadership usually expects in order to reach and maintain the desired level of awareness.

Summary

A successful free legal services plan involves designing a program, choosing the lawyers, and publicizing the plan. To learn more about these steps or to order a $25 how-to manual, call me at (519) 884-9901.

Sincerely,

Richard M. Ramos

Richard M. Ramos
Executive Director

pas

FIGURE 11.3 ■ Analytical Report—Memo Format

Tips for Memo Reports

- Use memo format for most short (10 or fewer pages) informal reports within an organization.

- Leave side margins of 1 to 1¼ inches.

- Sign your initials on the FROM line.

- Use an informal, conversational style.

- For direct analytical reports, put recommendations first.

- For indirect analytical reports, put recommendations last.

Atlantic Environmental, Inc.

Interoffice Memo

TO: Kermit Fox, President   **DATE:** March 7, 1996 ●——— Applies memo format for short, informal internal report

FROM: Cynthia M. Rashid, Environmental Engineer *CMR*

SUBJECT: INVESTIGATION OF MOUNTAIN PARK COMMERCIAL SITE

For Laurentian Realty, Inc., I've completed a preliminary investigation of its ●——— Uses first paragraph as introduction
Mountain Park property listing. The following recommendations are based on my
physical inspection of the site, official records, and interviews with officials and
persons knowledgeable about the site.

Presents recommendations first (direct pattern) because reader is supportive and familiar with topic ●———

Recommendations

To reduce its potential environmental liability, Laurentian Realty should take the
following steps in regard to its Mountain Park listing:

- Conduct an immediate asbestos survey at the site, including inspection of
  ceiling insulation material, floor tiles, and insulation around a gas-fired
  heater vent pipe at 2539 Mountain View Drive.

- Prepare an environmental audit of the generators of hazardous waste
  currently operating at the site, including Mountain Technology.

- Obtain lids for the dumpsters situated in the parking areas and ensure that
  the lids are kept closed.

Combines findings and analyses in short report ●———

Findings and Analyses

My preliminary assessment of the site and its immediate vicinity revealed rooms
with damaged floor tiles on the first and second floors of 2539 Mountain View Drive.
Apparently, in recent remodelling efforts, these tiles had been cracked and broken.
Examination of the ceiling and attic revealed further possible contamination from
asbestos. The insulation material surrounding the hot-water storage tank was in
poor condition.

Located on the property is Mountain Technology, a possible hazardous waste
generator. Although I could not examine its interior, this company has the potential
for producing hazardous-material contamination.

In the parking area large dumpsters collect trash and debris from several businesses.
These dumpsters were uncovered, thus posing a risk to the general public.

In view of the construction date of the structures on this property, asbestos-
containing building materials might be present. Moreover, this property is located
in an industrial part of the city, further prompting my recommendation for a
thorough investigation. Laurentian Realty can act immediately to eliminate one
environmental concern by covering the dumpsters in the parking area.

FIGURE 11.4 ■ Portion of Analytical Report—Manuscript Format

Tips for Manuscript Reports

- Use manuscript format for long, complex, or formal reports and proposals.
- Print the report on plain paper.
- Allow side and bottom margins of 1 to 1¼ inches.
- Display primary and secondary headings appropriately (see Chapter 12).
- Use single, line and a half, or double spacing, depending on your organization's preferences.
- Document your sources with appropriate citations.

REDUCING VEHICLE EMISSIONS
AND SMOG IN THE GREATER VANCOUVER AREA

Uses plain paper, title, and manuscript format for long, complex report

INTRODUCTION

Pacific Enterprises, Inc., is pleased to submit this report to the Vancouver Air Resources Board in response to its request of April 18. This report examines the problem of vehicle emission in the Greater Vancouver Area. Moreover, it reviews proposed solutions, analyzes some of the findings from California, and recommends a course of action that will lead to a significant reduction in emissions of hydrocarbon and nitrogen from older cars.

Background and Discussion of Problem

The air quality in the The Greater Vancouver Area has deteriorated in the past decade. Unless this problem is addressed, it will get worse with the growing population of the Fraser River Basin. There is a push towards the California-style emission standards from the government that would force the automotive industry to start selling zero-emission vehicles before the turn of the century. The big three automotive companies, General Motors, Ford, and Chrysler, are being pressured to produce electric vehicles (EVs); however, the costs are still prohibitive.

Therefore, other more cost-effective solutions must be sought. A recent California study (Rutman 37) estimated that 50 percent of the smog generated in Southern California comes from the older vehicles.

Cites source of data with author reference

Yet many of these vehicles are either undetected or exempted from meeting the clear-air standards. Little has been done to solve this problem because retrofitting these old cars with modern pollution control systems would cost more than many of them are worth. Two innovative solutions from California were recently proposed.

Uses single spacing to save paper and filing space

Reducing Smog by Eliminating Older Cars

Two large organizations, Unocal and Ford Motor Company, suggested a buy-out program to eliminate older cars. To demonstrate its effectiveness, the two firms bought more than 8000 pre-1975 cars in the Los Angeles area for $700 each. These cars were junked, and buyers were encouraged to purchase newer and cleaner cars. One of

RECOMMENDATIONS

Uses indirect organization, with recommendations last, to inform and persuade readers

Based on our findings and the conclusions discussed earlier, we submit the following recommendations to you:

1. Study the progress of Germany's attempt to reduce smog by retrofitting older vehicles with computer-controlled fuel-management systems.

2. Encourage Ford Motor Company and Unocal to continue their buy-out programs in exchange for temporary smog credits.

3. Invite Neutronics Enterprises in Toronto, Ontario, to test its Lamba emission-control system at your Fraser test centre.

Arranges recommendations from least important to most important

- **Memo format.** For short informal reports that stay within organizations, memo format is appropriate. Memo reports begin with TO, FROM, DATE, and SUBJECT, as shown in Figure 11.3. Like letter reports, memo reports differ from regular memos in length, use of headings, and deliberate organization.

- **Manuscript format.** For longer, more formal reports, use manuscript format. These reports are usually printed on plain paper instead of letterhead stationery or memo forms. They begin with a title followed by systematically displayed headings and subheadings, as illustrated in Figure 11.4.

- **Printed forms.** Prepared forms are often used for repetitive data, such as monthly sales reports, performance appraisals, merchandise inventories, and personnel and financial reports. Standardized headings on these forms save time for the writer. Preprinted forms also make similar information easy to locate and ensure that all necessary information is provided.

Writing Style

Like other business messages, reports can range from informal to formal, depending on their purpose, audience, and setting. Research reports sent to clients, such as those Peter Le Piane writes for DMR, tend to be rather formal. Such reports must give an impression of objectivity, authority, and impartiality. But a report to your boss describing a trip to a conference would probably be informal.

An office worker once called a grammar hot-line service with this problem: "We've just sent a report to our headquarters, and it was returned with this comment, 'Put it in the third person.' What do they mean?" The hot-line experts explained that apparently management wanted a more formal writing style, using third-person constructions (*the company* or *the researcher* instead of *we* and *I*). Figure 11.5, which compares characteristics of formal and informal report-writing styles, can help you decide the writing style that's appropriate for your reports.

Applying the 3 × 3 Writing Process to Reports

Because business reports are systematic attempts to answer questions and solve problems, the best reports are written methodically. The same 3 × 3 writing process that guided memo and letter writing can be applied to reports. Let's divide the process into seven specific steps:

- **Step 1:** Analyze the problem and purpose.

- **Step 2:** Anticipate the audience and issues.

- **Step 3:** Prepare a work plan.

- **Step 4:** Research the subject.

- **Step 5:** Organize, analyze, interpret, and illustrate the material.

- **Step 6:** Compose the first draft.

- **Step 7:** Revise, proofread, and evaluate.

How much time you spend on each step depends on the purpose of your report. A short informational report on a familiar topic might require a brief

FIGURE 11.5 ■ Report Writing Styles

	Formal Writing Style	**Informal Writing Style**
Use	Theses Research studies Controversial or complex reports (especially to outsiders)	Short, routine reports Reports for familiar audiences Noncontroversial reports Most reports for company insiders
Effect	Impression of objectivity, accuracy, professionalism, fairness Distance created between writer and reader	Feeling of warmth, personal involvement, closeness
Characteristics	Absence of first-person pronouns: use of third-person (*the researcher, the writer*) Absence of contractions (*can't, don't*) Use of passive-voice verbs (*the study was conducted*) Complex sentences; long words Absence of humour; figures of speech Reduced use of colourful adjectives, adverbs Elimination of "editorializing" (author's opinions, perceptions)	Use of first-person pronouns (*I, we, me, my, us, our*) Use of contractions Emphasis on active-voice verbs (*I conducted the study*) Shorter sentences, familiar words Occasional use of humour, metaphors Occasional use of colourful speech Acceptance of author's opinions and ideas

work plan, little research, and no analysis. A complex analytical report, on the other hand, might demand a comprehensive work plan, extensive research, and careful analysis of the data.

To illustrate the planning stages of a report, let us imagine that Diane Chong is preparing a report for her boss, Mike Rivers, at Mycon Pharmaceutical Laboratories. Mike asked Diane to investigate the problem of transportation for sales representatives. Currently, some Mycon reps visit customers (mostly doctors and hospitals) using company-leased cars. A few reps drive their own cars, receiving reimbursements for use. In three months Mycon's leasing agreement for 14 cars expires, and Mike is considering a major change. Diane's task is to investigate the choices and report her findings to Mike.

Analyzing the Problem and Purpose

The first step in writing a report is to understand the problem or assignment clearly. For complex reports it's wise to prepare a written problem statement. In analyzing her report task, Diane had many questions. Is the problem that Mycon is spending too much money on leased cars? Does Mycon wish to invest in owning a fleet of cars? Is Mike unhappy with the paperwork involved in reimbursing sales reps when they use their own cars? Does he suspect that reps are submitting inflated mileage figures? Before starting research for the report, Diane talked with Mike to define the problem. She learned several dimensions of the situation and wrote the following statement to clarify the problem—both for herself and for Mike.

Before beginning a report, identify the problem to be solved in a clear statement.

Smart researchers save themselves heartache and wasted time by determining the purpose of a report well before they start collecting data. Talking over the scope of a problem, the problem's significance, and any report limitations helps a researcher organize an entire project.

Problem Statement: The leases on all company cars will be expiring in three months. Mycon must decide whether to renew them or develop a new policy regarding transportation for sales reps. Expenses and paperwork for employee-owned cars seem excessive.

Diane further defined the problem by writing a specific question that she would try to answer in her report:

Problem Question: What plan should Mycon follow in providing transportation for its sales reps?

Now Diane was ready to concentrate on the purpose of the report. Again, she had questions. Exactly what did Mike expect? Did he want a comparison of costs for buying cars and leasing cars? Should she conduct research to pinpoint exact reimbursement costs when employees drive their own cars? Did he want her to do all the legwork, present her findings in a report, and let him make a decision? Or did he want her to evaluate the choices and recommend a course of action?

After talking with Mike, Diane was ready to write a simple purpose statement for this assignment.

A simple purpose statement defines the focus of a report.

Simple Statement of Purpose: To recommend a plan that provides sales reps with cars to be used in their calls.

Preparing a written purpose statement is a good idea because it defines the focus of a report and provides a standard that keeps the project on target. In writing useful purpose statements, choose active verbs telling what you intend to do: *analyze, choose, investigate, compare, justify, evaluate, explain, establish, determine,* and so on. Notice that Diane's statement begins with the active verb *recommend.*

Some reports require only a simple statement of purpose: *to investigate expanded teller hours, to select a manager from among four candidates, to describe the position of accounts supervisor.* Many assignments, though, demand additional focus to guide the project. An expanded statement of purpose considers three additional factors:

- **Scope.** What issues or elements will be investigated? To determine the scope, Diane brainstormed with Mike and others to pin down her task. She learned that Mycon had enough capital to consider purchasing a fleet of cars outright. Mike also told her that employee satisfaction was almost as important as cost-effectiveness. Moreover, he disclosed his suspicion that employee-owned cars were costing Mycon more than leased cars. Diane had many issues to sort out in setting the boundaries of her report.

- **Significance.** Why is the topic worth investigating at this time? Some topics, after initial examination, turn out to be less important than originally thought. Others involve problems that cannot be solved, making a study useless. For Diane and Mike the problem was important because Mycon's leasing agreement would expire shortly and decisions had to be made about a new policy for transportation of sales reps.

- **Limitations.** What conditions affect the generalizability and utility of a report's findings? In Diane's case her conclusions and recommendations might apply only to reps in her Edmonton sales district. Her findings would probably not be reliable for reps in Rimouski, Windsor, or Brandon. Another limitation for Diane is time. She must complete the report in four weeks, thus restricting the thoroughness of her research.

Diane decides to expand her statement of purpose to define the scope, significance, and limitations of the report.

> **Expanded Statement of Purpose:** The purpose of this report is to recommend a plan that provides sales reps with cars to be used in their calls. The report will compare costs for three plans: outright ownership, leasing, and compensation for employee-owned cars. It will also measure employee reaction to each plan. The report is significant because Mycon's current leasing agreement expires April 1 and an improved plan could reduce costs and paperwork. The study is limited to costs for sales reps in the Edmonton district.

An expanded purpose statement considers scope, significance, and limitations.

After preparing a statement of purpose, Diane checked it with Mike Rivers to be sure she was on target.

Anticipating the Audience and Issues

Once the purpose of a report is defined, a writer must think carefully about who will read the report. It is a mistake to concentrate solely on a primary reader. Although the report may have been solicited by one person, others within the organization may eventually read it, including upper management and people in other departments. A report to an outside client may first be read by someone who is familiar with the problem and then be distributed to others less familiar with it. Moreover, candid statements to one audience may be offensive to another audience. Diane could make a serious blunder, for instance, if she mentioned Mike's suspicion that sales reps were padding their mileage statements. If the report were made public—as it probably would be to explain a new policy—the sales reps could feel insulted that their integrity was questioned.

Report writers must take into account both primary and secondary readers.

As Diane considered her primary and secondary readers, she asked herself these questions:

- *What do my readers need to know about this topic?*

- *What do they already know?*

- *How will they react to this information?*

- *How can I make this information understandable and readable?*

Answers to these questions help writers determine how much background material to include, how much detail to add, whether to include jargon, what method of organization and presentation to follow, and what tone to use.

Major report problems
should be broken into
subproblems—or
factored—to highlight
possible solutions.

In the planning stages a report writer must also break the major investigative problem into subproblems. This process, sometimes called factoring, identifies issues to be investigated or possible solutions to the main problem. In this case Mycon must figure out the best way to transport sales reps. Each possible solution or issue that Diane considers becomes a factor or subproblem to be investigated. Diane came up with three tentative solutions to providing transportation for sales reps: (1) purchase cars outright, (2) lease cars, or (3) compensate employees for using their own cars. These three factors form the outline of Diane's study.

Diane continued to factor these main points into the following subproblems for investigation:

What plan should Mycon use to transport its sales reps?
I. Should Mycon purchase cars outright?
   A. How much capital would be required?
   B. How much would it cost to insure, operate, and maintain company-owned cars?
   C. Do employees prefer using company-owned cars?
II. Should Mycon lease cars?
   A. What is the best lease price available?
   B. How much would it cost to insure, operate, and maintain leased cars?
   C. Do employees prefer using leased cars?
III. Should Mycon compensate employees for using their own cars?
   A. How much has it cost in the past to operate employee-owned cars?
   B. How much paperwork is involved in reporting expenses?
   C. Do employees prefer being compensated for using their own cars?

Each subproblem would probably be further factored into additional subproblems. These issues may be phrased as questions, as Diane did, or as statements. In factoring a complex problem, prepare an outline showing the initial problem and its breakdown into subproblems. Make sure your divisions are consistent (don't mix issues), exclusive (don't overlap categories), and complete (don't skip significant issues).

Preparing a Work Plan

After analyzing the problem, anticipating the audience, and factoring the problem, you're ready to prepare a work plan. Preparing a plan forces you to evaluate your resources, set priorities, outline a course of action, and establish a timetable. Such a plan keeps you on schedule and also gives management a means of measuring your progress. A good work plan includes the following:

- Statement of the problem

- Statement of the purpose including scope, significance, and limitations

- Description of the sources and methods of collecting information

- Tentative outline

- Work schedule

A good work plan provides
an overview of a project:
resources, priorities, course
of action, and schedule.

A work plan gives a complete picture of a project. Because the usefulness and quality of any report rests primarily on its data, you'll want to allocate plenty of time to locating sources of information. For firsthand information you might interview people, prepare a survey, or even conduct a scientific experiment. You'll probably also want to search—either manually or electronically—printed materials like books and magazines. Your work plan describes how you expect to generate or collect data. Since data collection is a major part of report writing, the next section of this chapter treats the topic more fully.

Figure 11.6 shows a complete work plan for a report that studies safety seals for a food company's products. This work plan is particularly useful because it outlines the issues to be investigated. Notice that considerable thought and discussion—and even some preliminary research—are necessary before you can make a useful work plan.

Although this tentative outline guides the writer's investigations, it does not determine the content or order of the final report. You may, for example, study five possible solutions to a problem. If two prove to be useless, your report may discuss only the three winners. Moreover, you will organize the report to accomplish your goal and satisfy the audience. Remember that a busy executive who is familiar with a topic may prefer to read the conclusions and recommendations before a discussion of the findings.

If the report is authorized by someone, be sure to review the work plan with that individual (your manager, client, or professor, for example) before proceeding with the project.

Researching Report Data

One of the most important steps in the writing of a report is research. Because a report is only as good as its data, the remainder of this chapter describes how to find data and document it.

As you analyze your purpose and audience, you'll assess the kinds of facts needed to support your argument or explain your topic. Do you need statistics, background data, expert opinions, group opinions, or organizational data? Figure 11.7 lists five forms of data and provides questions to guide you in making your research accurate and productive.

Data fall into two broad categories, primary and secondary. Primary data result from firsthand experience and observation. Secondary data come from reading what others have experienced and observed. Coca-Cola and Pepsi-Cola, for example, produce primary data when they stage taste tests and record the reactions of consumers. These same sets of data become secondary after they have been published and, let's say, a newspaper reporter uses them in an article about soft drinks. Secondary data are easier and cheaper to develop than primary data, which might involve interviewing large groups or sending out questionnaires. Nearly every research project should begin with a search of secondary data. Often, something has already been written about your topic. Reviewing secondary sources can save time and effort and prevent you from reinventing the wheel.

Locating Secondary Data

A logical place to begin any research project is by examining relevant secondary data available in print and in databases. Your college, university, or municipal library should contain such data.

If you don't use the library often, begin your research by talking to a reference librarian about your project. These librarians won't do the research for you, but they will steer you in the right direction. And they are very accommodating. Many libraries have brochures, handouts, and workshops to help the public understand their cataloguing and retrieval systems.

In locating secondary data, researchers find librarians a prime resource.

FIGURE 11.6 ■ Work Plan for a Formal Report

Tips for Preparing a Work Plan

- Start early; allow plenty of time for brainstorming and preliminary research.
- Describe the problem motivating the report.
- Write a purpose statement that includes its scope, significance, and limitations.
- Describe data collection sources and methods.
- Divide the major problem into subproblems stated as questions to be answered.
- Develop a realistic work schedule citing dates for completion of major tasks.
- Review the work plan with whoever authorized the report.

Statement of Problem

Consumers worry that food and drug products are dangerous as a result of tampering. Our company may face loss of market share and potential liability if we don't protect our products. Many food and drug companies now offer tamper-resistant packaging, but such packaging is costly.

Statement of Purpose

The purpose of this study is to determine whether tamper-resistant packaging is necessary and/or feasible for our jams, jellies, and preserves. The study will examine published accounts of package tampering and evaluate how other companies have solved the problem. It will also measure consumers' interest in safety-seal packaging, as well as consumers' willingness to pay a slightly higher price for safety lids. We will conduct a market survey limited to a sample of 400 local consumers. Finally, the study will investigate a method for sealing our products and determine the cost for each unit we produce. This study is significant because safety seals could enhance the sales of our products and protect us from possible liability.

Defines purpose, scope, limits, and significance of report

Sources and Methods of Data Collection

Magazine and newspaper accounts of product tampering will be examined for the past 15 years. Articles describing tamper-resistant lids and other safe packaging devices for food and drug manufacturers will be studied. Moreover, our marketing staff will conduct a random telephone survey of local consumers, measuring their interest in safety seals. Finally, our production department will test various devices and determine the most cost-effective method to seal our product safely.

Describes primary and secondary data sources

Tentative Outline

I. Are consumers and producers concerned about product tampering?
   A. What incidents of tampering have been reported in the past 15 years?
   B. How did consumers react to tampering that caused harm?
   C. How did food and drug producers protect their products?
II. How do consumers react to safety seals on products today?
   A. Do consumers prefer food and drug products with safety seals?
   B. Would consumers be more likely to purchase our products if safety-sealed?
   C. Would consumers be willing to pay a few cents extra for safety seals?
III. What kind of safety seal is best for our products?
   A. What devices are other producers using—plastic "blister" packs, foil seals over bottle openings, or bands around lids?
   B. What device would work for our products?
   C. How much would each device cost per unit?
IV. Should we proceed with safety seals?

Factors problem into manageable chunks

Work Schedule

Investigate newspaper and magazine articles	Oct. 1-10
Examine safety-seal devices on the market	Oct. 8-18
Interview 400 local consumers	Oct. 8-24
Develop and test devices for our products	Oct. 15-Nov.14
Interpret and evaluate findings	Nov. 15-17
Compose first draft of report	Nov. 18-20
Revise draft	Nov. 21-23
Submit final report	Nov. 24

Estimates time needed to complete report tasks

FIGURE 11.7 ■ Selecting Report Data

Form of Data	Questions to Ask
Statistical	What is the source?
	How were these figures derived?
	In what form do I need the statistics?
	Must they be converted?
	How recent are they?
Background or historical	Has this topic been explored before?
	What have others said about it?
	What sources did they use?
Expert opinion	Who are the experts?
	Are their opinions in print?
	Can they be interviewed?
	Do we have in-house experts?
Individual or group opinion	Do I need to interview or survey people (such as consumers, employees, or managers)?
	Do good questionnaires already exist?
	Can parts of existing test instruments be used or combined?
Organizational	What are the proper channels for obtaining in-house data?
	Are permissions required?
	How can I find data about public and private companies?

For a business report you'll probably use the following in searching for secondary information: (1) books, (2) periodicals and newspapers, and (3) electronic catalogues and databases.

Books. Although quickly outdated, books contain excellent historical, in-depth information. Books can be found through print or computer listings.

- **Card catalogue.** Some libraries still maintain card catalogues with all books indexed on 3-by-5 cards alphabetized by author, title, or subject.

- **On-line catalogue.** Most libraries have by now computerized their card catalogues. Some systems are fully automated, thus allowing you to learn not only whether the library has a book but also whether it is available.

- **Search strategies.** If you are unfamiliar with the on-line catalogue, don't hesitate to ask a clerk or librarian for help. Generally you can search by author, title, or subject. Be sure to read the help screens to learn how to conduct keyword searches.

Periodicals. Magazines, pamphlets, and journals are called *periodicals* because they are published recurrently or periodically. Journals, by the way, are compilations of scholarly articles. Articles in journals and other periodicals will be extremely useful to you because they are concise, current, and limited in scope, and they can supplement information in books.

- **Print indexes.** *The Readers' Guide to Periodical Literature* is a valuable index of general-interest magazine article titles. It includes such magazines as *Time, Newsweek, Maclean's,* and *The Canadian Forum.* More useful to business writers, though, will be articles appearing in business and industrial magazines (such as *Canadian Business, Canadian Banker, and Business Quarterly.)* For an index of these publications, consult the *Business Periodicals Index.* The *Canadian Business Index* lists articles from over 200 Canadian business periodicals.

- **CD-ROM indexes and databases.** Automated indexes similar to the print indexes just described are stored in CD-ROM (short for *Compact Disc, Read Only Memory*) databases. Many libraries now provide such CD-ROM databases for computer-aided retrieval of references, abstracts, and some full-text articles from magazines, journals, and newspapers, such as *The Globe and Mail.* CD-ROM database collections are appealing because users do not have to pay for on-line hookups to relatively expensive information services. The collections are stored on high-capacity disks that are regularly replaced with updated disks.

- **Search strategies.** When using CD-ROM indexes, follow the on-screen instructions or ask for assistance from a librarian. It's a good idea to begin with a subject search because that generally turns up more relevant citations than keyword searches (especially when you are searching for names of people or companies). Once you locate usable references, print a copy of your findings and then check the shelf listings to see if the publications are available. If they aren't, ask the librarian if they can be ordered from another library.

Other electronic resources. Your computer modem can deliver a world of information directly to your computer screen. Vast reserves of information are now stored in computerized databases around the world. With your computer you can search for bibliographies, check references, confirm statistics, quote experts, locate specific publications, and, in some instances, read entire documents. Electronic resources are rapidly becoming the principal source of secondary research information today. By learning to use these resources, you will enhance your communication skills and make yourself a valuable knowledge worker. Although information technology is a volatile field and on-line services are constantly emerging from new directions, we'll try to pin down three of the best current resources: (1) specialized information retrieval services, (2) generalized on-line services, and (3) the Internet.

- **Specialized information retrieval services.** Business organizations and professionals are likely to find information through services such as Lexis/Nexis, Dow Jones News/Retrieval Service, and DIALOG Information Retrieval Service. These collections of databases contain legal, scientific, scholarly, and business information. Some provide reference titles and bibliographic data only, while others provide full-text articles. Well-stocked and well-organized, these specialized collections can nevertheless be frustrating and expensive to use. You will need skill in selecting keywords (or descriptors), as well as experience in exploring a particular database. Thus, you may wish to ask reference librarians or information retrieval professionals for assistance.

- **Generalized on-line services.** CompuServe Information Service, Prodigy, and America Online are three major providers of electronic information services. Canadian sources include InfoGlobe, Informart, Newstext, and Québec Actualité. For a flat monthly fee you can access many basic services, like E-mail, news headlines, news articles, weather reports, sports results, and travel news. For additional fees you can access various specialized databases, including some described earlier (like Lexis/Nexis and DIALOG), as well as special-interest forums. Suppose you wanted to learn about financing a home business. An inquiry posted to one of the home office forums could bring valuable information and advice from someone who has firsthand experience. If you need information only occasionally, it may be more economical and efficient to use one of the generalized on-line services than to subscribe to a specialized service. NewsEdge, a Toronto electronic clipping service, makes searching for information very comprehensive. Users post the information they need to know, and NewsEdge automatically scans information from participating news and information sources and posts them to the user's computer. Hoover, a similar service, automatically selects information from on-line services.

- **The Internet.** Canada's Marshall McLuhan called the information super-highway the "tom-tom drums" of the "Global Village." The Internet is an ever-expanding international nonprofit collection of linked networks combining educational, research, and government facilities. The Internet is an exciting collection of voluntarily linked networks (over 25 000 at the time of writing). These loosely connected networks enable scientists, professors, students, librarians, universities, governments, and, most recently, business organizations to exchange information electronically. Using such search utilities as gopher clients or Web browsers, you can access the Internet through local network gateways or through generalized services like Prodigy. Figure 11.8 shows how Lisa, a marketing student, uses a text-based gopher client (or program) to gather Internet information about the effectiveness of in-store coupons.

World Wide Web. The fastest-growing segment of the Internet is the World Wide Web (WWW).[2] With new user-friendly browsing programs like NCSA Mosaic and Netscape's Navigator, any PC user can access WWW homepages.[3] Homepages are hypertext (electronic cross-referenced) documents that contain multimedia information as well as links to other pages on the Internet containing related information.

A number of service-oriented companies are beginning to use the Web in simple ways to provide automated customer service. Federal Express and United Parcel Service, for example, both maintain homepages that enable customers to check the whereabouts of mailed packages.[4] And Apple Computer allows customers to download software updates through its Web homepage.

However, researchers who use the Web are usually more interested in exploiting the more complex multimedia resources (imaginative graphics, real-istic photographs, sound clips, movies, and so forth) that are attached to many of the Web pages available on the Internet. The browsers these researchers use, unlike merely text-based clients (such as gopher, ftp, and Lynx), can display textual information in enhanced ways as well as attached graphics, illustrative movies, and sound effects. To help you visualize better how a researcher could use a browser to gain access to the rich resources of the Web, let's observe student researcher Alan at work. In Figure 11.9 you can follow his search for Web information about recycling.

FIGURE 11.8 ■ Internet Session: Typical Gopher Research Sequence

The computer ("coyote") of marketing student Lisa awaits her commands.

```
coyote%
```

Lisa tells computer to connect with a gopher server at the University of Manitoba.

```
coyote% gopher gopher.cc.umanitoba.ca
```

The gopher server at the University of Manitoba responds by transmitting a general menu to Lisa's computer screen.

```
                    Internet Gopher Information Client 2.0 p16

                    Root gopher server: gopher.cc.umanitoba.ca

1.   ----------- Welcome to UMinfo --------------------
2.   Visitors -- Please Sign Our Guestbook... <TEL>
3.   Academic and Staff Services/
4.   University Statistics and Information/
5.   Ancillary Services/Student Services and Research/
6.   Student Associations/
7.   1995-1996 General Calendar/
8.   Computer Services/
9.   Faculties and Departments/
10.  Libraries/
11.  University News and Public Affairs/
12.  World News and Weather/
13.  Selected Internet Resources/
14.  Finding People/
15.  Search Tools/
16.  Gateway to Other Gopher and Information Servers/
17.  UMinfo World Wide Web
```

Lisa moves the screen cursor (arrow) to the "Search Tools" line and presses the keyboard Enter key.

The gopher server at the University of Manitoba responds by transmitting a "Search Tools" menu to Lisa's computer screen.

```
                    Internet Gopher Information Client 2.0 p16

                                 Search Tools

1.   How to do searches using Jughead.
2.   Search UMinfo Contents (JUGHEAD) <?>
3.   About VERONICA.
4.   FAQ: Frequently Asked Questions About Veronica. <?>
5.   Search Gopherspace by Keyword (VERONICA at U. Manitoba) <?>
6.   Search Gopherspace by Keyword (VERONICA at AARNet, Australia) <?>
7.   Search Gopherspace by Keyword (VERONICA at CNIDR) <?>
8.   Search Gopherspace by Keyword (VERONICA at Imperial College, UK) <?>
9.   Search Gopherspace by Keyword (VERONICA at Keio U, Japan) <?>
10.  Search Gopherspace by Keyword (VERONICA at ManchesterU, UK) <?>
11.  Search Gopherspace by Keyword (VERONICA at U. NYSERNET) <?>
12.  Search Gopherspace by Keyword (VERONICA at U. PSINet) <?>
13.  Search Gopherspace by Keyword (VERONICA at U. SUNET) <?>
14.  Search Gopherspace by Keyword (VERONICA at U. of Nevada) <?>
15.  Search Gopherspace by Keyword (VERONICA at U.Cologne, Germany) <?>
16.  Search Gopherspace by Keyword (VERONICA at U.Texas, Dallas) <?>
17.  Search Gopherspace by Keyword (VERONICA at UNINETT) <?>
18.  Archie: Archive Server Listing Service/
```

After deciding to use the "Veronica" search tool at Manchester University, Lisa moves the screen cursor to line 10 and presses the Enter key.

FIGURE 11.8 ■ Internet Session: Typical Gopher Research Sequence continued

```
·············Search Gopherspace by Keyword (Veronica at Manchester, UK) ···········
  Words to search for
```
— A dialogue box opens on Lisa's computer screen.

```
·············Search Gopherspace by Keyword (Veronica at Manchester, UK) ···········
  Words to search for      coupons
```
— Lisa tells the gopher server at Manchester University to search throughout the world for Internet computer files with the word "coupons" in their titles.

```
              Internet Gopher Information Client 2.9 p16

Search Gopherspace by Keyword (Veronica at ManchesterU, UK): coupons

 1.  Effective Price Discrimination Using In-Store Coupons.
 2.  Coupons.
 3.  Student Loan Payment Coupons.
 4.  Student Loan Payment Coupons.
 5.  Student Loan Payment Coupons.
 6.  952-45 Food Stamps/Coupons.
 7.  alt.coupons/
 8.  Adobe Type Manager Coupons.
 9.  F> Discount Coupons.
10.  Riverside Park Discount Coupons.
11.  Subject: CITY OK'S DRUG COUPONS.
12.  Coupons: Good Business or Bad Business.
13.  One-day Coupons.
14.  Purchasing Coupons.
15.  TELL 154 Coping Using Coupons.
16.  Adobe Type Manager Coupons.
17.  Adobe Type Manager Coupons.
18.  coupons/
```
— Veronica at Manchester University responds by transmitting a menu listing relevant documents.

— Lisa moves the screen cursor to the first line of the menu and presses the Enter key.

```
Effective Price Discrimination Using In-Store Coupons
------------------------------------------------------

Sanjay Dhar
Stephen J. Hoch

Firms can always be more profitable if they can successfully price discrim-
inate.  We analyze the effectiveness of in-store coupons as a price
discrimination mechanism. In five field tests, we find that,
compared to straight off-the-shelf discounts (bonus buys), in-store
coupons lead to a 25% greater increase in sales volume.  And because
redemption rates hover around 55%, in-store coupons produce a 100%
greater increase in dollar profits.  We develop a simple model of the
process and show that optimal discount levels always are higher with
coupons, that it is in the best interests of the retailer to
pass-through larger amounts of a trade-deal when using an in-store
coupon. As a consequence, at the optimal dicount level, unit sales and
```
— The Manchester University computer connects with a University of Chicago computer, which responds by transmitting to Lisa's computer screen an abstract of the selected document.

Alan starts his search for information about recycling by accessing Netscape's "Internet Search" page (address or URL: "http//home.mcom.com/home/internet-search.html).

EXPLORING THE NET

INTERNET SEARCH

If you're trying to find a particular site or document on the Internet or just looking for a resource list on a particular subject, you can use one of the many available on-line search engines. These engines allow you to search for information in many different ways - some search titles or headers of documents, others search the documents themselves, and still others search other indexes or directories.

SEARCH ENGINES

INFOSEEK SEARCH

InfoSeek is a comprehensive and accurate WWW search engine. You can type your search in plain English or just enter key words and phrases. You can also use special query operators:

[   ]

[Run Query] [Clear Query Text]

THE LYCOS HOME PAGE: HUNTING WWW INFORMATION

This search engine, served by Carnegie Mellon University, will allow you to search on document titles and content. Its May 1 database contains 3.75 million link descriptors and the keywords from 767,000 documents. The Lycos index is built by a Web crawler that can bring in 5000 documents per day. The index searches document title, headings, links, and keywords it locates in these documents.

WEBCRAWLER SEARCHING

This engine allows searches by document title and content. It is part of the WebCrawler project, managed by Brian Pinkerton at the University of Washington, which collects documents from the Web.

Alan decides to use WebCrawler for his search and therefore, with his mouse, clicks on the appropriate underlined phrase. (All underlined phrases or "links" on page are "clickable.")

SEARCH ENGINE SEARCH

If you still haven't found what you're looking for and you'd like to try out other available search engines, check out these other lists of search engines:

W3 SEARCH ENGINES

Published by the University of Geneva, this list of search engines covers a wide variety of topics and subjects but isn't updated very often.

CUSI (CONFIGURABLE UNIFIED SEARCH INTERFACE)

Nexor U.K. offers this tool, a single form to search a large number of different WWW engines for documents, people, software, dictionaries, and more.

 SEARCH | SPONSOR INDEX | CONTACT INFO | NETSCAPE STORE | TABLE OF CONTENTS | DOWNLOAD SOFTWARE | NETSCAPE GALLERIA | FEEDBACK

Find out more about Netscape at info@netscape.com, or call 415/528-2555.
Copyright © 1995 Netscape Communications Corporation

FIGURE 11.9 ■ Screen 2

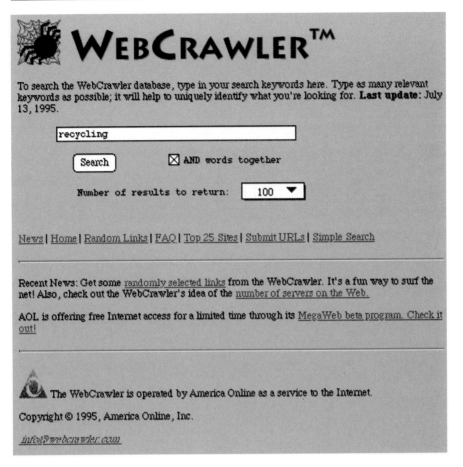

To search the WebCrawler database, type in your search keywords here. Type as many relevant keywords as possible; it will help to uniquely identify what you're looking for. **Last update**: July 13, 1995.

recycling

Search   ☒ AND words together

Number of results to return: 100 ▼

News | Home | Random Links | FAQ | Top 25 Sites | Submit URLs | Simple Search

Recent News: Get some randomly selected links from the WebCrawler. It's a fun way to surf the net! Also, check out the WebCrawler's idea of the number of servers on the Web.

AOL is offering free Internet access for a limited time through its MegaWeb beta program. Check it out!

The WebCrawler is operated by America Online as a service to the Internet.

Copyright © 1995, America Online, Inc.

info@webcrawler.com

Alan browser's displays a "WebCrawler" form for his use.

Alan types "recycling," his research topic, in this field.

Last, Alan clicks "Search" button.

Generating Primary Data

Although you'll begin a business report by probing for secondary data, you'll likely also need primary data to give a complete picture. Because business reports typically solve specific current problems, they rely heavily on primary, firsthand data. If, for example, management wants to discover the cause of increased employee turnover in its Vancouver office, it must investigate and collect information. Providing answers to business problems often means generating primary data through surveys, interviews, observation, or experimentation.

Research projects often draw on primary data from surveys and interviews.

Surveys. Surveys collect data from groups of people. When companies develop new products, for example, they often survey consumers to learn their needs. The advantages of surveys are that they gather data economically and efficiently. Mailed surveys reach big groups nearby or at great distances. Moreover, people responding to mailed surveys have time to consider their answers, thus improving the accuracy of the data.

Surveys yield efficient and economical primary data for reports.

FIGURE 11.9 ■ Screen 3

WebCrawler Search Results

The query "recycling" found 365 documents and returned 100:

```
1000  http://gargoyle.tiac.net/ne_greenbase.txt
0963  http://www.awinc.com/OCPRI/
0921  Recycling Our Built Heritage
0781  Environment
0637  General Information about Virginia Tech
0629  Carnegie Mellon ECE FARQ
0625  Ribbon-Jet Tek
0572  Q Recycling Company Home Page
0473  Goodwill Recycling
0469  Thomson-Shore Green Pages
0398  Electric Recycling System
0394  Recyler's World
0346  The Home Page of Global Recycling Network
0299  GRC Guide to Ribbons and Cartridges
0295  LS HA - Lehre
0295  Information
0261  Environmental Management homepage
0251  The World-Wide Web Virtual Library: Environment - Subject Tree
0244  Vital Visions Corporation
0236  St. Louis Life Magazine
0222  http://fergus.cfa.org:7700/1/FF/Employment/Even%20More%20Labor%20Positions/
0212  EcoWeb
0200  What's New
0196  Gopher Menu
0196  DEPARTMENT OF CONSERVATION
0192  The Integral Fast Reactor (IFR)
0188  San Francisco Business to Business Pages
0188  Tecnotes
0180  Alberta SuperNet: Cartridge Charge Canada
0178  Overview
0176  Cartridge Care & Inks Direct
0176  AGRA Earth & Enviromental's Garbage Page
0168  the zweblö underground fan cult online catalog
```

Alan's browser displays results of WebCrawler search as "clickable" links.

From the 100 sources returned by WebCrawler search engine, Alan chooses one ("EcoWeb") by clicking on it with his mouse.

Although mailed surveys may suffer low response rates, they are still useful in generating primary data.

Mailed questionnaires, of course, have disadvantages. Most of us rank them with junk mail, so response rates may be no higher than 10 percent. Furthermore, those who do respond may not represent an accurate sample of the overall population, thus invalidating generalizations from the group. Let's say, for example, that an insurance company sends out a questionnaire asking about provisions in a new policy. If only older people respond, the questionnaire data cannot be used to generalize what people in other age groups might think. A final problem with surveys has to do with truthfulness. Some respondents exaggerate their incomes or distort other facts, thus causing the results to be unreliable.

Nevertheless, surveys may be the best way to generate data for business and student reports. In preparing a survey, consider these pointers:

- **Explain why the survey is necessary.** In a cover letter or an opening paragraph, describe the need for the survey. Suggest how someone or something other than you will benefit. If appropriate, offer to send recipients a copy of the findings.

FIGURE 11.9 ■ Screen 4

Welcome to EcoWeb at U.Va.

 EcoSystems

Are the environmental information systems which run on EcoSys.

 The Program

Is a tour through U.Va.'s Recycling Program: materials we recycle, etc.

 Links

Is the World Wide Web Virtual Library Environment Subject Page

 Exploration

Will lead you to some of the many other interesting internet resources accessible via EcoWeb.

 Perform a keyword search of all the hyper-text on EcoWeb.

 Perform a keyword search of the images on EcoWeb.

Alan's browser displays EcoWeb "Welcome" page.

Alan clicks on "The Program" link.

- **Consider incentives.** If the survey is long, persuasive techniques may be necessary. Response rates can be increased by offering money, coupons, gift certificates, free books, or other gifts.

- **Limit the number of questions.** Resist the temptation to ask for too much. Request only information you will use. Don't, for example, include demographic questions (income, gender, age, and so forth) unless the information is necessary to evaluate responses.

- **Use questions that produce quantifiable answers.** Check-off, multiple-choice, yes-no, and scale (or rank-order) questions (illustrated in Figure 11.10) provide quantifiable data that are easily tabulated. Responses to open-ended questions (*What should the bookstore do about plastic bags?*) reveal opinions that are interesting, but difficult to quantify.[5] To obtain workable data, give interviewees a list of possible responses (as shown in items 5–8 of Figure 11.10). For scale and multiple-choice questions, try to present all the possible answers. To be safe, add an "Other" or "Don't know" category in case the choices seem insufficient to the respondent. Many surveys use scale questions because they capture degrees of feelings. Typical scale headings are "agree strongly," "agree somewhat," "neutral," "disagree somewhat," and "disagree strongly."

Effective surveys target appropriate samples and ask a limited number of specific questions with quantifiable answers.

FIGURE 11.9 ■ Screen 5

EcoWeb **_The Program_**

U.Va. has added many different resources to the resource recovery and recycling program since its inception in 1991. Implementation of the program takes place in phases, and there are various methods of operation of the recycling program. When areas are to be implemented with the program, one of the major steps is the formation of Area Recycling Committees (ARCs).

Paper recycling is divided into two grades of paper, 'revenue' and 'non-revenue'. The first is called 'revenue' because it is white ledger paper which is sold to a vendor. The sale of revenue paper helps pay for the recycling of both grades, and of course lowers tipping fee expenses. When the program is implemented in a building, instructions for sorting the paper are distributed and basic environmental education is provided.

Other materials are also recycled at U.Va., including aluminum, glass, and plastic.

For U.Va.'s 1993 efforts, the Virginia Department of Environment Quality recognized the Office of Recycling and Environmental Information as one of the leaders in state agency recycling.

Spend a virtual week with U.Va. Recycling a report by Flossie Steele

Recycling Factoids

Recycling Centers

- Audio and Visual

- **Avoid leading or ambiguous questions.** The wording of a question can dramatically affect responses to it, as shown in a *New York Times*/CBS national poll.[6] When respondents were asked "Are we spending too much, too little, or about the right amount on *assistance to the poor* [emphasis added]?" 13 percent responded "too much." When the same respondents were asked "Are we spending too much, too little, or about the right amount on *welfare*[emphasis added]?" 44 percent responded "too much." To obtain accurate information, you must strive to use objective language and pilot-test your questions with typical respondents. Stay away from questions that suggest an answer (*Don't you agree that the salaries of CEOs are obscenely high?*). Instead, ask neutral questions (*Do CEOs earn too much, too little, or about the right amount?*). Also avoid questions that really ask two or more things (*Should the salaries of CEOs be reduced or regulated by government legislation?*). Instead, break them into separate questions (*Should the salaries of CEOs be regulated by government legislation? Should the salaries of CEOs be reduced by government legislation?*).

- **Select the survey population carefully.** Many surveys question a small group of people (a sample) and project the findings to a larger population. Let's say that a survey of your class reveals that the majority prefer deep-dish pizza. Can you then say with confidence that all students on your campus (or in the nation) prefer deep-dish pizza? To be able to generalize from a survey, you need to make the sample as large as possible. In addition, you need to determine if the sample is like the larger population. For important surveys you will want to consult books or experts in sampling

FIGURE 11.9 ◼ Screen 6

 EcoWeb The Program

A Week in the Life of U.Va. Recycling

This report was written by Flossie Steele, a Budget Analyst at Facilities Management. She spent a week with the Office of Recycling and Environmental Information in the summer of 1994.

DAY ONE

Smack. Splat. I slapped at the mosquitoes that were attacking me. At 6:45AM the heat and humidity in the Recycling trailer was oppressive. Maybe this wasn't such a great idea, spending a week in the Office of Recycling and Environmental Information.

People were arriving at work. Everyone ignored me. I could hear signs of activity coming from the rear office of the trailer. Sonny Beale, Operations Supervisor was dispatching workers to buildings designated for Monday pickup. Details of the days operation were being discussed by loud voices. The single large truck owned by the Recycling Office, suitable for collection of recyclable paper, cardboard, cans rumbled off the site. It was quiet again.

Finally, Sonny closed the trailer doors and started the air conditioner. The mosquitoes retreated as I scratched furiously. How would I survive a week of this? Fritz Franke, the Director of the Recycling Office would not be coming in today. He was needed at home to care for the two youngest children who were suffering from chicken pox.

I was considering abandoning the whole experiment of "cross-training"and retreating to my budget analyst's air-conditioned cubicle when Tom Rowe , Manager of Environmental Information arrived.

Tom operates Ecosys ,a computer that tracks recyclables and dispatches information related to recycling and environmental preservation programs to students, faculty, and anyone on the planet who possesses an electronic mail address. Ecosys is sophisticated, comprehensive. Tom calls it a work in progress.

During the course of a normal work day Tom explores the outer reaches of computer technology. Users of Ecosys can query the system as to how many thousand pounds of glass were recycled last year by the University of Virginia or how many tons of revenue-grade paper were recovered during a six month period. It's menu-driven and easy to use. The complicated technology lurking behind Ecosys has been tamed and repackaged by Tom so that people like me can use it.

Tom's latest project is a juggling program known as Mosaic. Mosaic pulls files from the internet, translates them to graphics, sound, and animation for the user to enjoy. In the Recycling Department, the norm is to share information. Tom asked Sonny and me to schedule a training session with him to become acquainted with Mosaic.

Continuing the morning's instruction, Tom explained the use of Lynx, a new system of hypertext written with the ability to connect with other systems using the html, or hyper-text markup language. Hypertext allows the user to link to offsite sources of information by clicking an onscreen icon. A short- term goal is to produce a hypertext version of the earlier Ecogopher menus which contain text only. The result will be a sort of Alice-in-Wonderland journey through a maze of environmental data. And Tom will personally introduce many new users, as is his custom.

Alan's browser displays first page of "virtual week" report. He can now read (and print out, if he wishes) the complete report by Flossie Steele.

By clicking "Tom Rowe," Alan can command his browser to display Tom Rowe's résumé. (Résumé includes a clickable link to an audio clip.)

techniques. The Career Skills box on page 332 discusses basic sampling procedures.

- **Conduct a pilot study.** Try the questionnaire with a small group so that you can remedy any problems. For example, in the survey shown in Figure 11.10, a pilot study revealed that female students generally favoured cloth book bags and were willing to pay for them. Male students opposed purchasing cloth bags. By adding a sex category, researchers could verify this finding. The pilot study also revealed the need to ensure an appropriate representation of male and female students in the survey.

Interviews. Some of the best report information, particularly on topics about which little has been written, comes from experts in the field. Consider both in-house and outside experts for business reports. Tapping these sources will call for in-person or telephone interviews. To elicit the most useful data, try these techniques:

- **Find an expert**. Ask managers and other people in the field whom they consider to be most knowledgeable. Check membership lists of professional

Interviews with experts yield useful report data, especially when little has been written about a topic.

FIGURE 11.10 ■ Preparing a Survey

The Three Phases of the Writing Process

1

Analyze
The purpose is to help the bookstore decide if it should replace plastic bags with cloth bags for customer purchases.

Anticipate
The audience will be busy students who will be initially uninterested.

Adapt
Because students will be unwilling to participate, the survey must be short and simple. Its purpose must be significant and clear.

2

Research
Ask students how they would react to cloth bags. Use their answers to form question response choices.

Organize
Open by explaining the survey's purpose and importance. In the body ask clear questions that produce quantifiable answers. Conclude with appreciation and instructions.

Compose
Write the first draft of the questionnaire.

3

Revise
Try out the questionnaire with small, representative group. Revise unclear questions.

Proofread
Read for correctness. Be sure that answer choices do not overlap and that they are complete. Provide "other" category if appropriate (as in No. 9).

Evaluate
Is the survey clear, attractive, and easy to complete?

North Shore College Bookstore
STUDENT SURVEY

The North Shore College Bookstore wants to do its part in protecting the environment. Each year we give away 45 000 plastic bags for students to carry off their purchases. We are considering changing from plastic to cloth bags or some other alternative, but we need your views. ● — Explains need for survey (use cover letter for longer surveys)

Please place checks below to indicate your responses.

1. How many units are you carrying right now?
    ___ 15 or more units   ___ Male
    ___ 9 to 14 units   ___ Female
    ___ 8 or fewer units

Uses groupings that do not overlap (not 9 to 15 and 15 or more)

2. How many times have you visited the bookstore this semester?
    ___ 0 times   ___ 1 time   ___ 2 times   ___ 3 times   ___ 4 or more times

3. Indicate your concern for the environment.
    ___ Very concerned   ___ Concerned   ___ Unconcerned

4. To protect the environment, would you be willing to change to another type of bag when buying books?
    ___ Yes
    ___ No

Indicate your feeling about the following alternatives.

	Agree	Undecided	Disagree
For major purchases the bookstore should			
5. Continue to provide plastic bags.	___	___	___
6. Provide no bags; encourage students to bring their own bags.	___	___	___
7. Provide no bags; offer cloth bags at reduced price (about $3).	___	___	___
8. Give a cloth bag with each major purchase, the cost to be included in registration fees.	___	___	___
9. Consider another alternative, such as			

Uses scale questions to channel responses into quantifiable alternatives, as opposed to posing an open-ended question

Allows respondent to add an answer in case choices provided seem insufficient

_____

Please return the completed survey form to your instructor or to the survey box at the North Shore College Bookstore exit. Your opinion counts. ● — Tells how to return survey form

Thanks for your help!

organizations, and consult articles about the topic or related topics. Most people enjoy being experts or at least recommending them.

- **Prepare for the interview.** Learn about the individual you're interviewing as well as the background and terminology of the topic. Let's say you're interviewing a corporate communication expert about producing an in-house newsletter. You should be familiar with terms like *font* and with software like Quark Xpress, Aldus PageMaker, and Ventura. In addition, be prepared by making a list of questions. Ask the interviewee if you may record the talk.

- **Make your questions objective and friendly.** Don't get into a debate with the interviewee. And remember that you're there to listen, not to talk! Use open-ended, rather than yes-or-no, questions to draw experts out.

- **Watch the time.** Tell your interviewee in advance how much time you expect to need for the interview. Don't overstay your appointment.

- **End graciously.** Conclude the interview with a general question, such as "Is there anything you'd like to add?" Express your appreciation, and ask permission to telephone later if you need to verify anything.

Observation and experimentation. Some kinds of primary data can be obtained only through firsthand observation and investigation. How long does a typical caller wait before a customer service rep answers the call? How is a new piece of equipment operated? Are complaints of sexual harassment being taken seriously? Observation produces rich data, but that information is especially prone to charges of subjectivity. One can interpret an observation in many ways. Thus, to make observations more objective, try to quantify them. For example, record the time that customers wait on the telephone for 60-minute periods at different times throughout a week. Or compare the number of sexual harassment complaints made with the number of investigations undertaken and the resulting action.

Experimentation produces data suggesting causes and effects. Informal experimentation might be as simple as a pre-test and post-test in a college course. Did students expand their knowledge as a result of the course? More formal experimentation is undertaken by scientists and professional researchers who control variables to test their effects. Assume, for example, that Neilson Cadbury wants to test the hypothesis (which is a tentative assumption) that chocolate lifts people out of the doldrums. An experiment testing the hypothesis would separate depressed individuals into two groups: those who ate chocolate (the experimental group) and those who did not (the control group). What effect did chocolate have? Such experiments are not done haphazardly, however. Valid experiments require sophisticated research designs and careful matching of the experimental and control groups.

Documenting Data

Documenting data means revealing and crediting your information sources. Careful documentation in a report serves three purposes:

- **Strengthens your argument.** Including good data from reputable sources will convince readers of your credibility and the logic of your reasoning.

Documenting data lends credibility, aids the reader, and protects the writer from plagiarism.

331

SURVEY SAMPLING AT A GLANCE

Let's assume your school wants to add a new eating facility on campus, and you've been asked to find out whether students want a fast-food hamburger stand or a health-food bar. Your first idea might be to survey all 20 000 students to ask what they prefer. Such a survey, however, would obviously require a lot of time and money. A better plan would be to question only a portion, or sample, of the student body. Sampling is the process used to select a small group of individuals to represent an entire population. Most samples can be separated into two groups: probability samples and nonprobability samples.

PROBABILITY SAMPLES. In probability samples every person in the population has a known chance of being selected. Such samples allow researchers to estimate how closely the sample represents the population from which it is drawn. To determine what kind of food stand students prefer, you might consider one of the following probability samples.

Simple Random Sample. The easiest way to select a simple random sample is to use a random number generator program—say, from the university's computer system. The program might select 2000 students from the 20 000 enrolled. Thus, each student has a 10 percent chance of being selected.

Stratified Random Sample. To select a stratified random sample, you simply divide the population into subgroups and randomly select individuals from each subgroup. Our 20 000 students, might for example, be divided into their class levels. The random number generator might select 650 names from the 8 500 first-year students, 550 from the 5500 second-year students, 450 from the 4500 third-year students, and 350 from the 3500 fourth-year students. Thus, the total sample represents 10 percent of each class. Such samples are particularly useful for comparing responses between subgroups. A stratified sample will be more accurate than a simple random sample.

Cluster Sample. Cluster samples fall into two categories: system clusters and area clusters. In a cluster/system random sample, every *n*th individual is selected. For example, to select a sample of 2000, the number generator would begin at a random point on the list of 20 000 student names and then select every tenth name. In a cluster/area random sample, the population is divided into subgroups or clusters, often on a geographic basis. For our sample the 20 000 students might be divided into 10 home postal code clusters. A number generator randomly selects five postal codes from the 10, and 400 students in each cluster are selected to make up the sample of 2000.

NONPROBABILITY SAMPLES. When random samples cost too much or are impossible to obtain, researchers may use nonprobability samples. And the resulting data may be quite useful. But generalizations from such samples are usually not as representative as those from probability samples. That's why ethical researchers always reveal their survey methods. Nonprobability samples include judgment, convenience, and quota samples.

Judgment Sample. A judgment sample consists of non-randomly selected persons who appear to have the appropriate knowledge related to the survey topic. For example, only students who frequently eat at hamburger stands or health-food bars ("food experts") are surveyed about which eating spot all students would prefer.

Convenience Sample. Sometimes a sample is chosen solely on the basis of its convenience to the researcher. Interviewers might stand outside the campus cafeteria, for example, and question the first 2000 students who walk by. One form of convenience samples is the self-selected sample. MTV, for instance, asks viewers to choose recording artists, such as Celine Dion or Bryan Adams. Since the callers are not selected randomly, their choices may not reflect the feelings of all viewers.

Quota Sample. In a quota sample, individuals are selected from subgroups—but they are not randomly selected. For example, you could question the first 350 fourth-year students you meet, thus filling your 10 percent quota.

Career Track Application

Your class wants to survey 10 percent of the Fortune 500 companies (a list is available at your library). In teams of three or four, select a cluster/system random sample. Discuss how you could develop a stratified random sample and a cluster/area random sample.

- **Protects you.** Acknowledging your sources keeps you honest. It's unethical and illegal to use others' ideas without proper documentation. The Ethics box on page 336 lists specific ways to avoid plagiarism.

- **Instructs the reader.** Citing references enables readers to pursue a topic further and make use of the information themselves.

Three Documentation Formats

You may choose from three formats to document your data. Select a format that suits your needs and those of your instructor or organization. Many organizations have their own in-house documentation styles, which are often a variation of those shown here. Regardless of the format selected, stay with it throughout your report.

References are usually cited in two places: (1) a brief citation appears in the text and (2) a complete citation appears in a footnote, an endnote, and/or a bibliography at the end of the report. The three most common formats for citations and bibliographies are the following: (1) *The Chicago Manual of Style* format, (2) the Modern Language Association (MLA) format, and (3) the American Psychological Association (APA) format. Each has its own style for textual references and bibliography lists, illustrated in Figure 11.11.

The Chicago Manual of Style **Format.** Report writers who prefer to cite references with a small superscript (raised) number in the text generally follow the format prescribed in *The Chicago Manual of Style*. The superscript refers the reader to the foot of the page, where the complete source appears, as shown in Format 1 of Figure 11.11. At the end of the report, a bibliography lists all the references cited in the report (and perhaps all the references consulted).

An alternative to footnotes is endnotes. Instead of citing references at the bottom of each page, the writer lists them under the heading "Notes" at the end of the report. This method is certainly easier to prepare than footnotes, and the pages are less cluttered. The references, however, are less convenient for the readers. Computers have made both footnotes and endnotes much easier to create.

Modern Language Association Format. Writers in the humanities frequently use the MLA format, illustrated in Figure 11.11. In parentheses close to the textual reference appear the author's name and the page cited. If no author is known, a shortened version of the source title is enclosed. At the end of the report, the writer lists alphabetically all references in a bibliography called "Works Cited." This format is somewhat more efficient than the Chicago style because complete references appear only once—in "Works Cited." Appendix C contains additional information about the MLA format. To see a long report illustrating MLA documentation, turn to Figure 14.4 in Chapter 14.

American Psychological Association Format. Like the MLA style, the APA style, illustrated in Figure 11.11, inserts the author's name in the text where the reference appears. The APA format, however, includes the publication data and "p." before the page number of the reference cited. Other variations occur in bibliography formats, the most notable being the emphasis on publication dates in the APA style. For more details about the APA style, see Appendix C. You may see a business report illustrating the APA reference style by turning to Figure 13.6 in Chapter 13.

FIGURE 11.11 ■ Three Reference and Bibliography Formats

Tips for Documentation — Chicago Manual of Style

- Use footnotes to place complete references at the bottom of each report page, or use endnotes to place references in a list at the end of the report.

- Place a superscript (raised) number at the end of a sentence citing a reference.

- Include in the note the author's name, title of publication, date, and page cited.

- Number citations consecutively throughout.

- For footnotes, separate them from the text with a 1 1/2-inch line. Leave one blank line above and below the separating line.

Format 1
Chicago Manual of Style **Documentation Style**
Footnotes or Endnotes

Text Page

In 1987, 24 nations gathered in Montreal to sign an agreement to cooperatively reduce the consumption of chloroflurocarbons (CFCs). Since then more than 40 nations have joined to sign the "Montreal Protocol" whose main purpose is to protect the ozone layer.[1] Ozone depletion is a major health concern with the risks associated with ultraviolet radiation. For example, Canadians have experienced an increase in skin cancer rates in the past two decades, with an estimated outlook of 60 000 newly diagnosed skin cancer cases in 1995.[2] According to Anne Landrey, Canadian developer of a new sunscreen product, "The level of awareness in the American population is about the same as it is here (Canada). But the difference is that exposure to the sun in some places is year-round."[3]

[1]Ruth Caplan, Our Earth, Ourselves (Toronto: Bantam Books, 1990), 61.

[2]"Managing the Message: Health Canada Focuses on the Hazards of Ultraviolet Radiation," Cosmetics 23 (1) (January 1995): 20.

[3]Robert Burg, "Clean Up on a Hot Idea," The Toronto Star (9 August 1995): C3.

Tips for a Bibliography — Chicago Manual of Style

- Make the bibliography the last page of a report.

- Centre the heading in all capitals 2 inches from the top of the page.

- Include all the references cited in the report and, optionally, all references consulted in your research.

- Arrange items alphabetically by authors' last names or by the first entry of the reference.

- Single-space within and double-space between references.

- Indent the second and succeeding lines of references.

Bibliography

BIBLIOGRAPHY

Burg, Robert. "Clean Up on a Hot Idea." The Toronto Star (9 August 1995): C1, C3.

Caplan, Ruth. Our Earth, Ourselves. Toronto: Bantam Books, 1990.

"Managing the Message: Health Canada Focuses on the Hazards of Ultraviolet Radiation." Cosmetics 23 (1) (January 1995): 20.

Format 2
Modern Language Association Documentations Style, Parenthetic Notes, Works Cited

Text Page

In 1987, 24 nations gathered in Montreal to sign an agreement to cooperatively reduce the consumption of chloroflurocarbons (CFCs). Since then more than 40 nations have joined to sign the "Montreal Protocol" whose main purpose is to protect the ozone layer (Caplan 61). Ozone depletion is a major health concern with the risks associated with ultraviolet radiation. For example, Canadians have experienced an increase in skin cancer rated in the past two decades, with an estimated outlook of 60,000 newly diagnosed skin cancer cases in 1995 ("Managing the Message" 20). According to Anne Landrey, Canadian developer of a new sunscreen product, "The level of awareness in the American population is about the same as it is here (Canada). But the difference is that exposure to the sun in some places is year-round" (Burg C3).

Works Cited

Works Cited

Burg, Robert. "Clean Up on a Hot Idea." The Toronto Star 9 August 1995: C1, C3.

Caplan, Ruth. Our Earth, Ourselves. Toronto: Bantam Books, 1990.

"Managing the Message: Health Canada Focuses on the Hazards of Ultraviolet Radiation." Cosmetics Jan. 1995: 20.

Format 3
American Psychological Association Documentation Style, Parenthetic Notes, References

Text Page

In 1987, 24 nations gathered in Montreal to sign an agreement to cooperatively reduce the consumption of chloroflurocarbons (CFCs). Since then more than 40 nations have joined to sign the "Montreal Protocol" whose main purpose is to protect the ozone layer (Caplan, 1990, p. 61). Ozone depletion is a major health concern with the risks associated with ultraviolet radiation. For example, Canadians have experienced an increase in skin cancer rated in the past two decades, with an estimated outlook of 60 000 newly diagnosed skin cancer cases in 1995 ("Managing the Message," 1995, p. 20). According to Anne Landrey, Canadian developer of a new sunscreen product, "The level of awareness in the American population is about the same as it is here (Canada). But the difference is that exposure to the sun in some places is year-round" (Burg, 1995, p. C3).

References

References

Burg, R. (1995, August 9). Cleaning up on a hot idea. The Toronto Star, C1, C3.

Caplan, R. (1990). Our earth, ourselves. Toronto: Bantam Books.

Managing the message: Health Canada focuses on the hazards of ultraviolet radiation. (1995, January) Cosmetics, 23 (1), 20.

ETHICS

HOW TO AVOID UNINTENTIONAL PLAGIARISM

Whether you quote directly or paraphrase (put someone else's ideas into your own words), you must acknowledge the source. Using another person's words or ideas without citing the source is plagiarism, a serious offence in the academic world and elsewhere. Students who plagiarize risk a failing grade in a course and even expulsion. Businesspeople, professionals, and politicians caught plagiarizing lose not only their credibility but often their jobs. For example, a member of Parliament was relieved of his post when a legal credential listed on his résumé was questioned and found to be false.

Unskilled researchers can unintentionally plagiarize if they're not careful. Here are some suggestions that might prevent an embarrassing moment for you.

- **Take excellent notes.** When you find a good data source, write complete notes on cards or separate sheets of paper. Mark the author's ideas and words carefully. Put your own remarks in parentheses or use a different colour. Be sure you distinguish your notes and ideas from the author's.

- **Know what should be documented.** Information that is common knowledge requires no documentation. For example, the statement *The Globe and Mail is a popular business newspaper* would require no footnote or documentation. Statements that are not common knowledge, however, must be documented. For example, if you were to name a specific newspaper as being "the largest daily newspaper in Canada," you would require a note because most people do not know this fact. Also use footnotes to document direct quotations and ideas that you summarize or paraphrase in your own words. Moreover, cite sources for proprietary information such as statistics organized and reported by a newspaper or magazine.

- **Use quotations sparingly.** Wise writers and speakers use direct quotations to (1) provide objective background data and establish the severity of a problem as seen by experts, (2) repeat identical phrasing because of its precision, clarity, or aptness, or (3) duplicate exact wording before criticizing it. Avoid the tendency of untrained report writers to overuse quotations. Documents that contain pages of spliced-together quotations carry a hidden message: these writers have few ideas of their own.

- **Introduce quotations.** When you must use a long quotation, try to summarize and introduce it in your own words. Readers want to know the gist of a quotation before they tackle it. For example, to introduce a quotation discussing the future of urban centres, you should precede it with your words: *In predicting employment trends, Frank Feather believes work will become decentralized from urban centres with the suburbs housing many service-related companies and departments.*

- **Cite quotations and sources properly.** Use quotation marks to enclose exact quotations, such as this: "It goes without saying," writes Frank Feather, "that the best jobs will go to those who prepare for them. Future trends challenge all of us to find a new set of lenses through which to manage our careers in the new information economy." Select a documentation format, such as superscripts or parenthetic notes, and use it consistently.

Career Track Application

Examine two or more research articles from a professional journal in your career field. How do the writers cite references? Are many quotations used? How are they introduced?

Summary of Learning Goals

1. **Describe nine typical business reports.** (1) Periodic reports monitor and control business operations, (2) situational reports describe one-time activities, (3) investigative reports examine problems and supply facts without making recommendations, (4) compliance reports satisfy laws and regula-

tions, (5) justification reports analyze problems and make recommendations, (6) yardstick reports evaluate alternatives by using consistent criteria, (7) feasibility reports analyze the practicality of alternatives, (8) research studies examine problems scientifically, and (9) proposals offer to solve problems.

2. **Distinguish between informational and analytical reports.** Informational reports collect and organize facts but offer little analysis and no recommendations. Analytical reports contain data, analyses, conclusions, and, if requested, recommendations.

3. **Identify four report formats.** Reports may be written like letters (using company stationery and letter format), like memos (opening with TO, FROM, DATE, and SUBJECT), like manuscripts (on plain paper beginning with a title), and on printed forms (with data inserted in appropriate spots).

4. **Apply the writing process to reports.** Report writers begin by analyzing a problem and writing a problem statement, which may include the scope, significance, and limitations of the project. Writers then analyze the audience and define major issues. They prepare a work plan, including a tentative outline and work schedule. They collect, organize, interpret, and illustrate their data. Then they compose the first draft. Finally, they revise (perhaps many times), proofread, and evaluate.

5. **Conduct research by locating secondary data.** Secondary data may be found by searching for books, periodicals, and newspapers through print or electronic indexes. Using CD-ROM and on-line databases, researchers may find titles or full-text articles. Some companies may use specialized information collection services such as Lexis/Nexis and Dow Jones News/Retrieval Service. Generalized on-line services—like CompuServe, Prodigy, and Infoglobe—offer selected databases, special-interest forums, and access to the Internet.

6. **Generate primary data for research projects.** Researchers generate firsthand, primary data through surveys, interviews, observation, and experimentation. Surveys are most economical and efficient for gathering information from large groups of people. Interviews are useful when working with an expert in a field.

7. **Describe three formats for documenting sources.** All data sources must be documented. *The Chicago Manual of Style* format uses superscript figures in the text and footnotes or endnotes to record the complete reference. A bibliography at the end of the report lists all references alphabetically. The Modern Language Association gives the author's name and page reference in parentheses following the citation or a quotation. A complete list of references, "Works Cited," appears at the end of the report. The American Psychological Association method shows the author, date, and page number in parentheses near the reference. A bibliography at the end of the report is called "References." All three formats have specific sequence and capitalization styles, which must be used consistently.

CHAPTER REVIEW

1. What purpose do most reports serve? (Goal 1)

2. List nine kinds of typical business reports. (Goal 1)

3. How do informational and analytical reports differ? (Goal 2)

4. How do the direct and indirect patterns of development differ? (Goal 2)

5. Under what circumstances would an analytical report be organized directly? Indirectly? (Goal 2)

6. Identify four common report formats. (Goal 3)

7. List the seven steps in the report-writing process. (Goal 4)

8. What is factoring? (Goal 4)

9. How do primary data differ from secondary data? Give an original example of each. (Goals 5, 6)

10. Should data collection for most business reports begin with primary or secondary research? Why? (Goal 5)

11. What major sources of print and electronic data could you expect to find in most libraries today? (Goal 5)

12. Name four major sources of primary data. (Goal 6)

13. In questionnaires what kind of questions produce quantifiable answers? (Goal 6)

14. What is documentation, and why is it necessary in reports? (Goal 7)

15. What kind of data require no documentation? (Goal 7)

DISCUSSION

1. What kinds of reports typically flow upward in an organization? What kinds flow downward? Why? (Goal 1)

2. Discuss this statement, made by three well-known professional business writers: "Nothing you write will be completely new."[7] (Goals 5, 6)

3. For long reports, why is it a wise idea to have a written work plan? (Goal 4)

4. How can a researcher improve the generalizability of collected data? (Goal 6)

5. **Ethical Issue:** Discuss this statement: "Let the facts speak for themselves." Are facts always truthful?

EXERCISES

11.1 Report Types, Functions, Writing Styles, and Formats (Goals 1, 2, 3)

For the following reports, (1) name the report's primary function (informational or analytical), (2) recommend a direct or indirect pattern of development, and (3) select a report format (memo, letter, or manuscript).

a. A persuasive proposal from a construction firm to the Ontario College of Art describing the contractor's bid to renovate and convert the school's newly purchased 1930s art deco office building into offices, studios, and classrooms.

b. A situational report submitted by a sales rep to her manager describing her attendance at a sports products trade show, including the reactions of visitors to a new noncarbonated sports drink.

c. A recommendation report from a technical specialist to the vice-president, Product Development, analyzing ways to prevent piracy of the software company's latest game program. The vice-president values straight talk and is familiar with the project.

d. A progress report from a location manager to a Hollywood production company describing safety, fire, and environmental precautions taken for the shooting of a stunt involving blowing up a boat off Toronto Island.

e. A feasibility report prepared by an outside consultant examining whether a company should invest in a health and fitness centre for its employees.

f. A compliance report from a national moving company telling provincial authorities how it has improved its safety program so that its trucks now comply with provincial regulations. The report describes but doesn't interpret the program.

11.2 Collaborative Project: Report Portfolio (Goals 1, 2, 3)

In student teams of four or five, collect four or more sample business reports illustrating at least three report types described in this chapter. (Don't forget corporate annual reports.) For each report identify and discuss the following characteristics:

a. Type

b. Function (informational or analytical)

c. Pattern (primarily direct or indirect)

d. Writing style (formal or informal)

e. Format (memo, letter, manuscript, preprinted form)

f. Effectiveness (clarity, accuracy, expression)

In an informational memo report to your instructor, describe your findings.

11.3 Data Forms and Questions (Goals 5, 6)

In conducting research for the following reports, name at least one form of data you will need and the questions you should ask to determine if that set of data is appropriate (see Figure 11.7).

a. A report evaluating the relocation of a Montreal company to Toronto. You find figures in a *Toronto Life* article showing the average cost of housing for 60 cities, including Montreal and Toronto.

b. A market research report to assess fan support for a name ("Raptors") and logo (a dinosaur holding a basketball) just selected for a new professional basketball team in Toronto.

c. A report examining the effectiveness of ethics codes in Canadian businesses.

11.4 Problem and Purpose Statements (Goal 4)

The following situations require reports. For each situation write (a) a concise problem question and (b) a simple statement of purpose.

a. The Confederation Bank is losing money on its Webster branch. A number of branches are being targeted for closure. Management authorizes a report that must recommend a course of action for the Webster branch.

b. New federal regulations have changed the definitions of common terms such as *fresh, fat-free, low in cholesterol*, and *light*. The Big Deal Bakery worries that it must rewrite all its package labels. Big Deal doesn't know whether to hire a laboratory or a consultant for this project.

c. Customers placing telephone orders for clothing with James River Enterprises typically order only one or two items. JRE wonders if it can train telephone service reps to motivate customers to increase the number of items ordered per call.

11.5 Problem and Purpose Statements (Goal 4)

Identify a problem in your current job or a previous job (such as inadequate equipment, inefficient procedures, poor customer service, poor product quality, or personnel problems). Assume your boss agrees with your criticism and asks you to prepare a report. Write (a) a two- or three-sentence statement describing the problem, (b) a problem question, and (c) a simple statement of purpose for your report.

11.6 Factoring and Outlining a Problem (Goal 4)

Japan Airlines has asked your company, Connections International, to prepare a proposal for a training school for tour operators. JAL wants to know if Victoria would be a good spot for its school. Victoria interests JAL but only if nearby entertainment facilities can be used for tour training. JAL also needs an advisory committee consisting, if possible, of representatives of the travel community and perhaps executives of other major airlines. The real problem is how to motivate these people to cooperate with JAL.

You've heard that CBC Studios in Victoria offers training seminars, guest speakers, and other resources for tour operators. You wonder if Magic Mountain in Vancouver would also be willing to cooperate with the proposed school. And you remember that Griffith Park is nearby and might make a good tour training spot. Before JAL will settle on Victoria as its choice, it wants to know if access to air travel is adequate. It's also concerned about available school building space. Moreover, JAL wants to know whether city officials in Victoria would be receptive to this tour training school proposal.

To guide your thinking and research, factor this problem into an outline with several areas to investigate. Further divide the problem into subproblems, phrasing each entry as a question. (See the tentative outline in Figure 11.6).

11.7 Developing a Work Plan (Goal 4)

Select a report topic from Problems 13.5–13.19 or 14.1–14.18. For that report prepare a work plan that includes the following:

a. A statement of the problem

b. An expanded statement of purpose (including scope, limitations, and significance)

c. Sources and methods

d. A tentative outline

e. A work schedule (with projected completion dates)

11.8 Using Secondary Sources (Goals 5, 6)

Conduct research in a library. Prepare a bibliography of the most important magazines and professional journals in your major field of study. Your instructor may ask you to list the periodicals and briefly describe their content, purpose, and audience. In a covering memo to your instructor, describe your bibliography and your research sources (manual or computerized indexes, databases, CD-ROM, and so on).

11.9 Developing Primary Data: Collaborative Survey (Goal 6)

In teams of three to five, design a survey for your associated student body council. The survey seeks student feedback in addressing the parking problem on campus. Students complain bitterly about lack of parking spaces for them, distance of parking lots from classrooms, and poor condition of the lots. Some solutions have been proposed: limiting parking to full-time students, using auxiliary parking lots farther away with a shuttle bus to campus, encouraging the use of bicycles and mopeds and reducing the number of spaces for visitors. Discuss these solutions and add at least three other possibilities. Then prepare a questionnaire to be distributed on campus. If possible, pilot-test the questionnaire before submitting it to your instructor. Be sure to consider how the results will be tabulated and interpreted.

Report Organization and Presentation

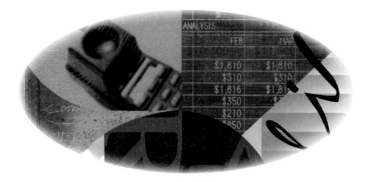

1 Use tabulating and statistical techniques to sort and interpret report data.

2 Draw meaningful conclusions from report data.

3 Prepare practical report recommendations.

4 Organize the report logically.

5 Provide cues to aid report readability.

6 Develop visual aids that create meaning and interest.

7 Incorporate visual aids into reports effectively.

The Fraser Institute

When Fazil Mihlar writes a report for the Fraser Institute, he takes much of his direction from the eighteenth-century Scottish economist Adam Smith, the father of free trade. A policy analyst with the Vancouver-based think tank, Fazil is part of a national, nonprofit research and educational organization that was founded in 1974 with a goal of drawing public attention to the role free markets can play in providing for the economic and social well-being of Canadians.

But Fazil's job goes well beyond writing on topics ranging from social policy to health care to taxation, to include public relations duties. "You've got to be flexible enough to deal with calls from the media, various government ministries, and the general public. The work has to be communicated, that's the key," says the 29-year-old. "One has to be accessible. People want to know what we have done, what the research suggests, what has been done in other parts of the world … what has worked and what has not."

"Our work is all based on research, and we make no inflammatory statements—only statements that we can substantiate."

Fazil graduated from the Chartered Institute of Marketing in London, England, Simon Fraser University in B.C. (economics), and in 1994, from Carleton University, where he studied public policy, especially as it applies to industry. He joined the Fraser Institute in 1994. One of some 20 full-time employees he is charged with looking at issues from a market perspective. "That is the prism, the starting premise for us—classical economic thought—and we clearly state that at the outset," says Fazil. "We have a strong opinion, but we report what the research says. Our work is all based on research, and we make no inflammatory statements—only statements that we can substantiate." Getting broad economic and social theory out to the general public in a manner that is both informative and interesting requires reports that "minimize the theory" and are written in everyday language rather than anything too technical. "From the average person on the street to academics to parliamentarians and policymakers, our audience is rather broad; therefore we write reports that can be understood by everybody.

"It's a pretty good starting premise to say you are dealing with short attention spans," says Fazil. As a result, he frequently puts things in point form to get a message across more quickly and clearly. The bulk of his reports is, however, written in prose. Here, he says, sentences must be clear, lucid, and short. "It's important to economize on the number of words, because people do not have time to read through hundreds of pages." Needless to say, good grammar and spelling are crucial to a professional presentation, adds Fazil.

When it comes to structuring a report, he underscores the importance of good transitions "from paragraph to paragraph and section to section." As for the layout of a report,

the essential components are proper spacing of material on the page, fonts selected for their readability, graphs and graphics, and an executive summary, which is particularly important when a report is long. (Recently Fazil composed a 50-page document, the first three pages of which were devoted to summarizing 81 recommendations spread across 14 policy areas.)

Clearly understanding a report's objective has helped Fazil Mihlar prepare a well-organized summary that introduces the elements of a thorough report. Colleagues at the Frazer Institute are routinely asked to check over reports for errors and to double-check facts and figures. This process ensures a professional presentation.

This sort of summarization is not unusual for the Fraser Institute. In fact, Fazil routinely uses the first two pages of a long report to do five things: (1) define the problem, (2) set the context, (3) describe proposed solutions, (4) tell the reader what the objectives of the report are, and finally, (5) tell the reader what information to expect from reading the report.

"But before I start writing the report—in what I call the thinking stage—I try to identify the issue or problem and narrow it down. I do not want to take on the world; I want to take on a very specific issue, so I can provide a narrow, detailed analysis." In addition, Fazil points out that report writers must know their audience and "be clear in their own heads" about the report's objective. Finally, he says, "have a broad outline of the issues you are going to deal with, and write them down."

Before the report goes out the door, Fazil makes a point of asking others at the Fraser Institute to look it over. He advises: "Get critiques and take them seriously. Double-check all the figures and facts. Check all the quotations carefully. And make sure that it's a very professional presentation, one that people can read easily." But even after all this is done, there's one last, big step: "In order to convince someone that a report is great, you need strong public speaking and presentation skills."

Finally, because he has as many as five projects on his desk at one time, Fazil finds that it's crucial to be organized. This, in turn, allows him the time to entertain new ideas, which "keeps me ahead of the game, or at least on a par"—no simple task when the issues of the day are as many and as weighty the ones the Fraser Institute tackles.

Clear communication is the key, especially when you're in the "ideas business," says Fazil. "Ours is an educational role. We say, 'Here is the evidence.' Then we leave it up to the policymakers and politicians to decide on the best course of action."[1] ■

Interpreting Data

Interpreting data means sorting, analyzing, combining, and recombining to yield meaningful information.

After collecting data for a report, you must sort it and make sense out of it. For informational reports you may organize the facts into a logical sequence, illustrate them, and present a final report. For analytical reports, though, the process is more complex. You'll also interpret the data, draw conclusions, and, if asked, make recommendations.

The information you've collected probably faces you in a jumble of printouts, note cards, copies of articles, interview notes, questionnaire results, and statistics. You might feel like a contractor who allowed suppliers to dump all the building materials for a new house in a monstrous pile.[2] Like the contractor you must sort the jumble of raw material into meaningful, usable groups. Unprocessed facts become meaningful information through sorting, analysis, combination, and recombination. You'll be examining each item to see what it means by itself and what it means when connected with other facts. You're looking for meanings, relationships, and answers to the research questions posed in your work plan.

Tabulating and Analyzing Responses

Numerical data must be tabulated and analyzed statistically to bring order out of chaos.

If you've collected considerable numerical and other information, you must tabulate and analyze it. Fortunately, several tabulating and statistical techniques can help you create order from the chaos. These techniques simplify, summarize, and classify large amounts of data into meaningful terms. From the condensed data you're more likely to be able to draw valid conclusions and make reasoned recommendations.

Tables permit easy comprehension of quantitative information as well as informed conclusions.

Tables. Numerical data from questionnaires or interviews are usually summarized and simplified in tables. Using systematic columns and rows, tables make quantitative information easier to comprehend. After assembling your data, you'll want to prepare preliminary tables to enable yourself to see what the information means. Here is a table summarizing the response to one question from a campus survey about student parking:

Question: Should student fees be increased to build parking lots?

	Number	Percentage	
Strongly agree	76	11.5	} *(To simplify the table, combine these items.)*
Agree	255	38.5	
No opinion	22	3.3	
Disagree	107	16.1	} *(To simplify the table, combine these items.)*
Strongly disagree	203	30.6	
Total	**663**	**100.0**	

Notice that this preliminary table includes both a total number of responses and a percentage for each response. (To calculate a percentage, divide the figure for each response by the total number of responses and multiply by 100.) To simplify the data and provide a broad overview, you can join categories. For example, combining "strongly agree" (11.5 percent) and "agree" (38.5 percent) reveals that 50 percent of the respondents supported the proposal to finance new parking lots with increased student fees.

Sometimes data become more meaningful when *cross-tabulated*. This process allows analysis of two or more variables together. By breaking down our

student survey data into male and female responses, as shown in the following table, we make an interesting discovery.

Cross-tabulating allows the analysis of two or more variables together.

Question: Should student fees be increased to build parking lots?

	Total		Male		Female	
	Number	Percentage	Number	Percentage	Number	Percentage
Strongly agree	76	11.5	8	2.2	68	22.0
Agree	255	38.5	54	15.3	201	65.0
No opinion	22	3.3	12	3.4	10	3.2
Disagree	107	16.1	89	25.1	18	5.8
Strongly disagree	203	30.6	191	54.0	12	4.0
Total	**663**	**100.0**	**354**	**100.0**	**309**	**100.0**

Although 50 percent of all student respondents supported the proposal, among women the approval rating was much stronger. Notice that 87 percent of female respondents (combining 22 percent "strongly agree" and 65 percent "agree") endorsed the proposal to increase fees for new parking lots. But among male students, *only 17 percent agreed with the proposal.* You naturally wonder why such a disparity exists. Are female students more unhappy than males with the current parking? If so, why? Is safety a reason? Are male students more concerned with increased fees than females? By cross-tabulating the findings, you sometimes uncover data that may help answer your problem question or that may prompt you to explore other possibilities. Don't, however, undertake cross-tabulation just to satisfy your curiosity.

Tables also help you compare multiple data collected from questionnaires and surveys. Figure 12.1 shows, in raw form, responses to several survey items. To convert these data into a more usable form, you need to calculate percentages for each item. Then you can arrange the responses in some rational sequence, such as largest percentage to smallest.

Once the data are displayed in a table, you can more easily draw conclusions. As Figure 12.1 shows, Midland College students apparently are not interested in public transportation or shuttle buses from satellite lots. They want to park on campus, with restricted visitor parking; and only half are willing to pay for new parking lots.

The three Ms: mean, median, mode. Tables help you organize data, and the three Ms help you describe it. These statistical terms—mean, median, and

FIGURE 12.1 ■ Converting Survey Data Into Finished Tables

Tips for Converting Raw Data

- Tabulate the responses on a copy of the survey form.
- Calculate percentages (divide the score for an item by the total for all responses to that item; for example, for Item 1, divide 331 by 663 and multiply by 100).
- Round off figures to one decimal point or to whole numbers.
- Arrange items in a logical order, such as largest to smallest percentage.
- Prepare a table with a title that tells such things as who, what, when, where, and why.
- Include the total number of respondents.

Raw Data from Survey Item

INDICATE YOUR FEELINGS TOWARD THE FOLLOWING PROPOSED SOLUTIONS TO THE STUDENT PARKING PROBLEM ON CAMPUS.

	Agree	No opinion	Disagree
1. Increase student fees to build parking lots	331	22	310
2. Limit student parking to satellite lots, providing shuttle buses to campus	52	31	580
3. Offer incentives to use public transportation	111	29	523
4. Restrict visitor parking	612	15	36

Shows raw figures from which percentages are calculated

Finished Table

REACTIONS OF MIDLAND COLLEGE STUDENTS TO FOUR PROPOSED SOLUTIONS TO CAMPUS PARKING PROBLEM*
Spring, 1995
N = 663 students

	Agree	No opinion	Disagree
Restrict visitor parking	92.3%	2.3%	5.4%
Increase student fees to build parking lots	49.9	3.3	46.8
Offer incentives to use public transportation	16.7	4.4	78.9
Limit student parking to satellite lots, providing shuttle buses to campus	7.8	4.7	87.5

*Figures may not equal 100 percent because of rounding.

Orders items from highest to lowest "Agree" percentages

Uses percent sign only at beginning of column

Avoids cluttering the table with number of responses

Three statistical concepts— mean, median, and mode— help you describe data.

mode—are all occasionally used loosely to mean "average." To be safe, though, you should learn to apply these statistical terms precisely.

When people say *average*, they usually intend to indicate the *mean*, or arithmetic average. Let's say that you're studying the estimated starting salaries of graduates from different disciplines, as shown here:

Education	$24 000	
Sociology	25 000	
Humanities	27 000	
Biology	30 000	
Health sciences	31 000	Median (middle point in continuum)
Engineering	33 000	Mode (figure occurring most frequently)
Business	33 000	
Law	35 000	Mean (arithmetic average)
Medicine	77 000	

To find the mean, you simply add up all the salaries and divide by the total number of items ($315 000 ÷ 9 = $35 000). Thus, the mean salary is $35 000. Means are very useful to indicate central tendencies of figures, but they have one major flaw: extremes at either end cause distortion. Notice that the $77 000 figure makes the mean salary of $35 000 deceptively high. It does not represent a valid average for the group. Because means can be misleading, you should use them only when there are no extreme figures.

The *median* is the midpoint in a group of figures arranged from lowest to highest (or vice versa). In our list of salaries, the median is $31 000 (health sciences). In other words, half the salaries are above this point and half are below it. The median is useful when extreme figures may warp the mean. Whereas salaries for medicine distort the mean, the median, at $31 000, is still a representative figure.

The *mode* is simply the value that occurs most frequently. In our list $33 000 (for engineering and business) represents the mode since it occurs twice. The mode has the advantage of being easily determined—just a quick glance at a list of arranged values reveals it. Although mode is not often used by researchers, knowing the mode is useful in some situations. Let's say 7-Eleven sampled its customers to determine what size of drink they preferred: 12-ounce, 16-ounce, or Big-Gulp 24-ounce. Finding the mode—the most frequently named figure— makes more sense than calculating the median, which might yield a size that 7-Eleven doesn't even offer. (To remember the meaning of *mode*, think about fashion; the most frequent response, the mode, is the most fashionable.)

Mean, median, and mode figures are especially helpful when the range of values is also known. *Range* represents the span between the highest and lowest values. To calculate the range, you simply subtract the lowest figure from the highest. In starting salaries for graduates, the range is $53 000 (77 000–24 000). Knowing the range enables readers to put mean and median figures into perspective. This knowledge also prompts researchers to wonder why such a range exists, thus stimulating hunches and further investigation to solve problems.

Correlations. In tabulating and analyzing data, you may see relationships among two or more variables that help explain the findings. If your data for graduates' starting salaries also included years of schooling, you would doubt-less notice that graduates with more years of education received higher salaries. For example, beginning teachers, with four years of schooling, earn less than beginning physicians, who have completed nine or more years of education. Thus, a correlation may exist between years of education and starting salary.

Intuition suggests correlations that may or may not prove to be accurate. Is there a relationship between studying and good grades? Between new office computers and increased productivity? Between the rise and fall of hemlines and the rise and fall of the stock market (as some newspaper writers have suggested)? If a correlation seems to exist, can we say that one event *caused* the other? Does studying cause good grades? Does more schooling guarantee increased salary? Although one event may not be said to *cause* another, the busi-ness researcher who sees a correlation begins to ask why and how the two vari-ables are related. In this way, apparent correlations stimulate investigation and suggest possible solutions to the original problem.

In reporting correlations, you should avoid suggesting that a cause-and-effect relationship exists when none can be proved. Only sophisticated research methods can statistically *prove* correlations. Instead, present a correlation as a *possible* relationship (*The data suggest that beginning salaries are related to years of*

The mean is the arithmetic average; the median is the midpoint in a group of figures; the mode is the most frequently occurring figure.

Correlations between variables suggest possible relationships that will explain research findings.

FIGURE 12.2 ■ Grid to Analyze Complex Verbal Data with Multiple Factors

	Point 1	Point 2	Point 3	Point 4	Overall Reaction
Vice-President 1	Disapproves. "Too little, too late."	Strong support. "Best of all points.	Mixed opinion. "Must wait and see market."	Indifferent.	Optimistic, but "hates to delay expansion for 6 months."
Vice-President 2	Disapproves. "Creates credit trap.	Approves.	Strong disapproval.	Approves. "Must improve receivable collections."	Mixed support. "Good self-defence plan."
Vice-President 3	Strong disapproval.	Approves. "Key to entire plan."	Indifferent.	Approves, but with "caveats."	"Will work only with sale of unproductive fixed assets."
Vice-President 4	Disapproves. "Too risky now."	Strong support. "Start immediately."	Approves, "but may damage image."	Approves. "Benefits far outweigh costs."	Supports plan. Suggests focus on Pacific Rim markets.

education). Cautious statements followed by explanations gain you credibility and allow readers to make their own decisions.

Grids permit analysis of raw verbal data by grouping and classifying.

Grids. Another technique for analyzing raw data—especially verbal data—is the grid. Let's say you've been asked by the CEO to collect opinions from all vice presidents about the CEO's four-point plan to build cash reserves. The grid shown in Figure 12.2 enables you to summarize the vice-presidents' reactions to each point. Notice how this complex verbal information is transformed into concise, manageable data; readers can see immediately which points are supported and opposed. Imagine how long you could have struggled to comprehend the meaning of this verbal information before plotting it on a grid.

Arranging data in a grid also works for projects like feasibility studies that compare many variables. Assume you must recommend a new printer to your manager. To see how four models compare, you could lay out a grid with the names of printer models across the top. Down the left side, you would list such significant variables as price, warranty, service, capacity, compatibility, and specifications. As you fill in the variables for each model, you can see quickly which model has the lowest price, longest warranty, and so forth. *Consumer Reports* often uses grids to show information.

In addition, grids help classify employment data. For example, suppose your boss asked you to recommend one person from among many job candidates. You could arrange a grid with names across the top and distinguishing characteristics—experience, skills, education, and other employment interests —down the left side. When you had summarized each candidate's points, you'd have a helpful tool for drawing conclusions and writing a report.

Drawing Conclusions in Reports

The most-read parts of a report are the conclusions and recommendations. Knowledgeable readers go straight to the conclusions to see what the writer thinks the data mean. Because conclusions summarize and explain the findings, they represent the heart of a report. Your value in an organization rises considerably if you can draw conclusions that analyze information logically and show how the data answer questions and solve problems.

Any set of data can produce a variety of conclusions. Always bear in mind, though, that the audience for a report wants to know how these data relate to the problem being studied. What do the findings mean in terms of solving the original report problem?

For example, the Marriott Corporation recognized a serious problem among its employees. Conflicting home and work requirements seemed to be causing excessive employee turnover and decreased productivity. To learn the extent of the problem and to consider solutions, Marriott surveyed its staff.[3] It learned, among other things, that nearly 35 percent of its employees had children under age 12, and 15 percent had children under age 5. Another finding, shown in Figure 12.3, was that one-third of its staff with young children took time off because of child-care difficulties. Moreover, many current employees left previous jobs because of work and family conflicts. The survey also showed that managers did not consider child-care or family problems to be suitable topics for discussion at work.

A sample of possible conclusions that could be drawn from these findings is shown in Figure 12.3. Notice that each conclusion relates to the initial report problem. Although only a few possible findings and conclusions are shown here, you can see that the conclusions try to explain the causes for the home/work conflict among employees. Many report writers would expand the conclusion section by explaining each item and citing supporting evidence. Even for simplified conclusions, such as those shown in Figure 12.3, you will want to number each item separately and use parallel construction (balanced sentence structure).

Although your goal is to remain objective, drawing conclusions naturally involves a degree of subjectivity. Your goals, background, and frame of reference all colour the inferences you make. When Federal Express, for example, tried to expand its next-day delivery service to Europe, it racked up a staggering loss of $1.2 billion in four years of operation.[4] The facts could not be disputed. But what conclusions could be drawn? The CEO might conclude that the competition is greater than anticipated but that FedEx is making inroads; patience is all that is needed. The board of directors and stockholders, however, might conclude that the competition is too well entrenched and that it's time to pull the plug on an ill-fated operation. Findings will be interpreted from the writer's perspective, but they should not be manipulated to achieve a preconceived purpose.

Effective report conclusions are objective and bias-free.

You can make your report conclusions more objective if you use consistent evaluation criteria. Let's say you are comparing computers for an office equipment purchase. If you evaluate each by the same criteria (such as price, specifications, service, and warranty), your conclusions are more likely to be unbiased.

You also need to avoid the temptation to sensationalize or exaggerate your findings or conclusions. Be careful of words like *many*, *most*, and *all*. Instead of *Many of the respondents felt...*, you might more accurately write *Some of the respondents...* Examine your motives before drawing conclusions. Don't let preconceptions or wishful thinking colour your reasoning.

FIGURE 12.3 ■ Report Conclusion and Recommendations

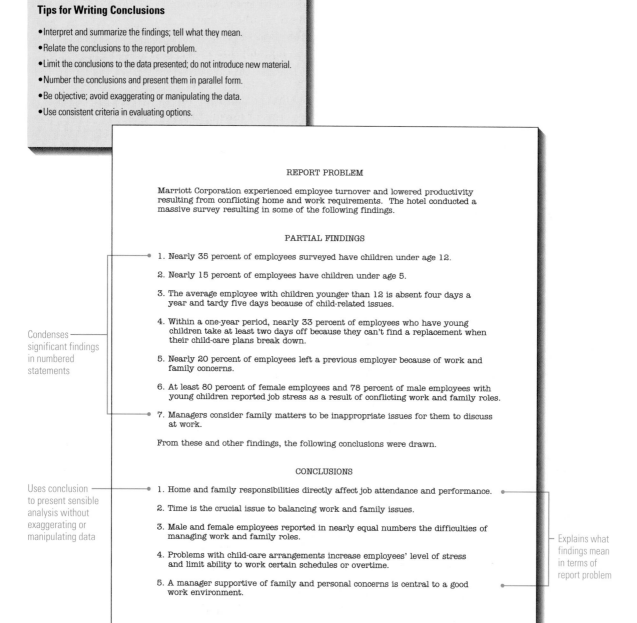

Tips for Writing Conclusions

• Interpret and summarize the findings; tell what they mean.

• Relate the conclusions to the report problem.

• Limit the conclusions to the data presented; do not introduce new material.

• Number the conclusions and present them in parallel form.

• Be objective; avoid exaggerating or manipulating the data.

• Use consistent criteria in evaluating options.

REPORT PROBLEM

Marriott Corporation experienced employee turnover and lowered productivity resulting from conflicting home and work requirements. The hotel conducted a massive survey resulting in some of the following findings.

PARTIAL FINDINGS

1. Nearly 35 percent of employees surveyed have children under age 12.

2. Nearly 15 percent of employees have children under age 5.

3. The average employee with children younger than 12 is absent four days a year and tardy five days because of child-related issues.

4. Within a one-year period, nearly 33 percent of employees who have young children take at least two days off because they can't find a replacement when their child-care plans break down.

5. Nearly 20 percent of employees left a previous employer because of work and family concerns.

6. At least 80 percent of female employees and 78 percent of male employees with young children reported job stress as a result of conflicting work and family roles.

7. Managers consider family matters to be inappropriate issues for them to discuss at work.

From these and other findings, the following conclusions were drawn.

CONCLUSIONS

1. Home and family responsibilities directly affect job attendance and performance.

2. Time is the crucial issue to balancing work and family issues.

3. Male and female employees reported in nearly equal numbers the difficulties of managing work and family roles.

4. Problems with child-care arrangements increase employees' level of stress and limit ability to work certain schedules or overtime.

5. A manager supportive of family and personal concerns is central to a good work environment.

Condenses significant findings in numbered statements

Uses conclusion to present sensible analysis without exaggerating or manipulating data

Explains what findings mean in terms of report problem

Writing Recommendations

Effective recommendations offer specific suggestions on how to solve a problem.

Recommendations, unlike conclusions, make specific suggestions for actions that can solve the report problem. Consider the following examples:

Conclusion

Our investments are losing value because the stock market continues its decline. The bond market shows strength.

RECOMMENDATIONS

1. Provide managers with training in working with personal and family matters.

2. Institute a flextime policy that allows employees to adapt their work schedules to home responsibilities.

3. Investigate opening a pilot child development centre for preschool children of employees at company headquarters.

4. Develop a child-care resource program to provide parents with professional help in locating affordable child care.

5. Offer a child-care discount program to help parents pay for services.

6. Authorize weekly payroll deductions, using pre-tax dollars, to pay for child care.

7. Publish a quarterly employee newsletter devoted to family and child-care issues.

Arranges actions to solve problems from most important to least important

Recommendation

Withdraw at least half of our investment in stocks, and invest it in bonds.

Conclusion

The cost of constructing multilevel parking structures for student on-campus parking is prohibitive.

Recommendation

Explore the possibility of satellite parking lots with frequent shuttle buses to campus.

Notice that the conclusions explain what the problem is, while the recommendations tell how to solve it. Most readers prefer specific recommendations. They want to know exactly how to implement the suggestions. In addition to recommending satellite parking lots for campus parking, for example, the writer could have discussed sites for possible satellite lots and the cost of running shuttle buses.

The specificity of your recommendations depends on your authorization. What are you commissioned to do, and what does the reader expect? In the planning stages of your project, you anticipate what the reader wants in the report. Your intuition and your knowledge of the audience indicate how far your recommendations should be developed.

In the recommendations section of the Marriott employee survey, shown in Figure 12.3, many of the suggestions are summarized. In the actual report each recommendation could have been backed up with specifics and ideas for implementing them. For example, the child-care resource recommendation would be explained: it provides parents with names of agencies and professionals who specialize in locating child care across the country.

A good report makes practical recommendations that are agreeable to the audience. In the Marriott survey, for example, report researchers knew that the company wanted to help employees cope with conflicts between family and work obligations. Thus, the report's conclusions and recommendations focused on ways to resolve the conflict. If the goal of Marriott had been merely to reduce employee absenteeism and save money, the recommendations could have been quite different.

If possible, make each recommendation a command. Note in Figure 12.3 that each recommendation begins with a verb. This structure sounds forceful and confident and helps the reader comprehend the information quickly. Avoid words like *maybe* and *perhaps*; they suggest conditional statements that reduce the strength of the recommendations.

Experienced writers may combine recommendations and conclusions. And a short report may omit conclusions and move straight to recommendations. The important thing about recommendations, though, is that they include practical suggestions for solving the report problem.

▉ Organizing Data

The direct pattern is appropriate for informed or receptive readers; the indirect pattern is appropriate when informing or persuading.

After collecting sets of data, interpreting them, and drawing conclusions, you're ready to organize the parts of the report into a logical framework. Poorly organized reports lead to frustration. Readers will not understand, remember, or be persuaded. Wise writers know that reports rarely "just organize themselves." Instead, organization must be imposed on the data.

Informational reports typically are organized in three parts, as shown in Figure 12.4. Analytical reports usually contain four parts and may be organized directly or indirectly. For readers who know about the project, are supportive, or are eager to learn the results quickly, the direct method is appropriate. Conclusions—and recommendations, if requested—appear at the beginning. For readers who must be informed or persuaded, the indirect method works better. Conclusions and recommendations appear last, after the findings have been presented and analyzed.

Although every report is different (you'll learn specifics for organizing informal and formal reports in Chapters 13 and 14), the overall organizational patterns described here usually hold true. The real challenge, though, lies in (1) organizing the facts and findings and the discussion and analysis sections and (2) providing cues for the reader.

Ordering Information Logically

Whether you're writing informational or analytical reports, the information you've collected must be arranged coherently. Five common organizational methods are by time, component, importance, criteria, or convention. Regardless of the method you choose, be sure that it helps the reader understand the data. Reader comprehension, not writer convenience, should govern organization.

Organization by time, component, importance, criteria, or convention helps readers comprehend data.

Time. Ordering data by time means establishing a chronology of events. Agendas, minutes of meetings, progress reports, and procedures are usually

FIGURE 12.4 ■ Organizing Informational and Analytical Reports

| | Analytical Reports | |
Informatinal Reports	Direct Pattern	Indirect Pattern
I. Introduction/background II. Facts/findings III. Summary/conclusion	I. Introduction/problem II. Conclusions/recommendations III. Facts/findings IV. Discussion/analysis	I. Introduction/problem II. Facts/findings III. Dicussion/analysis IV. Conclusions/recommendations

organized by time. For example, a report describing an eight-week training program would most likely be organized by weeks. A plan for step-by-step improvement of customer service would be organized by each step. A monthly trip report submitted by a sales rep might describe customers visited Week 1, Week 2, and so on. Beware of overusing time chronologies, however. Although this method is easy and often mirrors the way data are collected, chronologies—like the sales rep's trip report—tend to be boring, repetitive, and lacking in emphasis. The readers can't always pick out what's important.

Component. Especially for informational reports, data may be organized by components such as location, geography, division, product, or part. For instance, a report detailing company expansion might divide the plan into Pacific, Central, and Maritime expansion. The report could also be organized by division: personal products, consumer electronics, and household goods. A report comparing profits among makers of athletic shoes might group the data by company: Reebok, Nike, L.A. Gear, and so forth. Organization by components works best when the classifications already exist.

Importance. Organization by importance involves beginning with the most important item and proceeding to the least important—or vice versa. For example, a report discussing the reasons for declining product sales would present the most important reason first followed by less important ones. The Marriott report describing work/family conflicts might begin by discussing child care if the writer considered it the most important issue. Using importance to structure findings involves a value judgment. The writer must decide what is most important, always keeping in mind the readers' priorities and expectations. Busy readers appreciate seeing important points first; they may skim or skip other points. On the other hand, building to a climax by moving from least important to most important enables the writer to focus attention at the end. Thus, the reader is more likely to remember the most important item. Of course, the writer also risks losing the attention of the reader along the way.

Organizing by level of importance saves the time of busy readers and increases the odds that key information will be retained.

Criteria. Establishing criteria by which to judge helps writers to treat topics consistently. Let's say your report compares health plans A, B, and C. For each plan you examine the same standards: Criterion 1, cost per employee; Criterion 2, amount of deductible; and Criterion 3, patient benefits. The resulting data could then be organized either by plans or by criteria:

To evaluate choices or plans fairly, apply the same criteria to each.

By Plan	By Criteria
Plan A	Criterion 1
Criterion 1	Plan A
Criterion 2	Plan B
Criterion 3	Plan C
Plan B	Criterion 2
Criterion 1	Plan A
Criterion 2	Plan B
Criterion 3	Plan C
Plan C	Criterion 3
Criterion 1	Plan A
Criterion 2	Plan B
Criterion 3	Plan C

Although you might favour organizing the data by plan (because that's the way you collected the data), the better way is by criterion. When you discuss patient benefits, for example, you would examine all three plans' benefits together. Organizing a report around criteria helps readers make comparisons, instead of forcing them to search through the report for similar data.

Organizing by convention simplifies the organizational task and yields easy-to-follow information.

Convention. Many operational and recurring reports are structured according to convention. That is, they follow a prescribed plan that everyone understands. For example, an automotive parts manufacturer might ask all sales reps to prepare a weekly report with these headings: *Competitive observations* (competitors' price changes, discounts, new products, product problems, distributor changes, product promotions), *Product problems* (quality, performance, needs), and *Customer service problems* (delivery, mailings, correspondence). Management gets exactly the information it needs in easy-to-read form.

Like operating reports, proposals are often organized conventionally. They might use such categories as background, problem, proposed solution, staffing, schedule, costs, and authorization. As you might expect, reports following these conventional, prescribed structures are much simpler to organize.

Providing Reader Cues

When you finish organizing a report, you probably see a neat outline in your mind: major points, supported by subpoints and details. However, your readers don't know the material as well as you; they cannot see your outline. To guide them through the data, you need to provide the equivalent of a map and road signs. For both formal and informal reports, devices like introductions, transitions, and headings prevent readers from getting lost.

Good openers tell readers what topics will be covered in what order and why.

Introductions. The best way to point a reader in the right direction is to provide an introduction that does three things:

- Tells the purpose of the report
- Describes the significance of the topic
- Previews the main points and the order in which they will be developed

The following paragraph includes all three elements in introducing a report on computer security:

The purpose of this report is to examine the security of our current computer operations and present suggestions for improving security. Lax computer security could mean loss of information, loss of business, and damage to our equipment and systems. Because many former employees, released during recent downsizing efforts, know our systems, major changes must be made. To improve security, I will present three recommendations: (1) begin using smart cards that limit access to our computer system, (2) alter sign-on and log-off procedures, (3) move central computer operations to a more secure area.

This opener tells the purpose (examining computer security), describes its significance (loss of information and business, damage to equipment and systems), and outlines how the report is organized (three recommendations). Good openers in effect set up a contract with the reader. The writer promises to cover certain topics in a specified order. Readers expect the writer to fulfil the contract. They want the topics to be developed as promised—using the same wording and presented in the order mentioned. For example, if in your introduction you state that you will discuss the use of *smart cards*, don't change the heading for that section to *access cards*. Remember that the introduction provides a map to a report; switching the names on the map will ensure that readers get lost. To maintain consistency, delay writing the introduction until after you have completed the report. Long, complex reports may require introductions for each section.

Transitions. Expressions like *on the contrary*, *at the same time*, and *however* show relationships and help reveal the logical flow of ideas in a report. These *transitional expressions* enable writers to tell readers where ideas are headed and how they relate. Notice how abrupt the two following sentences sound without a transition: *North American car manufacturers admired Toyota's just-in-time inventory practices. Adopting a JIT system [however] means total restructuring of assembly plants.*

> Transitional expressions inform readers where ideas are headed and how they relate.

The following expressions (see Figure 4.7 for a complete list) enable you to show readers how you are developing your ideas.

To Present Additional Thoughts: additionally, again, also, moreover, furthermore

To Suggest Cause and Effect: accordingly, as a result, consequently, therefore

To Contrast Ideas: at the same time, but, however, on the contrary, though, yet

To Show Time and Order: after, before, first, finally, now, previously, then, to conclude

To Clarify Points: for example, for instance, in other words, that is, thus

In using these expressions, recognize that they don't have to sit at the head of a sentence. Listen to the rhythm of the sentence, and place the expression where a natural pause occurs. Used appropriately, transitional expressions serve readers as guides; misused or overused, they can be as distracting and frustrating as too many road signs on a highway.

Headings. Good headings are another structural cue that assist readers in comprehending the organization of a report. They highlight major ideas, allowing busy readers to see the big picture in a glance. Moreover, headings provide resting points for the mind and for the eye, breaking up large chunks of text into manageable and inviting segments.

> Good headings provide organizational cues and spotlight key ideas.

Report writers may use functional or talking headings. *Functional headings* (for example, *Background, Findings, Personnel, and Production Costs*) describe functions or general topics. They show the outline of a report but provide little insight for readers. Functional headings are useful for routine reports. They're also appropriate for sensitive topics that might provoke emotional reactions. By keeping the headings general, experienced writers hope to minimize reader opposition or response to controversial subjects. *Talking headings* (for example, *Two Sides to Campus Parking Problem* or *Survey Provides Support for Parking Fees*) provide more information and interest. Unless carefully written, however, talking headings can fail to show readers the organization of a report. With some planning, though, headings can be both functional and talking, such as *Parking Recommendations: Shuttle and New Structures.*

Headings should be brief, parallel, and ordered in a logical hierarchy.

To create the most effective headings, follow a few basic guidelines:

- **Use appropriate heading levels.** The position and format of a heading indicate its level of importance and relationship to other points. Figure 12.5 both illustrates and discusses a commonly used heading format for business reports.

- **Capitalize and underline carefully.** Most writers use all capital letters (without underlining) for main titles, such as the report, chapter, and unit titles. For first- and second-level headings, they capitalize only the first letter of main words—that is, the first and last word and all other words with the exception of articles (*the, a, an*), coordinate conjunctions (*and, but, or, nor*), and prepositions (*in, on, at, by, with*, etc.). For additional emphasis, they underline these headings, as shown in Figure 12.5.

- **Balance headings within levels.** All headings at a given level should be grammatically equivalent. For example, *Developing Quality Circles* and *Presenting Plan to Management* are balanced, but *Development of Quality Circles* is not parallel with *Presenting Plan to Management.*

- **For short reports use first- or second-level headings.** Many business reports contain only one or two levels of headings. For such reports use first-level headings (centred, underlined) and if needed, second-level headings (flush left, underlined). See Figure 12.5.

- **Include at least one heading per report page.** Headings increase the readability and attractiveness of report pages. Use at least one per page to break up blocks of text.

- **Keep headings short but clear.** One-word headings are emphatic but not always clear. For example, the heading *Budget* does not adequately describe figures for a summer project involving student interns for an oil company in Alberta. Try to keep your headings brief (no more than eight words), but make sure they are understandable. Experiment with headings that concisely tell who, what, when, where, and why.

- **Integrate headings gracefully.** Try not to repeat the exact wording from the heading in the sentence immediately following. Also avoid using the heading as an antecedent to a pronoun. For example, don't follow the heading *New Office Systems* with *These will be installed ...*

▦ Illustrating Data

Effective graphics clarify numerical data and simplify complex ideas.

After collecting information and interpreting it, you need to consider how best to present it to your audience. Whether you are delivering your report orally or in writing to company insiders or to outsiders, it will be easier to understand and remember if you include suitable visual aids. Appropriate graphics make numerical data meaningful, simplify complex ideas, and provide visual interest. In contrast, readers tend to be bored and confused by text paragraphs packed

FIGURE 12.5 ■ Levels of Headings in Reports

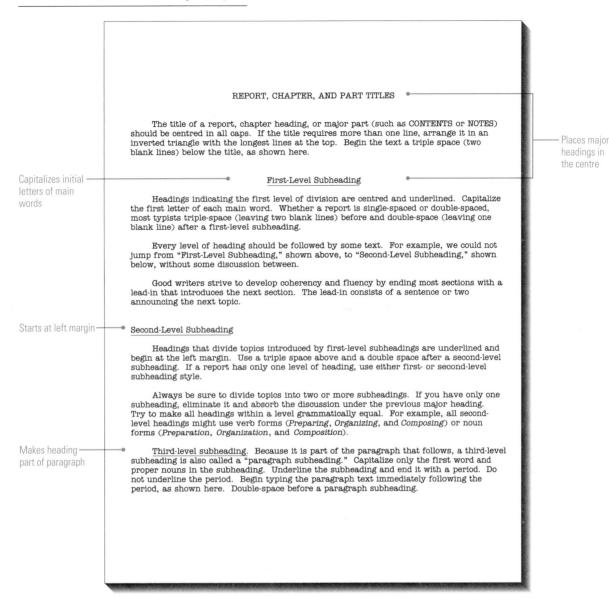

with complex data and numbers. The same information summarized in a table or chart becomes clear. Tables, charts, graphs, pictures, and other visuals perform three important functions:

- They clarify data.
- They condense and simplify data.
- They emphasize data.

Because the same data can be shown in many different forms (for example, in a chart, table, or graph), you need to recognize how to match the appropriate visual with your objective. In addition, you need to know how to incorporate visuals in your reports.

Matching Visuals and Objectives

In developing the best visuals, you must first decide what data you want to highlight. Chances are you will have many points you would like to show in a table or chart. But which visuals are most appropriate to your objectives? Tables? Bar charts? Pie charts? Line charts? Surface charts? Flow charts? Organization charts? Pictures? Figure 12.6 summarizes appropriate uses for each type of visual; the following text discusses each visual in more detail.

Tables permit systematic presentation of large amounts of data, while charts enhance visual comparisons.

Tables. Probably the most frequently used visual in reports is the table. Because a table presents quantitative or verbal information in systematic columns and rows, it can clarify large quantities of data in small spaces. You may have made rough tables to help you organize the raw data collected from literature, questionnaires, or interviews. In preparing tables for your readers or listeners, though, you'll need to pay more attention to clarity and emphasis. Here are tips for making good tables, one of which is illustrated in Figure 12.7:

- Provide clear headings for the rows and columns.

- Identify the units in which figures are given (percentages, dollars, units per worker hour, and so forth) in the table title, in the column or row heading, with the first item in a column, or in a note at the bottom.

- Arrange items in a logical order (alphabetical, chronological, geographical, highest to lowest) depending on what you need to emphasize.

- Use *N/A* (not available) for missing data.

- Make long tables easier to read by shading alternate lines or by leaving a blank line after groups of five.

- Print the title in upper and lower case (not all capitals).

Bar charts enable readers to compare related items, see changes over time, and understand how parts relate to a whole.

Bar charts. Although they lack the precision of tables, bar charts enable you to make emphatic visual comparisons. Bar charts can be used to compare related items, illustrate changes in data over time, and show segments as part of a whole. Figures 12.8 through 12.11 show vertical, horizontal, grouped, and segmented bar charts that highlight some of the data shown in the fictional MPM Entertainment Company table (Figure 12.7). Note how the varied bar charts present information in differing ways.

Many suggestions for tables also hold true for bar charts. Here are a few additional tips:

- Keep the length of each bar and segment proportional.

- Include a total figure in the middle of a bar or at its end if the figure helps the reader and does not clutter the chart.

- Start dollar or percentage amounts at zero.

- Avoid showing too much information, thus producing clutter and confusion.

Line charts illustrate trends and changes in data over time.

Line charts. The main advantage of line charts is that they show changes over time, thus indicating trends. Figures 12.12 through 12.14 show line charts that reflect income trends for the three divisions of MPM. Notice that line charts do not provide precise data, such as the 1996 MPM Videos income. Instead, they give an overview or impression of the data. Experienced report writers use

FIGURE 12.6 ■ Matching Visual Aids to Objectives

Visual Aid		Purpose
Table	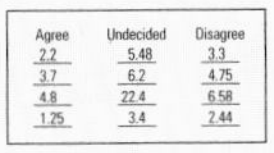	To show exact figures and values
Bar Chart		To compare one item with others
Line Chart		To demonstrate changes in quantitative data over time
Pie Chart		To show a whole unit and the proportions of its components
Flow Chart	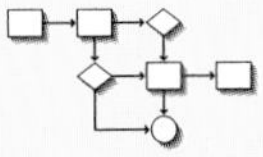	To display a process or procedure
Organization Chart	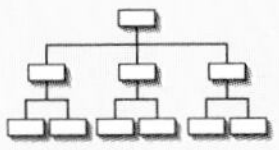	To define a hierarchy of elements
Photograph, Map, Illustration		To create authenticity, to spotlight a location, and to show an item in use

FIGURE 12.7 ■ Table Summarizing Precise Data

FIGURE 1
MPM ENTERTAINMENT COMPANY
Income by Division (in millions of dollars)

	Theme Parks	Motion Pictures	Video	Total
1993	$15.8	$39.3	$11.2	$66.3
1994	18.1	17.5	15.3	50.9
1995	23.8	21.1	22.7	67.6
1996	32.2	22.0	24.3	78.5
1997 (projected)	35.1	21.0	26.1	82.2

Source: *AET Predictors Research* (Toronto: CompDat, 1996), 225.

FIGURE 12.8 ■ Vertical Bar Chart

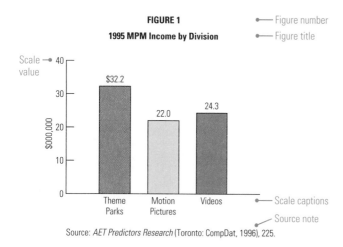

FIGURE 1

1995 MPM Income by Division

Figure number
Figure title

Scale value — 40

$000,000

$32.2
22.0
24.3

Theme Parks   Motion Pictures   Videos

Scale captions
Source note

Source: *AET Predictors Research* (Toronto: CompDat, 1996), 225.

FIGURE 12.9 ■ Horizontal Bar Chart

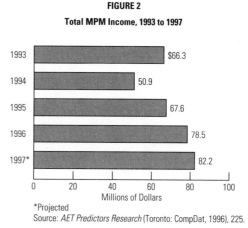

FIGURE 2

Total MPM Income, 1993 to 1997

1993 — $66.3
1994 — 50.9
1995 — 67.6
1996 — 78.5
1997* — 82.2

Millions of Dollars

*Projected
Source: *AET Predictors Research* (Toronto: CompDat, 1996), 225.

FIGURE 12.10 ■ Grouped Bar Chart

FIGURE 3

**MPM Income by Division
1993, 1995, and 1997**

Millions of Dollars

1993
1994
1995
(projected)

Theme Parks: $15.8 (1993), 23.8 (1995), 35.1 (1997)
Motion Pictures: 39.3 (1993), 21.1 (1995), 21.0 (1997)
Videos: 11.2 (1993), 22.7 (1995), 26.1 (1997)

Source: *AET Predictors Research* (Toronto: CompDat, 1996), 225.

FIGURE 12.11 ■ Segmented 100% Bar Chart

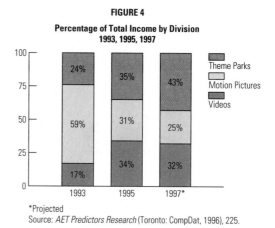

FIGURE 4

**Percentage of Total Income by Division
1993, 1995, 1997**

Theme Parks
Motion Pictures
Videos

1993: 24%, 59%, 17%
1995: 35%, 31%, 34%
1997*: 43%, 25%, 32%

*Projected
Source: *AET Predictors Research* (Toronto: CompDat, 1996), 225.

tables to list exact data; they use line charts or bar charts to spotlight important points or trends.

Simple line charts (Figure 12.12) show just one variable. Multiple-line charts combine several variables (Figure 12.13). Segmented line charts (Figure 12.14), also called *surface* charts, illustrate how the components of a whole change over time. Notice how Figure 12.14 helps you visualize the shift in total MPM income from motion pictures to videos and theme parks. By contrast, tables don't permit such visualization.

Here are tips for preparing a line chart:

• Begin with a grid divided into squares.

• Arrange the time component (usually years) horizontally across the bottom; arrange values for the other variable vertically.

• Draw small dots at the intersections to indicate each value at a given year.

• Connect the dots and add colour if desired.

USING YOUR COMPUTER TO PRODUCE CHARTS

Designing effective bar charts, pie charts, figures, and other images has never been easier than it is now with the use of computer graphics programs.

Spreadsheet programs—such as Lotus 1-2-3, Excel, and QuattroPro—and presentations graphics programs—such as Harvard Graphics, Microsoft PowerPoint, and Lotus Freelance Graphics—allow even nontechnical people to design quality graphics. These graphics can be printed directly on paper for written reports or used for transparency masters and slides for oral presentations. The benefits of preparing visual aids on a computer are near-professional quality, shorter preparation time, and substantial savings in preparation costs.

To prepare a computer graphic, begin by assembling your data, usually in table form. Let's say you work for Dynamo Products, and you prepared the accompanying table showing the number of Dynamo computers sold in each region for each quarter of the fiscal year.

Next, you must decide what type of chart you want: pie chart, grouped bar chart, vertical bar chart, horizontal bar chart, organization chart, or some other graphic. To make a pie chart showing total computers sold by division for the year, key in the data or select the data from an existing file. Add a title for the chart, indicate the horizontal and vertical axes (reference lines or beginning points). Most programs will automatically generate legends for figures. If you wish, however, you can easily customize titles and legends.

The finished chart can be printed on paper or imported into your word processing document to be printed with your finished report. The pie chart and bar chart shown here were created in a spreadsheet program and then imported into a word processing program.

Another useful feature of most word processing programs involves linking and importing tables. Our table showing the total number of disks sold could be created by importing a Lotus 1-2-3 or QuattroPro worksheet into WordPerfect's table feature. The result is a nicely arranged, easy-to-read table. The table can also be "linked" to the spreadsheet program so that the latest changes made in the worksheet will be automatically reflected in the tables as it appears in the word processing document.

Career Track Application

Visit your local software dealer and ask for a demonstration of how to create a pie or bar chart using a computer graphics program. Ask the salesperson to print out a copy of the visual (on a colour printer, if available) for you to bring to class for discussion.

TABLE 1

DYNAMO PRODUCTS
Number of Computers Sold

Region	1st Qtr.	2nd Qtr.	3rd Qtr.	4th Qtr.	Yearly Totals
Maritime	13,302	15,003	15,550	16,210	60,065
Central	12,678	11,836	10,689	14,136	49,339
Mountain	10,345	11,934	10,899	12,763	45,941
Pacific	9,345	8,921	9,565	10,256	38,087
Total	45,670	47,694	46,703	53,365	193,432

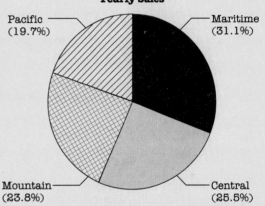

Figure 1
Dynamo Products
Yearly Sales

Pacific (19.7%) · Maritime (31.1%) · Mountain (23.8%) · Central (25.5%)

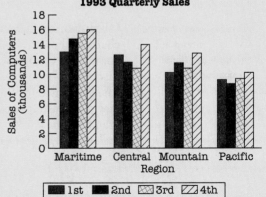

Figure 2
Dynamo Products
1993 Quarterly Sales

Sales of Computers (thousands) — Region: Maritime, Central, Mountain, Pacific

Legend: 1st Qtr. · 2nd Qtr. · 3rd Qtr. · 4th Qtr.

- To prepare a segmented (surface) chart, plot the first value (say, video income) across the bottom; add the next item (say, motion picture income) to the first figures for every increment; for the third item (say, theme park income) add its value to the total of the first two items. The top line indicates the total of the three values.

Pie Charts. Pie, or circle, charts enable the reader to see a whole and the proportion of its components, or wedges. Although less versatile than bar or line charts, pie charts are useful for showing percentages, as Figure 12.15 illustrates. Notice that a wedge can be "exploded" or popped out for special emphasis.

For the most effective pie charts, follow these suggestions:

- Begin at the 12 o'clock position, drawing the largest wedge first. (Computer software programs don't always observe this advice, but if you're drawing your own charts, you can.)

- Include, if possible, the actual percentage or absolute value for each wedge.

- Use four to eight segments for best results; if necessary, group small portions into one wedge called "Other."

- Distinguish wedges with colour, shading, or cross-hatching.

- Keep all the labels horizontal.

Many software programs help you prepare professional-looking charts with a minimum of effort. See the Technology box on page 361 for more information.

Flow charts. Procedures are simplified and clarified by diagramming them in a flow chart, as shown in Figure 12.16. Whether you need to describe the procedure for handling a customer's purchase order or outline steps in solving a problem, flow charts help the reader visualize the process. Traditional flow charts use the following symbols:

- Ovals to designate the beginning and end of a process

- Diamonds to denote decision points

- Rectangles to represent major activities or steps

Organization charts. Many large organizations are so complex that they need charts to show the chain of command, from the boss down to line managers and employees. Organization charts like the one in Figure 12.17 provide such information as who reports to whom, how many subordinates work for each manager (the span of control), and what channels of official communication exist. They may also illustrate a company's structure (by function, customer, or product, for example), the work being performed in each job, and the hierarchy of decision making. Organization charts improve reports by helping readers clarify an organization's structure and environment.

Photographs, maps, and illustrations. Some business reports include photographs, maps, and illustrations to serve specific purposes. Pictures, for example, add authenticity and provide a visual record. Dusty Richter, a location manager for a motion picture company, includes pictures in all his scouting reports; and Eliza Cohn, an environmental engineer, documents hazardous sites

FIGURE 12.12 ▣ Simple Line Chart

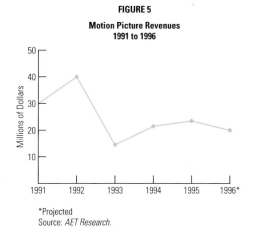

FIGURE 5

**Motion Picture Revenues
1991 to 1996**

*Projected
Source: *AET Research.*

FIGURE 12.13 ▣ Multiple Line Chart

FIGURE 6

**Comparison of Division Revenues
1991 to 1996**

*Projected
Source: *AET Research.*

FIGURE 12.14 ▣ Segemented Line (Surface) Chart

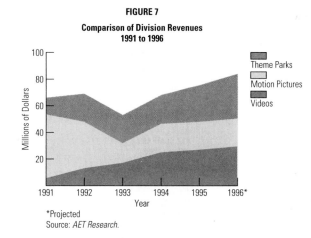

FIGURE 7

**Comparison of Division Revenues
1991 to 1996**

*Projected
Source: *AET Research.*

FIGURE 12.15 ▣ Pie Chart

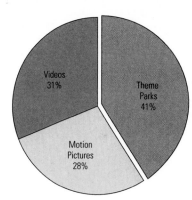

FIGURE 8

1996 MPM Income by Division

Source: *AET Research.*

with her own photographs. With today's computer technology, photographs and images can be scanned directly into business reports.

Maps enable report writers to depict activities or concentrations geographically, such as dots indicating sales reps across the country. Your reports might show where an organization's new products will be introduced. Office supply stores sometimes carry blank provincial, national, and global maps; and many computer programs provide maps that you can fill in to highlight locations discussed in your reports.

Illustrations and diagrams are useful in indicating how an object looks or operates. A drawing showing the parts of a VCR with labels describing their functions, for example, is more instructive than a photograph or verbal description. Artists can emphasize critical points and delete distracting details.

Incorporating Visuals in Reports

Used appropriately, visuals make reports more interesting and easier to understand. In putting visuals into your reports, follow these suggestions for best effects.

Computer technology permits photographs, maps, and illustrations to be scanned directly into a report.

FIGURE 12.16 ■ Flow Chart

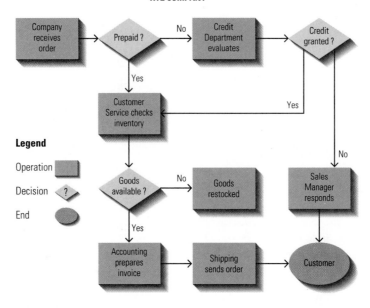

FLOW OF CUSTOMER
ORDER THROUGH
XYZ COMPANY

FIGURE 12.17 ■ Organization Chart

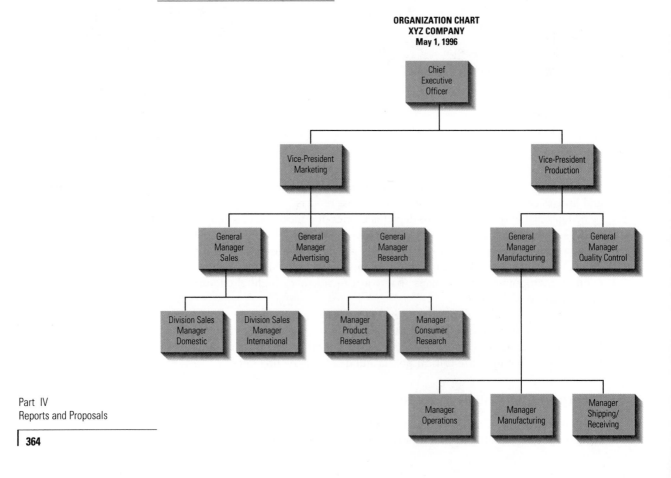

ORGANIZATION CHART
XYZ COMPANY
May 1, 1996

MAKING ETHICAL CHARTS AND GRAPHICS

Business communicators must present visual aid data in the same ethical, honest manner required for all other messages. Remember that the information shown in your charts and graphics will be used to inform others or help them make decisions. If this information is not represented accurately, the reader will not be correctly informed; any decisions based on the data are likely to be faulty. And mistakes in interpreting such information may have serious and long-lasting consequences.

Chart data can be distorted in many ways. Figure 1 shows advertising expenses displayed on an appropriate scale. Figure 2 shows the same information, but the horizontal scale, from 1991 to 1996, has been lengthened. Notice that the data have not changed, but the increases and decreases are smoothed out, so changes in expenses appear to be slight. In Figure 3 the vertical scale is taller and the horizontal scale is shortened, resulting in what appear to be sharp increases and decreases in expenses.

To avoid misinterpretating data, keep the following pointers in mind when designing your visual aids:

- Use an appropriate type of chart or graphic for the message you wish to convey.

- Design the chart so that it focuses on the appropriate information.

- Include all relevant or important data; don't arbitrarily leave out necessary information.

- Don't hide critical information by including too much data in one graphic.

- Use appropriate scales with equal intervals for the data you present.

Career Skill Application

Choose one or two visual aids from a newspaper, magazine article, or annual report. Analyze the strengths and weaknesses of each visual aid. Is the information presented accurately? Select a bar or line chart. Sketch the same chart but change the vertical or horizontal scales on the graphic. How does the message of the chart change?

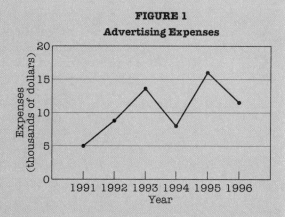

FIGURE 1
Advertising Expenses

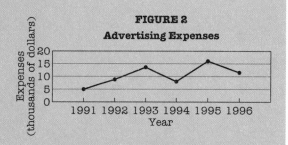

FIGURE 2
Advertising Expenses

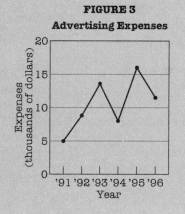

FIGURE 3
Advertising Expenses

Effective visuals are
accurate and ethical, avoid
overuse of colour or
decorations, and include
titles.

- **Evaluate the audience.** Size up your readers to determine how many visuals are appropriate. Six charts in an internal report to an executive may seem like overkill; but in a long technical report to outsiders, six may be too few. Evaluate the reader, the content, your schedule, and your budget (graphics take time and money to prepare) in deciding how many visuals to use.

- **Use restraint.** Don't overuse colour or decorations. Although colour can effectively distinguish bars or segments in charts, too much colour can be distracting and confusing. Remember, too, that colours themselves sometimes convey meaning: red suggests deficits or negative values, blue suggests coolness, and orange may mean warmth. Also, use decorations (sometimes called "dingbats" or "chartjunk") sparingly, if at all.

- **Be accurate and ethical.** Double-check all visuals for accuracy of figures and calculations. Be certain that your visuals aren't misleading—either accidentally or intentionally. Manipulation of a chart scale can make trends look steeper and more dramatic than they really are. To avoid giving a false picture, experiment with different scales. Then judge whether the resulting trend looks accurate and honest. Also, be sure to cite sources when you use someone else's facts. The previous Ethics box discusses in more detail how to make ethical graphs.

Textual visual aids should
be introduced by
statements that help
readers interpret the aids.

- **Introduce a visual meaningfully.** Refer to every visual in the text, and place the visual close to the point where it is mentioned. Most important, though, help the reader understand the significance of a visual. You can do this by telling the reader what to look for or by summarizing the main point of a visual. Don't assume the reader will automatically draw the same conclusions you reached from a set of data. Instead of *The findings are shown in Figure 3*, tell the reader what to look for: *Two-thirds of the responding employees, as shown in Figure 3, favour a flextime schedule.* The best introductions for visuals interpret them for readers.

- **Choose a suitable caption or title style.** Like reports, visuals may use "talking" titles or generic, descriptive titles. "Talking" titles are more persuasive; they tell the reader what to think. Descriptive titles describe the facts more objectively.

Talking Title	**Descriptive Title**
Average Annual Health Care Costs per Worker Rise Steeply As Workers Grow Older	Average Annual Health Care Costs per Worker As Shown by Age Groups

Judge the style you should use by your audience and your company's preferences. Regardless of the style, make the titles consistent and specific.

Summary of Learning Goals

1. **Use tabulating and statistical techniques to sort and interpret report data.** Report data become more meaningful when sorted into tables or when analyzed by mean (the arithmetic average), median (the midpoint in a group of figures), and mode (the most frequent response). Range represents a span between the highest and lowest figures. Grids help organize complex data into rows and columns.

2. **Draw meaningful conclusions from report data.** Conclusions tell what the survey data mean—especially in relation to the original report problem. They summarize key findings and may attempt to explain what caused the report problem. They are usually enumerated.

3. **Prepare practical report recommendations.** In reports that call for recommendations, the writer makes specific suggestions for actions that can solve the report problem. Recommendations should be feasible and potentially agreeable to the audience. They should all relate to the initial problem. Recommendations may be combined with conclusions.

4. **Organize the report logically.** Reports may be organized in many ways, including (1) by time (establishing a chronology or history of events), (2) by component (discussing a problem by geography, division, or product), (3) by importance (arranging data from most important to least important, or vice versa), (4) by criteria (comparing items by standards), or (5) by convention (using an already established grouping).

5. **Provide cues to aid report readability.** Good writers help their readers understand the organization of the report by using introductions (to spell out topics), transitional expressions (to indicate where a topic is headed), and headings (to highlight major ideas).

6. **Develop visual aids that create meaning and interest.** Good visual aids improve reports by clarifying, simplifying, and emphasizing data. Tables organize precise data into rows and columns. Bar and line charts enable data to be compared visually. Line charts are especially helpful in showing changes over time. Pie charts show a whole and the proportion of its components. Organization charts, pictures, maps, and illustrations each serve specific purposes.

7. **Incorporate visual aids into reports effectively.** In choosing or crafting visuals, good writers evaluate their audience, purpose, topic, and budget to determine the number and kind of visuals. These writers are accurate, ethical, and restrained in their use of visuals. And they are consistent in writing "talking" titles (telling readers what to think about the visual) or "descriptive" titles (summarizing the topic objectively).

CHAPTER REVIEW

1. What is the word for a form that uses systematic columns and rows to enable you to summarize and simplify numerical data from questionnaires and interviews? (Goal 1)

2. What is cross-tabulation? Give an example. (Goal 1)

3. Calculate the mean, median, and mode for these numbers: 3, 4, 4, 4, 10. (Goal 1)

4. How can a grid help classify material? (Goal 1)

5. What are the two most widely read sections of a report? (Goal 2)

6. How do conclusions differ from recommendations? (Goals 2, 3)

7. When reports have many recommendations, how should they be presented? (Goal 3)

8. What are the three parts of a typical information report? (Goal 4)

9. Analytical reports may be organized directly or indirectly. How do the organizational patterns differ? (Goal 4)

10. Name five methods for organizing a report. Be prepared to discuss each. (Goal 4)

11. What three devices can report writers use to prevent readers from getting lost in the text? (Goal 5)

12. Briefly compare the advantages and disadvantages of illustrating data with charts (bar and line) versus tables. (Goal 6)

13. What is the major advantage of using pie charts to illustrate data? (Goal 6)

14. What visual aid is best for illustrating a process or procedure? (Goal 6)

15. Describe two kinds of captions or titles for visual aids. (Goal 7)

DISCUSSION

1. Why is audience analysis particularly important in making report recommendations? (Goal 3)

2. Why is anticipation of the audience's response less important in an informational report than in an analytical report? (Goals 2, 3)

3. Should all reports be organized so that they follow the sequence of investigation—that is, description of the initial problem, analysis of issues, data collection, data analysis, and conclusions? Why or why not? (Goal 4)

4. Why is it important for reports to contain structural cues clarifying their organization? (Goal 5)

5. **Ethical Issue:** Discuss the ethics of an annual report that disguises a company's net operating loss by using deceptive graphs. The actual figures, as audited by a CA, show the loss; but they are buried in long tables within the report. By starting with a base figure below 0, the graphics suggested a profit instead of a loss. The graphics were not audited.

EXERCISES

12.1 Collaborative Tabulation and Interpretation of Survey Results (Goal 1)

a. Assume your business communication class at North Shore College was asked by the college bookstore manager, Larry Krause, to conduct a survey (see Figure 11.10). Concerned about the environment, Krause wants to learn students' reactions to eliminating plastic bags, of which 45 000 are given away annually by the bookstore. Students were questioned about a number of proposals, resulting in the following raw data. In groups of four or five, convert the data into a table (see Figure 12.1) with a descriptive title. Arrange the items in a logical sequence.

For major purchases the bookstore should	AGREE	UNDECIDED	DISAGREE
5. Continue to provide plastic bags	132	17	411
6. Provide no bags; encourage students to bring their own bags	414	25	121
7. Provide no bags; offer cloth bags at a reduced price (about $3)	357	19	184
8. Give a cloth bag with each major purchase, the cost to be included in registration fees	63	15	482

b. How could these survey data be cross-tabulated? Would cross-tabulation serve any purpose?

c. Given the conditions of this survey, name at least three conclusions that could be drawn from the data.

d. Prepare three to five recommendations to be submitted to Mr. Krause. How could they be implemented?

12.2 Evaluating Conclusions (Goal 2)

Read an article (of 800 or more words) in *Newsweek, Canadian Business, Maclean's,* or the *Financial Post Magazine.* What conclusions does the author draw? Are the conclusions valid, based on the evidence presented? In a memo to your instructor, summarize the main points in the article and analyze the conclusions. What conclusions would you have drawn from the data?

12.3 Distinguishing between Conclusions and Recommendations (Goals 2, 3)

For each of the following statements, say whether it could be classified as a conclusion or recommendation.

a. In times of recession, people spend less money on meals away from home.

b. Our restaurant should offer a menu featuring a variety of low-priced items in addition to the regular menu.

c. Absenteeism among employees with families decreases when they have adequate child care.

d. Nearly 80 percent of our business comes from only 20 percent of our customers.

e. Datatech Company should concentrate its major sales effort on its largest accounts.

f. The length of vacations for employees across the country is directly correlated with their length of employment.

g. The employee vacation schedule of Datatech Company compares favorably with the averages of other similar Canadian companies.

h. Offering outplacement service (assistance in finding jobs) tends to defuse the anger that goes with involuntary separation (being released from a job).

12.4 Data Organization (Goal 4)

How could the findings in the following reports be best organized? Consider these methods: time, component, importance, criteria, and convention.

a. A report comparing three sites for a company's new production plant. The report presents figures on property costs, construction costs, proximity to raw materials, taxes, labour availability, and shipping distances.

b. A report describing the history of the development of dwarf and spur apple trees, starting with the first genetic dwarfs discovered about 100 years ago and progressing to today's grafted varieties on dwarfing rootstocks.

c. An informational brochure for job candidates that describes the types of employment offered by your company: accounting, finance, information systems, operations management, marketing, production, and computer-aided design.

d. A monthly sales report submitted to the sales manager.

e. A recommendation report, to be submitted to management, presenting four building plans for improving access to your building, in compliance with provincial regulations. The plans range considerably in feasibility and cost.

f. A progress report submitted six months into the process of planning the program for your organization's convention.

g. An informational report describing a company's expansion plans for South America, Europe, Australia, and Southeast Asia.

h. An employee performance appraisal submitted annually.

12.5 Evaluating Headings and Titles (Goals 5, 7)

Identify the following report headings and titles as "talking" or "functional/descriptive." Discuss the usefulness and effectiveness of each.

a. Problem

b. Need for Tightening Computer ID System

c. Annual Budget

d. How to Implement Quality Circles That Work

e. Case History: King's Palace Hotel Focuses on Improving Service to Customers

f. Solving Our Records Management Problems

g. Comparing Copier Volume, Ease of Use, and Speed

h. Alternatives

12.6 Selecting Visual Aids (Goal 6)

What is the best kind of visual aid to illustrate the following data?

a. Instructions for workers telling them how to distinguish between workplace accidents that must be reported to federal and provincial agencies and those that need not be reported.

b. Figures showing what proportion of every provincial tax dollar is spent on education, social services, transportation, debt, and other expenses.

c. Data showing the academic, administrative, and operation divisions of a university, from the president to department chairs and division managers.

d. Figures comparing the sales of VCRs, colour TVs, and personal computers over the past 10 years.

e. Figures showing the operating profit of a company for the past five years.

f. Data showing areas in North America most likely to have earthquakes.

g. Percentages showing the causes of forest fires (lightning, 73 percent; arson, 5 percent; campfires, 9 percent; and so on) in the Rocky Mountains.

h. Figures comparing the cost of basic TV cable service in 10 areas of Canada for the past 10 years (the boss wants to see exact figures).

12.7 Evaluating Visual Aids (Goals 6, 7)

Select five visual aids from newspapers or magazines. Look in *The Globe and Mail*, *The Economist*, *Canadian Business*, *The Financial Post*, or other business news publications. In a memo to your instructor, critique each visual on the basis of what you have learned in this chapter.

12.8 Drawing a Bar Chart (Goal 6)

Draw a bar chart comparing the tax rates of eight industrial countries: Canada, 34 percent; France, 42 percent; Germany, 39 percent; Japan, 26 percent; the Netherlands, 48 percent; Sweden, 49 percent; the United Kingdom, 37 percent; the United States, 28 percent. These figures represent a percentage of the gross domestic product for each country. The sources of the figures are the International Monetary Fund and the Japanese Ministry of Finance. Arrange the entries logically. Write two titles: a talking title and a descriptive title. What conclusion might you draw from these figures? What should be emphasized in the graph and title?

12.9 Drawing a Line Chart (Goal 6)

Draw a line chart showing the sales of Sidekick Athletic Shoes, Inc., for these years: 1995, $6.7 million; 1994, $5.4 million; 1993, $3.2 million; 1992, $2.1 million; 1991, $2.6 million; 1990, $3.6 million. In the chart title highlight the trend you see in the data.

12.10 Studying Visuals in Annual Reports (Goals 6, 7)

In a memo to your instructor, evaluate the effectiveness of visual aids in three to five corporate annual reports. Critique their readability, clarity, and success in visualizing data. How were they introduced in the text? What suggestions would you make for improving them?

Typical Business Reports

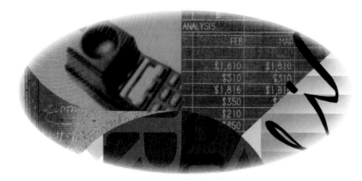

LEARNING GOALS

After studying this chapter, you should be able to

1 Distinguish between informational and analytical reports.

2 Define periodic reports and describe their major components.

3 Discuss the forms and content of situational reports.

4 Distinguish between investigative and compliance reports.

5 Compare direct and indirect justification and recommendation reports.

6 Describe the purpose and content of feasibility reports.

7 Define yardstick reports and describe their major components.

8 Discuss the content of research reports.

Toronto Raptors

Fresh out of school, James Paterson walked into what his friends tell him is a "dream job." The special assistant to the president of Toronto Raptors Basketball Club Inc. spends his days in the high-profile business of professional sports. But James says that working for Canada's first entry into the National Basketball Association is anything but easy. In fact, he says his days are extremely fast-paced and he's having to learn the business as he goes.

Ironically, the right-hand man to Raptors boss John I. Bitove says, "I am not really on the organizational chart, but I am often exposed to more information than anyone in the company aside from the president. I know the direction of the company better than anybody else, yet I don't have a specific niche … at times it can make for a bit of an identity crisis."

The 24-year-old native of Toronto joined the Raptors in May 1994 after completing an honour's degree in geography at Queen's University in Kingston, Ontario (where he was part of the university football squad that won the Vanier Cup in 1992). And though the chance to work alongside such legends of the game as the Raptor's vice-president of basketball, Isiah Thomas, might put stars in the eyes of many other employees, James says there's no time to be awe-struck—all his energy and attention are needed to help the team through its first few seasons.

"It's as if the world has become an executive summary. If you write a report that goes on for pages and pages, it may have all this wonderful detail, but today's executives don't have the time to read all that."

Seated in the Raptors' bustling and colourful downtown office, James explains that a large part of his work involves the writing of a monthly business report that is distributed to all members of the team's board of directors and shareholders (a circulation of about 12). The document is a compilation of material he receives from the various Raptor vice-presidents in charge of such divisions as finance, marketing, stadium operations, and basketball. "Each department gives me a summary of what's going on, and I take that information and compile it into a monthly report. It's a six- or seven-page report that contains an introduction, executive summary, information by department, and a table or appendix outlining the main projects, key people, dates of accomplishment, issues, strategy and status of each project."

The reports do not contain certain pieces of information for reasons of time or confidentiality, says Paterson, but what they do all contain is prose that paints a clear picture of what the team has accomplished to date and where the club is headed. The pressure of bringing together such disparate bodies of information with exacting detail requires a writing style that is not wordy or flowery—clear and concise is the name of the game.

"What I think was my weakness in university may be a strength in business," says James, who does not consider himself a particularly strong writer. "My weakness in university was being too short and trying to write using the least number of words while still getting the message across clearly. In the business community, when you write anything from a memo to a report, no one has the time to read something that goes on and on in detail. It's one-two-three-bang."

Making sure that Toronto Raptors president John I. Bitove is well-informed about the status of every department including finance, marketing, stadium operations, and basketball requires that James Paterson write effective monthly reports. When the Raptors' new home, the Air Canada Centre, begins construction, keeping all areas of the organization informed will require effective reports, memos, and executive summaries.

"It's as if the world has become an executive summary. If you write a report that goes on for pages and pages, it may have all this wonderful detail, but today's business executives don't have the time to read all that."

The structure of these monthly reports is also at the top of his mind when James sits down at his computer. "Sometimes it's expanding on an issue, and in some cases it's deleting information, such as a personal recommendation, and in some instances it's a case of leaving it in." Regardless of how much editing he does, James puts his personal stamp on each report. "Rather than just taking what they've written and photocopying and binding it, I try to create a fluid report for the board of directors and one that is all formatted the same way."

Consistency, coupled with the demands of having to meet a monthly deadline, requires that another set of eyes proofread his written work; the company president, Bitove, has final approval over each of Paterson's reports. "In some instances it is drastically worked over, and in some cases it's barely touched," says the boss's assistant

This attention to detail, along with massive amounts of energy, will be essential for the NBA expansion franchise to compete with the 27 other established clubs (as well as Canada's second entry into the league, the Vancouver Grizzlies). "Our goal is not to be like anyone else, we want to be *better* than anyone else," says James.

Twelve good men on the court, a solid coaching staff, and a stadium full of fans will go a long way toward achieving that goal. In the case of the latter, fans will spend the first two seasons watching dunks and fast-breaks in the SkyDome, home of Toronto's professional baseballers and footballers, the Blue Jays and Argonauts. The tip-off of the 1997–98 season is expected to take place in the 22 500-seat Air Canada Centre, which is being erected on the site of the old Post Office building near Toronto's waterfront.

With new uniforms, a new logo, and a new stadium in the works, the Raptors are off to a flying start. But, like the reports James Paterson generates, there is no formula for success.[1]

Informational Reports

Informational reports provide data on periodic and situational activities for readers who do not need to be persuaded.

Coordinating a project in business may require a tremendous amount of research, organization, and communication. Nearly all business operations and decisions are based on the same kinds of activity, and much of this activity results in reports. This chapter examines both informational and analytical reports.

Informational reports generally present information and answer questions without offering recommendations or much analysis. In these reports the emphasis is on facts. Informational reports describe periodic, recurring activities (like monthly sales or weekly customer calls) as well as situational, nonrecurring events (such as trips, conferences, and special projects). They also include routine operating, compliance, and investigative reports. What they have in common is that they report information to readers who do not have to be persuaded. Readers of informational reports usually are neutral or receptive.

You can expect to write many informational reports as an entry-level or middle-management employee. Because these reports generally deliver nonsensitive data and thus will not upset the reader, they are organized directly. Often they need little background material or introductory comments since readers are familiar with the topics. Although they're generally conversational and informal, informational reports should not be so casual that the reader struggles to find the important points. Main points must be immediately visible. Headings, lists, bulleted items, and other graphic highlighting, as well as clear organization, enable readers to grasp major ideas immediately. The Career Skills box on page 380 provides additional pointers on design features and techniques that can improve your reports.

Periodic Reports

Periodic reports keep management informed of operations and activities.

Most businesses—especially larger ones—require periodic reports to keep management informed of operations. These recurring reports are written at regular intervals—weekly, monthly, yearly—so that management can monitor and, if necessary, remedy business strategies. Some periodic reports simply contain figures, such as sales volume, number and kind of customer service calls, shipments delivered, accounts payable, and personnel data. More challenging periodic reports require description and discussion of activities. In preparing a narrative description of their activities, employees writing periodic reports usually do the following:

- Summarize regular activities and events performed during the reporting period.

- Describe irregular events deserving the attention of management.

- Highlight special needs and problems.

Managers naturally want to know that routine activities are progressing normally. They're often more interested, though, in what the competition is doing and in how operations may be affected by unusual events or problems. In companies with open lines of communication, managers expect to be informed of the bad news along with the good news.

Let's assume Jim Chrisman, sales rep for a West Coast sprinkler manufacturer, worked with a group of fellow sales reps and managers to produce the format for the periodic report shown in Figure 13.1. In Jim's words, "We used to write three- and four-page weekly activity reports that, I hate to admit,

FIGURE 13.1 ■ Periodic Report

The Three Phases of the Writing Process

1

Analyze
The purpose of this report is to inform management of the week's activities, customer reactions, and the rep's needs.

Anticipate
The audience is a manager who wants to be able to pick out the report highlights quickly. His reaction will probably be neutral or positive.

Adapt
Introduce the report data in a direct, straightforward manner.

2

Research
Verify data for the landscape judging test. Collect facts about competitors. Double-check problems and needs.

Organize
Make lists of items for each of the four report categories. Be sure to distinguish between problems and needs. Emphasize needs.

Compose
Write and print first draft on a computer.

3

Revise
Look for ways to eliminate wordiness. For greater emphasis use a bulleted list for *Competition Update* and for *Needs*. Make all items parallel.

Proofread
Run spell checker. Adjust white space around headings.

Evaluate
Does this report provide significant data in an easy-to-read format?

TO: Steve Schumacher

FROM: Jim Chrisman *JC*

DATE: March 15, 1996

SUBJECT: Weekly Activity Report

Activity Summary

Highlights of my activities for the week ending March 14 follow:

Sherbrooke. On Thursday and Friday I demonstrated our new Rain Stream drip systems at a vendor fair at Benbrook Farm Supply, where over 500 people walked through.

Frontenac College. Over the weekend I was a judge for the Quebec Landscape Technician test given at the college. This certification program ensures potential employers that a landscaper is properly trained. Applicants are tested in such areas as irrigation theory, repair, trouble-shooting, installation, and controller programming. The event proved to be very productive. I was able to talk to my distributors and to several important contractors whose crews were taking the tests.

Competition Update

- Toronado can't seem to fill its open sales position in the Eastern Townships.
- RainCo tried to steal the Trinity Country Club golf course contract from us by waiting until the job was spec'd our way and then submitting a lower bid. Fortunately, the Trinity people saw through this ploy and awarded us the contract nevertheless.
- Atlas has a real warranty problem with its 500 series in this area. One distributor had over 200 controllers returned in a seven-week period.

Product Problems, Comments

A contractor in Drummondville told me that our Rain Stream No. 250 valves do not hold the adjustment screw in the throttled-down position. Are they designed to do so?

Our Remote Streamer S-100 is generating considerable excitement. Every time I mention it, people come out of the woodwork to request demos. I gave four demos last week and have three more scheduled this week. I'm not sure, though, how quickly these demos will translate into sales because contractors are waiting for our six-month special prices.

Needs

- More information on irrigation training.
- French training videos showing our products.
- Spray nozzle to service small planter areas, say 6 to 8 feet.

Presents internal informational report in memo format

Condenses weekly activity report into topics requested by management

Summarizes needs in abbreviated, easy-to-read form

rambled all over the place. When our managers complained that they weren't getting the information they wanted, we sat down together and developed a report form with four categories: (1) activity summary, (2) competition update, (3) product problems and comments, and (4) needs. Then one manager wrote several sample reports that we studied. Now, my reports are shorter and more focused. I try to hit the highlights in covering my daily activities, but I really concentrate on product problems and items that I must have to do a better job. Managers tell us that they need this kind of detailed feedback so that they can respond to the competition and also develop new products that our customers want."

Situational Reports

Situational reports cover nonrecurring events.

Reports covering nonrecurring situations—trips, conventions, conferences, event planning, and progress—are a little more difficult to write than periodic reports. Because samples are generally unavailable to serve as models, you'll probably devote more attention to organizing your material. Like other informational reports, situational reports are generally prepared as memos. The tone of these reports is informal. The length depends on the reader's expectations and on the actual situation, but shorter is usually better. Before writing, if possible, ask the person who authorized the report how much detail should be included and how long the report should be. You have nothing to lose by clarifying the assignment. Situational reports usually need introductions (to familiarize the reader with the topic) and closings (to give a sense of ending).

Trip, convention, and conference reports should be organized by topic—usually no more than five.

Trip, convention, and conference reports. Employees sent on business trips or to conventions and conferences must usually submit reports when they return. Organizations want to know that their money was well spent in funding the travel. These reports inform management about new procedures, equipment, and laws, and supply information affecting products, operations, and service.

The hardest part of writing these reports is selecting the most relevant material and organizing it coherently. Generally, it's best not to use chronological sequencing (*in the morning we did X, at lunch we heard Y, and in the afternoon we did Z*). Instead, you should focus on three to five topics in which your reader will be interested. These items become the body of the report. Then simply add an introduction and closing, and your report is organized. Here is a general outline for trip, conference, and convention reports:

- Begin by identifying the event (exact date, name, and location) and listing the topics to be discussed.

- Summarize in the body three to five main points that might benefit the reader.

- Itemize your expenses, if requested, on a separate sheet.

- Close by expressing appreciation, suggesting action to be taken, or synthesizing the value of the trip or event.

Jeff Marchant was recently named employment coordinator in the Human Resources Department of an electronics appliance manufacturer headquartered in central Ontario. Recognizing his lack of experience in interviewing job applicants, he asked permission to attend a one-day conference on the topic. His boss, Angela Taylor, encouraged Marchant to attend, saying, "We all need to

FIGURE 13.2 ■ Conference Report

TO: Angela Taylor
FROM Jeff Marchant *JM*
DATE: April 22, 1996
SUBJECT: TRAINING CONFERENCE ON EMPLOYMENT INTERVIEWING

I enjoyed attending the "Interviewing People" training conference sponsored by the National Business Foundation. This one-day meeting, held in Toronto on April 19, provided excellent advice that will help us strengthen our interviewing techniques. Although the conference covered many topics, this report concentrates on three areas: structuring the interview, avoiding common mistakes, and responding to new legislation.

Identifies topic and explains how the report is organized

STRUCTURING THE INTERVIEW

Job interviews usually have three parts. The opening establishes a friendly rapport with introductions, a few polite questions, and an explanation of the purpose for the interview. The body of the interview consists of questions controlled by the interviewer. The interviewer has three goals: (a) educating the applicant about the job, (b) eliciting information about the applicant's suitability for the job, and (c) promoting goodwill about the organization. In closing, the interviewer should encourage the applicant to ask questions, summarize main points, and indicate what actions will follow.

Sets off major topics with centred headings

AVOIDING COMMON MISTAKES

Probably the most interesting and practical part of the conference centred on common mistakes made by interviewers, some of which I summarize here:

1. Not taking notes at each interview. Recording important facts enables you to remember the first candidate as easily as you remember the last—and all those in between.

2. Losing control of the interview. Keep control of the interview by digging into the candidate's answers to questions. Probe for responses of greater depth. Don't move on until a question has been satisfactorily answered.

Covers facts that will most interest and help reader

3. Not testing the candidate's communication skills. To be able to evaluate a candidate's ability to express ideas, ask the individual to explain some technical jargon from his or her current position—preferably, something mentioned during the interview.

4. Having departing employees conduct the interviews for their replacements. Departing employees may be unreliable as interviewers because they tend to hire candidates not quite as strong as they are. Their hidden agenda may be to keep the door open in case the new job fails.

5. Failing to check references. As many as 15 percent of all résumés may contain falsified data. The best way to check references is to network: ask the person whose name has been given to suggest the name of another person.

Angela Taylor   April 22, 1996   Page 2

RESPONDING TO NEW LEGISLATION

Recently enacted provisions of the Human Rights Code prohibit interviewers from asking candidates—or even their references—about candidates' disabilities. A question we frequently asked ("Do you have any physical limitations which would prevent you from performing the job for which you are applying?") would now break the law. Interviewers should also avoid asking about medical history, prescription-drug use, prior workers' compensation claims, work absenteeism due to illness, and past treatment for alcoholism, drug use, or mental illness. Questions must pertain to the job itself.

CONCLUSION

This conference provided me with valuable training that I would like to share with other department members at a future staff meeting. Let me know when it can be scheduled.

brush up on our interviewing techniques. Come back and tell us what you learned." When he returned, Marchant wrote the conference report shown in Figure 13.2. Here's how he describes its preparation: "I know my boss values brevity, so I worked hard to make my report no more than a page and a quarter. The conference saturated me with great ideas, far too many to cover in one brief report. So, I decided to discuss three topics that would be most useful to our staff. Although I had to be brief, I nonetheless wanted to provide as many details—especially about common interviewing mistakes—as possible. By the third draft, I had compressed my ideas into a manageable size without sacrificing any of the meaning."

Progress and interim reports describe continuing projects to both internal and external readers.

Progress and interim reports. Continuing projects often require progress or interim reports to describe their status. These reports may be external (informing customers regarding the headway of their projects) or internal (informing management of the status of activities). Progress reports typically follow this pattern of development:

- Specifies in the opening the purpose and nature of the project.

- Provides background information if the audience needs filling in.

- Describes the work completed.

- Explains the work currently in progress, including personnel, activities, methods, and locations.

- Anticipates problems and possible remedies.

- Discusses future activities and gives the expected completion date.

As a location manager in the film industry, Sheila Ryan frequently writes progress reports, such as the one shown in Figure 13.3. Producers want to be informed of what she's doing, and a phone call doesn't provide a permanent record. Here's how she describes her reasoning behind the progress report in Figure 13.3: "I usually include background information in my reports because a director doesn't always know or remember exactly what specifications I was given for a location search. Then I try to hit the high points of what I've completed and what I plan to do next, without getting bogged down in minute details. Although it would be easier to skip them, I've learned to be honest with any problems that I anticipate. I don't tell how to solve the problems, but I feel duty-bound at least to mention them."

Investigative Reports

Investigative or information reports present information for a specific situation—without offering interpretation or recommendations. These nonrecurring reports are generally arranged in a direct pattern with three segments: introduction, body, and summary. The body—which contains the facts, findings, or discussion—may be organized by time, component, importance, criteria, or convention. What's important is to divide the topic into logical segments, say, three to five areas that are roughly equal and don't overlap.

The subject matter of the report usually suggests the best way to divide and organize it. Beth Givens, an information specialist for a national health care consulting firm, was given the task of researching and writing an investigative report for St. John's Hospital. Her assignment: study the award-winning patient-service program at Good Samaritan Hospital, and report how it

FIGURE 13.3 ■ Progress Report

Tips for Writing Progress Reports

- State the purpose and the nature of the project immediately.
- Supply background information only if the reader must be educated.
- Describe the work completed.
- Discuss the work in progress, including personnel, activities, methods, and locations.
- Identify problems and possible remedies.
- Consider future activities.
- Close by telling the expected date of completion.

QuaStar Productions

Interoffice Memo

TO: Rick Willens, Executive Producer

FROM: Sheila Ryan, Location Manager *SR*

DATE: January 7, 1996

SUBJECT: Sites for "Bodega Bay" Telefilm

Identifies project and previews report →

This memo describes the progress of my search for an appropriate rustic home, villa, or ranch to be used for the wine country sequences in the telefilm "Bodega Bay." Three sites will be available for you to inspect on January 21, as you requested.

Background: In preparation for this assignment, I consulted Director Dave Durslag, who gave me his preferences for the site. He suggested a picturesque ranch home situated near vineyards, preferably with a scenic background. I also consulted Producer Teresa Silva, who told me that the site must accommodate 55 to 70 production crew members for approximately three weeks of filming. Ben Waters, telefilm accountant, requested that the cost of the site not exceed $24 000 for a three-week lease.

Saves space by integrating headings into paragraphs →

Work Completed: For the past eight days I have searched the Niagara Escarpment area in the Southern Ontario wine country. Possible sites include turn-of-the-century estates, Victorian mansions, and rustic farmhouses in the Welland/St. Catharines area. One exceptional site is the Country Meadow Inn, a 97-year-old farmhouse nestled among vineyards with a breathtaking view of valleys and distant hills.

Work to Be Completed: In the next five days, I'll search the Niagara countryside. Many wineries contain charming structures that may present exactly the atmosphere and mystery we need. These wineries have the added advantage of easy access. I will also inspect possible structures in and around Niagara-on-the-Lake. Finally, I've made an appointment with the director of provincial parks to discuss our project, use of provincial lands, restrictions, and costs.

Anticipated Problems: You should be aware of two complications for filming in this area.

Tells the bad news as well as the good →

1. Property owners are very familiar with the making of films in this area and expect to receive substantial amounts for short-term leases.
2. The trees won't have leaves again until May. You may wish to change the filming schedule somewhat.

Concludes by giving completion date and describing what follows →

By January 14 you'll have my final report describing the three most promising locations. Arrangements will be made for you to visit these sites January 21.

TEN TIPS FOR DESIGNING BETTER DOCUMENTS

Desktop publishing packages, high-level word processing programs, and laser printers now make it possible for you to turn out professional-looking documents. The temptation, though, is to overdo it by incorporating too many features in one document. Here are 10 tips for applying good sense and good design principles in "publishing" your documents.

- **Analyze your audience.** Sales brochures and promotional letters can be flashy—with colour print, oversized type, and fancy borders—to attract attention. But such effects are out of place for most conservative business documents. Also consider whether your readers will be reading painstakingly or merely browsing. Lists and headings help those readers who are in a hurry.

- **Choose an appropriate type size.** For most business memos, letters, and reports, the type size used for the body text should be 10 or 11 points (a point is $\frac{1}{72}$ of an inch). Larger type looks amateurish, and smaller type is hard to read.

- **Use a consistent type font.** Although your software may provide a variety of fonts, stay with a single family of type within one document—at least until you become more expert. Two of the most popular fonts are Times Roman and Courier. For emphasis and contrast, you can vary the font size and weight with **bold**, *italic*, ***bold italic***, and other selections.

- **Generally, don't justify right margins.** Textbooks, novels, newspapers, magazines, and other long works are usually set with justified (even) right margins. However, for shorter works ragged-right margins are recommended because such margins add white space and help readers find the beginnings of new lines. Slower readers find ragged-right copy more legible.

- **Separate paragraphs and sentences appropriately.** The first line of a paragraph should be indented or preceded by a blank line. To separate sentences, typists have traditionally left two spaces. This spacing is still acceptable for most business documents. If you are preparing a newsletter or brochure, however, you may wish to adopt printer's standards, leaving one space after end punctuation.

- **Design readable headlines.** Presenting headlines and headings in all uppercase letters is generally

discouraged because solid blocks of capital letters interfere with recognition of word patterns. For contrast with the text you may want to use a sans serif typeface (one without cross strokes or embellishment), such as Helvetica.

- **Strive for an attractive page layout.** In designing title pages or visual aids, provide for a balance between print and white space. Also consider placing the focal point (something that draws the reader's eye) at the optical centre of a page—about three lines above the actual center. Moreover, remember that the average reader scans a page from left to right and top to bottom in a Z pattern. Plan your visuals accordingly.

- **Use graphics and clip art with restraint.** Images created with spreadsheet or graphics programs can be imported into documents. Original drawings, photographs, and clip art can also be scanned into documents. Use such images, however, only when they are well drawn, relevant, purposeful, and appropriately sized.

- **Avoid amateurish results.** Many beginning writers, eager to display every graphic device a program offers, produce busy, cluttered documents. Too many typefaces, ruled lines, oversized headlines, and images will overwhelm readers. Strive for simple, lean, and forceful effects.

- **Develop expertise.** Learn to use the desktop publishing features of your current word processing software, or investigate one of the special programs, such as Ventura, PageMaker, Harvard Graphics, PowerPoint, or CorelDraw. Although the learning curve for many of these programs is steep, such effort is well spent if you will be producing newsletters, brochures, announcements, visual aids, and promotional literature.

Career Track Application

Buy a book or two on designing documents, and select ten tips that you could share with the class. In teams of three or four, analyze the design and layout of three or four annual reports. Evaluate the appropriateness of typeface and type size, white space, headings, and graphics.

improved its patient satisfaction rating from 6.2 to 7.8 in just one year. Beth collected data and then organized her findings into four parts: management training, employee training, patient services, and follow-up program. Although we don't show Beth's complete report here, you can see a similar one in Figure 11.2.

Compliance Reports

Government agencies at local, provincial, and federal levels increasingly require organizations to submit reports verifying compliance with laws. Some of these reports—like those covering employment equity, profit and loss, taxation, and occupational safety—consist primarily of data and figures entered on prepared forms. When you must explain actions and operations without the convenience of printed forms, follow these suggestions:

- Collect and report the specific information requested.

- Ensure the accuracy of the data.

- Submit the desired data in an appropriate format and on time.

Imagine that Mark Thomas, vice-president of Associated Trucking in Kingston, found his company in the position of responding to an unsatisfactory safety rating from the Ontario Ministry of Transportation. In preparation for a hearing, Mark wrote a letter report, shown in Figure 13.4, to the Crown attorney explaining the steps his company was taking to achieve and maintain compliance with the law. In explaining his report, Mark said: "An 'unsatisfactory' safety rating … is a very serious matter for any trucking company. We immediately shifted into high gear and completely revamped our driver and equipment safety programs. My goal in the report was to show the swift and extensive changes we had made. But I couldn't just talk about the changes. I also had to demonstrate them, so I sent examples of all our new inspection routines, equipment checks, and driver reports. I organized the report around the three main areas of change: education, preventive maintenance, and record keeping."

Mark's compliance report and other informational reports apply most of the suggestions found in the following checklist.

▰ Checklist for Writing Informational Reports

Introduction

✓ **Begin directly.** Identify the report and its purpose.

✓ **Provide a preview.** If the report is over a page long, give the reader a brief overview of its organization.

✓ **Supply background information.** When readers are unfamiliar with the topic, briefly fill in the necessary details.

Body

✓ **Divide the topic.** Strive to group the facts or findings into three to five roughly equal segments that do not overlap.

FIGURE 13.4 ■ Compliance Report

ASSOCIATED TRUCKING, INC.
668 Highland Road
Kingston, ON K6M 5E2

October 17, 1996

Mr. John R. Arthur
Crown Attorney
1330 Courthouse Road
Kingston, ON K7L 6N8

Dear Mr. Arthur:

SUBJECT: IMPROVED SAFETY COMPLIANCE PROGRAM

After Associated Trucking received an "unsatisfactory" rating on the Ontario Highway Patrol Safety Compliance Report dated June 15, senior management took immediate action. We initiated systematic procedures to achieve and maintain compliance with provincial safety regulations. This report describes our three-stage program, including (1) education, (2) preventive maintenance, and (3) accurate record keeping. The report is accompanied by numerous examples of records that illustrate our compliance with provincial and federal safety laws.

STAGE 1: EDUCATION

Our first step in developing an improved safety program was education. We reviewed publications from (1) the Ministry of Transportation, (2) Transport Canada, and (3) the Canadian Automobile Association. Several meetings included not only truck drivers and senior management but also middle management, vehicle dispatchers, and mechanics. Then we developed and implemented a safety program with two important components: preventive maintenance and improved record keeping.

STAGE 2: PREVENTIVE MAINTENANCE

Transportation safety depends in large part on precautions taken before vehicles are driven. We have developed a rigorous three-part preventive maintenance program that requires drivers' and mechanics' inspections, as well as careful inspection documentation.

Drivers' Inspections

All drivers will submit a documented daily vehicle inspection report before the vehicle is driven on the highway. All reports will be carefully examined, with all defects corrected <u>before</u> the driver leaves for daily deliveries. An example of one of last month's reports is enclosed.

Mechanics' Inspections

In order to ensure the safe operation of our vehicles, Associated mechanics will inspect our trucks and trailers every 30 days (see enclosed schedule). We are aware that a maximum inspection interval of 90 days is the norm; however, we feel that a 30-day interval best suits our current needs.

Provides brief background data because reader is unfamiliar with topic

Previews three major sections of report

Supplies headings that clearly show outline of ideas

Improves readability with ample white space

✓**Arrange the subtopics logically.** Consider organizing by time, component, importance, criteria, or convention.

✓**Use clear headings.** Supply functional or talking headings (at least one per page) that describe each important section.

✓**Determine degree of formality.** Use an informal, conversational writing style unless the audience expects a more formal tone.

✓**Enhance readability with graphic highlighting.** Make liberal use of bullets, numbered and lettered lists, headings, underlined items, and white space.

Copies of recent mechanics' inspections are enclosed. Please note that all four required systems are being inspected:

   a. Brake adjustment
   b. Brake system components and leaks
   c. Steering and suspension systems
   d. Tires and wheels

— Increases credibility by sending copies of relevant documents

STAGE 3: RECORD KEEPING AND COMPLIANCE SYSTEMS

To enable Associated Trucking to be certain that it is complying with all local, provincial, and federal regulations, we have improved our record keeping in three specific areas.

MTO Pull Notices

All Associated drivers are entered and participate in the Ministry of Transportation Pull Notice Program. All pull notice reports are now reviewed, signed, and dated before they are filed. In addition, a new computerized monthly review of current drivers allows us to double-check for the enrolment of new or current drivers and/or the deletion of drivers no longer employed. Current pull notice reports are enclosed for review.

Driver Hours of Service

All driver logs and/or time cards are now continually reviewed in an attempt to adhere to federal and provincial regulations regarding duty time and rest periods. Moreover, all driver logs and time cards are cross-referenced to ensure accurate recording of driving and duty times. Driver and dispatcher education have been very helpful in achieving and maintaining these objectives. A sample of recent logs and time cards is enclosed.

Driving Proficiency Records

We now keep on file all records of the different types and combinations of vehicles each employee is certified to drive. Samples are enclosed.

CONCLUSION

We at Associated Trucking believe that the implementation of this three-stage program has helped us attain our twin goals of driver safety and equipment reliability. Should you have questions about this report, please call me at (613) 383-2290.

— Summarizes report objective and adds concluding thought

                    Sincerely,

                    Mark W. Thomas

                    Mark W. Thomas
                    Vice-President

MWT:eeg
Enclosures

Summary or Conclusion

✓ **When necessary, summarize the report.** Briefly review the main points and discuss what action will follow.

✓ **Offer a concluding thought.** If relevant, express appreciation or describe your willingness to provide further information.

Analytical Reports

Analytical reports differ significantly from informational reports. Although both seek to collect and present data clearly, analytical reports also analyze the data and typically try to persuade the reader to accept the conclusions and act on the recommendations. Informational reports emphasize facts; analytical reports emphasize reasoning and conclusions.

For some readers analytical reports may be organized directly with the conclusions and recommendations near the beginning. Directness is appropriate when the reader has confidence in the writer, based on either experience or credentials. Putting the recommendations at the beginning also works when the topic is routine or familiar and the reader is supportive.

Directness can backfire, though. If you announce the recommendations too quickly, the reader may immediately object to a single idea, one that you had no suspicion would trigger a negative reaction. Once the reader is opposed, changing an unfavourable mind-set may be difficult or impossible. A reader may also think you have oversimplified or overlooked something significant if you lay out all the recommendations before explaining how you arrived at them. When the reader must be led through the process of discovering the solution or recommendation, use the indirect method: present conclusions and recommendations last.

Most analytical reports answer questions about specific problems. How can we boost sales to baby boomers? Should we close the Bradford plant? Should we buy or lease company cars? How can we improve customer service? Four typical analytical reports answer business questions: justification or recommendation reports, feasibility reports, yardstick reports, and research studies. Because these reports all solve problems, the categories are not mutually exclusive. What distinguishes them is their goals and organization.

Justification and Recommendation Reports

Both managers and employees must occasionally write reports that justify or recommend something, such as buying equipment, changing a procedure, hiring an employee, consolidating departments, or investing funds. Large organizations sometimes prescribe how these reports should be organized; they use forms with conventional headings. When you are free to select an organizational plan yourself, however, let your audience and topic determine your choice of direct or indirect structure.

Direct pattern. For nonsensitive topics and recommendations that will be agreeable to your readers, you can organize directly according to the following order:

- State the problem or need briefly.

- Announce the recommendation, solution, or action concisely and with action verbs.

- Explain more fully the benefits of the recommendation or steps to be taken to solve the problem.

- Include a discussion of pros, cons, and costs.

- Conclude with a summary specifying the recommendation and action to be taken.

Here's how Justin Brown applied the process in justifying a purchase. Justin is operations manager in charge of a fleet of trucks for a large parcel delivery company in Moncton. When he heard about a new Goodyear smart tire with an electronic chip, Justin thought his company should give the new tire a try. Because new tires would represent an irregular purchase and because they would require a pilot test, he wrote the justification/recommendation report, shown in Figure 13.5, to his boss. Justin describes his report in this way: "As more and more parcel delivery systems crop up, we have to find ways to cut costs so that we can remain competitive. Although more expensive initially, smart tires may solve a lot of our problems and save us money in the long run. I knew Bill Montgomery, operations vice-president, would be interested in them, particularly if we went slowly and purchased only 24 for a pilot test. Because Bill would be most interested in what they could do for us, I concentrated on benefits. In my first draft the benefits were lost in a couple of long paragraphs. Only after I read what I had written did I see that I was really talking about four separate benefits. Then I looked for words to summarize each one as a heading. So that Bill would know exactly what he should do, I concluded with specifics. All he had to do was say 'Go.'"

Indirect pattern. When a reader may oppose a recommendation or when circumstances suggest caution, don't be in a hurry to reveal your recommendation. Consider using the following sequence for an indirect approach to your recommendations:

- Make a general reference to the problem, not to your recommendation, in the subject line.

- Describe the problem or need your recommendation addresses.

- Use specific examples, supporting statistics, and authoritative quotes to lend credibility to the seriousness of the problem.

- Discuss alternative solutions, beginning with the least likely to succeed.

- Present the most promising alternative (your recommendation) last.

- Show how the advantages of your recommendation outweigh its disadvantages.

- Summarize your recommendation. If appropriate, specify the action it requires.

- Ask for authorization to proceed, if necessary.

> The indirect pattern is appropriate for justification or recommendation reports on sensitive topics and for potentially unreceptive audiences.

Assume Diane Adams, an executive assistant at a large petroleum and mining company in Lethbridge, Alberta, received a challenging research assignment. Her boss, the director of human resources, asked her to investigate ways to persuade employees to quit smoking. Here's how she describes her task: "We banned smoking many years ago inside our buildings, but we never tried very hard to get smokers to actually kick their habit. My job was to gather information about the problem and how other companies have helped workers stop smoking. The report would go to my boss, but I knew he would pass it along to the management council for approval. If the report were just for my boss, I would put my recommendation right up front, because I'm sure he would support it. But the management council is another story. They need persuasion because of the costs involved—and because some of them are smokers. Therefore, I put the alternative I favoured last. To gain credibility, I footnoted my sources. I had enough material for a 10-page report, but I kept it to two pages in keeping with our company report policy."

> Footnoting sources lends added credibility to justification or recommendation reports.

Diane single-spaced her report, shown in Figure 13.6, because that's her company's preference. Some companies prefer the readability of line-and-a-half or double spacing. Be sure to check with your organization for its preference before printing out your reports.

FIGURE 13.5 ■ Justification or Recommendation Report: Direct Pattern

The Three Phases of the Writing Process

1

Analyze
The purpose of this report is to persuade the manager to authorize the purchase and pilot testing of smart tires.

Anticipate
The audience is a manager who is familiar with operations but not with this product. He will probably be receptive to the recommendation.

Adapt
Present the report data in a direct, straightforward manner.

2

Research
Collect data on how smart tires could benefit operations.

Organize
Discuss the problem briefly. Introduce and justify the recommendation by noting its cost-effectiveness and paperwork benefits. Explain the benefits of smart tires. Describe the action to be taken.

Compose
Write and print first draft.

3

Revise
Revise to break up long paragraphs about benefits. Isolate each benefit in an enumerated list with headings.

Proofread
Double-check all figures. Be sure all headings are parallel.

Evaluate
Does this report make its request concisely but emphatically? Will the reader see immediately what action is required?

TO: Bill Montgomery, Vice-President
FROM: Justin Brown, Operations Manager *JB*
DATE: July 19, 1996
SUBJECT: Pilot Testing Smart Tires

Next to fuel, truck tires are our biggest operating cost. Last year we spent $211 000 replacing and retreading tires for 495 trucks. This year the costs will be greater because prices have jumped at least 12 percent and because we've increased our fleet to 550 trucks. Truck tires are an additional burden since they require labour-intensive paperwork to track their warranties, wear, and retread histories. To reduce our long-term costs and to improve our tire tracking system, I recommend that we do the following:

— *Introduces problem briefly*

■ Purchase 24 Goodyear smart tires.
■ Begin a one-year pilot test on six trucks.

— *Presents recommendations immediately*

How Smart Tires Work

Smart tires have an embedded computer chip that monitors wear, performance, and durability. The chip also creates an electronic fingerprint for positive identification of a tire. By passing a hand-held sensor next to the tire, we can learn where and when a tire was made (for warranty and other identification), how much tread it had originally, and its serial number.

— *Justifies recommendation by explaining product and benefits*

How Smart Tires Could Benefit Us

Although smart tires are initially more expensive than other tires, they could help us improve our operations and save us money in four ways:
1. <u>Retreads</u>. Goodyear believes that the wear data is so accurate that we should be able to retread every tire three times, instead of our current two times. If that's true, in one year we could save at least $27 000 in new tire costs.
2. <u>Safety</u>. Accurate and accessible wear data should reduce the danger of blowouts and flat tires. Last year, despite our rigorous maintenance program, drivers reported six blowouts.
3. <u>Record keeping and maintenance</u>. Smart tires could reduce our maintenance costs considerably. Currently, we use an electric branding iron to mark serial numbers on new tires. Our biggest headache is manually reading those serial numbers, decoding them, and maintaining records to meet safety regulations. Reading such data electronically could save us thousands of dollars in labour.
4. <u>Theft protection</u>. The chip can be used to monitor each tire as it leaves or enters the warehouse or yard, thus discouraging theft.

— *Explains recommendation in more detail*

Summary and Action

Specifically, I recommend that you do the following:
■ Authorize the special purchase of 24 Goodyear smart tires at $450 each, plus one electronic sensor at $1200.
■ Approve a one-year pilot test in our Quebec territory that would equip six trucks with smart tires and track their performance.

— *Specifies action to be taken*

This greenhouse at the famous Keukenhof Gardens in Holland became a key point in the justification report of a tour organizer. In supporting his inclusion of the Keukenhof in a proposed itinerary for a North American travel company, the writer argued that tourists can never be rained out. In addition to the 70 acres of outdoor gardens, thousands of flowers bloom under glass. Persuasive justification reports explain fully all the benefits of a recommendation and also anticipate possible reader objections.

Feasibility Reports

Feasibility reports examine the practicality and advisability of following a course of action. They answer this question: Will this plan or proposal work? Feasibility reports typically are internal reports written to advise on matters such as consolidating departments, offering a wellness program to employees, or hiring an outside firm to handle a company's accounting or computing operations. These reports may also be written by consultants called in to investigate a problem. The focus in these reports is on the decision: stopping or proceeding with the proposal. Since your task is not to persuade the reader to accept the decision, you'll want to present the decision immediately. In writing feasibility reports, consider these suggestions:

Feasibility reports analyze whether a proposal or plan will work.

- Announce your decision immediately.

- Provide a description of the background and problem necessitating the proposal.

- Discuss the benefits of the proposal.

- Describe the problems that may result.

- Calculate the costs associated with the proposal, if appropriate.

- Show the time frame necessary for implementing the proposal.

Elizabeth Webb, customer service manager for a large insurance company in Surrey, British Columbia, wrote the feasibility report shown in Figure 13.7. She describes the report thus: "We had been losing customer service reps (CSRs) after they were trained and were most valuable to us. When I talked with our vice president about the problem, she didn't want me to take time away from my job to investigate what other companies were doing to retain their

A typical feasibility report presents the decision, background information, benefits, problems, costs, and a schedule.

FIGURE 13.6 ■ Justification or Recommendation Reports: Indirect Pattern

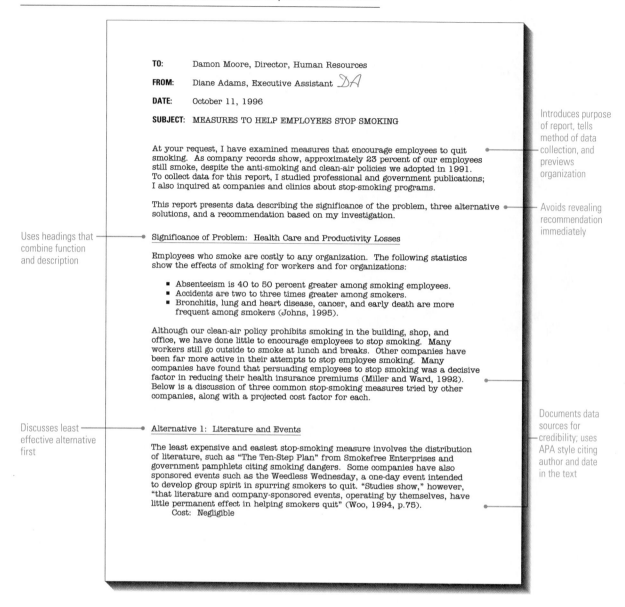

Uses headings that combine function and description

Discusses least effective alternative first

Introduces purpose of report, tells method of data collection, and previews organization

Avoids revealing recommendation immediately

Documents data sources for credibility; uses APA style citing author and date in the text

TO: Damon Moore, Director, Human Resources

FROM: Diane Adams, Executive Assistant _DA_

DATE: October 11, 1996

SUBJECT: MEASURES TO HELP EMPLOYEES STOP SMOKING

At your request, I have examined measures that encourage employees to quit smoking. As company records show, approximately 23 percent of our employees still smoke, despite the anti-smoking and clean-air policies we adopted in 1991. To collect data for this report, I studied professional and government publications; I also inquired at companies and clinics about stop-smoking programs.

This report presents data describing the significance of the problem, three alternative solutions, and a recommendation based on my investigation.

Significance of Problem: Health Care and Productivity Losses

Employees who smoke are costly to any organization. The following statistics show the effects of smoking for workers and for organizations:

- Absenteeism is 40 to 50 percent greater among smoking employees.
- Accidents are two to three times greater among smokers.
- Bronchitis, lung and heart disease, cancer, and early death are more frequent among smokers (Johns, 1995).

Although our clean-air policy prohibits smoking in the building, shop, and office, we have done little to encourage employees to stop smoking. Many workers still go outside to smoke at lunch and breaks. Other companies have been far more active in their attempts to stop employee smoking. Many companies have found that persuading employees to stop smoking was a decisive factor in reducing their health insurance premiums (Miller and Ward, 1992). Below is a discussion of three common stop-smoking measures tried by other companies, along with a projected cost factor for each.

Alternative 1: Literature and Events

The least expensive and easiest stop-smoking measure involves the distribution of literature, such as "The Ten-Step Plan" from Smokefree Enterprises and government pamphlets citing smoking dangers. Some companies have also sponsored events such as the Weedless Wednesday, a one-day event intended to develop group spirit in spurring smokers to quit. "Studies show," however, "that literature and company-sponsored events, operating by themselves, have little permanent effect in helping smokers quit" (Woo, 1994, p.75).
   Cost: Negligible

CSRs. Instead, we hired a consultant who suggested that we use a CSR career progression schedule. The vice president then wanted to know if the consultant's plan was feasible. Although my report is only one page long, it provides all necessary information: approval, background, benefits, problems, costs, and schedule."

Yardstick Reports

Yardstick reports consider alternative solutions to a problem by establishing criteria against which to weigh options.

Yardstick reports examine problems with two or more solutions. To evaluate the best solution, the writer establishes criteria by which to compare the alternatives. The criteria then act as a yardstick against which all the alternatives are measured. This yardstick approach is effective when companies establish specifications for equipment purchases, and then compare each manufacturer's

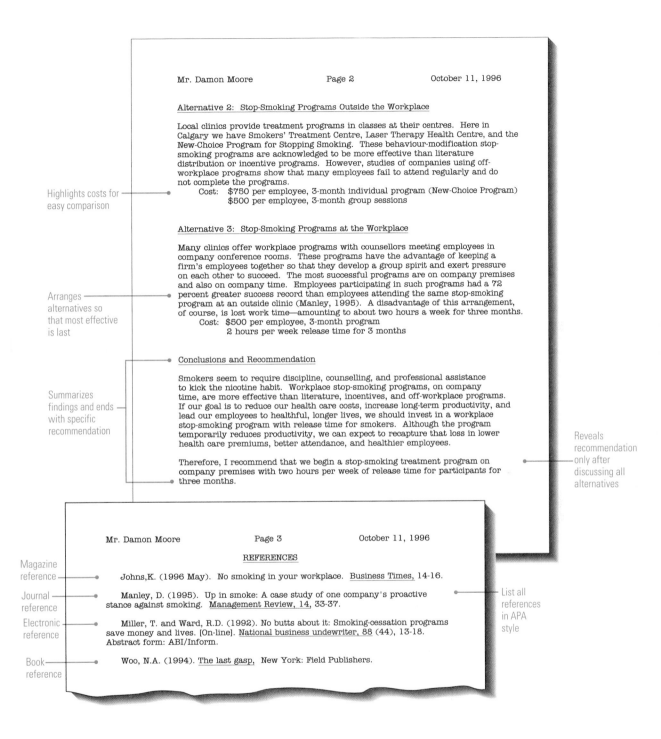

Mr. Damon Moore   Page 2   October 11, 1996

Alternative 2: Stop-Smoking Programs Outside the Workplace

Local clinics provide treatment programs in classes at their centres. Here in Calgary we have Smokers' Treatment Centre, Laser Therapy Health Centre, and the New-Choice Program for Stopping Smoking. These behaviour-modification stop-smoking programs are acknowledged to be more effective than literature distribution or incentive programs. However, studies of companies using off-workplace programs show that many employees fail to attend regularly and do not complete the programs.

Highlights costs for easy comparison

        Cost: $750 per employee, 3-month individual program (New-Choice Program)
                $500 per employee, 3-month group sessions

Alternative 3: Stop-Smoking Programs at the Workplace

Many clinics offer workplace programs with counsellors meeting employees in company conference rooms. These programs have the advantage of keeping a firm's employees together so that they develop a group spirit and exert pressure on each other to succeed. The most successful programs are on company premises and also on company time. Employees participating in such programs had a 72 percent greater success record than employees attending the same stop-smoking program at an outside clinic (Manley, 1995). A disadvantage of this arrangement, of course, is lost work time—amounting to about two hours a week for three months.

Arranges alternatives so that most effective is last

        Cost: $500 per employee, 3-month program
              2 hours per week release time for 3 months

Conclusions and Recommendation

Smokers seem to require discipline, counselling, and professional assistance to kick the nicotine habit. Workplace stop-smoking programs, on company time, are more effective than literature, incentives, and off-workplace programs. If our goal is to reduce our health care costs, increase long-term productivity, and lead our employees to healthful, longer lives, we should invest in a workplace stop-smoking program with release time for smokers. Although the program temporarily reduces productivity, we can expect to recapture that loss in lower health care premiums, better attendance, and healthier employees.

Summarizes findings and ends with specific recommendation

Reveals recommendation only after discussing all alternatives

Therefore, I recommend that we begin a stop-smoking treatment program on company premises with two hours per week of release time for participants for three months.

Mr. Damon Moore   Page 3   October 11, 1996

REFERENCES

Magazine reference

Johns,K. (1996 May). No smoking in your workplace. Business Times, 14-16.

Journal reference

Manley, D. (1995). Up in smoke: A case study of one company's proactive stance against smoking. Management Review, 14, 33-37.

List all references in APA style

Electronic reference

Miller, T. and Ward, R.D. (1992). No butts about it: Smoking-cessation programs save money and lives. [On-line]. National business undewriter, 88 (44), 13-18. Abstract form: ABI/Inform.

Book reference

Woo, N.A. (1994). The last gasp, New York: Field Publishers.

product with the established specifications. The yardstick approach is also effective when exact specifications cannot be established. For example, a major company relocating might evaluate cities like Montreal, Toronto, Vancouver, Halifax, and Edmonton. For each of these sites, the company would compare labour costs, land availability and costs, tax breaks, and housing costs. It would also weigh other criteria such as access to markets and transportation costs for raw materials. It might set up exact specifications for each category; it might

FIGURE 13.7 ■ Feasibility Report

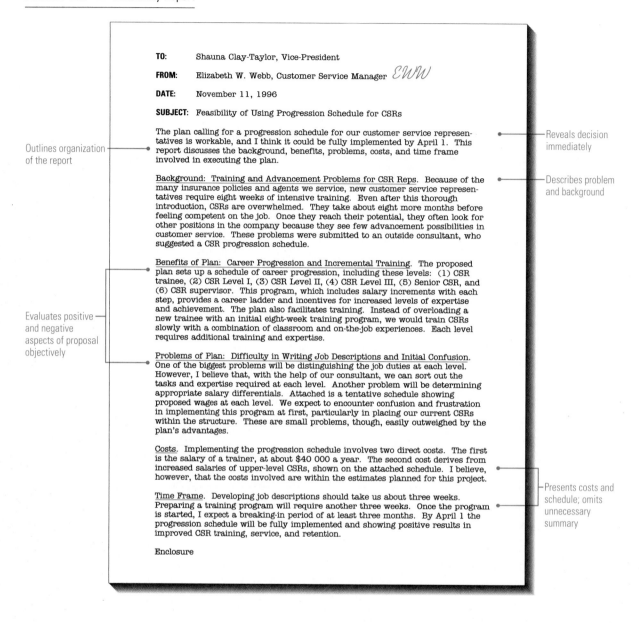

TO: Shauna Clay-Taylor, Vice-President

FROM: Elizabeth W. Webb, Customer Service Manager *EWW*

DATE: November 11, 1996

SUBJECT: Feasibility of Using Progression Schedule for CSRs

The plan calling for a progression schedule for our customer service representatives is workable, and I think it could be fully implemented by April 1. This report discusses the background, benefits, problems, costs, and time frame involved in executing the plan.

↳ *Outlines organization of the report*
↳ *Reveals decision immediately*

Background: Training and Advancement Problems for CSR Reps. Because of the many insurance policies and agents we service, new customer service representatives require eight weeks of intensive training. Even after this thorough introduction, CSRs are overwhelmed. They take about eight more months before feeling competent on the job. Once they reach their potential, they often look for other positions in the company because they see few advancement possibilities in customer service. These problems were submitted to an outside consultant, who suggested a CSR progression schedule.

↳ *Describes problem and background*

Benefits of Plan: Career Progression and Incremental Training. The proposed plan sets up a schedule of career progression, including these levels: (1) CSR trainee, (2) CSR Level I, (3) CSR Level II, (4) CSR Level III, (5) Senior CSR, and (6) CSR supervisor. This program, which includes salary increments with each step, provides a career ladder and incentives for increased levels of expertise and achievement. The plan also facilitates training. Instead of overloading a new trainee with an initial eight-week training program, we would train CSRs slowly with a combination of classroom and on-the-job experiences. Each level requires additional training and expertise.

↳ *Evaluates positive and negative aspects of proposal objectively*

Problems of Plan: Difficulty in Writing Job Descriptions and Initial Confusion. One of the biggest problems will be distinguishing the job duties at each level. However, I believe that, with the help of our consultant, we can sort out the tasks and expertise required at each level. Another problem will be determining appropriate salary differentials. Attached is a tentative schedule showing proposed wages at each level. We expect to encounter confusion and frustration in implementing this program at first, particularly in placing our current CSRs within the structure. These are small problems, though, easily outweighed by the plan's advantages.

Costs. Implementing the progression schedule involves two direct costs. The first is the salary of a trainer, at about $40 000 a year. The second cost derives from increased salaries of upper-level CSRs, shown on the attached schedule. I believe, however, that the costs involved are within the estimates planned for this project.

↳ *Presents costs and schedule; omits unnecessary summary*

Time Frame. Developing job descriptions should take us about three weeks. Preparing a training program will require another three weeks. Once the program is started, I expect a breaking-in period of at least three months. By April 1 the progression schedule will be fully implemented and showing positive results in improved CSR training, service, and retention.

Enclosure

---

merely compare each city in these various categories. The real advantage to yardstick reports is that alternatives can be measured consistently using the same criteria.

Reports using a yardstick approach typically are organized this way:

- Begin by describing the problem or need.

- Explain possible solutions and alternatives.

- Establish criteria for comparing the alternatives; tell how they were selected or developed.

- Discuss and evaluate each alternative in terms of the criteria.

- Draw conclusions and make recommendations.

Kelly Smythe, benefits administrator for computer manufacturer CompuTech, was called on to write a report comparing outplacement agencies. These agencies counsel discharged employees and help find new positions; fees are paid by the former employer. Kelly knew that times were bad for CompuTech and that extensive downsizing would take place in the next two years. Her task was to compare outplacement agencies and recommend one to CompuTech.

After collecting information, Kelly's biggest problem was organizing the data and developing a system for making comparisons. All the outplacement agencies she investigated seemed to offer the same basic package of services. Here's how she described her report, shown in Figure 13.8.

"With the information I gathered about three outplacement agencies, I made a big grid listing the names of the agencies across the top. Down the side I listed general categories—such as services, costs, and reputation. Then I filled in the information for each agency. This grid, which began to look like a table, helped me organize all the bits and pieces of information. After studying the grid, I saw that all the information could be grouped into four categories: counselling services, secretarial/research services, reputation, and costs. I made these the criteria I would use to compare agencies. Next, I divided my grid into two parts, which became Table 1 and Table 2. In writing the report, I could have made each agency a separate heading, followed by a discussion of how it measured up to the criteria. Immediately, though, I saw how repetitious that would become. So I used the criteria as headings and discussed how each agency met that criteria—or failed to meet it. Making a recommendation was easy once I had the tables made and could see how the agencies compared."

Grids are a useful way to organize and compare data for a yardstick report.

Research Studies

In some business reports the emphasis is on the research. These studies examine a problem, collect data to solve the problem, and reach conclusions growing out of the findings. This scientific approach leads the reader through all the steps to discovering the answer, positive or negative, to a problem. The answer comes as a result of assembling facts and evidence. Throughout the report the emphasis is on educating the reader with objective facts and reasoning.

For example, the cable TV industry hired a research firm to investigate this question: What effect will direct broadcast satellites have on cable TV? Direct broadcast satellite (DBS) systems employ high-power satellites to permit reception by small home-receiving terminals (dishes). Researchers developed three hypotheses. Cable operators would face severe competition if (1) DBS became the first national distributor of high-definition television programs, (2) DBS succeeded in providing low-cost small-antenna home receivers, and (3) DBS was able to offer major network programming. Each of these hypotheses was studied, and data were collected. Researchers described their findings and drew conclusions. One conclusion stated that DBS did, indeed, represent a considerable threat to the cable industry. That cable owners should consider buying into DBS was a natural recommendation following from this conclusion.

In this kind of research study, the reader must be informed and guided through the research so that the conclusions seem rational. Although an executive summary may reveal the conclusions and recommendations first, the report itself follows an indirect development pattern so that readers can follow the discovery of the answer. This means that the report begins with discussion of the problem and is followed by exploration of possible solutions. It ends with reasons explaining the selection of one course of action.

Research studies educate readers through scientific data collection and analysis.

Research studies follow the indirect patten to guide the reader through the research process to the conclusions.

FIGURE 13.8 ■ Yardstick Report

TO: George O. Dawes, Vice-President   DATE: April 28, 1996

FROM: Kelly Smythe, Benefits Administrator *KS*

SUBJECT: CHOICE OF OUTPLACEMENT SERVICES

Here is the report you requested April 1 investigating the possibility of CompuTech's use of out-placement services. It discusses the problem of counselling services for discharged staff and establishes criteria for selecting an out-placement agency. It then evaluates three prospective agencies and presents a recommendation based on that evaluation.

Introduces purpose and gives overview of report organization

PROBLEM: COUNSELLING DISCHARGED STAFF

In an effort to reduce costs and increase competitiveness, CompuTech will begin a program of staff reduction that will involve releasing up to 20 percent of our workforce over the next 12 to 24 months. Many of these employees have been with us for 10 or more years, and they are not being released for performance faults. These employees deserve a severance package that includes counselling and assistance in finding new careers.

Discusses background only briefly because readers already know the problem

SOLUTION AND ALTERNATIVES: OUT-PLACEMENT AGENCIES

Uses dual headings, giving function and description

Numerous out-placement agencies offer discharged employees counselling and assistance in locating new careers. This assistance minimizes not only the negative feelings related to job loss but also the very real possibility of litigation. Potentially expensive lawsuits have been lodged against some companies by unhappy employees who felt they were unfairly released.

In seeking an out-placement agency, we should find one that offers advice to the sponsoring company as well as to dischargees. Frankly, many of our managers need help in conducting termination sessions. A suitable out-placement agency should be selected soon so that we can learn about legal termination procedures and also have an agency immediately available when employees are discharged. Here in the metropolitan area, I have located three potential outplacement agencies appropriate to serve our needs: Gray & Associates, Right Access, and Careers Plus.

Announces solution and the alternatives it presents

ESTABLISHING CRITERIA FOR SELECTING AGENCY

Tells how criteria were selected

In order to choose among the three agencies, I established criteria based on professional articles, discussions with officials at other companies using outplacement agencies, and interviews with agencies. Here are the four groups of criteria I used in evaluating the three agencies:

1. Counselling services—including job search advice, résumé help, crisis management, corporate counselling, and availability of full-time counsellors

2. Secretarial and research assistance—including availability of secretarial staff, librarian, and personal computers

3. Reputation—based on a telephone survey of former clients and listing with a professional association

4. Costs—for both group programs and executive services

Creates four criteria to use as yardstick in evaluating alternatives

---

In writing the results of a research study, follow this organizational plan:

- Discuss the purpose, problem, or need objectively.
- Define the significance, scope, research methodology, and limitations of the project.
- Present the information collected, organizing it around reasons leading to the conclusions.
- Draw conclusions that result naturally from the findings.
- Make recommendations if requested.

An example of a long research study is shown in Chapter 14.

DISCUSSION: EVALUATING AGENCIES BY CRITERIA

Each agency was evaluated using the four criteria just described. Data comparing the first three criteria are summarized in Table 1.

Table 1

A COMPARISON OF SERVICES AND REPUTATIONS
FOR THREE LOCAL OUTPLACEMENT AGENCIES

	Gray & Associates	Right Access	Careers Plus
Counselling services			
Résumé advice	Yes	Yes	Yes
Crisis management	Yes	No	Yes
Corporate counselling	Yes	No	No
Full-time counselors	Yes	No	Yes
Secretarial, research assistance			
Secretarial staff	Yes	Yes	Yes
Librarian, research library	Yes	No	Yes
Personal computers	Yes	No	Yes
Listed by National Association of Career Consultants	Yes	No	Yes
Reputation (telephone survey of former clients)	Excellent	Good	Excellent

Counselling Services

All three agencies offered similar basic counselling services with job-search and résumé advice. They differed, however, in three significant areas.

Right Access does not offer crisis management, a service that puts the discharged employee in contact with a counsellor the same day the employee is released. Experts in the field consider this service especially important to help the dischargee begin "bonding" with the counsellor immediately. Immediate counselling also helps the dischargee through the most traumatic moments of one of life's great disappointments and helps him or her learn how to break the news to family members. Crisis management can be instrumental in reducing lawsuits because dischargees immediately begin to focus on career planning instead of concentrating on their pain and need for revenge. Moreover, Right Access does not employ full-time counsellors; it hires part-timers according to demand. Industry authorities advise against using agencies whose staff members are inexperienced and employed on an "as-needed" basis.

In addition, neither Right Access nor Careers Plus offers regular corporate counselling, which I feel is critical in training our managers to conduct terminal interviews. Careers Plus, however, suggested that it could schedule special workshops if desired.

Secretarial and Research Assistance

Both Gray & Associates and Careers Plus offer complete secretarial services and personal computers. Dischargees have access to staff and equipment to assist them in their job searches. These agencies also provide research libraries, librarians, and databases of company information to help in securing interviews.

Margin annotations:
- Summarizes complex data in table for easy reading and reference
- Highlights the similarities and differences among the alternatives
- Places table close to spot where it is first mentioned
- Does not repeat obvious data from table

▨ Checklist for Writing Analytical Reports

Introduction

✓ **Identify the purpose of the report.** Explain why the report is being written. For research studies also include the significance, scope, limitations, and methodology of the investigation.

✓ **Preview the organization of the report.** Especially for long reports, explain to the reader how the report will be organized.

FIGURE 13.8 ■ (continued)

Vice-President Dawes   Page 3   April 28, 1996

Reputation

Discusses objectively how each agency meets criteria

To assess the reputation of each agency, I checked its listing with the National Association of Career Consultants. This is a voluntary organization of out-placement agencies that monitors and polices its members. Gray & Associates and Careers Plus are listed; Right Access is not.

For further evidence I conducted a telephone survey of former agency clients. The three agencies supplied me with names and telephone numbers of companies and individuals they had served. I called four former clients for each agency. Most of the individuals were pleased with the out-placement services they had received. I asked each client the same questions so that I could compare responses.

Costs

All three agencies have two separate fee schedules, summarized in Table 2. The first schedule is for group programs intended for lower-level employees. These include off-site or on-site single-day workshop sessions, and the prices range from $1000 a session (at Right Access) to $1500 per session (at Gray & Associates). An additional fee of $40 to $50 is charged for each participant.

Selects most important data from table to discuss

The second fee schedule covers executive services. This counselling is individual and costs from 10 percent to 18 percent of the dischargee's previous year's salary. Since CompuTech will be forced to release numerous managerial staff members, the executive fee schedule is critical. Table 2 shows fees for a hypothetical case involving a manager who earns $60 000 a year.

Table 2

A COMPARISON OF COSTS FOR THREE AGENCIES

	Gray & Associates	Right Access	Careers Plus
Group programs	$1500/session, $45/participant	$1000/session, $40/participant	$1400/session, $50/participant
Executive services	15% of previous year's salary	10% of previous year's salary	18% of previous year's salary plus $1 000 fee
Manager at $60,000/year	$9000	$6000	$11 800

CONCLUSIONS AND RECOMMENDATIONS

Gives reasons for making recommendation

Although Right Access has the lowest fees, it lacks crisis management, corporate counselling, full-time counsellors, library facilities, and personal computers. Moreover, it is not listed by the National Association of Career Consultants. Therefore, the choice is between Gray & Associates and Careers Plus. Since they have similar services, the deciding factor is costs. Careers Plus would charge nearly $3000 more for counselling a manager than would Gray & Associates. Although Gray & Associates has fewer computers available, all other elements of its services seem good. Therefore, I recommend that CompuTech hire Gray & Associates as an out-placement agency to counsel discharged employees.

Narrows choice to final alternative

✓**Summarize the conclusions and recommendations for receptive audiences.** Use the direct pattern only if you have the confidence of the reader.

Findings

✓**Discuss pros and cons.** In recommendation and justification reports evaluate the advantages and disadvantages of each alternative. For unreceptive audiences consider placing the recommended alternative last.

✓ **Establish criteria to evaluate alternatives.** In yardstick studies create criteria to use in measuring each alternative consistently.

✓ **Support the findings with evidence.** Supply facts, statistics, expert opinion, survey data, and other proof from which you can draw logical conclusions.

✓ **Organize the findings for logic and readability.** Arrange the findings around the alternatives or the reasons leading to the conclusion. Use headings, enumerations, lists, tables, and visual aids to focus emphasis.

Conclusions and Recommendations

✓ **Draw reasonable conclusions from the findings.** Develop conclusions that answer the research question. Justify the conclusions with highlights from the findings.

✓ **Make recommendations, if asked.** For multiple recommendations prepare a list. Use action verbs. Explain needed action.

Summary of Learning Goals

1. **Distinguish between informational and analytical reports.** Informational reports provide data and answer questions without offering recommendations or analysis. They may report sales, routine operations, trips, conferences, or compliance. Analytical reports organize data, draw conclusions, and often make recommendations. They may include justification/recommendation, feasibility, yardstick, and research reports.

2. **Define periodic reports and describe their major components.** Periodic reports—such as sales, accounts payable, and personnel reports—generally summarize regular activities occurring during the reporting period. They also describe irregular events demanding attention and highlight special needs and problems.

3. **Discuss the forms and content of situational reports.** Trip, convention, and conference reports often specify the event, summarize three to five main points of interest to the reader, itemize expenses, and close with appreciation or a suggestion for action. Progress and interim reports identify a project, provide background data, explain the work currently in progress, anticipate problems and remedies, and discuss future activities. Progress reports should always include an expected completion date.

4. **Distinguish between investigative and compliance reports.** Investigative reports examine a topic (such as a production problem) but do not draw conclusions or make recommendations. Compliance reports present data in compliance with local, provincial, and federal laws. These reports should be honest, accurate, and prompt.

5. **Compare direct and indirect justification and recommendation reports.** Justification and recommendation reports organized directly identify a problem, immediately announce a recommendation or solution, explain and discuss its merits, and summarize the action to be taken. Justification and recommendation reports are organized indirectly to

describe a problem, discuss alternative solutions, prove the superiority of one solution, and ask for authorization to proceed with that solution.

6. **Describe the purpose and content of feasibility reports.** Feasibility reports study the advisability of following a course of action. They generally announce the author's proposal immediately. Then they describe the background, advantages and disadvantages, costs, and schedule for implementing the proposal.

7. **Define yardstick reports and describe their major components.** Yardstick reports compare two or more solutions to a problem by measuring each against a set of established criteria. They usually describe a problem, explain possible solutions, establish criteria for comparing alternatives, evaluate each alternative in terms of the criteria, draw conclusions, and make recommendations. The advantage of yardstick reports is consistency in comparing various alternatives.

8. **Discuss the content of research reports.** Research reports identify a problem, collect data to solve the problem, and reach conclusions drawn from the findings. These scientific reports generally discuss a problem or need objectively; define the significance, scope, methodology, and limitations of the study; gather information; present the data; draw conclusions; and make recommendations, if requested.

CHAPTER REVIEW

1. Name four categories of informational reports. (Goal 1)

2. Describe periodic reports and what they generally contain. (Goal 2)

3. Describe situational reports and give two examples. (Goal 3)

4. What should a progress report include? (Goal 3)

5. How can the body of an investigative or other informational report be organized? (Goal 4)

6. What are compliance reports? (Goal 4)

7. Informational reports emphasize facts. What do analytical reports emphasize? (Goals 1, 5)

8. When should an analytical report be organized directly? (Goal 5)

9. How can directness backfire? (Goal 5)

10. What sequence should a direct recommendation/justification report follow? (Goal 5)

11. What sequence should an indirect recommendation/justification report follow? (Goal 5)

12. What is a feasibility report? (Goal 6)

13. Are feasibility reports usually intended for internal or external audiences? (Goal 6)

14. What is a yardstick report? (Goal 7)

15. How do research studies differ from other problem-solving reports? (Goal 8)

DISCUSSION

1. Do most reports flow upward or downward? Why? (Goals 1–7)

2. Why are large companies more likely to require reports than smaller ones? (Goals 1–7)

3. If you were doubtful about writing a report directly or indirectly, which pattern would be safer? Why? (Goal 5)

4. What are the major differences between informational and analytical reports? (Goals 1, 5)

5. **Ethical Issue:** Discuss the ethics of using persuasive tactics to persuade a report's readers to accept its conclusions. Is it ethical to be persuasive only when you believe in the soundness and truth of your conclusions?

EXERCISES

13.1 Periodic Reports (Goal 2)

In a business you know, name five situations that would require periodic reports. If you've had little business experience, imagine a large department store. What kinds of periodic reports would management require of department managers, buyers, and operations staff? Describe how one report might be organized.

13.2 Convention, Conference, and Seminar Reports (Goal 3)

Select an article from a business publication (such as *Canadian Business*, *Maclean's* or the *Financial Post Magazine*) describing a convention, conference, or seminar. Imagine that you attended that meeting for your company. Outline a report to your boss describing the meeting.

13.3 Situational and Investigative Reports (Goals 3, 4)

For each of the following situations, suggest a report type and briefly discuss how the report would be organized.

a. The mail centre could save over $10 000 a year if the company would allow it to invest in reusable nylon mail pouches to deliver customer insurance policies to branch offices.

b. The manager wants a quick overview of quality circles—just to keep her informed. She sees no direct need for the information immediately.

c. Home Depot is considering using shrink wrapping to secure merchandise stored on racks that range from 8 to 16 feet high. Management is concerned about the safety of employees and customers.

d. King Grocery must implement a worker-incentive wage program. This plan would establish standards for warehouse workers and generously reward those who exceed the standard with extra pay and time off. The current wage program pays everyone the same, causing dissension and underachievement. Other wage plans, including a union three-tier system, have drawbacks. Expect management to oppose the worker-incentive plan.

e. Your convention committee has chosen a site, set up a tentative program, and is now working on keynote speakers and exhibitors. Report your progress to the organization president.

f. The New Carlisle assembly plant is plagued by high absenteeism and worker turnover. What can be done about eliminating these problems?

13.4 Yardstick Report Criteria (Goal 7)

Assume you are a benefits analyst who has been assigned the task of investigating three health care plans for your company. You must recommend a plan that the company can afford and that will satisfy employees. Your company is facing a 45 percent increase in its basic major medical plan. After doing some research, you find two other options: a health maintenance organization and MedicPlus, a plan that offers choice and is somewhat cheaper than your present carrier. You decide to compare the three plans using the yardstick approach. What criteria could you use to compare plans? How would you organize the final report?

PROBLEMS: INFORMATIONAL REPORTS

13.5 Periodic Report: Filling in the Boss (Goal 2)

Write a report of your month's accomplishments addressed to your boss. For a job that you currently hold or a previous one, describe your regular activities, discuss irregular events that management should be aware of, and highlight any special needs or problems. Use memo format.

13.6 Conference Report: In Your Dreams (Goal 3)

From a business periodical select an article describing a conference, seminar, convention, or trip (preferably to an exotic spot) connected with your major area of study. The article must be at least 500 words long. Assume that you attended the meeting or took the trip at the expense of your company. Prepare a memo report to your supervisor.

13.7 Progress Report: Heading Toward that Degree (Goal 3)

Assume you have made an agreement with your parents (or spouse, relative, or significant friend) that you would submit a progress report at this time describing your headway toward your educational goal (such as employment, degree, or diploma). List your specific achievements, and outline what you have left to complete. Prepare a report in letter format.

13.8 Progress Report: Checking In (Goal 3)

If you are preparing a long report (see Chapter 14), write a progress report informing your instructor of your work. Briefly describe the project (its purpose, scope, limitations, and methodology), work you have completed, work yet to be completed, problems encountered, future activities, and expected completion date. Address the memo report to your instructor.

13.9 Investigative Report: All You Ever Wanted to Know (Goal 4)

Investigate a company listed in *100 Best Companies to Work For in Canada* for which you might like to work. Describe its major product, service, or emphasis. Find its ranking, its current stock price (if listed), and its high and low range for the year. Include its profit-to-earnings ratio. Describe its latest marketing plan, promotion, or product. Give its home office, president's name, and number of employees. Provide a short history of the company. Address a memo report to your professor or instructor.

13.10 Investigative Report: Selling Abroad (Goal 4)

You have been asked to help write the sales section in a training manual for North American companies doing business with [select a country]. Collect data from the library and from the country's embassy in Ottawa. Interview an on-campus international student from your assigned country or a recent business visitor to the country. Collect information about formats for written communication, observance of holidays, customary greetings, business ethics (for example, business bribes), and other topics of interest to business-people. Remember that your report should promote business, not tourism. Prepare a memo report addressed to Kelly Johnson, editor.

13.11 Investigative Report: Between the Covers (Goal 4)

As a research assistant in an advertising agency, you must maintain data files about various magazines in which your clients may place ads. Select a business-oriented magazine and examine four to six issues. Collect information about articles (length, seriousness of topics, humour), readability (word, sentence, and paragraph length; formal or informal tone), format and design (colour, white space, glamour), and pictures and graphics. Examine the ads (advertisers, products and services, appeals). Does the magazine accept liquor ads? At what audience is the magazine aimed (sex, education, age, income, interests)? Consider other charac-

teristics in which your clients may be interested. Address a memo report to Judy Gold, print media coordinator.

PROBLEMS: ANALYTICAL REPORTS

13.12 Justification/Recommendation Report: We Need It (Goal 5)

Choose a piece of equipment that should be purchased or replaced (photocopier, fax, VCR, computer, printer, camera, or the like). Write a memo report addressed to your boss. Assume that you can be direct and straightforward about this request.

13.13 Justification/Recommendation Report: Time for a Change (Goal 5)

Identify a problem or a procedure that must be changed at your job (such as poor scheduling of employees, outdated equipment, slow order processing, failure to encourage employees to participate fully, restrictive rules, inadequate training, or disappointed customers). Using an indirect pattern, write a recommendation report suggesting one or more ways to solve the problem. Address the memo report to your boss.

13.14 Collaborative Justification/Recommendation Report: Solving a Campus Problem (Goal 5)

In groups of three to five, investigate a problem on your campus, such as inadequate parking, slow registration, poor class schedules, inefficient bookstore, weak job-placement program, unrealistic degree/diploma requirements, or lack of internship programs. Within your group develop a solution to the problem. After reviewing persuasive techniques discussed in Chapter 9, write a group or individual justification or recommendation report(s) addressed to the proper campus official. Depending on how you expect the reader to react to your recommendation, decide whether to use the direct or indirect pattern. With your instructor's approval, send the report.

13.15 Feasibility Report: International Organization (Goal 6)

For an assignment in one of your courses you have been asked to submit a letter report to the dean evaluating the feasibility of starting an organization of international students on campus. Find out how many international students there are, what nations they represent, how one goes about starting an organization, and whether a faculty sponsor is needed. Assume that you conducted an informal survey of international students. Of the 39 who filled out the survey, 31 said they would be interested in joining.

13.16 Feasibility Report: Improving Employee Fitness (Goal 6)

Your company is considering ways to promote employee fitness and morale. Select a possibility that seems reasonable for your company (softball league, bowling teams, basketball league, lunchtime walks, lunchtime fitness speakers and demos, company-sponsored health club memberships, workout room, fitness centre, fitness director, and so on). Assume that your boss has tentatively agreed to one of the programs and has asked you to write a memo report investigating its feasibility.

13.17 Feasibility Report: Reducing, Reusing, and Recycling (Goal 6)

As a management trainee for a large hotel chain, you have been asked to investigate the feasibility of saving energy and reducing waste within the hotel chain. Your task is to learn how other hotels are improving their environmental record. Bayshore Hotel in Vancouver has special guest rooms with economical fluorescent lighting, bulk shampoo and lotion, water-saving shower heads and toilets, and the option of keeping towels longer than a day. Hotel Vancouver became the first hotel in North America to replace chlorine in swimming pools with non-stinging baking soda and salt. Days Inn in Fort Myers, Florida, shreds wastepaper for compost mulch. Hotel Inter-Continental, with 100 hotels in 47 countries, has prepared a checklist of 134 actions to help employees "reduce, reuse,

and recycle." Your task is not to present specifics on implementing a hotel environmental program, but rather to decide if such a program is feasible. What are the benefits of environmental programs for hotels? You could begin your research by looking at "Saving by Recycling: Greening of the Grand Hotel," *New York Times*, 8 August 1992, Y17. Address your memo report to Leland Jeffrey, Operations.

13.18 Yardstick Report: Evaluating Equipment (Goal 7)

You recently complained to your boss that you were unhappy with a piece of equipment that you use (printer, computer, copier, fax, or the like). After some thought, the boss decided you were right and told you to go shopping. Compare at least three different manufacturers' models and recommend one. Since the company will be purchasing 10 or more units and since several managers must approve the purchase, write a careful report documenting your findings. Establish at least five criteria for comparing the models. Submit a memo report to your boss.

13.19 Yardstick Report: Measuring the Alternatives (Goal 7)

Consider a problem where you work or in an organization you know. Select a problem with several alternative solutions or courses of action (retaining the present status could be one alternative). Develop criteria that could be used to evaluate each alternative. Write a report measuring each alternative by the yardstick you have created. Recommend a course of action to your boss or to the organization head.

Proposals and Formal Reports

L E A R N I N G   G O A L S

After studying this chapter, you should be able to

1 Discuss the parts of an informal proposal.

2 Discuss the special parts of a formal proposal.

3 Distinguish between proposals and formal reports.

4 Name the parts of a formal report that precede the introduction.

5 Outline topics that might be covered in the introduction of a formal report.

6 Describe the parts of a formal report that follow the introduction.

7 Specify some tips that aid writers of formal reports.

Hewlett-Packard

First, you must find a customer's "hot buttons." That's the most important step in putting together any proposal," says Mary Piecewicz.

As a technical editor at the Hewlett-Packard Proposal Center in Burlington, Massachusetts, Mary knows what she's talking about. She has helped write hundreds of successful proposals selling large installations of HP computers to banks, brokerage houses, hotel chains, clothing manufacturers, and insurance companies.

Pushing customers' "hot buttons" involves finding out exactly what they want in a computer purchase. Often buyers are looking for more than low price and high performance. "Some customers are interested primarily in support. They want to be sure we'll walk them through the whole installation and train their employees. Others want a solid company that promises to stay with them for the long haul. "You can't really put a dollar value on these warm and fuzzy things," observes Mary. "But they are critical issues and must be recognized early so that they can be addressed in a proposal."

"To conquer writer's block, begin with a bulleted list of what the customer is looking for. This list ... gets you started and keeps you headed in the right direction."

Like many businesspeople, Mary Piecewicz eventually became an expert in a field that she knew nothing about when she was a student. After graduating from Boston College (with a degree in sociology), she took a job in marketing. Building on a strong foundation of basic language skills, she enrolled in technical writing courses at local universities. Mary also developed on-the-job writing skills at an electronics company, later joining Hewlett-Packard as an editor of proposals.

Proposals (written offers to sell services and equipment) are so important that Hewlett-Packard has an in-house department devoted wholly to developing them. "Competition today is tough," notes Mary. "Customers are shopping around—especially for big purchases. They want to compare apples with apples, and proposals allow them to do that. Big corporations are now going the proposal route simply because money is tight, and they want to get the most for their dollar. Companies are also trying to protect themselves. Since a proposal is a legally binding document, whatever you put down on paper you have to be able to supply. Proposals allow companies to find the best deal while at the same time giving them protection."

At the HP Proposal Center, all projects are team efforts. "No proposal is ever written in isolation. If you can't work with others or if you have a sensitive ego, you're lost in this field. I've learned to be a kind of Lady Teflon," laughs Mary. A team usually consists of a sales representative familiar with the client, an HP technical consultant who knows the

hardware, and support and contracts personnel. The proposal production coordinator and a proposal manager pull the whole project together.

One of the biggest problems for HP sales representatives working on a proposal team is writer's block. Untrained in writing, they often just can't get started. Since they are responsible for writing the executive summary of the proposal (the most important section), Mary generally offers some coaching.

"To conquer writer's block, begin with a bulleted list of what the customer is looking for. This list ... gets you started and keeps you headed in the right direction."

Staying tuned in to the customer's concerns is Mary's number one focus in writing proposals. "Much of the time you think you're focusing on the customer, but you're really just singing your own song. For example, a customer wants a cost-effective solution to a problem, and you try to describe a wonderful solution. But all you talk about is your state-of-the-art technology, performance, and reputation—without mentioning costs. You weren't really listening to what the customer said. It's like writing a term paper. You've found all this great stuff that you want to use, and whether it's relevant or not, you're going to use it." Ready-made, all-purpose answers are not very persuasive in proposals.

How do you know what customers really want? Mary recalls one proposal written for an international hotel chain that wanted to upgrade its reservations system. But all it sent out was an informal one-page request with few details. Fortunately, HP's sales representative had previously talked extensively with the chain's hotel managers and had a good idea of what they really needed—even though these wants were not spelled out in their vague request. The resulting successful proposal zeroed in on two "hot buttons": corporate reliability and long-term service. "They wanted to know that HP wouldn't leave them high and dry after the equipment was installed."

In organizing proposals, HP always responds to the customer's outline. If the customer doesn't specify a plan, proposals are arranged as follows: Section 1 contains the executive summary and management overview. Section 2 covers specifications and technical descriptions. Section 3 lists costs, terms, conditions. Section 4 presents supplemental literature.

Because of its importance, the executive summary gets special attention. It may open with a brief history of HP, but its primary focus is on the customer's needs. "We address every customer issue and specify our 'differentiators.' What makes HP different from our competitors? What makes us stand out? The executive summary is really the selling tool in our proposals, and we spend the most time on it."[1] ■

This Hewlett-Packard Media Applications Learning Laboratory is one of 50 HP learning centres around the world. The centres emphasize self-paced, interactive training. These research and development laboratories enable HP to study the technology and documentation support materials of its products. HP also uses the labs to formulate and improve curricula for teaching computer studies.

Writing Formal and Informal Proposals

Proposals are persuasive offers to solve problems, provide services, or sell equipment.

Proposals are written offers to solve problems, provide services, or sell equipment. Although some proposals are internal, often taking the form of justification and recommendation reports, most proposals are external. The external proposals that Mary Piecewicz helps write at Hewlett-Packard are an important means of generating income for the giant computer company.

Because proposals are vital to their success, some businesses hire consultants or maintain specialists, like Mary, who do nothing but write proposals. Such proposals tell how a problem can be solved, what procedure will be followed, who will do it, how long it will take, and how much it will cost.

Government agencies and large companies use requests for proposals (RFPs) to solicit competitive bids on projects.

Proposals may be solicited or unsolicited. When firms know exactly what they want, they prepare a request for proposal (RFP) specifying their requirements. Government agencies and large companies are likely to use RFPs to solicit competitive bids on their projects. As Mary noted, companies today want to be able to compare "apples with apples," and they also want the protection offered by proposals, which are legal contracts. Unsolicited proposals are written when an individual or firm sees a problem to be solved and offers a proposal to do so. Clean-Up Technology, an American waste disposal firm, will be submitting several proposals, for example, to government agencies and firms in Mexico. Explaining his bid for Mexican business, the waste disposal company president said, "There's obviously a lot of clean-up work to be done in Mexico, and there's not a lot of expertise in our business."[2] Unsolicited proposals, like those of Clean-Up Technology, seize opportunities and capitalize on potential.

The most important point to remember about proposals—whether solicited or unsolicited—is that they are sales presentations. They must be persuasive, not merely mechanical descriptions of what you can do. Among other things, you may recall, effective persuasive sales messages (1) emphasize benefits for the reader, (2) "toot your horn" by detailing your expertise and accomplishments, and (3) make it easy for the reader to understand and respond.

Proposals may be formal or informal; they differ primarily in length and format. Notice in Figure 14.1 that formal proposals, described shortly, have many more parts than informal proposals.

Components of Informal Proposals

Informal proposals may contain an introduction, background information, the proposal, staffing requirements, a budget, and authorization.

Informal proposals may be presented in short (two- to four-page) letters. Sometimes called "letter proposals," they may contain six main parts: introduction, background, proposal, staffing, budget, and authorization. As you can see in Figure 14.1, both formal and informal proposals contain these six basic parts. Figure 14.2, an informal letter proposal to a London dentist to improve patient satisfaction, illustrates the six parts of letter proposals.

Introduction. Most proposals begin by briefly explaining the reasons for the proposal and by highlighting the writer's qualifications. To make your introduction more persuasive, you need a "hook" to capture the interest of the reader. One proposal expert suggests these possibilities:[3]

- Hint at extraordinary results with details to be revealed shortly.

- Promise low costs or speedy results.

- Mention a remarkable resource (well-known authority, new computer program, well-trained staff) available exclusively to you.

FIGURE 14.1 ■ Components in Formal and Informal Proposals

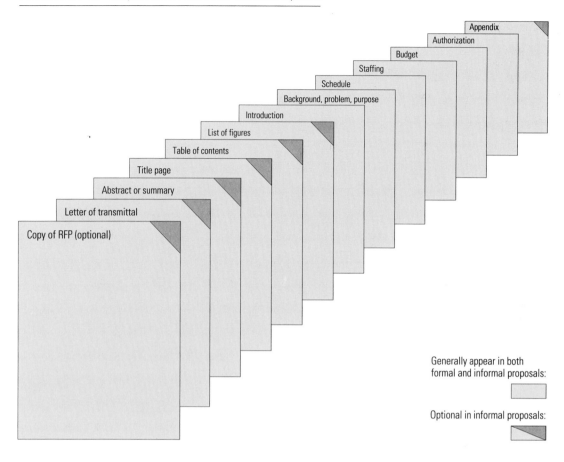

Generally appear in both
formal and informal proposals:

Optional in informal proposals:

- Identify a serious problem (worry item) and promise a solution, to be explained later.

- Specify an issue or benefit that you feel is the heart of the proposal.

For example, Jeffrey Myers, in the introduction for his proposal shown in Figure 14.2, focused on a key benefit. In his proposal to conduct a patient satisfaction survey, Jeffrey thought that Dr. Calloway would be most interested in specific recommendations for improving service to his patients. But Jeffrey didn't hit on this hook until he had written a first draft and had come back to it later. Indeed, it's often a good idea to put off writing the introduction until after you have completed other parts. For longer proposals the introduction also describes the scope and limitations of the project, as well as outlining the organization of the material to come.

Effective proposal openers "hook" the readers by promising extraordinary results or resources or by identifying key benefits, issues, or outcomes.

Background, problem, purpose. The background section states the problem and discusses the goals or purposes of the project. In an unsolicited proposal your goal is to convince the reader that a problem exists. Thus, you must present the problem in detail, discussing such factors as monetary losses, failure to comply with government regulations, or loss of customers. In a solicited proposal your aim is to persuade the reader that you understand the problem completely. Thus, if you are responding to an RFP, this means repeating its language. For example, if the RFP asks for the *design of a maintenance program for high-speed mail-sorting equipment*, you would use the same language in

FIGURE 14.2 ■ Informal Proposal

The Three Phases of the Writing Process

1

Analyze
The purpose is to persuade the reader to accept this proposal.

Anticipate
The reader must be convinced that this survey project is worth its hefty price.

Adapt
Because the reader will be resistant at first, use a persuasive approach that emphasizes benefits.

2

Research
Collect data about the reader's practice and other surveys of patient satisfaction.

Organize
Identify four specific purposes (benefits) of this proposal. Specify the survey plan. Promote the staff, itemize the budget, and ask for approval.

Compose
Prepare for revision by composing on a computer.

3

Revise
Revise to emphasize benefits. Improve readability with functional headings and lists. Remove jargon and wordiness.

Proofread
Check spelling of client's name. Verify dates and calculation of budget figures. Recheck all punctuation.

Evaluate
Is this proposal convincing enough to sell your product or service?

MYERS RESEARCH CONSULTANTS

One Riverview Plaza
London, ON N6H 2V7
(519) 356-4300

May 16, 1996

Dr. Matthew M. Calloway
286 Old Bridge Road
London, ON N6H 4K4

Dear Dr. Calloway:

I enjoyed talking to you several days ago, Dr. Calloway, about your successful general dentistry practice in downtown London. Myers Research Consultants is pleased to submit the following proposal outlining our plan to analyze your patients and suggest ways to improve your service to them.

— Uses opening paragraph in place of introduction

— Grabs attention with "hook" that focuses on key benefit

Background and Purposes

We understand that you have been incorporating a total quality management system in your practice. Although you have every reason to believe your patients are pleased with the service you provide, you would like to give them an opportunity to discuss what they like and possibly don't like about your service. Specifically, your purposes are to survey your patients to (1) determine the level of their satisfaction with you and your staff, (2) elicit their suggestions for improvement, (3) learn more about how they discovered you, and (4) compare your "preferred" and "standard" patients.

— Identifies four purposes of survey

Proposed Plan

On the basis of our experience in conducting many local and national customer satisfaction surveys, Myers Research proposes the following plan to you.

— Announces heart of proposal

Survey. We will develop a short but thorough questionnaire probing the data you desire. Although the survey instrument will include both open-ended and closed questions, it will concentrate on the latter. Closed questions enable respondents to answer easily; they also facilitate systematic data analysis. The questionnaire will measure patient reactions to such elements as courtesy, professionalism, accuracy of billing, friendliness, and waiting time. After you approve it, the questionnaire will be sent to a carefully selected sample of 300 patients whom you have separated into groupings of "preferred" and "standard."

— Divides total plan into logical segments for easy reading

— Describes procedure for solving problem or achieving goals

Analysis. Data from the survey will be analyzed by demographic segments, such as patient type, age, and gender. Our experienced team of experts, using state-of-the-art computer systems and advanced statistical measures, will study the (a) degree of patient satisfaction, (b) reasons for satisfaction or dissatisfaction, and (c) relationship between responses of your "preferred" and "standard" patients. Moreover, our team will report to you specific suggestions for making patient visits more pleasant.

Report. You will receive a final report with the key findings clearly spelled out, Dr. Calloway. Our expert staff will also draw conclusions based on these findings. The report will include tables summarizing all responses, broken down into groups of preferred and standard patients.

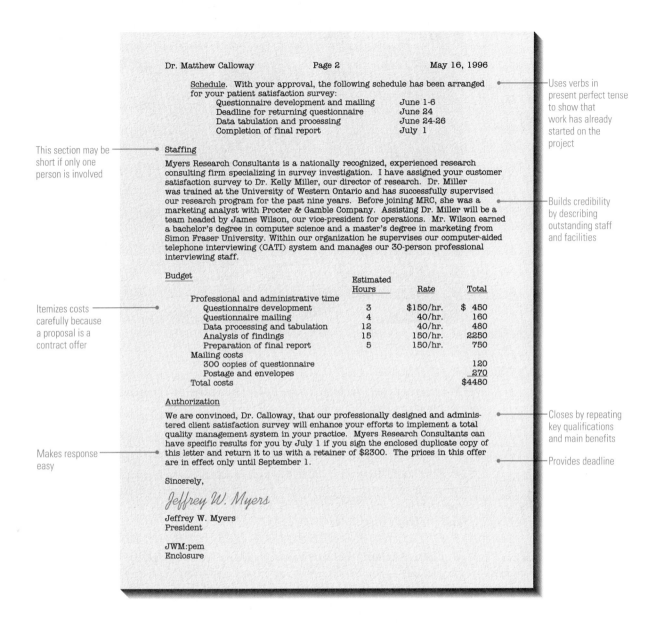

Dr. Matthew Calloway   Page 2   May 16, 1996

Schedule. With your approval, the following schedule has been arranged for your patient satisfaction survey:

Questionnaire development and mailing	June 1-6
Deadline for returning questionnaire	June 24
Data tabulation and processing	June 24-26
Completion of final report	July 1

(annotation: Uses verbs in present perfect tense to show that work has already started on the project)

Staffing

(annotation: This section may be short if only one person is involved)

Myers Research Consultants is a nationally recognized, experienced research consulting firm specializing in survey investigation. I have assigned your customer satisfaction survey to Dr. Kelly Miller, our director of research. Dr. Miller was trained at the University of Western Ontario and has successfully supervised our research program for the past nine years. Before joining MRC, she was a marketing analyst with Procter & Gamble Company. Assisting Dr. Miller will be a team headed by James Wilson, our vice-president for operations. Mr. Wilson earned a bachelor's degree in computer science and a master's degree in marketing from Simon Fraser University. Within our organization he supervises our computer-aided telephone interviewing (CATI) system and manages our 30-person professional interviewing staff.

(annotation: Builds credibility by describing outstanding staff and facilities)

Budget

(annotation: Itemizes costs carefully because a proposal is a contract offer)

	Estimated Hours	Rate	Total
Professional and administrative time			
Questionnaire development	3	$150/hr.	$ 450
Questionnaire mailing	4	40/hr.	160
Data processing and tabulation	12	40/hr.	480
Analysis of findings	15	150/hr.	2250
Preparation of final report	5	150/hr.	750
Mailing costs			
300 copies of questionnaire			120
Postage and envelopes			270
Total costs			$4480

Authorization

We are convinced, Dr. Calloway, that our professionally designed and administered client satisfaction survey will enhance your efforts to implement a total quality management system in your practice. Myers Research Consultants can have specific results for you by July 1 if you sign the enclosed duplicate copy of this letter and return it to us with a retainer of $2300. The prices in this offer are in effect only until September 1.

(annotation: Closes by repeating key qualifications and main benefits)

(annotation: Provides deadline)

(annotation: Makes response easy)

Sincerely,

Jeffrey W. Myers

Jeffrey W. Myers
President

JWM:pem
Enclosure

explaining the purpose of your proposal. This section might include segments entitled *Basic Requirements*, *Most Critical Tasks*, and *Most Important Secondary Problems*.

Proposal, plan, schedule. In the proposal section itself, you should discuss your plan for solving the problem. In some proposals this is tricky because you want to disclose enough of your plan to secure the contract without giving away so much information that your services are unneeded. Without specifics, though, your proposal has little chance, so you must decide how much to reveal. Tell what you propose to do and how it will benefit the reader. Remember, too, that a proposal is a sales presentation. Sell your methods, product, and "deliverables"—items that will be left with the client. In this section some writers specify how the project will be managed and how its progress will be audited.

The actual proposal section must give enough information to secure the contract but not so much detail that the services are no longer needed.

Many proposals are written by teams who collaborate in developing a plan to sell products and services that solve a client's problem. The most successful teams avoid "canned" solutions. Instead, they gather information to understand a particular client's needs. They work together to customize a "bid package" with all the information necessary to respond to the client's RFP.

Most writers also include a schedule of activities or timetable showing when events take place.

Staffing. The staffing section of a proposal describes the credentials and expertise of the project leaders. It may also describe the size and qualifications of the support staff, along with other resources such as computer facilities and special programs for analyzing statistics. In longer proposals, résumés of key people may be provided. The staffing or personnel section is a good place to endorse and promote your staff.

Budget. A central item in most proposals is the budget, a list of proposed project costs. You need to prepare this section carefully because it represents a contract; you can't raise the price later—even if your costs increase. You can—and should—protect yourself with a deadline for acceptance. In the budget section some writers itemize hours and costs; others present a total sum only. A proposal to install a complex computer system might, for example, contain a detailed line-by-line budget. Similarly, Jeffrey Myers felt that he needed to justify the budget for his firm's patient satisfaction survey, so he itemized the costs, as shown in Figure 14.2. But the budget contained in a proposal to conduct a one-day seminar to improve employee communication skills might be a lump sum only. Your analysis of the project will help you decide what kind of budget to prepare.

> Because a proposal is a legal contract, the budget must be carefully researched.

Authorization. Informal proposals often close with a request for approval or authorization. In addition, the closing should remind the reader of key benefits and motivate action. It might also include a date beyond which the offer is invalid.

Special Parts of Formal Proposals

Formal proposals differ from informal proposals not in style but in size and format. Formal proposals respond to big projects and may range from 5 to 200 or more pages. To facilitate comprehension and internal references, they are organized into many parts, as shown in Figure 14.1. In addition to the six basic parts just described, formal proposals may contain some or all of the following front and end parts.

Formal proposals might also contain a copy of the RFP, a letter of transmittal, an abstract, a title page, a table of contents, a list of figures, and an appendix.

Copy of RFP. A copy of the RFP may be included in the opening parts of a formal proposal. Large organizations may have more than one RFP circulating, and identification is necessary.

Letter of transmittal. A letter of transmittal, usually bound inside a formal proposal, addresses the person who is designated to receive the proposal or who will make the final decision. The letter describes how you learned about the problem or confirms that the proposal responds to the enclosed RFP. This persuasive letter briefly presents the major features and benefits of your proposal. Here, you should assure the reader that you are authorized to make the bid, and mention the time limit for which the bid stands. You may also offer to provide additional information, and ask for action, if appropriate.

Abstract or executive summary. An abstract is a brief summary (usually about one page) of a proposal's highlights intended for specialists or for technical readers. An executive summary also reviews the proposal's highlights, but it is written for managers and so should be less technical. Formal proposals may contain one or both summaries.

An abstract summarizes a proposal's highlights for specialists; an executive summary does so for managers.

Title page. The title page includes the following items, generally in this order: title of proposal, name of client organization, RFP number or other announcement, date of submission, author's name, and/or his or her organization.

Table of contents. Because most proposals don't contain an index, the table of contents becomes quite important. Tables of contents should include all headings and their beginning page numbers. Items that appear before the contents (copy of RFP, letter of transmittal, abstract, and title page) are not listed in the contents. However, any appendices should be listed.

List of figures. Proposals with many tables and figures often contain a list of figures. This list contains the title and page number of each figure or table. If you have just a few figures or tables, however, you may omit this list.

Appendix. Ancillary material of interest to some readers goes in appendices. Appendix A might contain résumés of the principal investigators or letters of testimonial. Appendix B might contain examples or a list of previous projects. Other appendices could contain audit procedures, technical graphics, or professional papers cited in the body of the proposal.

Well-written proposals win contracts and business for companies and individuals. In fact, many companies depend entirely on proposals to generate their income, so proposal writing becomes critical. The following checklist summarizes the main parts of proposals.

Checklist for Writing Proposals

Introduction

✓ **Indicate the purpose.** Specify why the proposal is being made.

✓ **Develop a persuasive "hook."** Suggest excellent results, low costs, or exclusive resources. Identify a serious problem or name a key issue or benefit.

Background, Problem, Purpose

✓ **Give necessary background.** Discuss the significance of the proposal and its goals or purposes.

✓ **Introduce the problem.** For unsolicited proposals convince the reader that a problem exists. For solicited proposals show that you fully understand the problem and its ramifications.

Proposal, Plan, Schedule

✓ **Explain the proposal.** Present your plan for solving the problem or meeting the need.

✓ **Discuss plan management and evaluation.** If appropriate, tell how the plan will be implemented and evaluated.

✓ **Outline a timetable.** Furnish a schedule showing what will be done and when.

Staffing

✓ **Promote the qualifications of your staff.** Explain the specific credentials and expertise of the key personnel for the project.

✓ **Mention special resources or equipment.** Show how your support staff and resources are superior to the competition.

Budget

✓ **Show project costs.** For most projects itemize costs. Remember, however, that proposals are contracts.

✓ **Include a deadline.** Here or in the conclusion present a date beyond which the bid figures are no longer valid.

Authorization

✓ **Ask for approval.** Make it easy for the reader to authorize the project (for example, *Sign and return duplicate copy*).

Writing Formal Reports

Formal reports are similar to formal proposals in length, organization, and serious tone. Instead of making an offer, however, formal reports represent the end

FIGURE 14.3 ■ Components in Formal and Informal Reports

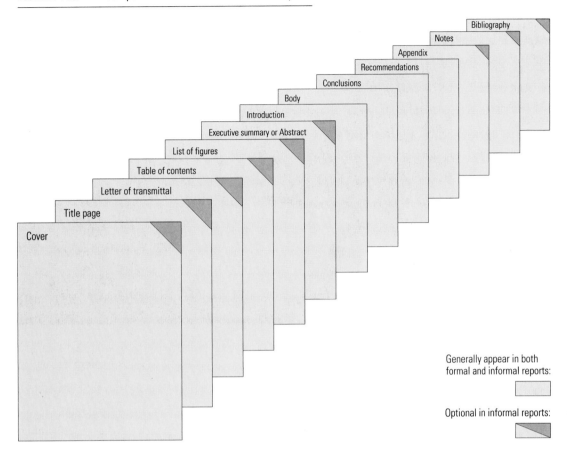

Generally appear in both formal and informal reports:

Optional in informal reports:

product of thorough investigation and analysis. They present ordered information to decision-makers in business, industry, government, or education. In many ways formal reports are extended versions of the analytical business reports presented in Chapter 13. Figure 14.3 shows the parts of a typical formal report, their normal sequence, and parts that might be omitted in informal reports.

Formal reports discuss the results of a process of thorough investigation and analysis.

Components of Formal Reports

A number of front and end items lengthen formal reports but enhance their professional tone and serve their multiple audiences. Formal reports may be read by many levels of managers, along with technical specialists and financial consultants. Therefore, breaking a long formal report into small segments makes its information more accessible and easier to understand for all readers. These segments are discussed here and also illustrated in the model report shown later in the chapter (Figure 14.4). This analytical report studies the recycling program at West Coast College and makes recommendations for improving its operation.

Like proposals, formal reports are divided into many segments to make information comprehensible and accessible.

Cover. Formal reports are usually enclosed in vinyl or heavy paper binders to protect the pages and to give them a professional appearance. Some companies have binders imprinted with their name and logo. The title of the report may appear through a cut-out window or may be applied with an adhesive label.

Corporate training programs typically begin with proposals for funding. No matter how well-intentioned, such programs can't get off the ground without persuasive proposals. Once completed, such programs often require formal reports to describe the project, summarize results, and evaluate success. Future funding is often determined by the effectiveness of the project, as expressed by the accuracy and thoroughness of the concluding report.

Good stationery and office supply stores usually stock an assortment of report binders and labels.

Title page. A report title page, as illustrated in the Figure 14.4 model report, begins with the name of the report typed in uppercase letters (no underlining and no quotation marks). Next comes *Presented to* (or *Submitted to*) and the name, title, and organization of the individual receiving the report. Lower on the page is *Prepared by* (or *Submitted by*) and the author's name plus any necessary identification. The last item on the title page is the date of submission. All items after the title are typed in a combination of upper- and lowercase letters.

A letter of transmittal gives a personalized overview of a formal report.

Letter or memo of transmittal. Generally written on organization stationery, a letter or memorandum of transmittal introduces a formal report. You will recall that letters are sent to outsiders and memos to insiders. A transmittal letter or memo follows the direct pattern and is usually less formal than the report itself (for example, the letter or memo may use contractions and the first-person pronouns *I* and *we*). The transmittal letter or memo (1) announces the topic of the report and tells how it was authorized; (2) briefly describes the project; (3) highlights the report's findings, conclusions, and recommendations if the reader is expected to be supportive; and (4) closes with appreciation for the assignment, instruction for the reader's follow-up actions, acknowledgment of help from others, or an offer to answer questions. If a report is going to different readers, a special transmittal letter or memo should be prepared for each, anticipating what each reader needs to know in using the report.

Table of contents. The table of contents shows the headings in a report and their page numbers. You should wait to prepare the table of contents until after you've completed the report. For short reports you should include all headings. For longer reports you might want to list only first- and second-level headings.

Leaders (spaced or unspaced dots) help guide the eye from the heading to the page number. Or the page number may be typed right after the heading (usually following a comma and a space). Items may be indented in outline form or typed flush with the left margin.

List of figures. For reports with several figures or illustrations, you may wish to include a list of figures to help your readers find them. This list may appear on the same page as the table of contents, space permitting. For each figure or illustration, give the title and page number. Some writers distinguish between tables and all other illustrations, which are called figures. If you make this distinction, you should also prepare separate lists of tables and figures. Because the model report in Figure 14.4 has few illustrations, the writer labelled them all "figures," a method that greatly simplifies numbering.

Executive summary or abstract. Executives and other readers appreciate a summary or abstract that highlights the findings, conclusions, and recommendations of the report. Like proposals, report abstracts are aimed at technical experts and may contain specialized language; executive summaries concentrate on what management needs to know, omitting technical jargon. Whether you are writing an abstract or an executive summary, its length and complexity will be determined by the report. For example, a 100-page report might require a 10-page summary. A 10-page report might need only a 1-page summary—or no summary at all. Longer abstracts may include headings and visual aids to highlight main points. Although the executive summary in Figure 14.4 is only one page long, it includes headings to help the reader see the main divisions immediately. Let your organization's practices guide you in determining the length and form of a summary or abstract.

> **The length and complexity of the abstract or executive summary depend on the length of and audience for the report.**

Introduction. Formal reports begin with an introduction that sets the scene and announces the subject. Because they contain many parts serving different purposes, formal reports have a degree of redundancy. The same information may be contained in the letter of transmittal, summary, and introduction. To avoid sounding repetitious, try to present the information slightly differently. But don't skip the introduction just because you've included some of its information elsewhere. You can't be sure that your reader saw the information earlier. A good report introduction typically covers the following elements, although not necessarily in this order:

- **Background**. Describes events leading up to the problem or need.

- **Problem or purpose**. Explains the report topic and specifies the problem or need that motivated the report.

- **Significance**. Tells why the topic is important. You may wish to quote experts or cite newspapers, journals, books, and other secondary sources to establish the importance of the topic.

- **Scope**. Clarifies the boundaries of the report, defining what will be included or excluded.

- **Organization**. Helps readers by giving them a road map that previews the structure of the report.

Beyond these minimal introductory elements, consider adding any of the following information that is relevant for your readers:

- **Authorization**. Says who commissioned the report. If no letter of transmittal is included, also tell why, when, by whom, and to whom the report was written.

- **Literature review**. Summarizes what other authors and researchers have published on this topic, especially for academic and scientific reports.

- **Sources and methods**. Describes your secondary sources (periodicals, books, databases). Also explain how you collected primary data, including survey size, sample design, and statistical programs used.

- **Definitions of key terms**. Defines words that may be unfamiliar to the audience. Also defines terms with special meanings, such as *small business* when it specifically means businesses with fewer than a specified number of employees.

Body. The principal section in a formal report is the body. It discusses, analyzes, interprets, and evaluates the research findings or solution to the initial problem. This is where you show the evidence that justifies your conclusions. Organize the body into main categories following your original outline or using one of the patterns described earlier (such as time, component, importance, criteria, or convention).

Although we refer to this section as the "body," it doesn't carry that heading. Instead, it contains clear headings that explain each major section. Headings may be functional or talking. Functional headings (such as *Results of the Survey, Analysis of Findings,* or *Discussion*) help the reader recognize the purpose of the section but don't reveal what's in it. Such headings are useful for routine reports or for sensitive topics that may upset readers. Talking headings (for example, *Recycling Habits of Campus Community*) are more informative and interesting, but they don't help readers see the organization of the report. The model report in Figure 14.4 uses functional headings for organizational sections requiring identification ("Introduction," "Conclusions," and "Recommendations") and talking headings to divide the body.

Conclusions. This important section tells what the findings mean, particularly in relation to the original problem. Some writers prefer to intermix their conclusions with the analysis of the findings—instead of presenting the conclusions separately. Other writers place the conclusions before the body so that busy readers can examine the significant information immediately. Still others combine the conclusions and recommendations. Most writers, though, present the conclusions after the body because readers expect this structure. In long reports this section may include a summary of the findings. To improve comprehension, you may present the conclusions in a numbered or bulleted list.

The recommendations section of a formal report offers specific suggestions for solving a problem.

Recommendations. When requested, you should submit recommendations that make precise suggestions for actions to solve the report problem. Recommendations are most helpful when they are practical and reasonable. Naturally, they should evolve from the findings and conclusions. Don't introduce new information in the conclusions or recommendations. As with conclusions, the position of recommendations is somewhat flexible. They may be combined with conclusions, or they may be presented before the body, especially when the audience is eager and supportive. Generally, though, in formal reports they come last.

Recommendations require an introductory sentence, such as *The findings and conclusions in this study support the following recommendations*. When making many recommendations, number them and phrase each as a command, such as *Begin an employee fitness program with a workout room available five days a week*. If appropriate, add information describing how to implement each recommendation. Some reports include a timetable describing the who, what, when, where, and how for putting each recommendation into operation.

Appendix. Incidental or supporting materials belong in appendices at the end of a formal report. These materials are relevant to some readers but not to all. Appendices may include survey forms, copies of other reports, tables of data, computer printouts, and related correspondence. When there is more than one appendix, they are named *Appendix A, Appendix B*, and so forth.

Footnotes, Endnotes, Works Cited, References or Bibliography. Readers look in the notes or bibliography section to find the sources of ideas mentioned in a report. If you use the MLA method of documentation, all citations would be listed alphabetically in the "Works Cited." If you use the APA style, your list would be called "References." With the *Chicago Manual of Style* method, you would cite your references in footnotes or endnotes. Regardless of which method you choose, you must include the author, title, publication, date of publication, page number, and other significant information for all ideas or quotations used in your report. For electronic references include the preceding information plus a description of the electronic address or path leading to the citation. Also include the date on which you located the electronic reference. To see electronic and other citations, examine the list of references at the end of Figure 14.4. Appendix C contains additional information about documentation.

> The reference or bibliography section of a formal report lists the sources of ideas mentioned in the report.

Final Writing Tips

Formal reports are not undertaken lightly. They involve considerable effort in all three phases of writing, beginning with analysis of the problem and anticipation of the audience (as discussed in Chapter 3). The second phase of the writing consists of researching the data, organizing it into a logical presentation, and composing the first draft (Chapter 4). The third phase consists of revising, proofreading, and evaluating (Chapter 5). Although everyone approaches the writing process somewhat differently, the following tips offer advice with problems faced by most writers of formal reports.

> Formal reports require careful attention to all phases of the 3 × 3 writing process.

- **Allow sufficient time**. The main reason given by writers who are disappointed with their reports is "I just ran out of time." Develop a realistic timetable and stick to it.

- **Finish data collection**. Don't begin writing until you've collected all the data and drawn the primary conclusions. Starting too early often means backtracking. For reports based on survey data, compile the tables and figures first.

- **Work from a good outline**. A big project like a formal report needs the order and direction provided by a clear outline, even if the outline has to be revised as the project unfolds.

- **Provide a proper writing environment**. You'll need a quiet spot where you can spread out your materials and work without interruption. Formal reports demand blocks of concentration time.

> Smart report writers allow themselves plenty of time, research thoroughly, draw up a useful outline, and work on a computer.

- **Use a computer**. Writing a report on a computer enables you to keyboard quickly, revise easily, and, with most programs, check spelling and find synonyms readily. A word of warning, though: save your document often and print occasionally so that you have a hard copy. Take these precautions to guard against the grief caused by lost files, power outages, and computer malfunctions.

- **Write rapidly; revise later**. Experts advise writers to record their ideas quickly and save revision until after the first draft is completed. They say that quick writing avoids wasted effort spent in polishing sentences and even sections that may be cut later. Moreover, rapid writing encourages fluency and creativity. However, a "quick-and-dirty" first draft doesn't work for everyone. Some business writers prefer a more deliberate writing style, so consider this advice selectively.

- **Save hard sections**. If some sections are harder to write than others, save them until you've developed confidence and rhythm working on easier topics.

Effective formal reports maintain consistency in verb tenses, avoid first-person pronouns, and use the active voice.

- **Be consistent in verb tense**. Use past-tense verbs to describe completed actions (for example, *the respondents said* or *the survey showed*). Use present-tense verbs, however, to explain current actions (*the purpose of the report is, this report examines, the table shows,* and so forth). Don't switch back and forth between present and past tense in describing related data.

- **Generally avoid *I* and *we***. To make formal reports seem as objective and credible as possible, most writers omit first-person pronouns. This formal style sometimes results in the overuse of passive-voice verbs (for example, *periodicals were consulted* and *the study was conducted*). Look for alternative constructions (*periodicals indicated* and *the study revealed*). It's also possible that your organization allows first-person pronouns, so check before starting your report.

- **Let the first draft sit**. After completing the first version, put it aside for a day or two. Return to it with the expectation of revising and improving it. Don't be afraid to make major changes.

- **Revise for clarity, coherence, and conciseness**. Read a printed copy out loud. Do the sentences make sense? Do the ideas flow together naturally? Can wordiness and flabbiness be cut out? Try reading it aloud to look for awkward or unnatural constructions and unintentional rhymes or alliterations. See Chapter 5 for specific suggestions for revisions.

- **Proofread the final copy three times**. First, read a printed copy slowly for meaning and content. Then read the copy again for spelling, punctuation, grammar, and other mechanical errors. Finally, scan the entire report to check its formatting and consistency (page numbering, indenting, spacing, headings, and so forth).

Putting It All Together

Formal reports in business generally aim to study problems and recommend solutions. Suppose that Alan Christopher, business senator to the Office of Associated Students (OAS) at West Coast College, was given a campus problem to study, resulting in the formal report shown in Figure 14.4.

The campus recycling program, under the direction of Cheryl Bryant and supported by the OAS, was not attracting as much participation as expected. As the campus recycling program began its second year of operation, Cheryl and the OAS wondered if campus community members were sufficiently aware of the program. They also wondered how participation could be increased. Alan volunteered to investigate the problem because of his strong support for environmental causes. He also needed to conduct a research project for one of his business courses, and he had definite ideas for improving the campus OAS recycling program.

Alan's report illustrates many of the points discussed in this chapter. Although it's a good example of typical report format and style, it's not the only way to present a report. There is wide variation in reports.

The following checklist summarizes the report-writing process and the parts of a report in one handy list.

Checklist for Writing Formal Reports

Report Process

✓ **Analyze the report problem and purpose**. Develop a problem question (*Is sexual harassment affecting employees at DataTech?*) and a purpose statement (*The purpose of this report is to investigate sexual harassment at DataTech and recommend remedies*).

✓ **Anticipate the audience and issues**. Consider primary and secondary audiences. What do they already know? What do they need to know? Divide the major problem into subproblems for investigation.

✓ **Prepare a work plan**. Include problem and purpose statements, as well as a description of the sources and methods of collecting data. Prepare a tentative project outline and a work schedule with anticipated dates of completion for all segments of the project.

✓ **Collect data**. Begin by searching secondary sources (books, magazines, journals, newspapers, electronic databases) for information on your topic. Then, if necessary, gather primary data by surveying, interviewing, observing, and experimenting. To ensure accuracy in your documentation, photocopy the title page of all the books, magazines, and other print materials you use.

✓ **Document data sources**. Prepare note cards or separate sheets of paper citing all references (author, date, source, page, and quotation). Select a method of documentation (Chapter 11) and use it consistently.

✓ **Interpret and organize the data**. Arrange the collected information in tables, grids, or outlines to help you visualize relationships and interpret meanings. Organize the data into an outline (Chapter 4).

✓ **Prepare visual aids**. Make tables, charts, graphs, and illustrations—but only if they serve a function. Use visual aids to help clarify, condense, simplify, or emphasize your data.

✓ **Compose the first draft**. At a computer write the first draft from your outline. Use appropriate headings as well as transitional expressions (such as *however*, *on the contrary*, and *in addition*) to guide the reader through the report.

✓**Revise and proofread**. Revise to eliminate wordiness, ambiguity, and redundancy. Look for ways to improve readability, such as bulleted or numbered lists. Proofread three times for (1) word and content meaning, (2) grammar and mechanical errors, and (3) formatting.

✓**Evaluate the product**. Examine the final report. Will it achieve its purpose? Encourage feedback so that you can learn how to improve future reports.

Parts of the Report

✓**Title page**. Balance the following lines on the title page: (1) name of the report (in all caps); (2) name, title, and organization of the individual receiving the report; (3) author's name, title, and organization; and (4) date submitted.

✓**Letter of transmittal**. Announce the topic of the report and explain who authorized it. Briefly describe the project and preview the conclusions, if the reader is supportive. Close by expressing appreciation for the assignment, suggesting follow-up actions, acknowledging the help of others, or offering to answer questions.

✓**Table of contents**. Show the beginning page number where each report heading appears in the report. If you type the page numbers flush right, use leaders (spaced dots) to connect them with the headings.

✓**List of illustrations**. Include a list of tables, illustrations, or figures showing the title of the item and its page number. If space permits, put these lists on the same page with the table of contents.

✓**Executive summary or abstract**. Summarize the purpose, findings, conclusions, and recommendations of the report. The length of the summary will be determined by the length of the report and by your organization's practices.

✓**Introduction**. Explain the purpose of the report; describe its background and significance. Clarify the scope and limitations of the report. Optional items include a review of relevant literature and a description of data sources, methods, and key terms. Close by previewing the report's organization.

✓**Body**. Discuss, analyze, and interpret the research findings or the proposed solution to the problem. Arrange the findings in logical segments following your outline. Use clear, descriptive headings.

✓**Conclusions and recommendations**. Explain what the findings mean in relation to the original problem. If requested, make enumerated recommendations that suggest actions for solving the problem.

FIGURE 14.4 ■ Model Formal Report

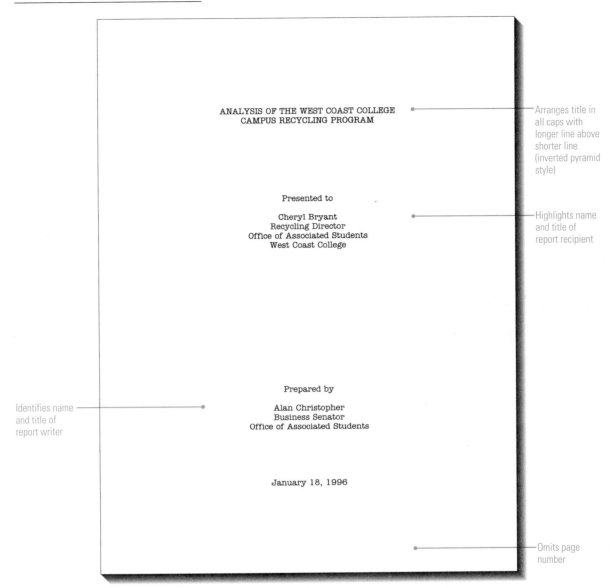

ANALYSIS OF THE WEST COAST COLLEGE
CAMPUS RECYCLING PROGRAM

Presented to

Cheryl Bryant
Recycling Director
Office of Associated Students
West Coast College

Prepared by

Alan Christopher
Business Senator
Office of Associated Students

January 18, 1996

Arranges title in all caps with longer line above shorter line (inverted pyramid style)

Highlights name and title of report recipient

Identifies name and title of report writer

Omits page number

Alan arranges the title page so that the amount of space above the title is equal to the space below the date. If a report is to be bound on the left, move the left margin and centre point ¹/₄ inch to the right. Notice that no page number appears on the title page, although it is counted as page i.

Be careful to avoid anything unprofessional (such as too many type fonts, oversized print, and inappropriate graphics).

FIGURE 14.4 ■ (continued)

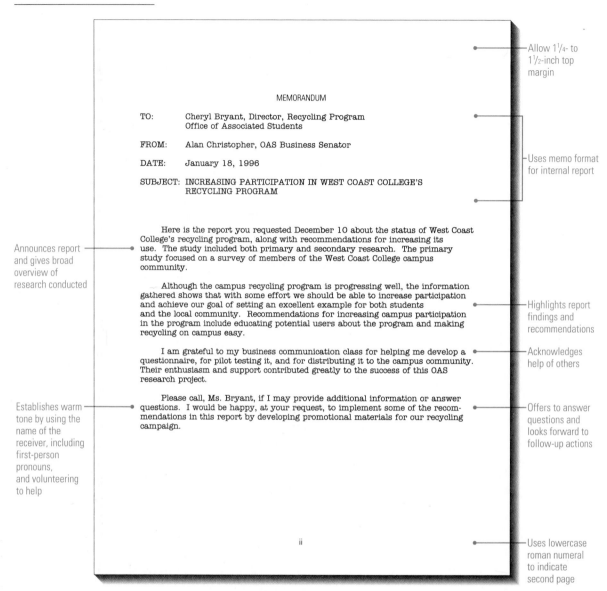

Allow 1¼- to 1½-inch top margin

MEMORANDUM

TO: Cheryl Bryant, Director, Recycling Program
           Office of Associated Students

FROM: Alan Christopher, OAS Business Senator

DATE: January 18, 1996

SUBJECT: INCREASING PARTICIPATION IN WEST COAST COLLEGE'S
           RECYCLING PROGRAM

Uses memo format for internal report

Here is the report you requested December 10 about the status of West Coast College's recycling program, along with recommendations for increasing its use. The study included both primary and secondary research. The primary study focused on a survey of members of the West Coast College campus community.

Announces report and gives broad overview of research conducted

Although the campus recycling program is progressing well, the information gathered shows that with some effort we should be able to increase participation and achieve our goal of setting an excellent example for both students and the local community. Recommendations for increasing campus participation in the program include educating potential users about the program and making recycling on campus easy.

Highlights report findings and recommendations

I am grateful to my business communication class for helping me develop a questionnaire, for pilot testing it, and for distributing it to the campus community. Their enthusiasm and support contributed greatly to the success of this OAS research project.

Acknowledges help of others

Please call, Ms. Bryant, if I may provide additional information or answer questions. I would be happy, at your request, to implement some of the recommendations in this report by developing promotional materials for our recycling campaign.

Establishes warm tone by using the name of the receiver, including first-person pronouns, and volunteering to help

Offers to answer questions and looks forward to follow-up actions

ii

Uses lowercase roman numeral to indicate second page

Because this report is being submitted within his own organization, Alan uses a memorandum of transmittal. Formal organization reports submitted to outsiders would carry a letter of transmittal printed on company stationery.

The margins for the transmittal should be the same as for the report, about 1¼ inches on all sides. If a report is to be bound, add an extra ¼ inch to the left margin.

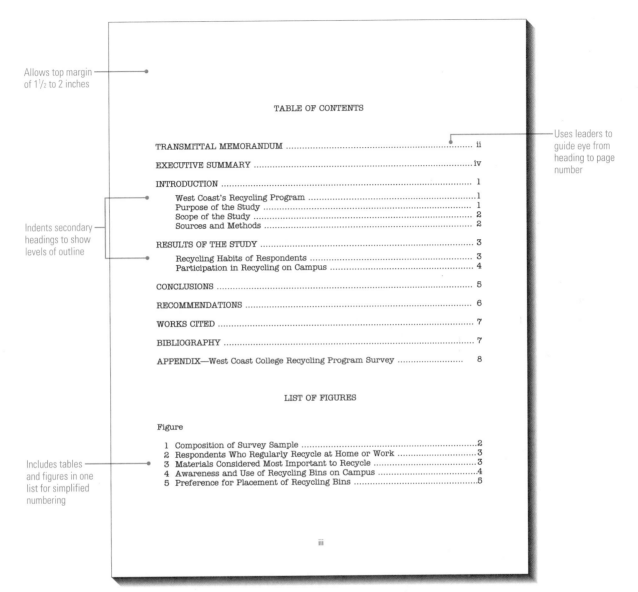

Allows top margin of 1½ to 2 inches

TABLE OF CONTENTS

Uses leaders to guide eye from heading to page number

Indents secondary headings to show levels of outline

LIST OF FIGURES

Figure

Includes tables and figures in one list for simplified numbering

iii

Because Alan's table of contents and list of figures are small, he combines them on one page. Notice that he uses all caps for the titles of major report parts and a combination of upper- and lowercase letters for first-level headings. This duplicates the style within the report.

Some computer programs enable you to generate a table of contents automatically, including leaders and accurate page numbering—no matter how many times you revise!

FIGURE 14.4 ▪ (continued)

EXECUTIVE SUMMARY

Purpose of the Report

The purposes of this report are to (1) determine the West Coast College campus community's awareness of the campus recycling program and (2) recommend ways to increase participation. West Coast's recycling program was intended to respond to the increasing problem of waste disposal, to fulfill its social responsibility as an educational institution, and to meet the demands of legislation requiring individuals and organizations to recycle.

A questionnaire survey was conducted to learn about the campus community's recycling habits and to assess participation in the current recycling program. A total of 220 individuals responded to the survey. Since West Coast College's recycling program includes only aluminum, glass, paper, and plastic at this time, these were the only materials considered in this study.

Recycling at West Coast

Most survey respondents recognized the importance of recycling and stated that they do recycle aluminum, glass, paper, and plastic on a regular basis either at home or at work. However, most respondents displayed a low level of awareness and use of the on-campus program. Many of the respondents were unfamiliar with the location of the bins around campus and, therefore, had not participated in the recycling program. Other responses indicated that the bins were not conveniently located.

The results of this study show that more effort is needed to increase participation in the campus recycling program.

Recommendations for Increasing Recycling Participation

Recommendations for increasing participation in the program include (1) relocating the recycling bins for greater visibility, (2) developing incentive programs to gain the participation of individuals and on-campus student groups, (3) training student volunteers to give on-campus presentations explaining the need for recycling and the benefits of using the recycling program, and (4) increasing advertising about the program.

iv

Tells purpose of report and briefly describes survey

Summarizes findings of survey

Draws primary conclusion

Concisely enumerates four recommendations using parallel (balanced) phrasing

Numbers pages that precede the body with lowercase roman numerals

For readers who want a quick picture of the report, the executive summary presents its most important elements. Alan has divided the summary into three sections for increased readability.

Executive summaries generally contain little jargon or complex statistics; they condense what management needs to know about a problem and its study. Report abstracts, sometimes written in place of summaries, tend to be more technical and are aimed at specialists rather than management.

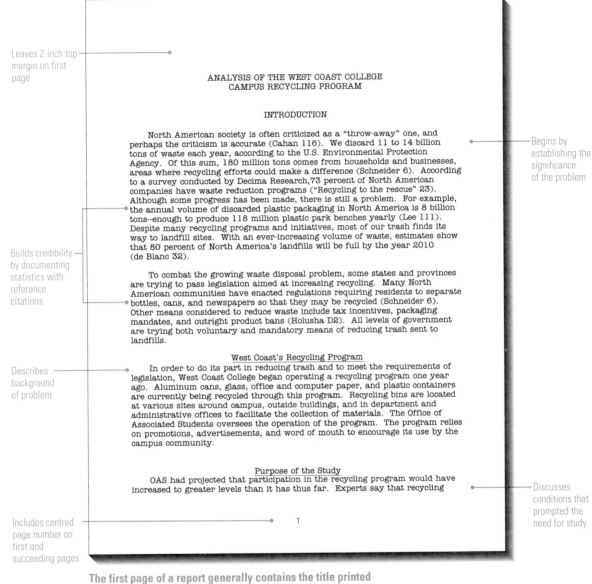

Leaves 2-inch top margin on first page

Begins by establishing the significance of the problem

Builds credibility by documenting statistics with reference citations

Describes background of problem

Discusses conditions that prompted the need for study

Includes centred page number on first and succeeding pages

ANALYSIS OF THE WEST COAST COLLEGE
CAMPUS RECYCLING PROGRAM

INTRODUCTION

North American society is often criticized as a "throw-away" one, and perhaps the criticism is accurate (Cahan 116). We discard 11 to 14 billion tons of waste each year, according to the U.S. Environmental Protection Agency. Of this sum, 180 million tons comes from households and businesses, areas where recycling efforts could make a difference (Schneider 6). According to a survey conducted by Decima Research, 73 percent of North American companies have waste reduction programs ("Recycling to the rescue" 23). Although some progress has been made, there is still a problem. For example, the annual volume of discarded plastic packaging in North America is 8 billion tons--enough to produce 118 million plastic park benches yearly (Lee 111). Despite many recycling programs and initiatives, most of our trash finds its way to landfill sites. With an ever-increasing volume of waste, estimates show that 80 percent of North America's landfills will be full by the year 2010 (de Blanc 32).

To combat the growing waste disposal problem, some states and provinces are trying to pass legislation aimed at increasing recycling. Many North American communities have enacted regulations requiring residents to separate bottles, cans, and newspapers so that they may be recycled (Schneider 6). Other means considered to reduce waste include tax incentives, packaging mandates, and outright product bans (Holusha D2). All levels of government are trying both voluntary and mandatory means of reducing trash sent to landfills.

West Coast's Recycling Program

In order to do its part in reducing trash and to meet the requirements of legislation, West Coast College began operating a recycling program one year ago. Aluminum cans, glass, office and computer paper, and plastic containers are currently being recycled through this program. Recycling bins are located at various sites around campus, outside buildings, and in department and administrative offices to facilitate the collection of materials. The Office of Associated Students oversees the operation of the program. The program relies on promotions, advertisements, and word of mouth to encourage its use by the campus community.

Purpose of the Study

OAS had projected that participation in the recycling program would have increased to greater levels than it has thus far. Experts say that recycling

1

The first page of a report generally contains the title printed 2 inches from the top edge. Titles for major parts of a report (such as *Introduction, Results, Conclusion,* and so forth) are centred in all caps. First-level headings are underlined and printed with upper- and lowercase letters. Second-level headings begin at the side. For illustration of heading formats, see Figure 12.5.

Notice that Alan's report is single-spaced. Many businesses prefer this space-saving format. However, some organizations prefer double-spacing, especially for preliminary drafts. Page numbers may be centred 1 inch from the top or bottom of the page or placed 1 inch from the upper right corner at the margin.

FIGURE 14.4 ■ (continued)

programs generally must operate at least a year before results become apparent (de Blanc 33). The OAS program has been in operation one year, yet gains are disappointing. Therefore, OAS authorized this study to determine the campus community's awareness and use of the program. Recommendations for increasing participation in the campus recycling program will be made to the OAS based on the results of this study.

Scope of the Study

This study investigates potential participants' attitudes toward recycling in general, their awareness of the campus recycling program, their willingness to recycle on campus, and the perceived convenience of the recycling bins. Only aluminum, glass, paper, and plastic are considered in this study, as they are the only materials being recycled on campus at this time. The costs involved in the program were not considered in this study, since a recycling program generally does not begin to pay for itself during the first year. After the first year, the financial benefit is usually realized in reduced disposal costs (Steelman, Desmond, and Johnson 145).

Describes what the study includes and excludes

Sources and Methods

Current business periodicals and newspapers were consulted for background information and to learn how other organizations are encouraging use of in-house recycling programs. In addition, a questionnaire survey (shown in the appendix) of administrators, faculty, staff, and students at West Coast College campus was conducted to learn about this group's recycling habits. In all, a convenience sample of 220 individuals responded to the self-administered survey. The composition of the sample closely resembles the makeup of the campus population. Figure 1 shows the percentage of students, faculty, staff, and administrators who participated in the survey.

Discusses how the study was conducted

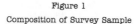

Figure 1

Composition of Survey Sample

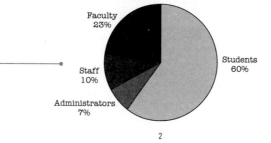

Uses computer-generated pie chart to illustrate makeup of survey

2

Because Alan wants this report to be formal in tone, he avoids "I" and "we." Notice, too, that he uses present-tense verbs to describe his current writing *(this study investigates)*, but past-tense verbs to indicate research completed in the past *(newspapers were consulted)*.

If you use figures or tables, be sure to introduce them in the text. Although it's not always possible, try to place them close to the spot where they are first mentioned. If necessary to save space, you can print the title of a figure at its side.

RESULTS OF THE STUDY

Introduces body of report with functional head

The findings of the study will be presented in two categories: recycling habits of the respondents and participation in the West Coast College recycling program.

Recycling Habits of Respondents

Interprets and discusses results of survey

A major finding of the survey reveals that most respondents are willing to recycle even when not required to do so. Data tabulation shows that 72 percent of the respondents live in an area where neither the city nor the region requires separation of trash. Yet 80 percent of these individuals indicated that they recycle aluminum on a regular basis at home or at work, while another 55 percent said that they recycle paper on a regular basis. Although the percentages are somewhat smaller, many of the respondents also regularly recycle glass (46 percent) and plastic (45 percent). These results, summarized in Figure 2, clearly show that campus respondents are accustomed to recycling the four major materials targeted for the West Coast College recycling program.

Introduces figure as part of another statement

Summarizes findings of survey question in table

Figure 2

Respondents Who Regularly
Recycle at Home or Work

Material	Percentage
Aluminum	80%
Paper	55
Glass	46
Plastic	45

Respondents were asked to rank the importance of recycling the materials collected in the West Coast program. Figure 3 shows that they felt aluminum was most important, although most respondents also ranked the other materials (glass, paper, and plastic) either "extremely important" or "somewhat important" to recycle. Respondents were also asked what materials they actually recycled most frequently, and aluminum again ranked first.

Figure 3

Materials Considered Most Important to Recycle

Presents bar chart for visual comparison of responses to survey question

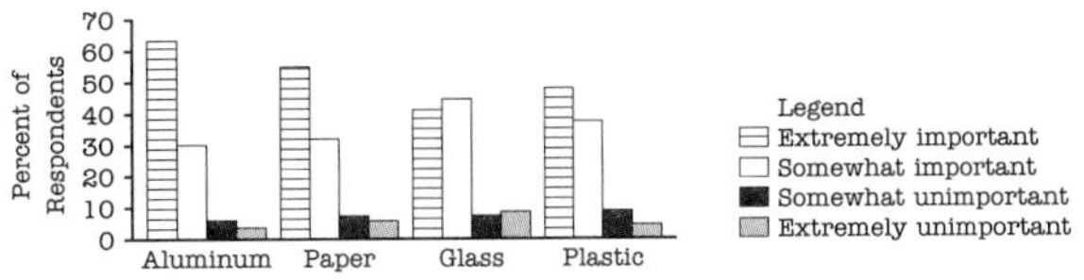

Legend
Extremely important
Somewhat important
Somewhat unimportant
Extremely unimportant

(Percent of Respondents / Aluminum, Paper, Glass, Plastic)

3

Alan selects the most important survey findings to interpret and discuss for readers. Notice that he continues to use present-tense verbs *(the survey reveals* and *these results clearly show)* to discuss the current report.

Because he has few tables and charts, Alan labels them all as "Figures." Notice that he numbers them consecutively, and places the label above each figure. Report writers with a great many tables, charts, and illustrations may prefer to label and number them separately. Tables are labelled as such; everything else is generally called a figure. When tables and figures are labelled separately, tables may be labelled above the table, and figures below the figure.

FIGURE 14.4 ◼ (continued)

Adds personal interpretation

When asked how likely they would be to go out of their way to deposit an item in a recycling bin, 29 percent of the respondents said "very likely," and 55 percent said "somewhat likely." Thus, respondents showed a willingness--at least on paper--to recycle even if it means making a special effort to locate a recycling bin.

Participation in Recycling on Campus

For any recycling program to be successful, participants must be aware of the location of recycling centres and must be trained to use them (de Blanc 33). Another important ingredient in thriving programs is convenience to users. If recycling centres are difficult for users to reach, these centres will be unsuccessful. To collect data on these topics, the survey included questions assessing awareness and use of the current bins. The survey also investigated reasons for not participating and the perceived convenience of current bin locations.

Introduces more findings and relates them to the report's purpose

Student Awareness and Use of Bins

Two of the most significant questions in the survey asked whether respondents were aware of the OAS recycling bins on campus and whether they had used the bins. Responses to both questions were disappointing, as Figure 4 illustrates.

Figure 4

Awareness and Use of Recycling Bins on Campus

Arranges responses from highest to lowest with "unaware" category placed last

Location	Awareness of bins at this location	Use of bins at this location
Cafeteria	38%	21%
Bookstore	29	12
Administration building	28	12
Computer labs	16	11
Library	15	7
Student union	9	5
Classrooms	8	6
Department and administrative offices	6	3
Athletic centre	5	3
Unaware of any bins; have not used any bins	20	7

Only 38 percent of the respondents, as shown in Figure 4, were aware of the bins located outside the cafeteria. Even fewer were aware of the bins outside the bookstore (29 percent) and outside the administration building (28 percent). Equally dissatisfying, only 21 percent of the respondents had used the most visible recycling bins outside the cafeteria.

Clarifies and emphasizes meaning of findings

4

In discussing the results of the survey, Alan highlights those that have significance for the purpose of the report.

As you type a report, avoid widows and orphans (ending a page with the first line of a paragraph or carrying a single line of a paragraph to a new page). Strive to start and end pages with at least two lines of a paragraph, even if a slightly larger bottom margin results.

Other recycling bin locations were even less familiar to the survey respondents and, of course, were little used. These responses plainly show that the majority of the respondents in the West Coast campus community have a low awareness of the recycling program and an even lower record of participation.

Reasons for Not Participating

Respondents offered several reasons for not participating in the campus recycling program. Forty-five percent said that the bins are not convenient to use. Thirty percent said that they did not know where the bins were located. Another 25 percent said that they are not in the habit of recycling. Although many reasons for not participating were listed, the primary one appears to centre on convenience of bin locations.

Discusses results of other survey questions not represented in tables or charts

Location of Recycling Bins

When asked specifically how they would rate the location of the bins currently in use, only 13 percent of the respondents felt that the bins were extremely convenient. Another 35 percent rated the locations as somewhat convenient. Over half the respondents felt that the locations of the bins were either somewhat inconvenient or extremely inconvenient. Recycling bins are currently located outside nearly all the major campus rooms or buildings, but respondents clearly considered these locations inconvenient or inadequate.

In indicating where they would like recycling bins placed (see Figure 5), 42 percent of the respondents felt that the most convenient locations would be inside the cafeteria. Placing more recycling bins near the student union seemed most convenient to another 33 percent of those questioned, while 15 percent stated that they would like to see the bins placed near the vending machines. Ten percent of the individuals responding to the survey did not seem to think that the locations of the bins would matter to them.

Clarifies results of another survey question with textual discussion accompanied by table

Figure 5

Preference for Placement of Recycling Bins

Inside the cafeteria	42%
More in student union	33
Near vending machines	15
Does not matter	10

CONCLUSIONS

Based on the findings of the recycling survey of members of the West Coast College campus community, the following conclusions are drawn:

1. Most members of the campus community are already recycling at home or at work without being required to do so.

5

After completing a discussion of the survey results, Alan articulates what he considers the five most important conclusions to be drawn from this survey. Some writers combine the conclusions and recommendations, particularly when they are interrelated. Alan separated them in his study because the survey findings were quite distinct from the recommendations he would make based on them.

Notice that it is unnecessary to start a new page for the conclusions.

FIGURE 14.4 ■ (continued)

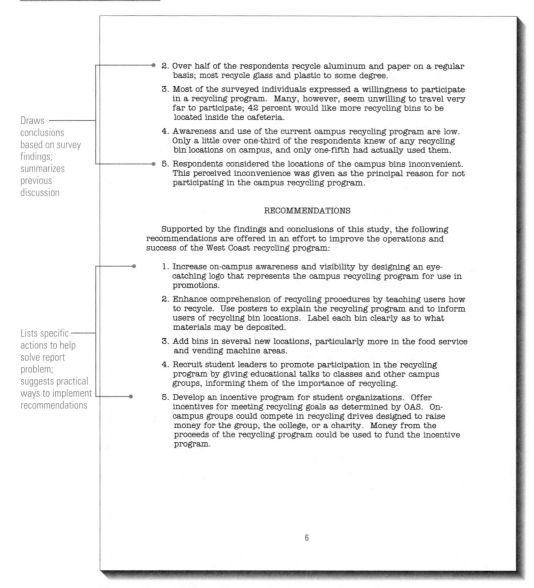

Draws conclusions based on survey findings; summarizes previous discussion

2. Over half of the respondents recycle aluminum and paper on a regular basis; most recycle glass and plastic to some degree.

3. Most of the surveyed individuals expressed a willingness to participate in a recycling program. Many, however, seem unwilling to travel very far to participate; 42 percent would like more recycling bins to be located inside the cafeteria.

4. Awareness and use of the current campus recycling program are low. Only a little over one-third of the respondents knew of any recycling bin locations on campus, and only one-fifth had actually used them.

5. Respondents considered the locations of the campus bins inconvenient. This perceived inconvenience was given as the principal reason for not participating in the campus recycling program.

RECOMMENDATIONS

Supported by the findings and conclusions of this study, the following recommendations are offered in an effort to improve the operations and success of the West Coast recycling program:

Lists specific actions to help solve report problem; suggests practical ways to implement recommendations

1. Increase on-campus awareness and visibility by designing an eye-catching logo that represents the campus recycling program for use in promotions.

2. Enhance comprehension of recycling procedures by teaching users how to recycle. Use posters to explain the recycling program and to inform users of recycling bin locations. Label each bin clearly as to what materials may be deposited.

3. Add bins in several new locations, particularly more in the food service and vending machine areas.

4. Recruit student leaders to promote participation in the recycling program by giving educational talks to classes and other campus groups, informing them of the importance of recycling.

5. Develop an incentive program for student organizations. Offer incentives for meeting recycling goals as determined by OAS. On-campus groups could compete in recycling drives designed to raise money for the group, the college, or a charity. Money from the proceeds of the recycling program could be used to fund the incentive program.

6

The most important parts of a report are its conclusions and recommendations. To make them especially clear, Alan enumerated each conclusion and recommendation. Notice that each recommendation starts with a verb and is stated as a command for emphasis and readability.

Report recommendations are most helpful to readers when they not only make suggestions to solve the original research problem but also describe specific actions to be taken. Notice that this report goes beyond merely listing ideas; instead, it makes practical suggestions for ways to implement the recommendations.

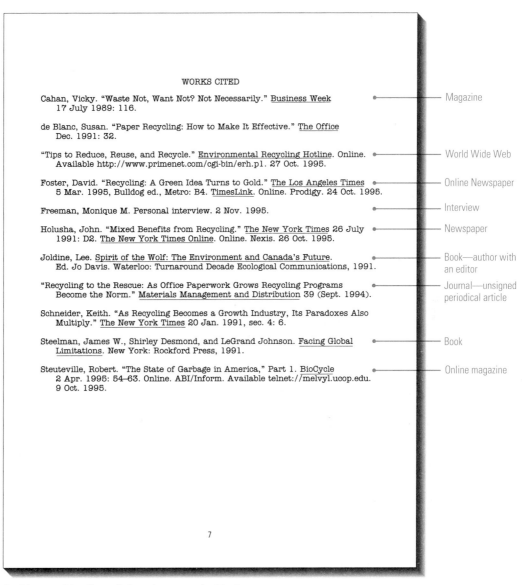

WORKS CITED

Cahan, Vicky. "Waste Not, Want Not? Not Necessarily." <u>Business Week</u>
    17 July 1989: 116. ●————— Magazine

de Blanc, Susan. "Paper Recycling: How to Make It Effective." <u>The Office</u>
    Dec. 1991: 32.

"Tips to Reduce, Reuse, and Recycle." <u>Environmental Recycling Hotline</u>. Online. ●————— World Wide Web
    Available http://www.primenet.com/cgi-bin/erh.pl. 27 Oct. 1995.

Foster, David. "Recycling: A Green Idea Turns to Gold." <u>The Los Angeles Times</u> ●————— Online Newspaper
    5 Mar. 1995, Bulldog ed., Metro: B4. <u>TimesLink</u>. Online. Prodigy. 24 Oct. 1995.

Freeman, Monique M. Personal interview. 2 Nov. 1995. ●————— Interview

Holusha, John. "Mixed Benefits from Recycling." <u>The New York Times</u> 26 July ●————— Newspaper
    1991: D2. <u>The New York Times Online</u>. Online. Nexis. 26 Oct. 1995.

Joldine, Lee. <u>Spirit of the Wolf: The Environment and Canada's Future</u>. ●————— Book—author with
    Ed. Jo Davis. Waterloo: Turnaround Decade Ecological Communications, 1991.   an editor

"Recycling to the Rescue: As Office Paperwork Grows Recycling Programs ●————— Journal—unsigned
    Become the Norm." <u>Materials Management and Distribution</u> 39 (Sept. 1994).   periodical article

Schneider, Keith. "As Recycling Becomes a Growth Industry, Its Paradoxes Also
    Multiply." <u>The New York Times</u> 20 Jan. 1991, sec. 4: 6.

Steelman, James W., Shirley Desmond, and LeGrand Johnson. <u>Facing Global</u> ●————— Book
    <u>Limitations</u>. New York: Rockford Press, 1991.

Steuteville, Robert. "The State of Garbage in America," Part 1. <u>BioCycle</u> ●————— Online magazine
    2 Apr. 1995: 54–63. Online. ABI/Inform. Available telnet://melvyl.ucop.edu.
    9 Oct. 1995.

7

On this page Alan lists all the references cited in the text as well as others that he examined during his research. (Some authors list only those works cited in the report.) Alan formats his citations following the MLA referencing style. Notice that all entries are arranged alphabetically. He underlines book and periodical titles, but italics could be used. When referring to on-line items, he shows the full name of the citation and then identifies the path leading to that reference as well as the date on which he accessed the electronic reference.

Most word processing software today automatically updates citation references within the text and prints a complete list for you. For more information about documentation styles, see Chapter 12 and Appendix C.

FIGURE 14.4 ■ (continued)

Includes copy of survey questionnaire so that report readers can see actual questions

Explains why survey is necessary, emphasizing "you" view

Provides range of answers that will be easy to tabulate

APPENDIX

WEST COAST COLLEGE RECYCLING PROGRAM SURVEY

West Coast College recently implemented a recycling program on campus. Please take a few minutes to answer the following questions so that we can make this program as convenient and helpful as possible for you to use.

1. Please indicate which items you recycle on a regular basis at home or at work.
   (Check *all* that apply.)
   ☐ Aluminum
   ☐ Glass
   ☐ Paper
   ☐ Plastic

2. Do you live in an area where the city/municipality requires separation of waste?
   ☐ Yes   ☐ No

3. How important is it to you to recycle each of the following:

	Extremely Important	Somewhat Important	Somewhat Unimportant	Extremely Unimportant
Aluminum				
Glass				
Paper				
Plastic				

4. How likely would it be for you to go out of your way to put something in a recycling bin?

Very Likely	Somewhat Likely	Somewhat Unlikely	Very Unlikely

5. Which of the following items do you recycle *most* often? (Choose *one* item only.)
   ☐ Aluminum
   ☐ Glass
   ☐ Paper
   ☐ Plastic
   ☐ Other

6. The following are locations of the recycling bins on campus.
   (Check *all* those of which you are aware.)
   ☐ Administration building   ☐ Library
   ☐ Bookstore   ☐ Classrooms
   ☐ Athletic centre   ☐ Student union
   ☐ Computer labs   ☐ Department and administrative offices
   ☐ Cafeteria   ☐ I'm unaware of any of these recycling bins.

8

Alan had space to add the word "Appendix" to the top of the survey questionnaire. If space were not available, he could have typed a separate page with that title on it. If more than one item were included, he would have named them Appendix A, Appendix B, and so on.

Notice that the appendix continues the report pagination.

7. Which of the following recycling bins have you actually used? (Check *all* that you have used.)

- [ ] Administration building
- [ ] Bookstore
- [ ] Athletic centre
- [ ] Computer labs
- [ ] Cafeteria
- [ ] Library
- [ ] Classrooms
- [ ] Student union
- [ ] Department and administrative offices
- [ ] I've not used any of these recycling bins.

8. If you don't recycle on campus, why don't you participate?

- [ ] I'm not in the habit of recycling.
- [ ] I don't know where the bins are.
- [ ] The bins aren't convenient to me.
- [ ] Other _____

9. How do you rate the convenience of the bins' locations?

- [ ] Extremely convenient
- [ ] Somewhat convenient
- [ ] Somewhat inconvenient
- [ ] Extremely inconvenient

10. Which of the following possible recycling bin locations would be most convenient for you to use? (Check *one* only.)

- [ ] Outside each building
- [ ] Near the food service facilities
- [ ] Near the vending machines
- [ ] Does not matter
- [ ] Other _____

11. Please indicate:

- [ ] Student
- [ ] Faculty
- [ ] Administrator
- [ ] Staff

COMMENTS:

Thank you for your responses! Please return the questionnaire in the enclosed, stamped envelope to West Coast College, School of Business, Rm. 321. If you have any questions, please call (555) 450–2391.

9

Anticipates responses but also supplies "Other" category

Uses scale questions to capture degrees of feeling

Requests little demographic data to keep survey short

Offers comment section for explanations and remarks

Concludes with appreciation and instructions

✓ **Appendix**. Include items of interest to some, but not all, readers, such as a survey questionnaire or computer printouts.

✓ **References and bibliography**. If you did not use footnotes in the text, list all references in a section called "Endnotes," "Works Cited," or "References." As an option, include a bibliography showing all the works cited (and perhaps all those consulted) arranged alphabetically by author.

◼ Summary of Learning Goals

1. **Discuss the parts of an informal proposal**. Most informal proposals contain (1) a persuasive introduction that explains the purpose of the proposal and qualifies the writer, (2) background material identifying the problem and project goals, (3) a proposal, plan, or schedule outlining the project, (4) a section describing staff qualifications, (5) a budget showing expected costs, and (6) a request for approval or authorization.

2. **Discuss the special parts of a formal proposal**. Beyond the six components generally contained in informal proposals, formal proposals may include these additional parts: (1) copy of the RFP (request for proposal), (2) letter of transmittal, (3) abstract or executive summary, (4) title page, (5) table of contents, (6) list of illustrations, and (7) appendix.

3. **Distinguish between proposals and formal reports**. Proposals offer to solve problems, provide services, or sell equipment. Formal reports present ordered information to decision-makers in business, industry, government, and education.

4. **Name the parts of a formal report that precede the introduction**. Formal reports may include these beginning parts: (1) vinyl or heavy paper cover, (2) title page, (3) letter of transmittal, (4) table of contents, (5) list of illustrations, and (6) executive summary or abstract.

5. **Outline the topics that might be covered in the introduction of a formal report**. The introduction to a formal report sets the scene by discussing some or all of the following topics: background material, problem or purpose, significance of the topic, scope and organization of the report, authorization, review of relevant literature, sources and methods, and definitions of key terms.

6. **Describe the parts of a formal report that follow the introduction**. The body of a report discusses, analyzes, interprets, and evaluates the research findings or solution to a problem. The conclusion tells what the findings mean and how they relate to the report's purpose. The recommendations tell how to solve the report problem. The last portions of a formal report are the appendix, references, and bibliography.

7. **Specify some tips that aid writers of formal reports**. Before writing, develop a realistic timetable and collect all necessary data. During the writing process, work from a good outline, work in a quiet place, and use a computer. Also, try to write rapidly, revising later. While writing, use verb tenses consistently, and avoid *I* and *we*. A few days after completing the first draft, revise to improve clarity, coherence, and conciseness. Proofread the final copy three times.

CHAPTER REVIEW

1. Proposals are written offers to do what? (Goal 1)
2. What is an RFP? (Goals 1, 2)
3. What are the six principal parts of a letter proposal? (Goal 1)
4. What is a "worry item" in a proposal? (Goal 1)
5. Why should a proposal budget be prepared very carefully? (Goal 1)
6. What is generally contained in a letter of transmittal accompanying a formal report? (Goal 3)
7. What label can a report writer use to describe all illustrations and tables? (Goal 4)
8. How is an abstract different from an executive summary? (Goals 2, 4)
9. What does "scope" mean in relation to a formal report? (Goal 5)
10. Should the body of a report include the heading *Body*? Explain your answer. (Goal 6)
11. What are the advantages of functional headings? Of talking headings? (Goal 6)
12. In a formal report where do most writers place the conclusions? (Goal 6)
13. What kind of materials go in an appendix? (Goal 6)
14. What kind of environment enhances writing? (Goal 7)
15. How should a formal report be proofread? (Goal 7)

DISCUSSION

1. Why are proposals important to many businesses? (Goal 1)
2. How do formal reports differ from informal reports? (Goals 4–6)
3. Why do some parts of formal reports tend to be redundant? (Goals 3, 5)
4. Discuss the three phases of the writing process in relation to formal reports. What activities take place in each phase? (Goals 3–7)
5. **Ethical Issue:** Is it ethical to have someone else proofread a report that you will be turning in for a grade?

PROBLEMS

Consult your instructor to determine the length, format, and emphasis for the following report projects. Some require additional research; others do not.

14.1 Proposal: Outsourcing (Goals 1–3)

Businesses today are doing more "outsourcing" than ever before. This means that they are going outside to find specialists to handle some aspect of their business, such as billing, shipping, or advertising. They're also hiring experts with special training and equipment to solve problems for which they lack the necessary talent and staff. For a business where you have worked or an organization you know, select a problem. Here are some possibilities: poor handling of customer orders, inefficient payroll practices, inadequate computer equipment or software, unsatisfactory inventory control, poor use of sales staff, bad scheduling of employees, poorly trained employees, sexual harassment on the job, and poor telephone techniques. Assume the boss has asked you as a consultant to either solve the problem or study it and tell the organization what to do. Write an informal proposal describing your plan to solve the problem or perform a service. Decide how much you will charge and what staff you will need. Send your letter proposal to your boss.

14.2 Proposal: Profiting from Someone Else's Mistakes (Goals 1–3)

"It's amazing," says the owner of one of the country's largest trucking companies. "Companies will require a vice-president to sign a cheque for over $50, but the guy or girl in the back can sign for a half million dollars worth of raw material." Freight transportation experts claim that business owners may be losing millions of dollars a year in their shipping and receiving departments. Poorly trained and paid workers make costly blunders that anger customers and eat away at profits.

Your company, United Traffic Services (UTS), offers solutions, especially for businesses without a transportation specialist on the payroll. UTS audits freight bills and provides consulting services. Specifically, you and your staff of nine check all shipping charges (monthly or quarterly) to ensure that trucking companies are charging the correct rates. You also give advice on how to get the lowest shipping rates. You know that, because of competitiveness in the trucking industry, any company that is not getting at least a 50 percent discount is paying too much. You work with both outbound and inbound shipments. One of your services involves selecting a good carrier. Because of your expertise and research capabilities, you can advise any company about the most financially stable and reliable truckers. You also advise businesses about packing and labelling to avoid problems. You know that 98 percent of actual freight claims start at the point of origin because cartons are marked incorrectly.

In addition to auditing shipments, you file freight claims for your clients as well as fight wrongful claims against them. You have saved companies thousands of dollars. Two years ago, an Ajax, Ontario, auto products manufacturer was hit by a claim from a trucking company. "In one fell swoop," said the director of operations, "UTS saved us $29 000. We would have owed twice that amount if we didn't have UTS on our side."

Your fee is one half of whatever you save clients on their shipping transactions. They pay nothing if you don't save them money. Write a letter proposal to Steve Hershey, President, Club Enterprises, 468 Industry Avenue, Montreal, QC H1H 4W8 proposing your services. Club Enterprises makes a security device for locking the steering column of a car. Club ships out 2 million pounds of products annually, and it receives 1.5 million pounds of raw materials—most of it by truck. Mr. Hershey has heard of your service and wants to learn more.[4]

14.3 Proposal: Strangers in a Strange Land (Goals 1–3)

"Probably between $2 billion and $2.5 billion a year is lost from expatriate burnout and failed assignments," said an international personnel expert. Businesses suffer this loss when expatriate employees sent on foreign assignments fail to adjust and pack their bags to come home prematurely. As a result, many cross-cultural training programs are being offered by enterprising consultants. North American businesses "are dumb if they don't use cross-cultural training," observed the personnel vice-president for overseas branches of Reynolds Metals Company. The expatriate burnout rate for his company dropped to almost zero after it began using cross-cultural training programs.

Global Visions, a consulting firm in Toronto, offers a number of training programs for employees being sent to other countries. Global provides previsit orientations, career path counselling, foreign language training, and family cultural immersion programs. Mimi Sams, senior partner in

Global Visions, has recently learned that General Motors plans to open a vehicle assembly plant in Kenya. Although the Kenyan government will own 51 percent of the plant and will supply most of the labour force, the plant will be run by GM managers and engineers. Anticipating the need for training the transported staff, Mimi talks to the director of international personnel at GM. He recognizes the benefits of training and would like to consider Global Visions, but he wants a brief written proposal describing the program.

As assistant to Mimi Sams, you have been asked to compose a two-page letter proposal to GM for her approval. Describe your African Total Immersion cross-cultural program. This crash course, conducted at your headquarters in Toronto, includes three full days of intensive training for the employee's entire family. It totally immerses the family, with both group and individual sessions, in African political history, business practices, social customs, and nonverbal communication. The training helps the entire family grasp cultural differences and anticipate symptoms of culture shock such as depression and self-pity.

Because the family's reaction causes more failure of foreign transfers than a manager's work performance, Global Visions focuses on family adjustment. Children and teenagers receive separate training from that of their parents. They sample Indian food, popular in Kenya, and learn how to ride Nairobi public buses and how to speak a little Swahili.

The staff for your African Total Immersion program includes senior trainer Jackson Fox, who was a CUSO official in Nigeria for 12 years, responsible for training hundreds of new recruits. In addition, you have Idi Midamba, adjunct professor of international relations at McMaster University and son of a Kenyan political leader. Rounding out the staff of African specialists is Innawati Witowalidi, a Kenyan who received an M.S. degree in psychology from the University of Toronto. She specializes in the psychological phases of the process of adjustment. This staff has conducted many successful training sessions for U.S. managers and their families heading for Africa. As part of the program, a former expatriate to Kenya shares his experiences with participants.

Global Visions will tailor a three-day program expressly for the GM managers being sent to Kenya. The sum of $8 000 covers training for four people, with $500 for each additional person. The maximum number of trainees for any program is 10. This price includes meals for three days and two nights of lodging at the Lakefront Hilton. It also includes a guidebook to African social and business customs, along with a Swahili primer. For Mimi Sams's signature write a proposal to Jim Rymers, Director, International Programs, General Motors, Ltd., 1900 Colonel Sam Drive, Oshawa, ON L1H 8Q3.[5]

14.4 Proposal: Don't Give Up Your Day Job (Goals 1–3)

As a struggling student, displaced homemaker, or budding entrepreneur, you decide to start your own part-time word processing business in your home. Select a company or professional in your city that might need your services. Often, businesses, medical centres, lawyers, and other professionals have overload transcribing or word processing to farm out to a service. Assess your expertise and equipment. Check out the competition. What do other word processing services offer, and what do they charge? Although many apply a flat hourly rate, you may decide to charge more for items that require much revision. Find out what a particular company needs. Write a letter proposal addressed to a specific individual outlining your plan to offer your services.

14.5 Proposal: Surf's Up in New Brunswick! (Goals 1–3)

Amusement parks around the country are constantly searching for sensational new rides to draw crowds. Theme park giants like Canada's Paramount Wonderland employ their own staffs to develop hot new rides, but smaller parks can't afford such research. Yet they need fresh entertainment to attract new thrill-seekers and keep old customers coming back. "The general theory is that you must add a major new ride every two years and a minor one in between," claims one amusement park expert.

Wave Madness, a one-man Nepean company, designs and installs water-related amusement rides. An enormous success for the young company has been Flow Rider, a surfing machine that shoots water against a curved wall creating a wave effect for riders to "surf" down on their stomachs or on boards. At the WaterWorld Family Water Park in Morden, Manitoba, attendance rose 24 percent, to about 60 000 people, after Flow Rider was installed.

Wave Madness has been approached by the owners of Chatham Fun Park in New Brunswick. For next year's summer season, they want a new water ride, similar to the Flow Rider or Waimea Wave, which is popular at the Raging Waters Park in Edmundston, New Brunswick. But they have a limited budget as well as space and energy restrictions. Although water is scarce, they feel that a scaled-down version of Flow Rider or Waimea Wave might

be possible. Michael Larson, owner and sole proprietor of Wave Madness, is definitely interested in working with the Chatham people, but he's afraid that he would scare them off if he quoted a price for one of his rides outright. Therefore, he decides to submit a proposal outlining his services as a consultant. At $200 an hour he would be able to talk to them about what they need and how best it can be achieved. If they decide to install one of his rides, his consultation fees would be waived.

In his proposal Larson wants to describe one of his new rides: Master Blaster, a roller coaster using a high-powered stream of water to carry people along. The feeling of being pushed uphill is eerie and exciting, according to users at another park. This new ride is less expensive to install and operate than Flow Rider. On the other hand, he could possibly scale down Flow Rider, which is very popular because of its speed. The surfer moves at only two or three miles an hour down the face of the wall. But the water races past at 20 miles an hour, twice as fast as an ocean wave.

Because the Chatham Fun Park owners want action quickly, Larson develops a tentative schedule. Conferring with the owners would probably take about two days; examining the site and working out the placement of a ride would take about one week; installation of a new ride usually requires 30 working days, weather permitting; testing and adjusting the ride requires two weeks.

Michael Larson comes to you, a writing specialist, to help him with his proposal. His background includes a law degree and experience as a surfer and real estate developer. When he began developing water rides, he obtained technical help at Scripps Institution of Oceanography, a research facility in La Jolla, California. His greatest success thus far has been Flow Rider. He designs and tests every ride himself, never leaving a project until it is installed and working successfully.

Work out a schedule that ensures the ride would be ready for the park's opening on May 1. For Michael Larson's signature write a proposal addressed to William Langford, Chatham Entertainment, Ltd., 37 Elizabeth Street, Chatham, NB E1N 3P5.[6]

14.6 Research Report: Car Insurance (Goals 4–7)

Costs for car insurance and levels of customer satisfaction vary greatly from one company to another. One of your tasks as a research analyst for Consumers Union is tracking insurance data for provincial automobile associations. From the most current *Consumer Reports* magazine article on car insurance, select five representative or well-known insurance carriers that operate in your province. Assume that James Michelin, director of your provincial automobile association, has asked you to report on these five companies. He's interested in the degree of customer satisfaction, claims problems, nonclaims problems, delayed payments, drop rates, and annual premiums. To investigate and compare premiums, use the figures provided by *Consumer Reports* for typical urban customers. Draw conclusions about these five insurance carriers. Make recommendations to Mr. Michelin, who will be distributing your information to members of the automobile association. Address your report to James Michelin, Director, Provincial Automobile Association in the capital of your province.

14.7 Research Report: Quality Circles (Goals 4–7)

Research shows that 60 percent of Fortune 500 firms either have implemented or are experimenting with different types of employee involvement programs, such as work teams, quality circles, and workplace democracy councils. In large and small firms these programs are thought to reap many benefits—from increasing production to boosting morale. Mike Rivera, vice-president of operations at DataTech, which employs about 80 electronics assemblers and 30 supporting employees, wants to learn more about these programs. He asks you, his executive assistant, to prepare a report that investigates how other companies have used them. He's particularly interested in safety applications. Could quality circles or work teams improve DataTech's safety record? How are such programs operated at other companies? Collect secondary data, analyze it, draw conclusions, and make recommendations in a letter report to Mike Rivera.

14.8 Formal Report: Breaking Through the Glass Ceiling (Goals 4–7)

Only 3 to 5 percent of all senior executives in corporate North America are women. Some observers suggest that a glass ceiling prevents women from breaking through into upper management. You have been asked by the Canadian Management Association to investigate the success of efforts made in the past decade to train and promote female executives. Does a glass ceiling exist? Discuss some of the programs involving mentoring, coaching, women's councils, and management incentives. Develop recommendations directed toward female students majoring in business or management. Suggest how they can improve their chances of moving up the career ladder when they enter the work world. Address your report to Barbara M. Loring, Chair, Women's Advisory Council, CMA.[7]

14.9 Formal Report: Entrepreneurial Women (Goals 4–7)

By the year 2000, 40 to 50 percent of all businesses will be owned by women. As an intern at the North American Association of Women in Business, you have been asked to collect information for a booklet to be distributed to women who inquire about starting businesses. Specifically, you have been asked to find articles describing three or four women who have started their own businesses. Examine why they started their businesses, how they did it, and how successful they were. In your report draw conclusions about what kinds of women start businesses, why they do it, what kinds of businesses they are likely to start, and what difficulties they face. Speculate on the dramatic increase in the number of female business owners. Make recommendations to women about starting businesses. Use your research skills to prepare a report to Rochelle Robinson, Director, North American Association of Women in Business.

14.10 Collaborative Formal Report: Lending a Helping Hand to the Student Council (Goals 4–7)

Volunteer your class to conduct research aimed at a specific problem facing your campus student council. Ask the president of your campus council to visit your class to discuss a problem that requires research. Most student councils want to learn what students think about their activities, projects, and use of resources. However, councils generally lack the expertise and staff needed to gather reliable data. Question the council president to isolate the issues to be investigated. For example, the council may want students to prioritize activities deserving support. With a limited budget, what activities should the council fund: concerts, lectures, intramural sports, movies, a country store, or something else? Other questions may face the leadership: Should the student council set up a recycling centre? Should it sponsor an adult literacy volunteer program? How should these programs be implemented?

Once a problem for investigation has been selected, divide into groups of three to five to draw up a survey questionnaire. Evaluate each group's questionnaire in class, and select the best one. Pilot-test the questionnaire. Administer the revised questionnaire to a targeted student group. Tabulate the findings. In teams of three to five or individually, write a report to the council president discussing your findings, conclusions, and recommendations.

FIGURE 14.5 ■ 21st Century Insurance Company Policyholder Survey

Response to statement "I am able to read and understand the language and provisions of my policy."					
Age Group	Strongly Agree	Agree	Undecided	Disagree	Strongly Disagree
18–34	2%	9%	34%	41%	14%
35–49	2	17	38	33	10
50–64	1	11	22	35	31
65+	1	2	17	47	33

14.11   Formal Report: Fast-Food Checkup (Goals 4–7)

Select a fast-food franchise in your area. Assume that the national franchising headquarters has received complaints about the service, quality, and cleanliness of the unit. You have been sent to inspect and to report on what you see. Visit on two or more occasions. Make notes on how many customers were served, how quickly they received their food, and how courteously they were treated. Observe the number of employees and supervisors working. Note the cleanliness of observable parts of the restaurant. Inspect the washroom as well as the exterior and surrounding grounds. Sample the food. Your boss is a stickler for detail; he has no use for general statements like *The washroom was not clean*. Be specific. Draw conclusions. Are the complaints justified? If improvements are necessary, make recommendations. Address your report to Lawrence C. Kelsey, President.

14.12   Formal Report: Readability of Insurance Policies (Goals 4–7)

The 21st Century Insurance Company is concerned about the readability of its policies. Provincial legislators are beginning to investigate complaints of policyholders who say they can't understand their insurance policies. One judge lambasted insurers, saying, "The language in these policies is bureaucratic gobbledegook, jargon, double-talk, a form of officialese, bureaucratese, and insurancese that does not qualify as English. The burden upon organizations is to write policies in a manner designed to communicate rather than to obfuscate." Taking the initiative in improving its policies, 21st Century hires you as a consultant to study its standard policy and make recommendations.

Examine a life, fire, or health insurance policy that you own or one from a friend or relative. Select one that is fairly complex. Determine its readability level by calculating its Fog Index (Chapter 5) for several selections. Study the policy for jargon, confusing language, long sentences, long words and unclear antecedents. Evaluate its format, print size, paper and print quality, amount of white space, and use of headings. Does it have an index or glossary? Are difficult terms defined? How easy is it to find specifics, should a policyholder want to check something?

In addition to the information you collect from your own examination of the policy, 21st Century gives you the data shown in Figure 14.5 from a recent policyholder survey. Prepare a report for Heather Kwan, Vice-President, 21st Century Insurance Company, discussing your analysis, conclusions, and recommendations for improving its basic policy.

14.13   Formal Report: Doing Your Own Thing (Goals 4–7)

In a business, organization, or field you know, think about a problem or issue that needs to be investigated. Assume that a president, owner, supervisor, or executive asks you to examine the problem or issue and analyze its causes and ramifications. Consider ways to solve the problem or define the issue. Draw conclusions based on your analysis. Make specific recommendations for implementing changes necessary to achieve the solution. You may need to design a questionnaire and circulate it. Be sure to narrow the problem down enough so that it can be broken into three to five segments or factors.

14.14 Collaborative Formal Report: Intercultural Communication (Goals 4–7)

North American businesses are expanding into foreign markets with manufacturing plants, sales offices, and branch offices abroad. Unfortunately, many North Americans have little knowledge of or experience with people from other cultures. To prepare for participation in the global marketplace, collect information for a report focused on a Pacific Rim, Latin American, or European country where English is not spoken. Before selecting the country, though, consult your campus international student program for volunteers who are willing to be interviewed. Your instructor may make advance arrangements seeking international student volunteers.

In teams of three to five, collect information about your target country from the library and other sources. Then invite an international student representing your target country to be interviewed by your group. In your primary and secondary research, investigate the topics listed in Figure 14.6. Confirm what you learn in your secondary research by talking to your interviewee. When you complete your research, write a report for the CEO of your company (make up a name and company). Assume that your company plans to expand its operations abroad. Your report should advise the company's executives of social customs, family life, attitudes, religions, education, and values in the target country. Remember that your company's interests are business-oriented; don't dwell on tourist information. Write your report individually or in teams.[8]

14.15 Formal Reports Requiring Secondary Research (Goals 4–7)

Select one of the following topics for a report. Discuss with your instructor its purpose, scope, length, format, audience, and data sources. For each topic analyze your findings, draw conclusions, and make logical recommendations. Your instructor may ask teams to do the secondary research.

a. How does the compensation of North American executives compare with that of Japanese executives?

b. How are corporations managing drug and alcohol abuse among employees?

c. Are corporate fitness programs worth their costs?

d. Has the image of women in advertisements today changed from that shown 15 years ago?

e. How are businesses dealing with computer fraud and malice?

f. Should McDonald's expand its company-owned and franchise restaurants in Latin America and Asia?

g. Should environmentalists engage in junk-mail promotions to advertise their causes?

h. What is the best way for you to invest $100 000?

i. Should you invest in an event-planning franchise that specializes in children's parties?

j. Of three locations, which is the best for a new McDonald's (or Dairy Queen, Subway, or franchise of your choice)?

k. What magazines represent the best advertising choice for Reebok (or a product with which you are familiar)?

l. What effects do aromas have on the senses, and how can aromas be used to advantage in the workplace?

14.16 Formal Reports Requiring Primary Research (Goals 4–7)

Select one of the following topics for a report. Discuss with your instructor its purpose, scope, length, format, audience, and data sources. For each topic analyze your findings, draw conclusions, and make logical recommendations. Your instructor may ask teams to complete the primary research.

a. How can your community improve its image and attract new businesses?

b. How can your community improve its recycling efforts?

c. Does your campus need to add or improve a student computer lab?

d. How can the associated student organization (or a club of your choice) increase its membership and support on this campus?

e. Can the registration process at your college or university be improved?

f. Are the requirements for your degree realistic and relevant?

g. How can drug and alcohol abuse be reduced in your community?

h. What is a significant student problem on your campus, and how can it be solved?

i. What does an analysis of local and national newspapers reveal about employment possibilities for college and university graduates?

j. What demographic characteristics (age, sex, income, major, socioeconomic status, family, employment, interests, and so forth) does the typical student have on your campus?

FIGURE 14.6 ■ Intercultural Interview Topics and Questions

Social Customs

1. What is the reaction of people to strangers? Friendly? Hostile? Reserved?
2. How do people greet each other?
3. What are the proper etiquette when you enter a room? Bow? Nod? Shake hands with everyone?
4. How are names used for introductions? Is it proper to inquire about a person's occupation or family?
5. What are the attitudes toward touching?
6. How does one express appreciation for an invitation to someone's home? Take a gift? Send flowers? Write a thank-you note? Are any gifts taboo?
7. Are there any customs related to how or where one sits?
8. Are any facial expressions or gestures considered rude?
9. How close do people stand when talking?
10. What is the attitude toward punctuality in social situations? In business situations?
11. What is the etiquette about looking people in the eye?
12. What gestures indicate agreement? Disagreement?

Family Life

1. What is the basic unit of social organization? Basic family? Extended family?
2. Do women work outside of the home? In what occupations?

Housing, Clothing, and Food

1. Are there differences in the kind of housing used by different social groups? Differences in location? Differences in furnishings?
2. What occasions require special clothing?
3. Are some types of clothing considered taboo?
4. What is appropriate business attire for men? For women?
5. How many times a day do people eat?
6. What types of places, food, and drink are appropriate for business entertainment? Where is the seat of honour at a table?

Class Structure

1. Into what classes is society organized?
2. Is social status determined by racial, religious, or economic factors?
3. Are there any minority groups? What is their social standing?

Political Patterns

1. Are there any immediate threats to the political survival of the country?
2. How is political power manifested?
3. What channels are used for expressing popular opinion?
4. What information media are important?
5. Is it polite to talk politics in social situations?

FIGURE 14.6 ■ (continued)

Religion and Folk Beliefs

1. To which religions do people belong? Is one predominant?

2. Do religious beliefs influence daily activities?

3. Which places have sacred value? Which objects? Which events?

4. How do religious holidays affect business activities?

Economic Institutions

1. What are the country's principal products?

2. Are workers organized into unions?

3. How are businesses owned? By family units? By large public corporations? By the government?

4. What is the standard work schedule?

5. Is it appropriate to do business by telephone?

6. Is participatory management used?

7. Are there any customs related to exchanging business cards?

8. What shows status in an organization? Private office? Secretary? Furniture?

9. Are businesspeople expected to socialize before conducting business?

Value Systems

1. Is competitiveness or cooperation more prized?

2. Is thrift or enjoyment of the moment more valued?

3. Is politeness more important than factual honesty?

4. What are the attitudes toward education?

5. Do women own or manage businesses? If so, how are they treated?

6. What are people's views of North Americans? Do North Americans offend you? What has been hardest for you to adjust to in Canada? How could Canadians make this adjustment easier for you?

14.17 Formal Report: The Perfect Résumé (Goals 4–7)

What do personnel administrators and recruiters really want to see in the résumés of job applicants? Assume that the Canadian Association of Personnel Administrators conducts continuing research to answer that very question. Each year this organization samples its members regarding résumé preferences. Some of the data collected for 1985, 1990, and 1995 are shown in Figure 14.7. The CAPA uses a stratified random sample ensuring that an appropriate number of personnel administrators from small, medium, and large businesses are included (small businesses employ fewer than 100 people; medium, 100–999; and large, 1000 plus). Each year 500 questionnaires are sent; this year 378 usable questionnaires were returned, and this figure is similar to that received in previous surveys.

As a research assistant for the CAPA, analyze the data and prepare a report to be submitted to your boss, Dr. Nancy M. Taylor. Eventually, the report will be distributed to CAPA members, college and university placement offices, and the news media. The CAPA résumé report has become a popular tool among colleges and universities, which use it to keep their students informed of current résumé practices. Your boss expects you to interpret the findings and speculate about why personnel administrators have responded as they have. Dr. Taylor may add her ideas to the report later, but she wants your analysis first. In addition to the data for 1985, 1990, and 1995, the most recent survey (1995) posed two new questions, shown in Figures 14.8 and 14.9. These questions dealt with correctness and length of résumés as well as the average time each personnel administrator spends reading a résumé.

FIGURE 14.7 ■ CAPA Survey on the Importance of Résumé Items and Formats

Résumé Item	Percentage of respondents who considered résumé items important		
	1985	**1990**	**1995**
Name, address, telephone number	100%	100%	100%
Degree	100	100	100
Name of college	100	100	100
Titles of jobs held	99	99	100
Names of previous employers	98	97	100
Special aptitudes, skills	90	91	95
Job, career objective	73	84	92
Awards, scholarships, honours, achievements	88	89	91
Grade point average	85	89	91
Willingness to relocate	74	82	90
Workplace achievements (learning, contributions, accomplishments)	72	81	89
Professional organizations	67	74	84
College or university activities	85	83	84
References shown on résumé	79	51	32
Note saying that references would be supplied on request	35	21	20
Summary of qualifications	25	42	72
Reasons for leaving jobs	54	37	29
Name of high school	20	14	4
High school grades	18	15	5
High school activities, awards	19	14	5
List of college and university courses completed	42	34	21
Social insurance number	32	35	18
Religion, race	10	5	1
Photograph	16	11	2
Marital status	30	19	2
Height and weight	13	8	0
Church involvement	13	8	0
Birthdate	21	17	3
Health	34	19	6
Résumé Format			
Preference for traditional, reverse-chronological format	78	81	88
Preference for functional, skills-oriented format	22	19	12

FIGURE 14.8 ■ CAPA Survey on Résumé Correctness and Length

Factor	Strongly Agree	Agree	Neutral	Disagree	Strongly Disagree	Not Sure
Response to statement "The following factor would cause me to lose interest in a candidate."						
Poor grammar	63%	34%	1%	1%	0%	1%
More than one spelling error	51	42	4	2	0	1
Incorrect word choice	15	51	26	6	0	2
One spelling error	13	37	31	18	1	0
Use of abbreviations	4	18	49	22	4	3
More than one typing error	39	44	10	6	0	1
Poorly reproduced	21	44	25	7	1	2
Poor margins	7	30	42	13	4	4
One typing error	11	27	41	18	2	1
Poor organization	26	52	18	2	1	1
Too long	23	33	30	11	1	2
Too condensed	11	35	35	13	1	5

FIGURE 14.9 ■ CAPA Survey on Average Reading Time per Résumé

Time in Seconds	Percentage of Recruiters
1–29	1%
30–60	26
61–90	15
91–120	16
121–180	28
181+	11
No response	3

Draw conclusions and make recommendations for job applicants. Define any terms that students, a primary audience for the report, may not understand. Write a memo report to Dr. Nancy M. Taylor, Director of Research.

14.18 Formal Report: Writing Skills for CGAs (Goals 4–7)

For years practitioners from all types and sizes of accounting firms have complained about the weak communication skills of those entering the profession. Assume that the Canadian Association of Certified General Accountants recently conducted a study investigating the communication skills of new accountants. In a survey questionnaire distributed to managing partners of 150 of the largest accounting firms in Canada, 97 partners responded. Some of the results from the study are shown in Figure 14.10.

As a research analyst for the CACGA, interpret the findings and make recommendations to the association.

Two issues are particularly important to the CACGA, although these issues were not addressed directly in the survey. The first issue concerns the essay portion of the CGA examination. The exam currently contains essay questions covering auditing theory and business laws, as well as accounting problems for which narrative solutions must be written. Critics want to eliminate all essay questions, contending that the exam is too long, too expensive to administer, and too subjective. A second issue concerns recommendations for colleges offering accounting education. Should the CACGA recommend accounting curricula to colleges and universities that include more or fewer communication courses? In your analysis consider the profession as a whole in addition to the two issues presented here. Address your report to Richard M. Tarsky, Executive Director, Canadian Association of Certified General Accountants.

FIGURE 14.10 ▓ Survey Results of Canadian Association of CGAs

1. How important are the following communication tasks and skills for "new" accountants?

	Very Important	Somewhat Important	Somewhat Unimportant	Totally Unimportant	Don't Know No Response
Written Communication					
Audit reports	11%	18%	34%	12%	25%
Articles for publication	9	10	43	21	17
Memos	31	48	11	4	6
Reports	42	38	10	3	7
Letters	28	31	25	6	10
Proposals	16	23	42	13	6
Oral Communication					
Meeting, conference skills	45	33	13	4	5
Interviewing	38	35	16	7	4
Presentations	24	38	21	11	6
Formal speechmaking	7	14	49	23	7

2. Evaluate the level of communication ability of the "new" accountants who have joined your firm.

	Very Important	Somewhat Important	Somewhat Unimportant	Totally Unimportant	Don't Know No Response
Written Communication					
Reports	79%	10%			11%
Memos	55	31	5%		9
Letters	53	39			8
Proposals	81	7			12
Audit reports	71	18			11
Articles for publication	86	2	2		10
Oral Communication					
Speeches	52	31	5		12
Presentations	39	45	7		9
Meetings/conferences	47	39	5		9
Client interviews	58	34			8

3. Indicate your agreement with the following statement:

	Agree	Disagree	No Opinion
The primary mission of accounting education should be			
a. preparation for the CGA examination	14%	80%	6%
b. development of well-rounded individuals	91	4	5

4. If you could design a course or program to develop communication skills, what would it contain?

Representative answers "More emphasis on writing," "extensive case studies requiring brief, concise explanations," "require considerably more nontechnical classes to prepare the accountant for his environment as part of graduation requirement for a 5-year curriculum," "courses to develop written and oral communication skills in college and continued in training sessions by employers in workshop fashion," "more required written reports in schools to be graded skillfully and critically by competent teachers." The overall emphasis was on "more communication course work."

Presentation Skills

Speaking Skills

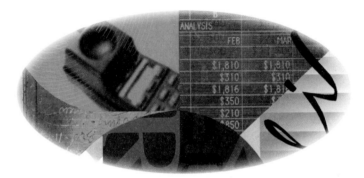

Walt Disney Imagineering

Jon Georges felt his palms growing sweaty. He surveyed the room packed with 50 Japanese financiers and managers gathered on a sultry, grey morning in Tokyo to hear his presentation. His stomach flip-flopped when he remembered how many employees back in Los Angeles were depending on him and his team to win approval for this project, an extensive addition to Tokyo Disneyland.

The proposal was to add three new attractions based on classic Disney animated films. One of the planned attractions would be a major children's ride similar to the perennial Disneyland favourite, "Dumbo the Flying Elephant." Another would feature an outdoor garden maze, with a network of hedge passageways for children to wander through. For the past year Jon and a Walt Disney Imagineering design team had been working intensively on these ideas.

Preparations and all work would stop, though, without a successful presentation before this group, the owners and operators of Tokyo Disneyland. Jon and the entire team had to convince the assembled Japanese that these new feature attractions, as well as associated merchandise shops and a large restaurant, would be exciting and profitable additions to the existing theme park.

> *"Before every formal presentation I ... suffer butterflies. But now I'm able to channel my surging adrenalin ... it actually helps me perform better."*

At some point everyone in business has to sell his or her ideas, and such persuasion is usually done in person. Like most of us, Jon does not consider himself a professional speaker. "I was so afraid of public speaking that I totally avoided such classes in high school," he admits. "In college I started a couple of speech courses but always dropped out. Finally, though, I faced the medicine and took a night class. A lot of fear surfaced, but the experience was very helpful." For Jon poise and confidence grew as he found more opportunities to perform while progressing in his career.

Immediately after graduating from UCLA, Jon was hired by Walt Disney Imagineering as an exhibit coordinator. One of his first tasks was working with a pre-Columbian art exhibit for Epcot Center in Florida. Then he was promoted to assistant show producer and finally to show producer. As leader of a creative team, he now develops new ideas for theme park rides and attractions.

In this position Jon makes both formal and informal presentations. He enjoys the informal meetings that require him to describe a current design project to a vice president who may drop in for a quick update. "Ninety percent of our presentations are done informally," observes Jon. "These presentations require little planning because they simply grow out of what we've been doing." Formal presentations, however, are an entirely differ-

ent story. They require careful preparation, particularly when they are part of a collaborative effort with an important project riding on the outcome.

Understanding the audience and anticipating its reaction are integral parts of Jon's preparations for formal presentations. For the Tokyo Disneyland project Jon and the Disney Imagineering team wanted to present their concepts in broad terms to see if the financiers liked the total idea. But Jon also knew that this audience would want details. Therefore, he and the project managers had to be prepared to answer specific questions involving engineering facts, such as the durability of the metal used in the track to make the children's ride. "Even when a project is in the design stages," says Jon, "Japanese businessmen tend to want particulars like the colour of the concrete, the number of restrooms, and the exact location of an exit."

Other adaptations Jon made for the Tokyo presentation involved choice of language and presentation style. Carefully avoiding Disney and design jargon, Jon consciously used common words and simple sentences, which the interpreter had little trouble translating into Japanese. While the interpreter delivered a sentence, Jon mentally shaped the next one to eliminate words and phrases that might cause misunderstandings.

In readying his part of the Tokyo presentation, Jon kept in mind these important elements: organization, visuals, and focus. After a year's preparatory work on this project, he had thousands of details he would have been delighted to share with listeners. He also understood, though, the importance of simplicity in his oral presentation. To be effective, his presentation demanded a powerful focus. And that focus wasn't hard to find. He had to convince his Japanese listeners that this new children's "land" would enhance the value of Tokyo Disneyland and would draw more visitors through the turnstiles. Every aspect of his presentation had to emphasize this benefit for his audience.

Although Jon and his team scored a big triumph in Tokyo, he admits to having felt quite nervous. "Before every formal presentation," he confesses, "I always, always suffer butterflies. But now I'm able to channel my surging adrenalin into an increased level of excitement. It's no longer fear; I look upon it as enthusiasm, and it actually helps me perform better."

Like Jon Georges, many future businesspeople fail to take advantage of opportunities to develop speaking skills when they are students. Yet, such skills often play an important role in a successful career. This chapter develops skills in making oral presentations, using telephones and voice mail, and participating in meetings and conferences.[1] ■

The concepts of Main Street, U.S.A., and Cinderella Castle are easily transported to Tokyo Disneyland, but verbal and visual jokes do not translate as easily. Jon Georges and other Imagineers work closely with local comedy writers to reinterpret humour that works in North America but falls flat in Japan. Today's global economy increasingly challenges communicators to learn about local cultures and shape messages accordingly.

Oral Presentations

"This speech would have been a lot easier if y'all hadn't shown up today," confesses a student as she begins her required classroom presentation.[2] She's certainly not alone in her feelings. Faced with making a speech, most of us feel great stress. The physiological responses that you experience are much like those triggered by a car accident or a narrow escape from a dangerous situation.[3] But giving oral presentations is a common requirement for businesspeople. You might, for example, need to describe your company's expansion plans to your banker or persuade management to support your proposed marketing strategy. You might have to make a sales pitch before customers or speak to a professional gathering.

For any presentation you can reduce your fears and lay the foundation for a professional performance by concentrating on four things: preparation, organization, visual aids, and delivery.[4]

Preparing an Effective Oral Presentation

Getting ready for an oral presentation is similar to the prefatory process for writing a report. That process begins with serious thinking about your purpose and your audience.

Preparing for an oral presentation means identifying the purpose and knowing the audience.

Knowing your purpose. Deciding what you want to accomplish in a presentation is the most important part of your preparation. Do you want to persuade management to install networked computers? Do you want to inform customer service reps of three important ways to prevent miscommunication? Whether your goal is to persuade or to inform, you must have a clear idea of where you are going. At the end of your presentation, what do you want your listeners to remember or do?

Suppose that Eric Evans, a loan officer at Dominion Trust, had to answer such questions as he planned a talk for a class in small business management. Eric's former business professor had asked him to return to campus and give the class advice about borrowing money from banks in order to start new businesses. Because Eric knew so much about this topic, he found it difficult to extract a specific purpose statement for his presentation. After much thought he narrowed his purpose to this: *To inform potential entrepreneurs about three important factors that loan officers consider before granting start-up loans to launch small businesses.* His entire presentation focused on ensuring that the class understood and remembered three principal ideas.

Audience analysis issues include size, age, gender, experience, attitude, and expectations.

Knowing your audience. A second key element in preparation is to analyze your audience, anticipating its reactions and making appropriate adaptations. Jon Georges adjusted his message and presentation style (using common words and simple sentences, and supplying technical details) in anticipation of the needs of his Japanese audience.

Many factors influence a presentation. A large audience, for example, usually requires a more formal and less personal approach. Other elements, such as the audience's age, gender, education, experience, and attitude toward the subject, will also affect your style and message content. Analyze these factors to determine your strategy, vocabulary, illustrations, and level of detail. Here are specific questions to consider:

- *How will this topic appeal to this audience?*

- *How can I relate this information to their needs?*

- *How can I earn respect so that they accept my message?*

- *Which of the following would be most effective in making my point? Statistics? Graphic illustrations? Demonstrations? Case histories? Analogies? Cost figures?*

- *What must I do to ensure that this audience remembers my main points?*

Organizing the Content

Once you have decided your purpose and analyzed the audience, you're ready to collect information and organize it logically. Good organization and conscious repetition are the two most powerful tools for ensuring that your audience understands and remembers your presentation. In fact, many speech experts recommend the following admittedly repetitious, but effective, plan:

- **Step 1:** Tell them what you're going to say.

- **Step 2:** Say it.

- **Step 3:** Tell them what you've just said.

In other words, repeat your main points in the introduction, body, and conclusion of your presentation. Although it sounds deadly, this strategy works surprisingly well. Let's examine how to construct the three parts of a presentation and add verbal signposts to ensure that listeners understand and remember.

Introduction. The opening of your presentation should strive to accomplish three specific goals:

- Capture listeners' attention and get them involved.

- Identify yourself and establish your credibility.

- Preview your main points.

If you're able to appeal to your listeners and involve them in your presentation right from the start, you're more likely to hold their attention until the finish. Consider some of the same techniques that you used to open sales letters: a question, a startling fact, a joke, a story, or a quotation. Some speakers achieve involvement by opening with a question or command that requires the audience to raise their hands or stand up. Additional techniques to gain and keep audience attention are presented in the Career Skills box on page 452.

To establish your credibility, you need to describe your position, knowledge, or experience—whatever qualifies you to speak. Try also to connect with your audience. Listeners are particularly drawn to speakers who reveal something of themselves and identify with them. A consultant addressing office workers might reminisce about how she started as a clerk-typist; a CEO might tell a funny story in which the joke is on himself.

After capturing attention and establishing yourself, you'll want to preview the main points of your topic, perhaps with a visual aid. You may wish to put off actually writing your introduction, however, until after you have organized the rest of the presentation and crystallized your principal ideas.

Take a look at Eric Evans's introduction, shown in Figure 15.1, to see how he integrated all the elements necessary for a good opening.

Attention-grabbing openers include questions, stating facts, jokes, anecdotes, and quotations.

NINE TECHNIQUES FOR CAPTURING AND KEEPING THE AUDIENCE'S ATTENTION

Experienced speakers know how to capture the attention of an audience and how to keep that attention during a presentation. Here are nine proven techniques.

- **A promise.** Begin with a promise that keeps the audience expectant (for example, "By the end of this presentation I will show you how you can increase your sales by 50 percent").

- **Drama.** Open by telling a moving story or by describing a serious problem that involves the audience. Throughout your talk include other dramatic elements, such as a long pause after a key statement. Change the tone or pitch of your voice. Professionals use intense emotions like anger, joy, sadness, and excitement.

- **Eye contact.** As you begin, command attention by surveying the entire audience to take in all listeners. Take two to five seconds to make eye contact with as many people as possible.

- **Movement.** Leave the lectern area whenever possible. Walk around the conference table or between the aisles of your audience. Try to move toward your audience, especially at the beginning and end of your talk.

- **Questions.** Keep your listeners active and involved with rhetorical questions. Ask for a show of hands to get each listener thinking. The response will also give you a quick gauge of the audience's attentiveness.

- **Demonstrations.** Include a member of the audience in a demonstration (for example, "I'm going to show you

exactly how to implement our four-step customer courtesy process, but I need a volunteer from the audience to help me").

- **Samples and samples gimmicks.** If you're promoting a product, consider having samples to toss out to the audience or to award as prizes to volunteer participants. You can also pass around samples or promotional literature. Be careful, though, to maintain control.

- **Visuals.** Give your audience something to look at besides you. Use a variety of visual aids in a single session. Also consider writing the comments made by your listeners on a flipchart or on the board as you go along.

- **Self-interest.** Review your entire presentation to ensure that it meets the critical "What's-in-it-for-me?" audience test. Remember that people are most interested in things that benefit them.

Career Track Application

Watch a lecture series speaker on campus, a department store sales presentation, a TV "infomercial," or some other speaker. Note and analyze specific techniques used to engage and maintain the listener's attention. Which techniques would be most effective in a classroom presentation? Before your boss or work group?

The best oral presentations focus on a few key ideas.

Body. The biggest problem with most oral presentations is a failure to concentrate on a few principal ideas. Thus, the body of your short presentation (20 minutes or less) should include a small number of main points, say, two to four. Develop each main point with adequate, but not excessive, explanation and details. Too many details can obscure the main message, so keep your presentation simple and logical. Remember, listeners have no pages to leaf back through should they become confused.

When Eric Evans began planning his presentation, he realized immediately that he could talk for hours on his topic. He also knew that listeners are not good at separating major and minor points. Thus, instead of submerging his listeners in a sea of information, he sorted out a few principal ideas. In the mortgage business, loan officers generally ask the following three questions of each applicant for a small business loan: (1) Are you ready to "hit the ground running" in starting your business? (2) Have you done your homework? and (3) Have you made realistic projections of potential sales, cash flow, and equity investment? These questions would become his main points, but Eric wanted to

FIGURE 15.1 ■ Oral Presentation Outline

The Three Phases of the Development Process

1

Analyze
The purpose of this report is to inform listeners of three critical elements in securing business loans.

Anticipate
The audience members are aspiring businesspeople who are probably unfamiliar with loan operations.

Adapt
Because the audience will be receptive but uninformed, explain terms and provide examples. Repeat the main ideas to ensure comprehension.

2

Research
Analyze previous loan applications; interview other loan officers. Gather critical data.

Organize
Group the data into three major categories. Support with statistics, details, and examples. Plan visual aids.

Compose
Prepare a sentence outline. Consider composing a rough draft at a computer.

3

Revise
Develop transitions between topics. Prepare note cards.

Practice
Rehearse the entire talk and time it. Practice enunciating words and projecting your voice. Develop natural hand motions.

Evaluate
Tape-record or videotape a practice session to evaluate your movements, voice tone, enunciation, and timing.

What Makes a Loan Officer Say "Yes"?

I. INTRODUCTION

  A. *(Captures attention)* How many of you expect one day to start your own businesses? How many of you have all the cash available to capitalize that business when you start?

  B. *(Involves audience)* Like you, nearly every entrepreneur needs cash to open a business, and I promise you that by the end of this talk you will have inside information on how to make a loan application that will be successful.

  C. *(Identifies speaker)* As a loan officer at Dominion Trust, which specializes in small-business loans, I make decisions on requests from entrepreneurs like you applying for start-up money.
    Transition: Your professor invited me here today to tell you how you can improve your chances of getting a loan from us or from any other lender. I have suggestions in three areas: *(Previews three main points)* experience, preparation, and projection.

II. BODY

  A. *(Establishes main points)* First, let's consider experience. You must show that you can hit the ground running.
    1. Demonstrate what experience you have in your proposed business.
    2. Include your résumé when you submit your business plan.
    3. If you have little experience, tell us whom you would hire to supply the skills that you lack.
    Transition: In addition to experience, loan officers will want to see that you have researched your venture thoroughly.

  B. My second suggestion, then, involves preparation. Have you done your homework?
    1. Talk to local businesspeople, especially those in related fields.
    2. Conduct traffic counts or other studies to estimate potential sales.
    3. Analyze the strengths and weaknesses of the competition.
    Transition: Now that we've discussed preparation, we're ready for my final suggestion.

  C. *(Develops coherence with planned transitions)* My last tip is the most important one. It involves making a realistic projection of your potential sales, cash flow, and equity.
    1. Present detailed monthly cash-flow projections for the first year.
    2. Describe "what-if" scenarios indicating both good and bad possibilities.
    3. Indicate that you intend to supply at least 25 percent of the initial capital yourself.
    Transition: The three major points I've just outlined cover critical points in obtaining start-up loans. Let me review them for you.

III. CONCLUSION

  A. *(Summarizes main points)* Loan officers are most likely to say "Yes" to your loan application if you do three things: (1) prove that you can hit the ground running when your business opens, (2) demonstrate that you've researched your proposed business seriously, and (3) project a realistic picture of your sales, cash flow, and equity.

  B. *(Provides final focus)* Experience, preparation, and projection, then, are the three keys to launching your business with the necessary start-up capital so that you can concentrate on where your customers, not your funds, are coming from.

streamline them further so that his audience would be sure to remember them. He capsulized the questions in three words: *experience*, *preparation*, and *projection*. As you can see in Figure 15.1, Eric prepared a sentence outline showing these three main ideas. Each is supported by examples and explanations.

How to organize main ideas may not be immediately obvious when you begin working on a presentation. Let's review the five organizational methods employed for written reports in Chapter 12, because those methods are equally useful for oral presentations. You could arrange your ideas by the following elements:

- **Time** (for example, a presentation describing the history of a problem, organized from the first sign of trouble to the present)
- **Component** (a report on sales organized by divisions or products)
- **Importance** (a report describing operating problems arranged from the least important to the most)
- **Criteria** (a presentation evaluating equipment by comparing each model against a set of specifications)
- **Conventional groupings** (a report comparing asset size, fees charged, and yields of mutual funds arranged by these existing categories)

In his presentation Eric arranged the main points by importance, placing the most important point last where it had maximum effect.

In organizing any presentation, prepare a little more material than you think you will actually need. Experienced speakers always have something useful in reserve (such as an extra handout, transparency, or idea)—just in case they finish early.

Conclusion You should prepare the conclusion carefully because this is your last chance to drive home your main points. Don't end limply with comments like "I guess that's about all I have to say." Skilled speakers use the conclusion to review the main themes of the presentation and focus on a goal. They concentrate on what they want the audience to do, think, or remember. Even though they were mentioned earlier, important ideas must be repeated. Notice how Eric Evans, in the conclusion shown in Figure 15.1, summarized his three main points and provided a final focus for his listeners.

When they finish, most speakers encourage questions. If silence ensues, you can prime the pump with "One question that I'm frequently asked is … " You can also remark that you will be happy to answer questions individually after the presentation.

Verbal signposts. Speakers must remember that listeners, unlike readers of a report, cannot control the rate of presentation or flip back through pages to review main points. As a result, listeners get lost easily. Knowledgeable speakers help the audience recognize the organization and main points in an oral message with verbal signposts. They keep their listeners on track by including helpful previews, summaries, and transitions, such as these:

To Preview

The next segment of my talk presents three reasons for …

Let's now consider the causes of …

Main ideas can be organized according to time, component, importance, criteria, or conventional groupings.

Effective conclusions summarize main points and focus on a goal.

To Summarize

Let me review with you the major problems I've just discussed ...

You see, then, that the most significant factors are ...

To Switch Directions

Thus far we've talked solely about ... ; now let's move to ...

I've argued that ... and ... , but an alternative view holds that ...

You can further improve any oral presentation by including transitional expressions such as *first, second, next, then, therefore, moreover, on the other hand, on the contrary*, and *in conclusion*. These expressions lend emphasis and tell listeners where you are headed. Notice in Eric Evans' outline, in Figure 15.1, the specific transitional elements designed to help listeners recognize each new principal point.

Knowledgeable speakers use verbal signposts to point out organization and key ideas.

Planning Visual Aids and Handouts

Before you make a business presentation, consider this wise Chinese proverb: "Tell me, I forget. Show me, I remember. Involve me, I understand." Because your goals as a speaker are to make listeners understand, remember, and act on your ideas, include visual aids to get them interested and involved. Some authorities suggest that we acquire 85 percent of all our knowledge visually. Therefore, an oral presentation that incorporates visual aids is far more likely to be understood and remembered than one lacking visual enhancement.

Good visual aids have many purposes. They emphasize and clarify main points, thus improving comprehension and retention. They increase the audience's interest, and they make the presenter appear more professional, better prepared, and more persuasive. Furthermore, research shows that the use of visual aids actually shortens meetings.[5] Visual aids are particularly helpful for inexperienced speakers because the audience concentrates on the aid rather than on the speaker. Good visuals also serve to jog the memory of a speaker, thus improving self-confidence, poise, and delivery.

Fortunately for today's speakers, many forms of visual media are available to enhance a presentation. Figure 15.2 describes a number of visual aids and compares their cost, formality, and other considerations. Three of the most popular visuals are overhead transparencies, slides, computer visuals, and handouts.

Visual aids clarify points, improve comprehension, and aid retention.

Overhead transparencies. Student and professional speakers alike use the overhead projector for many reasons. Most meeting areas are equipped with projectors and screens. Moreover, acetate transparencies for the overhead are cheap, easily prepared on a computer or copier, and simple to use. And, because the room need not be darkened, a speaker using transparencies can maintain eye contact with the audience. A word of caution, though: stand to the side of the projector so that you don't obstruct the audience's view.

Computer visuals. With today's greatly improved software programs (like PowerPoint, Charisma, and Persuasion), you can create colourful presentations with your computer, as described in the Technology box on page 457. The output from these programs may be projected through slide projectors or, increasingly, shown on a computer monitor, a TV monitor, or an LCD (liquid crystal display) panel. With a little expertise and advanced equipment, you can

FIGURE 15.2 ■ Presentation Enhancers

Medium	Cost	Audience Size	Formality Level	Advantages (✓) and Disadvantages (x)
Overhead projector	Low	2–200	Formal or informal	✓ Transparencies are easy and inexpensive to produce. Speaker keeps contact with audience.
Flipchart	Low	2–200	Informal	✓ Easels and charts are readily available and portable. Speaker can prepare the display in advance or on the spot.
Whiteboard	Medium	2–200	Informal	✓ Porcelain-on-steel surface replaces messy blackboard. Speaker can wipe clean with cloth.
Slide projector	Medium	2–500	Formal	✓ Slides provide excellent graphic images. Darkened room may put audience to sleep. Slides demand expertise, time, and equipment to produce.
Video monitor	High	2–100	Formal or informal	✓ A VCR display features motion and sound. X Videos require skill, time, and equipment to prepare.
Computer visuals	High	2–200	Formal or informal	X Computers generate slides, transparencies, or multimedia visuals. Presentation software programs are easy to use and they create dazzling results.
Handouts	Varies	Unlimited	Formal or informal	✓ Audience appreciates take-home items like outlines, tables, charts, reports, brochures, or summaries. X Handouts can divert attention from speaker.

create a multimedia presentation that includes stereo sound and videos. Many business speakers are switching to computer presentations because the visuals are easy to make, economical, and flexible—changes can be made right up to the last minute. Most important, though, such presentations make even amateurs look like real professionals.

Handouts. You can enhance and complement your presentations by distributing pictures, outlines, brochures, articles, charts, summaries, or other supplements. Timing their distribution, though, is tricky. If given out during a presentation, your handouts tend to distract the audience, causing you to lose control. Thus, it's probably best to discuss most handouts during the presentation but delay distributing them until after you finish.

Using Visual Aids Effectively. Whenever possible, then, you'll want to incorporate visual aids in a presentation; but keep a few points in mind:

- **Avoid overkill.** Use visual aids only for major points or for information that requires clarification. Excessive or unnecessary visuals dull their effectiveness.

- **Keep all visuals simple.** Spotlight main points. Don't, for example, put the outline for your entire presentation on a transparency.

HOW YOU AND YOUR COMPUTER CAN MAKE COLOURFUL MULTIMEDIA PRESENTATIONS

Don't underestimate the power of a compelling presentation. It may be the sizzle that sells the steak—whether you're persuading upper management to fund a project or pitching a new product to prospective buyers.

The latest Windows-based presentation graphics programs let even amateurs produce remarkable results. These programs contain sophisticated tutorials and templates that are the ultimate in ease of learning and ease of use. Your productions can now include special transition effects such as "wipes," "glitter," and "rain" to give your presentation coherence and pizzazz. With a little advanced know-how and special equipment, you can add the latest and snazziest technologies like graphics, video, and sound to produce professional-quality slide shows. Moreover, you can print handouts and speaker's notes from the slide frames you prepare.

Three of the top presentation software programs are PowerPoint, Charisma, and Persuasion. These programs enable you to produce 35 mm slides, black-and-white printouts, or transparencies. Increasingly popular are on-screen presentations, displayed on a computer, an LCD projection panel, or a TV monitor.

All three software programs let you use automatic-build slides. This means that bulleted points are added one at a time for the most dramatic unveiling of your ideas. Below are tips for producing a dazzling presentation.

- **Using an outliner.** Most people plan a presentation with an "outliner,": a software feature that helps you divide your topic into main and subpoints. For example, a travel agency presentation might contain four main headings, two of which are (1) international tours and (2) domestic tours. The outliner would prompt you in developing each main heading. International tours might include three subheadings such as (a) cruise adventures, (b) horticultural explorations, and (c) excursions in the Orient.

- **Building bullet points.** You can then easily translate the outline into headings and bullet points. Each main topic becomes a slide heading, as shown in the attached slide. Subheadings become bullet points. Experts recommend no more than five levels of subtopics for any presentation. Each bulleted item should contain no more than seven words. The purpose of the bulleted text is to prompt you as well as to emphasize and visualize the information you want the audience to remember. Bullet points summarize: they don't tell the whole story.

- **Making master slides.** "Slide" is the term used for each formatted frame, whether it takes the form of a transparency, 35 mm slide, or computer screen. A master slide has common graphic elements, such as your company name or logo or perhaps the overall name of the presentation. Select appropriate colours (usually from a template) for good contrast. Retain some of the unifying elements from the master slide (colour combination, logo, and so forth) for all frames that develop the same subtopic.

- **Avoiding information overload.** The best presentation slides contain no more than thirty-five-digit numbers or thirty-six words arranged in no more than six lines. If you crowd the slide, the audience strains to read it and the impact of the presentation dwindles. Each slide, including text and title, should fill two-thirds to three-quarters of the screen. Use upper- and lowercase rather than all capitals. Use solid fonts in a wide bold style.[6]

Career Track Application

Invite a businessperson, classmate, faculty member, friend, or vendor to make a presentation before your class with visual aids made from a software presentation program. Learn how the frames were constructed. Write a memo to your instructor summarizing how such software could be helpful to you in your presentations.

- **Ensure visibility.** Be sure everyone in your audience can see the visual aids.

- **Enhance comprehension.** Give the audience a moment to study a visual before explaining it. Then, paraphrase it instead of reading it word for word.

- **Practise using them.** Rehearse your talk, perfecting your handling of the visuals. Be sure you talk to the audience and not to the visual.

Polishing Your Delivery

Once you've organized your presentation and prepared visuals, you're ready to practise delivering it. Here are suggestions for selecting a delivery method, along with specific techniques to use before, during, and after your presentation.

Delivery method. Inexperienced speakers often feel that they must memorize an entire presentation to be effective. Unless you're an experienced performer, however, you will sound wooden and unnatural. Moreover, forgetting your place can be disastrous! Therefore, it is not recommended that you memorize an entire oral presentation. However, memorizing significant parts—the introduction, the conclusion, and perhaps a meaningful quotation—can be dramatic and impressive.

If memorizing won't work, should you read your presentation? Definitely not! Reading to an audience is boring and ineffective. Because reading suggests that you don't know your topic very well, the audience loses confidence in your expertise. Reading also prevents you from looking at the audience. You can't see their reactions; consequently, you can't benefit from feedback.

Neither memorizing nor reading creates very convincing presentations. The best plan, by far, is to use notes. Plan your presentation carefully and talk from note cards or an outline containing key sentences and major ideas. By preparing and then practising with your notes, you can talk to your audience in a conversational manner. Your notes should be neither entire paragraphs nor single words. Instead, they should contain a complete sentence or two to introduce each major idea. Below the topic sentence(s), outline subpoints and illustrations, as shown in the sample note card in Figure 15.3. Note cards will keep you on track and prompt your memory, but only if you have rehearsed the presentation thoroughly.

Stage fright is both natural and controllable.

Delivery techniques. Nearly everyone has some stage fright when speaking before a group. Canadian speaker and author Peter Urs Bender asserts that 99 percent of speakers are nervous before they start their presentation, but that anxiety creates the adrenalin that adds energy to the presentation.[7] Being afraid is quite natural and results from actual physiological changes occurring in your body. Faced with a frightening situation, your body responds with the fight-or-flight syndrome, discussed more fully in the Career Skills box on page 460. You can learn to control and reduce stage fright, as well as to incorporate techniques for effective speaking, by using the following strategies before, during, and after your presentation.

Before Your Presentation

- **Prepare thoroughly.** One of the best ways of reducing stage fright is to know your subject thoroughly. Research your topic diligently and prepare a careful sentence outline. Those who try to "wing it" usually suffer the worst butterflies—and make the worst presentations.

FIGURE 15.3 ■ Note Card for Oral Presentation

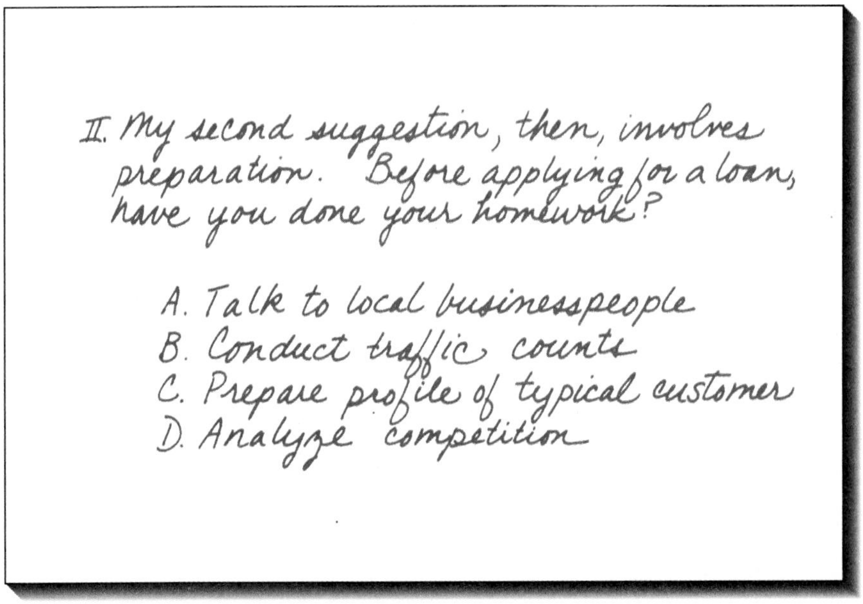

II. My second suggestion, then, involves preparation. Before applying for a loan, have you done your homework?

A. Talk to local businesspeople
B. Conduct traffic counts
C. Prepare profile of typical customer
D. Analyze competition

- **Rehearse repeatedly.** When you rehearse, practise your entire presentation, not just the first half. Put each outline sentence on a separate card. You may also wish to include transitional sentences to help you move to the next topic. Use these cards as you practise, and include your visual aids in your rehearsal. Record your rehearsal on audio or videotape so that you can evaluate your effectiveness.

- **Time yourself.** Most audiences tend to get restless during long talks. Thus, try to complete your presentation in no more than 20 minutes. Set a timer during your rehearsal to measure your speaking time.

- **Request a lectern.** Every beginning speaker needs the security of a high desk or lectern from which to deliver a presentation. It serves as a note holder and a convenient place to rest wandering hands and arms.

- **Check the room.** Before you talk, make sure that a lectern has been provided. If you are using sound equipment or a projector, be certain it is working. Check electrical outlets and the position of the viewing screen. Ensure that the seating arrangement is suitable.

- **Practice stress reduction.** If you are nervous while you are waiting to speak, use stress reduction techniques, such as deep breathing. Additional techniques to help you conquer stage fright are presented in the Career Skills box on page 460.

Thorough preparation, extensive rehearsal, and stress-reduction techniques can lessen stage fright.

During Your Presentation

- **Begin with a pause.** When you first approach the audience, take a moment to adjust your notes and make yourself comfortable. Establish your control of the situation.

HOW TO AVOID STAGE FRIGHT

Ever get nervous before giving a speech? Everyone does! And it's not all in your head, either. When you face something threatening or challenging, your body reacts in what psychologists call the *fight-or-flight response*. This response provides your body with increased energy to deal with threatening situations. It also creates those sensations—dry mouth, sweaty hands, increased heartbeat, and stomach butterflies—that we associate with stage fright. The fight-or-flight response arouses your body for action—in this case, giving a speech.

Since everyone feels some form of apprehension before speaking, it's impossible to eliminate the physiological symptoms altogether. But you can help reduce their effects with the following techniques:

- Use deep breathing to ease your fight-or-flight symptoms. Inhale to a count of 10, hold this breath to a count of 10, and exhale to a count of 10. Concentrate on your counting and your breathing; both activities reduce your stress.

- Don't view your sweaty palms and dry mouth as evidence of fear. Interpret them as symptoms of exuberance, excitement, and enthusiasm to share your ideas.

- Feel confident about your topic. Select a topic that you know well and that is relevant to your audience.

- Remind yourself that you know your topic and are prepared. Tell yourself that the audience is on your side—because it is!

- Shift the spotlight to your visuals. At least some of the time the audience will be looking at your transparencies, handouts, or whatever you have prepared—and not at you.

- Ignore any stumbles. Don't apologize or confess your nervousness. If you keep going the audience will forget any mistakes quickly.

When you're finished, you'll be surprised at how good you feel. You can take pride in what you've accomplished, and your audience will reward you with applause and congratulations. And, of course, your body will call off the fight-or-flight response and return to normal!

Career Track Application

Interview someone in your field or in another business who must make oral presentations. How did he or she develop speaking skills? What advice can this person suggest to reduce stage fright? When you next make a class presentation, try some or all of the techniques described above and note which are most effective for you.

Eye contact, a moderate tone of voice, and natural movements enhance a presentation.

- **Present your first sentence from memory.** By memorizing your opening, you can immediately establish rapport with the audience through eye contact. You'll also sound confident and knowledgeable.

- **Maintain eye contact.** If the size of the audience overwhelms you, pick out two people on the right and two on the left. Talk directly to these people.

- **Control your voice and vocabulary.** This means speaking in moderated tones but loudly enough to be heard. Eliminate verbal static, such as *ah, er, you know,* and *um.* Silence is preferable to meaningless fillers when you are thinking of your next idea.

- **Put the brakes on.** Many novice speakers talk too rapidly, displaying their nervousness and making it very difficult for the audience to understand their ideas. Slow down and listen to what you are saying.

- **Move naturally.** You can use the lectern to hold your notes so that you are free to move about casually and naturally. Avoid fidgeting with your notes, your clothing, or items in your pockets. Learn to use your body to express a point.

- **Use visual aids effectively.** You should discuss and interpret each visual aid for the audience. Move aside as you describe it so that it can be seen fully. Use a pointer if necessary.

- **Avoid digressions.** Stick to your outline and notes. Don't suddenly include clever little anecdotes or digressions that occur to you on the spot. If it's not part of your rehearsed material, leave it out so that you can finish on time. Remember, too, that your audience may not be as enthralled with your topic as you are.

- **Summarize your main points.** Conclude your presentation by reiterating your main points or by emphasizing what you want the audience to think or do. Once you have announced your conclusion, proceed to it directly. Don't irritate the audience by talking for 5 or 10 more minutes.

After Your Presentation

- **Distribute handouts.** If you prepared handouts for the audience, pass them out when you finish.

- **Encourage questions.** If the situation permits a question-and-answer period, announce it at the beginning of your presentation. Then, when you finish, ask for questions. Set a time limit for questions and answers.

- **Repeat questions.** Although the speaker may hear the question, the rest of the audience often does not. Begin each answer by repeating the question. This also gives you time to think. Then, direct your answer to the entire audience.

- **Reinforce your main points.** You can use your answers to restate your primary ideas ("I'm glad you brought that up because it gives me a chance to elaborate on ... "). In answering questions, avoid becoming defensive or debating with the questioner.

- **Keep control.** Don't allow one individual to take over. Keep the entire audience involved.

- **End with a summary and appreciation.** To signal the end of the session before you take the last question, say something like "We have time for just one more question." As you answer the last question, try to work it into a summary of your main points. Then, express appreciation to the audience for the opportunity to talk with them.

The preparation and organizing of an oral presentation, as summarized in the concluding checklist, requires attention to content and strategy. Along with the care you devote to preparing your talk, consider also its ethics, so that you won't be guilty of committing the "worst deadly sin" spotlighted in the Ethics box on page 462.

The time to answer questions, distribute handouts, and reiterate main points is after a presentation.

Adapting to International and Cross-Cultural Audiences

Every good speaker adapts to the audience, and cross-cultural presentations call for special adjustments and sensitivity. When working with an interpreter or speaking before people who don't know much English, you'll need to be very careful about your language. As Jon Georges did in Tokyo, you'll want to speak slowly, use simple English, avoid slang, jargon, and clichés, and use short sentences.

THE "WORST DEADLY SIN" IN A PRESENTATION

ETHICS

Audiences appreciate speakers with polished delivery techniques, but they are usually relatively forgiving when mistakes occur. One thing they don't suffer gladly, though, is unethical behaviour. Executives in a comprehensive research survey agreed that the "worst deadly sin" a speaker can commit in a presentation is demonstrating a lack of integrity.[8]

What kinds of unethical behaviour do audiences reject? They distrust speakers who misrepresent, exaggerate, and lie. They also dislike cover-ups and evasiveness. Everyone expects a speaker who is trying to "sell" a product or idea to emphasize its strong points. Promotion, however, becomes unethical when the speaker intentionally seeks to obscure facts or slant issues to deceive the audience. The following situations clearly signal trouble for speakers because of the unethical actions involved:

- A sales representative, instead of promoting his company's products, suggests that his competitor's business is mismanaged, is losing customers, or offers seriously flawed products.

- A manager distorts a new employee insurance plan, underemphasizing its deficiencies and overemphasizing its strengths.

- An accountant for a charity suggests that management should authorize loose bookkeeping practices in order to mislead the public regarding the use of donors' money.

- A sales representative fabricates an answer to a tough question instead of admitting ignorance.

- A financial planner tries to prove her point by highlighting an irrelevant statistic.

- A real estate broker compares dissimilar properties and locations to inflate the value of some property.

- A speaker deliberately uses excessively technical language to make an idea or proposal seem more important and complex than it is.

- A project manager claims personal credit for a proposal developed largely by consultants.

How can you make certain that your own presentations are ethical? The best strategy, of course, is to present your information honestly, fairly, and without deception. Be aware of your own biases and prejudices so that you don't unconsciously distort data. Remember that the goals of an ethical communicator, discussed in Chapter 3, include telling the truth, labelling opinions so that they can be distinguished from facts, being objective, writing clearly, and giving credit when you use someone else's ideas or words.

Career Track Application

Watch TV or read news stories about parliamentary debates. Note how members of the government and of the opposition each present their views in a positive light and cast their opponents' views in a negative light. Make notes of any unethical presentation techniques.

Addressing cross-cultural audiences requires a speaker to consider audience expectations and cultural conventions.

Beyond these basic language adaptations, however, more fundamental sensitivity is often necessary. In organizing a presentation for a cross-cultural audience, think twice about delivering your main idea at the beginning. Many people (notably those from Japan, Latin America, and Arabic cultures) consider such directness to be brash and inappropriate. Remember that others may not share our cultural emphasis on straightforwardness.

Also consider breaking your presentation into short, discrete segments. In Japan, Jon divided his talk into three distinct topics: theme park attractions, merchandise shops, and food services. He developed each topic separately, encouraging discussion periods after each. Such organization enables participants to ask questions and digest what has been presented. This technique is especially effective in cultures where people communicate in "loops." In the Middle East, for example, Arab speakers "mix circuitous, irrelevant (by North American standards) conversations with short dashes of information that go directly to the point." Presenters who are patient, tolerant, and "mature" (in the eyes of the audience) will make the sale or win the contract.[9]

Remember, too, that some cultures prefer greater formality than North Americans do. Writing on a flipchart or transparency seems natural and spontaneous in this country. Abroad, though, such informal techniques may suggest that the speaker does not value the audience enough to prepare proper visual aids in advance.[10]

This caution aside, you'll still want to use visual aids to convey your message. These visuals should be written in both languages, so that you and your audience understand them. Never use numbers without writing them out for all to see. If possible, say numbers in both languages. Distribute translated handouts, summarizing your important information, when you finish. Finally, be careful of your body language. Looking people in the eye suggests intimacy and self-confidence in this country, but in other cultures it may be considered disrespectful.

■ Checklist for Preparing and Organizing Oral Presentations

Getting Ready to Speak

✓ **Identify your purpose.** Decide what you want your audience to believe, remember, or do when you finish. Aim all parts of your talk toward this purpose.

✓ **Analyze the audience.** Consider how to adapt your message (its organization, appeals, and examples) to your audience's knowledge and needs.

Organizing the Introduction

✓ **Get the audience involved.** Capture the audience's attention by opening with a promise, story, startling fact, question, quote, relevant problem, or self-effacing joke.

✓ **Establish yourself.** Demonstrate your credibility by identifying your position, expertise, knowledge, or qualifications.

✓ **Preview your main points.** Introduce your topic and summarize its principal parts.

Organizing the Body

✓ **Develop two to four main points.** Streamline your topic so that you can concentrate on its major issues.

✓ **Arrange the points logically.** Sequence your points chronologically, or from most important to least important (or vice versa) or by comparison and contrast, or by some other strategy.

✓ **Prepare transitions.** Between each major point write "bridge" statements that connect the previous item to the next one. Use transitional expressions as verbal signposts (*first, second, then, however, consequently, on the contrary,* and so forth).

✓ **Have extra material ready.** Be prepared with more information and visuals in case you have additional time to fill.

Organizing the Conclusion

✓ **Review your main points.** Emphasize your main ideas in your closing so that your audience will remember them.

✓ **Provide a final focus.** Tell how your listeners can use this information, why you have spoken, or what you want them to do.

Designing Visual Aids

✓ **Select your medium carefully.** Consider the size of your audience, degree of formality desired, cost and ease of preparation, and effectiveness.

✓ **Highlight main ideas.** Use visual aids to illustrate major concepts only. Keep them brief and simple.

✓ **Use aids skilfully.** Talk to the audience, not to the visuals. Paraphrase their contents. Remove each visual as soon as you finish with it.

▣ Meetings and Conferences

The trend toward worker teams, benchmarking, and employee empowerment means employees will spend more time in meetings.

Whether you like attending them or not, meetings and conferences are becoming increasingly important in business today. Many organizations are progressing toward team-oriented management; they're reorganizing the rank and file along team lines. Much of this shift toward employee empowerment has resulted from the "total quality" movement. Facing stiff global competition, companies realized that they had to provide both quality products and service. But quality goals in any organization can't be achieved without a key ingredient: involved employees with a commitment to the organization's goals. Three central strategies have emerged from the total quality movement: (1) worker teams (with control of their projects), (2) benchmarking (studying and emulating the best ideas of top companies), and (3) employee empowerment (authority to resolve customers problems). Such trends toward greater employee involvement and team decisions suggest that you'll probably be attending more meetings and conferences than ever before.

Meetings differ from conferences in that they are smaller and less formal. We'll concentrate on meetings in this discussion, although most of the advice holds for conferences as well.

Meetings consist of three or more individuals who gather to pool information, clarify policy, seek consensus, and solve problems. It's important to note that meetings also differ from speeches, where one person talks at an audience. In meetings people are expected to *exchange* ideas; emphasis should be on interaction.

From an organization's viewpoint meetings are occasions for a productive exchange of information. From your own personal viewpoint, though, meetings should represent opportunities. At meetings judgments are formed and careers

Members of this quality control team meet regularly to discuss ways to improve their procedures and product. Greater emphasis on worker teams and employee involvement in the 1990s means more meetings and conferences.

are made. Therefore, instead of treating them as thieves of your valuable time, see them as golden opportunities to demonstrate your leadership and communication skills. Jon Georges, at Walt Disney Imagineering, wisely recognized presentations and meetings as chances to impress management. So that you, too, can make the most of these opportunities, here are techniques for planning, conducting, and participating in successful meetings. Before studying the following techniques, though, take a look at the two meetings described in Figures 15.4 and 15.5. The "bad" meeting, unfortunately, is typical of many conducted by untrained managers. The "good" meeting, on the other hand, shows how preparation and proper management can transform a "meeting from hell" into a productive gathering.

Planning Meetings

Successful meetings begin with planning. This means deciding on a goal or an objective, and then determining whether a meeting is the best way to achieve that goal. If, for example, the goal is to announce a new policy regarding flexible work schedules, a meeting may be unnecessary. Perhaps a memo or electronic mail message would be better. Or if the goal is to inform management of department or project progress, reports sent directly to specific managers might work better than an update meeting.

When a meeting is necessary, your first task is to prepare an agenda of items to be discussed. The best agendas list each topic, an estimate of time for each item, and an ending time. They also include the names of individuals who are responsible for presenting topics or for performing some action. To keep meetings productive, limit the number of items on the agenda. Remember, the narrower the focus, the greater the success. Send the agenda (and perhaps the minutes of the previous meeting) at least two days before meeting. Finally, include only those people directly concerned with the matter at hand. Let the purpose of your meeting determine its ideal size, as shown in Figure 15.6.

FIGURE 15.4 ■ Scenario of a Bad Meeting

Preparation

As manager of Customer Service, Mark must call a meeting to generate ideas for departmental cost cutting. Because he is rushed with other tasks, he forgets to send out a notice of the meeting until the day before the meeting. His brief note announces the time and topic but nothing else.

Opening

Mark delays starting the meeting for 15 minutes because three key service reps are late. While waiting for the meeting to begin, many members grumble about the short notice and having to change their plans. Others vow to come to future meetings at least 15 minutes late because that's when the meeting will probably begin. When everyone is finally assembled, Mark doesn't give any background of the need for cost cutting or possible solutions to the company's problem because he is now pushed for time.

Meeting management

Having called the meeting to order, Mark launches right into the subject, asking whether anyone has ideas for cutting the budget. Rachel delivers a long-winded lecture lambasting management for its poor decisions, which she feels caused the need for budget cuts. When Rachel pauses briefly, Robert begins a proposal for budget cutting—only to be interrupted by Rachel. Lisa tries to explain and expand on Robert's suggestion but cannot be heard because Robert and Rachel are arguing loudly between themselves. As at all meetings, Scott begins to preach on his favourite topic: the need for updated computer software to handle incoming calls from customers. Mark finally takes over the meeting and outlines his own plans for departmental budget cuts. After one and a half hours, some people get up and say they have to leave. More suggestions for budget cutting, some practical and some silly, are outlined and then discussed. No decisions are made.

Conclusion

After two hours most participants are tired, irritable, and discouraged. Mark therefore adjourns the meeting. Because no notes were taken and no consensus reached, it is difficult to say what, if anything, has been accomplished.

Conducting Meetings

Meetings should follow an agenda, permit a free exchange of ideas, and begin and end on time.

To avoid wasting time and irritating the participants, you should always start meetings on time—even if some people are missing. Delays can ruffle some feathers. Those who came on time resent waiting for latecomers. Moreover, it sets a bad precedent. People may fail to be on time for future meetings because they assume that the chair won't be punctual.

Meetings should begin with a three-to-five minute introduction that includes the following: (1) goal and length of the meeting, (2) background of the problem, (3) possible solutions and constraints, (4) tentative agenda, and (5) procedures to be followed. At this point you can ask if the participants agree with you thus far.

The next step is to assign one person to take minutes. It's impossible for the chair to direct a meeting and record its proceedings at the same time. Then you can open the discussion; from that point forward, say as little as possible. One meeting specialist says that an effective chair is "a lot like a talk show host, making sure that each panel member gets some air time while no one member steals the show."[11] Remember that the purpose of a meeting is to *exchange* views, not to hear one person, even the chair, do all the talking.

It's also important to adhere to the agenda and the timetable. When the group seems to have reached a consensus, summarize it in your own words and check to see whether everyone agrees. Finally, end the meeting at the agreed-

FIGURE 15.5 ■ Scenario of a Good Meeting

Preparation

As department manager, Mark circulates a message announcing a meeting to be held on budget cutting. His announcement goes out a week before the meeting date. It not only tells the date, starting time, ending time, and location of the meeting but also includes a detailed agenda. Mark asks each person to come to the meeting with at least three practical suggestions for cutting expenditures.

Opening

Mark starts on time, although employees are late. He appoints a note taker, who is to summarize the main points on a flipchart. As latecomers arrive, they are able to see what has been discussed without interrupting the meeting. Mark focuses on the main topic of the meeting with a brief discussion of the background to cut the budget. He also offers a few suggestions to "prime the pump." Finally, he outlines two ground rules for the meeting: (1) discussion will be limited to agenda items and (2) each person will have five minutes to speak. Mark asks if everyone understands the purpose of the meeting and the ground rules.

Meeting management

After his opening statement, Mark manages the meeting but does not participate himself. When Rachel begins an attack on management, Mark asks her to frame a suggestion for solving the problem. Mark does not allow Rachel to interrupt others who wish to talk. Although two departmental members tend to be quite vocal, Mark does not let them dominate the meeting or carry on a dialogue between themselves. When speakers drift toward unrelated topics, Mark tactfully brings them back to the agenda. Moreover, he encourages quiet members to contribute, making statements like "Theresa, we'd like to hear what you think about ..." Mark is able to stick to the timetable for each agenda item by telling speakers how much time remains for the topic. When the group seems to reach a consensus on any point, he offers a summary of the group's position and asks whether the members agree with his summary.

Conclusion

Just before the ending time, Mark looks at the flipchart and summarizes all the points of agreement. He thanks the group and promises that all members will receive a copy of the minutes

upon time. At this point you can summarize what you have accomplished, thank the group, and announce that a report of the proceedings will be sent to everyone.

Participating in Meetings

As a participant you can get the most out of a meeting and best contribute to its success by coming prepared. This means reading the agenda and gathering any relevant information: the problem, its causes, possible solutions, and so on. Careful preparation and knowledgeable participation at meetings can provide a real impetus to the careers of upwardly mobile employees.

Once you arrive at the meeting (on time or even a little early), be ready to speak on an issue. At the same time, however, consider your timing. You might want to let others speak first so that you can shape your remarks to best advantage. If you have a significant proposal or point to make, wait for the best moment. One corporation president compared the challenge of picking the best time to jumping aboard a moving train. "Jump too soon," he said, "and the train may run over you; jump too late and you'll miss it."[12] If you're sure of your evidence and feel confident, raise your point as soon as it is relevant. If you're less confident, hold off until you can introduce it as a logical outgrowth to the discussion. For the best reception, encourage the group to assist you in refining your idea.

Successful meetings result from a planned agenda and a tight focus.

FIGURE 15.6 ■ Meeting Purpose and Number of Participants

Purpose	Ideal Size
Intensive problem solving	5 or fewer
Problem identification	10 or fewer
Information reviews and presentations	Up to 30
Motivational meetings	Unlimited

In addition to contributing your own ideas, you can help the chair keep the discussion on target. When a participant strays, you might remark, "Yes, Jeffrey, we're all pleased with the new company banking plan, but right now we're most concerned with how to solve this problem. Has anyone considered … ?"

Videoconferencing

Video and teleconferences are electronic meetings that enable people to conduct business without actually getting together physically. Although the technology has been available since the late 1970s, videoconferencing didn't boom until the early 1990s.[13]

Videoconferencing saves money and forces participants to listen to one another.

Videoconferences are possible in most major metropolitan areas where long-distance telephone companies have completed the fibre-optic networks required to transmit digital signals. Meetings take place in specially designed rooms, which are steadily becoming cheaper and more abundant. Hotels also rent public video rooms; but many organizations, taking advantage of falling equipment prices, are now installing their own.

Most companies start videoconferencing because it saves travel costs. Employees at Novocor Chemicals (Canada) Ltd. of Sarnia use videoconferences rather than travel to meetings. There are video systems set up at seven sites, using relatively inexpensive equipment. Not only did the equipment pay for itself in the first year, but Novocor saved more than $500 000 in travel costs.[14]

However, there are also many other benefits. Engineers at Neill and Gunter Limited of Fredericton, New Brunswick, can tour a multimillion-dollar project in Singapore without leaving their offices. The company also uses videoconferencing as a sales tool. According to the chair of Neill and Gunter, "We've put terminals in a number of clients' offices and it's a big selling point. We can tell them it's much more cost-effective to hire us than to have their own engineers, and that our very best people are accessible just as quickly and easily as if they were in their office."[15]

Surprisingly, videoconferencing has produced other unexpected benefits. American Greetings Corporation reports that decisions are reached more quickly. Why? More employees participate in the high-tech meetings, thus reducing the time spent communicating ideas and decisions upward and downward. At Hewlett-Packard videoconferences have accelerated product development by 30 percent. That's because videoconferences, which must be more structured than face-to-face meetings, are 20 to 30 percent shorter.[16] Moreover, videoconference participants are more polite. Because the transmission format creates a slight delay, speakers can't interrupt one another. As a result, says one

Videoconferencing allows groups in distant locations to see each other and exchange ideas without the fatigue and disruption of travel. As equipment costs decline, companies are increasingly using videoconferences to replace face-to-face meetings.

expert, "It's back to *Robert's Rules of Order*. People actually have to listen to each other now.[17]

Telephones and Voice Mail

The telephone is the most universal—and, some would say, the most important—piece of equipment in offices today.[18] The telephone has spawned an entire new industry—voice mail systems, which are rapidly replacing switchboards and receptionists. These computerized message systems save labour costs and provide sophisticated capabilities and flexibility unavailable in the past. Regardless of their advanced technology, though, telephones and voice mail are valuable business tools only when they generate goodwill and increase productivity. Poor communication techniques can easily offset any benefits arising from improved equipment. What good is an extensive voice mail system if callers hang up in frustration after waiting through a long list of menu options without learning what they need? Here are suggestions for helping business communicators make the best use of telephone and voice mail equipment.

Telephones and voice mail should promote goodwill and increase productivity.

Making Productive Telephone Calls

Before making a telephone call, decide whether the intended call is really necessary. Could you find the information yourself? If you wait a while, would the problem resolve itself? Perhaps your message could be delivered more efficiently by some other means. One West Coast company found that telephone interruptions consumed about 18 percent of staff members' workdays. Another study found that two-thirds of all calls were less important than the work they interrupted.[19] Alternatives to telephone calls include electronic mail (E-mail) messages, memos, and calls to voice mail systems. If a telephone call must be made, consider using the following suggestions to make it fully productive.

Making productive telephone calls means having an agenda, identifying the purpose, being courteous and cheerful, and avoiding rambling.

- **Plan a mini-agenda.** Have you ever been embarrassed when you had to make a second telephone call because you forgot an important item the first time? Before placing a call, jot down all the topics you need to discuss. Having an agenda guarantees not only a complete call but also a quick one. You'll be less likely to wander from the business at hand while rummaging through your mind trying to remember everything.

- **Use a three-point introduction.** When placing a call, immediately (1) name the person you are calling, (2) identify yourself and your affiliation, and (3) give a brief explanation of your reason for calling. For example: "May I speak to Larry DaSilva? This is Hillary Dahl of Sebastian Enterprises, and I'm seeking information about a software program called 'Power Presentations.'" This kind of introduction enables the person answering the phone to respond immediately without asking further questions.

- **Be cheerful and accurate.** Let your voice show the same kind of animation that you radiate when you greet people in person. In your mind try to envision the individual answering the telephone. A smile can certainly affect the tone of your voice, so smile at that person. Moreover, be accurate about what you say. "Hang on a second; I'll be right back" is rarely true. Better to say, "It may take me two or three minutes to get that information. Would you prefer to hold or have me call you back?"

- **Bring it to a close.** The responsibility for ending a call lies with the caller. This is sometimes difficult to do if the other person rambles on. You may need to use suggestive closing language, such as "I've certainly enjoyed talking with you," "I've learned what I needed to know, and now I can proceed with my work," "Thanks for your help," or "I must go now, but may I call you again in the future if I need ... ?"

- **Avoid telephone tag.** If you call someone who's not in, ask when it would be best for you to call again. State that you will call at a specific time—and do it. If you ask a person to call you, give a time when you can be reached—and then be sure you are in at that time.

- **Leave complete voice mail messages.** Remember that there's no rush when you leave a voice mail message. Always enunciate clearly. And be sure to provide a complete message, including your name, telephone number, and the time and date of your call. Explain your purpose so that the receiver can be ready with the required information when returning your call.

Receiving Productive Telephone Calls

With a little forethought you can make your telephone a productive, efficient work tool. Good telephone manners also reflect well on you and on your organization.

- **Identify yourself immediately.** In answering your telephone or someone else's, give your name, title or affiliation, and, possibly, a greeting. For example, "Larry DaSilva, Proteus Software. How may I help you?" Force yourself to speak clearly and slowly. Remember that the caller may be unfamiliar with what you are saying and fail to recognize slurred syllables.

- **Be responsive and helpful.** If you are in a support role, be sympathetic to callers' needs. Instead of "I don't know," try "That's a good question; let me investigate." Instead of "We can't do that," try "That's a tough one; let's see what we can do." Avoid "No" at the beginning of a sentence. It sounds especially abrasive and displeasing because it suggests total rejection.

- **Be cautious when answering calls for others.** Be courteous and helpful, but don't give out confidential information. Better to say, "She's away from her desk" or "He's out of the office" than to report a colleague's exact whereabouts.

- **Take messages carefully.** Few things are as frustrating as receiving a phone message that is illegible. Repeat the spelling of names and verify telephone numbers. Write messages legibly and record their time and date. Promise to give the messages to intended recipients, but don't guarantee return calls.

- **Explain what you're doing when transferring calls.** Give a reason for transferring, and identify the extension to which you are directing the call in case the caller is disconnected.

Making the Best Use of Voice Mail

Voice mail links a telephone system to a computer that digitizes and stores incoming messages. Some systems also provide functions like automated attendant menus, allowing callers to reach any associated extension by pushing specific buttons on a touch-tone telephone. Interactive systems allow callers to receive verbal information from a computer database. For example, a ski resort might use voice mail to answer routine questions that once were routed through an operator: "Welcome to Snow Paradise. For information on accommodations, touch 1; for snow conditions, touch 2; for ski equipment rental, touch 3," and so forth.

Voice mail serves many functions, but the most important is message storage. Because half of all business calls require no discussion or feedback (according to AT&T estimates), the messaging capabilities of voice mail can mean huge savings for businesses. Incoming information is delivered without interrupting potential receivers and without all the niceties that most two-way conversations require. Stripped of superfluous chit-chat, voice mail messages allow communicators to focus on essentials. Voice mail also eliminates telephone tag, inaccurate message-taking, and time-zone barriers. Critics complain, nevertheless, that automated systems seem cold and impersonal and are sometimes confusing and irritating.

In any event, here are some ways that you can make voice mail work more effectively for you.

- **Announce your voice mail.** If you rely principally on a voice mail message system, identify it on your business stationery and cards. Then, when people call, they will be ready to leave a message.

- **Prepare a warm and informative greeting.** Make your mechanical greeting sound warm and inviting, both in tone and content. Identify yourself and your organization so that callers know they have reached the right number. Thank the caller and briefly explain that you are unavailable. Invite the caller to leave a message or, if appropriate, call back. Here's a typical voice mail greeting: "Hi! This is Larry DaSilva of Proteus Software, and I appreciate your call. You've reached my voice mailbox because I'm either working with customers or talking on another line at the moment. Please leave your name, number, and reason for calling so that I can be prepared when I return your call." Give callers an idea of when you will be available, such as "I'll be back at 2:30" or "I'll be out of my office until Wednesday, May 20." If you screen your calls as a time-management

> Voice mail eliminates telephone tag, inaccurate message taking, and time-zone barriers; it also allows communicators to focus on essentials.

technique, try this message: "I'm not near my phone right now, but I should be able to return calls after 3:30."

- **Test your message.** Call your number and assess your message. Does it sound inviting? Sincere? Understandable? Are you pleased with your tone? If not, says one consultant, have someone else, perhaps a professional, record a message for you.

■ Summary of Learning Goals

1. **Discuss the most important steps in preparing an effective oral presentation.** First, decide what your purpose is and what you want the audience to believe or do so that you can aim the entire presentation toward your goal. Second, know your audience so that you can adjust your message and style to its knowledge and needs.

2. **Explain the parts of an effective oral presentation.** The introduction of a good presentation should capture the listener's attention, identify the speaker, establish credibility, and preview the main points. The body should discuss two to four main points, with appropriate explanations, details, and verbal signposts to guide listeners. The conclusion should review the main points and provide a final focus.

3. **Describe appropriate visual aids and handouts for a presentation.** Use simple, easily understood visual aids to emphasize and clarify main points. Choose transparencies, flipcharts, slides, or other visuals depending on audience size, degree of formality desired, and budget. Generally, it's best to distribute handouts after a presentation.

4. **Specify delivery techniques for use before, during, and after a presentation.** Before your talk prepare a sentence outline on note cards and rehearse repeatedly. Check the room, lectern, and equipment. During the presentation consider beginning with a pause and presenting your first sentence from memory. Make eye contact, control your voice, speak and move naturally, and avoid digressions. After your talk distribute handouts and answer questions. End gracefully and express appreciation.

5. **Discuss effective techniques for adapting oral presentations to cross-cultural audiences.** In presentations before groups whose English is limited, speak slowly, use simple English, avoid slang, jargon, and clichés, and use short sentences. Consider building up to your main idea rather than announcing it immediately. Also consider breaking the presentation into short segments to allow participants to ask questions and digest small parts separately. Beware of appearing too spontaneous and informal. Use visual aids to help communicate your message, but also distribute translated handouts summarizing the most important information.

6. **Plan, conduct, and participate in effective meetings and conferences.** In planning a successful meeting or conference, determine a goal, prepare an agenda with a small number of items, and allocate time for each item to be discussed. In conducting a meeting, start on time, introduce the goal of the meeting, assign a note taker, and encourage a balanced discussion. Follow the agenda and stop on time. As a participant at meetings, do research to prepare for the topic, arrive on time, and consider the best strategy for introducing your ideas.

7. **Explain videoconferencing and its uses.** Videoconferences use fibre-optic networks and video screens to enable people to meet electronically instead of in person. They greatly reduce costs, fatigue, and time lost in travelling to meetings.

8. **List techniques for improved telephone and voice-mail effectiveness.** You can improve your telephone calls by planning a mini-agenda and using a three-point introduction (name, affiliation, and purpose). Be cheerful and responsive, and use closing language to end a conversation. Avoid telephone tag by leaving complete messages. In answering calls, identify yourself immediately, avoid giving out confidential information when answering for others, and take careful messages. In setting up an automated-attendance voice mail menu, limit the number of choices. For your own message prepare a warm and informative greeting. Tell when you will be available. Evaluate your message by calling it yourself.

CHAPTER REVIEW

1. In planning an oral presentation what two things should you think about first? (Goal 1)

2. Name three goals to be achieved in the introduction of an oral presentation. (Goal 2)

3. For a 30-minute presentation, how many main points should be developed? (Goal 2)

4. What should the conclusion to an oral presentation include? (Goal 2)

5. Why are visual aids particularly useful to inexperienced speakers? (Goal 3)

6. Why are transparencies a favourite visual aid? (Goal 3)

7. What delivery method is most effective for speakers? (Goal 4)

8. Why should a speaker deliver the first sentence from memory? (Goal 4)

9. How might presentations before international or cross-cultural audiences be altered to be most effective? (Goal 5)

10. How do meetings differ from speeches? (Goal 6)

11. What items should the agenda of a meeting include? (Goal 6)

12. How should the chair of a meeting begin? (Goal 6)

13. Why are businesses increasingly using video conferences for meetings between distant groups? (Goal 7)

14. What is a three-point introduction for a telephone call? (Goal 8)

15. What is voice mail? (Goal 8)

DISCUSSION

1. Why is it necessary to repeat key points in an oral presentation? (Goals 1, 2, 4)

2. How can a speaker make the most effective use of visual aids? (Goal 3)

3. Discuss effective techniques for reducing stage fright. (Goal 4)

4. How are meetings important to a person's career advancement? (Goal 6)

5. **Ethical Issue:** How can business communicators ensure that their oral presentations are ethical?

ACTIVITIES

15.1 Critiquing a Speech (Goals 1–4)

Visit your library and select a speech from *Canadian Speeches: Issues of the Day*. Write a memo report to your instructor critiquing the speech under the following categories:

a. Effectiveness of the introduction, body, and conclusion

b. Evidence of effective overall organization

c. Use of verbal signposts to create coherence

d. Emphasis on two to four main points

e. Effectiveness of supporting facts (use of examples, statistics, quotations, and so forth)

15.2 Preparing an Oral Presentation from an Article (Goals 1, 2, 4)

Select a newspaper or magazine article and prepare an oral report based on it. Submit your outline, introduction, and conclusion to your instructor, or present the report to your class.

15.3 Overcoming Stage Fright (Goal 4)

In a class discussion develop a list of reasons for being fearful when making a presentation before class. What makes you nervous? Being tongue-tied? Fearing all eyes on you? Messing up? Forgetting your ideas and looking silly? Then, in groups of three or four discuss ways to overcome these fears. Your instructor may ask you to write a memo (individual or collective) summarizing your suggestions, or you may break out of your small groups and report your best ideas to the entire class.

15.4 Investigating Oral Communication in Your Field (Goals 1–4)

Interview one or two people in your professional field. How is oral communication important in this profession? Does the need for oral skills change as one advances? What suggestions can these people make to newcomers to the field for becoming proficient at oral communication? Discuss your findings with your class.

15.5 Outlining an Oral Presentation (Goals 1, 2)

One of the hardest parts of preparing an oral presentation is making the outline. Select an oral presentation topic from the list in Activity 15.6 or suggest an original topic. Prepare an outline for your presentation using the following format.

Title
Purpose

	I.	INTRODUCTION
Gain attention of audience		A.
Involve audience		B.
Establish credibility		C.
Preview main points		D.
Transition		

	II.	BODY
Main point		A.
Illustrate, clarify, contrast		1.
		2.
		3.
Transition		
Main point		B.
Illustrate, clarify, contrast		1.
		2.
		3.
Transition		
Main point		C.
Illustrate, clarify, contrast		1.
		2.
		3.
Transition		
	III.	CONCLUSION
Summarize main points		A.
Provide final focus		B.
Encourage questions		C.

15.6 Choosing a Topic for an Oral Presentation (Goals 1–5)

Select a topic from the list below or from the report topics in Exercise 14.15 for a 5- to 10-minute oral presentation. Imagine you are an expert who has been called in to explain some aspect of the topic before a group of interested people. Since your time is limited, prepare a concise yet forceful presentation with effective visual aids.

a. What kinds of employment advertisements are legal, and what kinds are potentially illegal?

b. What aspects of Japanese management techniques might work in this country?

c. What graphics package should your fellow students use to prepare visual aids for reports?

d. What is the employment outlook in three career areas of interest to you?

e. What is telecommuting, and for what kind of workers is it an appropriate work alternative?

f. How much choice should parents have in choosing schools for their young children (within their municipality, district, etc.)?

g. What travel location would you recommend for students at Christmas (or another holiday or in summer)?

h. What is the economic outlook for a given product (such as domestic cars, laptop computers, economy cameras, fitness equipment, or a product of your choice)?

I. How can your institution (or company) improve its image?

j. Why should people invest in a company or scheme of your choice?

k. What brand and model of computer and printer are the best buy for students today?

l. What franchise would offer the best investment opportunity for an entrepreneur in your area?

m. How should a job candidate dress for an interview?

n. Why should you be hired for a position for which you have applied?

o. How do the accounting cycles in manual and computerized systems compare?

p. How is an administrative assistant different from a secretary?

q. Where should your organization hold its next convention?

r. What is your opinion of the statement "Advertising steals our time, defaces the landscape, and degrades the dignity of public institutions"?[20]

s. How can individuals reduce their income tax?

t. What is the outlook for real estate (commercial or residential) investment in your area?

u. What are the pros and cons of videoconferencing for [name an organization]?

15.7 Planning a Meeting (Goal 6)

Assume that the next meeting of your student organization will discuss preparations for a careers day in the spring. The group will hear reports from committees working on speakers, business recruiters, publicity, reservations of campus space, setup of booths, and any other matters you can think of. As president of the organization, prepare an agenda for the meeting. Compose your introductory remarks to open the meeting. Your instructor may ask you to submit these two documents or use them in staging an actual meeting in class.

15.8 Analyzing a Meeting (Goal 6)

Attend a structured meeting of a college, social, business, or other organization. Compare the conduct within the meeting with the suggestions presented in this chapter. Why did the meeting succeed or fail? Prepare a memo for your instructor or be ready to discuss your findings in class.

15.9 Improving Telephone Skills by Role Playing (Goal 8)

Your instructor will divide the class into pairs. For each scenario take a moment to read and rehearse your role silently. Then play the role with your partner. If time permits, repeat the scenarios, changing roles.

Partner 1

A. You are the personnel manager of Datatronics, Inc. Call Elizabeth Franklin, office manager at Computers Plus. Inquire about a job applicant, Chelsea Kostas, who listed Ms. Franklin as a reference.

B. Call Ms. Franklin again the following day to inquire about the same job applicant, Chelsea Kostas. Ms. Franklin answers today, but she talks on and on, describing the applicant in great detail. Tactfully close the conversation.

C. You are now the receptionist for Tom Wing, of Wing Imports. Answer a call for Mr. Wing, who is working in another office, at ext. 134, where he will accept calls.

D. You are now Tom Wing, owner of Wing Imports. Call your lawyer, Michael Murphy, about a legal problem. Leave a brief, incomplete message.

E. Call Mr. Murphy again. Leave a message that will prevent telephone tag.

Partner 2

You are the receptionist for Computers Plus. The caller asks for Elizabeth Franklin, who is home sick today. You don't know when she will be able to return. Answer the call appropriately.

You are now Ms. Franklin, office manager. Describe Chelsea Kostas, an imaginary employee. Think of someone with whom you've worked. Include many details, such as her ability to work with others, her appearance, her skill at computing, her schooling, her ambition, and so forth.

You are now an administrative assistant for lawyer Michael Murphy. Call Tom Wing to verify a meeting date Mr. Murphy has with Mr. Wing. Use your own name in identifying yourself.

You are now the receptionist for lawyer Michael Murphy. Mr. Murphy is skiing at Whistler and will return in two days, but he doesn't want his clients to know where he is. Take a message.

Take a message again.

Employment Messages

LEARNING GOALS

After studying this chapter, you should be able to

1 Evaluate your assets, career paths, and the job market in preparation for employment.

2 Compare and contrast chronological, functional, and combination résumés.

3 Organize, format, and produce a persuasive résumé.

4 Identify techniques that prepare a résumé for computer scanning and for faxing.

5 Write a persuasive letter of application to accompany your résumé.

6 Write effective employment follow-up letters and other messages.

7 Evaluate successful job interview strategies.

Vector Design

When Michael Robertson opens the mail and finds a résumé, he immediately looks beyond the words on the page to the person making the application. It might sound like an odd way of assessing job hunters, but the 36-year-old creative director of Vector Design, Inc., of Toronto knows exactly what he's after. "It's not something that can be manufactured ... I'm looking for *real* intelligence."

This hire-smart approach has stood Vector Design in good stead since the company was founded in 1987 by Michael, a graduate of the University of Toronto's Faculty of Arts and a self-taught designer who began dabbling in desktop publishing at the time Macintosh computers and laser printers were first introduced. Since then Vector Design, which handles print communication ranging from advertising to editorial design work, has blossomed from one employee and a shoestring budget, into a organization with a full-time staff of seven (and one part-timer) and annual revenues of more than $1 million.

> *"We are very concerned with words and accuracy: our reputation is built on it. So if I get a résumé with a mistake in it, that person is not getting an interview."*

Because business is good, Michael hires new employees in order to address the demands of a client list that includes Merisel Canada, Xerox Canada, The Body Shop, SAS Institute Canada, and *The Globe and Mail*. When it comes time to expand, he puts attitude ahead of all else. "First of all we want good, responsible people, who have a positive outlook. That chemistry is as important as their talent."

In less than traditional manner, the hiring at Vector Design is a collective effort by the whole staff. (This hire-by-committee approach may become more common in a marketplace where downsizing has produced smaller corporations, many of which are owner-operated.) Because "everybody is involved," Michael admits that the interview can be quite intimidating. But he says this unusual hiring technique is not about scaring people: it's about getting the right person for the job. The idea is to find people that work well with the larger group and fit well into the "family atmosphere" Michael fosters at Vector Design.

The interview is very revealing. "Proper body language, good speaking ability, and a good grasp of current events are all important for job seekers today," says Michael. "We want people who can communicate with the client on a number of different levels."

This is all part of what Michael calls the "new work environment," where employees are given more authority. But, he warns, with that freedom come added responsibilities. "You hear a lot of talk about the deadwood at companies—people who are just going through the motions and collecting a paycheque every two weeks. Employers want people who can pull their weight."

Picking the person who's right for the job requires that Michael first scrutinize hundreds of résumés. It is at this stage that presentation and attention to detail can make or break a candidate's chance of being given a second look. "We are very concerned with words and accuracy: our reputation is built on it. So if I get a résumé with a mistake in it, that person is not getting an interview. The door is closed because mistakes indicate a lack of concern for presentation," says Michael, whose business involves copy writing as well as design work. "You are either meticulous, or you're not."

When approaching the job market, having a well-written résumé will increase your chances of getting an interview. It is important to specifically tailor your résumé to the job for which you are applying by outlining your related skills and work experience. Michael Robertson at Vector Design looks first for brief, "punchy," and error-free résumés.

For Michael, this attention to detail doesn't affect the length of a résumé or application. If a résumé runs longer than one page, that's all right, he says, so long as the information is relevant and interesting. He warns that people who pad their résumés with work experience that is not related to the position at hand, stand out as poor communicators.

When it comes to previous experience, this is difficult for students entering the workforce for the first time. "The jury is still out on this one," says Michael, who gets around the problem by hiring fourth-year undergraduates part-time during the school year as a way of examining the quality of their work and deciding whether they are able to function as part of a small design team.

Clear, tight writing is important in the covering letter that goes with an application, as well. Mistake-free, punchy, and to the point, this one-page lead-in to a résumé is a chance to make a good first impression. "It's a demonstration of professionalism," says Michael, who adds that, along the same lines, thank-you letters after an interview are a good idea as well. "It shows a level of consideration and thoughtfulness that should be there if someone wants to be part of a team. It's another little bit of polish."

In a field where presentation is everything, Michael knows the value of professionalism and attention to detail better than most. But the bottom line of an application process is honesty and integrity. "Don't exaggerate," he says, "because sooner or later it will be found out." If all this sounds a bit nebulous, Michael has some inside information to share. He says most employers have one trait in common: "We don't fall for anyone's bluff."

As someone familiar with finding and creating jobs in the so-called "new economy," where technology rules and the only constant is change, Michael Robertson's advice to aspiring businesspeople is to "create your own opportunities. Don't expect somebody to hand you that job."[1] ∎

Preparing for Employment

Finding a satisfying career means learning about yourself, the job market, and the employment process.

Learning how to evaluate your assets and how to manage the entire employment process demands preparation. Whether you are looking for an internship, applying for a permanent position, competing for a promotion, or changing careers, you must invest time and effort preparing yourself. You can't hope to find the position of your dreams without first (1) knowing yourself, (2) knowing the job market, and (3) knowing the employment process. Learning about yourself involves identifying your interests, preferences, and goals so that you choose a satisfying career. Your self-evaluation should also include assessing your qualifications and skills. In addition, you must obtain career information and choose a specific job objective. At the same time, you should be studying the job market. Finally, you'll need to compose a persuasive résumé and letter of application. If you follow the steps summarized in Figure 16.1 and described in this chapter, you will have a master plan for getting the job you want.

Identifying Your Interests

Answer specific questions to help yourself choose a career.

The employment process begins with introspection. This means looking inside yourself to analyze what you like and dislike so that you can make good employment choices. Career counsellors charge large sums for helping individuals learn about themselves. You can do the same kind of self-examination—without spending a dime. For guidance in choosing a field that eventually proves to be satisfying, answer the following questions. If you have already chosen a field, think carefully about how your answers relate to that choice.

- *Do I enjoy working with people, information, or things?*
- *How important is it to be my own boss?*
- *How important are salary, benefits, and job stability?*
- *How important are working environment, colleagues, and job stimulation?*
- *Would I rather work for a large or small company?*
- *Must I work in a specific city, geographical area, or climate?*
- *Am I looking for security, travel opportunities, money, power, or prestige?*
- *How would I describe the perfect job, boss, and co-workers?*

Evaluating Your Qualifications

In addition to your interests, assess your qualifications. As Michael Robertson at Vector Design pointed out, employers want to find people that work well with the group and who can communicate with the client on a variety of levels. Your responses to the following questions will target your thinking as well as prepare a foundation for your résumé. Remember, though, that employers seek more than empty assurances; they will want proof of your qualifications.

- *What skills have I acquired in school, on the job, or through other activities?* Employers are especially interested in communication and computer skills.
- *Do I work well with people?* What proof can I offer? Consider extracurricular activities, clubs, and jobs.
- *Am I a leader, self-starter, or manager?* What evidence can I offer?

FIGURE 16.1 ■ The Employment Search

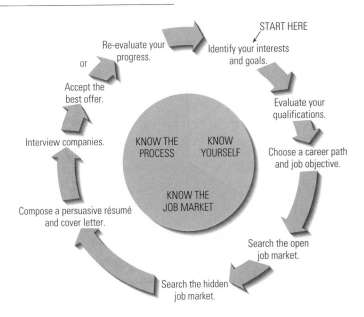

START HERE

Identify your interests and goals.

Re-evaluate your progress.

or

Accept the best offer.

Interview companies.

Evaluate your qualifications.

Choose a career path and job objective.

KNOW THE PROCESS

KNOW YOURSELF

KNOW THE JOB MARKET

Compose a persuasive résumé and cover letter.

Search the open job market.

Search the hidden job market.

- *Do I speak, write, or understand another language?*

- *Do I learn quickly? Am I creative?* How can I demonstrate these characteristics?

- *Do I speak and write well?* How can I verify these talents?

Choosing a Career Path

As a result of job trends and personal choices, the average employee changes careers at least three times in a lifetime. Some of you probably have not settled on your first career choice yet; others are returning to college to retrain for a new career. You'll make the best career decisions when you can match your interests and qualifications with the requirements and rewards in specific careers. But where can you get specific information about careers? Here are some suggestions:

- **Visit your campus career centre**. Most have literature, inventories, and software programs that allow you to investigate such fields as accounting, finance, office administration, hotel management, and so forth.

- **Power up your computer.** There are now many software programs for job candidates. Job Power Source, for example, is a highly rated CD-ROM multimedia training course. It helps users discover their work styles, set career goals, and find jobs.[2]

- **Use your library**. Several publications are especially helpful. Consult the latest edition of the *Blue Book of Canadian Business, Canadian Key Business Directory*, and *Financial Post Selects the 100 Best Companies to Work for in Canada*. Read the *Scott's Directory* for the geographical area of your search.

- **Take a summer job, internship, or part-time position in your field.** Nothing is better than trying out a career by actually working in it or an

Career information can be obtained at campus career centres and libraries, in classified ads, and from professional organizations.

Preparing for a career begins long before you search the classified ads and write your résumé. Some of the best ways to learn about career paths involve taking a summer job, internship, or part-time position in the area of your interest. Most often these positions don't just fall in your lap. They require determination and effort.

Summer and part-time jobs and internships are good opportunities to learn about different careers.

allied area. Many companies offer internships and temporary jobs to begin training students and to develop relationships with them. These relationships sometimes blossom into permanent positions. Jon Georges, profiled in Chapter 15, commuted 90 minutes each way to work at Disneyland while in high school and college. That tenacity undoubtedly helped his résumé stand out from the hundreds Disney Imagineering had received.

- **Interview someone in your chosen field.** People are usually flattered when asked to describe their careers. Inquire about needed skills, required courses, financial and other rewards, benefits, working conditions, future trends, and entry requirements.

- **Monitor the classified ads.** Early in your college or university career, begin scanning want ads in your career area. Check job availability, qualifications sought, duties, and salary range. Don't wait until you're about to graduate to see how the job market looks.

- **Join professional organizations in your field.** Frequently, they offer student membership status and reduced rates. You'll get an inside track on issues, career news, and possibly jobs.

Searching the Job Market

A job-search campaign might include checking classified ads and announcements in professional publications, contacting companies, and developing a network of contracts.

Finding the perfect job, even when the economy is flourishing, requires an early start and a determined effort. Some American colleges and universities now require first- and second-year students to take an employment seminar called "Reality 101." Students are told early on that a college degree alone doesn't guarantee a job. They are cautioned that grade-point averages make a difference to employers. And they are advised of the importance of experience and an aggressive job search campaign, including some or all of the following steps:

- **Check classified ads in local and national newspapers.** Be aware, though, that classified ads are only one small source of jobs, as discussed in the accompanying Career Skills box.

NETWORKING TO EXPLORE THE HIDDEN JOB MARKET

When you look in the classified ads, you see only a fraction of the jobs that really exist. Amazingly, the "hidden" job market—those positions never advertised or announced publicly—accounts for two-thirds to three-fourths of all positions available!

Employers don't advertise job openings for many reasons. For one thing, such advertisements are expensive and time-consuming. One employer, for example, advertised for a receptionist and had 80 applicants, tying up phone lines and disrupting normal business considerably. Moreover, employers dislike hiring "strangers." One personnel specialist explains, "If I'm in a hiring position, I'm first going to look around among my friends and acquaintances. If I can't find anybody, I'll look around for their friends and acquaintances. Only if I can't find anybody will I advertise."[3] Employers are much more comfortable hiring a person they know.

The real key to finding a good job, then, is converting yourself from a "stranger" into a known quantity. You can become a known quantity and cultivate your own personal network with a three-step plan.

STEP 1: MAKE A LIST. Make a list of anyone who would be willing to talk to you about finding a job. These people do not have to be in your career area. In fact, most won't be. List your friends, relatives, former employers, former co-workers, classmates from elementary school and high school, college friends, members of your church or place of worship, people in social and athletic clubs, present and former teachers, neighbours, and people who sell you things (such as services, insurance, and supplies). And don't overlook your parents—you often find a rich source of possibilities among their friends, colleagues, and so on.

STEP 2: MAKE CONTACTS. Call the people on your list or, even better, try to meet with them in person. A personal visit makes a much greater impression than a telephone call. To set up a meeting, you might say something like, "Hi, Aunt Jenny! I'm looking for a job and I wonder if you could help me out. When could I come over to talk about it?" During your visit be friendly, well organized, polite, and interested in what your contact has to say. Provide a copy of your résumé and try to keep the conversation centred on your job search area. Your goal is to get two or more referrals. In pinpointing your request, ask three questions. "Do you know of anyone who might have an opening for a person with my skills?" If not, "Do you know of anyone else who might know of someone who would?" If not, "Do you know someone who knows lots of people?"

STEP 3: FOLLOW UP ON YOUR REFERRALS. Call the people whose names are on your referral list. You might say something like, "Hello, I'm Carlos Ramos, a friend of Connie Cole's. She suggested that I call and ask you for help. I'm looking for a position as a marketing trainee, and she thought you might be willing to see me and give me a few ideas." Don't ask for a job. Most of the people you meet this way will not be in a position to offer a job, but they may know other people and be willing to refer you to them.

During your referral interview ask how the person got started in this line of work, what he or she likes best (or least) about the work, what career paths exist in the field, and what problems must be overcome by a newcomer. Most important, ask how a person with your background and skills might get started in the field.

Send an informal thank-you note to anyone who helps you in your job search, and stay in touch with the most promising contacts. Ask if you may call every three weeks or so during your job search.

Career Track Application

Begin developing your network. Conduct at least one referral interview. Take notes, and report your reactions and findings to your class.

- **Check announcements in publications of professional organizations.**
  If you do not have a student membership, ask your professors to lend you the current copies of professional journals, newsletters, and so on. Your college or university library is another good source.

- **Contact companies in which you're interested, even if you know of no current opening**. Write an unsolicited letter and include your résumé. Follow up with a telephone call.

- **Sign up for campus interviews with visiting company representatives**. Campus recruiters may open your eyes to exciting jobs and locations.

- **Ask for advice from your professors**. They often have contacts and ideas for expanding your job search.

- **Develop your own network of contacts**. According to Toronto career consultant Colleen Clarke, author of a self-help book on networking and founder of EARN (Executive Advancement Resource Network), about 80 percent of jobs are now found through networking. The other 20 percent of jobs are almost equally divided between those found through print ads and those found through recruiters.[4] Therefore, plan to spend the majority of your job search time developing a personal network. The Career Skills box gives you step-by-step instructions for cultivating a network and following through with referral interviews.

Above all, be creative and persistent in your job search. With unemployment running high, think of the following options. Create your own job; part-time your way to a full-time job; network effectively; upgrade your skills; and finally know your goals, but be flexible.[5]

The Persuasive Résumé

After learning about the employment market and getting job leads, your next step is to write a persuasive résumé. Such a résumé does more than merely list your qualifications. It packages your assets into a convincing advertisement that sells you for a specific job. The goal of a persuasive résumé is to win an interview. Even if you are not in the job market at this moment, preparing a résumé now has advantages. Having a current résumé makes you look well organized and professional should an unexpected employment opportunity arise. Moreover, preparing a résumé early helps you recognize weak qualifications and gives you two or three years in which to strengthen them.

Choosing a Résumé Style

Your qualifications and career goal will help you choose from among three résumé styles: chronological, functional, and combination.

Chronological. Most popular with recruiters is the chronological résumé, shown in Figure 16.2. It lists work history job by job, starting with the *most recent* position. Some recruiters favour the chronological style because such résumés quickly reveal a candidate's work stability and promotion record. Another corporate recruiter said, "I'm looking for applicable experience; chronological résumés are the easiest to assess."[6] The chronological style works well for candidates who have experience in their field of employment and for those who show steady career growth. But for many students and others without extensive experience, the functional résumé may be preferable.

Functional. The functional résumé, shown in Figure 16.3, draws attention to a candidate's skills rather than on past employment. Like a chronological

FIGURE 16.2 ■ Chronological Résumé

The Three Phases of the Writing Process

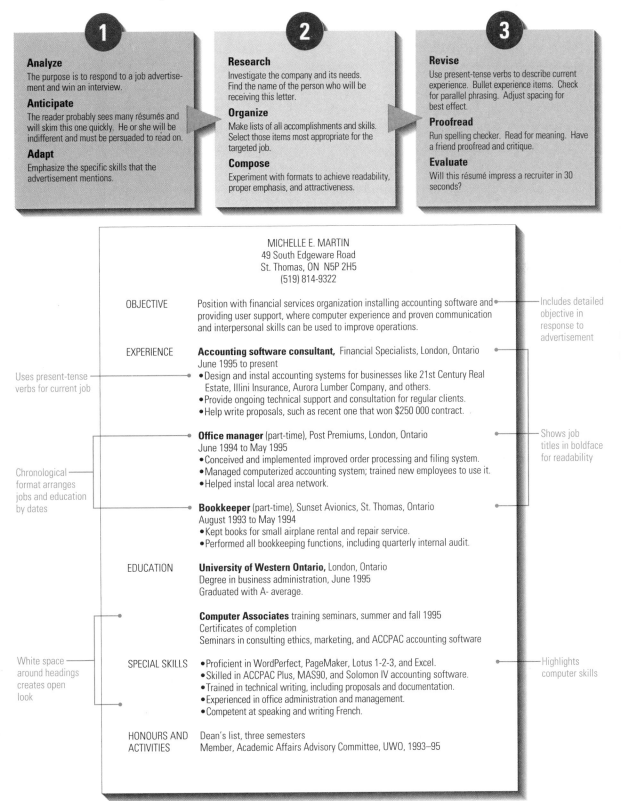

1

Analyze
The purpose is to respond to a job advertisement and win an interview.

Anticipate
The reader probably sees many résumés and will skim this one quickly. He or she will be indifferent and must be persuaded to read on.

Adapt
Emphasize the specific skills that the advertisement mentions.

2

Research
Investigate the company and its needs. Find the name of the person who will be receiving this letter.

Organize
Make lists of all accomplishments and skills. Select those items most appropriate for the targeted job.

Compose
Experiment with formats to achieve readability, proper emphasis, and attractiveness.

3

Revise
Use present-tense verbs to describe current experience. Bullet experience items. Check for parallel phrasing. Adjust spacing for best effect.

Proofread
Run spelling checker. Read for meaning. Have a friend proofread and critique.

Evaluate
Will this résumé impress a recruiter in 30 seconds?

MICHELLE E. MARTIN
49 South Edgeware Road
St. Thomas, ON N5P 2H5
(519) 814-9322

OBJECTIVE

Position with financial services organization installing accounting software and providing user support, where computer experience and proven communication and interpersonal skills can be used to improve operations.

Includes detailed objective in response to advertisement

EXPERIENCE

Accounting software consultant, Financial Specialists, London, Ontario
June 1995 to present
- Design and instal accounting systems for businesses like 21st Century Real Estate, Illini Insurance, Aurora Lumber Company, and others.
- Provide ongoing technical support and consultation for regular clients.
- Help write proposals, such as recent one that won $250 000 contract.

Uses present-tense verbs for current job

Office manager (part-time), Post Premiums, London, Ontario
June 1994 to May 1995
- Conceived and implemented improved order processing and filing system.
- Managed computerized accounting system; trained new employees to use it.
- Helped instal local area network.

Shows job titles in boldface for readability

Chronological format arranges jobs and education by dates

Bookkeeper (part-time), Sunset Avionics, St. Thomas, Ontario
August 1993 to May 1994
- Kept books for small airplane rental and repair service.
- Performed all bookkeeping functions, including quarterly internal audit.

EDUCATION

University of Western Ontario, London, Ontario
Degree in business administration, June 1995
Graduated with A- average.

Computer Associates training seminars, summer and fall 1995
Certificates of completion
Seminars in consulting ethics, marketing, and ACCPAC accounting software

SPECIAL SKILLS

- Proficient in WordPerfect, PageMaker, Lotus 1-2-3, and Excel.
- Skilled in ACCPAC Plus, MAS90, and Solomon IV accounting software.
- Trained in technical writing, including proposals and documentation.
- Experienced in office administration and management.
- Competent at speaking and writing French.

Highlights computer skills

White space around headings creates open look

HONOURS AND ACTIVITIES

Dean's list, three semesters
Member, Academic Affairs Advisory Committee, UWO, 1993–95

FIGURE 16.3 ■ Functional Résumé

Donald, a recent graduate, chose this functional format to de-emphasize his limited work experience and emphasize his potential in sales and marketing. He included an employment section to satisfy recruiters.

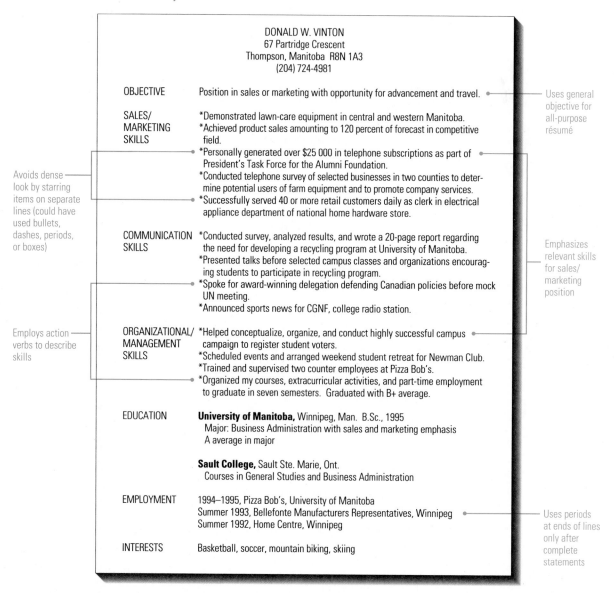

DONALD W. VINTON
67 Partridge Crescent
Thompson, Manitoba R8N 1A3
(204) 724-4981

OBJECTIVE — Position in sales or marketing with opportunity for advancement and travel. — Uses general objective for all-purpose résumé

SALES/ MARKETING SKILLS
*Demonstrated lawn-care equipment in central and western Manitoba.
*Achieved product sales amounting to 120 percent of forecast in competitive field.
*Personally generated over $25 000 in telephone subscriptions as part of President's Task Force for the Alumni Foundation.
*Conducted telephone survey of selected businesses in two counties to determine potential users of farm equipment and to promote company services.
*Successfully served 40 or more retail customers daily as clerk in electrical appliance department of national home hardware store.

Avoids dense look by starring items on separate lines (could have used bullets, dashes, periods, or boxes)

COMMUNICATION SKILLS
*Conducted survey, analyzed results, and wrote a 20-page report regarding the need for developing a recycling program at University of Manitoba.
*Presented talks before selected campus classes and organizations encouraging students to participate in recycling program.
*Spoke for award-winning delegation defending Canadian policies before mock UN meeting.
*Announced sports news for CGNF, college radio station.

Emphasizes relevant skills for sales/ marketing position

ORGANIZATIONAL/ MANAGEMENT SKILLS
*Helped conceptualize, organize, and conduct highly successful campus campaign to register student voters.
*Scheduled events and arranged weekend student retreat for Newman Club.
*Trained and supervised two counter employees at Pizza Bob's.
*Organized my courses, extracurricular activities, and part-time employment to graduate in seven semesters. Graduated with B+ average.

Employs action verbs to describe skills

EDUCATION
University of Manitoba, Winnipeg, Man. B.Sc., 1995
Major: Business Administration with sales and marketing emphasis
A average in major

Sault College, Sault Ste. Marie, Ont.
Courses in General Studies and Business Administration

EMPLOYMENT
1994–1995, Pizza Bob's, University of Manitoba
Summer 1993, Bellefonte Manufacturers Representatives, Winnipeg
Summer 1992, Home Centre, Winnipeg

Uses periods at ends of lines only after complete statements

INTERESTS — Basketball, soccer, mountain biking, skiing

Chronological résumés focus on past employment; functional résumés focus on skills.

Part V
Presentation Skills

résumé the functional résumé begins with the candidate's name, address, telephone number, job objective, and education. Instead of listing jobs, though, the functional résumé groups skills and accomplishments in special categories, such as *Supervisory and Management Skills* or *Retailing and Marketing Experience*. This résumé style highlights accomplishments and can de-emphasize a negative employment history. People who have changed jobs frequently or who have gaps in their employment records may prefer the functional résumé. Recent graduates with little employment experience often find the functional résumé useful.

FIGURE 16.4 ■ Combination Résumé

Because Susan wanted to highlight her skills and capabilities along with her experience, she combined the best features of functional and traditional résumés. This résumé style is becoming increasingly popular.

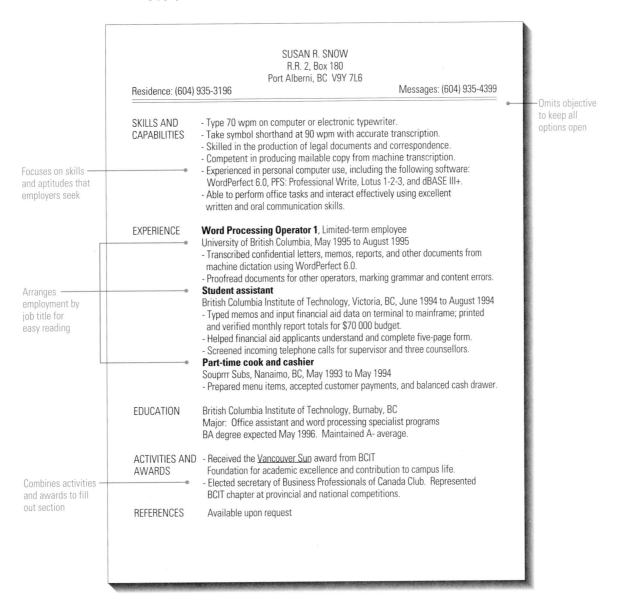

SUSAN R. SNOW
R.R. 2, Box 180
Port Alberni, BC V9Y 7L6

Residence: (604) 935-3196   Messages: (604) 935-4399

— Omits objective to keep all options open

SKILLS AND CAPABILITIES
- Type 70 wpm on computer or electronic typewriter.
- Take symbol shorthand at 90 wpm with accurate transcription.
- Skilled in the production of legal documents and correspondence.
- Competent in producing mailable copy from machine transcription.
- Experienced in personal computer use, including the following software: WordPerfect 6.0, PFS: Professional Write, Lotus 1-2-3, and dBASE III+.
- Able to perform office tasks and interact effectively using excellent written and oral communication skills.

Focuses on skills and aptitudes that employers seek

EXPERIENCE
Word Processing Operator 1, Limited-term employee
University of British Columbia, May 1995 to August 1995
- Transcribed confidential letters, memos, reports, and other documents from machine dictation using WordPerfect 6.0.
- Proofread documents for other operators, marking grammar and content errors.

Student assistant
British Columbia Institute of Technology, Victoria, BC, June 1994 to August 1994
- Typed memos and input financial aid data on terminal to mainframe; printed and verified monthly report totals for $70 000 budget.
- Helped financial aid applicants understand and complete five-page form.
- Screened incoming telephone calls for supervisor and three counsellors.

Part-time cook and cashier
Souprrr Subs, Nanaimo, BC, May 1993 to May 1994
- Prepared menu items, accepted customer payments, and balanced cash drawer.

Arranges employment by job title for easy reading

EDUCATION
British Columbia Institute of Technology, Burnaby, BC
Major: Office assistant and word processing specialist programs
BA degree expected May 1996. Maintained A- average.

ACTIVITIES AND AWARDS
- Received the Vancouver Sun award from BCIT Foundation for academic excellence and contribution to campus life.
- Elected secretary of Business Professionals of Canada Club. Represented BCIT chapter at provincial and national competitions.

Combines activities and awards to fill out section

REFERENCES   Available upon request

Functional résumés are also called "skill" résumés. Although the functional résumé of Donald Vinton shown here concentrates on skills, it does include a short employment section because recruiters expect it. Notice that Donald breaks his skills into three categories. An alternative—and easier—method is to make one large list, perhaps with a title such as *Areas of Accomplishment*, *Summary of Qualifications*, or *Areas of Expertise and Ability*.

Combination. The combination résumé style, shown in Figure 16.4, draws on the best features of the chronological and functional résumés. It emphasizes a candidate's capabilities while also including a complete job history. For recent graduates the combination résumé is a good choice because it enables them to profile what they can do for a prospective employer. If the writer has a specific job in mind, the items should be targeted to that job description.

Arranging the Parts

Although résumés have standard parts, their arrangement and content should be strategically planned. The most persuasive résumés emphasize skills and achievements aimed at a particular job or company. They show a candidate's most important qualifications first, and they de-emphasize any weaknesses. In arranging the parts, try to create as few headings as possible; more than six generally looks cluttered. No two résumés are ever exactly alike, but most writers consider the following parts.

Main heading. Your résumé should always begin with your name, address, and telephone number. If possible, include a number where messages may be left for you. Prospective employers tend to call the next applicant when no one answers. Avoid showing both permanent and temporary addresses; some specialists say that dual addresses immediately identify students who are about to graduate. Keep the main heading as uncluttered and simple as possible. And don't include the word *résumé;* it's like putting the word *letter* above correspondence.

Career objective. Opinion is divided on the effect of including a career objective on a résumé. Recruiters think such statements indicate that a candidate has made a commitment to a career. Moreover, career objectives make the recruiter's life easier by quickly classifying the résumé. But such declarations can also disqualify a candidate if the stated objective doesn't match a company's job description. One expert warned that putting a job objective on a résumé has "killed more opportunities for candidates ... than typos."[7]

You have three choices regarding career objectives. One option is to include a career objective when applying for a specific, targeted position. For example, the following responds to an advertised position: *Objective: To work in the health care industry as a human resources trainee with exposure to recruiting, training, and benefit administration.* A second choice—one that makes sense if you are preparing an all-purpose résumé—is to omit the career objective. A third possibility involves using a general statement, such as *Objective: Challenging position in urban planning* or *Job Goal: Position in sales/marketing.* Some consultants warn against using the words *entry-level* in your objective, as such words emphasize lack of experience.

Many aggressive job applicants today prepare individual targeted résumés for each company or position sought. Thanks to computers, the task is easy.

Résumés targeted to specific positions have the best chance of being read.

Education. The next part is your education—if it is more noteworthy than your work experience. In this section you should include the name and location of schools, dates of attendance, major fields of study, and degrees received. Your average and/or class ranking are important to prospective employers. One way to enhance your average is to calculate it in your major courses only (for example, *B+ average in major*). A list of completed courses makes dull reading; refer to courses only if you can relate them to the position sought. When relevant, include certificates earned, seminars attended, and workshops completed. Because employers are interested in your degree of self-sufficiency, you might wish to indicate the percentage of your education for which you paid. If your education is incomplete, include such statements as *B.Sc. degree expected 6/97* or *80 units completed in 120-unit program*. Entitle this section *Education, Academic Preparation*, or *Professional Training*.

Work experience. If your work experience is significant and relevant to the position sought, this information should appear before education. List your most recent employment first and work backwards, including only those jobs that you think will help you win the targeted position. A job application form may demand a full employment history, but your résumé may be selective. (Be aware, though, that time gaps in your employment history will probably be questioned in the interview.) For each position show the following:

- Employer's name, city, and province
- Dates of employment
- Most important job title
- Significant duties, activities, accomplishments, and promotions

Educational achievements should precede employment history on a résumé only when they are more noteworthy.

Describe your employment achievements concisely but concretely. Avoid generalities like *Worked with customers*. Be more specific, with statements such as *Served 40 or more retail customers a day, Successfully resolved problems about custom stationery orders*, or *Acted as intermediary between customers, printers, and suppliers*. If possible, quantify your accomplishments, such as *Conducted study of equipment needs of 100 small businesses in Halifax, Personally generated orders for sales of $90 000 annually, Keyboarded all the production models for a 250-page employee procedures manual*, or *Assisted editor in layout, design, and news writing for 12 issues of division newsletter*.

In addition to technical skills, employers seek communication, management, and interpersonal abilities. This means you'll want to select work experiences and achievements that illustrate your initiative, dependability, responsibility, resourcefulness, and leadership. Employers also want people who can work together in teams. Thus, include statements like *Collaborated with interdepartmental task force in developing 10-page handbook for temporary workers* and *Headed student government team that conducted most successful voter registration in campus history*.

Statements describing your work experience can be made forceful and persuasive by using "action" verbs, such as those listed in Figure 16.5 and demonstrated in Figure 16.6.

The work experience section of a résumé should list specifics and quantify achievements.

Capabilities and skills. Recruiters want to know specifically what you can do for their companies. Therefore, list your special skills, such as *Proficient in preparing correspondence and reports using Word for Windows*. Include your ability to use computer programs, office equipment, foreign languages, or sign language. Describe proficiencies you have acquired through training and experience, such as *Trained in computer accounting, including general ledger, accounts receivable, accounts payable, and payroll*. Use expressions like *competent in, skilled in, proficient with, experienced in*, and *ability to*; for example, *Competent in typing, editing, and proofreading reports, tables, letters, memos, manuscripts, and business forms*.

You'll also want to highlight exceptional aptitudes, such as working well under stress and learning computer programs quickly. If possible, provide

Emphasize the skills and aptitudes that recommend you for a specific position.

FIGURE 16.5 ■ Action Verbs for Persuasive Résumés*

Management Skills	Communication Skills	Research Skills	Technical Skills	Teaching Skills
administered	addressed	clarified	assembled	adapted
analyzed	arbitrated	collected	built	advised
consolidated	arranged	critiqued	calculated	clarified
coordinated	collaborated	diagnosed	computed	coached
delegated	convinced	evaluated	designed	communicated
developed	developed	examined	devised	coordinated
directed	drafted	extracted	engineered	developed
evaluated	edited	identified	executed	enabled
improved	explained	inspected	fabricated	encouraged
increased	formulated	interpreted	maintained	evaluated
organized	interpreted	interviewed	operated	explained
oversaw	negotiated	investigated	overhauled	facilitated
planned	persuaded	organized	programmed	guided
prioritized	promoted	summarized	remodeled	informed
recommended	publicized	surveyed	repaired	instructed
scheduled	recruited	systematized	solved	persuaded
strengthened	translated		upgraded	set goals
supervised	wrote			trained

*The **underlined** words are especially good for pointing out **accomplishments**.

details and evidence that back up your assertions; for example, *Mastered the Barrister computer program in 25 hours with little instruction.* Search for examples of your writing, speaking, management, organizational, and interpersonal skills—particularly those talents that are relevant to your targeted job.

For recent graduates, this section can be used to give recruiters evidence of your potential. Instead of *Capabilities*, the section might be called *Skills and Abilities.*

Awards, honours, and activities are appropriate for résumés; most personal data are not.

Awards, honours, and activities. If you have three or more awards or honours, highlight them by listing them under a separate heading. If not, put them with activities. Include awards, scholarships (financial and other), fellowships, honours, recognition, commendations, and certificates. Be sure to identify items clearly. Your reader may be unfamiliar, for example, with some professional organizations, honouraries, and awards; tell what they mean. Instead of saying *Recipient of Star award*, give more details: *Recipient of Star award given by Mount Allison University to outstanding graduates who combine academic excellence and extracurricular activities.*

It's also appropriate to include school, community, and professional activities. Employers are interested in evidence that you are a well-rounded person. This section provides an opportunity to demonstrate leadership and interpersonal skills. Strive to use action statements. For example, instead of saying *Treasurer of business club*, explain more fully: *Collected dues, kept financial records, and paid bills while serving as treasurer of 35-member business management club.*

Financial Skills	Creative Skills	Helping Skills	Clerical or Detail Skills	More Verbs for Accomplishments
administered	acted	assessed	approved	achieved
allocated	conceptualized	assisted	catalogued	expanded
analyzed	created	clarified	classified	improved
appraised	customized	coached	collected	pioneered
audited	designed	counseled	compiled	reduced (losses)
balanced	developed	demonstrated	generated	resolved (problems)
budgeted	directed	diagnosed	inspected	restored
calculated	established	educated	monitor	spearheaded
computed	founded	expedited	operated	transformed
developed	illustrated	facilitated	organized	
forecasted	initiated	familiarized	prepared	
managed	instituted	guided	processed	
marketed	introduced	motivated	purchased	
planned	invented	referred	recorded	
projected	originated	represented	screened	
researched	performed		specified	
	planned		systematized	
	revitalized		tabulated	

FIGURE 16.6 ■ Using Action Verbs to Strengthen Your Résumé

Identified weaknesses in internship program and **researched** five alternate programs.

Reduced delivery delays but an average of three days per order.

Streamlined filing system, thus reducing 400-item backlog to 0.

Organized holiday awards program for 1200 attendees and 140 awardees.

Created a 12-point checklist for managers to use when requesting temporary workers.

Designed five posters announcing new employee suggestions program.

Calculated shipping charges for overseas deliveries and **recommended** most economical rates.

Managed 24-station computer network linking data and employees in three departments.

Distributed and **explained** over 500 voter registration forms to prospective student voters.

Personal data. The trend in résumés today is to omit personal data, such as birth date, marital status, height, weight, and religious affiliation. Such information doesn't relate to genuine occupational qualifications, and recruiters are legally barred from asking for such information. Some job seekers do, however, include hobbies or interests (such as skiing or photography) that might catch the recruiter's attention or serve as conversation starters. Naturally, you wouldn't mention dangerous pastimes (such as bungee jumping or sports car racing) or time-consuming interests. But you should indicate your willingness to travel or to relocate, since many companies will be interested.

References. Some recruiters prefer to see references listed on a résumé; others do not.[8] Such a list takes up valuable space. Moreover, it is not normally instrumental in securing an interview—few companies check references before the interview. Instead, they prefer that a candidate take to the interview a list of people willing to discuss her or his qualifications. If you do list them, use parallel form. For example, if you show a title for one person *(Professor, Dr., Mrs.)*, show titles for all. Include addresses and telephone numbers.

Whether or not you include references on your résumé, you should have their names available when you begin your job search. Ask three to five instructors or previous employers whether they will be willing to answer inquiries regarding your qualifications for employment. Be sure, however, to provide them with an opportunity to refuse. No reference is better than a negative one. Do not include personal or character references, such as friends or neighbours, because recruiters rarely consult them; they are more interested in the opinions of someone objective.

One final note: personnel officers see little reason for including the statement *References furnished upon request.* "It's like saying the sun comes up every morning," remarked one human resources professional.[9]

Preparing for Computer Scanning

Thus far we've aimed our résumé advice at human readers. However, the first reader of your résumé may well be a computer. Hiring companies now use computer programs in two ways: to reduce the costs of hiring and to make résumé information more accessible.

Applicant-Tracking Programs

The first method involves software that helps large companies track incoming résumés. Sport shoe manufacturer Nike, for example, was deluged with thousands of unsolicited résumés. As a result, confesses Karen Cross, Nike employment specialist, "nobody ever looked at the résumé files because they were just too huge."[10] Then Nike installed a computer-based applicant-tracking program. This program uses optical-character recognition (OSR) to scan incoming résumés. Such programs scan résumés, identify job categories, and even rank applicants. Most programs then generate letters of rejection or prepare interview offers for the lucky applicants whose résumés match the job openings. Finally, these applicant-tracking programs store résumé information for future hiring. When a job opens up, a hiring manager tells the system what the position requires. The computer then searches to find résumés with words that match the request. Electronic searches offer ease and precision, unlike the hopelessness of searching manually through thousands of résumés in filing cabinets.

Résumé Databanks

A second way hiring companies use computers is through résumé databanks. Smaller companies can't afford money applicant-tracking software; they are therefore turning to résumé databanks. These databanks store thousands of electronic résumés submitted by eager job candidates. The companies no longer have to recruit, advertise, and interview extensively. Experts estimate that it costs an employer $35 000 to hire a professional or managerial person if a private recruiting firm is used. But an electronic search costs only a fraction of that sum. Small wonder that employers are increasingly using résumé banks to find new employees.[11]

Making Your Résumé Computer-Friendly

What does this all mean for you and your résumé? First, don't panic. It doesn't mean that you will have to hire a résumé specialist to write an entirely new résumé. It does mean, though, that you should consider the possibility that your résumé might be scanned. How can you know? One simple solution is to call any company where you plan to apply. Ask if it scans résumés electronically. What if you can't get a clear answer? If you have even the slightest suspicion that your résumé might be read electronically, you'll be smart to prepare a plain, scannable version. A scannable résumé must sacrifice many of the graphics possibilities that experienced writers employ. Computers aren't impressed by graphics; they prefer résumés that are free of graphics and fancy fonts. To make a computer-friendly résumé, you'll want to follow these suggestions about its physical appearance.

- **Avoid unusual typefaces, underlining, and italics**. Moreover, don't use boxes, shading, or other graphics to highlight text. These features don't scan well. Most applicant-tracking programs, however, can accurately read boldface, solid bullets, and asterisks.

- **Use 10- to 14-point type**. Because touching letters or unusual fonts are likely to be misread, it's safest to use a large, well-known font, such as 12-point Times Roman or Courier. This may mean that your résumé will require two pages. After printing, inspect your résumé to see if any letters touch—especially in your name.

- **Use smooth white paper, black ink, and high-quality printing**. Avoid coloured and textured papers as well as dot matrix printing.

- **Be sure that your name is the first line on the page**. Don't use fancy layouts that may confuse a scanner.

- **Provide white space**. To ensure separation of words and categories, leave plenty of white space. For example, instead of using parentheses to enclose a telephone area code, insert blank spaces, such as 613 799–2415. Leave blank lines around headings.

- **Avoid double columns**. When listing job duties, skills, computer programs, and so forth, don't tabulate items into two- or three-column lists. Scanners read across and may convert tables into gobbledegook.

- **Don't fold or staple your résumé**. Send it in a large envelope so that it doesn't need to be folded. Words that appear on folds may not be scanned correctly. Avoid staples because the indentions left after they are removed may cause pages to stick.

- **Use abbreviations carefully**. Minimize unfamiliar abbreviations, but maximize easily recognized abbreviations—especially those within your field, such as CAD, COBRA, or JIT. When in doubt, though, spell out! Computers are less confused by whole words.

Emphasize Key Words

In addition to paying attention to the physical appearance of your résumé, you must also be concerned with key words. These are usually nouns that describe what an employer wants. Suppose a supervisor at Nike wants to hire an administrative assistant with special proficiencies. That supervisor might submit the following key words to the company's applicant-tracking system: *Administrative Assistant, Computer Skills, Word for Windows, Self-starter, Report Writing, Proofreading, Communication Skills.* The system would then search through all the résumés on file to see which ones best match the requirements.

Joyce Lain Kennedy, nationally syndicated career columnist and author of *Electronic Resume Revolution*, suggests using a *key word* summary.[12] On your résumé this list of key words immediately follows your name and address.

A key word summary should contain your targeted job title and alternative labels, as well as previous job titles, skills, software programs, and selected jargon known in your field. It concentrates on nouns rather than on verbs or adjectives.

To construct your summary, go through your résumé and mark all relevant nouns. Also try to imagine what 8 to 10 words an employer might use to describe the job you want. Then select the 25 best words for your summary. Because interpersonal traits are often requested by employers, consult Figure 16.7. It shows the most frequently requested interpersonal traits, as reported by Resumix, one of the leaders in résumé-scanning software.

You may entitle your list "Key Word Summary," "Key Word Profile," or "Key Word Index." Here's an example of a possible key word summary for a junior accountant:

KEY WORD SUMMARY

Accountant: Public. Junior. Staff. Dipl. Conestoga College Business Administration. B.A., Waterloo University–Accounting. Payables. Receivables. Payroll Experience. Quarterly Reports. Unemployment Reports. Communication Skills. Computer Skills. Lotus 1-2-3. dBase. PCs. Mainframes. Networks. J.D. Edwards Software. Ability to learn software. Accurate. Dean's List. Award of Merit. Team player. Willing to travel. Relocate.

After an introductory keyword summary, your résumé should contain the standard parts discussed in this chapter. Remember that the key word section merely helps ensure that your résumé will be selected for inspection. Then human eyes take over. Therefore, you'll want to observe the other writing tips you've learned to make your résumé attractive and forceful. Figures 16.8 to 16.10 show additional examples of chronological and combination résumés. Notice that the scannable résumé in Figure 16.11 is not drastically different from the others. It does, however, include a key word summary.

Applying the Final Touches

Because your résumé is probably the most important message you will ever write, you'll revise it many times. With so much information in concentrated form and with so much riding on its outcome, your résumé demands careful polishing, proofreading, and critiquing.

FIGURE 16.7 ■ Interpersonal Keywords Most Requested by Employers Using Résumé Scanning Software*

Ability to delegate	Innovative
Ability to implement	Leadership
Ability to plan	Multitasking
Ability to train	Open communication
Accurate	Open-minded
Adaptable	Oral communication
Aggressive work	Organizational skills
Analytical ability	Persuasive
Assertive	Problem-solving
Communication skills	Public-speaking
Competitive	Results-oriented
Creative	Safety-conscious
Customer-oriented	Self-accountable
Detail-minded	Self-managing
Empowering others	Sensitive
Ethical	Setting priorities
Flexible	Supportive
Follow instructions	Takes initiative
Follow through	Team-building
Follow up	Team player
High-energy	Tenacious
Industrious	Willing to travel

*Reported by Resumix, one of the leading producers of résumé-scanning software.

As you revise, be certain to verify all the facts, particularly those involving your previous employment and education. Don't be caught in a mistake, or worse, distortion of previous jobs and dates of employment. These items likely will be checked. And the consequences of puffing up a résumé with deception or flat-out lies are simply not worth the risk. Other ethical traps you'll want to avoid are described in the following Ethics box.

As you continue revising, look for other ways to improve your résumé. For example, consider consolidating headings. By condensing your information into as few headings as possible, you'll produce a clean, professional-looking document. Study other résumés for valuable formatting ideas. Ask yourself what graphic highlighting techniques you can use to improve readability: capitalization, underlining, indenting, and bulleting. Experiment with headings and styles to achieve a pleasing, easy-to-read message. Moreover, look for ways to eliminate wordiness. For example, instead of *Supervised two employees who worked at the counter,* try *Supervised two counter employees.* Review Chapter 5 for more tips.

In addition to being well written, a résumé must be carefully formatted and meticulously proofread.

Chapter 16
Employment Messages

AVOIDING WRITING AN UNETHICAL RÉSUMÉ

A résumé is expected to showcase a candidate's strengths and minimize weaknesses. Recruiters expect a certain degree of self-promotion. But some résumé writers step over the line that separates honest self-marketing from deceptive half-truths and flat-out lies. Distorting facts on a résumé is unethical; lying is illegal. And either practice can destroy a career.

Although recruiters can't check everything, most will verify previous employment and education before hiring candidates. Over half will require official transcripts.[13] And after hiring, the checking process may continue. At a top accounting firm, the human resource director described their post-hiring routine: "If we find a discrepancy in GPA [grade point average] or prior experience due to an honest mistake, we meet with the new hire to hear an explanation. But if it wasn't a mistake, we terminate the person immediately. Unfortunately, we've had to do that too often.[14]

No job seeker wants to be in the unhappy position of explaining résumé errors or defending misrepresentation. Avoiding the following common problems can keep you off the hot seat:

- **Inflated education, grades, or honours.** Some job candidates claim to have degrees from colleges or universities when in fact they merely attended classes. Others increase their averages or claim fictitious honours. Any such dishonest report is grounds for dismissal when discovered.

- **Enhanced job titles.** Wishing to elevate their status, some applicants misrepresent their titles. For example, one technician called himself a "programmer" when he had actually programmed for only one project for his boss. A mail clerk who assumed added responsibilities conferred upon herself the title of "supervisor." Even when the description seems accurate, it's unethical to list any title not officially granted.

- **Puffed-up accomplishments.** Some job seekers inflate their employment experience or achievements. One clerk, eager to make her photocopying duties sound more important, said that she *assisted the vice-president in communicating and distributing employee directives*. A graduate who spent the better part of six months watching rented videos on his VCR described the activity as *Independent Film Study*. The latter statement may have helped win an interview, but it lost him

the job.[15] In addition to avoiding puffery, guard against taking sole credit for achievements that required many people. When recruiters suspect dubious claims on résumés, they nail applicants with specific—and often embarrassing—questions during their interviews.[16]

- **Altered employment dates.** Some candidates extend the dates of employment to hide unimpressive jobs or to cover up periods of unemployment and illness. Let's say that several years ago Cindy was unemployed for 14 months between working for Company A and being hired by Company B. To make her employment history look better, she adds seven months to her tenure with Company A and seven months to Company B. Now her employment history has no gaps, but her résumé is dishonest and is a potential bobby trap for her.

The employment process can easily lure you into ethical traps, such as those described in Chapter 3. Beware of these specific temptations:

- **The relative-filth trap:** "A little fudging on my GPA is nothing compared to the degrees that some people buy in degree mills."

- **The rationalization trap:** "I deserve to call myself 'manager' because that's what I really did."

- **The self-deception trap:** "Giving myself a certificate from the institute is OK because I really intended to finish the program, but I got sick."

These ethical traps can jeopardize your entire employment future. If your honest qualifications aren't good enough to get you the job you want, start working now to improve them.

Career Track Application

As a class, discuss the ethics of writing résumés. What's the difference between honest self-marketing and deception? What are some examples from your experience? Where could students go wrong in preparing their résumés? Is a new employee "home free" if an inflated résumé is not detected in the hiring process? Are job candidates obligated to describe every previous job on a résumé? How can candidates improve an unimpressive résumé without resorting to exaggeration?

Above all, make your résumé look professional. Avoid anything humorous or cute, such as a help-wanted poster with your name or picture inside. Eliminate the personal pronoun *I*. The abbreviated, objective style of a résumé precludes the use of personal pronouns. Use white, off-white, or buff-colored heavy bond paper (24-pound) and a first-rate printer.

After revising, proofread, proofread, and proofread again: for spelling and mechanics, for content, and for format. Then, have a knowledgeable friend or relative proofread it again. This is one document that must be perfect.

By now you may be thinking that you'd like to hire someone to write your résumé. Don't. First, you know yourself better than anyone else could know you. Second, you'll end up with either a generic or a one-time résumé. A generic résumé in today's highly competitive job market will lose out to a targeted résumé 9 times out of 10. Equally useless is a one-time résumé aimed at a single job. What if you don't get that job? Because you will need to revise your résumé many times as you seek a variety of jobs, be prepared to write (and rewrite) it yourself.

A final word about résumé-writing services. Some tend to produce eye-catching, elaborate documents with lofty language, fancy borders, and fuzzy thinking. Here's an example: "Seeking a position which will utilize academic achievements and hands-on experience while providing for career-development opportunities."[17] Save your money and buy a good interview suit instead.

Faxing Your Résumé

In this hurry-up world, employers increasingly want information immediately. If you must fax your résumé, take a second look at it. The key to success is SPACE. Without it, letters and characters blur. Underlining blends with the words above, and bold print looks like an ink blot.[18] How can you improve your chances of making a good impression when you must fax your résumé?

- **Select a font with adequate space between characters.** Thinner fonts—such as Times, Palatino, New Century Schoolbook, Courier, and Bookman—are clearer than thicker ones.

- **Use 12-point or larger font.** Larger fonts are less likely to blur.

- **Avoid underlining.** When faxed, underlines may look broken and choppy. Instead, you might use italics, bold, or capital letters—so long as the letters don't touch.

- **Verify transmission.** If you are using a mail centre, ask for a transmission report to ensure that all pages were received satisfactorily.

Nearly everyone writes a résumé by adapting a model, such as those in Figures 16.2 to 16.4 and 16.8 to 16.11. The chronological résumé for Rachel shown in Figure 16.10 is a typical résumé for candidates with considerable working experience. Although she describes four positions that span a 14-year period, she manages to fit her résumé on one page. However, two-page résumés are justified for people with long work histories.

As you prepare to write your current résumé, consult the following checklist to review the job search process and important résumé-writing techniques.

FIGURE 16.8 ■ Chronological Résumé

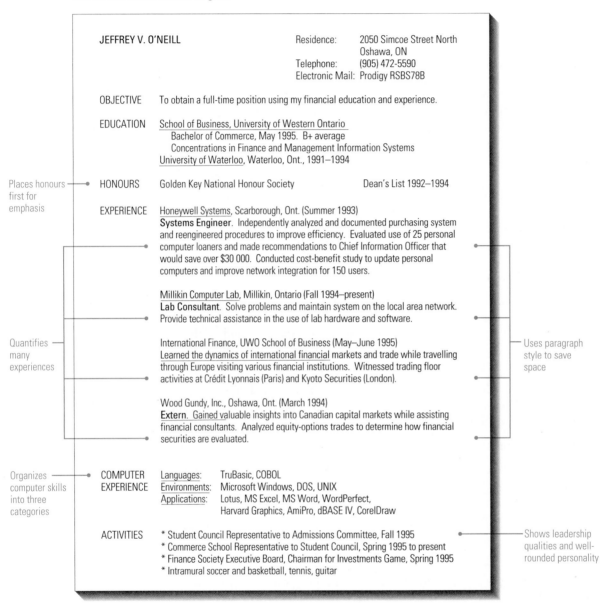

Although Jeffrey had little paid work experience off campus, his résumé looks impressive because of his relevant summer, campus, and extern experiences. He describes specific achievements related to finance, his career goal.

JEFFREY V. O'NEILL

Residence: 2050 Simcoe Street North
                          Oshawa, ON
Telephone: (905) 472-5590
Electronic Mail: Prodigy RSBS78B

OBJECTIVE   To obtain a full-time position using my financial education and experience.

EDUCATION   School of Business, University of Western Ontario
                              Bachelor of Commerce, May 1995. B+ average
                              Concentrations in Finance and Management Information Systems
                          University of Waterloo, Waterloo, Ont., 1991–1994

Places honours first for emphasis → HONOURS   Golden Key National Honour Society   Dean's List 1992–1994

EXPERIENCE   Honeywell Systems, Scarborough, Ont. (Summer 1993)
                              Systems Engineer. Independently analyzed and documented purchasing system and reengineered procedures to improve efficiency. Evaluated use of 25 personal computer loaners and made recommendations to Chief Information Officer that would save over $30 000. Conducted cost-benefit study to update personal computers and improve network integration for 150 users.

                          Millikin Computer Lab, Millikin, Ontario (Fall 1994–present)
                              Lab Consultant. Solve problems and maintain system on the local area network. Provide technical assistance in the use of lab hardware and software.

Quantifies many experiences → International Finance, UWO School of Business (May–June 1995)
                              Learned the dynamics of international financial markets and trade while travelling through Europe visiting various financial institutions. Witnessed trading floor activities at Crédit Lyonnais (Paris) and Kyoto Securities (London).

                          Wood Gundy, Inc., Oshawa, Ont. (March 1994)
                              Extern. Gained valuable insights into Canadian capital markets while assisting financial consultants. Analyzed equity-options trades to determine how financial securities are evaluated.

← Uses paragraph style to save space

Organizes computer skills into three categories → COMPUTER EXPERIENCE
                          Languages: TruBasic, COBOL
                          Environments: Microsoft Windows, DOS, UNIX
                          Applications: Lotus, MS Excel, MS Word, WordPerfect,
                                                    Harvard Graphics, AmiPro, dBASE IV, CorelDraw

ACTIVITIES   * Student Council Representative to Admissions Committee, Fall 1995
                          * Commerce School Representative to Student Council, Spring 1995 to present
                          * Finance Society Executive Board, Chairman for Investments Game, Spring 1995
                          * Intramural soccer and basketball, tennis, guitar

← Shows leadership qualities and well-rounded personality

■ Checklist for Writing a Persuasive Résumé

Preparation

✓ **Research the job market.** Learn about available jobs, common qualifications, and potential employers. The best résumés are written for specific jobs with specific companies.

FIGURE 16.9 ■ Combination Résumé

Rick's résumé responds to an advertisement specifying skills for a staff accountant. He uses the combination format to allow him to highlight the skills his education and limited experience have provided. To make the résumé look professional, he uses the italics, bold, and scalable font features of his word-processing program.

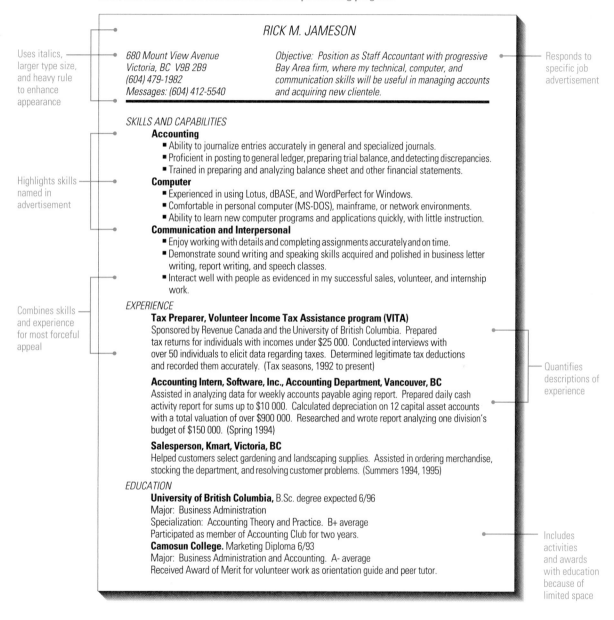

Uses italics, larger type size, and heavy rule to enhance appearance

Highlights skills named in advertisement

Combines skills and experience for most forceful appeal

Responds to specific job advertisement

Quantifies descriptions of experience

Includes activities and awards with education because of limited space

RICK M. JAMESON

680 Mount View Avenue
Victoria, BC V9B 2B9
(604) 479-1982
Messages: (604) 412-5540

Objective: Position as Staff Accountant with progressive Bay Area firm, where my technical, computer, and communication skills will be useful in managing accounts and acquiring new clientele.

SKILLS AND CAPABILITIES

Accounting
- Ability to journalize entries accurately in general and specialized journals.
- Proficient in posting to general ledger, preparing trial balance, and detecting discrepancies.
- Trained in preparing and analyzing balance sheet and other financial statements.

Computer
- Experienced in using Lotus, dBASE, and WordPerfect for Windows.
- Comfortable in personal computer (MS-DOS), mainframe, or network environments.
- Ability to learn new computer programs and applications quickly, with little instruction.

Communication and Interpersonal
- Enjoy working with details and completing assignments accurately and on time.
- Demonstrate sound writing and speaking skills acquired and polished in business letter writing, report writing, and speech classes.
- Interact well with people as evidenced in my successful sales, volunteer, and internship work.

EXPERIENCE

Tax Preparer, Volunteer Income Tax Assistance program (VITA)
Sponsored by Revenue Canada and the University of British Columbia. Prepared tax returns for individuals with incomes under $25 000. Conducted interviews with over 50 individuals to elicit data regarding taxes. Determined legitimate tax deductions and recorded them accurately. (Tax seasons, 1992 to present)

Accounting Intern, Software, Inc., Accounting Department, Vancouver, BC
Assisted in analyzing data for weekly accounts payable aging report. Prepared daily cash activity report for sums up to $10 000. Calculated depreciation on 12 capital asset accounts with a total valuation of over $900 000. Researched and wrote report analyzing one division's budget of $150 000. (Spring 1994)

Salesperson, Kmart, Victoria, BC
Helped customers select gardening and landscaping supplies. Assisted in ordering merchandise, stocking the department, and resolving customer problems. (Summers 1994, 1995)

EDUCATION

University of British Columbia, B.Sc. degree expected 6/96
Major: Business Administration
Specialization: Accounting Theory and Practice. B+ average
Participated as member of Accounting Club for two years.
Camosun College. Marketing Diploma 6/93
Major: Business Administration and Accounting. A- average
Received Award of Merit for volunteer work as orientation guide and peer tutor.

✓**Analyze your strengths.** Determine what aspects of your education, experience, and personal characteristics will be assets to prospective employers.

✓**Study models.** Look at other résumés for ideas for formatting and organization. Experiment with headings and styles to achieve an artistic, readable product.

FIGURE 16.10 ■ Chronological Résumé

Because Rachel has many years of experience and seeks high-level employment, she focuses on her experience. Notice how she includes specific achievements and quantifies them whenever possible.

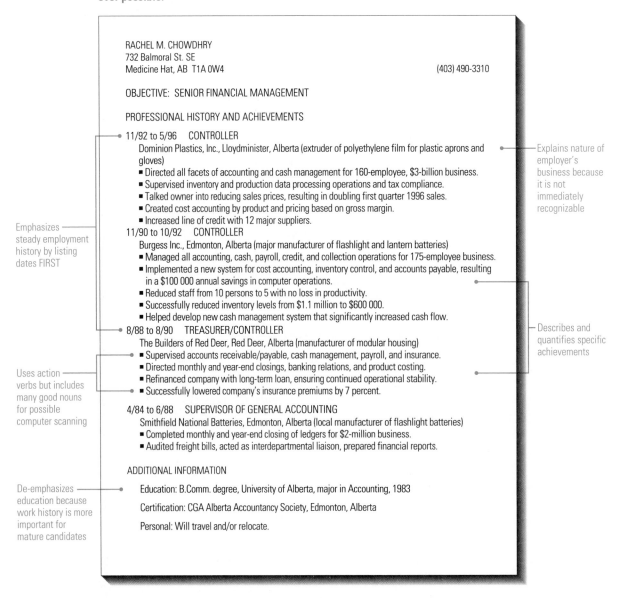

RACHEL M. CHOWDHRY
732 Balmoral St. SE
Medicine Hat, AB T1A 0W4   (403) 490-3310

OBJECTIVE: SENIOR FINANCIAL MANAGEMENT

PROFESSIONAL HISTORY AND ACHIEVEMENTS

11/92 to 5/96   CONTROLLER
Dominion Plastics, Inc., Lloydminister, Alberta (extruder of polyethylene film for plastic aprons and gloves)
- Directed all facets of accounting and cash management for 160-employee, $3-billion business.
- Supervised inventory and production data processing operations and tax compliance.
- Talked owner into reducing sales prices, resulting in doubling first quarter 1996 sales.
- Created cost accounting by product and pricing based on gross margin.
- Increased line of credit with 12 major suppliers.

11/90 to 10/92   CONTROLLER
Burgess Inc., Edmonton, Alberta (major manufacturer of flashlight and lantern batteries)
- Managed all accounting, cash, payroll, credit, and collection operations for 175-employee business.
- Implemented a new system for cost accounting, inventory control, and accounts payable, resulting in a $100 000 annual savings in computer operations.
- Reduced staff from 10 persons to 5 with no loss in productivity.
- Successfully reduced inventory levels from $1.1 million to $600 000.
- Helped develop new cash management system that significantly increased cash flow.

8/88 to 8/90   TREASURER/CONTROLLER
The Builders of Red Deer, Red Deer, Alberta (manufacturer of modular housing)
- Supervised accounts receivable/payable, cash management, payroll, and insurance.
- Directed monthly and year-end closings, banking relations, and product costing.
- Refinanced company with long-term loan, ensuring continued operational stability.
- Successfully lowered company's insurance premiums by 7 percent.

4/84 to 6/88   SUPERVISOR OF GENERAL ACCOUNTING
Smithfield National Batteries, Edmonton, Alberta (local manufacturer of flashlight batteries)
- Completed monthly and year-end closing of ledgers for $2-million business.
- Audited freight bills, acted as interdepartmental liaison, prepared financial reports.

ADDITIONAL INFORMATION

Education: B.Comm. degree, University of Alberta, major in Accounting, 1983

Certification: CGA Alberta Accountancy Society, Edmonton, Alberta

Personal: Will travel and/or relocate.

Annotations:

Explains nature of employer's business because it is not immediately recognizable

Describes and quantifies specific achievements

Emphasizes steady employment history by listing dates FIRST

Uses action verbs but includes many good nouns for possible computer scanning

De-emphasizes education because work history is more important for mature candidates

Heading and Objective

✓ **Identify yourself.** List your name, address, and telephone number. Skip the word *résumé*.

✓ **Include a career objective for a targeted job.** If this résumé is intended for a specific job, include a statement tailored to it (*Objective: Cost accounting position in the petroleum industry*).

FIGURE 16.11 ◼ Computer-Friendly Résumé

Cassandra prepared this computer-friendly résumé (free of graphics and fancy formatting) so that it would scan well if read by a computer. Notice that she begins with a key word summary that contains job titles, skills, traits, and other descriptive words. She hopes that some of these key words will match those submitted by an employer. To improve accurate scanning, she avoids italics, vertical and horizontal lines, and double columns.

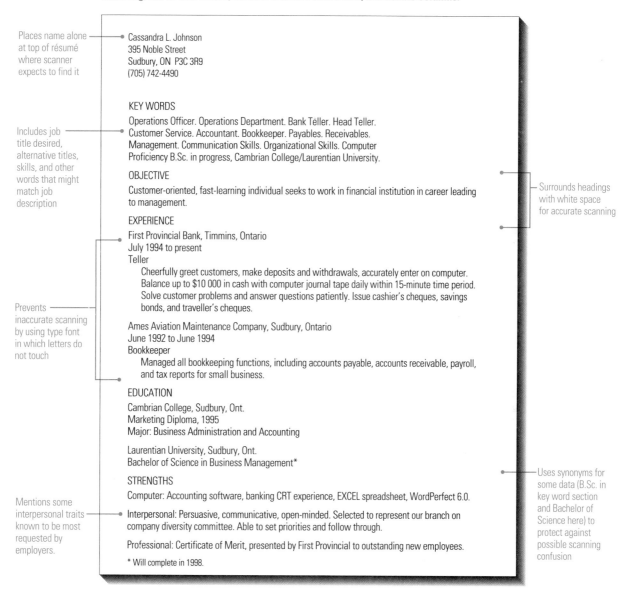

Places name alone at top of résumé where scanner expects to find it

Cassandra L. Johnson
395 Noble Street
Sudbury, ON P3C 3R9
(705) 742-4490

KEY WORDS

Includes job title desired, alternative titles, skills, and other words that might match job description

Operations Officer. Operations Department. Bank Teller. Head Teller. Customer Service. Accountant. Bookkeeper. Payables. Receivables. Management. Communication Skills. Organizational Skills. Computer Proficiency B.Sc. in progress, Cambrian College/Laurentian University.

OBJECTIVE

Customer-oriented, fast-learning individual seeks to work in financial institution in career leading to management.

Surrounds headings with white space for accurate scanning

EXPERIENCE

First Provincial Bank, Timmins, Ontario
July 1994 to present
Teller
   Cheerfully greet customers, make deposits and withdrawals, accurately enter on computer. Balance up to $10 000 in cash with computer journal tape daily within 15-minute time period. Solve customer problems and answer questions patiently. Issue cashier's cheques, savings bonds, and traveller's cheques.

Prevents inaccurate scanning by using type font in which letters do not touch

Ames Aviation Maintenance Company, Sudbury, Ontario
June 1992 to June 1994
Bookkeeper
   Managed all bookkeeping functions, including accounts payable, accounts receivable, payroll, and tax reports for small business.

EDUCATION

Cambrian College, Sudbury, Ont.
Marketing Diploma, 1995
Major: Business Administration and Accounting

Laurentian University, Sudbury, Ont.
Bachelor of Science in Business Management*

STRENGTHS

Uses synonyms for some data (B.Sc. in key word section and Bachelor of Science here) to protect against possible scanning confusion

Computer: Accounting software, banking CRT experience, EXCEL spreadsheet, WordPerfect 6.0.

Mentions some interpersonal traits known to be most requested by employers.

Interpersonal: Persuasive, communicative, open-minded. Selected to represent our branch on company diversity committee. Able to set priorities and follow through.

Professional: Certificate of Merit, presented by First Provincial to outstanding new employees.

* Will complete in 1998.

Education

✓**Name your degree, date of graduation, and institution.** Emphasize your education if your experience is limited.

✓**List your major and your average.** Give information about your studies, but don't list all your courses.

Work Experience

✓ **Itemize your jobs.** Start with your most recent job. Give the employer's name and city, dates of employment (month, year), and most significant job title.

✓ **Describe your experience.** Use action verbs to summarize achievements and skills relevant to your targeted job.

✓ **Present non-technical skills.** Give evidence of communication, management, and interpersonal talents. Employers want more than empty assurances; try to quantify your skills and accomplishments (*Collaborated with six-member task force in producing 20-page mission statement*).

Special Skills, Achievements, and Awards

✓ **Highlight computer skills.** Remember that nearly all employers seek employees who are proficient with word processing, databases, and spreadsheets.

✓ **Show that you are well-rounded.** List awards, experiences, and extracurricular activities—particularly if they demonstrate leadership, teamwork, reliability, loyalty, industry, initiative, efficiency, and self-sufficiency.

Final Tips

✓ **Consider omitting references.** Have a list of references available for the interview, but don't include them or refer to them unless you have a specific reason to do so.

✓ **Look for ways to condense your data.** Omit all street addresses except your own. Consolidate your headings. Study models and experiment with formats to find the most readable and efficient groupings.

✓ **Double-check for parallel phrasing.** Be sure that all entries use parallel construction, such as similar verb forms (*Organized files, trained assistants, scheduled events*).

✓ **Make your résumé scannable.** If there's a chance it will be read by a computer, add a key word summary, use a common font, and remove graphics.

✓ **Project professionalism and quality.** Avoid personal pronouns and humour. Use 24-pound bond paper and a high-quality printer.

✓ **Proofread, proofread, proofread.** Make this document perfect by proofreading at least three times.

▨ The Persuasive Letter of Application

To accompany your résumé, you'll need a persuasive letter of application (also called a *cover letter*). The letter of application has three purposes: (1) to introduce the résumé, (2) to highlight your strengths in terms of benefits to the reader, and (3) to obtain an interview. In many ways your letter of application is a sales letter; it sells your talents and tries to beat the competition. It will, accordingly, include many of the techniques you learned for sales presentations (see Chapter 9).

Letters of application introduce résumés, relate the writer's strengths to reader benefits, and seek an interview.

Personnel professionals disagree on how long to make the letter of application. Many prefer short letters with no more than four paragraphs; instead of concentrating on the letter, these readers focus on the résumé. Others desire longer letters that supply more information, thus giving them a better opportunity to evaluate a candidate's qualifications. The latter personnel professionals argue that hiring and training new employees is expensive and time-consuming; therefore, they welcome extra information to guide them in making the best choice the first time. Follow your judgment in writing a short or longer letter of application. If, for example, you need space to explain in more detail what you can do for a prospective employer, take it.

Regardless of its length, a letter of application should have three primary parts: (1) an opening that gains attention, (2) a body that builds interest and reduces resistance, and (3) a closing that motivates action.

Gaining Attention in the Opening

The first step in gaining the interest of your reader is addressing that person by name. Rather than sending your letter to the "Personnel Manager" or "Human Resources Department," try to find the name of the appropriate individual. Make it a rule to call the organization for the correct spelling and the complete address. This personal touch distinguishes your letter and demonstrates your serious interest.

The opener in a letter of application gains attention by addressing the receiver by name.

How you open your letter of application depends largely on whether the application is solicited or unsolicited. If an employment position has been announced and applicants are being solicited, you can use a direct approach. If you do not know whether a position is open and you are prospecting for a job, use an indirect approach. Whether direct or indirect, the opening should attract the attention of the reader. Strive for openings that are more imaginative than *Please consider this letter an application for the position of ...* or *I would like to apply for ...*

In applying for an advertised job, Nancy Sullivan James wrote the following solicited letter of application. Notice that her opening identifies the position and the newspaper completely so that the reader knows exactly what advertisement Nancy means. More challenging are unsolicited letters of application, such as Donald Vinton's shown in Figure 16.12. Because he hopes to discover or create a job, his opening must catch the reader's attention immediately. To do that, he capitalizes on company information appearing in the newspaper. Notice, too, that Donald purposely kept his cover letter short and to the point because he anticipated that a busy executive would be unwilling to read a long, detailed letter.

Donald's unsolicited letter, shown above, "prospects" for a job. Some job candidates feel that such letters may be even more productive than efforts to secure advertised jobs, since "prospecting" candidates face less competition.

Building Interest in the Body

Once you have captured the attention of the reader, you can use the body of the letter to build interest and reduce resistance. Keep in mind that your résumé emphasizes what you have *done;* your application letter stresses what you *can do* for the employer.

FIGURE 16.12 ■ Solicited Letter of Application

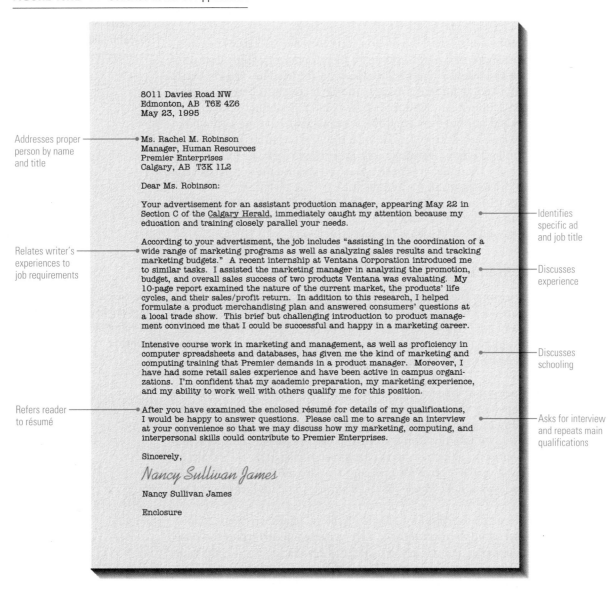

Addresses proper person by name and title

Relates writer's experiences to job requirements

Refers reader to résumé

8011 Davies Road NW
Edmonton, AB T6E 4Z6
May 23, 1995

Ms. Rachel M. Robinson
Manager, Human Resources
Premier Enterprises
Calgary, AB T3K 1L2

Dear Ms. Robinson:

Your advertisement for an assistant production manager, appearing May 22 in Section C of the <u>Calgary Herald</u>, immediately caught my attention because my education and training closely parallel your needs.

According to your advertisment, the job includes "assisting in the coordination of a wide range of marketing programs as well as analyzing sales results and tracking marketing budgets." A recent internship at Ventana Corporation introduced me to similar tasks. I assisted the marketing manager in analyzing the promotion, budget, and overall sales success of two products Ventana was evaluating. My 10-page report examined the nature of the current market, the products' life cycles, and their sales/profit return. In addition to this research, I helped formulate a product merchandising plan and answered consumers' questions at a local trade show. This brief but challenging introduction to product management convinced me that I could be successful and happy in a marketing career.

Intensive course work in marketing and management, as well as proficiency in computer spreadsheets and databases, has given me the kind of marketing and computing training that Premier demands in a product manager. Moreover, I have had some retail sales experience and have been active in campus organizations. I'm confident that my academic preparation, my marketing experience, and my ability to work well with others qualify me for this position.

After you have examined the enclosed résumé for details of my qualifications, I would be happy to answer questions. Please call me to arrange an interview at your convenience so that we may discuss how my marketing, computing, and interpersonal skills could contribute to Premier Enterprises.

Sincerely,

Nancy Sullivan James

Nancy Sullivan James

Enclosure

Identifies specific ad and job title

Discusses experience

Discusses schooling

Asks for interview and repeats main qualifications

The body of a letter of application should build interest, reduce resistance, and discuss relevant personal traits.

Your first goal is to relate your remarks to a specific position. If you are responding to an advertisement, you'll want to explain how your preparation and experience fill the stated requirements. If you are prospecting for a job, you may not know the exact requirements. Your employment research and knowledge of your field, however, should give you a reasonably good idea of what is expected for this position.

It's also important to emphasize reader benefits. In other words, you should describe your strong points in relation to the needs of the employer. In one employment survey many personnel professionals expressed the same view: "I want you to tell me what you can do for my organization. This is much more important to me than telling me what courses you took in college or what 'duties' you performed on your previous jobs."[19] Instead of *I have completed courses in business communication, report writing, and technical writing*, try this:

FIGURE 16.13 ■ Unsolicited Letter of Application

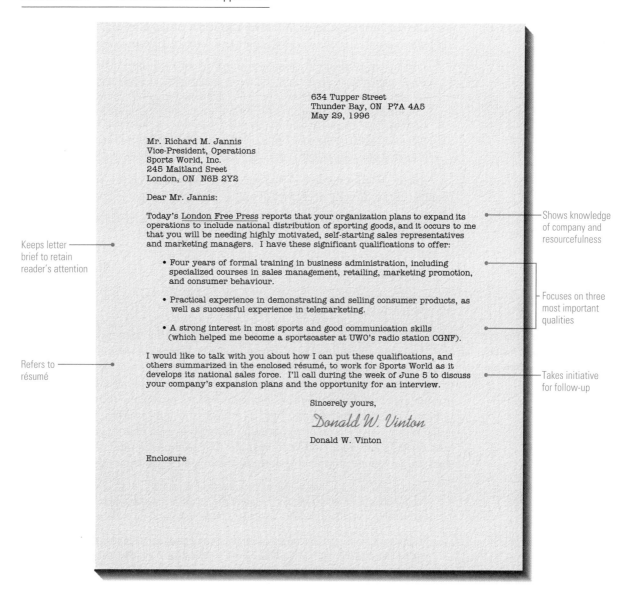

634 Tupper Street
Thunder Bay, ON P7A 4A5
May 29, 1996

Mr. Richard M. Jannis
Vice-President, Operations
Sports World, Inc.
245 Maitland Sreet
London, ON N6B 2Y2

Dear Mr. Jannis:

Today's London Free Press reports that your organization plans to expand its operations to include national distribution of sporting goods, and it occurs to me that you will be needing highly motivated, self-starting sales representatives and marketing managers. I have these significant qualifications to offer:

- Four years of formal training in business administration, including specialized courses in sales management, retailing, marketing promotion, and consumer behaviour.

- Practical experience in demonstrating and selling consumer products, as well as successful experience in telemarketing.

- A strong interest in most sports and good communication skills (which helped me become a sportscaster at UWO's radio station CGNF).

I would like to talk with you about how I can put these qualifications, and others summarized in the enclosed résumé, to work for Sports World as it develops its national sales force. I'll call during the week of June 5 to discuss your company's expansion plans and the opportunity for an interview.

Sincerely yours,

Donald W. Vinton

Donald W. Vinton

Enclosure

Annotations:
- Keeps letter brief to retain reader's attention
- Refers to résumé
- Shows knowledge of company and resourcefulness
- Focuses on three most important qualities
- Takes initiative for follow-up

> Courses in business communication, report writing, and technical writing have helped me develop the research and writing skills required of your technical writers.

Choose your strongest qualifications and show how they fit the targeted job. And remember, students with little experience are better off spotlighting their education and its practical applications, as these candidates did:

> Because you seek an architect's apprentice with proven ability, I submit a drawing of mine that won second place in the Holland College drafting contest last year.

> Successfully transcribing over 100 letters and memos in my college transcription class gave me experience in converting the spoken word into the written word, an exacting communication skill demanded of your administrative assistants.

Spotlighting reader benefits means matching personal strengths to employer needs.

In the body of your letter, you'll also want to discuss relevant personal traits. Employers are looking for candidates who, among other things, are team players, take responsibility, show initiative, and learn easily. Notice how the following paragraph uses action verbs to paint a picture of a promising candidate:

> In addition to developing technical and academic skills at Dalhousie University, I have gained interpersonal, leadership, and organizational skills. As vice president of the business students' organization, I helped organize and supervise two successful fundraising events. These activities involved conceptualizing the tasks, motivating others to help, scheduling work sessions, and coordinating the efforts of 35 diverse students in reaching our goal. I enjoyed my success with these activities and look forward to applying such experience in your management trainee program.

Finally, in this section or the next, you should refer the reader to your résumé. Do so directly or as part of another statement, as shown here:

> Please refer to the attached résumé for additional information regarding my education, experience, and references.

> As you will notice from my résumé, I will graduate in June with a bachelor's degree in business administration.

Motivating Action in the Closing

The closing of a letter of application should include a request for an interview.

After presenting your case, you should conclude with a spur to action. This is where you ask for an interview. If you live in a distant city, you may request an employment application or an opportunity to be interviewed by the organization's nearest representative. However, never ask for the job. To do so would be presumptuous and naive. In requesting an interview, suggest reader benefits or review your strongest points. Sound sincere and appreciative. Remember to make it easy for the reader to agree by supplying your telephone number and best times to call you. And keep in mind that some personnel directors prefer that you take the initiative to call them. Here are possible endings:

> I hope this brief description of my qualifications and the additional information on my résumé indicate to you my genuine desire to put my skills in accounting to work for you. Please call me at (705) 488–2291 before 10 a.m. or after 3 p.m. to arrange an interview.

> To add to your staff an industrious, well-trained word processing specialist with proven communication skills, call me at (705) 492–1433 to arrange an interview. I can meet with you at any time convenient to your schedule.

> Next week, after you have examined the attached résumé, I will call you to discuss the possibility of arranging an interview.

Final Tips

A letter of application should look professional and suggest quality.

As you revise your letter of application, notice how many sentences begin with *I*. Although it's impossible to talk about yourself without using *I*, you can reduce "I" domination with this writing technique. Make activities and outcomes, and not yourself, the subjects of sentences. For example, rather than *I took classes in word processing and desktop publishing*, say *Classes in word processing and desktop publishing prepared me to …* Instead of *I enjoyed helping customers*, say *Helping customers was a real pleasure*.

Like the résumé your letter of application must look professional and suggest quality. This means using a traditional letter style, such as block or modified block. Also, be sure to print it on the same bond paper as your résumé.

And, as with your résumé, proofread it several times yourself; then, have a friend read it for content and mechanics. The following checklist provides a quick summary of suggestions to review when you compose and proofread your cover letter.

▦ Checklist for Writing a Persuasive Letter of Application

Opening

✓ **Use the receiver's name.** Whenever possible, address the proper person by name.

✓ **Identify your information source, if appropriate.** In responding to an advertisement, specify the position advertised as well as the date and publication name. If someone referred you, name that person.

✓ **Gain the reader's attention.** Use one of these techniques: (1) tell how your qualifications fit the job specifications, (2) show knowledge of the reader's business, (3) describe how your special talents will be assets to the company, or (4) use an original and relevant expression.

Body

✓ **Describe what you can do for the reader.** Demonstrate how your background and training fill the job requirements.

✓ **Highlight your strengths.** Summarize your principal assets from education, experience, and special skills. Avoid repeating specific information from your résumé.

✓ **Openings for solicited jobs.** Here are some of the best techniques to open a letter of application for a job that has been announced:

- **Refer to the name of an employee in the company.** Remember that employers always hope to hire known quantities rather than complete strangers:

  Mitchell Sims, a member of your Customer Service Department, told me that DataTech is seeking an experienced customer service representative. The attached summary of my qualifications demonstrates my preparation for this position.

  At the suggestion of Ms. Jennifer Larson of your Human Resources Department, I submit my qualifications for the position of personnel assistant.

- **Refer to the source of your information precisely.** If you are answering an advertisement, include the exact position advertised and the name and date of the publication. For large organizations it's also wise to mention the section of the newspaper where the ad appeared:

  Your advertisement in Section C-3 of the June 1 *Daily News* for a junior accountant greatly appeals to me. With my accounting training and computer experience, I believe I could serve DataTech well.

  The September 10 issue of *The Globe and Mail* reports that you are seeking a mature, organized, and reliable administrative assistant with excellent communication skills.

> Susan Butler, placement director at Durham College, told me that DataTech has an opening for a technical writer with knowledge of desktop publishing techniques.

- **Refer to the job title and describe how your qualifications fit the requirements.** Personnel directors are looking for a match between an applicant's credentials and the job needs:

  > Will an honours graduate with a degree in recreation and two years of part-time experience organizing social activities for a convalescent hospital qualify for your position of activity director?

  > Because of my specialized training in computerized accounting at the University of Regina, I feel confident that I have the qualifications you described in your advertisement for a cost accountant trainee.

✓**Openings for unsolicited jobs.** If you are unsure whether a position actually exists, you may wish to use a more persuasive opening. Since your goal is to persuade this person to read on, try one of the following techniques:

- **Demonstrate interest in and knowledge of the reader's business.** Show the personnel director that you have done your research and that this organization is more than a mere name to you:

  > Since Signa HealthNet, Inc., is organizing a new information management team for its recently established group insurance division, could you use the services of a well-trained business administration graduate who seeks to become an information science professional?

- **Show how your special talents and background will benefit the company.** Personnel directors need to be convinced that you can do something for them:

  > Could your rapidly expanding publications division use the services of an editorial assistant who offers exceptional language skills, an honours degree from the University of P.E.I., and two years' experience in producing a campus literary publication?

✓ **Refer to your résumé.** In this section or the closing, direct the reader to the attached résumé. Do so directly or incidentally as part of another statement.

Closing

✓ **Ask for an interview.** Also consider reviewing your strongest points or suggesting how your assets will benefit the company.

✓ **Make it easy to respond.** Tell when you can be reached during office hours or announce when you will call the reader. Note that some personnel officers prefer that you call them.

Follow-up Letters and Other Employment Documents

Although the résumé and letter of application are your major tasks, other important letters and documents are often required during the employment process. You may need to make requests, write follow-up letters, or fill out employment applications. Because each of these tasks reveals something about you and your communication skills, you'll want to put your best foot forward. These documents often subtly influence company officials to extend an interview or offer a job.

Reference Request

Most employers expect job candidates at some point to submit names of individuals who are willing to discuss the candidates' qualifications. Before you list anyone as a reference, however, be sure to ask permission. Try to do this in person. Ask an instructor, for example, if he or she would be willing and has the time to act as your recommender. If you detect any sign of reluctance, don't force the issue. Your goal is to find willing people who think well of you.

What your recommenders need most is information about you. What should they stress to prospective employers? Let's say you're applying for a specific job that requires a letter of recommendation. Professor Smith has already agreed to be a reference for you. To get the best letter of recommendation from Professor Smith, help her out. Write a letter telling her about the position, its requirements, and the recommendation deadline. Include a copy of your résumé. You might remind her of a positive experience with you *(You said my report was well organized)* that she could use in the recommendation. Remember that recommenders need evidence to support generalizations. Give them ammunition, as the student has done in the following request:

> Dear Professor Smith:
>
> Recently I applied for the position of administrative assistant in the Human Resources Department of Host International. Because you kindly agreed to help me, I am now asking you to write a letter of recommendation to Host.
>
> The position calls for good organizational, interpersonal, and writing skills, as well as computer experience. To help you review my skills and training, I enclose my résumé. As you may recall, I earned an A in your business communication class; and you commended my long report for its clarity and organization.
>
> Please send your letter before July 1 in the enclosed stamped, addressed envelope. I'm grateful for your support, and I promise to let you know the results of my job search.

To get good letters of recommendation, find willing people and provide ample information about yourself.

Identify the target position and company. Tell immediately why you are writing.

Specify the job requirements so that the recommender knows what to stress. Supply data to jog the writer's memory.

Enclose a stamped, addressed envelope.

Application Request Letter

Some organizations consider candidates only when they submit a completed application form. To obtain a form, write a routine letter of request. But provide enough information about yourself, as shown in the following example, to assure the reader that you are a serious applicant:

> Dear Mr. Adams:
>
> Please send me an application form for work in your Human Resources Department. In June I will be completing my studies in psychology and communications at Waterloo University in Waterloo, Ontario. My program included courses in public relations, psychology, and communications.
>
> I would appreciate receiving this application by May 15 so that I may complete it before making a visit to your city in June. I'm looking forward to beginning a career in personnel management.

Because you expect a positive response, announce your request immediately.

Supply an end date, if it seems appropriate. End on a forward-looking note.

Application or Résumé Follow-up Letter

If your letter or application generates no response within a reasonable time, you may decide to send a short follow-up letter like the one below. Doing so (1) jogs the memory of the personnel officer, (2) demonstrates your serious interest, and (3) allows you to emphasize your qualifications or to add new information.

Dear Ms. Flynn:

Please know that I am still interested in becoming an administrative assistant with DataTech, Inc.

Since I submitted an application in May, I have completed my schooling and have been employed as a summer replacement for office workers in several downtown offices. This experience has strengthened my word processing and communication skills. It has also introduced me to a wide range of office procedures.

Please keep my application in your active file and let me know when I may put my formal training, technical skills, and practical experience to work for you.

Interview Follow-up Letter

After a job interview you should always send a brief letter of thanks. This courtesy sets you apart from other applicants (most of whom will not bother). Your letter also reminds the interviewer of your visit as well as suggesting your good manners and genuine enthusiasm for the job.

Follow-up letters are most effective if sent immediately after the interview.[20] In your letter refer to the date of the interview, the exact job title for which you were interviewed, and specific topics discussed. Avoid worn-out phrases, such as *Thank you for taking the time to interview me*. Be careful, too, about overusing *I*, especially to begin sentences. Most important, show that you really want the job and that you are qualified for it. Notice how the following letter conveys enthusiasm and confidence:

Dear Ms. Cogan:

Talking with you Thursday, May 23, about the graphic designer position was both informative and interesting.

Thanks for describing the position in such detail and for introducing me to Ms. Thomas, the senior designer. Her current project designing the annual report in four colours on a Macintosh sounds fascinating as well as quite challenging.

Now that I've learned in greater detail the specific tasks of your graphic designers, I'm more than ever convinced that my computer and creative skills can make a genuine contribution to your graphic productions. My training in Macintosh design and layout ensures that I could be immediately productive on your staff.

You will find me an enthusiastic and hard-working member of any team effort. I'm eager to join the graphics staff at your Kitchener headquarters, and I look forward to hearing from you soon.

Rejection Follow-up Letter

If you didn't get the job and you think it was perfect for you, don't give up. Employment consultant Patricia Windelspecht advises, "You should always respond to a rejection letter. ... I've had four clients get jobs that way." In a rejection follow-up letter, it's okay to admit you're disappointed. Be sure to add, however, that you're still interested and will contact them again in a month in case a job opens up. Then follow through for a couple of months—but don't overdo it. "There's a fine line between being professional and persistent and being a pest," adds consultant Windelspecht.[21] Here's an example of an effective rejection follow-up letter:

Dear Mr. Crenshaw:

Although I'm disappointed that someone else was selected for your accounting position, I appreciate your promptness and courtesy in notifying me.

Because I firmly believe that I have the technical and interpersonal skills needed to work in your fast-paced environment, I hope you will keep my résumé in your active file. My desire to become a productive member of your Trillium staff remains strong.

I enjoyed our interview, and I especially appreciate the time you and Mr. Samson spent describing your company's expansion into international markets. To enhance my qualifications, I've enrolled in a course in international accounting.

Should you have an opening for which I am qualified, you may reach me at (905) 579–4242. In the meantime, I will call you in a month to discuss employment possibilities.

Subordinate your disappointment to your appreciation at being notified promptly and courteously.

Emphasize your continuing interest. Express confidence in meeting the job requirements.

Refer to specifics of your interview. If possible, tell how you are improving your skills.

Take the initiative; tell when you will call for an update.

Application Form

Some organizations require job candidates to fill out job application forms instead of submitting résumés. This practice permits them to gather and store standardized data about each applicant. Here are some tips for filling out such forms:

- Carry a card summarizing those vital statistics not included on your résumé. If you are asked to fill out an application form in an employer's office, you will need a handy reference to the following data: social insurance number, graduation dates, beginning and ending dates of all employment; salary history; full names, titles, and present work addresses of former supervisors; and full names, occupational titles, occupational addresses, and telephone numbers of persons who have agreed to serve as references.

- Look over all the questions before starting. Fill out the form neatly, printing if your handwriting is poor.

- Answer all questions. Write *Not applicable* if appropriate.

- Be prepared for a salary question. Unless you know what comparable employees are earning in the company, the best strategy is to suggest a salary range or to write in *Negotiable* or *Open*.

- Ask if you may submit your résumé in addition to the application form.

▉ Interviewing for Employment

Job interviews, for most of us, are intimidating; no one enjoys being judged and, possibly, rejected. You can overcome your fear of the interview process by knowing how it works and how to prepare for it.

Trained recruiters generally structure the interview in three separate activities: (1) establishing a cordial relationship, (2) eliciting information about the candidate, and (3) giving information about the job and company. During the interview its participants have opposing goals. The interviewer tries to uncover any negative information that would eliminate a candidate. The candidate, of course, tries to minimize faults and emphasize strengths to avoid being eliminated.

You can become a more skillful player in the interview game if you know what to do before, during, and after the interview.

Before the Interview

- **Research the organization**. Never enter an interview cold. Visit the library or use your computer to search for information about the company or its field, service, or product. Call the company to request annual reports, catalogues, or brochures. Ask about the organization and possibly the interviewer. Learn something about the company's size, number of employees, competitors, reputation, and strengths and weaknesses.

- **Learn about the position**. Obtain as much specific information as possible. What are the functions of an individual in this position? What is the typical salary range? What career paths are generally open to this individual? What did the last person in this position do right or wrong?

- **Plan to sell yourself**. Identify three to five of your major selling points regarding skills, training, personal characteristics, and specialized experience. Memorize them; then in the interview be certain to find a place to insert them.

- **Prepare answers to possible questions**. Imagine the kinds of questions you may be asked and work out sample answers. Although you can't anticipate precise questions, you can expect to be asked about your education, skills, experience, and availability. The Career Skills box on page 514 shows 10 of the most common questions and suggests responses.

- **Prepare success stories**. Rehearse two or three anecdotes that you can relate about your accomplishments. These may concern problems you have solved, promotions you have earned, or recognition or praise you have received.

- **Arrive early**. Get to the interview 5 or 10 minutes early. If you are unfamiliar with the area where the interview is to be held, you might visit it before the scheduled day. Locate the building, parking facilities, and office. Time yourself.

- **Dress appropriately**. Heed the advice of one expert: "Dress and groom as the interviewer is likely to dress—but cleaner."[22] Don't overdo perfume, jewellery, or after-shave lotion. Avoid loud colours; strive for a coordinated, natural appearance. Favourite "power" colours for interviews are grey and dark blue. It's not a bad idea to check your appearance in a washroom before entering the office.

During the Interview

- **Establish the relationship**. Shake hands firmly. Don't be afraid to offer your hand first. Address the interviewer formally ("Hello, Mrs. Jones"). Allow the interviewer to put you at ease with small talk.

- **Act confidently but naturally**. Establish and maintain eye contact, but don't get into a staring contest. Sit up straight, facing the interviewer. Don't cross your arms and legs at the same time (review body language cues in Chapter 2). Don't play with things, like a pencil or keys, during the interview. Try to remain natural and at ease.

- **Don't criticize**. Avoid making negative comments about previous employers, instructors, or others. Such criticism may be taken to indicate a negative personality. Employers are not eager to hire complainers. Moreover, such criticism may suggest that you would do the same to this organization.

- **Continue to emphasize on your strengths**. If the interviewer asks a question that does not help you promote your strongest qualifications, answer briefly. Alternatively, try to turn your response into a positive selling point, such as this: "I have not had extensive paid training in that area, but I have completed a 50-hour training program that provided hands-on experience using the latest technology and methods. My recent training taught me to be open to new ideas and showed me how I can continue learning on my own. I was commended for being a quick learner."

- **Find out about the job early**. Because your time will be short, try to learn all you can about the job early in the interview. Ask about its responsibilities and the kinds of people who have done well in the position before. Knowing this information early will enable you to shape your responses to the job requirements.

- **Prepare for salary questions**. Remember that nearly all salaries are negotiable, depending on your qualifications. Knowing the typical salary range for the target position helps. The recruiter can tell you the salary ranges—but you will have to ask. If you've had little experience, you will probably be offered a salary somewhere between the low point and the midpoint in the range. With more experience you can negotiate for a higher figure. A word of caution, though. One personnel manager warns that candidates who emphasize money are suspect because they may leave if offered a few thousand dollars more elsewhere.

- **Be ready for inappropriate questions**. If you are asked a question that you think is illegal, politely ask the interviewer how that question is related to this job. Ask the purpose of the question. Perhaps there are valid reasons that are not obvious.

- **Ask your own questions**. Often, the interviewer concludes an interview with "Do you have any questions about the position?" Inquire about career paths, orientation or training for new employees, or the company's promotion policies. Have a list of relevant questions prepared. If the interview has gone well, ask the recruiter about his or her career in the company.

- **Conclude positively**. Summarize your strongest qualifications, show your enthusiasm for obtaining this position, and thank the interviewer for a constructive interview. Be sure you understand the next step in the employment process.

During an interview, applicants should act confidently, emphasize their strengths, and sell themselves.

After the Interview

- **Make notes on the interview**. While the events are fresh in your mind, jot down the main points—good and bad.

ANSWERING TEN FREQUENTLY ASKED INTERVIEW QUESTIONS

Interviewers want to learn about your job experiences and education so that they can evaluate who you are and predict how you might perform on the job. Study each of the following frequently asked interview questions and the strategies for answering them successfully.

- **Why do you want to work for us?** Questions like this illustrate the need for you to research an organization thoroughly before the interview. Do library research, ask friends, and read the company's advertisements and other printed materials. Describe your desire to work for them not only from your perspective but also from their point of view. What have you to offer them?

- **Why should we hire you?** Here is an opportunity for you to sell your strong points in relation to this specific position. Describe your skills, academic preparation, and relevant experience. If you have little experience, don't apologize—the interviewer has read your résumé. Emphasize strengths as demonstrated in your education, such as initiative and persistence in completing assignments, ability to learn quickly, self-sufficiency, and excellent attendance.

- **What can you tell me about yourself?** Use this chance to promote yourself. Stick to professional or business-related strengths; avoid personal or humorous references. Be ready with at least three success stories illustrating characteristics important to this job. Demonstrate responsibility you have been given; describe how you contributed as a team player.

- **What are your strongest (or weakest) personal qualities?** Stress your strengths, such as "I believe I am conscientious, reliable, tolerant, patient, and thorough." Add examples that illustrate these qualities: "My supervisor said that my research was exceptionally thorough." If pressed for a weakness, give a strength disguised as a weakness: "Perhaps my greatest fault is being too painstaking with details." Or, "I am impatient when tasks are not completed on time." Don't admit weaknesses, not even to sound human. You'll be hired for your strengths, not your weaknesses.

- **What do you expect to be doing 10 years from now?** Formulate a realistic plan with respect to your present age and situation. The important thing is to be prepared for this question.

- **Do you prefer working with others or by yourself?** This question can be tricky. Give a middle-of-the-road answer that not only suggests your interpersonal qualities but also reflects an ability to make independent decisions and work without supervision.

- **Have you ever changed your major during your education? Why?** Another tricky question. Don't admit weaknesses or failures. In explaining changes, suggest career potential and new aspirations awakened by your expanding education, experience, or maturity.

- **What have been your most rewarding or disappointing work (or school) experiences?** If possible, concentrate on positive experiences such as technical and interpersonal skills you acquired. Avoid dwelling on negative or unhappy topics. Never criticize former employers. If you worked for an ungrateful, penny-pinching slave driver in a dead-end position, say that you learned all you could from that job. Move the conversation to the prospective position and what attracts you to it.

- **Have you established any new goals lately?** Watch out here. If you reveal new goals, you may inadvertently admit deficiencies. Instead of "I've resolved to finally learn how to operate a computer," try "Although I'm familiar with basic computer applications, I'm now reading and studying more about computer applications in ..."

- **What are your long- and short-term goals?** Suggest realistic goals that you have consciously worked out before the interview. Know what you want to do with your future. To admit to an interviewer that you're not sure what you want to do is a sign of immaturity, weakness, and indecision.

Career Track Application

In teams of two to four, role-play an employment interview. Take turns playing interviewer and interviewee. Each student should answer four to five questions. Imagine a company where you'd like to work and answer accordingly.

- **Write a thank-you letter**. Immediately write a letter thanking the interviewer for a pleasant and enlightening discussion. Be sure to spell his or her name correctly.

Summary of Learning Goals

1. **Evaluate your assets, career paths, and the job market in preparation for employment**. The employment process begins with an analysis of your likes and your qualifications. Learn about career opportunities through your school, want ads, part-time employment, internships, professional organizations, and interviews. Develop a personal network by asking for referrals from friends and relatives.

2. **Compare and contrast chronological, functional, and combination résumés**. Chronological résumés, listing work and education by dates, rank highest with recruiters. Functional résumés, highlighting skills instead of jobs, appeal to people changing careers or those having weak employment histories. Combination résumés, including a complete job history along with skill areas, are increasingly popular.

3. **Organize, format, and produce a persuasive résumé**. Target your résumé for a specific job. Study models to arrange most effectively your main heading, career objective (optional), education, work experience, capabilities, awards and activities, personal data, and references (optional). Use action verbs to show how your assets will help the target organization.

4. **Identify techniques that prepare a résumé for computer scanning and for faxing**. Computer-friendly résumés avoid unusual typefaces, underlining, and italics. They use 10- to 14-point type, smooth white paper, and high-quality printing. The applicant's name appears on the first line. The résumé includes ample white space, avoids double columns, and is not folded or stapled. It emphasizes key words, which are nouns that an employer might use to describe the position and skills desired. Faxed résumés must also avoid small fonts and underlining. After faxing, verify transmission and follow up with a polished résumé.

5. **Write a persuasive letter of application to accompany your résumé**. Gain attention in the opening by mentioning the job or a person who referred you. Build interest in the body by stressing what you can do for the targeted company. Refer to your résumé, request an interview, and motivate action in the closing.

6. **Write effective employment follow-up letters and other messages**. Follow up all your employment activities with appropriate messages. After submitting your résumé, after an interview—even after being rejected—follow up with letters that express your appreciation and continuing interest.

7. **Evaluate successful job interview strategies**. Learn about the job and the organization. Prepare answers to possible questions and be ready with success stories. Act confidently and naturally. Be prepared to ask or answer salary questions. Have a list of your own questions, summarize your key strengths, and stay focused on your strong points. Afterwards, send a thank-you letter.

CHAPTER REVIEW

1. Before beginning an employment search, you should prepare by gathering information and insights in what three areas? (Goal 1)

2. List five sources of career information. (Goal 1)

3. How are most jobs likely to be found? Through classified ads? Employment agencies? Networking? (Goal 1)

4. What is the goal of your résumé? (Goal 2)

5. Describe a chronological résumé and discuss its advantages. (Goal 2)

6. Describe a functional résumé and discuss its advantages. (Goal 2)

7. What are the disadvantages of a functional résumé? (Goal 2)

8. When does it make sense to include a career objective on your résumé? (Goal 3)

9. On a chronological résumé what information should you include for the jobs you list? (Goals 2, 3)

10. In addition to technical skills, what traits and characteristics do employers seek? (Goals 2, 3)

11. What changes must be made in a typical résumé to make it suitable for computer scanning. (Goal 4)

12. What are the three purposes of a letter of application? (Goal 5)

13. How can you make it easy for a personnel director to reach you? (Goal 5)

14. Other than a letter of application, name five kinds of letters you might need to write in the employment process. (Goal 6)

15. On a company job application form, how should you respond to questions regarding salary? (Goal 7)

DISCUSSION

1. What kinds of questions should you ask yourself to identify your employment interests? (Goal 1)

2. How is a résumé different from a company employment application? (Goals 1, 2)

3. Some job candidates think that applying for unsolicited jobs can be more fruitful than applying for advertised openings. Discuss the advantages and disadvantages of letters that "prospect" for jobs. (Goal 5)

4. How do the interviewer and interviewee play opposing roles during job interviews? What strategies should the interviewee prepare in advance? (Goal 7)

5. **Ethical Issue:** Job candidate Karen accepts a position with Company A. One week later she receives a better offer from Company B. She wants very much to accept it. What should she do?

ACTIVITIES

16.1 Identifying Your Employment Interests (Goal 1)

In a memo addressed to your instructor, answer the questions in the section "Identifying Your Interests" at the beginning of the chapter. Draw a conclusion from your answers. What kind of career, company, position, and location seem to fit your self-analysis?

16.2 Evaluating Your Qualifications (Goals 1, 2, 3)

Prepare four worksheets that inventory your qualifications in these areas: employment, education, capabilities and skills, and honours and activities. Use verbs when appropriate.

a. *Employment.* Begin with your most recent job or internship. For each position list the following information: employer, job title, dates of employment, and three to five duties, activities, or accomplishments. Emphasize activities related to your job goal. Strive to quantify your achievements.

b. *Education.* List degrees, certificates, and training accomplishments. Include courses, seminars, or skills that are relevant to your job goal.

c. *Capabilities and skills.* List all capabilities and skills that recommend you for the job you seek. Use words like *skilled, competent, trained, experienced,* and *ability to.* Also list five or more qualities or interpersonal skills necessary for a successful individual in your chosen field. Write action statements demonstrating that you possess some of these qualities. Empty assurances aren't good enough; try to show evidence (*Developed teamwork skills by working with a committee of eight to produce a ...*).

d. *Awards, honours, and activities.* Explain any awards so that the reader will understand them. List campus, community, and professional activities that suggest you are well-rounded or possess traits relevant to your target job.

16.3 Choosing a Career Path (Goal 1)

Visit your college or university library, local library, or campus career centre. In bound form or on CD-ROM, consult the *Dictionary of Occupational Titles*. Find the description for a position for which you could apply in two to five years. Photocopy or print the pages from the *Occupational Outlook Handbook* that describe employment in the field in which you are interested. If your instructor directs, attach these copies to the letter of application you will write in Problem 16.9.

16.4 Searching the Job Market (Goal 1)

Clip a job advertisement from the classified section of a local or national newspaper. Select an ad describing the kind of employment you are seeking now or plan to seek when you graduate. Save this advertisement to attach to the résumé you will write in Problem 16.8.

16.5 Searching the Electronic Job Market (Goal 1)

Collect information about using your computer to search for employment. You might begin by looking for current newspaper or magazine articles describing electronic job hunting. You might also visit your school's career centre, local library, or major bookstore for the latest information. What's available through some of the computer services, such as Prodigy, CompuServe, or InfoGlobe? What's available on the Internet? Collect information about listing your résumé in a database as well as about employment opportunities. For example, Jobs Canada Inc. (1–800–268–JOBS) scans résumés into the National Employment Registry's database for $25, and the résumé stays on the system for six months.[23] In a class discussion consider how a job seeker can list a résumé in a databank. Evaluate the advantages and disadvantages of such a move. Your instructor may ask you to write a memo outlining electronic job resources currently available.

16.6 Draft Document: Résumé (Goals 2, 3)

Analyze the following résumé. Discuss its strengths and weaknesses. Your instructor may ask you to revise sections of this résumé before showing you an improved version.

Deborah M. Duchane
9 Ptarmigan Road
Yellowknife, NT
X1A 2J4
(403) 347–2290

EDUCATION
Northern College, Timmins, Ont.
Major: Office Technology. Diploma expected 5/96
Lakehead University, Thunder Bay, Ont.
Graduation 6/67 Major: General studies.

EXPERIENCE
- Clerk-typist, CANCO, Timmins, Ont. (1975–1977)
- CANCO, Thunder Bay, Ont. Worked as Management Analyst Technician. 1977-1980. Duties: Assisted in development of manpower staffing standards, statistical data gathered by on-site surveys, and analyzed data for accuracy.
- Employed two peak seasons for The Bay, Timmins, Ont. Duties: Input phone orders on CRT. 1989 and 1990.
- Financial Aid Office, NC, 1993–present. Duties: input data on computer, budget reconciliation, filing, letters and memos from oral dictation. Handle mail, telephone.
  Title: Office clerk.

CAPABILITIES
- Know PFS: Professional File, PFS: Professional Write, WordPerfect 6.0, and Lotus 1-2-3.
- Can function in IBM MS/DOS environment or with mainframe terminals.
- Competent in typing, editing, and/or proofreading reports, tables, letters, memos, manuscripts, and business forms.
  Type: 60 wpm.
- Have completed courses in accounting, business math, and word processing.
- Possess sound written and oral communication skills.

AWARDS, ACTIVITIES
- NC President's Award, 1993
- I served as officer (historian) for Business Professionals of North America.
- Keep books and records for my family's small retail business.

16.7 Draft Document: Letter of Application (Goal 5)

Analyze each section of the following letter of application written by an accounting major about to graduate.

Dear Human Resources Director:

Please consider this letter as an application for the position of staff accountant that I saw advertised in the *Whig*

Standard. Although I have had no paid work experience in this field, accounting has been my major in college and I'm sure I could be an asset to your company.

For four years I have studied accounting, and I am fully trained for full-charge bookkeeping as well as computer accounting. I have taken 36 units of college accounting and courses in business law, economics, statistics, finance, management, and marketing.

In addition to my course work, during the tax season I have been a student volunteer for VITA. This is a project to help individuals in the community prepare their income tax returns, and I learned a lot from this experience. I have also received some experience in office work and working with figures when I was employed as an office assistant for Copy Quick, Inc.

I am a competent and responsible person who gets along pretty well with others. I have been a member of some college and social organizations and have even held elected office.

I feel that I have a strong foundation in accounting as a result of my course work and my experience. Along with my personal qualities and my desire to succeed, I hope that you will agree that I qualify for the position of staff accountant with your company.

Sincerely,

PROBLEMS

16.8 Résumé (Goals 2, 3)

Using the data you developed in Activity 16.2, write your résumé. Aim it at a full-time job, part-time position, or internship. Attach a clipping if possible (from Activity 16.4). Use a computer. Revise your résumé until it is perfect.

16.9 Letter of Application (Goal 5)

Write a cover letter introducing your résumé. Again, use a word processor. Revise your cover letter until it is perfect.

16.10 Interview Follow-up Letter (Goal 6)

Assume you were interviewed for the position you seek. Write a follow-up thank-you letter.

16.11 Reference Request (Goal 6)

Assume that your favourite professor has agreed to recommend you. Write to the professor and request that he or she send a letter of recommendation to a company where you are applying for a job. Provide information about the job description and about yourself so that the professor can target its content.

16.12 Résumé Follow-up Letter (Goal 6)

A month has passed since you sent your résumé and letter of application in response to a job advertisement. Write a follow-up letter that doesn't offend the reader or damage your chances of employment.

16.13 Application Request

Select a company for which you'd like to work. Write a letter requesting an employment application, which they require for all job seekers.

16.14 Rejection Follow-up Letter (Goal 6)

Assume you didn't get the job. Although someone else was selected, you hope that other jobs may become available. Write a follow-up letter that will keep the door open.

Appendices

CLUE
(Competent Language Usage Essentials)

A Business Communicator's Guide

In the business word, people are often judged by the way they speak and write. Using the language competently can mean the difference between individual success and failure. Often a speaker sounds accomplished, but when that same person puts ideas on paper, errors in language usage destroy his or her credibility. One student observed, "When I talk, I get by on my personality, but when I write, the flaws in my communication show through. That's why I'm in this class."

What CLUE Is

This appendix provides a condensed guide to competence in language usage essentials (CLUE). Fifty guidelines review sentence structure, grammar, usage, punctuation, capitalization, and number style. These guidelines deal with the most frequently used—and abused—language elements. Presented from a business communicator's perspective, the guidelines also include realistic tips for application. And frequent exercises enable you to test yourself immediately. In addition to the 50 language guides in this appendix, you'll find a list of frequently misspelled words plus a quick review of selected confusing words.

The concentrated materials in this guide will help novice business communicators focus on the major areas of language use. The guide is not meant to teach or review all the principles of English grammar and punctuation. Instead, it deals with a limited number of language guidelines and troublesome words. Your goal should be to master these language principles and words, which represent a majority of the problems encountered by business writers.

For a more comprehensive treatment of grammar and punctuation consult a good reference book, such as Clark and Clark's *Handbook for Business Professionals*, or a business English textbook, such as Guffey's *Canadian Business English*.

How to Use CLUE

Your instructor may give you a language diagnostic test to help you assess your competence. After taking this test, read and work your way through the 50 guidelines. Concentrate on areas where you are weak. Memorize the spelling list and definitions for the confusing words located at the end of this appendix.

This book contains two kinds of exercises. (1) *Checkpoints*, located in this appendix, focus on a small group of language guidelines. Use them to test your comprehension as you complete each section. (2) *Review exercises*, in Chapters 1 to 10, cover all guidelines, spelling words, and confusing words. Use the review exercises to reinforce your language skills at the same time you are learning about the processes and products of business communication. In marking your revisions, you may wish to use the standard proofreading marks shown in Chapter 5 (see page 136) and Appendix D.

Guidelines: Competent Language Usage Essentials

Sentence Structure

GUIDE 1: Express ideas in complete sentences. You can recognize a complete sentence because it (a) includes a subject (a noun or pronoun that interacts with a verb), (b) includes a verb (a word expressing an action or a condition), and (c) makes sense (comes to a closure). A complete sentence is an independent clause. One of the most serious errors a writer can make is punctuating a fragment as if it were a complete sentence. A fragment is a broken-off part of a sentence.

Fragment	Improved
Because 90 percent of all business transactions involve written correspondence. Good writing skills are critical.	Because 90 percent of all business transactions involve written correspondence, good writing skills are critical.
The personnel director requested a writing sample. Even though the candidate seemed to communicate well.	The personnel director requested a writing sample, even though the candidate seemed to communicate well.

Tip. Fragments can often be recognized by the words that introduce them—words like *although, as, because, even, except, for example, if, instead of, since, so, such as, that, which, and when.* These words introduce dependent clauses (also called subordinate clauses). Make sure such clauses are always connected to independent clauses (also called principal or main clauses).

DEPENDENT CLAUSE   INDEPENDENT CLAUSE

Since she became supervisor,   she has had to write more memos and reports.

GUIDE 2: Avoid run-on (fused) sentences. A sentence with two independent clauses must be joined by a coordinating conjunction (*and, or, nor, but*) or by a semicolon (;). Without a conjunction or a semicolon, a run-on sentence results.

Run-on	Improved
Robin visited resorts of the rich and the famous he also dropped in on luxury spas.	Robin visited resorts of the rich and famous, and he also dropped in on luxury spas.
	Robin visited resorts of the rich and famous; he also dropped in on luxury spas.

GUIDE 3: Avoid comma-splice sentences. A comma splice results when a writer joins (splices together) two independent clauses—without using a coordinating conjunction (*and, or, nor, but*).

Comma Splice	Improved
Disney World operates in Orlando, Euro-Disney serves Paris.	Disney World operates in Orlando; Euro-Disney serves Paris.
	Disney World operates in Orlando, and EuroDisney serves Paris.
Visitors wanted a resort vacation, however they were disappointed.	Visitors wanted a resort vacation; however, they were disappointed.

Tip. In joining independent clauses, beware of using a comma and words like *consequently, furthermore, however, therefore, then, thus,* and so on. These conjunctive adverbs require semicolons.

✓ Checkpoint

Revise the following to rectify sentence fragments, comma splices, and run-ons.

1. When McDonald's tested pizza, Pizza Hut fought back. With aggressive ads ridiculing McPizza.

2. Aggressive ads can backfire, consequently, marketing directors consider them carefully.

3. Corporations study the legality of attack advertisements they also retaliate with counterattacks.

4. Although Pizza Hut is the No. 1 U.S. pizza chain. Domino's Pizza leads in deliveries.

5. About half of the 6600 outlets make deliveries, the others concentrate on walk-in customers.

The answers to all the Checkpoint sentences can be found at the end of Appendix A (page 542).

Grammar

Verb Tense

GUIDE 4: Use present tense, past tense, and past participle of verb forms correctly.

Present Tense	Past Tense	Past Participle
Today I _____	Yesterday I _____	I have _____
am	was	been
begin	began	begun
break	broke	broken
bring	brought	brought
choose	chose	chosen
come	came	come
dive	dived (or) dove	dived
do	did	done
give	gave	given
go	went	gone
know	knew	known
pay	paid	paid
see	saw	seen
steal	stole	stolen
take	took	taken
write	wrote	written

The package *came* yesterday, and they *knew* what to do with it.

If I *had seen* the shipper's bill, I *would have* paid it immediately.

I *know* the answer now; I with I *had known* it yesterday.

Tip: Probably the most frequent mistake in tenses results from substituting the past participle for the past tense. Notice that the past participle tense requires auxiliary verbs such as *has, had, have, would have,* and *could have.*

Faulty	Correct
When he *come* over last night, he *brung* a pizza.	When he *came* over last night, he *brought* a pizza.
If he *had came* earlier, we *could have saw* the video.	If he *had come* earlier, we *could have seen* the video.
If I *would have* worked harder, I *would of* passed.	If I *had* worked harder, I *would have* passed.

Verb Mood

GUIDE 5: Use the subjunctive mood to express hypothetical (untrue) ideas. The most frequent use of the subjunctive mood involves the use of *was* instead of *were* in clauses introduced by *if* and *as though* or containing *wish*. This use of *were* usually refers to the present, not the past.

> If I *were* (not *was*) you, I would take a business writing course.

> Sometimes I wish I *were* (not *was*) the manager of this department.

> He acts as though he *were* (not *was*) in charge of this department.

Tip. If the statement could possibly be true and if it refers to the past, use *was*.

> If I *was* to blame, I accept the consequences.

✓ Checkpoint

Correct faults in verb tenses and mood.

6. If I was in your position, I would have wrote the manager a letter.
7. You could have wrote a better résumé if you have read the chapter first.
8. When Trevor seen the want ad, he immediately contacted the company.
9. I wish I was able to operate a computer so that I could have went to work there.
10. If she had would have took more computer courses, Maria could of got a good job.

Verb Agreement

GUIDE 6: Make subjects agree with verbs despite intervening phrases and clauses. Become a detective in locating the subject. Don't be deceived by prepositional phrases and parenthetic words that often disguise the subject.

> Our study of annual budgets, five-year plans, and sales proposals *is* (not *are*) progressing on schedule. (The subject is *study*.)

> The budgeted item, despite additions proposed yesterday, *remains* (not *remain*) as submitted. (The subject is *item*.)

> A salesperson's evaluation of the prospects for a sale, together with plans for follow-up action, *is* (not *are*) what we need. (The subject is *evaluation*.)

Tip. Subjects are nouns or pronouns that control verbs. To find subjects, cross out prepositional phrases beginning with words like *about, at, by, for, from, of,* and *to*. Subjects of verbs are not found in prepositional phrases. Also, don't be tricked by expressions introduced by *together with*, *in addition to*, and *along with*.

GUIDE 7: Subjects joined by *and* require plural verbs. Watch for subjects joined by the conjunction *and*. They require plural verbs.

> The CEO and one of his assistants *have* (not *has*) ordered a limo.

> Kentucky Fried Chicken and Pizza Hut, although individual franchisees operate each unit, *are* (not *is*) owned by PepsiCo.

> Exercising in the gym and jogging every day *are* (not *is*) how he keeps fit.

GUIDE 8: Subjects joined by *or* or *nor* may require singular or plural verbs. The verb should agree with the closest subject.

> Either the software or the printer *is* (not *are*) causing the glitch. (The verb is controlled by closer subject *printer*.)

> Neither Montreal *nor* Calgary *has* (not *have*) a chance of winning. (The verb is controlled by Calgary.)

Tip. In joining singular and plural subjects with *or* or *nor*, place the plural subject closer to the verb. Then, the plural verb sounds natural. For example, *Either the manufacturer or the distributors are responsible.*

GUIDE 9: Use singular verbs for most indefinite pronouns. For example: *anyone, anybody, anything, each, either, every, everyone, everybody, everything, neither, nobody, nothing, someone, somebody*, and *something* all take singular verbs.

> Everyone in both offices *was* (not *were*) given a bonus.

> Each of the employees *is* (not *are*) being interviewed.

GUIDE 10: Use singular or plural verbs for collective nouns, depending on whether the members of the group are operating as a unit or individually. Words like *faculty, administration, class, crowd*, and *committee* are considered *collective* nouns. If the members of the collective are acting as a unit, treat them as singular subjects. If they are acting individually, it's usually better to add the word *members* and use a plural verb.

Correct

> The Finance Committee *is* working harmoniously. (*Committee* is singular because its action is unified.)

> The Planning Committee *are* having difficulty agreeing. (*Committee* is plural because its members are acting individually.)

Improved

> The Planning Committee members *are* having difficulty agreeing. (Add the word *members* if a plural meaning is intended.)

Tip. In Britain these collective nouns are generally considered plural. In the United States collective nouns are generally considered singular. In Canada, common sense and consistency prevail. Remember, as in spelling, to be consistent.

✓ Checkpoint

Correct the errors in subject-verb agreement.

11. A manager's time and energy has to be focused on important issues.

12. Promotion of women, despite managerial training programs and networking efforts, are disappointingly small.

13. We're not sure whether Mr. Murphy or Ms. Wagner are in charge of the program.

14. Each of the Fortune 500 companies are being sent a survey regarding women in management.

15. Our CEO, like other good executives, know how to be totally informed without being totally involved.

Pronoun Case

GUIDE 11: Learn the three cases of pronouns and how each is used. Pronouns are substitutes for nouns. Every business writer must know the following pronoun cases.

Nominative or Subjective Case	Objective Case	Possessive Case
Used for subjects of verbs and subject complements	Used for objects of prepositions and objects of verbs	Used to show possession
I	me	my, mine
we	us	our, ours
you	you	you, yours
he	him	his
she	her	her, hers
it	it	its
they	them	their, theirs
who, whoever	whom, whomever	whose

GUIDE 12: Use nominative case of pronouns as subjects of verbs and as complements. Complements are words that follow linking (or copula) verbs (such as *am, is, are, was, were, be, being,* and *been*) and rename the words to which they refer.

> *She* and *I* (not *her* and *me*) prefer easy-riding mountain bikes. (Use pronouns in the nominative case as the subjects of the verb *prefer.*)

> We think that *she* and *he* (not *her* and *him*) will win the race. (Use pronouns in the nominative case as the subjects of the verb *will win.*)

> It must have been *she* (not *her*) who called last night. (Use a pronoun in the nominative case as a subject complement.)

Tip. If you feel awkward using nominative pronouns after linking verbs, rephrase the sentence. Instead of *It is she who is the boss*, say *She is the boss.*

GUIDE 13: Use pronouns in the objective case as objects of prepositions and verbs.

> Please order stationery for *her* and *me* (not *she* and *I*). (The pronouns *her* and *me* are objects of the preposition *for.*)

The CEO appointed *him* (not *he*) to the position. (The pronoun *him* is the object of the verb *appointed*.)

Tip. When a pronoun appears in combination with a noun or another pronoun, ignore the extra noun or pronoun and the conjunction. Then, the case of the pronoun becomes more obvious.

Jason asked Jennifer and *me* (not *I*) to lunch. (Ignore *Jennifer and.*)

The waiter didn't know whether to give the bill to Jason or *her* (not *she*). (Ignore *Jason or.*)

Tip. Be especially alert to the following prepositions: *except*, *between*, *but*, and *like*. Be sure to use objective pronouns as their objects.

Just between you and *me* (not *I*), their mineral water comes from the tap.

Computer grammar checkers work well for writers like Lee and *him* (not *he*).

GUIDE 14: Use pronouns in the possessive case to show ownership. Possessive pronouns (such as *hers*, *yours*, *whose*, *ours*, *theirs*, and *its*) require no apostrophes.

All reports except *yours* (not *your's*) have to be rewritten.

The printer and *its* (not *it's*) fonts produce exceptional copy.

Tip. Don't confuse possessive pronouns and contractions. Contractions are shortened forms of subject-verb phrases (such as *it's* for *it is*, *there's* for *there is*, *who's* for *who is*, and *they're* for *they are*).

✓ Checkpoint

Correct errors in pronoun case.

16. Although my friend and myself are interested in this computer, it's price seems high.

17. Letters addressed to he and I were delivered to you and Ann in error.

18. Just between you and I, the mail room and its procedures need improvement.

19. Several applications were lost; your's and her's were the only ones delivered.

20. It could have been her who sent the program update to you and I.

GUIDE 15: Use pronouns ending in *self* only when they refer to the subject.

The president *himself* ate all the M & Ms.

If you exaggerate on your résumé, you will only harm *yourself*.

Send the package to Marcus or *me* (not *myself*).

Tip. Trying to sound modest, many people incorrectly substitute *myself* when they should use *I*. For example, "Jerry and *myself* (should be *I*) are cohosting the telethon."

GUIDE 16: Use *who* or *whoever* for nominative case constructions and *whom* or *whomever* for objective case constructions. In determining the correct choice, it's helpful to substitute *he* for *who* or *whoever* and *him* for *whom* or *whomever*.

> For *whom* was this software ordered? (The software was ordered for *him*.)
>
> *Who* did you say called? (You did say *he* called?)
>
> Give the supplies to *whoever* asked for them. (In this sentence the clause *whoever asked for them* functions as the object of the preposition *to*. Within the clause *whoever* is the subject of the verb *asked*. Again, try substituting *he*: *he* asked for them.)

✓ Checkpoint

Correct any errors in the use of *who*, *whom*, and pronouns ending in *self*.

21. The boss herself is willing to call whoever we nominate for the position.

22. Who would you like to see nominated?

23. These supplies are for whomever ordered them.

24. The meeting is set for Tuesday; however, Jeff and myself cannot attend.

25. Incident reports are to be written by whomever experiences a sales problem.

Pronoun Reference

GUIDE 17: Make pronouns agree in number and gender with the words to which they refer (their antecedents). When the gender of the antecedent is obvious, pronoun references are simple.

> One of the boys lost *his* (not *their*) pump-up tennis shoes. (The singular pronoun *his* refers to the singular *One*.)
>
> Each of the female nurses was escorted to *her car* (not *their cars*). (The singular pronoun *her* and singular noun *car* are necessary because they refer to the singular subject *Each*.)
>
> Somebody on the girls' team left *her* (not *their*) headlights on.

When the gender of the antecedent could be male or female, tactful writers today have a number of options.

Faulty	Improved
Every employee should receive *their* cheque on Friday. (The plural pronoun *their* does not agree with its singular antecedent *employee*.)	All employees should receive *their* cheques on Friday. (Make the subject plural so that the plural pronoun *their* is acceptable. This option is preferred by many writers today.)
Every employee should receive *their* cheque Friday.	All employees should receive cheques on Friday. (Omit the possessive pronoun entirely.)
	Every employee should receive *a* cheque on Friday. (Substitute *a* for a pronoun.)
	Every employee should receive *his* or *her* cheque on Friday. (Use the combination *his or her*. However, this option is wordy and should be used only occasionally.)

GUIDE 18: Be sure that pronouns like *it*, *which*, *this*, and *that* refer to clear antecedents. Vague pronouns confuse the reader because they have no clear antecedent. The most troublesome are *it*, *which*, *this*, and *that*. Replace vague pronouns with concrete nouns, or provide these pronouns with clear antecedents.

Faulty	Improved
Our office recycles as much paper as possible because *it* helps the environment. (Does *it* refer to *paper, recycling,* or *office*?)	Our office recycles as much paper as possible because *such efforts* help the environment. (Replace *it* with *such efforts*.)
The disadvantages of local area networks can offset their advantages, *which* merits further evaluation. (What merits evaluation: advantages, disadvantages, or offsetting of one by the other?)	The disadvantages of local area networks can offset their advantages, a *fact* which merits further evaluation. (*Fact* supplies a clear antecedent for *which*.)
Negotiators announced an expanded health care plan, reductions in dental coverage, and a proposal of on-site child care facilities. *This* caused employee protests. (What exactly caused employee protests?)	Negotiators announced an expanded health care plan, reductions in dental coverage, and a proposal of on-site child care facilities. *This* reduction in dental coverage caused employee protests. (The pronoun *This* now has a clear reference.)

Tip. Whenever you use the words *this, that, these,* and *those* by themselves, a red flag should pop up. These words are dangerous when they stand alone. Inexperienced writers often use them to refer to an entire previous idea, rather that to a specific antecedent, as shown in the preceding example. You can often solve the problem by adding another idea to the pronoun (as *this reduction*).

✓ Checkpoint

Correct the faulty and vague pronoun references in the following sentences. Numerous remedies are possible.

26. Every employee is entitled to have their tuition reimbursed.

27. Flexible working hours may mean slower career advancement, but it appeals to me anyway.

28. Any subscriber may cancel their subscription at any time.

29. Every voter must have their name and address verified at the polling place.

30. Obtaining agreement on job standards, listening to co-workers, and encouraging employee suggestions all helped to open lines of communication. This is particularly important in team projects.

Adjectives and Adverbs

GUIDE 19: Use an adverb, not an adjective, to describe or limit the action of a verb or another adverb.

Andrew said he did *well* (not *good*) on the exam.

After its tune-up, the engine is running *more smoothly* (not *smoother*).

Don't take the manager's criticism *personally* (not *personal*).

That was a *really* (not *real*) hard exam.

GUIDE 20: Hyphenate two or more adjectives that are joined to create a compound modifier before a noun.

> Follow the *step-by-step* instructions to construct the *low-cost* bookshelves.
>
> A *well-designed* keyboard is part of their *state-of-the-art* equipment.

Tip. Don't confuse adverbs ending in *-ly* with compound adjectives: *newly enacted* law and *highly regarded* CEO would not be hyphenated.

✓ Checkpoint

Correct any problems in the use of pronouns, adjectives, and adverbs.

31. My manager and myself prepared a point by point analysis of the proposal.

32. Because we completed the work so quick, we were able to visit the recently-opened snack bar.

33. If I do good on the placement exam, I qualify for many part time jobs and a few full time positions.

34. The vice president told Jim and I not to take the announcement personal.

35. In the not too distant future, we may enjoy interactive television.

▮ Punctuation

GUIDE 21: Use commas to separate three or more items (words, phrases, or short clauses) in a series.

> Downward communication delivers job instructions, procedures, and appraisals.
>
> In preparing your résumé, try to keep it brief, make it easy to read, and include only job-related information.
>
> The new ice cream flavours include cookie dough, chocolate raspberry truffle, cappuccino, and almond amaretto.

Tip. It is perfectly correct to omit the comma before *and*. However, many business writers prefer to retain it because it often prevents the last two items from being misread as one item. Notice in the example how the final two flavours could have been misread if the comma had been omitted.

GUIDE 22: Use commas to separate introductory clauses and some introductory phrases from independent clauses. This guideline describes the comma most often omitted by business writers. Sentences that open with dependent clauses (often introduced by words like *since, when, if, as, although,* and *because*) require commas to separate them from the main idea. The comma helps readers recognize where the introduction ends and the main idea begins. Long introductory phrases (of more than about half a dozen words) and phrases containing verbal elements also require commas.

> If you recognize introductory clauses, you will have no trouble placing the comma. (Comma separates introductory dependent clause from main clause.)
>
> When you have mastered this rule, half the battle with commas will be won.

As expected, additional explanations are necessary. (Use a comma after an introductory verbal phrase.)

In the spring of last year we opened our franchise. (No comma is needed after a short phrase.)

Having considered several alternatives, we decided to invest. (Use a comma after an introductory verbal phrase.)

To invest, we needed $100 000. (Use a comma after an introductory verbal phrase, regardless of its length.)

Tip. Short introductory prepositional phrases (four or fewer words) require no commas. Don't clutter your writing with unnecessary commas after introductory phrases such as *by 1998, in the fall,* or *at this time.*

GUIDE 23: Use a comma before the coordinating conjunction in a compound sentence. The most common coordinating conjunctions are *and, or, nor,* and *but.* Occasionally, *for, so,* and *yet* may also function as coordinating conjunctions. When coordinating conjunctions join two independent clauses, commas are needed.

The investment sounded too good to be true, *and* many investors were dubious. (Use a comma before the coordinating conjunction *and* in a compound sentence.)

Niagara Falls is the honeymoon capital of the world, *but* some newlyweds prefer to go to more exotic destinations.

Tip. Before inserting a comma, test the two clauses. Can each of them stand alone as a complete sentence? If either is incomplete, skip the comma.

Promoters said the investment offer was for a limited time and couldn't be extended even one day. (Omit a comma before *and* because the second part of the sentence is not a complete independent clause.)

Home is a place you grow up wanting to leave but grow old wanting to return to. (Omit a comma before *but* because the second half of the sentence is not a complete clause.)

✓ Checkpoint

Add appropriate commas.

36. Before he entered this class Jeff used to sprinkle his writing with commas semicolons and dashes.

37. After studying punctuation he learned to use commas more carefully and to reduce his reliance on dashes.

38. At this time Jeff is engaged in a strenuous body-building program but he also finds time to enlighten his mind.

39. Next spring Lauren may enrol in accounting and business law or she may work for a semester to earn money.

40. When she completes her degree she plans to apply for employment in Montreal Toronto or Ottawa.

GUIDE 24: Use commas correctly in dates, addresses, geographical names, academic degrees, and long numbers.

September 30, 1963, is her birthday. (For dates use commas before and after the year.)

Send the application to James Kirby, 3405 120 Ave. N.W., Edmonton, AB T5W 1M3, as soon as possible. (For addresses use commas to separate all units except the two-letter abbreviation of the province and the postal code.)

She expects to move from Salmon Arm, British Columbia, to Mississauga, Ontario, next fall. (For geographical names use commas to enclose the second element.)

Karen Mumson, CA, and Richard B. Larsen, Ph.D., were the speakers. (For professional designations and academic degrees following names, use commas to enclose each item.)

The latest census figures show the city's population to be 342,000. (In figures use commas to separate every three digits, counting from the right. The metric system uses a narrow space instead of a comma.)

GUIDE 25: Use commas to set off internal sentence interrupters. Sentence interrupters may be verbal phrases, dependent clauses, contrasting elements, or parenthetical expressions (also called transitional phrases). These interrupters often provide information that is not grammatically essential.

Medical researchers, working steadily for 18 months, developed a new cancer therapy. (Use commas to set off an interrupting verbal phrase.)

The new therapy, which applies a genetically engineered virus, raises hopes among cancer specialists. (Use commas to set off nonessential dependent clauses.)

Dr. James C. Morrison, who is one of the researchers, made the announcement. (Use commas to set off nonessential dependent clauses.)

It was Dr. Morrison, not Dr. Arturo, who led the team effort. (Use commas to set off a contrasting element.)

This new therapy, by the way, was developed from a herpes virus. (Use commas to set off a parenthetical expression.)

Tip. Parenthetical (transitional) expressions are helpful words that guide the reader from one thought to the next. Here are some representative parenthetical expressions that require commas:

as a matter of fact	in the meantime
as a result	nevertheless
consequently	of course
for example	on the other hand
in addition	therefore

Tip. Always use *two* commas to set off an interrupter, unless it begins or ends a sentence.

✓ Checkpoint

Insert necessary commas.

41. Sue listed 222 George Henry Blvd. Toronto ON M2J 1E6 as her forwarding address.

42. The personnel director felt nevertheless that the applicant should be given an interview.

43. Employment of paralegals which is expected to increase 32 percent next year is growing rapidly because of the expanding legal services industry.

44. The contract was signed April 1 1995 and remains in effect until January 1 1998.

45. As a matter of fact the average North American drinks enough coffee to require 12 pounds of coffee beans annually.

GUIDE 26: Avoid unnecessary commas. Do not use commas between sentence elements that belong together. Don't automatically insert commas before every *and* or at points where your voice might drop if you were saying the sentence out loud. Be sure you have a reason for every comma you use.

Faulty

Growth will be spurred by the increasing complexity of business operations, and by large employment gains in trade and services. (A comma unnecessarily precedes *and*.)

All students with high grades, are eligible for the honour society. (A comma incorrectly separates the subject and verb.)

One of the reasons for the success of the business honour society is, that it is very active. (A comma unnecessarily separates the verb and its complement.)

Our honour society has over 50 members, at this time. (A comma unnecessarily separates a prepositional phrase from the sentence.)

✓ Checkpoint

Remove unnecessary commas. Add necessary ones.

46. Businesspeople from all over the world, gathered in Windsor for the meeting.

47. When shopping for computer equipment consider buying products that have been on the market for at least a year.

48. The trouble with talking fast is, that you sometimes say something before you've thought of it.

49. We think on the other hand, that we must develop management talent pools with the aim of promoting women members of visible minorities and people with disabilities.

50. A powerful reason for mail-order purchasing is, that customers make big savings.

GUIDE 27: Use a semicolon to join closely related independent clauses. Mature writers use semicolons to show readers that two thoughts are closely associated. If the ideas are not related, they should be expressed as separate sentences. Often, but not always, the second independent clause contains a conjunctive adverb (such as *however, consequently, therefore,* or *furthermore*) to show the relation between the two clauses.

Learning history is easy; learning its lessons is almost impossible.

He was determined to complete his degree; consequently, he studied diligently.

Most people want to be delivered from temptation; they would like, however, to keep in touch.

Tip. Don't use a semicolon unless each clause is truly independent. Try the sentence test. Omit the semicolon if each clause could not stand alone as a complete sentence.

Faulty	**Improved**
There's no point in speaking; unless you can improve on silence. (The second half of the sentence is a dependent clause. It could not stand alone as a sentence.)	There's no point in speaking unless you can improve on silence.

Faulty	**Improved**
Although I cannot change the direction of the wind; I can adjust my sails to reach my destination. (The first clause could not stand alone.)	Although I cannot change the direction of the wind, I can adjust my sails to reach my destination.

GUIDE 28: Use a semicolon to separate items in a series when one or more of the items contains internal commas.

Representatives from as far away as Longueuil, Quebec; Vancouver, British Columbia; and Whitehorse, Yukon, attended the conference.

Stories circulated about Henry Ford, founder, Ford Motor Company; Lee Iacocca, CEO, Chrysler Motor Company; and Shoichiro Toyoda, chief, Toyota Motor Company.

GUIDE 29: Use a colon after a complete thought that introduces a list of items. Words such as *these*, *the following*, and *as follows* may introduce the list or they may be implied.

The following cities are on the tour: Toronto, Ottawa, and Montreal.

An alternative tour includes several western cities: Calgary, Saskatoon, and Edmonton.

Tip. Be sure that the statement before a colon is grammatically complete. An introductory statement that ends with a preposition (such as *by*, *for*, *at*, and *to)* or a verb (such as *is*, *are*, or *were*) is not complete. The list following a preposition or a verb actually functions as an object or as a complement to finish the sentence.

Faulty	**Improved**
Three Big Macs were ordered by: Pam, Jim, and Lee. (Do not use a colon after an incomplete statement.)	Three Big Macs were ordered by Pam, Jim, and Lee.
Other items that they ordered were: fries, Cokes, and salads. (Do not use a colon after an incomplete statement.)	Other items that they ordered were fries, Cokes, and salads.

GUIDE 30: Use a colon after business letter salutations and to introduce long quotations.

Gentlemen: Dear Mr. Wang: Dear Lisa:

The Asian consultant bluntly said: "North Americans tend to be too blabby, too impatient, and too informal for Asian tastes. To succeed in trade with Pacific Rim countries, North Americans must become more willing to adapt to native cultures."

Tip. Use a comma to introduce short quotations. Use a colon to introduce long one-sentence quotations and quotations of two or more sentences.

✓ Checkpoint

Add the necessary semicolons and colons.

51. My short-time goal is an entry-level job my long-term goal however is a management position.

52. Stelco interviewed the following candidates Joni Sims Simon Fraser University James Jones Wilfrid Laurier and Madonna Farr Ryerson Polytechnic University.

53. The recruiter was looking for three qualities initiative versatility and enthusiasm.

54. Stelco seeks experienced people however it will hire recent graduates who have excellent records.

55. Mississauga is an expanding area therefore many business opportunities are available.

GUIDE 31: To show possession (i.e. ownership), add an apostrophe plus *s* if the word does not end in an *s* sound.

We hope to show a profit in one year's time. (Add *'s* because the ownership word *year* does not end in an *s*.)

The company's assets rose in value. (Add *'s* because the ownership word *company* does not end in *s*.)

All the women's votes were counted. (Add *'s* because the ownership word *women* does not end in *s*.)

GUIDE 32: Add only an apostrophe to show possession if the word ends in an *s* sound—unless an extra syllable can be pronounced easily.

Some workers' benefits will be increased. (Add only an apostrophe because *workers* ends in an *s*.)

Several months' rent were paid in advance. (Add only an apostrophe because the ownership word *months* ends in an *s*.)

The boss's son got the job. (Add *'s* because an extra syllable can be pronounced easily.)

Tip. To determine whether an ownership word ends in an *s*, use it in an *of* phrase. For example, *one month's salary* becomes *the salary of one month*. By isolating the ownership word without its apostrophe, you can decide if it ends in an *s*.

GUIDE 33: Use *'s* to make a noun possessive when it precedes a gerund, a verb form used as a noun. Use a possessive case pronoun.

We all protested *Laura's* (not *Laura*) smoking.

His (not *Him*) talking interfered with the video.

I appreciate *your* (not *you*) answering the telephone while I was gone.

✓ Checkpoint

Correct erroneous possessives.

56. Both companies presidents received huge salaries, even when profits were falling.

57. Within one months time we were able to verify all members names and addresses.

58. Bryans supporters worry that there's little chance of him being elected.

59. The position requires five years experience in waste management.

60. Ms. Jackson car is serviced every six months.

GUIDE 34: Use a period to end a statement, command, indirect question, or polite request.

Everyone must row with the oars that he or she has. (Statement)

Send the completed report to me by June 1. (Command)

Stacy asked if she could use the car next weekend. (Indirect question)

Will you please send me an employment application. (Polite request)

Tip. Polite requests often sound like questions. If the request prompts an action, use a period. If it prompts a verbal response, use a question mark.

Faulty	Improved
Could you please correct the balance on my next statement? (This polite request prompts an action rather than a verbal response.)	Could you please correct the balance on my next statement.

GUIDE 35: Use a question mark after a direct question and after statements with questions appended.

Is it illegal to duplicate training videotapes?

Most of their training is in-house, isn't it?

GUIDE 36: Use a dash to (a) set off parenthetical elements containing internal commas, (b) emphasize a sentence interruption, or (c) separate an introductory list from a summarizing statement. The dash has legitimate uses. However, some writers use it whenever they know that punctuation is necessary but aren't sure exactly what. The dash can be very effective if not misused.

Three top students—Gene Engle, Donna Hersh, and Mika Sato—won awards. (Use dashes to set off elements with internal commas.)

Executives at IBM—despite rampant rumours in the stock market—remained quiet regarding dividend earnings. (Use dashes to emphasize a sentence interruption.)

IBM, Compaq, and Apple—these were the three leading computer manufacturers. (Use a dash to separate an introductory list from a summarizing statement.)

GUIDE 37: Use parentheses to set off nonessential sentence elements, such as explanations, directions, questions, or references.

Researchers find that the office grapevine (see Chapter 1 for more discussion) carries surprisingly accurate information.

Only two dates (February 15 and March 1) are suitable for the meeting.

Tip. Careful writers use parentheses to de-emphasize and the dash to emphasize parenthetical information. One expert said, "Dashes shout the news; parentheses whisper it."

GUIDE 38: Use quotation mark to (a) enclose the exact words of a speaker or writer, (b) distinguish words used in a special sense, such as slang, or (c) enclose titles of articles, chapters, or other short works.

"If you make your job important," said the consultant, "it's quite likely to return the favour."

The personnel director said that she was looking for candidates with good communication skills. (Omit quotation marks because the exact words of the speaker are not quoted.)

This office discourages "rad" hair styles and clothing. (Use quotes for slang.)

In Business Week I saw an article entitled "Communication for Global Markets." (Use quotation marks around the title of an article; use underlining or italics for the name of the publication.)

Tip. Never use quotation marks for emphasis, as in *Our "spring" sale starts April 1.*

✓ Checkpoint

Add the correct punctuation.

61. Will you please send me your latest catalogue as soon as possible

62. (Direct quote) The only thing you get in a hurry said the professor is trouble

63. (De-emphasize) Two kinds of batteries see page 16 of the instruction booklet may be used in this camera.

64. (Emphasize) The first three colours that we tested red, yellow, and orange were selected.

65. All letters with erroneous addresses were reprinted weren't they

▨ Capitalization

GUIDE 39: Capitalize proper nouns and proper adjectives. Capitalize the *specific* names of persons, places, institutions, buildings, religions, holidays, months, organizations, laws, races, languages, and so forth. Don't capitalize common nouns that make *general* references.

Proper Nouns	**Common Nouns**
Michelle DeLuca	the manufacturer's rep
Algonquin Provincial Park	the wilderness park
College of the Redwoods	the community college
the CN Tower	the downtown building

| the Department of the Environment | the federal department |
| Persian, Armenian, Hindi | modern foreign languages |

Proper Adjectives

French markets (*but* francophone, anglophone)	Italian dressing
Xerox copy	Japanese executives
Swiss chocolates	Rae days

GUIDE 40: Capitalize only specific academic courses and degrees.

Professor Jane Mangrum, Ph.D., will teach Accounting 121 next spring.

James Barker, who holds bachelor's and master's degrees, teaches business communications and marketing.

Jessica enrolled in classes in management, English, and business law.

GUIDE 41: Capitalize personal and business titles when they (a) precede names, (b) appear in addresses, salutations, and closing lines, and (c) represent high governmental rank or religious office.

Prime Minister Chrétien	Aunt Edna
Board Chairman Ames	Dr. Johnson
the Queen	Supervisor Valone
the Prime Minister of Canada	the Pope
the Premier of Newfoundland	the Liberal Senator

Do not capitalize a business title appearing alone or following a name unless it is part of an address.

The president met with our office manager and the supervisor today.

Dave Nichol, formerly of Loblaw Companies Limited, became the new partner of Cott Corporation.

Send the package to Amanda Haar, Advertising Manager, Kent Publishing Company, 20 Park Plaza, Saint John, NB.

GUIDE 42: Capitalize the principal words in the titles of books, magazines, newspapers, articles, movies, plays, songs, poems, and reports. Do *not* capitalize articles (*a, an, the*), coordinate conjunctions (*and, but, or, nor*), or prepositions of fewer than five letters (*in, to, by, for*) unless they begin or end the title.

I enjoyed the book <u>A Customer is More Than a Name</u>.

Did you read the article entitled "Companies in Europe Seeking Executives with Multinational Skills"?

We liked the article entitled "Advice from a Pro: How to Say it with Pictures."

(Note that the titles of books are underlined or italicized while the titles of articles and parts of a book are enclosed in quotation marks.)

GUIDE 43: Capitalize *north, south, east, west* and their derivatives only when they represent specific geographical regions.

| in the North | heading north on the highway |
| provinces in the West | west of the city |

GUIDE 44: Capitalize the names of departments, divisions, or committees within your own organization. Outside your organization capitalize only *specific* department, division, or committee names.

Lawyers in our Legal Assistance Department handle numerous cases.

Samsung offers TVs in its Consumer Electronics Division.

We volunteered for the Employee Social Responsibility Committee.

You might send an application to their human resources department.

GUIDE 45: Capitalize product names only when they refer to trademarked items. Don't capitalize the common names following manufacturers' names.

Pitney Bowes Dictaphone	Skippy peanut butter	NordicTrack
Eveready Energizer	Norelco razor	Kodak colour copier
Coca-Cola	Apple computer	Big Mac

GUIDE 46: Capitalize most nouns followed by numbers or letters (except in page, paragraph, line, and verse references).

Chapter 9	Exhibit A	Flight 12, Gate 43
Figure 2.1	Plan No. 1	Model Z2010

✓ Checkpoint

Capitalize as necessary.

66. vice-president ellis bought a toshiba computer for use on her trips to europe.

67. our director of research brought plan no. 1 with him to the meeting in our engineering research department.

68. proceed west on highway 10 until you reach the mt. vernon exit.

69. you are booked on air canada flight 164 leaving from gate 5 at mirabel airport.

70. to improve their english, many new canadians purchased the book entitled <u>the power of language is yours</u>.

▨ Number Usage

GUIDE 47: Use words to express (a) numbers nine and under and (b) numbers beginning sentences. Numbers nine and under should be expressed in words. Also use words for numbers that begin sentences. If the resulting number involves more than two words, however, try to recast the sentence so that the number does not fall at the beginning.

We answered *six* telephone calls for the *four* sales reps.

Fifteen customers responded to the *three* advertisements today.

A total of 155 cameras were awarded as prizes. (Avoid beginning the sentence with a long number such as *one hundred and fifty-five*.)

GUIDE 48: Use words to express general references to ages, small fractions, and approximate numbers.

When she reached twenty-one, she received *one-half* of the estate.

James owns a *one-third* interest in the electronics business. (Note that fractions are hyphenated except when the first word is *a*: *a third*.)

Several *thousand* demonstrators gathered outside the legislature.

Tip. Exact ages and specific business terms may be expressed in figures.

Both Meredith Jones, 55, and Jack Jones, 57, appeared in the article.

The note is payable in 60 days.

GUIDE 49: Use figures to express most references to numbers *10* and over.

Over *150* people from *53* companies attended the two-day workshop.

A four-ounce serving of Haagen-Dazs toffee crunch ice cream contains *300* calories and *19* grams of fat.

GUIDE 50: Use figures to express money, dates, clock time, decimals, and percentages. Use a combination of words and figures to express sums of 1 million and over.

One item cost only *$1.95*; most, however, were priced between *$20* and *$35*. (Omit the decimals and zeros in even sums of money.)

A total of *3 700* employees approved the contract on *May 12* at *3 p.m.*

When Canadian sales dropped *4.7* percent, net income fell *9.8* percent. (Use the word *percent* instead of the % symbol.)

Orion lost *$62.9 million* in the latest fiscal year on revenues of *$584 million*. (Use a combination of words and figures for sums of 1 million and over.)

Tip. To ease your memory load, concentrate on the numbers normally expressed in words: numbers *nine* and under, numbers at the beginning of a sentence, and small fractions. Nearly everything else in business is generally written with figures.

✓ Checkpoint

Correct any inappropriate expression of numbers.

71. McDonald's new McLean Deluxe, priced at two dollars and sixty-five cents, has only three hundred and ten calories and nine percent fat.

72. 175 employees will attend the meeting on January tenth at one p.m.

73. The Nordstrom family, which owns forty percent of the company's stock, recently added 4 co-presidents.

74. Our 3 branch offices, with a total of ninety-six workers, needs to add six computers and 9 printers.

75. On March eighth we paid thirty-two dollars a share to acquire one third of the stocks.

Answers to CLUE Checkpoint Exercises in Appendix A

This key shows all corrections. If you marked anything else, double-check the appropriate guideline.

1. Pizza Hut fought back with
2. backfire; consequently,
3. advertisements; they
4. chain, Domino's
5. deliveries; the

6. If I *were* ... I would have *written*
7. could have *written* ... if you *had* read
8. When Trevor *saw*
9. I wish I *were* ... could have *gone*
10. she had *taken* ... could *have got*

11. energy *have*
12. efforts, *is* disappointingly
13. Ms. Wagner *is* in charge
14. companies *is* being
15. *knows* how

16. my friend and *I* ... *its* price
17. to *him* and *me*
18. between you and *me*
19. *yours* and *hers*
20. could have been *she* ... to you and *me*

21. *whomever* we nominate
22. *Whom* would you
23. *whoever* ordered
24. Jeff and *I*
25. by *whoever* experiences

26. to have *his* or *her* tuition; to have *the* tuition; *All employees are entitled to have their tuition reimbursed; to be reimbursed for tuition*
27. but *this advancement plan* appeals (*Revise to avoid vague pronoun* it.)
28. may cancel *his* or *her* subscription; may cancel *the* subscription; *Subscribers may cancel their subscriptions*
29. *his* or *her* name and address; *All voters must have their names and addresses*
30. *These activities are* particularly important (*Revise to avoid the vague pronoun this.*)

31. my manager and *I* ... point-by-point

32. completed the work so *quickly ... recently opened* (*Omit hyphen.*)

33. If I do *well ... part-time ... full-time*

34. told Jim and *me ... personally*

35. *not-too-distant* future

36. class, Jeff ... commas, semicolons, and

37. punctuation, (*No comma before* and!)

38. program, but

39. business law, or

40. degree, she ... Montreal, Toronto, or

41. 222 George Henry Blvd., Toronto, ON M2J 1E6 as her

42. felt, nevertheless,

43. paralegals, which ... year,

44. April 1, 1995, ... January 1, 1998.

45. As a matter of fact,

46. (*Remove comma.*)

47. equipment,

48. (*Remove comma.*)

49. think, on the other hand, ... women, members of visible minorities, and

50. (*Remove comma.*)

51. entry-level job; my ... goal, however,

52. candidates: Joni Sims, Simon Fraser University; James Jones, Wilfrid Laurier University; and Madonna Farr, Ryerson Polytechnic University.

53. qualities: initiative, versatility, and

54. people; however,

55. area; therefore,

56. companies'

57. one month's time ... members'

58. Bryan's ... *his* being elected

59. years' experience

60. Jackson's car

61. possible.

62. "The only thing you get in a hurry," said the professor, "is trouble."

63. batteries (see page 16 of the instruction booklet) may be

64. tested—red, yellow, and orange—were selected.

65. reprinted, weren't they?

66. Vice-President Ellis ... Toshiba computer ... Europe

67. Our ... Plan No. 1 ... Engineering Research Department.

68. Proceed ... Highway 10 ... Mt. Vernon exit.

69. You ... Air Canada Flight 164 ... Gate 5 at Mirabel Airport.

70. To improve their English, new Canadians ... <u>The Power of Language Is Yours</u>.

71. priced at $2.65, has only 310 calories and 9 percent fat.

72. A total of 175 employees ... January 10 at 1 p.m.

73. 40 percent ... four co-presidents.

74. three branch offices, ... 96 workers ... nine printers.

75. March 8 ... $32 ... one-third.

CONFUSING WORDS

accede: to agree or consent
exceed: over a limit

advice: suggestion, opinion
advise: to counsel or recommend

affect: to influence
effect: (n.) outcome, result; (v.) to bring about, to create

all ready: prepared
already: by this time

all right: satisfactory
alright: unacceptable variant spelling

altar: structure for worship
alter: to change

appraise: to estimate
apprise: to inform

assure: to promise
ensure: to make certain
insure: to protect from loss

capital: (n.) city that is seat of government; wealth of an individual; (adj.) chief
Capitol: building that houses state legislature

cereal: breakfast food
serial: arranged in sequence

choose: present tense
chose: past tense

cite: to quote; to summon
site: location
sight: a view; to see

complement: that which completes
compliment: to praise or flatter

compose: the parts compose the whole
comprise: the whole comprises (*not* is comprised of) the parts

conscience: regard for fairness
conscious: aware

council: governing body
counsel: to give advice; advice

desert: arid land; to abandon
dessert: sweet food

device: invention or mechanism
devise: to design or arrange

disburse: to pay out
disperse: to scatter widely

elicit: to draw out
illicit: unlawful

every day: each single day
everyday: ordinary

farther: a greater distance
further: additional

formally: in a formal manner
formerly: in the past

hole: an opening
whole: complete

imply: to suggest indirectly
infer: to reach a conclusion

its: possessive of *it*
it's: contraction of *it is.* (Think of *he's, she's*)

liable: legally responsible
libel: damaging written statement

loose: not fastened
lose: to misplace

miner: person working in a mine
minor: a lesser item; person under age

patience: calm perseverance
patients: people receiving medical treatment

personal: private, individual
personnel: employees

precede: to go before
proceed: to continue

precedence: priority
precedents: events used as an example

principal: (n.) capital sum; school official; (adj.) chief
principle: rule of action

stationary: immovable
stationery: writing material

than: conjunction showing comparison
then: adverb meaning "at that time"

their: possessive form of *they*
there: at that place or point
they're: contraction of *they are*

to: a preposition; the sign of the infinitive
too: an adverb meaning "also" or "to an excessive extent"
two: a number

waiver: abandonment of a claim
waver: to shake or fluctuate

SOME FREQUENTLY MISSPELLED WORDS

absence
accommodate
acknowledgment *or*
   acknowledgement
achieve
across
adequate
advisable
all right
analyze
annually
appointment
argument
automatically
bankruptcy
becoming
beneficial
budget
business
calendar
cancelled
catalogue
column
changeable
committee
congratulate
conscience
conscious
consecutive
consensus
consistent
control
convenient
correspondence
courteous
criticize
decision
deductible
defendant
definitely
dependent

describe
destroy
desirable
development
disappoint
dissatisfied
division
efficient
embarrass
emphasis
emphasize
employee
envelope
equipped
especially
evidently
exaggerate
excellent
exempt
existence
extraordinary
fascinate
familiar
feasible
February
fiscal
foreign
forty
fourth
friend
genuine
government
grammar
grateful
guarantee
harass
height
hoping
immediate
incidentally
incredible

independent
interrupt
itinerary
indispensable
irrelevant
judgment (*or* judge-
   ment)
knowledgeable
legitimate
library
licence (n.)
license (v.)
maintenance
manageable
manufacturer
mileage
miscellaneous
mortgage
necessary
nevertheless
ninety
ninth
noticeable
occasionally
occurred
offered
omission
omitted
opportunity
opposite
ordinarily
paid
pamphlet
permanent
permitted
pleasant
practical
prevalent
privilege
probably
procedure

profited
prominent
qualify
quantity
questionnaire
receipt
receive
recognize
recommendation
referred
regarding
remittance
representative
restaurant
schedule
secretary
separate
similar
sincerely
software
succeed
sufficient
supervisor
surprise
tenant
therefore
thorough
though
through
truly
undoubtedly
unnecessarily
usable
usage
using
usually
valuable
volume
weekday
writing
yield

Guide to Document Formats

Business documents carry two kinds of messages. Verbal messages are conveyed by the words chosen to express the writer's ideas. Nonverbal messages are conveyed largely by the appearance of a document. If you compare an assortment of letters and memos from various organizations, you will notice immediately that some look more attractive and more professional than others. The nonverbal message of the professional-looking documents suggests that they were sent by people who are careful, informed, intelligent, and successful. Understandably, you're more likely to take documents seriously if they use attractive stationery and professional formatting techniques.

Over the years certain practices and conventions have arisen regarding the appearance of business documents. Although these conventions offer some choices (such as letter and punctuation styles), most business letters follow standardized formats. To ensure that your documents carry favourable nonverbal messages about you and your organization, you'll want to give special attention to the stationery and formatting of your letters, envelopes, memos, and fax cover sheets.

Stationery

Most organizations use high-quality stationery for business documents. This stationery is printed on select paper that meets two qualifications: weight and cotton-fibre content.

Paper is measured by weight and may range from 9 pounds (thin onionskin paper) to 32 pounds (thick card and cover stock). Most office stationery is in the 16- to 24-pound range. Lighter 16-pound paper is generally sufficient for internal documents, including memos. Heavier 20- to 24-pound paper is used for printed letterhead stationery.

Paper is also judged by its cotton-fibre content. Cotton fibre makes paper stronger, softer in texture, and less likely to yellow. Good-quality stationery contains 25 percent or more cotton fibre.

Letter Placement

The easiest way to place letters on the page is to use the default settings of your word processing program. These are usually set for side margins of 1 inch. Many companies today find these margins quite acceptable.

If you wish to adjust your margins so that letters are better balanced on the page, use the chart shown below.

Letter Length	Words in Body	Side Margins	Blank Lines After Date
Short	Under 100	2 inches	7 to 11 (12 pitch) 6 to 8 (10 pitch)
Medium	100 to 200	1½ inches	2 to 8 (12 pitch) 2 to 3 (10 pitch)
Long	Over 200	1 to 1¼ inches	2 to 8 (12 pitch) 2 to 3 (10 pitch)

Spacing. In preparing business documents on a typewriter or word processor, follow accepted spacing conventions. These conventions include double-spacing after all end punctuation marks (period, question mark, and exclamation point). Business typists also leave two spaces after a colon, except in the expression of time, as shown here:

Ann called at 3:15 yesterday. She wants to ask ...
It comes in three colours: amber, rust, and wheat.

Professional typographers leave only one space after all punctuation marks, as you will notice in books, magazines, and newspapers. Business writers, however, are not working within such tight space constraints. Leaving two spaces after end punctuation and colons helps readers separate ideas. It is essential if you are using a "typewriter" font, such as Courier, that does not have proportional spacing.

Justification. Many word processing programs automatically justify right margins to make all lines of text end evenly (as here). Justification usually adds unsightly extra space between words, a print feature you'll want to avoid for letters and memos. Moreover, experts tell us that justified right margins make documents more difficult to read, since the eye cannot easily see where individual lines end. Natural resting points for the eye are removed. And justified business letters look computer-generated and thus less personal. This is why smart communicators use ragged (i.e., unjustified) right margins for business letters and memos.

Justified right margins, however, are appropriate for special documents such as formal reports, brochures, newsletters, and announcements. But to avoid large, uneven gaps between words, you will need to turn on the hyphenation feature of your software.

◼ Parts of a Letter

Professional-looking business letters are arranged in a conventional sequence with standard parts. Following is a discussion of how to use these letter parts properly. Figure B.1 illustrates the parts in a block-style letter. (See Chapter 6 for additional discussion of letters and their parts.)

Letterhead. Most business organizations use 8½- by 11-inch paper printed with a letterhead displaying their official name, address, and telephone and fax numbers. The letterhead may also include a logo and an advertising message such as *Great Western Banking: A new brand of banking.*

Dateline. On letterhead paper you should place the date two lines below the last line of the letterhead or 2 inches from the top edge of the paper (line 13). On plain paper place the date immediately below your return address. Since the date goes on line 13, start the return address an appropriate number of lines above it. The most common dateline format is as follows: *June 9, 1996.* Don't use *th* (or *rd*) when the date is written this way. For European or military correspondence, use the following dateline format: *9 June 1996.* Notice that no commas are used.

Addressee and delivery notations. Delivery notations such as FAX TRANSMISSION, OVERNIGHT DELIVERY, CONFIDENTIAL, or CERTIFIED MAIL are typed in all capital letters two line spaces above the inside address.

Inside address. Type the inside address—that is, the address of the organization or person receiving the letter—single-spaced, starting at the left margin. The number of lines between the dateline and the inside address depends on the size of the letter body, the type size (point or pitch size), and the length of the typing lines. Generally, two to ten lines are appropriate.

Be careful to duplicate the exact wording and spelling of the recipient's name and address on your documents. Usually you can copy this information from the letterhead of the correspondence you are answering. If, for example, you are responding to *Jackson & Perkins Company*, don't address your letter to *Jackson and Perkins Corp.*

Always be sure to include a courtesy title such as *Mr.*, *Ms.*, *Mrs.*, *Dr.*, or *Professor* before a person's name in the inside address—for both the letter and the envelope. Although many women in business today prefer *Ms.*, you'll want to use whatever title the addressee prefers.

Remember that the inside address is not included for readers who already know who and where they are. It's there to help the writer accurately file a copy of the message.

In general, avoid abbreviations (such as *Ave.* or *Co.*) unless they appear in the printed letterhead of the document being answered.

Attention line. An attention line allows you to send your message officially to an organization but to direct it to a specific individual, officer, or department. However, if you know an individual's complete name, it's always better to use it as the first line of the inside address and avoid an attention line. Here are two common formats for attention lines:

```
MultiMedia Enterprises              MultiMedia Enterprises
27 Fairlane Blvd.                   Attention: Marketing Director
Nepean, ON K2E 5H3                  27 Fairlane Blvd.
                                    Nepean, ON K2E 5H3
ATTENTION MARKETING DIRECTOR
```

Attention lines may be typed in all caps or with upper- and lowercase letters. The colon following *Attention* is optional. Notice that an attention line may be placed two lines below the address block or printed as the second line of the inside address. You'll want to use the latter format if you're composing on a word processor because the address block may be copied to the envelope and the attention line will not interfere with the last-line placement of the postal code. (Mail can be sorted more easily if the postal code appears in the last line of a typed address.)

Whenever possible, use a person's name as the first line of an address instead of putting that name in an attention line. Some writers use an attention line because they fear that letters addressed to individuals at companies may be considered private. They worry that if the addressee is no longer with the company, the letter may be forwarded or not opened. Actually, unless a letter is marked "Personal" or "Confidential," it will very likely be opened as business mail. Figure B.2 shows more examples of attention lines.

Salutation. For most letter styles place the letter greeting, or salutation, two lines below the last line of the inside address or the attention line (if used). If the letter is addressed to an individual, use that person's courtesy title and last name (*Dear Mr. Lanham*). Even if you are on a first-name basis (*Dear Leslie*), be sure to add a colon (not a comma or a semicolon) after the salutation. Do not use an individual's full name in the salutation (not *Dear Mr. Leslie Lanham*) unless you are unsure of gender (*Dear Leslie Lanham*).

FIGURE B.1 ■ Block and Modified Block Letter Styles

Block style
Open punctuation

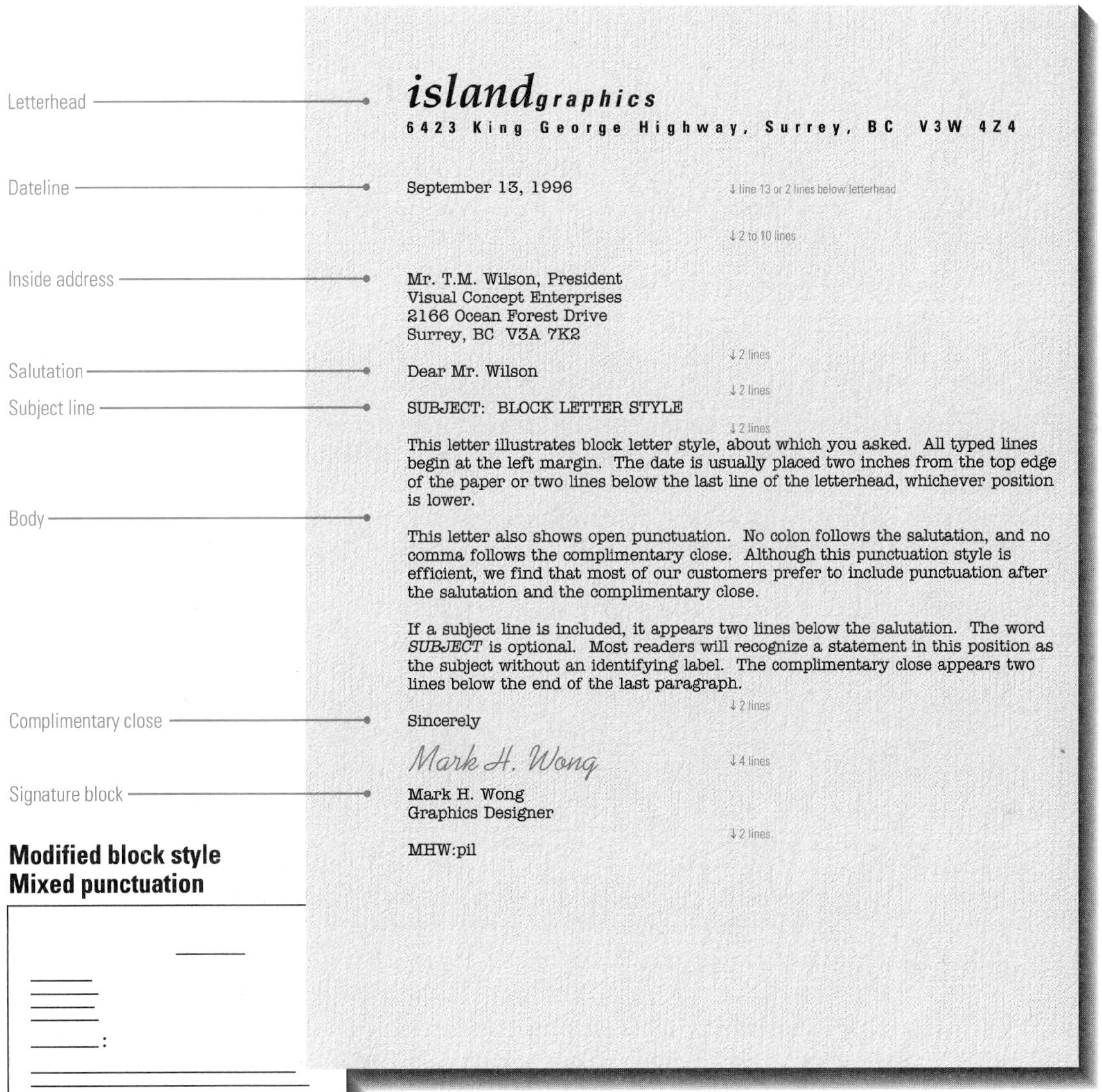

Letterhead ———————————————

*island*graphics
6423 King George Highway, Surrey, BC V3W 4Z4

Dateline ———————————————
September 13, 1996
↓ line 13 or 2 lines below letterhead

↓ 2 to 10 lines

Inside address ———————————————
Mr. T.M. Wilson, President
Visual Concept Enterprises
2166 Ocean Forest Drive
Surrey, BC V3A 7K2
↓ 2 lines

Salutation ———————————————
Dear Mr. Wilson
↓ 2 lines

Subject line ———————————————
SUBJECT: BLOCK LETTER STYLE
↓ 2 lines

This letter illustrates block letter style, about which you asked. All typed lines begin at the left margin. The date is usually placed two inches from the top edge of the paper or two lines below the last line of the letterhead, whichever position is lower.

Body ———————————————
This letter also shows open punctuation. No colon follows the salutation, and no comma follows the complimentary close. Although this punctuation style is efficient, we find that most of our customers prefer to include punctuation after the salutation and the complimentary close.

If a subject line is included, it appears two lines below the salutation. The word *SUBJECT* is optional. Most readers will recognize a statement in this position as the subject without an identifying label. The complimentary close appears two lines below the end of the last paragraph.
↓ 2 lines

Complimentary close ———————————————
Sincerely
↓ 4 lines

Mark H. Wong

Signature block ———————————————
Mark H. Wong
Graphics Designer
↓ 2 lines

MHW:pil

Modified block style
Mixed punctuation

In the modified block-style letter shown at the left, the date is centred or aligned with the complimentary close and signature block, which start at the centre. Mixed punctuation includes a colon after the salutation and a comma after the complimentary close, as shown at the left.

FIGURE B.2 ■ Letter Addresses and Salutations

Addressee	Salutation	Explanation
Individual Mrs. Leslie Lanham, CEO Atlantic Associates, Inc. 168 Elizabeth Drive Gander, NF A1V 1H5	Dear Mr. Lanham: Dear Leslie:	For specific individuals use a courtesy title (such as Mr. or Ms.) and the person's last name. For friends use a first-name greeting. When you are unsure of an addressee's gender, include the full name. (*Dear Leslie Lanham*). A helpful alternative is the simplified letter style, which omits a salutation.
Organization Pacific Builders Association Randall Building, Suite 303 555 Georgia Street West Vancouver, BC V6B 1Z6	Ladies and Gentlemen: Gentlemen: Ladies:	When females are part of management or if you are unsure, use *Ladies and Gentlemen*. If you know a company has only male managers, use *Gentlemen*. For a company with only female managers, use *Ladies*. An alternative that avoids this dilemma is the simplified letter style, which omits a salutation.
Individual Within Organization Thompson Fabricators, Inc. Attention: Ms. Lisa Jonas, Sales 1070 Cree Road Thompson, MB R8N 1R8	Ladies and Gentlemen:	Although an attention line is included here, the message is addressed to the the organization—hence the salutation *Ladies and Gentlemen*. However, when you know an individual's name, as in this case, it's better to use that name on the first line of the address without *Attention*. Then the salutation would be *Dear Ms. Jonas*.
Position or Department Within Organization Magnaflex Enterprises Inc. Attention: Marketing Manager 200 Main Street Newcastle, NB E1V 3E7	Ladies and Gentlemen:	When a letter is addressed to an organization for the attention of an individual in a specific position, the salutation should address the organization. If this salutation sounds awkward, use the simplified letter style and avoid a salutation.
Group of People Customers of individuals from a large database.	Dear Customer: Dear Policyholder:	When you are sending form letters to a large group and cannot use individual salutations, use an appropriate general salutation.

For letters with attention lines or those addressed to organizations, the selection of an appropriate salutation has become more difficult. Formerly, *Gentlemen* was used generally for all organizations. With increasing numbers of women in business management today, however, *Gentlemen* is problematic. Because no universally acceptable salutation has emerged as yet, you'll probably be safest with *Ladies and Gentlemen, Gentlemen and Ladies,* or *Dear Sir or Madam.*

One way to avoid the salutation dilemma is to address a document to a specific person. An alternative is to use the simplified letter style, which conveniently omits the salutation (and the complimentary close). Figure B.2 discusses and illustrates letter addresses and salutations.

Subject and reference lines. Although experts suggest placing the subject line two lines below the salutation, many businesses actually place it above the salutation. Use whatever style your organization prefers. Reference lines often show policy or file numbers; they generally appear two lines above the salutation.

Body. Most business letters and memoranda are single-spaced, with double line spacing between paragraphs. Very short messages may be double-spaced with indented paragraphs.

Complimentary close. Typed two lines below the last line of the letter, the complimentary close may be formal (*Very truly yours*) or informal (*Sincerely yours* or *Cordially*). The simplified letter style omits a complimentary close.

Signature block. In most letter styles the writer's typed name and optional identification appear three to four lines below the complimentary close. The combination of name, title, and organization information should be arranged to achieve a balanced look. The name and title may appear on the same line or on separate lines, depending on the length of each. Use commas to separate categories in the same line, but not to conclude a line. Women may choose to include *Ms., Mrs.,* or *Miss* before their names. Parentheses are optional. Men do not use *Mr.* before their names.

Sincerely yours,   Cordially yours,

Jeremy M. Wood, Manager   Casandra Baker-Murillo
Technical Sales and Services   Executive Vice-President

Some organizations include their names in the signature block. In such cases the organization name appears in all caps two lines below the complimentary close, as shown here.

Cordially,

LITTON COMPUTER SERVICES

Ms. Shelina A. Simpson
Executive Assistant

Reference initials. If used, the initials of the typist and writer are typed two lines below the writer's name and title. Generally, the writer's initials are capitalized and the typist's are lowercased, but this format varies.

Enclosure notation. When an enclosure or attachment accompanies a document, a notation to that effect appears two lines below the reference initials. This notation reminds the typist to insert the enclosure in the envelope, and it reminds the recipient to look for the enclosure or attachment. The notation may be spelled out (*Enclosure, Attachment*) or it may be abbreviated (*Enc., Att.*). It may indicate the number of enclosures or attachments, and it may also identify a specific enclosure (*Enclosure: Form 1099*).

Copy notation. If you make copies of correspondence for other individuals, you may use *cc* to indicate carbon copy, *pc* to indicate photocopy, or merely *c* for any kind of copy. A colon following the initial(s) is optional.

Second-page heading. When a letter extends beyond one page, use plain paper of the same quality and colour as the first page. Identify the second and succeeding pages with a heading consisting of the name of the addressee, the page number, and the date. Use either of the following two styles:

Ms. Rachel Ruiz
Page 2
May 3, 1996

Both headings appear on line 7 followed by two blank lines to separate them from the continuing text. Avoid using a second page if you have only one line or the complimentary close and signature block to fill that page.

Plain-paper return address. If you type a personal or business letter on plain paper, place your address immediately above the date. Do not include your name; you will type (and sign) your name at the end of your letter. If your return address contains two lines, begin typing it on line 11 so that the date appears on line 13. Avoid abbreviations except for a two-letter geographical abbreviation.

526 Frontenac Street
Kingston, ON K7K 4M2
December 14, 1996

Ms. Ellen Siemens
Escrow Department
Kingston Trust
1075 Johnson Street
Kingston, ON K7M 2N6

Dear Ms. Siemens:

For letters prepared in block style, type the return address at the left margin. For modified block-style letters, start the return address at the centre to align with the complimentary close.

Letter Styles

Business letters are generally prepared in one of three styles. The most popular is the block style, but the simplified style has much to recommend it.

Block style. In the block style, shown earlier in Figure B.1, all lines begin at the left margin. This style is popular because it is easy to format.

Modified block style. The modified block style differs from block style in that the date and closing lines appear in the centre, as shown at the bottom of Figure B.1. The date may be (1) centred, (2) begun at the centre of the page (to align with the closing lines), or (3) backspaced from the right margin. The signature block—including the complimentary close, writer's name and title, or organization identification—begins at the centre. The first line of each paragraph may begin at the left margin or may be indented 5 or 10 spaces. All other lines begin at the left margin.

Simplified style. Introduced by the Administrative Management Society a number of years ago, the simplified letter style, shown in Figure B.3, requires little formatting. Like the block style, all lines begin at the left margin. A subject line appears in all caps three lines below the inside address and three lines above

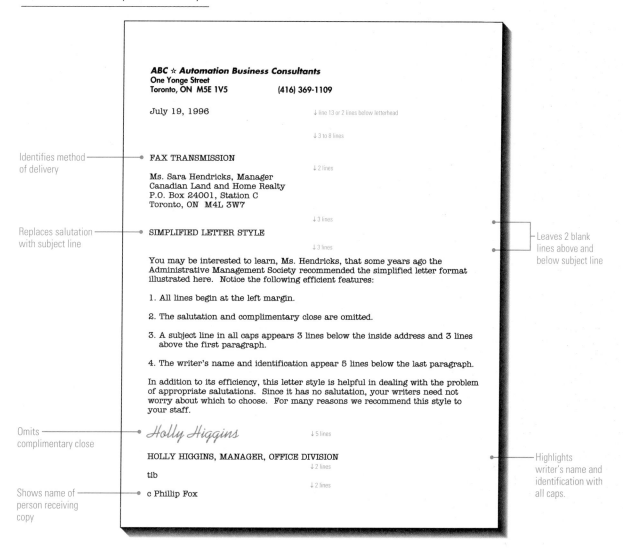

ABC ☆ Automation Business Consultants
One Yonge Street
Toronto, ON M5E 1V5   (416) 369-1109

July 19, 1996   ↓ line 13 or 2 lines below letterhead

                                                 ↓ 3 to 8 lines

Identifies method of delivery → ● FAX TRANSMISSION
                                                 ↓ 2 lines
Ms. Sara Hendricks, Manager
Canadian Land and Home Realty
P.O. Box 24001, Station C
Toronto, ON M4L 3W7

                                                 ↓ 3 lines
Replaces salutation with subject line → ● SIMPLIFIED LETTER STYLE

Leaves 2 blank lines above and below subject line

                                                 ↓ 3 lines
You may be interested to learn, Ms. Hendricks, that some years ago the
Administrative Management Society recommended the simplified letter format
illustrated here. Notice the following efficient features:

1. All lines begin at the left margin.

2. The salutation and complimentary close are omitted.

3. A subject line in all caps appears 3 lines below the inside address and 3 lines
   above the first paragraph.

4. The writer's name and identification appear 5 lines below the last paragraph.

In addition to its efficiency, this letter style is helpful in dealing with the problem
of appropriate salutations. Since it has no salutation, your writers need not
worry about which to choose. For many reasons we recommend this style to
your staff.

Omits complimentary close → ● *Holly Higgins*   ↓ 5 lines

HOLLY HIGGINS, MANAGER, OFFICE DIVISION
                                                 ↓ 2 lines
tib
                                                 ↓ 2 lines
Shows name of person receiving copy → ● c Phillip Fox

Highlights writer's name and identification with all caps.

---

the first paragraph. The salutation and complimentary close are omitted. The
signer's name and identification appear in all caps five lines below the last paragraph. This letter style is efficient and avoids the problem of appropriate salutations and courtesy titles.

■ Punctuation Styles

Two punctuation styles are commonly used for letters. *Open* punctuation, shown
with the block-style letter in Figure B.1, contains no punctuation after the salutation or complimentary close. *Mixed* punctuation, shown with the modified
block-style letter in Figure B.1, requires a colon after the salutation and a
comma after the complimentary close. Many business organizations prefer
mixed punctuation, even in a block-style letter.

If you choose mixed punctuation, be sure to use a colon—not a comma or
semicolon—after the salutation. Even when the salutation is a first name, the
colon should be used.

Envelopes

An envelope should be printed on the same quality and colour of stationery as the letter it carries. Because the envelope introduces your message and makes the first impression, you need to be especially careful in addressing it. Moreover, how you fold the letter is important.

Return address. The return address is usually printed in the upper left corner of an envelope, as shown in Figure B.4. In large companies some form of identification (the writer's initials, name, or location) may be typed above the company name and return address. This identification helps return the letter to the sender if it is not delivered.

On an envelope without a printed return address, single-space the return address in the upper-left corner. Beginning on line 3 on the fourth space (½ inch) from the left edge, type the writer's name, title, company, and mailing address.

Mailing address. On legal-sized No. 10 envelopes (4⅛ by 9½ inches), begin the address on line 13 about 4¼ inches from the left edge, as shown in Figure B.4. For small envelopes (3⅝ by 6½ inches), begin typing on line 12 about 2½ inches from the left edge.

Canada Post Corporation recommends that addresses be typed in all caps without any punctuation. This style, shown in the small envelope in Figure B.4, was originally developed to facilitate scanning by optical character readers (OCRs). Today's OCRs, however, are so sophisticated that they scan upper- and lowercase letters easily. Many companies today do not follow the Canada Post format because they prefer to use the same format on the envelope as for the inside address. If the same format is used, writers can take advantage of word processing programs to "copy" the inside address to the envelope, thus saving keystrokes and reducing errors. Having the same format on both the inside address and the envelope also looks more professional and consistent. For these reasons you may choose to use the familiar upper- and lowercase combination format. But you will want to check with your organization to learn its preference.

In addressing your envelopes for delivery in Canada or the United States, use the two-letter province and state abbreviations shown in Figure B.5. Notice that these abbreviations are in capital letters without periods.

Folding. The way a letter is folded and inserted into an envelope sends additional nonverbal messages about a writer's professionalism and carefulness. Most businesspeople follow the procedures shown here, which produce the least number of creases to distract the reader.

For large No. 10 envelopes, begin with the letter face up. Fold slightly less than one third of the sheet toward the top, as shown below. Then fold down the top third to within ⅛ inch of the bottom fold. Insert the letter into the envelope with the last fold toward the bottom of the envelope.

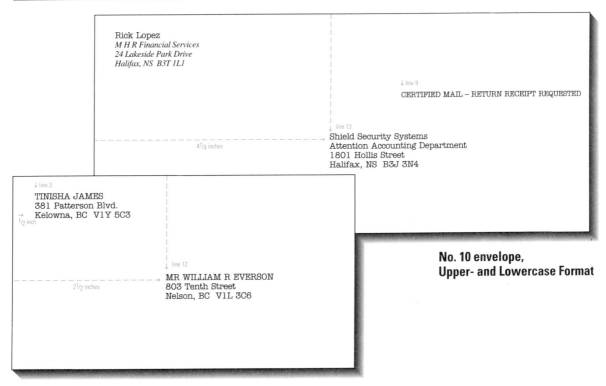

Rick Lopez
M H R Financial Services
24 Lakeside Park Drive
Halifax, NS B3T 1L1

↓ line 9
CERTIFIED MAIL – RETURN RECEIPT REQUESTED

↓ line 13
Shield Security Systems
Attention Accounting Department
1801 Hollis Street
Halifax, NS B3J 3N4

4¼ inches

↓ line 3
TINISHA JAMES
381 Patterson Blvd.
→ Kelowna, BC V1Y 5C3
½ inch

↓ line 12
MR WILLIAM R EVERSON
803 Tenth Street
Nelson, BC V1L 3C6

2½ inches

**No. 10 envelope,
Upper- and Lowercase Format**

No. 6¾ envelope, Canada Post Uppercase Format

For small No. 6¾ envelopes, begin by folding the bottom up to within ⅓ inch of the top edge. Then fold the right third over to the left. Fold the left third to within ⅓ inch from the last fold. Insert the last fold into the envelope first.

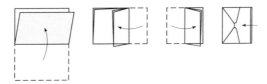

■ Memoranda

As discussed in Chapter 7, memoranda deliver messages within organizations. Many offices use memo forms imprinted with the organization name and, optionally, the department or division names, as shown in Figure B.6. Although the design and arrangement of memo forms vary, they usually include the basic elements of TO, FROM, DATE, and SUBJECT. Large organizations may include other identifying headings, such as FILE NUMBER, FLOOR, EXTENSION, LOCATION, and DISTRIBUTION.

Because of the difficulty of aligning computer printers with preprinted forms, many business writers store memo formats in their computers and call them up when preparing memos. The guide words are then printed with the message, thus eliminating alignment problems.

FIGURE B.5 ■ Abbreviations of Provinces, States, and Territories

Province or Territory	Two-Letter Abbreviation	American State or Territory	Two-Letter Abbreviation
Alberta	AB	Louisiana	LA
British Columbia	BC	Maine	ME
Manitoba	MB	Maryland	MD
New Brunswick	NB	Massachusetts	MA
Newfoundland	NF	Michigan	MI
Northwest Territories	NT	Minnesota	MN
Nova Scotia	NS	Mississippi	MS
Ontario	ON	Missouri	MO
Prince Edward Island	PE	Montana	MT
Quebec	QC	Nebraska	NE
Saskatchewan	SK	Nevada	NV
Yukon Territory	YT	New Hampshire	NH
		New Jersey	NJ

American State or Territory	Two-Letter Abbreviation	American State or Territory	Two-Letter Abbreviation
Alabama	AL	New Mexico	NM
Alaska	AK	New York	NY
Arizona	AZ	North Carolina	NC
Arkansas	AR	North Dakota	ND
California	CA	Ohio	OH
Canal Zone	CZ	Oklahoma	OK
Colorado	CO	Oregon	OR
Connecticut	CT	Pennsylvania	PA
Delaware	DE	Puerto Rico	PR
District of Columbia	DC	Rhode Island	RI
Florida	FL	South Carolina	SC
Georgia	GA	South Dakota	SD
Guam	GU	Tennessee	TN
Hawaii	HI	Texas	TX
Idaho	ID	Utah	UT
Illinois	IL	Vermont	VT
Indiana	IN	Virgin Islands	VI
Iowa	IA	Virginia	VA
Kansas	KS	Washington	WA
Kentucky	KY	West Virginia	WV
		Wisconsin	WI
		Wyoming	WY

If no printed or stored computer forms are available, memos may be typed on company letterhead or on plain paper, as shown in Figure B.7. On a full sheet of paper, start on line 13; on a half sheet, start on line 7. Double-space and type in all caps the guide words: TO:, FROM:, DATE:, SUBJECT:. Align all the fill-in information two spaces after the longest guide word (SUBJECT:). Leave three lines between the last line of the heading and the first line of the memo. Like business letters, memos are single-spaced.

Memos are generally formatted with side margins of 1¼ inches, or they may conform to the printed memo form. (For more information about memos, see Chapter 7.)

FIGURE B.6 ■ Printed Memo Forms

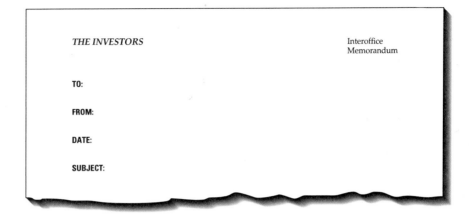

THE INVESTORS

Interoffice
Memorandum

TO:

FROM:

DATE:

SUBJECT:

TMB
Canada Inc.

Internal Memo

TO: **DATE:**

FROM: **FILE:**

SUBJECT:

FIGURE B.7 ■ Memo on Plain Paper

↓ line 10

MEMO

TO: Dawn Stewart, Manager   DATE: February 3, 1996
           Sales and Marketing

FROM: Jay Murray, Vice-President
           Operations

SUBJECT: TELEPHONE SERVICE REQUEST FORMS
           ↓ 3 lines

To speed telephone installation and improve service within the Bremerton facility,
we are starting a new application procedure.

Service request forms will be available at various locations within the three
buildings. When you require telephone service, obtain a request form at one of
the locations that is convenient for you. Fill in the pertinent facts, obtain approval
from your division head, and send the form to Brent White. Request forms are
available at the following locations:

FAX TRANSMISSION

DATE: _____

TO: _____ FAX NUMBER: _____

_____

_____

FROM: _____ FAX NUMBER: _____

_____

_____

NUMBER OF PAGES TRANSMITTED INCLUDING THIS COVER SHEET: _____

MESSAGE:

If any part of this fax transmission is missing or not received clearly, please call:

NAME: _____

PHONE: _____

■ Fax Cover Sheet

Documents transmitted by fax are usually introduced by a cover sheet, such as that shown in Figure B.8. As with memos, the format varies considerably. Important items to include are (1) the name and fax number of the receiver, (2) the name and fax number of the sender, (3) the number of pages being sent, and (4) the name and telephone number of the person to notify in case of unsatisfactory transmission.

When the document being transmitted requires little explanation, you may prefer to attach an adhesive note (such as a Post-it™ fax transmittal form) instead of a full cover sheet. These notes carry essentially the same information as shown in our printed fax cover sheet. They are perfectly acceptable in most business organizations and can save considerable paper and transmission costs.

Three Systems of Documentation

For many reasons careful writers take pains to document the information contained in their reports. Citing sources strengthens a writer's argument, as you learned in Chapter 11. Acknowledging sources also shields writers from charges of plagiarism. Moreover, good references help the reader pursue further research. Fortunately, word processing programs have taken much of the pain out of documenting data, particularly for footnotes and endnotes.

Before we discuss specific systems of documentation, you must understand the difference between *source* notes and *content* notes. Source notes identify the source of quotations, paraphrased passages, and ideas. They lead the reader to the sources of cited information, and they must follow a consistent style. Content notes, on the other hand, enable the writer to add comments, explain information not directly related to the text, or refer the reader to other sections of a report. Because content notes are generally infrequent, most writers identify them in the text with a raised asterisk (*). An asterisk should follow the statement to which it refers. At the bottom of the page, the asterisk is repeated with the content note following. If two content notes appear on one page, a double asterisk identifies the second reference.

Your real concern will be with source notes, which identify the sources of the quotations or paraphrased ideas in the text. Researchers have struggled for years to develop the perfect documentation system, one that is efficient for the writer and clear to the reader. As a result, there are many systems, each with its advantages. The important thing for you is to adopt one system and use it consistently.

Students frequently ask, "But what documentation system is most used in business?" Actually, no one method dominates. Many businesses have developed their own hybrid systems. These companies generally supply guidelines illustrating their in-house style to their employees. Before starting any research project on the job, you'll want to inquire about your organization's preferred documentation style. You can also look in the files for examples of previous reports.

To give you guidance for your academic papers, we'll concentrate on three common documentation formats: American Psychological Association (APA) style, Modern Language Association (MLA) style, and *The Chicago Manual of Style* (CMS), documentary style. These three systems have two primary goals: to cite sources of data, ideas, and quotations; and to interrupt the text as little as possible. Generally, a short citation is inserted into the text. It may be a superscript number or the author's name, year of publication, and reference page number. This in-text citation guides the reader either to a footnote (or endnote) or to a list of complete bibliographical references at the end of the work. But the reference formats differ in each of the three systems. The following discussion will show sample references illustrating (1) **in-text citations** and (2) **bibliography** references for all three systems.

An important development in documentation is the increasing use of electronic research. We'll show current formats, but remember that these formats may change as technology progresses and standards are introduced.

◼ APA Style—American Psychological Association

Popular in the social and physical sciences, the American Psychological Association (APA) documentation style uses parenthetic citations (sometimes called "author-date citations"). That is, each author reference is shown in parentheses when cited in the text. Below are selected distinguishing features of the APA style. For more information see the *Publication Manual of the American Psychological Association*, 4th edition (Washington: American Psychological Association, 1994).

In-text citation. In-text citations consist of the author's last name, year of publication, and pertinent page number(s). These items appear in parentheses, usually at the end of a clause or end of a sentence in which material is cited. This parenthetic citation, as shown in the following illustration, directs the reader to a reference list at the end of the report where complete bibliographic information is recorded.

> The strategy of chicken king Don Tyson was to expand aggressively into other "centre-of-the-plate" proteins, such as pork, fish, and turkey (Berss, 1994, p. 64).

Bibliography. All reference sources are alphabetized in a bibliography called a "Reference List." Below are selected guidelines summarizing important elements of the APA bibliographic format:

- Include authors' names with the last name first followed by initials, such as **Smith, M. A.** First and middle names are not used.

- Show the date of publication in parentheses such as **Smith, M. A. (1996).**

- Underline the titles of books and use "sentence-style" (sometimes called *down style*) capitalization. This means that only the first word of a title or the first word after an internal colon is capitalized. Book titles are followed by the place of publication and publisher's name: **Smith, M. A. (1996).** <u>**Communications for managers**</u>**. Elmsford, N.Y.: Pergamon Press.**

- Type the titles of magazine and journal articles without underlining or quotation marks. Use sentence-style capitalization for articles. However, underscore the names of magazines and journals and capitalize the initial letters of all important words. Also underscore the volume number: **Cheung, H. K., and Burn, J. M. (1994). Distributing global information systems resources in multinational companies—a contingency model.** <u>**Journal of Global Information Management, 2**</u> **(3), 14–27. ["2(3), 14–27" means volume 2, number 3, pages 14–27]**

- Space only once following periods and colons.

- For electronic references give the author, date of publication, title of article and/or name of publication, electronic medium [such as *on-line* or *CD-ROM*], volume, series, page, and path. The path should provide all the information necessary to retrieve an item: **Marmer, C. (1995, Jan.). Repatriation: Up, down, or out? [8 pages]** <u>**Personnel Journal**</u> **[On-line],** <u>**74**</u> **(1), 28. Available: Telnet:/melvyl.ucop.edu** [Do not end a path statement with a period because stray punctuation hinders retrieval.]

Figure C.1 shows the format of an APA Reference List as well as many sample references. To see a business report prepared using APA documentation, look at Figure 13.6 in Chapter 13.

FIGURE C.1 ■ Model APA Bibliography Sample References

References

Air Canada. (1995). <u>1995 Annual Report</u>. St. Laurent, QC.   Annual report

Berss, M. (1994, October 24). Protein man. <u>Forbes</u>, 64–66.   Magazine article

"Globalization often means that the fast track leads overseas."   Newspaper article, no author
(1996, June 16). <u>The Financial Post</u>, p. A1.

Huang, J. (1994). Solid waste disposal. <u>Microsoft Encarta '95</u>   CD-ROM encyclopedia
[CD-ROM]. Redmond, WA: Microsoft.   article, one author

Little, Bruce. (1995, August 9). Payroll taxes linked to job loss.   Newspaper article, one
<u>The Globe and Mail</u> (Metro edition), p. B1.   author

McDonald's Restaurants of Canada Ltd. (1994). <u>McDonald's food facts</u>   Brochure
[Brochure]. Toronto, ON: McDonald's Food Information.

Prewitt, M. (1995, January 2). Operators burn with anger as NYC   On-line newspaper
anti-smoking Bill passes. <u>Nation's Restaurant News</u> [On-line], <u>3</u>. ABI/INFORM.   article
Available: CompuServe.

Rivers, F., production manager, Waste Control Management, Inc.   Interview
(1996, January 16). Interview by author. Pickering, ON.

Rose, R. C., and Garrett, E. M. (1992). <u>How to make a buck and still be a decent</u>   Book, two authors
<u>human being.</u> New York: HarperCollins.

Statistics Canada. (1995). <u>A portrait of persons with disabilities: Target</u>   Government publication
<u>groups project.</u> Ottawa: Department of Industry, Science and Technology.

Steuteville, R. (1995, April). The state of garbage in America, Part 1.   On-line magazine article
<u>BioCycle</u> [On-line], <u>2</u>. Available: Telnet://melvyl.uncop.edu

Tips to reduce, reuse, and recycle. (1995). <u>Environmental Recycling Hotline</u>   Internet, World Wide Web
[On-line]. Available: http://www.primenet.com/cgi-bin/erh.pl
Cited 1995 Oct. 25.

Wetherbee, J. C., Vitalari, N. P., and Milner, A. (1994). Key trends in systems   Journal article with
development in Europe and North America. <u>Journal of Global Information</u>   volume and issue numbers
<u>Management, 3</u>(2), 5–20.

■ MLA Style–Modern Language Association

The MLA style is favoured by writers and researchers in the humanities. Like the APA documentation style, the MLA style uses parenthetic author references in the text. These in-text citations guide the reader to a bibliography called "Works Cited." For more information consult Joseph Gibaldi, *MLA Handbook for Writers of Research papers*, 4th ed. (New York: The Modern Language Association of America, 1995).

In-text citation. The author's last name and the year of publication appear in parentheses after the information cited, such as **(Smith 1996)**. Unlike in the APA style, the date and separating comma are omitted. Neither the word *page* nor the abbreviations *p.* or *pp.* are used. If the author's name is mentioned in the text, cite only the page number in parentheses.

Although listing your résumé with an electronic job bank is wise, don't stop there. George Crosby of the Human Resources Network says, "If you think just sending out your resume will get you a job, you're crazy. [These services are] just a supplement to a core strategy of networking your buns off" (Lancaster B1).

Bibliography. A bibliography called "Works Cited" lists all references cited in a report. Some writers also include all works consulted. Below is a summary of the MLA bibliographic style:

- Underline the titles of books and use "headline style" (up style) for capitalization. This means that all main words are capitalized: **Peters, Thomas J., and Robert H. Waterman, Jr. <u>In Search of Excellence</u>. New York: Warner Books, 1983.**

- For magazine articles include the date of publication but omit volume and issue numbers: **Lee, Mary M. "Investing in International Relationships." <u>Business Monthly</u> 18 Feb. 1996: 23–24.**

- For journal articles follow the same format as for magazine articles except include the volume number, issue number (if needed), and the year of publication inside parentheses: **Taylor, Chris L. "Nonverbal Communication." <u>The Journal of Business Ethics</u> 10.2 (1996): 23–29.** ["10.2" means volume 10, issue 2]

- For electronic reference to printed sources, provide author and publication data as well as the name of the electronic medium and the date of access: **Angier, Natalie. "Chemists Learn Why Vegetables Are Good for You." <u>New York Times</u> 13 Apr. 1993, late ed.: C1. <u>New York Times Online.</u> Online. Nexis. 10 Feb. 1994.**

- For electronic references to unprinted sources, provide an electronic address or pathway following the word *Available*.

Figure C.2 shows an MLA "Works Cited" bibliography and many sample references. To see a complete report using MLA documentation, turn to Figure 14.4 in Chapter 14.

Works Cited

Air Canada. <u>1995 Annual Report</u>. St. Laurent, QC.   Annual report

Barss, Marcia. "Protein Man." <u>Forbes</u> 24 Oct. 1994: 64–66.   Magazine article

"Globalization Often Means That the Fast Track Leads Overseas."   Newspaper article, no author
    <u>The Financial Post</u> 16 June 1996: A10.

Huang, Jerry Y. C. "Solid Waste Disposal." <u>Microsoft Encarta '95</u>. CD-ROM.   CD-ROM encyclopedia article,
    Redmond, WA: Microsoft, 1994.   one author

Little, Bruce. "Payroll Taxes Linked to Job Loss." <u>The Globe and Mail</u> 9 August 1995: B1.   Newspaper article, one author

McDonald's Restaurants of Canada Ltd. <u>McDonald's Food Facts</u>. Toronto: Brochure
    McDonald's Food Information, 1994.

Prewitt, Milford. "Operators Burn with Anger as NYC Anti-Smoking Bill Passes."   On-line magazine article
    <u>Nation's Restaurant News</u> 2 Jan. 1995: 3+. <u>ABI/Inform</u>. Online. CompuServe.
    25 Feb. 1995.

Rivers, Frank. Personal interview. 16 January 1996.   Interview

Rose, Richard C., and Echo Montgomery Garrett. <u>How to Make a Buck and Still</u>   Book, two authors
    <u>Be a Decent Human Being.</u> New York: HarperCollins, 1992.

Statistics Canada. <u>A Portrait of Persons with Disabilities Target Groups Project</u>.   Government publication
    Ottawa: Ministry of Industry, Science and Technology, 1995.

Steuteville, Robert. "The State of Garbage in America," Part 1. <u>BioCycle</u> 2 Apr. 1995: 54–63.   On-line magazine article
    On-line. Available telnet://melvyl.ucop.edu 25 Oct. 1995.

"Tips to Reduce, Reuse, and Recycle." <u>Environmental Recycling Hotline</u>. On-line.   Internet, World Wide Web
    World Wide Web. Available http://www.primenet com/cgi-bin/erh.pl 27 Oct. 1995.

Wetherbee, James C., Nicholas P. Vitalari, and Andrew Milner. "Key Trends in   Journal article with volume and issue
    Systems Development in Europe and North America." <u>Journal of Global Information</u>   numbers
    <u>Management</u> 3.2 (1994): 5–20.

■ CMS Style—The Chicago Manual of Style

The Chicago Manual of Style, which has guided writers and editors for many decades, shows two different systems of documentation. The first is the traditional documentary-note or humanities style. Favoured by many in literature, history, and the arts, this style employs superscript (raised) numbers in the text to mark references. The reader is directed to a complete bibliographic citation appearing in either a footnote or an endnote. Some readers like footnotes because the citations appear at the bottom of each page and are immediately available. Others dislike footnotes because they clutter the page. Instead of footnotes, many writers today use endnotes, which are all listed at the end of the report. Advanced word processing programs contain features that make footnotes or endnotes easy to handle.

A second method described in the *Chicago Manual* is an author-date system much like that used by APA and MLA. For our purposes, however, we will concentrate on the traditional documentary-note style and illustrate its in-text citation and bibliographic form. For more information see *The Chicago Manual of Style*, 14th ed., John Grossman, ed., pp. 487 to 635.

In-text citation. At the end of a quotation or reference, a superscript (raised) figure, shown below, marks the reference. It guides the reader to a complete reference given in a note, either at the bottom of the page or at the end of the report.

> Cross-border business alliances are difficult. "Simple things like scheduling meetings," said one manager, "became ballets of clashing customs."[4]

Endnote or footnote citation. This note refers the reader to a specific page or to an electronic screen showing the specific reference. These notes begin with the first name of the author. Incidentally, don't be alarmed if your word processing program numbers the endnotes in large numbers in parentheses instead of small superscript figures. Either form is acceptable.

> [4] *Frank Rivers, production manager, Waste Control Management, Inc. Interview with author, 16 January 1996. Pickering, Ont.*

Bibliography. If you use the Chicago style of footnotes or endnotes, a bibliography is not necessary since all the relevant information is contained in the notes. But if you wish you *may* include a bibliography, especially if there are a large number of notes and sources.

A bibliography must list all references *cited*, but it may also contain all references *consulted*. While endnotes are arranged in order of their appearance in the text, the bibliography is alphabetical by author. And the bibliography does not list the page numbers of the material cited in the text of your report. The following guidelines are for a Chicago style bibliography:

- Arrange entries alphabetically by author's last name. If no author is known, alphabetize by the first letter of the first important word in the title.

- Use hanging indented form with the second and succeeding lines indented.

- Enclose titles of magazine, newspaper, and journal articles in quotation marks and capitalize the first and last word and all other words except articles (*a, an, the*), coordinating conjunctions (*and, or, nor, but*), and prepositions (*in, of, on, for,* etc.)

- Italicize the names of books, newspapers, journals, and other complete publications. Capitalize as for articles.

- Identify electronic references in brackets, such as [On-line database] or [CD-ROM]. Explain how the reference can be reached, such as *Available from CompuServe*. For an on-line reference, tell when it was cited.

Figure C.3 shows a set of endnotes in the Chicago style; Figure C.4 shows a Chicago-style bibliography.

FIGURE C.3 ■ The Chicago Manual of Style Sample Endnotes or Footnotes

Endnotes

[1]Air Canada, *1995 Annual Report* (St. Laurent, QC), 7.

Annual report

[2]Milford Prewitt, "Operators Burn with Anger as NYC Anti-smoking Bill Passes," *Nation's Restaurant News* (2 January 1995): 3, in ABI/INFORM [on-line database, updated 1 February 1995; cited 25 February 1995; screen 2 of 9]; available from CompuServe.

On-line magazine article

[3]"Globalization Often Means That the Fast Track Leads Overseas," *The Financial Post,* 16 June 1996, A10.

Newspaper article, no author

[4]"Tips to Reduce, Reuse, and Recycle," *Environmental Recycling Hotline.* On-line, World Wide Web, cited 27 October 1995, available from http://www.primenet.com/cgi-bin/erh.pl

Internet, World Wide Web

[5]Bruce Little, "Payroll Taxes Linked to Job Loss," *The Globe and Mail* (Metro edition), 9 August 1995, B1.

Newspaper article, one author

[6]Frank Rivers, production manager, Waste Control Management, Inc. Interview with author, 16 January 1996. Pickering, ON.

Interview

[7]Marcia Berss, "Protein Man," *Forbes* (24 October 1994): 64–66.

Magazine article

[8]McDonald's Restaurants of Canada Ltd., *McDonald's Food Facts* (Toronto: McDonald's Food Information, 1994).

Brochure

[9]James C. Wetherbee, Nicholas P. Vitalari, and Andrew Milner, "Key Trends in Systems Development in Europe and North America," *Journal of Global Information Management* 3, no. 2 (Spring 1994): 6.

Journal article with volume and issue numbers

[10]Statistics Canada, *A Portrait of Persons with Disabilities: Target Groups Project.* (Ottawa: Department of Industry, Science and Technology 1995), 11.

Government publication

[11]Robert Steuteville, "The State of Garbage in America," Part 1, *BioCycle,* 2 April 1995, 54. [On-line, cited 25 October 1995], available from telnet://melvyl.ucop.edu

On-line magazine article

[12]Jerry Y. C. Huang, "Solid Waste Disposal," *Microsoft Encarta '95.* (Redmond, WA: Microsoft, 1994) [CD-ROM].

CD-ROM encyclopedia article, one author

[13]Richard C. Rose and Echo Montgomery Garrett, *How to Make a Buck and Still Be a Decent Human Being* (New York: HarperCollins, 1992), 168.

Book, two authors

FIGURE C.4 ▦ The Chicago Manual of Style Sample Bibliography

Bibliography

Air Canada. *1995 Annual Report*. St. Laurent, QC, 7. — Annual report

Berss, Marcia. "Protein Man." *Forbes* (24 October 1994): 64–66. — Magazine article

"Globalization Often Means That the Fast Track Leads Overseas."
    The Financial Post, 16 June 1996, A10. — Newspaper article, no author

Huang, Jerry Y. C. "Solid Waste Disposal." *Microsoft Encarta '95*. Redmond,
    WA: Microsoft, 1994. [CD-ROM]. — CD-ROM encyclopedia article, one author

Little, Bruce. "Payroll Taxes Linked to Job Loss." *The Globe and Mail*,
    9 August 1995, B1. — Newspaper article, one author

McDonald's Restaurants of Canada Ltd. *McDonald's Food Facts*. Toronto:
    McDonald's Food Information, 1994. — Brochure

Prewitt, Milford. "Operators Burn With Anger as NYC Anti-smoking Bill
    Passes." *Nation's Restaurant News*. 2 January 1995. In ABI/INFORM [full-text on-line
    database; updated 1 February 1995; cited 25 February 1995]. Available from CompuServe. — On-line magazine article

Rivers, Frank. Interview by author. Pickering, ON. 16 January 1996. — Interview

Rose, Richard C., and Echo Montgomery Garrett. *How to Make a Buck and Still
    Be a Decent Human Being*. New York: HarperCollins, 1992. — Book, two authors

Statistics Canada. *A Portrait of Persons with Disabilities: Target Groups Project*.
    Ottawa: Department of Industry, Science and Technology, 1995. — Government publication

Steuteville, Robert. "The State of Garbage in America," Part 1. *BioCycle*.
    2 April 1995, 54. [On-line, cited 25 October 1995]. Available from telnet://melvyl.ucop.edu — On-line magazine article

Wetherbee, James C., Nicholas P. Vitalari, and Andrew Milner. "Key Trends in
    Systems Development in Europe and North America," *Journal of Global Information
    Management*, 3, no. 2 (Spring 1994): 6. [Alternative form: *Journal of Global Information
    Management*, vol. 3, no. 2 (Spring 1994), 5–20.] — Journal article with volume and issue numbers

Correction Symbols

In marking your papers, your instructor may use the following symbols or abbreviations to indicate writing weaknesses. You'll find that studying these symbols and suggestions will help you understand your instructor's remarks. Knowing this information can also help you evaluate and improve your own letters, memos, reports, and other writing. For specific writing guidelines and self-help exercises, see Appendix A: Competent Language Usage Essentials (CLUE).

Strategy and Organization

Coh	Develop coherence between ideas. Repeat key idea or add transitional expression.
DS	Use direct strategy. Start with main idea or good news.
IS	Use indirect strategy. Explain before introducing main idea.
Org	Improve organization. Keep similar topics together.
Plan	Apply appropriate plan for message.
Trans	Include transition to join ideas.

Content and Style

Acc	Verify accuracy of names, places, amount, and other data.
AE	Use action ending that tells reader what to do.
ACE	Avoid copying examples.
ACP	Avoid copying case problems.
Act	Use active voice.
Awk	Rephrase to avoid awkward or unidiomatic expression.
Asn	Check assignment for instructions or facts.
Chop	Use longer sentences to avoid choppiness. Vary sentence patterns.
Cl	Improve clarity of ideas or expression.
Con	Condense into shorter form.
Emp	Emphasize this idea.
Eth	Use language that projects honest, ethical business practices.
Exp	Explain more fully or clearly.
Inc	Expand an incomplete idea.
Jar	Avoid jargon or specialized language that reader may not know.
Log	Remedy faulty logic.
Neg	Revise negative expression with more positive view.
Obv	Avoid saying what is obvious.
Par	Use parallel (balanced) expression.
PV	Express idea from reader's point of view.
RB	Show reader benefits. What's in it for reader?
Rdn	Revise to eliminate redundant idea or expression.
Rep	Avoid unintentional repetition of word, idea, or sound.
Sin	Use language that sounds sincere.
Spec	Develop idea with specific details.
Sub	Subordinate this point to lessen its impact.
SX	Avoid sexist language.
Tone	Use more conversational or positive tone.
You	Emphasize *you*-view.
Var	Vary sentences with different patterns.
Vag	Avoid vague pronoun. Don't use *they, that, this, which, it,* or other pronouns unless their references are clear.

Vb	Use correct verb tense. Avoid shift of tense.
W	Condense to avoid wordiness.
WC	Improve word choice. Find a more precise word.

Grammar and Mechanics

Abv	Avoid most abbreviations in text. Use correct abbreviation if necessary.
Agr	Make each subject and verb or pronoun and noun agree.
Apos	Use an apostrophe to show possession or contraction.
Art	Choose a correct article (*a*, *an*, or *the*).
Cap	Capitalize appropriately.
Cm	Use a comma.
CmConj	Use a comma preceding coordinating conjunction (*and, or, nor, but*) that joins independent clauses.
CmIntro	Use a comma following introductory dependent clause or long phrase.
CmSer	Use commas to separate items in a series.
CS	Rectify a comma splice by separating independent clauses with a period or a semicolon.
Div	Improve word division by hyphenating between syllables.
DM	Rectify a dangling modifier by supplying a clear subject for modifying element.
Exp	Avoid expletives such as *there is, there are*, and *it is*.
Frag	Revise fragment to form complete sentence.
Gram	Use correct grammar.
Hyp	Hyphenate a compound adjective.
lc	Use lower case instead of capital.
MM	Correct misplaced modifier by moving modifier closer to word it describes or limits.
Num	Express numbers in correct word or figure form.
Pn	Use correct punctuation.
Prep	Correct use of preposition.
RO	Rectify run-on sentence with comma or semicolon to separate independent clauses.
Sem	use semicolon to join related independent clauses.
Sp	Check spelling.
SS	Shorten sentences.
UnCm	Avoid unnecessary comma.

Format

Cen	Centre a document appropriately on the page.
DSp	Insert a double space, or double-space throughout.
F	Choose appropriate format for this item or message.
GH	Use graphic highlighting (bullets, lists, indentions, and headings to improve readability.
Mar	Improve margins to frame a document on the page.
SS	Insert a single space, or single-space throughout.
TSp	Insert a triple space.

PROOFREADING MARKS

Proofreading Mark	Draft Copy	Final Copy
═ Align horizontally	TO: Rick Munoz.	TO: Rick Munoz
‖ Align vertically	166.32 132.45	166.32 132.45
≡ Capitalize	Coca-cola runs on ms-dos	Coca-Cola runs on MS-DOS
⌒ Close up space	meeting at 3 p. m.	meeting at 3 p.m.
⊐⊏ Centre	⊐Recommendations⊏	Recommendations
⨍ Delete	in my final judgément	in my judgment
⋎ Insert apostrophe	our companys product	our company's product
⋏ Insert comma	you will of course	you will, of course,
⑈ Insert hyphen	tax free income	tax-free income
⊙ Insert period	Ms Holly Hines	Ms. Holly Hines
⋎ Insert quotation mark	shareholders receive a bonus.	shareholders receive a "bonus."
# Insert space	wordprocessing program	word processing program
/ Lowercase (remove capitals)	the Vice-President	the vice-president
	HUMAN RESOURCES	Human Resources
⊏ Move to left	⊏I. Labour costs	I. Labour costs
⊐ Move to right	A. Findings of study ⊐	A. Findings of study
◯ Spell out	aimed at ②depts	aimed at two departments
⁊ Start new paragraph	⁊Keep the screen height of your computer at eye level.	Keep the screen height of your computer at eye level.
⋯ (Stet) (don't delete)	officials talked openly	officials talked openly
∼ Transpose	accounts recievable	accounts receivable
𝓫𝓯 Use boldface	Conclusions 𝓫𝓯	**Conclusions**
𝑖𝑡𝑎𝑙 Use italics	The Perfect Résumé 𝑖𝑡𝑎𝑙	*The Perfect Résumé*

Key to CLUE Exercises

Revised words and punctuation are shown in bold type.

Chapter 1

1. After he **had** checked many statements**,** our **accountant** found the error in **Column** 2 of the balance sheet.

2. Because Mr. **Lockwood's** business owned considerable property**,** **we** were **surprised** by **its** lack of liquid assets.

3. The mortgage company checked all property titles **separately;** however, it found no discrepancies.

4. When Ms. Khan finished the audit**,** she wrote **three** letters **to apprise** the owners of her findings.

5. Just between you and **me, who** do you think could have ordered all this **stationery?**

6. Assets and liabilities **are** what the **four** buyers want to see**;** consequently, we are preparing this **year's** statements.

7. Next spring my brother and **I** plan to **enrol** in the following courses: marketing, **English**, and history.

8. Dan felt that he had done **well** on the exam**,** but he wants to do even better when it's given again next **fall**.

9. Our records show that your **end-of-the-month** balance was **$96.30.**

10. When the **principal** in the account grows **too** large**,** we must make annual withdrawals.

Chapter 2

1. To avoid **embarrassing** any employee**,** the **personnel** manager and **I have** decided to talk **personally** to each individual.

2. **Three** assistants were sent on a **search-and-destroy** mission in a conscious effort to remove at least **15 000** old documents from the files.

3. Electronic mail, now used by **three-quarters** of Canada's largest **companies,** will transmit messages instantly.

4. An article entitled **"What's New with Managers"** appeared in **Reader's Digest**, which is read by **2 million** Canadians.

5. Your account is now **60** days overdue**;** consequently, we have only **one** alternative left.

6. The marketing **manager's** itinerary listed the following three destinations: **Montreal, Winnipeg, and Victoria.**

7. Each of the **beautifully printed** [delete hyphen] books available at **Pickwick Book Company has** been reduced to **$30.**

8. We recommend**, therefore,** that a committee study our mail procedures for a **three-week** period and submit a report of **its** findings.

9. **They're** going to visit **their** relatives in Ottawa, Ontario, over the Victoria Day weekend.

10. The hotel can accommodate **300** convention guests, but it has parking facilities for only **100** cars.

Chapter 3

1. If I **were** you, I would schedule the conference for one of these cities: Ottawa, Kingston, or Montreal.

2. The **committee's** next meeting is scheduled for May **5** at **3** p.m. [omit comma] and should last about two hours.

3. **We're** not asking you to **alter** the figures; we are asking you to check **their** accuracy. [Or start a new sentence with "We are."]

4. Will you please fax me a list of our independent **contractors'** names and addresses.

5. The vacation **calendar** fills up **quickly** for the **summer** months; therefore, you should make your plans early.

6. After the inspector issues the **waiver,** we will be able to **proceed** with the **architect's** plan.

7. If we can't give out **necessary** information, what is the point in **our** answering the telephone**?**

8. **New employees** will receive their orientation **packets** [omit comma] and be told about parking **privileges**. [Or Every new employee will receive **an** orientation packet and be told about parking **privileges**. Or Every new employee will receive **his or her** orientation packet and be told about **his or her** parking **privileges.**]

9. About **85** percent of all new entrants into the workforce in the 1990s **are** expected to be [omit colon] women, **members of visible minorities,** and immigrants.

10. Our **vice-president** in the Human Resources Development Department asked the **manager** and **me** to come to her office at **3:30** p.m.

Chapter 4

1. Although [omit comma] we **formerly** used a neighbourhood printer for all our print jobs, we are now saving almost **$500** a month by using desktop publishing.

2. Powerful **software,** however, cannot **guarantee** a good final product.

3. To develop a better sense of design, we collected **desirable** samples from [omit colon] books, magazines, brochures, and newsletters.

4. We noticed that [omit comma] poorly [omit hyphen] designed projects often **were** filled with cluttered layouts, incompatible typefaces, and **too** many typefaces.

5. Our layout design **is** usually formal, but **occasionally** we use an informal layout design, which is shown in **Figure 6.**

6. We **usually** prefer a **black-and-white** design [omit semicolon] because colour printing is much more costly.

7. Expensive colour printing jobs are sent to foreign countries; for example, **China, Italy,** and **Japan.**

8. **Jeffrey's** article, which he entitled "The Shaping of a **Corporate Image,**" was **accepted** for publication in **The Journal of Communication**.

9. Every employee will **personally receive** a copy of **his or her performance evaluation,** which the **president** said will be the **principal** basis for promotion. [Or **All employees** will **personally receive** copies of their **performance evaluations. ...**]

10. We will print **350** copies of the newsletter [omit comma] to be sent to **whoever** is currently listed in our database.

Chapter 5

1. Business documents must be written **clearly** to **ensure** that readers comprehend the message **quickly.**

2. We expect Mayor Wilson to visit the premier in an attempt to increase the **city's** share of **provincial** funding.

3. The caller could have been **he,** but we don't know for sure [optional comma] since he didn't leave his name.

4. The survey was **cited** in an article entitled **"What's New in Software";** however, I can't locate it now.

5. All three of our **company's** auditors—Jim Lucus, Doreen Stein and Brad Kirby—**criticized their** accounting procedures.

6. **Any one** of the auditors **is** authorized to **proceed** with an **independent** action; however, only a member of the management **council** can alter policy.

7. Because our printer has been **broken every day** this week, **we're** looking at new models.

8. Have you **already** ordered the following: a dictionary, a reference manual, and a style book**?**

9. In the morning **Mrs.** Williams **ordinarily** opens the office; in the evening **Mr.** Williams **usually** closes it.

10. When you travel in **England** and **Ireland, I** advise you to charge purchases to your **Visa** [or **VISA**] credit card.

Chapter 6

1. The **extraordinary** increase in sales is related to **our** placing the staff on a commission basis, and the increase also **affected** our stock value.

2. She acts as if she **were** the only person who ever received a **compliment** about **his or her** business **writing**. [Or omit **his or her.**]

3. Karen is interested in working for the **Department of Foreign Affairs** [optional comma] since she is **hoping** to travel.

4. Major Hawkins, **who** I think will be elected, has **already** served three **consecutive** terms as a member of the **Oshawa City Council.**

5. After Mr. Freeman and **he** returned from lunch, the **customers** were handled more **quickly.**

6. Our new **employees'** cafeteria, which opened six months ago, has a salad bar that everyone **definitely** likes. [Or Our new **employee** cafeteria, ...]

7. On Tuesday **Ms.** Adams can see you at **2** p.m.; on Wednesday she has a full **schedule.**

8. His determination, courage, and sincerity could not be denied; however, his methods were often questioned.

9. After you have checked the matter **further,** report to the CEO and **me.**

10. Mr. Thomson and **she** advised me not to **desert** my employer at this time, **although** they were quite sympathetic to my **personal** problems.

Chapter 7

1. Mr. Krikorian always tries, however, to wear a tie and shirt that **have complementary** colours.

2. The **House of Commons Committee** on **Trade and Commerce is** holding hearings in **21 cities**.

3. Consumer buying and spending for the past **five** years [omit comma] **are** being studied by a **federal** team of analysts.

4. Because we recommend that students bring **their** own supplies, the total expense for the trip should be a **minor** amount.

5. **Wasn't** it **Mr.** Cohen, not **Ms.** Lyons, who asked for a tuition **waiver?**

6. As soon as we can verify the figures, either my sales manager or **I** will call you; nevertheless, you must continue to **disburse** payroll funds.

7. Our **Human Resources Department,** which was **formerly** in **Room** 35, has moved **its** offices to **Room** 5.

8. We have arranged interviews on the following dates**:** Wednesday at **3:30 p.m., Thursday** at **10:30 a.m.,** and Friday at **4:15 p.m.**

9. The **Bay News,** our local newspaper, featured as its **principal** article, a story entitled [omit comma] **"Smarter** E-Mail **Is Here."**

10. **Everyone** on the payroll, which includes all dispatchers and **supervisors, was** cautioned to maintain careful records **every day.**

Chapter 8

1. Your advertisement in the **June 2** edition of the **Montreal Gazette** [omit comma] caught my attention [omit semicolon] because my training and experience **match** your requirements.

2. **Undoubtedly,** the bank is closed at this hour, but **its** ATM will enable you to **receive** the cash you need.

3. A flow chart detailing all **sales** procedures in **four** divisions **was** prepared by our **vice-president.**

4. The computer and printer **were** working **well** yesterday [omit comma] and appeared to be **all right** this morning [omit semicolon] when I used **them** for my report.

5. If I **were** you, I would be more concerned with **long-term,** not **short-term,** returns on the invested **capital.**

6. We make a **conscious** effort, by the way, to find **highly qualified** individuals with **up-to-date** computer skills.

7. If your résumé had **come** earlier, it would have been **shown** to Mr. Sutton and **her** before your interview.

8. **Deborah's** report summary is [omit **more**] easier to read **than David's** because she used **consistent** headings and efficient writing techniques.

9. At McDonald's we ordered **four Big Macs, three** orders of french fries, and **five Coca-Colas** for lunch.

10. Because the budget cuts will severely **affect** all programs, the faculty **has** unanimously opposed **them.**

Chapter 9

1. **Two** loans made to **Consumer Products Corporation** must be repaid within 90 days, **or** the owners will be in default.

2. One loan was for property **appraised** at **$40 000;** the other was for property estimated to be worth **$10 000.**

3. Our **senior marketing director** and the sales manager are quite **knowledgeable** about communications hardware; therefore, they are **travelling** to the **computer** show in **North Bay.**

4. We **congratulate** you on winning the award [omit comma] and hope that you will continue to experience **similar** success [omit comma] in the future.

5. Mr. Salazar left **$3 million** to be divided among **four** heirs; one of whom is a successful **manufacturer.**

6. If the CEO and **he** had behaved more **professionally,** the chances of a **practical** settlement would be considerably greater.

7. Just inside the entrance [omit comma] **are** the desk of the receptionist and a complete directory of all **departments.**

8. **All** new **employees** must receive their **permits** to park in Lot 5–A, **or their cars** will be **cited.** [Or **Every** new **employee** must receive **a** permit to park in **Lot** 5–A, or **his or her** car will be **cited.**]

9. When we open our office in Montreal, we will need at least **three** people **who** are fluent in **French** and **English.**

10. Most **companies** can boost profits almost **100** percent by retaining just 5 **percent** more of **their permanent** customers.

Chapter 10

1. North American exports **have** increased by **76** percent in the past five years, and the trade deficit has **fallen** to **its** lowest level since 1974.

2. After years of downsizing and restructuring, Canada has now become one of the **world's** most competitive producers in many **industries.**

3. However, many **companies'** products still sell better at home **than** abroad [omit semicolon] because these **companies** lack overseas experience.

4. **Companies** like Amway [omit comma] discovered that **their** unique **door-to-door** selling method was very successful in **Japan.**

5. The **Ministry of Industry** and **Technology** asked Mr. Sato and **me** to describe the marketing of [omit colon] aircraft, high-tech products, and biomedical technology.

6. Some of the products most likely to succeed abroad are [omit colon] blue jeans, **Coke**, home appliances, and prepared foods.

7. As North American **companies** learn to **accommodate** global tastes, they will be expanding into vast new markets in **China, South America,** and **Europe.**

8. The seminar **emphasizing** exporting will cost **$300,** which seems expensive for a **newly formed** company.

9. The manager thinks that **your** attending the **three-day** seminar is a good idea; however, we must still check your work **calendar.**

10. Exports from small companies **have** increased, thereby **affecting** this **country's** trade balance positively.

Notes

CHAPTER 1

1. Mario Juarez, interviews with Mary Ellen Guffey, 3 October 1994, and 29 November 1994.

2. "Creating a Resilient Organization," *Canadian Business Review*, no. 2 (Summer 1994): 22–25.

3. Jason Siroonian, *Work Arrangements, Analytical Report 6* (Ottawa: Statistics Canada, 1993).

4. Nuala Beck, *Shifting Gears: Thriving in the New Economy* (Toronto: Harper Collins, 1992), 151.

5. "Creating a Resilient Organization," 3.

6. Beck, "Shifting Gears," 132.

7. Beck, "Shifting Gears," 49.

8. "The Rising Value of Brain Power," *The Globe and Mail*, metro edition, 8 September 1992, B18.

9. Peter Drucker, "New Realities, New Ways of Managing," *Business Month*, May 1989, 50–51.

10. Beck, "Shifting Gears," 430.

11. Hal Lancaster, "A New Social Contract to Benefit Employer and Employee," *The Wall Street Journal*, 29 November 1994, B1. See also Oren Harari, "An Open Letter to Job Seekers," *Management Review* (American Management Association), December 1994, 39.

12. Corporate Council on Education, *Employability Skills Profile*, (09/92), (Ottawa: The Conference Board of Canada, 1992).

13. Corporate Council on Education, *Employability Skills Profile*, 1992.

14. Harry Gaines, "Teaching Scientists to Talk Business," *New York Times*, 18 September 1994, F11.

15. Arthur Andersen and Co.; Arthur Young; Coopers and Lybrand; Deloitte, Haskins, and Sells; Ernst and Whinney; Peat, Marwick, and Co.; Price Waterhouse, and Touche Ross, *Perspectives on Education: Capabilities for Success in the Accounting Profession* (New York, 1989). See also A.R. Pustorino, "CPAs Need Better Communication Skills," *CPA Journal*, June 1989, 6, 10.

16. Barrett J. Mandel and Judith Yellen, "Mastering the Memo," *Working Woman*, September 1989, 135.

17. Barbara DePompa, "Start Your Engines," *Success*, December 1990, 24.

18. Lester Faigley and Thomas P. Miller, "What We Learn From Writing on the Job," *College English* 44 (1982), 557–69.

19. Cheryl Hamilton with Cordell Parker, *Communicating for Results* (Belmont, Calif.: Wadsworth, 1990), 8.

20. Jerry Sullivan, Naoki Karmeda, and Tatsuo Nobu, "Bypassing in Managerial Communication," *Business Horizons*, January/February 1991, 72.

21. "Delivering the Goods: With Expectations Running So High, Can Wal-Mart Possibly Succeed?" *Marketing*, no. 29, 1/8 August 1994, 17–18.

22. Warren R. Plunkett and Raymond F. Attner, *Introduction to Management* (Boston: PWS/Kent, 1988), 84.

23. Peter Drucker, *Managing the Non-Profit Organization: Practices and Principles* (New York: HarperCollins, 1990), 46.

24. "Who's Mayor of Toronto? Haw Parc Lai—in Chinese," *Toronto Star*, 26 June 1995, A6.

25. "Where West Meets East," *The Sunday Sun*, 30 July 1995, 16–17.

26. "The Written Word," *Success*, December 1990, 24.

27. Ray Killian, *Managing by Design ... for Executive Effectiveness* (New York: American Management Association, 1968), 255.

28. Peter Blau, *On the Nature of Organizations* (New York: Wiley, 1974), 7.

29. "Who Told You That?" *The Wall Street Journal*, 23 May 1985, 33.

30. Eugene Walton, "How Effective Is the Grapevine?" *Personnel* 28 (1961), 45–49; and Keith Davis, *Human Behavior at Work*, 5th ed. (New York: McGraw-Hill, 1977), 277–286.

31. Eugene Walton, "Communicating Down the Line: How They Really Get the Word," *Personnel* 28 (1961), 22–24.

32. Hamilton, *Communicating for Results*, 12–13.

33. Faye Rice, "Champions of Communication," *Fortune*, 3 June 1991, 111.

34. Paul Ingrassia and Bradley A. Stertz, "With Chrysler Ailing, Lee Iacocca Concedes Mistakes in Managing," *The Wall Street Journal*, 17 September 1990, A9.

35. "Management Styles (Four Food Industry Leaders Profiles)" *Food in Canada* 52, no. 2 (March 1992) 14–15.

36. "Achieving Excellence," *Maclean's*, 26 December 1994, 53.

37. "Kids Grill Irwin Execs," *Toronto Star* (Ontario edition), 13 June 1995, A1.

38. Rice, "Champions of Communication," 112.

39. Andrew S. Grove, "Managing for 'Just-in-Time Business,'" *Newsweek*, 11 May 1991, Management Digest section.

40. Gerald M. Goldhaber, *Organizational Communication*, 5th ed. (Dubuque, Iowa: William C. Brown, 1990), 5.

41. Matt Miller, "Psssst ... Have You Heard the Latest?" *Fortune*, May 1984, 2.

42. "New Worker-Survey Findings," *The Fact Finder*, March 1991, 4, reports study of Evan G. Bane, "1990 Deluxe Data Systems Employee Communications Survey."

43. John H. Bryan, CEO Sara Lee Corporation, speech before the Corporate Affairs Communications Conference, 21 May 1990, Chicago.

CHAPTER 2

1. Johanne Totta, interview with Amanda J. Lang, 5 August 1995.

2. Tom W. Harris, "Listen Carefully," *Nation's Business*, June 1989, 78.

3. Harris, "Listen Carefully," 78.

4. L.K. Steil, L.L. Barker, and K.W. Watson, *Effective Listening: Key to Your Success* (Reading, Mass.: Addison-Wesley, 1983).

5. Interview with John Sculley, "Pinnacle," Cable News Network, New York, 12 December 1987.

6. Eric H. Nelson and Jan Gypen, "The Subordinate's Predicament," *Harvard Business Review*, September/October 1979, 133.

7. Stephen Golen, "A Factor Analysis of Barriers to Effective Listening," *The Journal of Business Communication*, Winter 1990, 25–37.

8. Albert Mehrabian, *Silent Messages* (Belmont, Calif.: Wadsworth, 1971), 44.

9. J. Burgoon, D. Coker, and R. Coker, "Communicative Explanations," *Human Communication Research* 12 (1986), 463–494.

10. Ray Birdwhistel, *Kinesics and Context* (Philadelphia: University of Pennsylvania Press, 1970).

11. "In Athens, It's Palms In," *Newsweek*, 10 December 1990, 79Q.

12. Dean Allen Foster, *Bargaining Across Borders* (New York: McGraw-Hill, 1992).

13. "Understanding the Japanese," National Business Education Association newsletter *Keying In* (March 1993), 7.

14. Anne Russell, "Fine-Tuning Your Corporate Image," *Black Enterprise*, May 1992, 74.

15. Russell, "Fine-Tuning Your Corporate Image," 80.

16. "Wa: the Japanese Way: Canadians Doing Business in Japan Soon Learn That Group Harmony Is a Business Fundamental That Can't Be Ignored," *Financial Post*, 4–6 March 1995.

17. Endel-Jakob Kolde, *Environment of International Business*, 2nd ed. (Boston: PWS/Kent, 1985), 420–424.

18. Anthony Wilson-Smith, "A Quiet Passion," *Maclean's*, 1 July, 1995, 8–12.

19. Kathleen K. Reardon, *Where Minds Meet* (Belmont, Calif.: Wadsworth, 1987), 199.

20. Vivienne Luk, Mumtaz Patel, and Kathryn White, "Personal Attributes of American and Chinese Business Associates," *The Bulletin of the Association for Business Communication*, December 1990, 67.

21. Susan S. Jarvis, "Preparing Employees to Work South of the Border," *Personnel*, June 1990, 63.

22. Lennie Copeland and Lewis Griggs, *Going International* (New York: Penguin Books, 1985), 12.

23. Copeland and Griggs, *Going International*, 108.

24. Shari Caudron, "Training Ensures Success Overseas," *Personnel Journal*, December 1991, 29.

25. Robert McGarvey, "Foreign Exchange," *USAir Magazine*, June 1992, 61.

26. Jeff Copeland, "Stare Less, Listen More," *American Way*, American Air Lines, 15 December 1990.

27. Nancy Rivera Brooks, "Exports Boom Softens Blow of Recession," *Los Angeles Times*, 29 May 1991, D1.

28. Ted Holden and Jennifer Wiener, "Revenge of the 'Office Ladies,'" *Business Week*, 13 July 1992, 42–43.

29. Roger Axtell, *Do's and Taboos Around the World*, 2nd ed. (New York: Wiley, 1990), 171.

30. Bob Weinstein, "When in Rome," *Entrepreneur*, March 1991, 70.

31. William Horton, "The Almost Universal Language: Graphics for International Documents," *Technical Communication*, Fourth Quarter, 1993, 690.

32. Robert McGarvey, "Foreign Exchange," *USAir Magazine*, June 1992, 64.

CHAPTER 3

1. Angela Barker, interview with Jo Ann Napier, 5 September 1995.

2. Elizabeth Fisher, "Campaigners in the Communications War," *Accountancy*, December 1989, 98.

3. Earl N. Harbert, "Knowing Your Audience," in *The Handbook of Executive Communication*, ed. John

L. DiGaetani (Homewood, Ill.: Dow Jones/Irwin, 1986), 3.

4. Eugene E. Brussel, ed., *Dictionary of Quotable Definitions* (Englewood Cliffs, N.J.: Prentice-Hall, 1970), 622.

5. Mark Bacon, quoted in "Business Writing: One-on-One Speaks Best to the Masses," *Training*, April 1988, 95.

6. For more information, see Marilyn Schwartz, *Guidelines for Bias-Free Writing* (Bloomington: Indiana Press, 1994).

7. Leslie Matthies, quoted in Carl Heyel, "Policy and Procedure Manuals," *The Handbook of Executive Communication*, 212.

8. "Ethics as a Management Tool," *Canadian Business Review* 21, no. 2 (Summer 1994), 41–43.

9. James Gillies, *Boardroom Renaissance: Power, Morality and Performance in the Modern Corporation* (Toronto: McGraw-Hill Ryerson and National Centre for Management Research and Development, 1992), 175.

10. Robert C. Solomon and Kristine Hanson, *It's Good Business* (New York: Atheneum, 1985).

11. Mary E. Guy, *Ethical Decision Making in Everyday Work Situations* (New York: Quorum Books, 1990), 3.

12. Guy, *Ethical Decision Making*, 4.

13. Alison Bell, "What Price Ethics?" *Entrepreneurial Woman*, January/February 1991, 68.

14. Based on Michael Josephson's remarks reported in Bell, "What Price Ethics?" *Entrepreneurial Woman*, 68.

15. Gillies, *Boardroom Rennaissance*, 173.

16. Diane Cole, "Ethics: Companies Crack Down on Dishonesty," *The Wall Street Journal*, Spring 1991, Managing Your Career, sec. 8.

17. Eric Swetsky, "Truth in Advertising: the Robin Hood Case Strikes a Blow against False or Misleading Impressions," *Marketing*, 21 November 1994, 29.

18. Jane Applegate, "Women Starting Small Businesses Twice as Fast as Men," *The Washington Post*, 2 September 1991, WB10.

19. Parts of this section are based on Kristin R. Woolever's "Corporate Language and the Law: Avoiding Liability in Corporate Communications," *IEE Transactions on Professional Communication*, 2 June 1990, 94–98.

20. Swetsky, "Broken Promises: a Case of Sale Priced Goods Bait and Switch Advertising,"*Marketing*, 11 April 1994, 26.

21. Woolever, *IEE Transactions*, 96.

22. Woolever, *IEE Transactions*, 97.

23. Judy E. Pickens, "Communication: Terms of Equality: A Guide to Bias-Free Language," *Personnel Journal*, August 1985, 24.

24. "Faxpoll," *Business Month*, December 1989, 7.

CHAPTER 4

1. Harry Moore, interview with Jo Ann Napier, 6 September 1995.

2. Andrew Fluegelman and Jeremy Joan Hewes, "The Word Processor and the Writing Process," in *Strategies for Business and Technical Writing*, ed. Kevin J. Harty (San Diego: Harcourt Brace Jovanovich, 1989), 43.

3. Michael Granberry, "Lingerie Chain Fined $100,000 for Gift Certificates," *Los Angeles Times*, 14 November 1992, D3.

4. Advertisement appearing in *The New York Times*, 12 December 1992, 7.

5. Kim Foltz, "Scali Quits Volvo Account, Citing Faked Commercial," *The New York Times*, 14 November 1990, C1; and Stuart Elliott, "Volvo Says It's Crushed Over Misleading Ads," *USA Today*, 6 November 1990, B1.

6. Bruce Horovitz, "Ad Nauseam," *Los Angeles Times*, 10 December 1992, D1.

7. Horovitz, "Ad Nauseam," D1.

8. Robert W. Goddard, "Communication: Use Language Effectively," *Personnel Journal*, April 1989, 32.

9. Frederick Crews, *The Random House Handbook*, 5th ed. (New York: Random House, 1987), 152.

10. "Managing Change: Welcome to the Corporate Age of the Quick or the Dead," *B.C. Business Magazine*, March 1994, 37–44.

11. Lisa S. Ede and Andrea A. Lunsford, "Collaborative Learning: Lessons from the World of Work," *WPA: Writing Program Administration*, Spring 1986, 17–26.

12. Lester Faigley and Thomas P. Miller, "What We Learn From Writing on the Job," *College English* 44 (1982), 557–569; Barbara Couture and Jone Rymer, "Interactive Writing on the Job: Definitions and Implications of 'Collaboration'" in *Writing in the Business Professions*, ed. Myra Kogen (Urbana, Ill.: National Council of Teachers of English, 1989), 74.

CHAPTER 5

1. Joe Chidley, interview with Amanda J. Lang, 12 August 1995.

2. Peter Elbow, *Writing With Power: Techniques for Mastering the Writing Process* (Oxford: Oxford University Press, 1981); Michael E. Adelstein, *Contemporary Business Writing* (New York: Random House, 1971).

3. John S. Fielden, "What Do You Mean You Don't Like My Style?" *Harvard Business Review*, May/June 1982, 138.

4. Claire K. Cook, *Line by Line* (Boston: Houghton Mifflin, 1985), 17.

5. "Plainly Speaking, Rewrite Cost $10,500," *Toronto Star*, 28 July 1994, A9.

6. William Power and Michael Siconolfi, "Memo to: Mr. Ball, RE: Your Messages, Sir: They're Weird," *The Wall Street Journal*, 30 November 1990, 1.

7. *The Canadian Style: A Guide to Writing and Editing* (Toronto: Dundurn Press Limited, 1985).
8. Laurie Bildfell, "Standard time: the Canadian Style? Versatile and Not Pushy," *Quill and Quire*, December 1994, 12–13.
9. *The Canadian Style: A Guide to Writing and Editing* (1985).
10. Berle Haggblade, "Has Technology Solved the Spelling Problem?" *The Bulletin of the Association for Business Communication*, March 1988, 23.
11. Spell checker poem attributed to John Placona and acquired from Dr. Brian G. Wilson, College of Marin, Marin, California.
12. Malcolm Forbes, "How to Write a Business Letter," International Paper Company, reprinted in *Strategies for Business and Technical Writing*, 3rd ed., ed. Kevin J. Harty (San Diego, Calif.: Harcourt Brace Jovanovich, 1989), 115.

CHAPTER 6

1. Lise Andrews, interview with David Napier, 1 August 1995.
2. Malcolm Forbes, "How to Write a Business Letter," International Paper Company, reprinted in *Strategies for Business and Technical Writing*, 3rd ed., ed. Kevin J. Harty (San Diego, Calif.: Harcourt Brace Jovanovich, 1989), 115.
3. Sylvia Porter, "Dear Boss: Just What Was Your Memo Trying to Say?" *Los Angeles Daily News*, 28 April 1986.
4. *Business Week*, 6 July 1981, 107.
5. Eugene E. Brussell, *Dictionary of Quotable Definitions* (Englewood Cliffs, New Jersey: Prentice-Hall, 1970), 550.
6. "The Quality Imperative," *Business Week*, 25 October 1991, 7–16.
7. "Nixdorf Computer Corporation," *Excellence Achieved* (New York: Bureau of Business Practice, 1991), 141.
8. Steven N. Spertz and Glenda S. Spertz, *The Rule of Law: Canadian Business Law*, 2nd ed. (Toronto: Copp Clark Ltd., 1995), 289.
9. "Managing Change: Welcome to the Corporate Age of the Quick and the Dead," *B. C. Business Magazine*, no. 22(3), (March 1994), 37–44.
10. "Connecting Customer Loyalty to the Bottom Line," *Canadian Business Review*, no. 21 (4), (Winter 1994), 40–43.
11. Stanely Brown, "Honing our Focus on Customer Service: What Can Canadian Business Learn from US Companies about Improving Customer Satisfaction?" *Canadian Business Review*, no. 21 (4), (Winter 1994), 29–31.
12. Robert J. Aalberts and Lorraine A. Krajewski, "Claim and Adjustment Letters: Theory Versus Practice and Legal Implications," *The Bulletin of the Association for Business Communication*, September 1987, 2.
13. Saburo Haneda and Hirosuke Shima, "Japanese Communication Behavior as Reflected in Letter Writing," *The Journal of Business Communication*, 1 (1982), 29.
14. Wolfgang Manekeller, as cited in Iris I. Varner, "Internationalizing Business Communication Courses," *The Bulletin of the Association for Business Communication*, December 1987, 10.
15. Dr. Annette Luciani-Samec, French instructor, and Dr. Pierre Samec, French businessman, interviews with Mary Ellen Guffey, Palo Alto, California, November and December 1991.
16. Leonard Silk, "The New (Improved) Creed of Social Responsibility," *Business Month*, November 1988, 109.
17. Robert D. Haas, "Ethics—A Global Business Challenge," *Vital Speeches of the Day*, 60 (16), 1 June 1994, 506–509.
18. Retha H. Kilpatrick, "International Business Communication Practices," *The Journal of Business Communication*, Fall 1984, 42–43.
19. Larry Stevens, "Automating the Selection Process," *Personnel Journal*, November 1991, 59–60.
20. Based on articles by Frank Edward Allen, "McDonald's to Reduce Waste in Plan Developed With Environmental Group," *Wall Street Journal*, 17 April 1991, B1; Martha T. Moore, "McDonald's Trashes Sandwich Boxes," *USA Today*, 2 November 1990, 9B; and Michael Parrish, "McDonald's to Do Away with Foam Packages," *Los Angeles Times*, 2 November 1990, 1.
21. Based on the case of First Union National Bank of Charlotte, North Carolina, described in James L. Heskett, *Service Breakthroughs* (New York: Free Press), as reported in "How to Correct Service Mistakes without Losing Customers," *Boardroom Reports*, 15 March 1990, 2.

CHAPTER 7

1. Susan O'Brien, interview with David Napier, 29 August 1995.
2. See Anita S. Bednard and Robert J. Olney, "Communication Needs of Recent Graduates," *The Bulletin of the Association for Business Communication*, December 1987, 22; see also Mary K. Kirtz and Diana C. Reep, "A Survey of the Frequency, Types and Importance of Writing Tasks in Four Career Areas," *The Bulletin of the Association for Business Communication*, December 1990, 3.
3. Revealed by Robert Half International, as cited in Cynthia A. Barnes, *Model Memos* (Englewood Cliffs, New Jersey: Prentice-Hall, 1990), 4.
4. Bednard and Olney, "Communication Needs of Recent Graduates," 22.
5. Richard H. Needham, "First Job Survival Guide," *Managing Your Career, The Wall Street Journal*, Spring 1991, 7.

6. Rosalind Gold, " 'Reader-Friendly' Writing," *Supervisory Management*, January 1989, 40.

7. "E-mail Raises Confidentiality Issues," *Computer Dealer News*, 13 July 1994, 30, 42.

8. "E-mail Raises Confidentiality Issues," *Computer Dealer News*, 30, 42.

9. Marya W. Holcombe, "Wisdom or Information? Managerial Writing in the Office of the Future," in *The Handbook of Executive Communication*, ed. John L. DiGaetani (New York: Dow Jones/Irwin, 1986), 261.

10. Linda Himelstein, "Exhibit A: The Telltale Computer Tape," *Business Week*, 5 August 1994, 8; and Lawrence Dietz, "E-mail Is Wonderful But It Has Risks," *Bottom Line/Business* (published by Boardroom, Inc.), 15 June 1995, 3–4.

11. Leslie Helm, "The Digital Smoking Gun," *Los Angeles Times*, 16 June 1994, El.

12. David Angell and Brent Heslop, *The Elements of E-mail Style* (Reading, Mass.: Addison-Wesley, 1993), Chapter 1.

13. Jayne E. Pearl, "The E-mail Quandary," *Management Review* (July 1993), 49.

14. Pearl, "The E-mail Quandary," *Management Review*, 50.

15. John Fielden, "Clear Writing Is Not Enough," *Management Review*, April 1989, 51.

16. Based on Leslie Lamkin and Emily W. Carmain, "Crisis Communication at Georgia Power," *Personnel Journal*, January 1991, 35–37.

CHAPTER 8

1. Cathy Dial, interview with Mary Ellen Guffey.

2. Steven N. Spertz and Glenda S. Spertz, *The Rule of Law: Canadian Business Law*, 2nd ed., (Toronto: Copp Clark Ltd., 1995), 45.

3. Robert L. Mirguet, Information Security Manager, Eastern Kodak Co., Rochester, New York, cited in

"Telecommunicating," *Boardroom Reports*, 1 March 1995, 15.

4. Elizabeth A. McCord, "The Business Writer, the Law, and Routine Business Communication: A Legal and Rhetorical Analysis," *Journal of Business and Technical Communication*, April 1991, 183.

5. McCord, "The Business Writer," 183, 193.

6. "Letters to Lands' End," *February 1991 Catalog* (Dodgeville, Wis.: Lands' End, 1991), 100.

7. Based on Dana Milbank, "As Stores Scrimp More and Order Less, Suppliers Take On Greater Risks, Costs," *The Wall Street Journal*, 10 December 1991, B1.

8. Malcolm Forbes, "How to Write a Business Letter," International Paper Company, reprinted in *Strategies for Business and Technical Writing*, 3rd ed., ed. Kevin J. Harty (San Diego, Calif.: Harcourt Brace Jovanovich, 1989), 116.

9. Based on Lisa Driscoll, "The New King of the Forest: International Paper," *Business Week*, 28 October 1991, 140–141.

10. John Markoff, "Recent Novell Software Contains a Hidden Virus," *The New York Times*, 20 December 1991, C2.

CHAPTER 9

1. Elizabeth Clarke, interview with Jo Ann Napier, 11 September 1995.

2. Raymond A. Dumont and John M. Lannon, *Business Communications*, 3rd ed. (Glenview, Ill.: Scott, Foresman/Little, Brown, 1990), 33.

3. "How to Ask for—and Get— What You Want!" *Supervision*, February 1990, 11.

4. Kevin McLaughlin, "Words of Wisdom," *Entrepreneur*, October 1990, 101.

5. Kara Kuryllowicz, "How Entrepreneurs Can Boost Business by Using Direct Mail," *The Financial Post*, n.d.

6. Keith J. Tuckwell, *Canadian Advertising in Action*, (Scarborough: Prentice-Hall, 1995), 435.

7. Jeffrey Potts, "SBA Winner Profits From Survival Instinct," *USA Today*, 16 May 1991, B8.

8. Fitness Center Gets Couch Potatoes Moving," *The Wall Street Journal*, 12 April 1991, B1.

CHAPTER 10

1. Richard Peter, interview with Jo Ann Napier, 1 September 1995.

2. *Customer Service Manager's Letter*, Prentice-Hall Bureau of Business Practice, 25 January 1992, 6.

3. "Keeping Bad Taste in the Family," *Business Quarterly*, Spring 1995, 23–29.

4. William C. Himstreet, Wayne Murlin Baty, and Carol M. Lehman, *Business Communications*, 9th ed. (Belmont, Calif.: Wadsworth, 1993), 477.

5. James Carlisle, "Employer's Lack of Co-operation Increases Dismissal Award in Recent Ontario Court Decision in Han Lim Case," *Financial Post Daily*, 18 April 1995, 18.

6. "Many Canadian Firms Catching 'Reference Chill,'" *Daily Commercial News*, 21 September 1992, 1, 3.

7. "References Too Good to be True," *CA Magazine* 127 (9), November 1994, 14, 15.

8. Stephen B. Knouse, "Confidentiality and the Letter of Recommendation: A New Approach," *The Bulletin of the Association for Business Communication*, September 1987, 7.

9. Adapted from Terry McNally and Peter Schiff, *Contemporary Business Writing: A Problem-Solving Approach* (Belmont, Calif.: Wadsworth, 1986), 175–176.

10. Portions of this section are based on Rebecca Burnett Carosso, *Technical Communication* (Belmont, Calif.: Wadsworth, 1986), 354–374.

11. Based on "An Heirloom You Can Sit On," *Newsweek*, 23 December 1991, 61.

CHAPTER 11

1. Peter Le Piane, interview with David Napier, 14 August 1995.
2. Peter H. Lewis, "The World Wide Web: Open for Business," *Computer Shopper* (February 1995), 600.
3. Mary Ann Pike, Peter Kent, Kamran Husain, Dave Kinnaman, and David C. Menges, *Using Mosaic* (Indianapolis: Que Corporation, 1994), 32.
4. Laurie Flynn, "Companies Use Web Hoping to Save Millions," *The New York Times*, 17 July 1995, C5.
5. Christopher Velotta, "How to Design and Implement a Questionnaire," *Technical Communication*, Fall 1991, 390.
6. Robin Toner, "Politics of Welfare: Focusing on the Problems," *The New York Times*, 5 July 1991, 1.
7. Gerald J. Alred, Walter E. Oliu, and Charles T. Brusaw, *The Professional Writer* (New York: St. Martin's Press, 1992), 78.
8. Frank Feather, *Canada's Best Career Guide* (Toronto: Warwick Publishing Inc., 1995), 101.
9. Feather, *Canada's Best Career Guide*, 111.

CHAPTER 12

1. Fazil Mihlar, interview with David Napier, 29 August 1995.
2. Walter Wells, *Communications in Business* (Boston: PWS/Kent, 1988), 471.
3. Charlene Marmer Solomon, "Marriott's Family Matters," *Personnel Journal*, October 1991, 40–42.
4. Chuck Hawkins, "FedEx: Europe Nearly Killed the Messenger," *Business Week*, 25 May 1992, 124–126.

CHAPTER 13

1. James Paterson, interview with David Napier, 18 August 1995.

CHAPTER 14

1. Mary Piecewicz, interview with Mary Ellen Guffey, 31 March 1993. Other information from Hewlett-Packard, *1992 Annual Report* (Palo Alto, Calif.: Hewlett-Packard, 1992), 1–21.
2. Nancy Rivera Brooks and Jesus Sanchez, "U.S. Firms Map Ways to Profit From the Accord," *Los Angeles Times*, 13 August 1992, D1, D2.
3. Herman Holtz, *The Consultant's Guide to Proposal Writing* (New York: John Wiley, 1990), 188.
4. Based on Jane Applegate, "Weigh Freight Expenses Carefully," *Los Angeles Times*, 14 August 1992, D3.
5. Based on Joann S. Lublin, "Companies Use Cross-Cultural Training to Help Their Employees Adjust Abroad," *The Wall Street Journal*, 4 August 1992, B1.
6. Based on John R. Emshwiller, "Designer of Surfing Ride Catches a Wave of Success," *The Wall Street Journal*, 12 August 1992, B2.
7. Based on Barbara Ettorre, "Breaking the Glass ... or Just Window Dressing," *Management Review*, March 1992, 16–22.
8. Based on Karen S. Sterkel, "Integrating Intercultural Communication and Report Writing in the Communication Class," *The Bulletin of the Association for Business Communication*, September 1988, 14–16.

CHAPTER 15

1. Jon Georges, interview with Mary Ellen Guffey, 4 December 1992. Other information from The Walt Disney Company, *1991 Annual Report* (Burbank, Calif.: 1991), 1–44; Walt Disney Imagineering, *Walt Disney Imagineering* (Burbank, Calif.: Walt Disney Imagineering); and Anthony Hatch, "Walt Disney Imagineering Facts" (Glendale, Calif.: Walt Disney Imagineering), 1–6.
2. Steven Grubaugh, "Public Speaking," *The Clearing House*, February 1990, 255.
3. Rod Plotnik, *Introduction to Psychology* (Pacific Grove, Calif.: Brooks/Cole, 1993), 484.
4. Some of the information presented in this chapter originated in Mary Ellen Guffey's *Essentials of Business Communication*, 2nd ed. (Boston: PWS/Kent, 1991), Chapter 14.
5. Wharton Applied Research Center, "A Study of the Effects of the Use of Overhead Transparencies on Business Meetings, Final Report" (Philadelphia: University of Pennsylvania, 14 September 1981).
6. William Harrel, "Presentations without Pain," *PC World*, April 1994, 187–201; "Great Presentations Brought to Light," InFocus® Systems (Wilsonville, Oregon, 1994); Cate C. Corcoran, "Chisholm Projection Panels Leave Mark on Presentations," *MacWeek*, 5 December 1994, 6; Ripley Hotch, Making the Best of Presentations," *Nation's Business*, August 1992, 37–38; Lawrence Stevens, "The Proof Is in the Presentation," *Nation's Business*, July 1991, 32–33.
7. Peter Urs Bender, *Secret Powers of Presentations* (Toronto: The Achievement Group, 1991), 31.
8. Raymond Slesinski, "Giving a Topnotch Executive Presentation," *Management*, April 1990, 16.
9. Ronald E. Dulek, John S. Fielden, and John S. Hill, "International Communication: An Executive Primer," *Business Horizons*, January/February 1991, 23.
10. Dulek, Fielden, and Hill, "International Communication," *Business Horizons*, 22.
11. Kirsten Schabacker, "A Short, Snappy Guide to Meaningful

Meetings," *Working Woman*, June 1991, 73.

12. Andrew S. Grove, quoted in Walter Kiechell, III, "How to Take Part in a Meeting," *Fortune*, 26 May 1986, 178.

13. Thomas C. Hayes, "Doing Business Screen to Screen," *The New York Times*, 21 February 1991, C5.

14. "The Information Highway Special Supplement," *Business Quarterly* 58, no. 3 (Spring 1994), 71–125.

15. "Fredericton Firm Sees the Future: Desktop Video Conferencing," *Canadian Consulting Engineer*, November/December 1994, 19.

16. "Lights, Camera, Meeting: Teleconferencing Becomes a Time-Saving Tool," *The Wall Street Journal*, 21 February 1995, A1.

17. Anthony Ramirez, "Video Meetings Get Cheaper, and a Bit Better," *The New York Times*, 5 February 1992, C5.

18. Patricia A. La Rosa, "Voice Messaging Is Quality 'Lip Service,'" *The Office*, May 1992, 10.

19. "Did You Know That ...," *Boardroom Reports*, 15 August 1992, 15.

20. Michael Jacobson, quoted in "Garbage In, Garbage Out," *Consumer Reports*, December 1992, 755.

CHAPTER 16

1. Michael Robertson, interview with David Napier, 6 September 1995.

2. "Finding a New Career Digitally," *PC Magazine*, 28 June 1994, 205.

3. Judith Schroer, "Seek a Job With a Little Help From Your Friends," *USA Today*, 19 November 1990, B7.

4. "Fired but Flourishing: Profiles of 5 Women who Survived Layoffs," *Chatelaine*, May 1994, 60–61.

5. "Fired, but Flourishing," *Chateline*, 60–61.

6. Dan Moreau, "Write a Resume That Works," *Changing Times*, June 1990, 91.

7. H.B. Crandall quoted in Jacqueline Trace, "Teaching Résumé Writing the Functional Way," *The Bulletin of the Association for Business Communication*, June 1985, 41.

8. Robert Lorentz, James W. Carland, and Jo Ann C. Carland, "The Resume: What Value Is There in References?" *Journal of Technical Writing and Communication*, Fall 1993, 371.

9. James Bates, "Pitfalls of the Resume," *Los Angeles Times*, 16 September 1991, 18–19.

10. Margaret Mannix, "Writing a Computer-Friendly Resume," *U.S. News & World Report*, 26 October 1992, 90.

11. Stanley W. Angrist, "Looking for Work in the Information Age," *The Wall Street Journal*, 19 January 1994.

12. Joyce Lain Kennedy and Thomas J. Morrow, *Electronic Resume Revolution* (New York: John Wiley & Sons, Inc., 1994), Chapter 3.

13. "As Graduation Approaches ... ," *Personnel*, June 1991, 14.

14. Diane Cole, "Ethics: Companies Crack Down on Dishonesty," *The Wall Street Journal, Managing Your Career supplement*, Spring 1991, 8.

15. "Managing Your Career," *National Business Employment Weekly*, Fall 1989, 29.

16. Joan E. Rigdon, "Deceptive Resumes Can Be Door-Openers but Can Become an Employee's Undoing," *The Wall Street Journal*, 17 June 1992, B1.

17. Marc Silver, "Selling the Perfect You," *U.S. News & World Report*, 5 February 1990, 70–72.

18. Rhonda D. Findling, "The Resume Fax-periment," *Resume Pro Newsletter*, Fall 1994, 10.

19. Harriet M. Augustin, "The Written Job Search: A Comparison of the Traditional and a Nontraditional Approach," *The Bulletin of the Association for Business Communication*, September 1991, 13.

20. Kenneth J. Horn, "Personnel Administrators' Reactions to Job Application Follow-up Letters Regarding Extending Interviews and Offering Jobs," *The Bulletin of the Association for Business Communication* September 1991, 24.

21. Julia Lawlor, "Networking Opens More Doors to Jobs," *USA Today*, 19 November 1990, B7.

22. J. Michael Farr, *The Very Quick Job Search* (Indianapolis, Indiana: JIST Works, 1991), 158.

23. "A Machinist with No Accounting Experience? No problem. New Database System Matching Prospective Employers with Qualified Employees," *Profit: The Magazine for Canadian Entrepreneurs*, March 1994, 11.

Acknowledgments

Text and Figures

pp. 4–5: interview with Mario Juarez used with permission. **p. 21:** Figure 1.6 courtesy of Microsoft Corporation. **p. 26:** Ethics box based on an article that first appeared in *Working Woman*, December 1991. Written by Craig Dellinger and Dan Rice. Reprinted with permission of *Working Woman* Magazine Copyright © 1991 by W. W. T. Partnership. **pp. 36–37:** interview with Johanne Totta used with permission. **p. 41:** Career Skills Box based on Mary Elwart-Keys and Marjorie Horton, "Collaborating in the Capture Lab: Computer Support for Group Writing," *The Bulletin of the Association for Business Communication*, June 1990, 38–44; and Ruth G. Newman, "Collaborative Writing with Purpose and Style," *Personnel Journal*, April 1988, 37.

p. 44: Figure 2.3 based on "Understanding People Better Through 'Body Language,'" *The Book of Inside Information* (New York: Boardroom Classics, 1989), 192–193; Norma Carr-Ruffino, *The Promotable Woman* (Belmont, CA: Wadsworth, 1985), 191; and Walter Kiechel III, "How to Take Part in a Meeting," *Fortune*, 26 May 1986, 117–118. **p. 56:** Figure 2.5 adapted from William Horton, "The Almost Universal Language: Graphics for International Documents," *Technical Communication*, Fourth Quarter,

1993, 690. **pp. 64–65:** interview with Angela Barker used with permission. **pp. 92–93:** interview with Harry Moore used with permission. **pp. 100–101:** from interview with Susanne Tulley, Liz Claiborne, Inc., used with permission. **pp. 122–123:** interview with Joe Chidley used with permission. **p. 134:** Career Skills box based on information from *The Canadian Style: A Guide to Writing and Editing* (Toronto: Dundurn Press Limited, 1985) and *Editing Canadian English* (Toronto: Douglas McIntyre, 1987). **p. 137:** Technology box based on Howard Eglowstein, "Can a Grammar and Style Checker Improve Your Writing?" *Byte*, August 1991, 238–242; Jean Harmon, "Say It Write!" *WordPerfect: The Magazine*, August 1992, 69–72; Rubin Rabinovitz, "New Windows Grammar Checkers Improve Error-Catching Rates," *PC Magazine*, 16 June 1992, 42, 44; Rubin Rabinovitz, "RightWriter for Windows: Works Smarter, Gains Ground on Grammatik," *PC Magazine*, 31 March 1992, 52; and Corey Sandler, "WordPerfect 5.2: New Polish for an Old Classic," *Windows Sources*, April 1993, 159–161. **pp. 148–149:** interview with Lise Andrews used with permission. **p. 171:** Seagull Pewter Mission Statement used with permission. **pp. 182–183:** interview with Susan O'Brien used with

permission. **p. 196:** Career Skills box based on John Fielden, "Clear Writing Is Not Enough," *Management Review*, April 1989, 51; Hal Fanner, as cited in *Boardroom Reports*, 15 January 1991; and Barrett J. Mandel and Judith Yellen, "Mastering the Memo," *Working Woman*, September 1989, 135.

pp. 208–209: interview with Cathy Dial used with permission. **p. 229:** Cross Culture box based on Iris I. Varner, "Internationalizing Business Communication Courses," *The Bulletin of the Association for Business Communication*, December 1987, 9; Lennie Copeland and Lewis Griggs, *Going International* (New York: Penguin Group, Plume Books, 1986), 104, 109; and Roger E. Axtell, *The Do's and Taboos of International Trade* (New York: Wiley, 1989, 249–250).

pp. 240–241: interview with Elizabeth Clarke used with permission. **pp. 246–247:** Career Skills box based on David W. Ewing, "Strategies of Persuasion," *Writing for Results* (New York: Wiley, 1979). Used with permission of the publisher. **pp. 270–271:** interview with Richard Peter used with permission. **pp. 302–303:** interview with Peter Le Piane used with permission. **pp. 308–309:** Figure 11.2 based on William A. Bolger, "How to Start a Free Legal Services Plan for Your Group"

(Gloucester, VA: National Resource Center for Consumers of Legal Services, 1987). **p. 324:** Netscape Navigator screen courtesy of Netscape Communication Corporation, Copyright © 1995. **pp. 325–326:** WebCrawler search screens courtesy of America Online, Copyright © 1995. **pp. 327–329:** Eco Web "Welcome" page and "Program" pages courtesy of America Online, Copyright © 1995. **p. 336:** Ethics box based on data from Gregg Easterbrook, "The Sincerest Flattery," *Newsweek*, 29 July 1991, 45–46; and William A. Henry, III, "Recycling in the Newsroom," *Time*, 29 July 1991, 59. **pp. 342–343:** interview with Fazil Mihlar used with permission. **pp. 350–351:** Figure 12.3 based on Charlene Marmer Solomon, "Marriott's Family Matters," *Personnel Journal*, October 1991, 40–42; Suzanne Gordon, "Helping Corporations Care," *Working*

Woman, January 1993, 30; and Karen Matthes, "Companies Can Make It Their Business to Care," *HR Focus*, February 1992, 4. **pp. 372–373:** interview with James Paterson used with permission. **p. 377:** Figure 13.2 based in part on Robert Half, "Mistakes People Make Interviewing People," *Boardroom Reports*, 15 April 1991, 10. **p. 380:** Career Skills box based on Pat R. Graves and Jack E. Murray, "Enhancing Communication with Effective Page Design and Typography," *Delta Pi Epsilon* Instructional Strategies Series, Summer 1990. **pp. 402–403:** interview with Mary Piecewicz used with permission. **pp. 448–449:** interview with Jon Georges used with permission. **p. 452:** Career Skills box based on Bert Decker, "Successful Presentations: Simple and Practical," *HR Focus*, February 1992, 19; and Lawrence Stevens, "The Proof Is in the Presentation,"

Nation's Business, July 1991, 33. **p. 468:** Figure 15.6 based on "Better Meetings," *Boardroom Reports*, October 1, 1991. **pp. 480–481:** interview with Michael Robertson used with permission. **p. 485:** Career Skills box based on Michael J. Farr, *The Very Quick Job Search* (Indianapolis: JIST Works, Inc., 1991), Chapter Two. Copyright JIST Works, Inc. Used with permission of the publisher. **pp. 492–493:** Figure 16.5 based on Yana Parker, *The Damn Good Résumé Guide* (Berkeley, CA: Ten Speed Press, 1989), 55. Used with permission of the author. **p. 497:** Figure 16.7 from Joyce Lain Kennedy and Thomas J. Morrow, *Electronic Resume Revolution* (New York: John Wiley & Sons, 1994), 70. **p. 516:** Career Skills box based on Mary Ellen Guffey, *Essentials of Business Communication* (Boston: PWS-Kent Publishing Company, 1991), 329.

Photo Credits and Captions

p. 4: Courtesy of Mario Juarez. **p. 5:** Courtesy of Microsoft Corporation. **p. 11:** Barros & Barros, The Image Bank. **p. 24:** David W. Hamilton, The Image Bank. **p. 36:** Courtesy of Johanne Totta. **p. 37:** Courtesy of the Bank of Montreal. **p. 54:** L.D. Gordon, The Image Bank. **p. 64:** Courtesy of Angela Barker. **p. 65:** Courtesy of Western International Communications. **p. 70:** M. David de Lossy, The Image Bank. **p. 82:** J.P.H. Images, The Image Bank. **p. 92:** Courtesy of Harry Moore. **p. 93:** Courtesy of Seagull Pewter. **p. 101:** Courtesy of Liz Claiborne, Inc. **p. 104:** Patrick Doherty, Stockphotos, Inc. and The Image Bank. **p. 122:** Courtesy of Joe

Chidley. **p. 123:** Courtesy of *Maclean's* Magazine. **p. 128:** L.D. Gordon, The Image Bank. Photo caption based on Kathy M. Kristof, "mutual Funds Try Something New: Plain English," *Los Angeles Times*, 1 November 1992, D4. **p. 132:** Mel Digiacomo, The Image Bank. Photo caption based on Paul D. Zimmerman, "Neil Simon: Up From Success," *Newsweek*, 2 February 1970, 55. **p. 148:** Courtesy of Lise Andrews. **p. 149:** Courtesy of Tilley Endurables. **p. 161:** Real Life, The Image Bank. **p. 166:** Courtesy of The Body Shop. Photo caption based on The Body Shop promotional material. **p. 182:** Courtesy of Susan O'Brien. **p. 183:** Courtesy

of Moosehead Breweries. **p. 187:** L.D. Gordon, The Image Bank. **p. 194:** Janeart Ltd., The Image Bank. **p. 208:** Courtesy of Cathy Dial. **p. 209:** Courtesy of Pepsi-Cola Ltd. **p. 222:** David Jeffrey, The Image Bank. **p. 225:** M. David de Lossy, The Image Bank. **p. 240:** Courtesy of Elizabeth Clarke. **p. 241:** Courtesy of IWK Children's Hospital Foundation. **p. 243:** Steve Niedorf, The Image Bank. **p. 270:** Courtesy of Richard Peter. **p. 271:** Courtesy of Canadian Airlines. **p. 275:** Anne Rippy, The Image Bank. **p. 302:** Courtesy of Peter Le Piane. **p. 303:** Courtesy of DMR Group Inc. **p. 314:** Charles March, The Image Bank. **p. 342:** Courtesy

Index